P9-BJQ-068

Fundraising Basics

Fundraising Basics
A Complete Guide *Third Edition*

Barbara L. Ciconte, CFRE
Senior Vice President
Donor Strategies, Inc.
Chevy Chase, Maryland

Jeanne G. Jacob, CAE, CFRE
Executive Director
Goodwin House Foundation
Alexandria, Virginia

JONES & BARTLETT
LEARNING

World Headquarters
Jones & Bartlett Learning
5 Wall Street
Burlington, MA 01803
978-443-5000
info@jblearning.com
www.jblearning.com

Jones & Bartlett Learning books and products are available through most bookstores and online booksellers. To contact Jones & Bartlett Learning directly, call 800-832-0034, fax 978-443-8000, or visit our website, www.jblearning.com.

Substantial discounts on bulk quantities of Jones & Bartlett Learning publications are available to corporations, professional associations, and other qualified organizations. For details and specific discount information, contact the special sales department at Jones & Bartlett Learning via the above contact information or send an email to specialsales@jblearning.com.

Copyright © 2009 by Jones & Bartlett Learning, LLC, an Ascend Learning Company

All rights reserved. No part of the material protected by this copyright may be reproduced or utilized in any form, electronic or mechanical, including photocopying, recording, or by any information storage and retrieval system, without written permission from the copyright owner.

This publication is designed to provide accurate and authoritative information in regard to the subject matter covered. It is sold with the understanding that the publisher is not engaged in rendering legal, accounting, or other professional service. If legal advice or other expert assistance is required, the service of a competent professional person should be sought.

Production Credits
Publisher: Cathleen Sether
Acquisitions Editor: Jeremy Spiegel
Editorial Assistant: Maro Asadoorian
Production Director: Amy Rose
Senior Production Editor: Renée Sekerak
Production Assistant: Jill Morton
Associate Marketing Manager: Lisa Gordon
Manufacturing and Inventory Control Supervisor: Amy Bacus
Composition: Auburn Associates, Inc.
Senior Photo Researcher: Christine McKeen
Cover Design: Brian Moore
Printing and Binding: Edwards Brothers Malloy
Cover Printing: Edwards Brothers Malloy

Library of Congress Cataloging-in-Publication Data
Ciconte, Barbara L.
  Fundraising basics : a complete guide / by Barbara L. Ciconte and Jeanne G. Jacob.
     p. cm.
  Includes bibliographical references and index.
  ISBN 978-0-7637-4666-7 (pbk.)
  1. Fund raising.   I. Jacob, Jeanne Gerda.   II. Title.
  HG177.C53 2009
  658.15'224—dc22
                                                        2008022736

6048
Printed in the United States of America
17   16   15   14   13   10   9   8   7   6   5   4

To my parents, Barbara and Lou Buschlinger, who throughout my life have been a constant source of love and support, and to my husband, Tony Ciconte, without whose support, love, and understanding this book could not have been written.

Barbara L. Ciconte, CFRE

In memory of my mother, Clara Cypreansen Jacob, who always told me I could do anything. Her indomitable Norwegian strength and spirit instilled in me the desire to try all things and to do them all with the best of my ability. To my husband, Gerry Frank, without whose love, support, and patience, I would not have been able to write this book.

Jeanne G. Jacob, CAE, CFRE

Contents

Chapter 16   Association Foundation Fundraising

Chapter 17   Fundraising with Affiliates or Chapters

Unprecedented growth of philanthropy during the last years of the 20th century caused some to say that the beginning of the 21st century would be the golden age of philanthropy. But a cooling off of the stock market, the attacks of September 11, 2001, and other global conflicts slowed the growth of philanthropy. Only in 2005 did the rate of growth show a significant increase, growing from \$245.22 billion to \$260.28 billion (Giving USA Foundation, 2006). This growth continued through 2006 with a record-breaking \$295.02 billion in giving, a 4.2 percent increase from 2005. Even then, half of the growth in 2005, according to *Giving USA*, was due to the unprecedented outpouring of support for the Asian tsunami and Gulf Coast hurricanes. Approximately one-third of the growth in philanthropy in 2006 was also attributable to disaster relief giving. However, incomes continue to grow, the stock market has built wealth, and individuals are still forming new private foundations. Giving is now, and has been, above the long-term trend line since 1999.

The potential for philanthropy is great, but the environment for philanthropy is also challenged. There is the potential to repeal permanently the estate tax, with potential impact on philanthropy, especially planned giving. There is heightened interest in Congress to increase regulation of nonprofit organizations. New donors and funders are calling for higher levels of accountability, assessment, and impact analysis. The so-called new donors challenge many nonprofit organizations to do things differently. Their approaches are often unique, with many new donors doing things as differently from one another as from the previous generation of donors. New and unique models of giving are being practiced by an increasing number of philanthropists.

Institutional philanthropy has changed as well. The number of foundations has tripled since 1975 (Foundation Center, 2006). Bill Gates alone has established what is now the largest U.S. foundation, and Warren Buffett's pledge of more than \$30 billion to be distributed through the Gates Foundation has effectively doubled the size of the foundation. Thanks to the new foundations and increases in the equities market, foundations displaced bequests as the second largest source of philanthropic support in 1992 and this gap widens each year (American Association of Fundraising Counsel, 1993). New forms of philanthropy are evolving, including giving circles, women's funds, social investing, social entrepreneurship, and micro loans, among others.

Those beginning careers in fundraising today are entering a philanthropic environment much more complex than it was even seven years ago when the *Second Edition* of this text was published. Understanding the fundamental ethical and technical standards for success in fundraising is essential. Passion for a good cause is an excellent basis for doing fundraising work. But, it is no longer sufficient for achieving success. Applying good practice and maintaining high ethical standards are necessary complements to belief in the cause. In *Fundraising Basics: A Complete Guide*, Barbara Ciconte and Jeanne Jacob have provided an excellent introduction to the ethical and technical standards for those getting started in fundraising.

They open with an introduction that provides the tradition and context for American philanthropy. This is important grounding for every fundraiser. All of us have the responsibility not only to raise money for our organizations, but also to understand and enhance the tradition of volunteerism and philanthropy as well. The authors then take us through the elements of a total development program and the strategies and techniques for reaching success.

Following are two basic truths about ethical philanthropic fundraising:

- Fundraising is a privilege based on organizational mission.
- Successful fundraising begins with the board.

In Chapter 1, the authors stress the importance of developing mission-driven fundraising programs that articulate a clear and compelling case for support. While they return to the case for support in various aspects of fundraising, such as the role of annual giving, direct mail usage, major gifts, and corporate and foundation fundraising, they introduce the reader to the importance of the case for support early in the text. An organization must seek philanthropic support based on the values it expresses in fulfillment of community or public needs. The case for support elevates fundraising activity to a rational discussion of fulfilling community needs. In this edition, the authors provide expanded information on the case for support.

They also stress the importance of boards and volunteers. Chapter 2, "The Many Roles of Board, Staff, and Volunteers in Fundraising," explores the work of fundraising. In an era when there is increased pressure for staff members to conduct more fundraising activity, including gift solicitation on their own, it is refreshing to find the authors' discussion of the important role of boards and volunteers in fundraising before they introduce fundraising strategies and techniques. They add a new section here on board assessment.

In this text, these two respected fundraisers, authors, and teachers provide a comprehensive overview of the total development program, the sources of philanthropy, and the strategies for achieving success. There are separate chapters on annual giving, major gifts, capital campaigns, and planned giving. They introduce the reader to such strategies as direct mail and telemarketing, prospect research, personal solicitation, and special events. This *Third Edition* also includes updated information on e-philanthropy and its impact on raising funds plus the use of technology in communication. They help us think of technology as integrated to all we do in fundraising from prospect research to communications for gift solicitation to database management. And, they focus on individuals separately (prospect research), corporations, and foundations as sources of support. With separate chapters on each of the elements, the reader can return easily to find answers to specific questions.

The authors open this text with a context piece focused on the tradition of American philanthropy, and they end with a context piece on fundraising as a career. As we take up our work as fundraisers, it is helpful to know about our colleagues, and what their motivations and expectations are, and the dynamics and tensions in making a career in fundraising. The expanded section on ethics and accountability provides guidance on an essential element of building a successful career in fundraising. Each of us working in fundraising has a responsibility to all fundraising colleagues. In our study of fundraisers, Peg Duronio and I (Duronio and Tempel, 1997) asked this question about fundraising: "Why do the actions of so few have such a large impact on so many?"

Those of us who work in the nonprofit sector are stewards of the public trust. As such we must hold ourselves to a higher standard, to what Independent Sector calls "Obedience to the Unenforceable" (Independent Sector, 2002). In the nonprofit sector, especially in fundraising, the bad act of one is easily transferred by the public to all others. This continues to be true today. According to several recent studies, public trust in nonprofit is increasing but we still have much work to do in building the level of trust that will ensure philanthropic support. As we take up our work in fundraising, we must be committed to the notion that ethical philanthropic fundraising inspires trust in the nonprofit sector. We must be committed to high standards of technical practice and ethical behavior to help ensure this trust. Ciconte and Jacob give us directions for developing both.

Eugene R. Tempel, EdD, CFRE
President, Indiana University Foundation
Former Executive Director
The Center on Philanthropy, Indiana University

REFERENCES

American Association of Fundraising Counsel (AAFRC) Trust for Philanthropy. 1993. *Giving USA*. Indianapolis, IN: AAFRC Trust for Philanthropy.

AAFRC Trust for Philanthropy. 1999. *Giving USA*. Indianapolis, IN: AAFRC Trust for Philanthropy.

AAFRC Trust for Philanthropy. 2000. *Giving USA*. Indianapolis, IN: AAFRC Trust for Philanthropy.

Duronio, M. A., and E. R. Tempel. 1997. *Fund raisers: Their careers, stories, concerns, and accomplishments*. San Francisco: Jossey-Bass Nonprofit Sector Series.

Foundation Center. 2006. *Foundations today series, foundation yearbook: Facts and figures on private and community foundations*. New York: Foundation Center, 28, 33.

Giving USA Foundation. 2006. Overview of giving in 2005, Key findings. Glenview, IL: Giving USA Foundation, 11.

Giving USA Foundation. 2007. Glenview, IL: Giving USA Foundation.

Independent Sector. 2002. *Ethics and the nation's voluntary and philanthropic community: Obedience to the unenforceable*. Washington, DC: Independent Sector.

We are delighted with the overwhelmingly positive feedback we have received since *Fundraising Basics: A Complete Guide* was first published in 1997. During the past 11 years we have heard from fundraising professionals around the world who told us that our book was a tremendous help to them in developing successful fundraising programs for their organizations. Many professionals also let us know that our book was a terrific resource to use when reviewing for the Certified Fund Raising Executive examination. Fundraising consultants shared with us that they not only recommended our book to their clients but also found it useful themselves in serving their nonprofit clients. Workshop leaders and trainers thanked us for writing a book that is so easily put to use for their seminars and workshops. They especially liked the sample forms used throughout the chapters that are readily adaptable to nearly every organization's needs or circumstances. In this *Third Edition*, these forms also are included on a CD-ROM for even easier use. Our thanks to all who shared their thoughts and comments with us.

The idea for *Fundraising Basics*, more commonly known as the "purple" book (published by Jones and Bartlett Publishers), first arose from our need for a text that we could use with our students at The George Washington University's Center for Continuing Education in Washington, DC, and at other fundraising trainings and workshops. However, we know now that this book can also be used by all who wish to learn more about fundraising—those seeking to become development professionals, those raising money for or sitting on the boards of nonprofit organizations, and those who simply want to know how to raise money in a professional manner.

With more than 60 years of fundraising experience between us, this book is a collection of our own and our colleagues' personal experiences in capital campaigns, special events, annual campaigns, planned giving, sponsorship solicitation, board development, major gift solicitation, and managing the fundraising for supporting foundations. This book attempts to address all aspects of the development field to provide an overview for its readers. The extensive research undertaken provides insight into many successful fundraising programs, and the varied opportunities available to those wishing for a career in the development field. In this updated and expanded *Third Edition*, we include new areas such as ethics and accountability and national-affiliate relations as they relate to fundraising, as well as update the reader on the major impact technology has made in this field. The reader will find more case studies and examples that allow them to learn from the experiences of others—one of the best ways for fundraisers to gain knowledge of successful development opportunities.

The chapters remain purposely short, as the text is intended as an overview. For those wishing to read more extensively on a subject, additional resources are suggested in the bibliography. Since we believe a key trait of most development officers is a good sense of humor, we also continue to highlight the chapters with cartoons provided by Mark Litzler, Joseph Brown, and Carole Cable. Fundraising is not all work; it can be, should be, and most often is fun!

We welcome readers to the professional world of fundraising, a world we thoroughly enjoy. We hope we have again provided a useful guide to successful fundraising that you will want to add to your professional library and continue to use in your professional work.

Acknowledgments

We wish to acknowledge the many organizations we have served during our careers and continue to serve as staff, consultants, and volunteers for providing us with opportunities to grow and develop as fundraising professionals and to share our skills and talents to advance their varied missions.

In this updated and expanded *Third Edition* of *Fundraising Basics: A Complete Guide*, we wish to recognize a special group of colleagues who made significant contributions of their own knowledge, expertise, and experience to assist with some of the chapters. A very special thank you to the following fundraising experts:

- Tony Ciconte, Senior Vice President, Technical Services, Donor Strategies, Inc., Chevy Chase, Maryland
- Gerry Frank, President, *INN*dependent Management Group (IMG), Alexandria, Virginia
- James P. Gelatt, PhD, President, Prentice Associates, Lake Monticello, Virginia
- Tara L. Hoke, Esq., Assistant General Counsel, American Society of Civil Engineers, Reston, Virginia
- Kathleen E. Pavelka, CFRE, Founder and President, Telecomp, Inc., Rochester, New York
- Maria Semple, Principal, The Prospect Finder, Bridgewater, New Jersey
- Barbara Waldorf, CAE, PRC, Director of Customer Insight and Development, United States Bowling Congress, Greendale, Wisconsin
- Sandra Walter-Steinberg, Chief Strategist, Sandra M. Walter & Associates Consulting, Rockville, Maryland
- Peter C. Wolk, Esq., Founder and Executive Director, National Center for Nonprofit Law, Washington, DC
- M. Sue Woodward, CFRE, President, Woodward Associates, Potomac, Maryland

We also wish to acknowledge the many colleagues who submitted helpful information and resources to this new edition. You will find their names noted throughout the book in source lines.

Other important people to recognize are the students who participated in our training classes throughout the years, many of whom chose to pursue careers in development. Their eagerness to learn about fundraising and to become professional fundraisers inspires us to share with future students our knowledge and enthusiasm for our work. We are proud of the work they are undertaking as development professionals for various nonprofit organizations in the United States, Canada, and around the world.

We are indebted to others for their assistance with this project, especially the team at Jones and Bartlett Publishers. Our very special thanks to the staff of AFP, especially Jan Alfieri and the Resource Center staff who so willingly researched topics for us and were always cheerful in their assistance and to Ann Kashnikow for the hours of research she undertook to verify details for information available from the Internet.

Thanks also to Mark Litzler who provided so many of the cartoons in this book. Litzler's cartoons have appeared in numerous publications including *The Harvard Business Review, Barrons, The Wall Street Journal, The Chronicle of Higher Education,* and *The Chronicle of Philanthropy*. He is the Executive Director for the Saint Luke's Hospital Foundation in Kansas City, Missouri.

Also, our thanks once again to our husbands, Tony Ciconte and Gerry Frank, and to our many friends and family for their continued support, encouragement, patience, and understanding during our work on the book. We greatly appreciate the lasting friendships of the women in the Ladies of the Club (Carolyn Boyer, Janice Callahan Eisert, Ricki Green Harvey, Judith Hunter, Terry Kees, Carol Fenske Orenstein, Anne McGregor, Suzie Alexander Gauthier, Barbara Valentino, and Carolyn Zollar), and thank them for listening to us talk about writing each edition of the book and for understanding why we had to miss so many events during these times. Special thanks to all of the others who have lived through this *Third Edition* with us: the Baeders (Janet, Bill, Amanda, and Anna), the Chadbournes (Kathleen, MayBelle, and Tom), the Cicontes (Robert, Eun Ha, and Pamela), Alice Collier Cochran, Mary Fran Coffey, Karen Gardner, Susan Gaumont, Ricki and Ralph Harvey, Jean and Chuck McDanal, Melanie Miller, Helen Ross, Bobbie and Mark Ruschman, Marcia Saumweber, Barbara Valentino, and Barbara Waldorf.

BARBARA L. CICONTE, CFRE

Barbara L. Ciconte, CFRE, is Senior Vice President, Consulting Services, for Donor Strategies, Inc. (DSI), a professional and technical services firm providing consulting services in nonprofit management, fundraising, development planning, board and staff training, and information systems to the nonprofit sector. DSI also offers *MissionAssist*, a highly affordable, comprehensive fundraising database system for nonprofits. Ms. Ciconte works with local, regional, and national organizations in strategic planning and assists them in building more effective resource development programs in annual, capital, and endowment giving; major gifts; planned giving; corporate and foundation relations; special events; as well as training board members, volunteers and staff. Her clients include associations, healthcare institutions, educational organizations, human services agencies, and public policy organizations. A sampling of clients served include the National Association for the Education of Young Children (NAEYC), Association of Small Foundations (ASF), Inova Health System Foundation, Sibley Memorial Hospital, Foundation for National Institutes of Health (FNIH), Falls Church Education Foundation, The Washington Center for Internships and Academic Seminars, New Neighbors Education Center of Northern Virginia, Community Ministries of Rockville, Reston Interfaith, Northern Virginia Family Service, The Campagna Center, Joint Center for Political and Economic Studies, National Academy of Social Insurance, and the Pacific Council on International Policy.

Prior to becoming a consultant, she was the Associate Dean for Development and Alumni Relations at the Washington College of Law at American University (AU) where she was responsible for the overall development, alumni relations, and publication programs for the college. As the law school's Director of Development, she managed the college's successful $20 million capital campaign for a new facility and programs. Other positions held at AU during her 13-year tenure included Director of Major Gifts and Director of the Annual Fund. Before joining the staff of AU in 1986, she was Fundraising Projects Manager for a national advocacy organization, where she established the organization's first major gifts program.

Ms. Ciconte is a former member of the Board of the Association of Fundraising Professionals (AFP) and served for two years as Vice Chair for Professional Advancement, which is responsible for the overall AFP educational program. She has been involved over the years revising AFP's First Course in Fundraising and Survey Course, assisting in developing curricula for new AFP trainings and workshops, and serving on a variety of committees and task forces. A certified fundraising executive (CFRE) since 1988, she is a past president of the Greater Washington, DC, AFP Chapter, and in 1997, received the DC Chapter's Outstanding Fundraising Executive of the Year Award for her leadership and service to the profession. In 1999, she co-chaired with fellow author, Jeanne Jacob, the record-setting AFP/DC Fundraising Days Conference, a two-day educational conference held annually. As a graduate of the Center for Philanthropy at Indiana University/Association of Fundraising Professionals Faculty Training Academy, Ms. Ciconte holds the Master Teacher credential.

A leading national educator on fundraising and board development, Ms. Ciconte has served as an adjunct faculty member at George Mason University and American University and has published articles in *The Nonprofit Times* and *The Development Director's Letter*. She is a frequent speaker at international and national conferences and meetings and has led many fundraising training sessions for the: Association of Fundraising Professionals (AFP) and its chapters; American Society of Association Executives (ASAE); Association Foundation Group (AFG); Council of Engineering and Scientific Society Executives (CESSE); Destination Marketing Association International (DMAI) as well as such groups as the U.S. Golf Association, Child Welfare League of America, the Enterprise Foundation, and the National Trust for Historic Preservation. Ms. Ciconte was a guest presenter at the Fundraising Institute-Australia's 2003 International Conference in Canberra, Australia. She volunteers her time regularly as a trainer and instructor for nonprofit management assistance organizations such as Maryland Nonprofits, Cultural Alliance of Greater Washington, Center for Nonprofit Advancement, and the Institute of Policy Studies.

As a volunteer, Ms. Ciconte is President of the Board of Directors for Take Heart Association Project (THAP), an organization that helps disadvantaged Kenyan children with heart problems receive life-saving medical treatment by working with Kenyan hospitals to help build their capacity to provide excellent medical care through partnerships with U.S. medical personnel and other nonprofit organizations. In the past, she served on the boards of the YWCA of the National Capital Area, New York State Association of YWCAs, and the Binghamton, New York, YWCA.

Prior to her career in development, she taught for 11 years as an elementary school teacher in Whitney Point, New York, and a junior high school remedial reading and writing teacher in Owego, New York. She received her Bachelor of Arts degree in Education from the State University of New York (SUNY) at Oneonta and her Master of Arts degree in Education from SUNY Cortland.

JEANNE G. JACOB, CAE, CFRE

Jeanne G. Jacob is both a Certified Association Executive (CAE) and a Certified Fund Raising Executive (CFRE). A nationally recognized association foundation executive and not-for-profit fundraiser, she currently serves as Executive Director of the Goodwin House Foundation in Alexandria, Virginia. The Foundation's mission is to support Goodwin House Incorporated, a continuing care retirement community, with two campuses housing 850 residents. The mission of Goodwin House is to support, honor, and uplift the lives of older adults and the people who care for them through a faith-based, nonprofit organization affiliated with the Episcopal Church. As a supporting foundation, the Goodwin House Foundation generates resources for Goodwin House Incorporated through various fundraising programs, holds and manages endowment funds, and manages the following programs: Fellowship, Community Matching Gift, and Clinical and Pastoral education. Additionally, the Foundation produces a widely distributed yearly calendar that features resident art. Since joining the Goodwin House Foundation in 2007, Ms. Jacob has served on the Foundation Board and on Goodwin House Incorporated's Executive Leadership Team.

For 12 years (1995 to 2007), Ms. Jacob worked for the American Society of Civil Engineers (ASCE) Foundation in Washington, DC, and in Reston, Virginia. The ASCE Foundation owns and operates a six-story class-A office building housing the Foundation, ASCE, and its affiliates. As Executive Vice President, Ms. Jacob was responsible for the Foundation's overall operation, staff management, fundraising efforts, and generation of non-dues financial resources for the entire complex. Since the Foundation's inception in 1994, more than $20 million in gifts have been raised and an additional $22 million in rent generated for the ASCE and its affiliates. Fundraising efforts included: two capital campaigns, the first raising $4.6 million on a goal of $3.5 million and the second raising $6.7 million on a goal of $6 million. Ms. Jacob initiated the Foundation's first planned giving, annual appeal, major gifts, and sponsorship programs; launched its first donor newsletter; and, led its outside consulting efforts. Also, she served as Secretary and Treasurer of the Foundation's Board and on ASCE's Senior Leadership Team.

Prior to joining both Foundations, Ms. Jacob was Vice President for Public Affairs and Development with INNdependent Management Group (IMG), a consulting firm serving clients that include the American Association of University Women; Water Environment Federation; Women in Development Office of U.S.A.I.D.; American College of Nurse Mid-Wives; American Center for International Leadership; Greater Washington Society of Association Executives; National Conference of State Societies; and the National Technological University.

Previous to IMG, she served as Vice President for Public Affairs and Development at Cities in Schools, raising nearly $6 million annually, and as Director of Development for the National Academy of Engineering (NAE), where she directed a five-year capital campaign for NAE that raised $46 million on a goal of $30 million. Prior to NAE, she worked eight years for Youth for Understanding (YFU) International Student Exchange, where she established a regional office in Illinois and served as its director. Then, she managed six of YFU's regional offices covering 15 states and supervising 30 professionals and a volunteer force of more than 500. She traveled internationally providing training to YFU staff in Germany, the Netherlands, Norway, Japan, the Philippines, Brazil, and Colombia. It was at YFU where she began her development career.

In 2002, Ms. Jacob was selected as the Outstanding Fundraising Professional for the Greater Washington, DC, area for her leadership and service to the fundraising profession and was presented with this honor at the 2002 National Capital Philanthropy Day luncheon.

In her volunteer life, Ms. Jacob has served on the Board of the Illinois State Society (ISS) for more than 20 years. Founded in 1854, ISS is the oldest of the state societies in Washington, DC. As ISS President in 1989, she produced the Society's first Inaugural Ball, raising money to underwrite its activities for the next four years. Following this success, she expanded each following Gala to reach an attendance of nearly 8,000 and generating income of more than $1 million at the most recent Gala. She has served as Chair for five ISS Presidential Inaugural Galas (Bush in 1989, Clinton in 1993 and 1997, Bush in 2001 and 2005, and Obama in 2009).

Ms. Jacob's other volunteer activities have included serving on the boards of the Big Sisters of the Washington Metropolitan Area; American Center for International Leadership; Alexandria Symphony Orchestra League; Association Foundation Group (AFG) where she served as President in 2008–2009; and Association of Fundraising Professionals, Washington, DC, Chapter, where she held the office of Secretary. In 1998, she chaired AFP/DC's annual Members Reception, and in 1999, she co-chaired, with fellow author, Barbara Ciconte, the AFP/DC Fundraising Days Conference, a two-day educational conference with nearly 1,000 participants. In 2002 and 2003, she served on the Leadership Committee for the Greater Washington Area National Capital Philanthropy Day. In addition, Jacob served on the 2008 United Way Tocqueville Society Award Committee.

For eight years, Ms. Jacob taught the Fundamentals of Fund Raising course at The George Washington University's Center for Continuing Education as well as at the Support Center. She is a frequent speaker on philanthropy at international and national conferences and meetings and has led many fundraising training sessions for the Association of Fundraising Professionals (AFP); American Society of Association Executives (ASAE); Association Foundation Group (AFG); Council of Engineering and Scientific Society Executives (CESSE); Destination Marketing Association International (DMAI); and the American Association of Homes and Services for the Aging (AAHSA). Also, she actively supports the development efforts of her sorority Gamma Phi Beta and her husband's preparatory school in Pennsylvania, The Hill School.

Prior to her Foundation association and fundraising career, Ms. Jacob worked for five years in the field of college admissions for Mount Holyoke College in South Hadley, Massachusetts, and the University of Chicago in Chicago, Illinois. She was also a teacher of English at Glenbard West High School in Glen Ellyn, Illinois. She received her Bachelor of Arts degree in English from the University of Iowa in Iowa City, Iowa, where she received the Susan B. Hancher Award for the outstanding graduating senior woman.

Chapter 1

Ensuring the Future of Philanthropy—An American Tradition—Through Accountability and Ethical Fundraising

CHAPTER OUTLINE

- The Nonprofit Sector
- Definition of Philanthropy
- History of Philanthropy in America
- A Tradition of Volunteerism
- The Relationship Between Volunteering and Charitable Contributions
- How Generous We Are as a Nation

- Profile of the Changing Donor
- Indicators That Affect Giving and Volunteering
- How to Create a Philanthropic Environment
- The Accountable Nonprofit Organization
- Assess Your Organization's Accountability
- Ethical Standards and Practices

KEY VOCABULARY

- Accountability
- Charitable Giving
- Demographics
- Development
- Donor
- Ethics
- Nonprofit Sector
- Nonprofit or Not-for-Profit Organization
- Philanthropy
- Transparency
- Volunteerism

> "We make a living by what we get, but we make a life by what we give."
>
> —Winston Churchill

This quote by Winston Churchill captures the heart of the nonprofit sector and the strong sense of mission so prevalent among those who work within it. To successfully raise funds for a nonprofit organization, you must understand what philanthropy is and how it became an American tradition.

THE NONPROFIT SECTOR

The nonprofit landscape in America is a mosaic of diverse organizations that cover an astounding breadth of causes—from homeless shelters to the ivy-covered walls of colleges and universities. Its more than a million organizations include charities, arts and cultural organizations, social welfare organizations, religious institutions and faith-based organizations, academic institutions, foundations, and professional and trade associations. The *nonprofit sector* (or *independent sector*) is the collective name used to describe the institutions and organizations in American society that are neither government nor business. Other names often used include the *not-for-profit sector,* the *third sector,* the *philanthropic sector,* the *voluntary sector,* and the *social sector.* Outside the United States, nonprofits are often called *nongovernmental organizations* (NGO) or *civil society organizations.* Whatever the term used, their numbers are dramatically on the rise.

Each nonprofit distinguishes itself from others through its mission and contributions to society. Yet, together, all the organizations in the nonprofit sector continually shape and reshape the social order, create both the intellectual and social space for Americans to organize, and influence every aspect of the human condition. Through nonprofits, individuals can organize and exercise their rights to advocate for issues and causes in which they truly believe.

It is often said that the nonprofit sector is the heart and soul of society because it connects with communities and makes a difference in the lives of people by fulfilling unmet needs. The nonprofit sector serves as a forum for the discussion and dissemination of new ideas, an efficient vehicle for delivering social services, and a guardian of our environment, values, and heritage. Millions of volunteers and donors truly make the nonprofit sector a critical player in the world today.

DEFINITION OF PHILANTHROPY

The word *philanthropy* is Greek and means "love of mankind." According to the online dictionary of the Association of Fundraising Professionals (AFP) (Levy, 2006), philanthropy is (1) the love of humankind, usually expressed by an effort to enhance the well-being of humanity through personal acts of practical kindness or by financial support of a cause or causes, such as a charity (e.g., the American Red Cross), mutual aid or assistance (e.g., service clubs and youth groups), quality of life (e.g., arts, education, and the environment), and religion; and (2) any effort to relieve human misery or suffering, improve the quality of life, encourage aid or assistance, or foster the preservation of values through gifts, service, or other voluntary activity, any and all of which are external to government involvement or marketplace exchange. Philanthropy and volunteerism are uniquely American traditions, and their pervasive presence in our lives is often taken for granted.

HISTORY OF PHILANTHROPY IN AMERICA

American philanthropy as we know it today began during colonial times. People focused on religion and higher education during the 18th century. Gradually, health, civic, social causes, and the arts entered the picture as our young nation grew and prospered.

It is interesting to note that philanthropy in America before the American Revolution had its roots in necessity. It was the only means of building and sustaining the service institutions each community needed.

The philanthropic tradition of American life and culture has shaped Americans as a people and a nation. Through voluntary association, Americans have come together; through nonprofit organizations and philanthropy, they have demonstrated care and concern for others, therefore building community within a vastly diverse society. (Wagner, 2002)

A TRADITION OF VOLUNTEERISM

The practice of philanthropy includes volunteer service in addition to gifts. Even in today's world, with the many demands made on our time by family, work, study, and leisure activities,

> *Even in today's world, with the many demands made on our time by family, work, study, and leisure activities, people are undertaking volunteer work.*

people are undertaking volunteer work. The Corporation for National and Community Service, the federal agency in Washington, DC, that oversees AmeriCorps and other service programs, recently

"CHARITABLE GIVING ISN'T THE ULTIMATE TEST OF ONE'S HUMANITY BUT IT GIVES US SOME NUMBERS TO PLAY WITH."

Source: Copyright © Mark Litzler.

surveyed 60,000 households and found that levels of volunteerism in the United States have reached a 30-year high, as more teenagers, baby boomers, and older adults choose to give back to their communities. According to *Volunteer Growth in America: A Review of Trends Since 1974*, adult volunteerism increased more than 32 percent between 1989 and 2005, largely because of the involvement by three age groups—teenagers between the ages of 16 and 19 years, baby boomers and others aged 45 to 65 years, and older adults 65 years and over. Highlights of the report include the following:

- Almost 29 percent of Americans volunteered in 2005.
- Time volunteered by older teenagers (ages 16–19 years) has more than doubled since 1989.
- Older Americans have increased their volunteer time 64 percent since 1974.
- Baby boomers are volunteering at sharply higher rates than did their parents at mid-life.
- Educational and youth-service organizations received the largest increase in volunteers (63 percent) between 1989 and 2006.
- The largest percentage of Americans—almost 35 percent—volunteer at churches, mosques, or other religious groups.

- A greater percentage of women donate their time than men.
- Minorities routinely volunteer less than whites.
- Married persons and parents with children under 18 years of age volunteered at a higher rate than unmarried persons and persons without children of that age.
- The main activity volunteers performed were as follows: fundraising (10.9 percent); tutoring or teaching (10.8 percent). Men and women tended to engage in different main activities. Men who volunteered were most likely to engage in general labor (11.5 percent) or to coach, referee, or supervise sports teams (10.2 percent), while women volunteers were most likely to fundraise (12.5 percent) or tutor or teach (12.5 percent).

A key finding from this report for nonprofit organizations is that about 43 percent of volunteers became involved with their main organization after being asked to volunteer, most often by someone in the organization. A slightly smaller proportion, about two in five volunteers, became involved due to their own initiative of approaching the organization. Thus, it is important for nonprofit organizations to be proactive in outreach for recruiting volunteers.

THE RELATIONSHIP BETWEEN VOLUNTEERING AND CHARITABLE CONTRIBUTIONS

As you can see, "participation" is very much an element of the American philanthropic spirit. But how does one learn to participate or to volunteer? A review of the current research shows that positive volunteer experiences in youth tend to lead to generous giving and volunteering in later life. Adults who belonged to a youth group, volunteered as a youth, did door-to-door canvassing to raise money, or participated in student government are the most likely to give and to volunteer. Parents who volunteered and served as role models for their families are also significant influences, as are active involvement in religious organizations and frequency of attendance at religious services.

Data from many recent studies and surveys clearly establish a relationship between giving and volunteering. Independent Sector's most recent survey revealed that 89 percent of all households gave charitable contributions and that the average gift from households with volunteers was more than two times that of donor households whose members did not volunteer.

Current research also reveals the most frequently cited important motivations for contributing to an organization:

- believe in the cause or feeling it is the right thing to do
- believe contribution will make an impact
- believe money is being used as intended
- know someone who is affected or who will be a beneficiary of the donation

HOW GENEROUS WE ARE AS A NATION

Today, America's philanthropic spirit remains strong as seen in *Giving USA*, the yearbook of philanthropy published by the Giv-

ing USA Foundation™ and researched and written by the Center on Philanthropy at Indiana University. According to the latest issue of *Giving USA 2008*, American giving reached a record high, $306.39 billion for 2007, up 3.9 percent from 2006. Foundation grant making, which made up 12.5 percent of total giving, is the fastest growing source of charitable donations.

Figure 1–1 shows that individuals continue to account for an overwhelming majority of all contributions, estimated at $252.18 billion (including $23.15 billion in bequests), or 82.4 percent of all contributions. The remaining 17.6 percent was contributed by foundations ($38.52 billion, a 10.3 percent increase) and corporations ($15.69 billion, an increase of 1.9 percent over 2006).

Regarding the types of organizations or institutions that receive contributions, not much has changed since the 18th century. Religious institutions remain the major recipients, followed by educational institutions. The breakdown of support for issues and causes is shown in Figure 1–2.

PROFILE OF THE CHANGING DONOR

In recent years, a growing body of research shows what effects the changing demographics in the United States will have on philanthropic trends. Donors in the United States have become more diverse in age, ethnicity, race, religion, gender, sexual orientation, geography, and source of wealth. This has created both challenges and opportunities for nonprofits.

For most nonprofits, the traditional donor is white, non-Hispanic, female, religious, and a member of the World War II

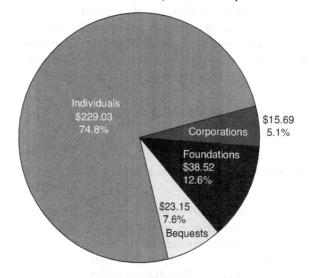

**2007 charitable giving
Total = $306.39 billion ($ in billions)**

Figure 1–1 Sources of Contributions
Source: Giving USA 2008, Giving USA Foundation.

Types of recipients of contributions, 2007
Total = $306.39 billion ($ in billions)

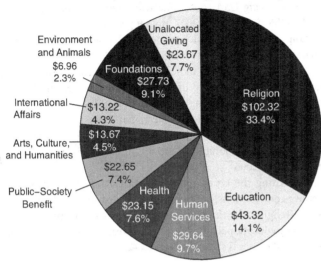

Figure 1–2 Contributions Received by Type of Recipient Organization
Source: Giving USA 2008, Giving USA Foundation.

generation. Because these donors are living longer, many non-profit organizations have not yet focused on bringing in new donors from Generations X and Y as well as the baby boomers. Due to the continuing rise in immigration among non-whites and Hispanics, the majority population in the United States eventually will consist of groups traditionally referred to as minorities. In order to engage these different generational and ethnic populations, nonprofit organizations must first look to the diversity of their staff, board, and volunteers. They need to utilize different communication styles, understand the different populations' views about money, and learn what they want to support. Opportunities to involve people from younger generations and ethnic populations as staff, board members, and volunteers are key to building a more diverse donor base.

INDICATORS THAT AFFECT GIVING AND VOLUNTEERING

Even though the American people have a strong tradition of volunteering and charitable giving, many factors can affect this tradition. They include

- an individual's current and future economic well-being
- the impact of changes in tax policy
- public trust and involvement
- management of charitable organization
- ethical and honest fundraising practices

HOW TO CREATE A PHILANTHROPIC ENVIRONMENT

As mentioned earlier in this chapter, an organization's mission and contribution to society is what distinguishes it from others within the nonprofit sector. The organization's mission defines its purpose and values as realized through its programs and services. To create an environment conducive to philanthropy, key messages that describe how the organization's mission is put into practice must be developed and used in all verbal and written communications. In other words, the organization's mission must be articulated in human terms. People are of primary importance; systems are secondary. If the organization remains focused on its mission, it will be able to build a stronger case for philanthropic support.

> *To create an environment conducive to philanthropy, key messages that describe how the organization's mission is put into practice must be developed and used in all verbal and written communications.*

To begin to build a philanthropic environment, an organization's board and staff leadership must first review the organization's mission statement. Questions to consider include these:

- Is the mission statement clear?
- Is the mission as vital to society today as it was when the organization was first founded?
- If the answer to the above question is no, does the mission statement need to be rewritten?
- Do the current programs and services reflect the mission?
- Do programs and services being planned reflect the mission?

Next, the organization's board and staff leadership should determine if the messages being used in communicating verbally and in writing with the general public clearly articulate the organization's mission and programs. Do the messages reflect the needs of the community, not the organization, and do they describe how people will benefit? Given the increasing competition for funds in the nonprofit sector, the organization needs to communicate how its approach to solving a problem or advancing an issue has been successful in human terms and will continue to be successful in the future. Donors want to know that their investment—their contribution—will have an impact on society.

Last, the organization's board and staff leadership should review current programs and services to see how they reflect the mission in practice. It may discover that, due to shifting societal needs and the interests of funding sources, some programs or services may not be as true to the mission as others. These programs and services should then undergo further review and analysis in order to help the organization advance its mission.

A philanthropic environment also focuses more attention on donor needs. See Appendix 1–A for A Donor Bill of Rights. Keep in mind that today's donors are looking for organizations that are focused on their mission, have identified priorities, are well managed, use resources wisely, and produce results. Since today's donors view themselves as "investors," they are more discerning and demand demonstrable accountability from the nonprofits they support.

THE ACCOUNTABLE NONPROFIT ORGANIZATION

Accountability in the nonprofit sector means being open and ready to answer to those who have invested their trust, faith, and money in your organization. Nonprofits are accountable to many stakeholders, including donors and funders; local, state, and federal agencies; volunteers; program recipients; and the general public. Everyone who works for a nonprofit shares a degree of responsibility for ensuring that the organization remains answerable to its constituents and true to its mission.

In general, nonprofits that are accountable are able to raise more money by building public confidence in the organization and by making processes more effective, as well as providing more time for focusing on delivering on the mission—the most important part.

Maintaining the public trust is paramount to the nonprofit sector. Recent surveys, however, show that public confidence that dropped after September 11, 2001, is rising slightly but still has not returned to the level of trust experienced before that day. According to *Confidence in Charitable Organizations, 2006,* a national telephone survey of 1,000 randomly selected adults, conducted in July 2006 by the Robert F. Wagner Graduate School of Public Service at New York University, 69 percent of Americans expressed a great deal or a fair amount of confidence in charities. That figure represents a 5-percent increase from the July 2005 survey and a 9-percent increase from the September 2002 survey. While the responses suggest that public confidence is beginning to rebound, the current level of trust is still significantly lower than the 90 percent of respondents who expressed a great deal of trust in charities pre-September 11, 2001.

Other findings included the following:

- 73 percent said charities have the right priorities but do not spend money wisely.
- 18 percent of Americans said charitable organizations do a very good job running their programs and services, compared with 19 percent in 2005.
- 18 percent said charitable organizations do a very good job being fair in their decisions, compared with 16 percent in 2005.

The study found that the most powerful predictor of confidence in charities was confidence and trust in the American Red Cross, followed by the second most powerful predictor, confidence and trust in the United Way of America. The major issues surrounding the American Red Cross's use of funds raised for the

September 11 victims' families seriously affected the public's confidence and trust not only in the American Red Cross but also raised doubts about how charities in their communities were using contributions. For that reason, nonprofit organizations must commit to the principles of honesty and transparency in order to live up to their role as stewards of the public trust.

Exhibit 1–1 is a statement of principles adopted more than a decade ago by the Board of Directors of the Association of Fundraising Professionals but still relevant and needed today. It outlines the operations and procedures a nonprofit undertakes to show it is accountable to donors, the people it serves, and the general public.

ASSESS YOUR ORGANIZATION'S ACCOUNTABILITY

Peter Wolk is the founder and executive director of the National Center for Nonprofit Law, a 501(c)(3) organization that conducts training seminars on a wide range of nonprofit organizational and legal topics. He also has a private law practice dedicated to creating, advising, and representing nonprofit organizations. He helps nonprofit organizations understand why they need to devote time and attention to the legal issues surrounding fundraising. According to Wolk, the first reason is because noncompliance can

Exhibit 1–1 The Accountable Nonprofit Organization

The accountable nonprofit organization is responsible for mission fulfillment, leadership on behalf of the public interest, stewardship, and quality.

The accountable nonprofit is also responsible for the following:

Mission fulfillment
- doing what it says it will do
- maintaining relevance by meeting needs in a changing environment

Leadership on behalf of the public interest
- enhancing the well-being of communities and society
- promoting inclusiveness, pluralism, and diversity within society
- educating the public, business, nonprofit organizations, and government, including appropriate advocacy and lobbying

Stewardship
- maintaining effective governance and management
- generating adequate resources, managing resources effectively, supporting and recognizing volunteers, and appropriately compensating staff
- avoiding conflict of interest and abuse of power

Quality
- striving for and achieving excellence in all aspects of the organization
- evaluating the total organization and its outcomes on an ongoing basis

Source: Courtesy of the Association of Fundraising Professionals (AFP), Arlington, Virginia.

cost money. Organizations can be fined for failure to file documents, be distracted by avoidable internal disputes, or be sued for failure to follow the applicable rules and laws. Second, noncompliance can cost an organization its good reputation. Third, related to these two reasons, noncompliance can cost an organization its effectiveness at securing future board members, program partners, and funds from the community. And finally, compliance is not particularly expensive, especially when compared to noncompliance. Nonprofit leaders that guide their organizations to serve charitable and educational purposes also have the opportunity—and some may say the obligation—to position their organization not only for minimal legal compliance, but to be a legal role model.

Today, nonprofits are operating in an environment of heightened expectations and accountability. An organization's failure to meet these expectations is increasingly likely to become known and can erode the confidence of its potential funders and supporters and invite government enforcement or audits. At a larger level, the nonprofit sector's failure to meet these expectations could invite the government to introduce new legal requirements and the bureaucratic compliance assurances that often accompany those requirements.

In Appendix 1–B, Peter Wolk highlights the most important steps nonprofit organizations should take to satisfy and exceed applicable legal expectations. It is presented in the form of an annotated checklist to identify and explain the salient points as a self-assessment so you can determine your organization's legal readiness to receive and properly expend gifts, grants, and other funding.

ETHICAL STANDARDS AND PRACTICES

As mentioned earlier in this chapter, a recent study showed that public confidence and trust in nonprofit organizations can often be related to the latest activities of nationally known organizations reported in the news. Because we rarely know when such news stories will appear, it is critical that a nonprofit organization establish ethical standards and practices to ensure maintaining the public trust. The Donor Bill of Rights in Appendix 1–A sets out key donor-focused guiding principles that today's donors expect from the organizations they support. A number of nonprofit boards of directors are taking an important step by adopting the Donor Bill of Rights as the ethical foundation of their development programs.

Nonprofits that practice ethical fundraising do the following:

- focus on the organization's mission
- educate as to their capacity to be effective
- are truthful in requests for funds
- use gifts for the purposes they are given
- respect confidentiality of information about gifts and donors

Staff whose primary role is raising funds must play a leading role in ensuring that their nonprofit organizations solicit funds ethically and legally. They serve as stewards to be certain that the intent of the donor is honestly fulfilled, which is why AFP adopted a Code of Ethical Principles for its members in 1964 and keeps it updated to reflect the latest best practices (see Chapter 18, Working with Consultants, Exhibit 18–5 for complete code). To become a member of AFP, an individual must agree to uphold the code by signing the membership form. Every year members recommit to complying with the code when they renew their membership.

Standards of professional practice focus on the following:

- not engaging in activities that will harm the organization, clients, or profession
- not exploiting relationships with various constituencies to benefit the member or member's organization
- complying with all applicable laws
- ensuring all solicitation materials are accurate and reflect the organization's mission, contributions are used in accordance with donors' intentions, and donors receive correct advice about value and tax implication of gifts
- understanding that donor information is privileged and should not be used to benefit other organizations
- not accepting compensation on the basis of percentage of contributions

Nonprofit leaders should encourage members of their development staff to join AFP and adhere to its code of ethics.

The American tradition of philanthropy enables the nonprofit sector to make a difference in people's lives, not only in the United States but indeed around the world. This tradition will endure if organizations are transparent in their actions, accountable to the public and their donors, and practice ethical fundraising.

REFERENCES

Association of Fundraising Professionals. www.afpnet.org, Public confidence in charities rebounds slightly. The Accountable Non-Profit Organization also on AFP Web site.

Corporation for National and Community Service. *Volunteer Growth in America: A Review of Trends Since 1974.* Washington, DC: U.S. Government Printing Office, 2006.

Giving USA Foundation. *Giving USA 2008.* Glenview, IL.

Levy, B.R., ed. *The AFP fundraising dictionary.* Association of Fundraising Professionals: Arlington, VA, 2006.

Light, Paul. *Confidence in Charitable Organizations, 2006.* New York: NYU Wagner, 2006. Available at: http://wagner.nyu.edu/performance/confidence/charities06.pdf.

The Foundation Center. Voluntarism hits 30-year high, study finds. *Philanthropy News Digest.* www.fdncenter.org. December 7, 2006.

Wagner, L. 2002. *Careers in fundraising.* New York: John Wiley & Sons, 15.

A Donor Bill of Rights

PHILANTHROPY is based on voluntary action for the common good. It is a tradition of giving and sharing that is primary to the quality of life. To assure that philanthropy merits the respect and trust of the general public, and that donors and prospective donors can have full confidence in the not-for-profit organizations and causes they are asked to support, we declare that all donors have these rights:

I.
To be informed of the organization's mission, of the way the organization intends to use donated resources, and of its capacity to use donations effectively for their intended purposes.

II.
To be informed of the identity of those serving on the organization's governing board, and to expect the board to exercise prudent judgement in its stewardship responsibilities.

III.
To have access to the organization's most recent financial statements.

IV.
To be assured their gifts will be used for the purposes for which they were given.

V.
To receive appropriate acknowledgement and recognition.

VI.
To be assured that information about their donations is handled with respect and with confidentiality to the extent provided by law.

VII.
To expect that all relationships with individuals representing organizations of interest to the donor will be professional in nature.

VIII.
To be informed whether those seeking donations are volunteers, employees of the organization or hired solicitors.

IX.
To have the opportunity for their names to be deleted from mailing lists that an organization may intend to share.

X.
To feel free to ask questions when making a donation and to receive prompt, truthful and forthright answers.

DEVELOPED BY

Association of Fundraising Professionals (AFP)
Association for Healthcare Philanthropy (AHP)
Council for Advancement and Support of Education (CASE)
Giving Institute: Leading Consultants to Non-Profits

ENDORSED BY
(in formation)
Independent Sector
National Catholic Development Conference (NCDC)
National Committee on Planned Giving (NCPG)
Council for Resource Development (CRD)
United Way of America

Source: Courtesy of the Association of Fundraising Professionals, Arlington, Virginia.

A Checklist: Selected Legal Precautions to Protect Your Organization and Distinguish It as a Potential Recipient of Gifts and Grants

This checklist is meant to help you identify and address issues in selected areas of concern. It is not a comprehensive list of all actions an organization must take to ensure compliance with all laws, but rather is an indication of significant legal issues for your organization to address when preparing itself for the scrutiny of potential grantors, board members, and individual donors.

A. Corporate Law Considerations.

1. Articles of Incorporation.

   Corporations, including nonprofit corporations, are only permitted to engage in activities within the scope of what is described in their Articles of Incorporation. The Bylaws cannot expand the scope of activities. Are you acting within these purposes, or should you amend your Articles to accommodate an expansion of your activities?

2. Bylaws.

   Some of the messiest nonprofit court cases have involved internal disputes in nonprofits about alleged non-compliance with Bylaws. Are you following your Bylaws by providing notice, conducting meetings, permitting voting, and electing leaders as stated? Or, should you amend your Bylaws to conform to your actual practice?

3. Corporate Standing and Registered Agents.

   Nonprofit corporations must file corporate reports with their State of incorporation. In addition, they must submit an application to do business in any other State where they have an office, and then file corporate reports thereafter. These report forms are sent to your organization's registered agent. Be sure that the registered agent on file for your organization is still at the listed address and is reliable. Otherwise, your organization might miss the report filing deadline and (worse!) could be sued by process served on your registered agent and lose a lawsuit without ever knowing about it. You can file with the State to change your registered agent.

4. Board Minutes.

   Every nonprofit corporation must keep minutes of its Board meetings. At a minimum, these minutes only have to identify the meeting, its time, the attendees, that a quorum attended, and any decisions made at the meeting. However, you may want to describe activity related to decisions (e.g., "after considerable debate, or following a committee report, the Board voted to approve...") to indicate the Board's attention to a particular issue. You do not have to—and really should not—tape record and treat each spoken word at your Board meeting as part of your Board minutes. Your minutes should be approved at the subsequent meeting. If you use an Executive Committee, it's a good idea to report its decisions to the Board and include them in the Board minutes.

B. Tax Considerations.

5. Form 1023 Tax Exemption Application.

   To obtain 501(c)(3) status, your organization filed Form 1023. In it, you described the intended activities, and based upon that description, the status was granted. If you have begun activities other than what was described, you have to disclose that on your Form 990 return, and if the changes are outside of the type of activities described in Form 1023, might have to obtain subsequent IRS approval of the new activities.

Source: © 2006. Peter C. Wolk, Esquire.

6. IRS 501(c)(3) Recognition Letter: Advance Rulings; Definitive Rulings.

 Please be sure that you have either a Definitive Ruling from the IRS, or an Advance Ruling whose date has not expired. Virtually all 501(c)(3) public charities begin with advance rulings but if they fail to file Form 8734 within the deadline after their Advance Ruling period expires, they can be reclassified by the IRS as 501(c)(3) private foundations.

7. Donor Substantiation/Quid Pro Quo.

 When we receive financial support, we have to comply with the tax rules on charitable substantiation, as follows. If a 501(c)(3) donor receives any goods or services in exchange for a donation over $75, the charity must tell the donor *in writing* in advance what portion of the donation is tax deductible. (E.g, Invitation to a Fundraising Dinner: "Amounts in excess of $60, the fair market value of this evening's dinner, are tax deductible.") With any charitable donation of $250 or more, the donor must have written substantiation or is prohibited from taking a charitable deduction for the donation. (A canceled check is not a sufficient receipt.)

8. Auctions and Raffles.

 The price paid at an auction must be over the Fair Market Value (FMV) of the item in order to be considered a contribution. If the price is under the FMV, nothing is deductible. If the contribution is for more than $75 and is greater then the FMV, then a disclosure statement is necessary. The purchase of raffle or lottery tickets is not deductible regardless of whether or not you win because the entire price of the ticket is considered a payment for services received—the opportunity to win a prize.

9. Lobbying.

 Your 501(c)(3) organization is permitted to lobby to an "insubstantial" degree. If you engage in lobbying, you should: (a) have a policy identifying who is authorized to speak on behalf of the organization and who decides which positions the organization will take; and (b) consider making the 501(h) Election (IRS Form 5768) so that only your lobbying expenditures, and not your volunteers' lobbying efforts, will be counted toward the "insubstantial" limit.

10. Campaign Activity.

 Your 501(c)(3) organization is <u>prohibited</u> from taking positions for or against any candidates for public office. You should have a policy to that effect, and advise your organizational leaders. Violation could cost your organization its 501(c)(3) its tax exemption.

11. State Tax Exemptions.

 Just as individuals pay State income taxes (in most States), so do corporations. But unlike commercial corporations, charitable organizations can obtain exemption from paying income tax and from paying sales tax on their purchases. You should obtain a copy of your States' tax exemption application and pursue both exemptions.

12. Private Inurement: Doing Business With Directors.

 You must treat doing business with directors as conflicts of interest. You must remove the conflicted Director from the balance of discussion and any voting on the issue. If Directors knowingly give another Director (or another organizational insider, such as a current or former leader) more in value than what the organization is receiving (e.g., spend more to buy computers from a Director's company than are available from other retailers or sources) the Board members conferring, and the Director receiving, the undue benefit can be held personally liable by the IRS under the Intermediate Sanctions law. Be sure to comparison shop and document your spending decisions before doing business with a Director.

13. Unrelated Business Income Taxation ("UBIT").

 For many groups, their financial future—and therefore their existence—is linked to their ability to diversify their funding sources. Your organization may be engaged in limited, substantial, or no revenue generation, but would benefit from such additional revenue. Knowing the law related to taxation of funds generated from activities unrelated to your mission can help you to either restructure your activities or to find exceptions that will allow your group to avoid taxation (and therefore save up to 35%; i.e., 35 cents from every dollar earned!). You may also find opportunities to license your name to generate untaxed royalty revenue (i.e., T-shirts, educational products, credit cards). You can pursue activities that are taxable, and just plan to pay taxes on that revenue (e.g., revenue from advertising on a website); you will have more revenue than when you started. However, such unrelated business activity can not be more than an insubstantial part of your group's work (or your group will change from nonprofit to for-profit, or have to move the unrelated activity into a for-profit subsidiary).

14. Form 990.

 Every 501(c)(3) nonprofit organization with more than $25,000 in income has to complete and file form 990 with the IRS. In it, among the most important points, the organization discloses: a) details about its financial activity; b) its fundraising costs (in ratio to the amounts spent on its mission and program); c) a description of the costs and outcomes of your programmatic efforts; d) compensation of the Directors, officers, and key employees. Beginning in 2008, even those groups that do not normally have $25,000 in income will be asked by the IRS to complete and submit what is being called a "990 Postcard Return." This is being used to identify which 501(c)(3) groups are still in existence (albeit with income normally less than $25,000) versus those that are no longer in existence at all. If your group does not receive such a form from the IRS, you will be able to retrieve it from the IRS website (www.irs.gov) for submission to the IRS.

15. Federal Tax Guidelines on Corporate Sponsorships.

Today, corporate contributions are an important source of funds. Typically, the corporate donor wants recognition of its donation. But there are rules about what and how the nonprofit can provide the recognition.

1. Corporation	supports ($$$) the Nonprofit organization	= OKAY
2. Nonprofit	acknowledges the Corporation's support by mentioning the donor's logo, locations, telephone numbers, and value-neutral descriptions of the donor's product/services	= OKAY it remains a nontaxable donation
3. Nonprofit	makes statements of comparison (e.g., this cola is the best"), price information (e.g., computers from our sponsor cost only $599), endorsement nonprofit's ("our favorite"), inducement or a call to ("buy one today!") taxable as advertising revenue	= NOT OKAY If the nonprofit does this, the actions are are considered advertising and the sponsorship amount becomes taxable.

   (a) Other examples:

   1. A 501(c)(3) organization organizes a marathon and walkathon at which it serves drinks and other refreshments provided by a national corporation. It recognizes the assistance of the corporation by listing the name of the corporation in promotional fliers, in newspaper advertisements, on T-shirts worn by participants, and by acknowledging prizes provided by the sponsor. The organization even changes the name of its event to include the name of the sponsor. These activities are acknowledgments of the sponsorship and not advertising.

   2. A local record shop supports your nonprofit organization's educational event in the park. You broadcast during the event: *This program has been underwritten by the Record Shop, where you can find all of your great hit music. The Record Shop is located at 123 Main Street. Give them a call today at 555-1234.* Because of encouraging people to call the Shop, the donation received from the record shop has to be treated as advertising and is taxable!

C. Other State and Federal Statutory Requirements.

16. Charitable Registrations.

As you may well know (and as noted in Appendix A in this book), over 40 States require nonprofits to register before seeking donations from citizens, corporations, and/or foundations in their State. A complete list of these requirements is kept quite current at www.nasconet.org.

17. Sarbanes-Oxley (SOX) Requirements.

This is a federal law that applies mainly to for-profit, publicly-traded organizations. Two provisions apply also to nonprofits. Your organization is expected to have a policy and procedures about:

a) Document/Records Retention and Destruction; and

b) Whistleblowers (to investigate complaints by—and prevent retaliation against—whistleblowers).

18. Sarbanes-Oxley (SOX): Suggested Actions.

Additional SOX requirements are being voluntarily adopted by nonprofits, making them the new de facto standards by which funders are evaluating grant applicants:

a) Have a Board audit committee:

   1) Choose the auditor.
   2) Have at least one member who is financially literate.
   3) Meet directly with the auditor, including at least once without the Executive Director.
   4) Have members who are not compensated by the organization in any capacity.

b) Use auditors who:

   1) Provide no, or limited consulting services to the organization.
   2) Meet with the audit committee for at least one meeting about the audit without the Executive Director present.
   3) Rotate the auditing partner every five–ten years.

c) Have a conflict of interest policy;

d) Prohibit loans or credit to any Directors, Officers, or organizational Executives;

e) Have adequate insurance and bonding for risks and to trigger volunteer immunity statutes;

f) Carefully develop corporate minutes;

g) Have the CEO and CFO certify:

    1) That the financial statements accurately depict the financial condition of the organization.

    2) That there are adequate internal controls regarding the handling of funds.

19. State Ethics Laws:

(1) California has gone beyond the Sarbanes-Oxley law and enacted a State law called The California Nonprofit Integrity Act of 2004, that:

    a) Requires groups with over $2M in gross revenues to:

        1) Have <u>and publicly-disclose</u> a financial audit;

        2) Have compensation of CEO and CFO approved by the Board or an authorized committee as just and reasonable.

    b) Requires there to be an audit committee:

        1) Whose chair is not a member of the finance committee, and 50% of whose members are not on the finance committee.

        2) That excludes staff and anyone with material interest in the organization to serve on the audit committee.

        3) Whose members, if paid, are paid no more than the amounts received by Directors for service on the Board.

        4) That recommends and negotiates the compensation of the independent auditor.

        5) That confers with the auditor and determines whether to accept the audit.

        6) Approves performance of any non-audit services provided by the audit firm.

    c) California is seeking to apply the Nonprofit Integrity Act to all charitable organizations conducting activities, qualified to do business, or holding property in California, but it does not apply to educational institutions, hospitals, cemeteries, and religious organizations.

(2) Other Ethics Laws: While New York's Attorney General, now Governor, Elliott Spitzer attempted (so far unsuccessfully) to have nonprofit integrity legislation enacted. In addition, the U.S. Senate Finance Committee members have held hearings and produced draft legislation—with the IRS—on nonprofit integrity. Proposed bills are expected.

    →   To exceed expectations, voluntarily comply with the California law.

(3) Other Nonprofit Governance Initiatives: Independent Sector established a Panel that has studied and made recommendations about procedures and additional requirements for charitable organizations. These recommendations can be obtained by going to www.independentsector.org.

D. Employment Considerations.

20. Employment Policies/Manual.

Perhaps the greatest source of liability for nonprofits is in the area of employment. You should be sure to have an employment manual that identifies those who are employed at-will, and that has policies with respect to their benefits, rights, and obligations.

21. Classifying Employees as Exempt/Non-Exempt.

If your employee is not an executive, administrative, professional, computer, or outside sales person as defined by the Fair Labor Standards Act, they are covered by (non-exempt from) the requirement that you pay overtime (time and a half) for more than 40 hours worked in any work week. If you think an IRS audit sounds bad, you don't want to go through a wage and hour audit, particularly if you do not have records showing that your non-exempt employees worked no more than 40 hours per week (or were paid overtime for doing so). If a covered employee works over 40 hours in a week, giving comp time the following week does not remove the employer's obligation to pay overtime pay.

22. Training about acceptable and unlawful application, screening, interviewing, hiring, promoting, terminating questions, criteria, and procedures.

23. Sexual Harassment avoidance training.

24. Classifying Workers as Independent Contractors Instead of Employees.

An employer has less financial paperwork to do if a worker is as an independent contractor instead of an employee, but not everyone qualifies as an independent contractor. Instead of withholding and making monthly or quarterly payments to the IRS, you only file one form (Form 1099) once at the end of the year, with a cover report form to the IRS. However, the IRS has rules on its website about when we can treat someone as an independent contractor. If we control aspects of where, when, and how workers do their work, they are likely to be employees and the employer must engage in the withholding, payments, and periodic reports to the IRS.

25. Insurance.

There are two main kinds of elective insurance for nonprofits: Comprehensive General Liability (CGL) Insurance and Directors and Officers (D&O) Insurance, which typically includes Employment Practices Insurance. Be sure your insurance agent is briefed on the scope of your operations (e.g., do you need publication insurance?) and that your staff and Board have worked together to secure the advisable insurance coverage that you can afford.

E.   Operational Considerations.

26. Conflict of Interest Policy.
    As noted above, your organization should have a conflict of interest policy that: (a) identifies conflicts of interest; (b) requires organizational leaders (Directors and key employees) to disclose if a conflict arises; (c) requires the Board (for Director conflicts) or the Executive Director (for employee conflicts) to determine how much the conflicted person can participate in the consideration and decision-making about the issue.

27. Intellectual Property Policy.
    Your employee handbook should explain that creations (e.g, articles, artwork, designs, web content) done by your employees within the scope of their duties are considered works for hire and owned by your organization. For those done outside the scope of their duties, you should have a policy and procedure for your employees (and volunteers) to assign their rights to your organization.

28. Financial Controls. Have you put into place arrangements for:

    a. The Board to review and approve the budget;
    b. Bonding (insurance against employee theft of organizational funds);
    c. Limits and procedures on check- and contract-signing authority; and,
    d. Handling of restricted funds.

29. Publications and Branding. Has your organization taken action to:

    a. Get assurances that authors' work is original and not infringing others' copyrights;
    b. Assert copyright protection over your organization's works; and,
    c. Secure ownership via trademark registration of the name(s) and logos by which your organization and its goods and services are known to others.

30. Internet Activities. Have you made provisions for:

    a. Copyright notices of the material on your website;
    b. User Agreements and disclaimers to avoid liability;
    c. Sufficient security to protect the privacy of your users/members' information and any transactional (i.e., internet sales activity) information.

Chapter 2

The Many Roles of Board, Staff, and Volunteers in Fundraising

CHAPTER OUTLINE

- Selection of Volunteers
- Volunteer Job Descriptions
- Knowing Who You Need on Your Board
- What to Look for When Recruiting Board Members
- Job Descriptions for Board Members
- Setting Clear Goals and Expectations for the Board
- Working with an Existing Board
- Techniques to Motivate the Board into Action

- Board Training and Development
- Advisory Committees to Boards for Fundraising
- Evaluating Board Members' Effectiveness
- How to Retire a Board Member
- Role of Staff in Fundraising
- Communications Between Board and Staff
- Staff Expectations for Board Members
- Board Members' Expectations for Staff

KEY VOCABULARY

- Advisory Committee
- Corporate Advisory Boards
- Corporate Advisory Programs
- Diversity
- Industry Councils
- Prospect
- The Three G's
- The Three W's
- Volunteer Bill of Rights

SELECTION OF VOLUNTEERS

Fundraising requires the use of volunteers at every level, from running the special event to chairing the board of the organization. Volunteers work with staff for the betterment of the organization, whether programmatically or financially. Just as well-trained staff perform their jobs better than staff who are untrained, volunteers who are trained will be more successful—and happier—than those who are left to their own devices. Therefore, it is as important to develop professional volunteers as it is to provide enrichment to the best professional staff.

Before individuals even begin to volunteer their time for an institution, they should be given job descriptions as well as information about the organization. If they are being asked to represent the organization to the public, they should be well-versed on the history, mission, vision, goals, and objectives of the organization and the department or event for which they will be volunteering. If they are serving on the board, they must be able to guide the organization to

> *Just as well-trained staff perform their jobs better than staff who are untrained, volunteers who are trained will be more successful—and happier—than those who are left to their own devices.*

the best of their abilities. Providing volunteers with appropriate information will make them more competent and thus more successful in their chosen volunteer roles.

Why People Volunteer

Most people volunteer because they are asked by a friend. They find fulfillment in the social interaction that volunteering can provide. Others are motivated by something in which they strongly believe. Perhaps they have had a friend or relative suffer from a disease, and they decide to volunteer in honor or memory of that person. Yet, others may volunteer because they desire to affect change. This often is the case for volunteering in political races. Older individuals often volunteer to learn new skills that could potentially lead to a new career for them.

Selecting the right volunteer for an organization or project is just as important as selecting the right person to fill a staff position. Just as people select careers for different reasons, so too do they volunteer for different reasons. The late Susan Church, a well-respected fundraising consultant in Chicago, stated, "It is worth spending some time thinking about why people volunteer at all. Motives vary somewhat from person to person, but generally people volunteer for one or more of the following reasons:

- They want to make a contribution to a cause in which they believe.
- They feel they need to fulfill business and/or social expectations.
- They are motivated by a desire for change.
- They want to have a sense of ownership and control that they can't find in a work situation.
- They want to learn new skills.
- They want to have fun and enjoy what they are about to do.

No longer is the average volunteer white, female, upper middle class, married, and nonworking. Today, volunteers come from a variety of backgrounds and include retirees (younger today than before because of military retirements, early retirement packages offered by corporations, and early retirement due to exorbitant wealth made in the stock market), minorities, youths, and even many of the actively employed. In the past, women were usually directed toward volunteering in hospitals or libraries whereas men sat on the boards of prep schools, colleges, universities, and major community charities. Women joined the Junior League, the PEO sisterhood, women's clubs, and other like organizations whereas men often volunteered under the auspices of membership clubs such as the Elks, Lions, Shriners, Rotary, and Kiwanis. Only when a community crisis or disaster brought them together did men and women tend to volunteer jointly for a cause. However, like the stereotypical roles in the workplace, the gender-specific roles of volunteering largely have disappeared. Service clubs are open to both sexes, and men are volunteering for organizations once thought to be solely of interest to women, while women are asking for money to support the organizations for which they volunteer, just like men did in the past.

Volunteerism is at the heart and soul of American culture. According to *The Chronicle of Philanthropy*, nearly half of all Americans (48 percent) volunteer! Some states even have offices and officials assigned to encourage volunteerism. The Web site listing state offices or centers of volunteerism appears in Appendix 2–A. The Web site was developed by the Points of Light Foundation, a nonprofit organization in Washington, DC, that encourages people to volunteer their help to charities. Appendix 2–B lists the state offices of volunteer service commissions developed by the Corporation for National Service.

Volunteering is considered unique to the culture of the United States. Europeans are less likely to volunteer than Americans, as are Asians, Africans, South Americans, and Australians. In a survey of nine European countries conducted for the Volunteer Center U.K. in London, about 27 percent of Europeans said they had volunteered to help a charitable cause. European attitudes toward volunteering diverged sharply from one country to the next, stemming from differences in the ways that each country developed politically, socially, and culturally.

> *Volunteerism is at the heart and soul of American culture.*

Currently, volunteerism in the United States is increasing among individuals in their twenties. The increase has been attributed to the growing number of members of this generation who live at home and thus have more wealth (money not spent on room and board) and time to volunteer (time not spent on homemaking). Also, this group has been raised by parents who, for the most part, have been more socially conscious than generations before and have encouraged their children to become involved in causes.

Whatever the motivating factors—nationality, sex, race, religion, or interests—of the potential volunteers, one thing they all have in common is the need to be recruited. The number of volunteer opportunities abound, and successful programs are looking for volunteers in new places, such as the Internet.

VOLUNTEER JOB DESCRIPTIONS

To recruit and keep volunteers, a detailed position description needs to be written. Job descriptions give volunteers ideas of definite work needed by the organization and provide the volunteer director with a guide for recruitment. Ask colleagues in similar nonprofit organizations for samples of their volunteer job descriptions. Then, ask those volunteers currently doing the work to help develop the description. Be sure to list the location, specific skills, and time needed to complete the job successfully. By listing the qualifications that are required as well as the number of hours/days expected, volunteers can self-select. If possible, divide the job into short- and long-term volunteer opportunities. It may be possible to find more than one person to undertake short-term commitments than to find just one to undertake a long-term volunteer role. For an example of a job description, refer to Exhibit 2–1.

In marketing your volunteer opportunities, make sure to include the advantages of volunteering for the organization. Use quotes from current volunteers and make sure those interested in volunteering meet with some of the organization's current volunteers during a volunteer open house. This gives prospective volunteers an opportunity to ask questions, to see the variety of volunteers on board, and to gain a better feel for the organization. Also, publicly recognizing and honoring volunteers who have done an exemplary job for the organization can help to focus positive attention on the organization and to recruit additional volunteers.

Exhibit 2–1 Job Description for the Arizona Children's Home Foundation Board of Trustees

Responsibilities:
- Review and approve the mission for this board.
- Serve as advisors for the positioning of the Arizona Children's Home Association (ACHA) in each community.
- Work with the support of the Executive Director and the Chief Executive Officer to sustain fundraising programs.
- For ACHA services, including such activities as:
  Prospect Identification
  Prospect Review
  Prospect Cultivation
  Prospect Solicitation
- Support the advocacy efforts of the ACHA Board of Directors.
- Develop a strategy, with the support of the Executive Director and development staff, for implementing a $5 million campaign by the year 2000.
- Respond to community interests and needs as related to the welfare of children in Arizona and the possible involvement of the ACHA.

The Mission:
The mission of this board is to generate funding to enable the Arizona Children's Home Association to provide therapy and services that will foster healing and promote the emotional well-being of families and children in Arizona.

Source: Courtesy of the Arizona Children's Home Foundation, Tucson, Arizona.

Criteria for Nomination:
- Individuals with visibility in the state and demonstrated commitment to children and families.
- Dedication to providing the optimum treatment programs for all children and families in need.
- Individuals with influence and ability to facilitate significant gifts.
- Individuals who represent cultural and ethnic diversity.

Member Responsibilities:
- Attendance at an orientation meeting or board retreat.
- Attendance at quarterly meetings.
- Commitment to serve on at least one committee.
- Willingness to serve as an advocate for the Arizona Children's Home Association.
- Involvement with the public relations program in your community.
- Commitment of an annual personal and/or corporate gift to the Foundation.
- Willingness to engage in friend raising and fundraising for ACHA.
- Participation in the annual Board evaluation.

Terms of Service:
- Each member will be eligible to serve three consecutive three-year terms. After three terms, a one-year hiatus is required before re-election.

Some say clever marketing devices or staff are the best recruiters of volunteers for an organization. The truth is that volunteers recruit other volunteers. Active, positive volunteers, excited about the work they are doing, will interest others in volunteering for the organization or the cause much more quickly

> *The truth is that volunteers recruit other volunteers.*

than ads placed in newspapers, announcements on the radio, or other traditional techniques. Personal contact is the best way in which to recruit volunteers. Most people won't say no when asked to volunteer by someone they know and respect, no matter what the cause!

Flexible time is especially important to volunteers today. Because many volunteers are employed full time, they must be able to fit their volunteer efforts into already tight schedules. Thus, they seek shorter term opportunities and may be drawn to organizations that offer them the opportunity to learn new skills. To attract these volunteers, organizations must eliminate barriers that would make them reluctant to volunteer. Important and insightful information on recruiting, training, motivating, and retaining volunteers may be obtained from the state office or center of volunteerism (Appendices 2–A and 2–B).

Fundraising Volunteers

If the goal is to find volunteers to assist in fundraising, make sure that this is stated up front. Also, provide volunteers with a job description. Include with the job description a copy of the Volunteer Bill of Rights (Exhibit 2–2). Susan Church always reminded development staff to increase volunteer leadership and participation in fundraising, development officers should do the following:

- Help provide a climate in which fundraising is a logical outgrowth of an exciting and productive organization's program;
- Ensure that volunteers are involved with other aspects of the organization—programs, policy development, etc.—along with fundraising;
- Recruit an ally (or allies) from the volunteer group to spearhead the revision of volunteer job descriptions and recruiting policies with special attention to specific expectations about fundraising;
- Ask volunteers to do what volunteers do best—don't waste the volunteers' limited time on work done more appropriately by staff;
- Give volunteers what they need to succeed (materials, training, practice, and recognition);
- Respect volunteer time—make requests specific and reasonable;
- Have a written fundraising plan, developed with volunteer participation. This plan should be specific as to what volunteers will do (and when) and what will be handled by staff; and
- Define success correctly. A volunteer who makes five calls that result in refusals is not a failure. He or she is a fundraiser.

Exhibit 2–2 Volunteer Bill of Rights

1. The right to be treated as a co-worker, not just as free help, not as a prima donna.
2. The right to a suitable assignment, with consideration for personal preference, temperament, life experience, education, and employment background.
3. The right to know as much about the organization as possible—its policies, its people, its programs.
4. The right to training for the job, thoughtfully planned and effectively presented training.
5. The right to continuing education on the job—as a follow-up to initial training—including information about new developments and training for greater responsibility.
6. The right to sound guidance and direction by someone who is experienced, well informed, patient, and thoughtful, and who has the time to invest in giving guidance.
7. The right to a place to work—an orderly, designated place, conducive to work and worthy of the job to be done.
8. The right to promotion and a variety of experiences—through advancement to assignments of more responsibility, through transfer from one activity to another, through special assignments.
9. The right to be heard—to have a part in planning, to feel free to make suggestions, to have respect shown for an honest opinion.
10. The right to recognition, in the form of promotion and awards, through day-by-day expressions of appreciation, and by being treated as a bona fide co-worker.

Source: Reprinted with permission from the Points of Light Foundation, 2007. For more information, call (202) 729-8000 or visit www.pointsoflight.org.

KNOWING WHO YOU NEED ON YOUR BOARD

Just as it is important to know how to recruit volunteers, it is equally important to know what to look for when recruiting volunteers for an organization's board. It is not always easy to identify potential board members, and in smaller communities, many organizations are competing for the same people. An article by Jacklyn P. Boice in *Advancing Philanthropy* (January/February 2006) referencing the Deloitte Volunteer IMPACT survey,

> revealed that 86 percent of employed Americans said volunteering can have a positive impact on their careers. Nearly four out of five respondents (78 percent) see volunteering as an opportunity to develop business skills including decision making, problem solving, and negotiating. Furthermore, of those respondents who serve on a nonprofit board of directors, nearly three-quarters (73 percent) strongly agreed that volunteering offers the opportunity to enhance leadership skills.

In the same article, Boice quotes Alice Korngold, author of *Leveraging Good Will: Strengthening Nonprofits by Engaging Businesses*, who states: "People looking to serve on a board are not just looking for something to add to their resume. In almost every case, they want to make a meaningful contribution and add value to the organization. They do not want to just write a check. They want to advance a cause they care about." In Exhibit 2–3, Korngold lists five tips for those thinking of serving on a nonprofit board.

Most board members are recruited for their wealth, but not all effective board members are wealthy. A successful board will comprise a diverse group of multi-talented people who have a variety of backgrounds, a strong desire to serve, and a keen interest in the organization.

Adding Diversity

As important as it is to have diversity on the board, it is equally important to be aware of all types of diversity. Diversity does not just mean ethnic backgrounds. It also means age, sex, geography, and economic levels. A successful board will comprise a diverse group of multi-talented people who have a variety of backgrounds, a strong desire to serve, and a keen interest in the organization.

> *Just as it is important to know how to recruit volunteers, it is equally important to know what to look for when recruiting volunteers for an organization's board.*

When selecting potential board members, be sure to include the following in the review and analysis.

Economic Diversity

Most board members are recruited for their wealth, but not all effective board members are wealthy. Although most board members are recruited on their ability to "give and get," not being wealthy should not keep someone from being on a fundraising committee or a nonprofit board. Having the insight of those from different backgrounds can provide fresh points of view. Working-class individuals have a lot to offer to a board, especially a different perspective.

Exhibit 2–3 Five Tips for Serving on a Nonprofit Board

1. Understand the mission and care about it.
2. Know what is being asked of you and understand what you are getting into—strategically, financially, and in terms of time required.
3. Know where the money comes from. Don't be afraid to ask!
4. Get a feel for the culture of the organization—attend a fundraising event, sit in on a board meeting, etc. Get to know the people involved.
5. Be prepared to be generous and make a difference and have a good time!

Source: Reprinted with permission by the Association of Fundraising Professionals (AFP) from the article "Top Notch" by Jacklyn P. Boice in *Advancing Philanthropy* (Jan/Feb 2006). List originally appeared in the book *Leveraging Good Will: Strengthening Nonprofits by Engaging Business* by Alice Korngold (Jossey-Bass, 2005).

Sex

Is there a fairly equal representation of women and men on the board? How will the rotation pattern of the term limits affect this representation? Has a list been composed of qualified candidates of both sexes?

Age

What is the average age of the current board members? Is there a balance between young, middle-aged, and senior members? What is the age of those who will be leaving the board each year as their terms expire? Have candidates of similar ages to those who have left or of ages needed to balance the representation on the board been identified to fill open positions?

Race or Ethnic Origin

Has a conscious effort been made to balance the membership of the board to reflect the race or ethnicity of the organization's membership or constituents? Have those of a different race or ethnicity who have the skills and qualities needed by your board to meet its mission been sought? Have individuals of different races and ethnic origins been identified to fill positions of current board members whose terms next expire? Are there board members who represent African Americans, Native Americans, Caucasians, Asians, Hispanics, Pacific Islanders, etc.?

Geographic Representation

Have members been selected from all parts of the United States or the world? Do the board members represent the geographic distribution of the organization's membership or constituents?

Expertise

Do the board members have the expertise needed to run the organization? Is there someone with a legal background? Is there a professional fundraiser? Does someone have a background in personnel management or human resources to assist in dealing with personnel issues? Is there a public relations or communications professional? Are there representatives from the community's corporate world?

Access

Do the board members have access to people with wealth? Are they leaders in the community and able to open doors to other leaders, groups, corporations, and foundations that can assist the organization?

WHAT TO LOOK FOR WHEN RECRUITING BOARD MEMBERS

Probably the most effective way to identify new board members is to ask those currently serving on the board who they think would make good board members. Give them an idea of the type of persons hoped to be recruited for the upcoming openings. List any desired age, sex, race, and geographic characteristics as well as the skills and access being sought. The number of potential board members identified by the current board probably will be surprising. Staff recommendations are another source of leads, as are recommendations by former clients of the organization.

Some boards have a nominating committee whose sole responsibility is to identify potential board members. It seeks recommendations from community and civic leaders, from other professionals in the field, and from active board members of similar organizations; it even invites the organization's constituencies to send in nominations. Often a questionnaire similar to Exhibit 2–4 is used.

JOB DESCRIPTIONS FOR BOARD MEMBERS

All volunteers, whether the board chair or "envelope stuffers," need to receive job descriptions. Just as a staff person would never be hired without a job description, a volunteer should never be brought on to do a task without a clearly defined written role.

> *All volunteers, whether the board chair or "envelope stuffers," need to receive job descriptions.*

Job descriptions give volunteers ideas of definite work needed by the organization and provide the volunteer director with a guide for recruitment. For an example of a job description, refer to Exhibit 2–1 and to Appendix 2–C. Also, it is important to be able to evaluate a volunteer's work. Having a written job description allows the volunteer's progress (or lack of progress) and successes and failures to be discussed. In addition, by reviewing a job description in advance, a volunteer is in a position to decide whether the project matches his or her skills or interests. It is better to know this in the beginning than after the project has begun, when it would be necessary to replace the volunteer and train someone new.

All volunteers should be interviewed to determine their interests, knowledge of the organization, skills, work habits, and attitudes. (Refer to Exhibit 2–5 for an example of a volunteer assessment form.) The interviewing may be done by the director of volunteers, if the organization is large enough to have a position such as this, or by the staff person needing the volunteers. It is imperative that the volunteers and staff supervising them have a good working rapport. The staff must be able to lead and motivate the volunteers, and those volunteering their time must feel positive and enthusiastic about the organization and its staff to work effectively. Just as members of the professional staff need to feel proud of their position within the organization, so, too, do the volunteers. Just as members of the staff need to be stimulated to maintain their motivation, so, too, do the volunteers. Just as members of the staff want to be promoted, so, too, do the volunteers. When establishing a volunteer program, approach the project as if new staff were being hired. Go through all of the

Exhibit 2–4 Board of Directors Member Questionnaire

NAME _____

HOME ADDRESS _____

CITY/STATE/ZIP CODE _____

TELEPHONE _____ FAX _____

E-MAIL ADDRESS _____

EMPLOYER _____

TITLE _____

OFFICE ADDRESS _____

_____

_____

CITY/STATE/ZIP _____

TELEPHONE _____ FAX _____

E-MAIL ADDRESS _____

PREVIOUS EMPLOYMENT DURING LAST TEN YEARS

          POSITION   COMPANY   LOCATION

_____

_____

_____

_____

_____

EDUCATION

SCHOOL/COLLEGE/UNIVERSITY/LOCATION/YEARS ATTENDED/DEGREES

_____

_____

_____

_____

HONORS/ACHIEVEMENTS

_____

_____

_____

_____

continues

Exhibit 2–4 Board of Directors Member Questionnaire (continued)

SOCIAL AFFILIATIONS/CLUBS/MEMBERSHIPS

_____

_____

_____

_____

PROFESSIONAL ORGANIZATIONS

_____

_____

_____

_____

BOARD MEMBERSHIPS

_____

_____

_____

_____

OTHER VOLUNTEER ROLES

_____

_____

_____

_____

CHILDREN

    NAME   AGE   SCHOOLS ATTENDING/GRADUATED FROM

_____

_____

_____

_____

PERSONAL INTERESTS/HOBBIES

_____

_____

_____

_____

_____

Exhibit 2–5 AFP/DC Volunteer Assessment

The AFP/DC chapter is one of the most active AFP chapters in the country, and we want to make this a rewarding affiliation for you. We have lots to offer with our informative monthly luncheons, educational roundtables, current job hotline, inspiring Fundraising Days in Washington, and the list goes on. What keeps us ahead is new talent and fresh ideas. Please tell us about your interests and abilities so we can match you with an appropriate opportunity within AFP/DC.

What expertise are you willing to share and which skills do you wish to develop?
(Please check those that apply.)

	EXPERTISE	INTEREST
• Organizing	_____	_____
• Telephoning	_____	_____
• Writing	_____	_____
• Interviewing in person	_____	_____
• Design and layout	_____	_____
• Meeting the public	_____	_____
• Advocacy	_____	_____
• Recruiting others	_____	_____
• Finance	_____	_____
• Facilitating	_____	_____
• Other	_____	_____

TIME
Many members are fully active volunteers by donating as little as three hours per month.
Please indicate your availability to support AFP/DC:

1–3   4–6   6+   hours/month

Please attach business card or complete the following:

Name: _____

Title: _____

Organization: _____

Address: _____

Telephone: (W) _____ (FAX) _____ (H) _____

E-mail: _____

Source: Courtesy of Carol Shaw, Association of Fundraising Professionals DC Chapter, Washington, DC.

steps—write the job description, place the ad, interview the applicants, "hire" the person, provide the proper introductions to the organization, train the person to be equipped to handle the position, evaluate the person's performance, provide motivation, and recognize and reward success.

SETTING CLEAR GOALS AND EXPECTATIONS FOR THE BOARD

Most members of nonprofit boards have been asked to be on their boards for one of three reasons: (1) their ability to bring in wealth, (2) their wisdom, or (3) their ability to work hard for the cause. These are commonly referred to as the "three W's" in fundraising. In his book *Fund Raising: The Guide to Raising Money from Private Sources,* Thomas E. Broce (1986) lists seven qualities that he looks for in good fundraising trustees:

1. a natural relationship with or interest in the institution
2. affluence or influence
3. a willingness to contribute sacrificially
4. enough interest in the organization to be willing to ask difficult questions and ensure that members of the staff are doing their homework in all areas of management and administration

5. an ability and a willingness to communicate enthusiastically to others
6. a willingness to be well informed about the institution's history, current operations, and future goals
7. a sense of urgency about the organization's mission

"Good trustees are precious commodities," states Broce. "Do not waste active people's time with busy work and show and tell. Involve them in the life of the organization in meaningful ways, and they will respond enthusiastically."

A properly trained, organized, and structured committee of volunteers is crucial to a successful organization. Equally important is the selection of the appropriate chairperson. With proper training, the chair will be able to lead and motivate the board or committee to the betterment of the organization. A well-written job description is crucial to a well-trained chair and to the success of the committee, board, or organization. Exhibit 2–6 provides a sample of an excellent job description for the Chair of the Board. It is taken from Kenneth N. Dayton's *Governance Is Governance,* published by Independent Sector. Appendix 2–D provides more information about Mr. Dayton, Independent Sector, and how to order the publication.

WORKING WITH AN EXISTING BOARD

Most development officers inherit their board and other volunteers. They do not have the luxury of recruiting them. Unfortunately, this can also mean that the board comes with preset attitudes regarding fundraising. It may mean that they were recruited with the understanding that they were *not* to raise funds. If it appears to be the situation, then the first step is to review the written job description for the board members. If it does not specify fundraising as part of the board members' roles, then the board must be convinced that the criteria for membership and the job description both should be changed. The development officer will need to rely upon help from the chairperson or other key volunteers to change the board's attitudes.

> *Most development officers inherit their board and other volunteers. They do not have the luxury of recruiting them.*

If a board is in place and actively involved in fundraising, the job of raising dollars will be much easier for the development office staff. If members of the board accept fundraising as their responsibility but just have not been doing it, and an active fundraising committee is not in place, much more work will be required to build an active fundraising effort among the board members.

The first step for the development office is to determine if the board members are accepting and acting upon their normal duties: making decisions on policies for the organization, ensuring the financial security of the organization, providing expertise and leadership in the necessary areas, keeping abreast of the mission and goals of the organization and representing them to the public, guiding the senior management of the organization when requested, remaining knowledgeable about the duties of the various staff and departments to evaluate the effectiveness of the organization, and so on. Appendix 2–E shows a sample of a Board of Directors Governing Mission. If the board is "on top" of the basics, then the development officer can begin to determine which of the board members would best lead or assist with the board's fundraising responsibilities. Usually, one or two board members will emerge as the natural leader(s) for this role. If not, then a member must be identified who can assume leadership for

---

Exhibit 2–6 Chair of the Board Responsibilities

Function
- As chair of the board, assure that the board of trustees fulfills its responsibilities for the governance of the institution.
- Be a partner to the CEO, helping to achieve the mission of the institution.
- Optimize the relationship between the board and management.

Responsibilities
- Chair meeting of the board. See that it functions effectively, interacts with management optimally, and fulfills all of its duties. Develop agendas in conjunction with the CEO.
- With the CEO, recommend composition of the board committees. Recommend committee chairs with an eye to future succession.
- Assist the CEO in recruiting board and other talent for volunteer assignments that are needed.

- Reflect any concerns management has in regard to the role of the board of trustees or individual trustees. Reflect to the CEO the concerns of the board of trustees and other constituencies.
- Present to the board an evaluation of the pace, direction, and organizational strength of the institution.
- Prepare a review of the CEO and recommend salary for consideration by the appropriate committee.
- Annually focus the board's attention on matters of institutional governance that relate to its own structure, role, and relationship to management. Make sure the board is satisfied that it has fulfilled all of its responsibilities.
- Act as another set of eyes and ears.
- Serve as an alternate spokesperson.
- Fulfill such other assignments as the chair and CEO agree are appropriate and desirable for the chair to perform.

Source: Reprinted with permission of Independent Sector, *Governance Is Governance,* by Kenneth N. Dayton, 2001.

fundraising by helping to develop the committee or by being a liaison between the existing board and the fundraising committee of the board (when it is established).

The fundraising committee of the board should do the following: set the standard for giving by making their personal gifts first—and generously; solicit major gifts from individual members and from the leadership in the corporate and foundation world; train incoming board members to be solicitors by taking them along on fundraising calls; write solicitation letters or lend their signatures to those written by staff; chair memorial or capital campaigns, special events, or planned giving efforts; and lead other members of the board in fundraising efforts.

TECHNIQUES TO MOTIVATE THE BOARD INTO ACTION

To motivate volunteers, staff must first empower them. Provide them with the training they need to succeed, the tools required to do their job, and the staff support necessary to complete the job successfully. Give credit to the volunteers for every success. Accept blame for every failure.

Staff members must provide the leadership and structure necessary for the volunteer effort to move forward; develop job descriptions for the volunteers so their performances may be evaluated; provide the volunteers with information that will help them with their assignments; give them copies of the case statement, all fundraising literature, and the strategic plans of the organization; and share with them what they need to know and whatever else that could make their roles more substantial and fun.

> *Volunteers want to be needed and want to perform tasks that make a difference.*

Volunteers want to be needed and want to perform tasks that make a difference. Training materials for volunteer development are available from volunteer centers in most states. See Appendix 2-A for the Web site listing a national network of volunteer centers and Appendix 2-B for a list of volunteer service centers.

Because most volunteers aren't comfortable asking for money, it is important for staff to train them in fundraising techniques. Use other board members to assist in the process. Send a new volunteer on a fundraising solicitation with a board member experienced in fundraising. Explain the reasons behind the campaign and take the volunteer on a site visit to see the work of the organization. Provide leadership and training. Review the volunteer's job description with them and provide time for feedback on their performance. Ask them for feedback. Keep an open channel of communication.

Don't attempt to manipulate volunteers to advance your own agenda. Never put a volunteer in the middle of an organization's turf war. Also, don't treat volunteers as a means to an end. They need to feel that what they are doing will make a difference; otherwise, they will lose interest.

Most important, give recognition for a job well done. This can be the number one method of motivation—peer recognition!

When a board member has done an exemplary job in soliciting a prospect, share this with the other members of the fundraising committee or board. Provide a regular format for recognizing efforts of the volunteers. Write thank-you letters, place articles in the organization's newsletter, or recognize the volunteers at a special event. In some way, say thank you for a job well done.

BOARD TRAINING AND DEVELOPMENT

After identifying board members' interests and determining their qualifications, appoint them to the appropriate committees. Provide them with the appropriate job description, and then train, train, and train again. Never assume that a volunteer will know what to do because he or she has done it before. The organization's fundraising needs may be completely different from those of the organization for which the board member had previously volunteered. Thoroughly explain the mission, goals and objectives, programs, and financial needs of the organization. Explain the time commitment necessary to perform the job at the level expected.

Remind board members up front that part of their job description is to set an exemplary pace for those who will be asked to donate. Board members must be willing to give a "stretch" gift to a specific campaign, and they must be willing to give annually to the organization. The organization's commitment to fundraising must start at the board level. Again, this message can be instilled through yearly training. Don't hesitate to bring in outside resources to train board members. It is important that they develop along

> *The well-trained and motivated volunteer will be the successful volunteer.*

with the organization. Just as staff members of the organization are encouraged to continually develop in their chosen field, so should the board member be offered development opportunities. Select a motivational speaker on a topic of interest to the board or bring in an expert on planned giving to show the board that it doesn't need to be complex and that they can present the concept to prospective donors. Show the board members new ways and techniques to do their jobs well. The well-trained and motivated volunteer will be the successful volunteer.

ADVISORY COMMITTEES TO BOARDS FOR FUNDRAISING

Board members are expected to raise money for their organizations as well as to set policy. The most effective way for a board to raise money is through a development or fundraising committee. Those who have the strongest skills and interest in fundraising work with the organization's development staff to direct and focus the fundraising efforts for the other board members and committees. The members of this group should have previous fundraising experience or strong ties with the corporate community. The development staff provide professional expertise to the committee and help the committee establish

"HEEEERE WE GO. BOARD RETREAT STRENGTH PAIN RELIEVER."

Source: Copyright © Mark Litzler.

tee are from the corporate or private foundation community and are brought on specifically to help the organization increase its financial coffers. Commonly called *corporate advisory boards, corporate advisory programs,* or *industry councils,* these committees' goals are primarily of a fundraising nature but also include improving the communications network between the organization and the general public. Just as members of the board are given job descriptions, so should all members of the fundraising advisory committee be given job descriptions.

An example of a job description for a development committee can be found in Exhibit 2–7.

As mentioned before, most individuals are selected to become members of nonprofit boards because they can bring wealth, work, and wisdom to the board. You will also hear the phrase "the three G's" used in reference to nonprofit boards. The three G's are Give, Get, or Get off! Board members are expected to give of their own personal wealth, get money from others for the organization, or get off the board. Nonprofit boards cannot afford to have members who don't raise money in some way. In addition to having a job description, it is a sound idea to have all board members sign commitment forms for both the amount of money they will personally give *and* what they will solicit from others. Exhibit 2–8 provides a sample format for this form.

> *Most individuals are selected to become members of nonprofit boards because they can bring wealth, work, and wisdom to the board.*

goals. A job description should be provided to every member of the committee (as well as to all board members) so they know what is expected of them in their role as a fundraiser. In Appendix 2–F there is an article titled *Developing an Effective Fundraising Board* written by co-author Barbara L. Ciconte, CFRE. Use it as an easy reference to help build boards that are comfortable and successful at fundraising.

If the committee is large, strong, and sophisticated enough in fundraising, you may wish to establish subcommittees in specialized fundraising areas. For example, if a member of the committee has a background in banking or law and is familiar with wills, estates, and trusts, you may wish to focus his or her energies on planned giving. If another one or two members have strong ties to the corporate world, their energies might be best directed toward raising money solely from corporations. The most important point to remember is that board and committee members must know what their roles are and that these roles should not only be clearly defined but be provided to members in a written job description.

If the board does not have members with the necessary experience to raise funds effectively, it may wish to develop fundraising committees that include nonboard members. This is one way of expanding the volunteer base of the board to assist with fundraising without increasing the overall membership of the board. Usually, the members of an advisory board or a commit-

Exhibit 2–7 Job Description for a Development Committee of the Board

The nonprofit board should establish a fundraising or development committee to assist the board with its fundraising responsibilities. The committee should consist of a chair and at least three to four members, all of whom have experience in raising funds for a nonprofit entity. The Chair of the Development Committee should be a member of the organization's board, but the committee members do not need to be part of the board. The committee can be selected from the membership of the organization or identified by the chair of the development committee as individuals who would be an asset to the committee.

Responsibilities of the Development Committee include:

1) Actively promote the organization and its mission.
2) Make a personal donation of an appropriate amount each year to the organization.
3) Identify, solicit, and cultivate prospects for gifts to the organization.
4) Develop long-range and short-range fundraising goals for the organization along with the lead paid development staff person.
5) Identify prospective members for the development committee and the board.
6) Serve as an example for the board regarding fundraising, including training the board members in fundraising, if necessary.

Exhibit 2–8 Board Member Personal Financial Commitment Form

Board Member Personal Financial Commitment Form

Name: _____

Contact information: _____

My personal financial pledge for the year is $ _____.

I will pay by:

_____ Check (enclosed)

_____ Credit Card (circle one):

American Express   Master Card   Visa

Card Number: _____

Card Expiration Date: _____

Instead of one payment, I wish to make multiple payments of: _____ per:

_____ Quarter   _____ Month   _____ Week

I agree personally to raise $ _____ from others this year to help reach the development goals of the organization.

In addition to my personal gift and what I will raise from others, I agree to:

☐ Serve on one event committee per year and will solicit gifts for that event from sources both known and new to the organization.

☐ Increase the volunteer pool for the organization by identifying at least one new volunteer for the organization each year.

☐ Identify new members to serve on the board by providing at least one new name each year.

Signature: _____

Date: _____

EVALUATING BOARD MEMBERS' EFFECTIVENESS

Volunteers need feedback. They need to know if what they are doing is correct or incorrect. They need both praise and guidance. Most organizations develop and use an evaluation form with their volunteers and find that their volunteers think the effort is worthwhile. Appendix 2–G provides a sample evaluation instrument to use with a nonprofit board. Some organizations averse to "performance reviews" for volunteers call their evaluations "progress reviews." Others just don't like the term "evaluation" and instead call it "feedback." Whatever the name, evaluations are important because they help not only the volunteers but also the organization's staff. An evaluation is an opportunity for the volunteer to assess his or her own role within the organization and for the organization to assess its ability to select, guide, train, and motivate volunteers. Evaluation is a two-way street—the volunteer often sees things needing improvement that staff members don't and can help staff members redefine volunteer job descriptions that may not be manageable.

How can evaluations help remove "dead weight" from a board—the volunteer who doesn't follow through on his or her commitments or who exhibits passive-aggressive behavior? Establishing structure is the most effective way to resolve this type of problem. If there aren't board term limits, set them. If job descriptions don't exist, write them. If performance evaluations are not being done, initiate them. If every board member is evaluated according to his or her job description, and if a discussion is held regarding the progress made or not made, it opens the way for correcting the lack of progress, reassigning the person to a different responsibility, or having the person leave the board or at least not serve for a second term.

"*Committee work? Fund raising? Public accountability?*
You didn't tell me it was gonna be that kind of board!"

Source: Copyright © Mark Litzler.

HOW TO RETIRE A BOARD MEMBER

At some point in every development officer's career, he or she will have to confront a board member who is no longer an active leader, who no longer produces for the organization—effectively, efficiently, or at all. Many times, a lack of action is not noticed at first but is discovered gradually as the board member is "carried along" by the other members. Sometimes the "awareness" will surface quickly, usually when an issue is brought before the board with which the member does not agree or cannot endorse for whatever reasons. Or it could just be the changing times—the board member cannot or will not change direction and move forward with the organization. The question is, what should you do when this happens to you?

Most organizations have defined term limits and a set percentage of members retiring each year from their positions. Usually, terms are set at three years, with one-third of the board rotating off each year. Some organizations have rules that allow board members to be reelected for two consecutive terms but require them to "sit out" before being elected again. Other institutions will not allow board members to serve more than two terms. Some unfortunate organizations have no term limits and thus can find themselves with individuals who have been members of the board for 10, 20, or 30 years. Why is this bad?

No organization can afford to have dead weight on its board. How to ask board members to leave who have fulfilled their usefulness as well as their terms is as important as selecting members for the board. One method is to evaluate board members on a regular basis. Paid employees are usually first evaluated after their probationary period (three to six months) and then yearly after that, on or near the anniversary of their employment. Similarly, volunteers should be given a probationary period, followed by an evaluation, and then be evaluated yearly after that.

ROLE OF STAFF IN FUNDRAISING

The vice president of development, director of development, or chief development officer has the role of leading the fundraising efforts. He or she is responsible for carrying out the work authorized by the board and making the day-to-day decisions of the office. This person is the liaison or bridge between the staff and the board and consults the board for direction and guidance. The director should be knowledgeable of all types of fundraising, including annual campaigns, capital campaigns, major gift solicitation, proposal writing, special events, direct mail, planned giving, etc. In addition, the director manages the functional responsibilities of the development office. He or she must be capable of leading the staff through the various phases of the fundraising operation—planning and marketing; public relations; volunteer management and training; donor identification and solicitation; gift processing, reporting, and management; donor renewal, upgrading, recognition; etc. The director is expected to lead and motivate the staff to complete the tasks required to meet the department's goals.

As all department heads have budgetary responsibilities, so too does the development director. He or she must ensure that the work of the office is completed in a timely, efficient, cost-effective, and ethical manner. The director sets the tone for the office and motivates the staff as well as the volunteers. He or she is also responsible for keeping the executive director or president of the organization and board informed of the activities of the department. There should be no "surprises" to report. Depending upon the size of the institution, there may be others to assist the director with office work.

COMMUNICATIONS BETWEEN BOARD AND STAFF

It is important that open communications exist between the board and staff. As mentioned previously, a development director should not even consider a position in which he or she is not given direct access to the board of the organization at any time. Use this access wisely. Know the difference between relevant and irrelevant information. Call upon the board members when there is a specific task for them to perform. Always follow through on what has been committed and within the time frame promised. Likewise, if asking a board member to perform a task, provide clear direction and give a timetable for the results.

> *A development director should not even consider a position in which he or she is not given direct access to the board of the organization at any time.*

Ensuring that there are regularly scheduled meetings with board members is also important for keeping open communications between the board and development staff. Highly evolved boards will most likely use Robert's Rules of Order to keep their meetings structured and running smoothly. Smaller, less formally structured boards may find this type of parliamentary procedure constraining and daunting. Those staff and board members who wish to simplify laborious meetings and heavy formal structures may wish to use a new method to make decisions—*Roberta's Rules of Order (Who Is Robert and Why Do We Still Follow His Rules Anyway?)* This is a book that "challenges nonprofit leaders and anyone who runs meetings to adopt a simpler, friendlier, and more effective method for conducting meetings." Appendix 2–H shows the cover of *Roberta's Rules of Order*, which provides information on how to help staff and boards "sail through meetings for stellar results without the gavel."

The director of development should meet at least once a year with every member of the board. Be sure to have an agenda—review fundraising goals with a new member, ask an experienced board fundraiser to attend a fundraising conference with you, seek advice on a problem or opportunity, or introduce a board member to some facet of your operation that gives him or her new insight into the strength of your and your staff's work.

Most important of all, listen to what the board members have to say. They may provide the resolution to a problem with which the staff has been struggling for months or at least offer an idea or insight that may help solve it. They may have new ways of doing things that can work!

STAFF EXPECTATIONS FOR BOARD MEMBERS

Staff members can expect board members to do the following: be loyal and committed to the organization and its mission and purposes; attend all regularly scheduled board meetings; give generously of their own wealth and solicit funds from others to support the organization; enthusiastically support and represent the organization to the public; act as a liaison with the organization's many publics; maintain confidentiality; and actively participate in fundraising activities, including special events, gift evaluations, resource prospecting, developing a case statement for the organization, and soliciting prospective donors.

It is the staff's responsibility to make sure that the board is provided with adequate training to accomplish the previously mentioned tasks. If the board is not performing up to the expectations of the staff, then the staff must first look at itself to see if board members have been provided with the tools that they need to be successful.

BOARD MEMBERS' EXPECTATIONS FOR STAFF

Just as the staff has expectations of its board, so does the board have expectations of the staff. The board can expect the staff to know the nonprofit world and be able to guide the organization to reach its fundraising goals successfully by use of strategic planning, which should direct the organization through many mazes and obstacles. The board will expect the staff to do the following: be professional, design the overall fundraising plan, develop all materials needed in the fundraising effort, provide adequate orientation and training for the board and other volunteers, assist the board in making solicitation calls, provide the necessary materials to board members to solicit a prospect, establish the criteria necessary to accept and evaluate gifts to the organization, follow up on all contacts made by board members, develop an acknowledgment procedure, and generally support the activities of the board. Board members and other volunteers can succeed only if they are provided with the proper training, motivation, and support by the staff.

Successful fundraising requires a team effort from both staff members and volunteers—a team effort requiring full energy on both sides. Just as in sports, fundraising requires a well thought out and well-executed plan. The plan is developed by the staff in cooperation with the board, as its members will also want to have ownership. The meetings organized by the staff for the board should be planned well in advance, fit the schedules of most members, be organized so that time is not wasted, and include items to be discussed on which the board will take action or make decisions. Respect the time of the volunteers. Use it wisely. Don't ask too much of one group of volunteers and neglect others. Watch for overuse or "burnout." Volunteers who are kept informed, whose time is used judiciously, and who are respected for the talent they bring to the board will more often remain active and loyal to the organization than those whose time has been abused and whose interests have been ignored.

REFERENCES

Boice, J.P. 2006. Top notch. *Advancing Philanthropy* (January/February).

Broce, T.E. 1986. *Fund raising. The guide to raising money from private sources.* 2nd ed. Norman, OK: University of Oklahoma Press.

Cochran, A.C. 2004. *Roberta's rules of order—Who is Robert and why do we still follow his rules anyway?* San Rafael, CA: Jossey-Bass.

Dayton, K.N. 2001. *Governance is governance.* Independent Sector, Washington, DC.

Points of Light Foundation—Directory of Volunteer Centers

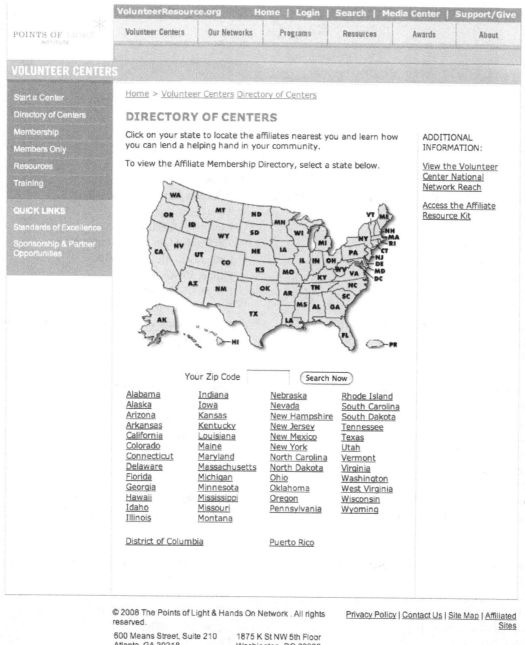

© 2008 The Points of Light & Hands On Network . All rights reserved.

Privacy Policy | Contact Us | Site Map | Affiliated Sites

600 Means Street, Suite 210
Atlanta, GA 30318
Tel: 404-979-2900
Fax: 404-979-2901
E-mail:
info@handsonnetwork.org

1875 K St NW 5th Floor
Washington, DC 20006
Tel: 202-729-8000
Fax: 202-729-8100
E-mail:
Info@PointsofLight.org

Source: Reprinted with permission from the Points of Light Foundation, www.pointsoflight.org/centers/find_center.cfm. © 2007, The Points of Light Foundation.

State Volunteer Service Commissions

ALABAMA

Governor's Office of Faith-Based and Community Initiatives
Sydney Hoffman
Executive Director
RSA Union Building, Suite 134
100 North Union Street
Montgomery, AL 36130-9534
Phone: 334-242-7110
Fax: 334-242-2885
E-mail: Sydney.Hoffman@ServeAlabama.gov
Web site: http://www.ServeAlabama.gov

ALASKA

Alaska State Community Service Commission
Elsa Sargento
Executive Director
550 W. 7th Ave., Suite 1770
Anchorage, AK 99501-3510
Phone: 907-269-4659
Fax: 907-269-5666
E-mail: Americorps@dced.state.ak.us
Web site: http://www.dced.state.ak.us/ascsc/home.htm

ARIZONA

**Arizona Governor's Commission on Service and
    Volunteerism**
Tammy Paz-Combs
Executive Director
1700 West Washington, Suite 101
Phoenix, AZ 85007-2806
Phone: 602-542-3489
Fax: 602-542-3423
E-mail: tcombs@az.gov
Web site: http://www.volunteerarizona.org

ARKANSAS

Arkansas Service Commission
Albert Schneider
Executive Director
700 South Main Street, Slot S230
Little Rock, AR 72201-4608
Phone: 501-682-6724
Fax: 501-682-1623
E-mail: al.schneider@arkansas.gov
Web site: http://www.arkansas.gov/dhhs/adov/New%20
Version/nsprograms.htm

CALIFORNIA

California Service Corps
Karen Baker
Executive Director
1110 K Street, Suite 210
Sacramento, CA 95814-3905
Phone: 916-323-7646
Fax: 916-323-3227
E-mail: karen.baker@csc.ca.gov
Web site: http://www.csc.ca.gov

COLORADO

Colorado Governor's Commission on Community Service
Nancy J. Brown
Executive Director
1600 Broadway, Suite 1030
Denver, CO 80202
Phone: 303-866-2572
Fax: 303-866-2525
E-mail: governors.commission@state.co.us
Web site: http://www.colorado.gov/gccs

Source: Reprinted from the Corporation for National and Community Service, 2007 Corporation for National Service, www.nationalservice.org/about/contact/statecommission.asp.

CONNECTICUT

Connecticut Commission on Community Service
Jacqueline Johnson
Executive Director
Department of Higher Education
61 Woodland Street
Hartford, CT 06105-2326
Phone: 860-947-1827
Fax: 860-947-1310
E-mail: jjohnson@ctdhe.org
Web site: http://servect.ctdhe.org

DELAWARE

Delaware Community Service Commission
Elisa C. Diller
Administrator
Charles Debnam Building, Herman Holloway Campus
1901 North Dupont Highway
New Castle, DE 19720-1100
Phone: 302-255-9881
Fax: 302-255-4462
E-mail: elisa.diller@state.de.us

DISTRICT OF COLUMBIA

District of Columbia Commission on National and Community Service
James E. Cooper, Jr.
Executive Director
441 4th Street, N.W. #1040
Washington, DC 20001
Phone: 202-727-9461
Fax: 202-727-9198
E-mail: james.cooper@dc.gov
Web site: http://www.serve.dc.gov

FLORIDA

Volunteer Florida
Wendy Spencer
Chief Executive Officer
401 South Monroe Street
Tallahassee, FL 32301-2034
Phone: 850-921-5172
Fax: 850-921-5146
E-mail: ysonde@volunteerflorida.org
Web site: http://www.volunteerflorida.org

GEORGIA

Georgia Commission for Service and Volunteerism
James P. Marshall, Jr.
Executive Director
60 Executive Park South, NE
Atlanta, GA 30329-2296
Phone: 404-327-6844
Fax: 404-327-6848
E-mail: jmarshal@dca.state.ga.us

HAWAII

Hawaii Commission on National and Community Service
Isaac Watson
Executive Director
Office of Community Services
2600 Campus Road, Room 405
Honolulu, HI 96822-2205
Phone: 808-956-8145
Fax: 808-956-9219
E-mail: hicncs@hawaii.edu
Web site: http://www.hawaii.edu/americorpshawaii

IDAHO

Serve Idaho
Kelly Houston
Executive Director
1299 North Orchard Street, Suite 110
Boise, ID 83706-2265
Phone: 208-658-2000
Fax: 208-327-7470
E-mail: khouston@corr.state.id.us
Web site: http://www.serveidaho.org

ILLINOIS

Illinois Commission on Volunteerism and Community Service
Scott Kimmel
Executive Director
Illinois Department of Human Services - Division of Community Health & Prevention
535 W. Jefferson Street, 3rd Floor
Springfield, IL 62702
Phone: 800-592-9896
Fax: 217-557-0515
E-mail: scott.kimmel@illinois.gov
Web site: http://www.illinois.gov/volunteer

INDIANA

Office of Faith-Based and Community Initiatives
Ms. Paula Parker-Sawyers
Executive Director
302 West Washington Street, Room E220
Indianapolis, IN 46204-4701
Phone: 317-233-4273
Fax: 317-233-5660
E-mail: PMSawyers@ofbci.IN.gov
Web site: http://www.state.in.us/iccsv

IOWA

Iowa Commission on Volunteer Service
Adam Lounsbury

Executive Director
200 East Grand Avenue
Des Moines, IA 50309-1856
Phone: 515-242-5466
Fax: 515-242-4809
E-mail: icvs@iowalifechanging.com
Web site: http://www.volunteeriowa.org

KANSAS

Kansas Volunteer Commission
Patricia P. Kells
Executive Director
120 SE 10th Avenue
Topeka, KS 66612-1103
Phone: 785-368-6207
Fax: 785-368-6284
E-mail: pkells@ksde.org
Web site: http://www.kanserve.org

KENTUCKY

**Kentucky Commission on Community Volunteerism
and Service**
Eileen Cackowski
Executive Director
275 East Main Street—Mail Stop 3W-F
Frankfort, KY 40621-0001
Phone: 502-564-7420 or 800/239-7404
Fax: 502-564-7478
E-mail: kccvs@ky.gov
Web site: http://http://volunteerky.ky.gov

LOUISIANA

Louisiana Serve Commission
Brook Smith
Executive Director
263 Third Street, Suite 610-B
Baton Rouge, LA 70801-1306
Phone: 225-342-6289
Fax: 225-342-0106
E-mail: bsmith@crt.state.la.us
Web site: http://www.crt.state.la.us/laserve

MAINE

Maine Commission for Community Service
Maryalice Crofton
Executive Director
Maine State Planning Office
187 State Street—38 State House Station
Augusta, ME 04333-0038
Phone: 207-287-5313
Fax: 207-287-8059
E-mail: service.commission@maine.gov
Web site: http://www.maine.gov/communityservice

MARYLAND

**Maryland Governor's Office on Service and
Volunteerism**
Keith Hart
Director
State Office Building
300 West Preston Street, Suite 608
Baltimore, MD 21201
Phone: 410-767-4803
Fax: 410-333-5957
E-mail: khart@dbm.state.md.us
Web site: http://www.gosv.state.md.us

MASSACHUSETTS

Massachusetts Service Alliance
Melanie Tavares
Acting Executive Director
100 North Washington Street, 3rd Floor
Boston, MA 02114
Phone: 617-542-2544 x217
Fax: 617-542-0240
E-mail: mtavares@mass-service.org
Web site: http://www.msalliance.org

MICHIGAN

Michigan Community Service Commission
Paula Kaiser Van Damm
Interim Executive Director
1048 Pierpont, Suite #4
Lansing, MI 48913
Phone: 517-335-1013
Fax: 517-373-4977
E-mail: kaiserp@michigan.gov
Web site: http://www.michigan.gov/mcsc

MINNESOTA

Serve Minnesota!
Audrey Suker
Executive Director
431 South 7th Street, #2540
Minneapolis, MN 55415
Phone: 612/333-7740
Fax: 612/333-7758
E-mail: audrey@serveminnesota.org
Web site: http://www.serveminnesota.org

MISSISSIPPI

Mississippi Commission for Volunteer Service
Marsha Meeks Kelly
Executive Director
3825 Ridgewood Road, Suite 601
Jackson, MS 39211-6463
Phone: 601-432-6790

Fax: 601-432-6790
E-mail: marsha@mcvs.org
Web site: http://www.mcvs.org

MISSOURI
Missouri Community Service Commission
Linda F. Jackson
Executive Director
Harry S Truman Building, Suite 770
P.O. Box 118
Jefferson City, MO 65102
Phone: 573-751-7488 or 877-210-7611
Fax: 573-526-0463
E-mail: linda.jackson@ded.mo.gov
Web site: http://www.movolunteers.org

MONTANA
Montana Commission on Community Service
Linda Carlson
Executive Director
Office of the Governor - Office of Community Service
1301 Lockey Avenue, 3rd Floor
P.O. Box 200801
Helena, MT 59620-0801
Phone: 406-444-2573
Fax: 406-444-4418
E-mail: lcarlson@mt.gov
Web site: http://www.mt.gov/mcsn

NEBRASKA
Nebraska Volunteer Service Commission
Gale Jungemann-Schulz
Program Officer
State Capitol - 6th Floor
P.O. Box 98927
Lincoln, NE 68509-4848
Phone: 402-471-6249
Fax: 402-471-6286
E-mail: gale.jungemannschulz@hhss.ne.gov
Web site: http://www.state.ne.us/home/NVSC

NEVADA
Nevada Commission for National and Community Service
Ms. Shawn R. Lecker-Pomaville
Executive Director
137 Keddie Street
Fallon, NV 89406
Phone: 775-423-1461 or 888-338-9759
Fax: 775-423-8039
E-mail: shawn@americorpsnevada.org
Web site: http://www.americorpsnevada.org

NEW HAMPSHIRE
Volunteer NH!
Tim Dupre
Executive Director
117 Pleasant Street
Dolloff Building, 4th Floor
Concord, NH 03301-3852
Phone: 603-271-7202
Fax: 603-721-7203
E-mail: Timdupre@volunteernh.org
Web site: http://www.volunteernh.org

NEW JERSEY
New Jersey Commission on National and Community Service
Rowena Madden
Executive Director
New Jersey State Department of Education - Office of Community Services
100 Riverview Complex, P.O. Box 500
Trenton, NJ 08625-0500
Phone: 609-633-9627
Fax: 609-777-2939
E-mail: rmadden@doe.state.nj.us
Web site: http://www.state.nj.us/njded/americorps

NEW MEXICO
New Mexico Commission for Community Volunteerism
Gregory Webb
Executive Director
Children, Youth and Family Department
3401 Pan American Freeway, NE
Albuquerque, NM 87107-4785
Phone: 505-841-4841
Fax: 505-841-4839
E-mail: gwebb@cyfd.state.nm.us
Web site: http://www.newmexserve.org

NEW YORK
New York Commission for National and Community Service, Inc.
Claire Strohmeyer
Executive Director
NYS Office of Children & Family Services
52 Washington Street, Capital View Office Park
Room 309, South
Rensselaer, NY 12144-2796
Phone: 518-473-8882
Fax: 518-402-3817
E-mail: Claire.Strohmeyer@ocfs.state.ny.us
Web site: http://www.ocfs.state.ny.us/main/youth/nyscncs

NORTH CAROLINA
North Carolina Commission on Volunteerism and
Community Service
William Lindsay
Executive Director
Governor's Office of Citizen Affairs
20312 Mail Service Center
Raleigh, NC 27699-0312
Phone: 919-715-3470
Fax: 919-715-8677
E-mail: volcommission@ncmail.net
Web site: http://www.volunteernc.org

NORTH DAKOTA
North Dakota Workforce Development Council -
State Commission on National and Community Service
Jim Hirsch
Executive Director
Department of Commerce
1600 East Century Avenue, Suite 2
P.O. Box 2057
Bismarck, ND 58502-2057
Phone: 701-328-5345
Fax: 701-328-5320
E-mail: jhirsch@nd.gov
Web site: http://www.ndcommerce.com

OHIO
Ohio Community Service Council
Katherine A Burcsu
Executive Director
51 North High Street, Suite 800
Columbus, OH 43215
Phone: 614-728-2916
Fax: 614-728-2921
E-mail: kitty.burcsu@ocsc.state.oh.us
Web site: http://www.serveohio.org

OKLAHOMA
Oklahoma Community Service Commission
Nancy Deaver Sharrock
Executive Director
1401 N. Lincoln Blvd.
Oklahoma City, OK 73104
Phone: 405-235-7278
Fax: 405-235-7036
E-mail: nsharrock@okamericorps.com
Web site: http://www.okamericorps.com

OREGON
Oregon Commission for Voluntary Action and Service
Kathleen A. Joy
Executive Director
1600 SW Fourth Avenue

Suite 850
Portland, OR 97201-5522
Phone: 503-725-5903
Fax: 503-725-8335
E-mail: info@oregonvolunteers.org
Web site: http://www.oregonvolunteers.org

PENNSYLVANIA
PennSERVE: The Governor's Office of Citizen Service
Karen Kaskey
Executive Director
1306 Labor and Industry Building
7th and Forster Streets
Harrisburg, PA 17120
Phone: 717-787-1971
Fax: 717-705-4215
E-mail: pennserve@state.pa.us
Web site: http://www.pennserve.state.pa.us

PUERTO RICO / VIRGIN ISLANDS
Puerto Rico State Commission on Community Service
Olga Aldrich
Executive Director
Department of Education
10th Floor, Box 190759
Calle Calaf #38
San Juan, PR 00919-0759
Phone: 787-759-8910, ext. 229
Fax: 787-751-6192
E-mail: aldrich_o@de.gobierno.pr

RHODE ISLAND
Rhode Island Service Alliance
Rick Benjamin
Executive Director
143 Prairie Avenue
P.O. Box 72822
Providence, RI 02907
Phone: 401-331-2298 x18
Fax: 401-331-2273
E-mail: rick@riservicealliance.org
Web site: http://www.riservicealliance.org

SOUTH CAROLINA
South Carolina Commission on National and
Community Service
Cherry Daniel
Acting Executive Director
3710 Landmark Drive, Suite 200
Columbia, SC 29204-4062
Phone: 803-734-8071
Fax: 803-734-4825
E-mail: cldaniel@sde.state.sc.us
Web site: http://www.servicesc.org

TENNESSEE

Tennessee Commission on National and Community Service

Carol C. White
Executive Director
William R. Snodgrass Tennessee Tower
312 8th Avenue North, Suite 1200
Nashville, TN 37243-0001
Phone: 615-532-9416
Fax: 615-532-6950
E-mail: carol.white@state.tn.us
Web site: http://www.state.tn.us/finance/rds/tcncs.html

TEXAS

OneStar National Service Commission

Susan Weddington
President/CEO
816 Congress Avenue, Suite 900
Austin, TX 78701
Phone: 512-473-2140 x204
Fax: 512-473-8228
E-mail: susan@onestarfoundation.org
Web site: http://www.onestarfoundation.org

UTAH

Utah Commission on Volunteers

Kathy Hyde
Executive Director
324 South State Street, Suite 500
Salt Lake City, UT 84111
Phone: 801-538-8644
Fax: 801-538-8690
E-mail: khyde@utah.gov
Web site: http://www.volunteers.utah.gov

VERMONT

Vermont Commission on National and Community Service

Susie Hudson
Executive Director
Office of the Governor
109 State Street
Montpelier, VT 05609-4801
Phone: 802-828-4982
Fax: 802-828-4988
E-mail: susie.hudson@state.vt.us
Web site: http://www.state.vt.us/cncs

VIRGINIA

Virginia Commission on National and Community Service

Nikki Nicholau
Executive Director
7 North Eighth Street, 5th Floor
Richmond, VA 23219-3301
Phone: 804-726-7620
Fax: 804-726-7024
E-mail: nikki.nicholau@dss.virginia.gov
Web site: http://www.vaservice.org

WASHINGTON

Washington Commission on National and Community Service

William C. Basl
Executive Director
P.O. Box 43113
Olympia, WA 98504-3113
Phone: 360-902-0663
Fax: 360-586-3964
E-mail: bill.basl@ofm.wa.gov
Web site: http://www.ofm.wa.gov/servewa

WEST VIRGINIA

West Virginia Commission for National and Community Service

Jean Ambrose
Executive Director
601 Delaware Avenue
Charleston, WV 25302
Phone: 304-558-0111 or 800-WV-HELPS
Fax: 304-558-0101
E-mail: jambrose@mail.state.wv.us
Web site: http://www.volunteerwv.org

WISCONSIN

Wisconsin National and Community Service Board

Thomas H. Devine
Executive Director
1 West Wilson Street - Room 456
Madison, WI 53703
Phone: 608-261-6716 or 800-620-8307
Fax: 608-266-9313
E-mail: devinth@dhfs.state.wi.us
Web site: http://www.servewisconsin.org

WYOMING

ServeWyoming–Wyoming Commission on National and Community Service

Rachel A. Chadderdon
Executive Director
P.O. Box 1271
229 East 2nd Street
Casper, WY 82602
Phone: 307-234-3428 or 866-737-8304 (toll free)
Fax: 307-234-3438
E-mail: rachel@servewyoming.org

Web site: where to find all this information:
http://www.nationalservice.gov/home/site_map/index.asp

Samples of Board Job Descriptions

A. Sample Job Description from FORE, the Foundation of Research and Education of AHIMA in Chicago, Illinois.

Foundation of Research
and Education of AHIMA

Job Description for a FORE Board Member

General Expectations

- Understand and articulate FORE'S mission, vision, values, strategies, policies, programs, services and strengths.
- Perform duties of board membership responsibly and uphold the values of FORE.
- Suggest possible nominees for the board.
- Support an atmosphere in which every member of the board can actively and fully participate.
- Serve in leadership positions and undertake special assignments willingly and enthusiastically.
- Represent FORE when called upon to do so.
- Become informed about and follow relevant trends in healthcare and HIM.
- Refer matters of potential significance to the Board chair and the Foundation's executive director.
- Bring good will and a sense of humor to the board's deliberations.
- Express opinions for the good of FORE, rather than to advance one's personal agenda.
- Serve on one Board committee.
- Communicate between regularly scheduled meetings, by
    - Participating in conference calls collectively or as part of a team
    - Checking the FORE Board Community of Practice
    - Answering correspondence promptly

Meetings

- Attend the majority of board meetings, committee meetings and FORE events.
- Prepare for and participate in board, committee and other meetings.
- Ask timely and substantive questions at board, committee and other meetings consistent with your conscience and convictions.
- Support the majority decision on issues decided by the board.

Avoiding Conflicts

- Serve FORE as a whole rather than any special interest group or constituency.
- Avoid even the appearance of a conflict of interest that might embarrass the board or FORE, and disclose any possible conflicts to the board in a timely fashion.
- Maintain independence and objectivity and do what a sense of fairness, ethics, and personal integrity dictate.
- Understand and fully comply with the terms and spirit of AHIMA's conflicts and dualities and confidentiality and nondisclosure agreements.

Fiduciary Responsibilities

- Consider the impact of each recommendation and decision on FORE resources.
- Adhere to expense guidelines and expense reporting procedures.
- Read and understand the FORE financial statements and status, and otherwise help the board fulfill its fiduciary responsibility.

Fundraising

- Give a meaningful annual gift to FORE, according to personal means.
- Assist the Foundation and staff by supporting fundraising strategies through personal influence with others (corporations, individuals, foundations).

Source: Courtesy of Eileen M. Murray, MM, CFRE, CAE, Vice President and Executive Director Foundation of Research and Education, AHIMA, 233 N Michigan Avenue, Chicago, Illinois.

B. Sample of Board of Trustees Responsibilities

Function

- As representatives of the public, be the primary force pressing the institution to the realization of its opportunities for service and the fulfillment of its obligations to all its constituencies.

Duties

Planning

- Approve the institution's philosophy and review management's performance in achieving it.
- Annually assess the ever-changing environment and approve the institution's strategy in relation to it.
- Annually review and approve the institution's plans for funding its strategy. Review and approve the institution's five-year financial goals.
- Annually review and approve the institution's budget.
- Approve major policies.

Organizational

- Elect, monitor, appraise, advise, stimulate, support, reward and, if deemed necessary or desirable, change top management. Regularly discuss with the CEO matters that are of concern to him or her or to the board.
- Be assured that management succession is properly being provided.
- Be assured that the status of organizational strength and human resources planning is equal to the requirements of the long-range goals.
- Approve appropriate compensation and benefit policies and practices. Propose a slate of directors to members and fill vacancies as needed.
- Annually approve the performance review of the CEO and establish his or her compensation based on recommendations of the personnel committee and chair of the board.
- Determine eligibility for and appoint board committees in response to recommendations of the nominating committee.
- Annually review the performance of the board and take steps (including its composition, organization, and responsibilities) to improve its performance.

Operations

- Review the results achieved by management as compared with the institution's philosophy, annual and long-range goals, and the performance of similar institutions.
- Confirm that the financial structure of the institution is adequate for its current needs and its long-range strategy.
- Provide candid and constructive criticism, advice and comments. Approve major actions of the institution, such as capital expenditures on all projects over authorized limits and major changes in programs and services.

Audit

- Ensure that the board and its committees are adequately and currently informed—through reports and other methods—of the condition of the institution and its operations.
- Confirm that published reports properly reflect the operating results and financial condition of the institution.
- Ascertain that management has established appropriate policies to define and identify conflicts of interest throughout the institution, and is diligently administering and enforcing those policies.
- Appoint independent auditors subject to approval by members.
- Review compliance with relevant material laws affecting the institution.

Source: Courtesy of Independent Sector, *Governance Is Governance,* by Kenneth N. Dayton, 2001.

An Excellent Resource on Board Governance

GOVERNANCE IS GOVERNANCE

KENNETH N. DAYTON

INDEPENDENT SECTOR

Source: Courtesy of Independent Sector, *Governance Is Governance,* by Kenneth N. Dayton, 2001.

About the Author

Kenneth N. Dayton is the former chairman and chief executive officer of the Dayton Hudson Corporation and is currently president of the Oakleaf Foundation in Minneapolis. He has served on the boards of a number of nonprofit organizations including major institutions such as the Rockefeller Foundation, the Mayo Foundation, Carnegie Hall, and the J. Paul Getty Trust, and as chairman of American Public Radio. He was also a founding trustee, and later vice chairperson of INDEPENDENT SECTOR. As chairperson of INDEPENDENT SECTOR's Task Force on Measurable Growth in Giving and Volunteering, he presided over the deliberations that resulted in a campaign to boost giving and volunteering nationwide.

INDEPENDENT SECTOR

INDEPENDENT SECTOR is a nonprofit, nonpartisan coalition of more than 700 national nonprofit organizations, foundations, and corporate philanthropy programs, collectively representing tens of thousands of charitable groups in every state across the nation. Our mission is to promote, strengthen, and advance the nonprofit and philanthropic community to foster private initiative for the public good.

This timeless commentary was originally a speech by Kenneth N. Dayton to an INDEPENDENT SECTOR Leadership/ Management Forum in 1986. It was first published as a monograph in 1987, then updated in 1998 and again in 2001. Governance Is Governance is one of the most popular INDEPENDENT SECTOR publications to date.

©2001, INDEPENDENT SECTOR
ISBN: 0-929556-08-9

Sample of a Board of Directors Governing Mission

FORE Board of Directors Governing Mission

The primary responsibility of the FORE Board of Directors is to set the vision and mission of FORE and guide their successful realization. Governing—the primary work of the FORE Board of Directors—essentially means to play the leading role (working closely with the Foundation Executive Director and Executive Staff) in continuously answering 3 preeminent questions that determine what the FORE Foundation is all about:

(1) Where should the FORE Foundation be headed—and what should the Foundation become—over the long run?
(2) What should the FORE Foundation be now and in the near term in terms of programs/services, resources, and expenditure targets?
(3) How is the FORE Foundation performing in terms of realizing its vision and carrying out its strategic and operational plans?

The ultimate goal of the Board is to insure that the FORE Foundation is a financially self-sustaining entity that provides resources for national leadership and innovation in health information management for the healthcare industry and its consumers.

The Board carries out its responsibilities by:

- Serving as the steward and guardian of the FORE Foundation's values, vision, mission, and resources.
- Playing a leading, proactive role in the FORE Foundation's strategic decision making, and in setting strong, clear strategic directions and priorities for the Foundation, within the framework of AHIMA's vision, mission, priorities, and strategies.
- Making sure that the working relationship between AHIMA and FORE Foundation is close, positive, and productive and that it is characterized by full, open communication and careful coordination.
- Monitoring FORE's operational performance against clearly defined performance targets.
- Ensuring that the FORE Foundation's relationships with key stakeholders are positive and that they contribute to the Foundation's success.
- Making sure that FORE Foundation possesses the financial and other resources necessary to realize its vision and carry out its mission fully.
- Striving to ensure that the Board's composition is diverse and that its members possess the attributes and qualifications required for strong governance.
- Ensuring that Board members are fully engaged in the governance process and that the resources they bring to the Board are fully utilized in governing.
- Taking accountability for its own performance as a governing body.
- Working in close partnership with the Foundation Executive Director, ensuring that clear, detailed Executive Director performance targets are set, and periodically assessing Executive Director performance against these targets.

Source: Courtesy of Eileen M. Murray, MM, CFRE, CAE, Vice President and Executive Director, Foundation of Research and Education, AHIMA, Chicago, Illinois.

Developing an Effective Fundraising Board

A senior development professional shares tips on how to motivate even the most reluctant
Board members to become successful fundraisers.

By

Barbara L. Ciconte, CFRE

Senior Vice President, Donor Strategies, Inc.

Introduction

Fundraising is not a one-person job even though there are still nonprofit boards of directors that believe that fundraising is the responsibility of the Executive Director or the Director of Development if the organization has one. It never was and given today's competitive fundraising environment we see that nonprofits with board members actively engaged in raising funds are indeed having greater success in raising funds to fulfill their missions.

One might ask - How did these nonprofits find board members who were willing to do fundraising? Are they just lucky? Or do they focus on educating and training their board members to be more comfortable and confident in soliciting funds? There may be a bit of luck involved, but what I have seen in my 25+ years in the nonprofit sector is that effective fundraising boards are created by committed staff and volunteer leaders who understand that fundraising is everyone's responsibility!

"My Board Won't Raise Funds"

As a fundraising consultant who works with various types of nonprofits, I often hear from clients that their boards won't raise funds. When I hear this statement, I ask the following questions:

- Do they have a clear idea of their roles and responsibilities as board members?
- Were they told they are responsible for raising funds before joining the Board?
- Do they know they are expected to make an annual gift?
- Do you feel the Board knows the organization's mission, goals and objectives, programs and financial needs?
- Are there established Board committees, including a Development or Fundraising Committee?
- Are there opportunities to train the Board in fundraising?
- Is the Board chair, Development Committee chair, or a key volunteer willing to take the lead in changing the current attitude of the Board?

Oten it is clear from the answers given that the reason the board can't or won't raise funds is due to the fact that they were not properly informed of their duties prior to joining the Board, have not been adequately educated about the organization's mission, programs, and financial needs since joining the Board, and have had little or no opportunity to receive fundraising training. Is it any wonder that the Board feels the way it does?

How to Build a Fundraising Board

How can an executive director or development director help prevent creating the "Won't" or "Can't" Board of Directors?

Step One

The first step is to work with the committee of the Board who is responsible for identifying and recruiting new Board members. For some organizations, this committee is known as the "Nominating Committee." For others, a new title of "Board Development Committee" is now used that includes not only identifying and recruiting new Board members, but also reviewing and evaluating current Board members' service. No matter what title is used, one needs to understand that this committee is extremely important to building an effective nonprofit organization.

In order for this Committee to recruit individuals who will assist with fundraising, it needs the following:

- A written document outlining a Board Member's roles and responsibilities clearly stating the Board's role in fundraising and expectations for giving
- Staff and volunteer suggestions for new board members who are current donors, volunteers, and community leaders that have experience in fundraising
- A chairperson who understands the importance of adding Board members who have affluence and influence among different populations

Step Two

Another way to build a fundraising board is to work with several current Board members who are participating in fundraising-related activities to serve as examples to other Board members. Ask them to share their experiences at Board meetings about calls and meetings they had with prospective and current donors, especially if their contact resulted in a contribution or increased gift. By taking the mystery out of what "fundraising" means, often you will discover that some of the more reluctant "fundraisers" will understand that they could do what John or Jean is doing for the organization. Be certain to publicly thank these board members for their fundraising assistance. This effort certainly builds confidence among board members.

Step Three

Board members do respond best to other board members, rather than staff. For that reason, it is important to create a Development Committee of the Board that can take the lead in fundraising efforts. It can provide peer support to the Board.

The Development Committee:

- Works with staff to develop the fundraising plan and necessary policies and procedures for fundraising
- Educates the Board on program plans and the funds needed to implement plans
- Reports on the status of fundraising activities at Board meetings
- Helps train the Board on activities to raise funds
- Solicits Board members for their gifts
- Identifies, cultivates and solicits major gift prospects

Keep in mind that the Development Committee can also include non-Board members. Invite special event volunteers, current donors, and community leaders to join the Development Committee with the specific purpose of raising funds for the organization. Active Development Committee members are excellent candidates for the Board of Directors.

Ways to Motivate Board Members to Become Successful Fundraisers

Board members who have the information, education and training they need will be more assured and confident, resulting in greater success in raising funds for the organizations they serve.

Here are some tips to motivate even your most reluctant Board member:

Tip #1: Identify the organization's expectations for Board members

Keep in mind Board members' primary family and professional responsibilities when identifying expectations for what Board members should do for the organization. Be realistic! Do not expect Board members to perform typical staff functions.

Tip #2: Outline the roles and responsibilities in a written Board position description.

A staff person would not accept a position without seeing a job description. This is also true for Board members who should be able to review the specific roles and responsibilities of Board service before making a decision to join your Board. Be certain you include the role of the Board in fundraising and giving to your organization.

Tip #3: Educate them that development is a process of building relationships, not just asking.

Most board members see fundraising and development related activities as only asking for money. For this reason, I urge my clients to educate their Board members that development is the process of building relationships and fundraising is the number of activities we use to ask for funds – direct mail, telephone, in person and on-line. There are many things that a Board member can do that are key to fundraising in advance of any type of solicitation. Examples include:

- Inviting someone to an event
- Making a thank you call
- Adding a personal note to an appeal letter
- Arranging for the executive director to meet with a business or community colleague to educate that individual about a particular problem addressed by the organization

Tip #4: Illustrate how fundraising is directly related to the mission, programs and services of the organization.

Staff and board members do not solicit funds just for the dollars. Instead, funds are solicited to support the specific programs and services that fulfill the organization's mission. Be certain Board members know which programs and services are priorities for the organization during a certain period of time. Linking funds raised to the ability to implement programs and services is an effective way for Board members to understand the organization's financial needs.

Tip #5: Provide the necessary tools and information for Board members to carry out their fundraising duties.

It is important to create a Solicitor's Kit that includes materials and information that Board members can use. A typical Solicitor's Kit includes:

- An organization's brochure articulating the organization's case for support
- Information on how to make a gift – to whom to make the check payable, how to make a gift of appreciated stock, who to contact at the organization if additional information is needed
- Pledge card/envelope
- Information on prospects to be contacted, e.g., past giving, programs and services supported and involvement with the organization

Tip #6: Train them on the basics of fundraising, methods and best practices that insure greater success.

A half-day Board retreat is an excellent way to cover fundraising basics. Training, however, should not conclude with the retreat but be incorporated into regularly scheduled board meetings in order to continue the Board's knowledge and education in fundraising.

Tip #7: Use the Development Committee to encourage and coach them in their duties.

This tip was covered earlier in the article. Once again keep in mind that Board members respond best to peers—the Development Committee or individual members of the Board of the Directors.

Tip #8: Recognize and reward Board member and volunteer efforts.

All of us respond to being recognized and thanked for what we do. This is also true of your board members!

In my experience if you follow these steps and tips, you, too, can be on the path to developing an effective fundraising board for your organization.

This article was adapted for The Public Manager Mini-Forum from a presentation at the December 2004 Northern Virginia Conference on Nonprofit Management for executive directors, board of director members, and development staff.

Nonprofit Board of Directors Evaluation Instrument

5 = Excellent; 4 = Good; 3 = Fair; 2 = Needs Work; 1 = Needs Considerable Work

I. Board Structure and Organization

1.1.	The Board has clear performance objectives and a work plan to guide its activities.	1 2 3 4 5
1.2.	The Board meets an appropriate number of times to conduct its business.	1 2 3 4 5
1.3.	Board meetings focus on issues and policies, and not on minor matters.	1 2 3 4 5
1.4.	Board meetings are efficient, informative, and productive.	1 2 3 4 5
1.5.	Board members receive sufficient orientation on the organization to do their job effectively.	1 2 3 4 5
1.6.	The Board is diverse in terms of race and ethnicity, skill sets, gender, and work setting.	1 2 3 4 5
1.7.	The Board's size is appropriate to complete its tasks.	1 2 3 4 5
1.8.	Board meetings are well attended and Board members come well prepared.	1 2 3 4 5
1.9.	The nominations and elections process is objective, designed to attract the best talent.	1 2 3 4 5

Maximum points this section = 45 points   Total points: _____

II. The Board and CEO

2.1.	The Board works well with its chief executive officer. There is a clear division of responsibilities between Board and staff.	1 2 3 4 5
2.2	The Board has made its expectations of the CEO clear, with a job description reflective of the organization's mission.	1 2 3 4 5
2.3.	Individual Board members invest time between board meetings to keep current and assist the CEO and staff.	1 2 3 4 5
2.4.	Board members are regularly available to the CEO and other staff to cultivate and make contact with donors.	1 2 3 4 5
2.5.	The Board conducts a regular evaluation of the CEO in a manner that allows for input, including by the CEO.	1 2 3 4 5

Maximum points this section = 25 points   Total points: _____

III. The Board and Committees

3.1.	Much of the work of the organization is delegated to committees empowered to make decisions and take action.	1 2 3 4 5
3.2.	The Board respects the work of committees and does not redo committee work.	1 2 3 4 5
3.3.	Committees are adequately staffed to do their work.	1 2 3 4 5
3.4.	Committees are used as a means of identifying and cultivating leadership.	1 2 3 4 5
3.5.	Board members demonstrate and express support for committee work.	1 2 3 4 5
3.6.	Committees function in a timely and efficient manner.	1 2 3 4 5

Maximum points this section = 30 points   Total points: _____

IV. Planning and Implementation

4.1.	There is a consensus about and clear understanding of the organization's mission.	1 2 3 4 5
4.2.	There is a current strategic plan.	1 2 3 4 5
4.3.	The strategic plan drives board decisions and activities.	1 2 3 4 5
4.4.	The strategic plan is reviewed at least annually.	1 2 3 4 5
4.5.	Planning is based in part on input from constituencies and stakeholders.	1 2 3 4 5
4.6.	There is an annual leadership retreat that gives full consideration to important issues.	1 2 3 4 5
4.7.	The organization's planning takes into account the environments in which the organization operates.	1 2 3 4 5

Maximum points this section = 35 points   Total points: _____

V. Financial

5.1.	The Board establishes realistic financial goals and objectives for the organization.	1 2 3 4 5
5.2.	The Board exercises its fiduciary responsibilities and carefully monitors the organization's finances.	1 2 3 4 5
5.3.	Financial planning is integrated with strategic planning.	1 2 3 4 5
5.4.	The Board contributes philanthropically with 100% participation.	1 2 3 4 5
5.5.	Board members make available their own personal networks in order to effectively raise funds.	1 2 3 4 5

Maximum points this section = 25 points   Total points: _____

VI. Ethics

6.1.	Board members at all times act in a manner that reflects favorably on the organization.	1 2 3 4 5
6.2.	Board members recuse themselves from involvement in any activity or decision that might be a conflict of interest.	1 2 3 4 5
6.3.	Board members put the success of the organization ahead of their own personal gain.	1 2 3 4 5

Maximum points this section = 15 points   Total points: _____

Summary

I. Board structure and organization   _____
II. Board and CEO   _____
III. Board and committees   _____
IV. Planning and Implementation   _____
V. Financial   _____
VI. Ethics   _____

Scoring Range

160–175 Excellent
140–159 Above Average
105–139 Adequate, But Improvement Needed
70–104 Inadequate, Significant Work Needed
35–69 Seriously Inadequate; Major Work Needed

Source: Copyright © Prentice Associates, Rockville, Maryland.

Source: © 2004 by Alice Collier Cochran. Reprinted with permission by John Wiley & Sons, Inc.

WHO IS ROBERT

AND WHY DO WE STILL FOLLOW HIS RULES ANYWAY?

This one-of-a-kind book challenges nonprofit leaders (and anyone who runs meetings) to retire Robert's Rules of Order and adopt a simpler, friendlier, and more effective method for conducting meetings—*Roberta's Rules of Order.*

Using traditional sailing ships as a metaphor, meetings and governance expert Alice Collier Cochran helps groups make the journey from the "shore" that represents the culture of Robert's Rules—procedural formality, debate, simple majority rule—to the opposite "shore" of Roberta's Rules—informality, dialogue, and decision-making options. In doing so, she helps them to conduct friendlier, more effective meetings and to take the first step toward creating flexible, democratic organizations.

Cochran outlines practical principles for effective meetings and governance. She shows leaders a new way to run effective meetings, improve the way their organizations are governed, and more successfully achieve their mission and goals.

THE AUTHOR

Alice Collier Cochran, an independent consultant, conducts workshops on Roberta's Rules of Order for nonprofit management support organizations such as BoardSource, CompassPoint, and Marin Nexus in California. She has been a member of the board of the San Francisco chapters of the American Society for Training and Development, the Bay Area Organization Development Network, and the local Guild of the International Association of Facilitators.

MANAGEMENT/REFERENCE

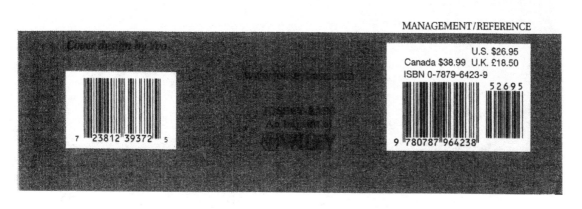

U.S. $26.95
Canada $38.99 U.K. £18.50
ISBN 0-7879-6423-9

52695

7 23812 39372 5

9 780787 964238

Chapter 3

Building a Professional Development Operation

KEY VOCABULARY

- Back-up
- Central Processing Unit (CPU)
- Hardware
- High-Speed Internet Connection
- Inkjet Printer
- Laser Printer
- Megs
- Memory
- Monitor
- Multitasking
- Office Suite
- RAM
- ROM
- Slug
- Software
- Strategic Plan
- Surge Protector

THE NEED FOR A DEVELOPMENT OFFICE

The development operation within an organization should manage all of the fundraising activities of that organization. Not only do the staff members coordinate all of the development efforts of the various departments within the organization, but they also manage all of the office operations that support fundraising. The development office is an integral part of a nonprofit organization's operation. It is one of the main sources of revenue for the organization, along with the membership, program support, conventions and meetings, continuing education, and publishing department. The development office should be considered a profit center for the organization and managed as such.

Many nonprofit organizations claim they have no financial need for a development office. For example, organizations with large membership bases may bring in enough money from their dues to support their operations and thus think they have no need for fundraising. When particular departments within an organization decide to expand their operations, they usually take on the fundraising responsibilities themselves—often with little or no coordination or cooperation from other departments or direction from the senior management staff. This can work effectively for a long time, until, suddenly, there is a crisis that requires a need for coordination. This is usually brought about when one department contacts a

> *The development office should be considered a profit center for the organization and managed as such.*

corporation or foundation that is being solicited concurrently by another department within the same organization. The prospective donor will often ask, "Which one of your programs (or departments) do you want us to support?" Usually, at this point in time, the executive director or a member of the senior management staff is called upon to decide which department should continue to solicit funding from that particular potential donor and which should step aside.

When this has occurred several times, staff members affected by the situation will request or demand that the organization find someone to coordinate these efforts so such conflicts will not happen again. Often at the same time, staff members will suggest that the organization hire a person to act not only as coordinator but also as the initiator of gift solicitation. Staff members want someone hired to raise funds so they can attend to the jobs for which they were hired and also expand the activities of their departments without diverting their energies from their day-to-day responsibilities and department operations. This is often how development offices are born.

Another reason a development office might be created is the institution has decided to embark upon a major fundraising effort—a capital campaign to construct a new building, to underwrite programs, to increase the number of scholarships, or to build an endowment. Thus, a development office may be started with no history of fundraising within the organization. Depending upon the reason for fundraising, having no history can be a major obstacle to overcome.

The size of the development operation can vary widely. Some organizations function for many years with a one-person development office. Others soon require three- or five-person operations. Yet others may employ more than 20 fundraising staff. This chapter will focus mainly on small to mid-size development operations. Larger operations, usually located within universities, have much more complex structures than this chapter will address.

The development functions should be an integral part of the organization's overall strategic plan. The fundraising effort will depend upon the organization's having a well-thought-out mission statement and goals as well as programs to support them. Development office staff members will then use these items to develop their fundraising plans. These plans must be accepted and supported by the institution's board and senior management as part of the entire organization's efforts.

Development office staff members will perform various duties, including the following: research prospects and solicit gifts; process gifts received; maintain donor records; produce numerous reports to distribute among various audiences; write proposals; write acknowledgment letters for gifts; write articles to promote fundraising efforts; develop a Web site for fundraising purposes; plan special events to raise money, promote institutional awareness, or enhance donor relations; train board members or other volunteers in fundraising methods; plan and organize major gift and planned giving efforts; and provide support for superiors when asked.

MAJOR FUNCTIONS OF THE DEVELOPMENT OFFICE AND STAFF AND RESOURCES NEEDED

Staff and resources for a development office will vary depending upon the functions of the office as well as the size of the organization. There are no set rules that dictate what number of staff or what size of office space will be needed for the development operation. Most organizations start small and grow only as money is raised. The same applies to development offices. Following are brief summaries of the functions of a development operation and what staff requirements are necessary to perform those functions successfully.

Active Fundraising

Most development departments are organized around annual giving, sponsorship, direct mail, special event, capital campaign, and planned giving activities. Board or trustee-led committees, along with other volunteers, will perform many of these activities with development staff. It is important that all activities be coordinated throughout the year by the development staff to seek maximum gift income for approved projects and programs.

Gift Processing, Recording, and Reporting

The development and finance departments are responsible for complying with IRS and American Institute of Certified Public Accountants (AICPA) guidelines. A single processing procedure should be used regardless of the number of different solicitation programs in operation. Each gift goes through a process of deposit, data entry, fund account assignment, and acknowledgment. Gifts received can include cash, checks, securities (stocks and bonds), works of art, jewelry, real estate, planned gifts (bequests, charitable remainder trusts, gift annuities etc.), and gifts-in-kind. The types of gifts that will be accepted by the organization must be decided in advance.

Reports listing gifts by source, purpose, and program must be produced on a regular basis. These reports which include unrestricted, restricted, annual fund, capital campaign, endowment, scholarship, research, and education will remain confidential and be circulated only to those who need them. Pledges will be recorded and follow-up invoicing will be conducted.

Permanent donor records will be maintained electronically and also, in certain cases, in paper files. A donor record will include giving history and contacts relating to gifts and pledges. Research information on donors and prospects will also be collected. In all of these activities, sensitive personal data must be kept in confidence by development staff and others who are given access to this information.

Acknowledgment and Recognition of Gifts

Each organization should have a gift policies and procedures manual so staff will know how to accept, record, acknowledge (thank), and recognize gifts properly. It is critical that all gifts are recorded in accordance with donors' wishes, especially when they are restricted gifts or are designated for special purposes.

Following the IRS guidelines for properly acknowledging gifts is a key responsibility of development staff. See sample acknowledgment letters in Appendix 3–A and 3–B. Recording of gifts should be undertaken as soon as they are received. Donors should be thanked for their gifts within 24 to 48 hours if possible. At the latest, each gift should be acknowledged within five business days.

Procedures for how donors will be recognized for their contributions should be established by the development staff and approved by the CEO and board. Creating a formal donor recognition policy will insure donor intent is followed, and donor privacy is maintained. Recognition is often given to donors for their gifts by publicizing the gift giving on a donor wall in a facility, in newsletters, in annual reports, or at a public event. Be certain your organization provides donors the opportunity to inform the organization that they do not wish to have their name appear in public or prefer to be listed as anonymous.

Donor Relations and Communications

The development department has the primary responsibility for donor relations, which involves donor recognition and communications. Maintaining regular communication with donors about the board and organization's activities and progress is key to building relationships with donors that will ensure their continued support.

Keep in mind that donors today expect the following:

- an organization to keep accurate records
- an acknowledgment of their gift and the appropriate recognition
- a report on how funds are used
- invitations to organization's public events
- access to information about programs, services, and financial affairs

Services to the Organization's Other Departments and Staff

Personnel in the development department are available to the organization's administrative and departmental staff for professional assistance on projects appropriate for fundraising. Often development staff are also available to the organization's chapters/affiliates to assist them with their development programs. Prospect research, proposal writing, prospect clearance, active solicitation, etc. are all duties development department staff can perform. Only the organization's programs or projects with greatest priority can command use of the development office budget for fundraising. All other projects may need to be funded by the department requesting assistance.

DEVELOPMENT POLICIES AND PROCEDURES

As mentioned in Chapter 1, nonprofit organizations today must be accountable and transparent in their actions in order to maintain the public trust, so critical to building successful donor relationships. Nonprofits must comply with all federal and state regulations pertaining to fundraising, especially being registered in those states where solicitations are conducted. See Appendix A for compliance information an organization needs.

In addition, written policies and procedures approved by the organization's board of directors are required to show that organizations adhere to ethical fundraising practices, to enhance relations with donors and funders, and to improve development staff efficiency and effectiveness. Exhibit 3–1 is a checklist of the types of development office policies and procedures an organization needs. Exhibits 3–2 and 3–3 are two sample policies.

THE BASIC REQUIREMENTS FOR SETTING UP A DEVELOPMENT OFFICE

Setting Up the Office

The development office serves not only as the fundraising arm of the organization but often as the public relations operation as well. Therefore, the appearance of the office to the public can often times be as important as what it does. If other organization staff members, potential donors, or outside guests visit the office, they should be able to enter the space and view a highly effective, organized, and clean office with a staff that exudes professionalism, energy, organization, and effectiveness. Everything that is displayed within the office or produced by the office

> *The development office serves not only as the fundraising arm of the organization but often as the public relations operation as well.*

staff should exhibit the highest level of quality. This office represents the organization and may be the first or only contact that a donor has with the organization.

Equipment

When establishing a development office, it is often tempting to purchase all the equipment and supplies at one time. Before embarking upon this method, consider first what can be shared with or obtained from other departments within the organization. Also, it may be possible to obtain equipment on loan from affiliate agencies or from firms associated with the organization through its volunteers. Leasing (or leasing with an option to buy) is another option to consider before purchasing.

The following basic equipment is needed to set up a development office.

Exhibit 3–1 Development Office Policies and Procedures Checklist

Does your organization have the following:		
1. a gift solicitation and acceptance policy	Yes _____	No _____
2. a policy and/or procedure for:		
– gifts of securities	Yes _____	No _____
– gifts of personal property	Yes _____	No _____
– gifts of real estate	Yes _____	No _____
– gifts of intellectual property	Yes _____	No _____
– restricted gifts	Yes _____	No _____
– establishing endowments	Yes _____	No _____
3. a donor privacy policy	Yes _____	No _____
4. a donor recognition policy	Yes _____	No _____
5. a written procedure for entering or recording gifts	Yes _____	No _____
6. a written procedure for acknowledging gifts	Yes _____	No _____
7. IRS language on receipts and thank yous	Yes _____	No _____
8. state disclosure statement on letters	Yes _____	No _____
9. a confidentiality policy pertaining to donor records and information	Yes _____	No _____
10. a permission policy for sending e-mail communications to members or donors	Yes _____	No _____

Exhibit 3–2 Sample Gift Acceptance Policy and Procedure

- The XYZ Organization seeks outright gifts and future gift commitments that are consistent with its mission. Donations generally will be accepted from individuals, partnerships, corporations, organizations, government agencies, or other entities without limitations—unless acceptance of gifts from a specific source is inconsistent with the organization's beliefs, values, and mission. The XYZ Organization will not accept gifts from companies whose products may be harmful to our clients or from donors whose requests for public recognition are incompatible with our philosophy of appreciation.

- In processing, all gifts will be coded in the donor database for the constituency source from which the gifts were given (e.g., individual, corporation, foundation, organization, etc.).

- Multi-year pledges for major gifts are encouraged, but for no more than three to five years. Donors should complete and sign a gift agreement or pledge commitment letter detailing the purpose of the gift, payment schedule, and how they wish their name to appear in donor recognition materials.

- Donors are encouraged to support areas reflecting their interests. The XYZ Organization's priorities include gifts for unrestricted, restricted, and endowment purposes.

- A selection of named or commemorative gift opportunities may be made available to each donor. Such opportunities represent a tangible means of demonstrating an individual donor's investment in the XYZ Organization.

- When gifts with restrictions are accepted, restrictions will be honored. These restrictions will be detailed in the donor's gift or pledge commitment letter.

- Donor information that should be private and confidential will not be made public.

Certain types of gifts must be reviewed prior to their being accepted because they will create liabilities or impose special obligations on the XYZ Organization. The types of gifts which will require review are as follows:

• Publicly Traded Securities

Stocks, bonds, and other securities may be accepted only upon approval of the executive director. A gift of stocks or bonds held more than six months, which has grown in value, not only qualifies for a charitable-contribution deduction (based on the fair market value) but also avoids tax on the appreciated portion of the gift. Valuation of stocks and bonds will be determined as the mean between the high and the low price on the date of the gift. The date of the gift will be calculated as: 1) the date the certificate is personally handed to a representative of XYZ Organization; 2) the date on the certificate if changed to the name of the XYZ Organization or its designated fiscal agent; or 3) the postmark date if mailed or the date and time of transfer if electronically transferred to an account at the XYZ Organization's broker's office.

• Closely Held Securities

Nonpublicly-traded securities may be accepted after a consultation with the treasurer and/or legal counsel. A qualified appraiser must determine the fair market value of the securities. Prior to acceptance, the XYZ Organization should explore methods of immediate liquidation of the securi-

continues

Exhibit 3–2 Sample Gift Acceptance Policy and Procedure (continued)

ties through redemption or sale. No commitment for repurchase or sale of closely held securities should be made prior to completion of the gift of the securities, as the transaction might be viewed by the IRS as a sale rather than a gift, with adverse tax consequences for the donor.

- **Real Estate**

Gifts of real estate should be reviewed by the XYZ Organization's board of directors or gift acceptance committee before acceptance. The donor should be responsible for obtaining and paying for an appraisal of the fair market value and an environmental audit of the property. Prior to presentation to the board or gift acceptance committee, a member of the staff must conduct a visual inspection of the property. If the property is located in a geographically isolated area, a local real estate broker can substitute for a member of the staff in conducting the visual inspection. Property that is encumbered by a mortgage should not be accepted.

- **Life Insurance**

The executive director of the XYZ Organization can accept a life insurance policy as a gift only when the organization is named as the owner and beneficiary of the policy.

- **Tangible Personal Property**

Gifts of tangible property to the XYZ Organization should have use related to the organization's tax-exempt purposes. Gifts of jewelry, artwork, collections, equipment and software may be accepted after approval by the gift acceptance committee. Such gifts of tangible personal property defined above shall be used by or sold for the benefit of the organization. The organization must follow all IRS requirements in connection with disposing of gifts of tangible personal property and filing of appropriate tax reporting forms. An authorized appraisal of the contributed property paid for by the donor is required for any gift over $5,000. The board will have final approval for acceptance of all gifts of personal property.

The XYZ Organization may elect to refuse gifts of cash, securities, real estate, or other items of value if there is reason to believe that such gifts are incompatible with the mission of the organization, conflict with its core values or would create financial, administrative, or programmatic burden. The executive director is directed to refer questionable gifts to the executive committee or the board of directors for guidance on a case-by-case basis.

Planned Giving: While an outright gift is always best for the XYZ Organization, some donors may find that they can support the organization at a more substantial level with a planned gift. Mechanisms such as charitable remainder trusts, unitrusts, charitable gift annuities, bequests, and gifts of life insurance policies often provide the donor with significant tax relief while at the same time providing for the future of the XYZ Organization.

The following gifts offer benefits to the donor that may include receiving an income or passing assets onto heirs.

- **Charitable Gift Annuity**—a contract between the XYZ Organization and the donor paying a guaranteed lifetime income to one or two beneficiaries in return for a gift of cash, securities, or real estate. The rate of payout on gift annuities will follow the rates established by the American Council on Gift Annuities. There shall be no more than two beneficiaries. The minimum gift accepted to establish a charitable gift annuity is $10,000. No income beneficiary for a charitable gift annuity shall be younger than 50 years of age.
- **Deferred Gift Annuity**—an annuity tailored to meet the needs of the donor who prefers to receive income at a future date (at least one year after the date of the gift), but who claims a substantial charitable contribution in the year of the gift. The principal value of a charitable deferred gift annuity can be pledged over a period of years prior to when payments are scheduled to begin. The donor will not receive income until the entire pledge is fulfilled. There will be no more than two beneficiaries. The minimum gift accepted to establish a deferred gift annuity is $10,000. No income beneficiary for a deferred gift annuity shall be younger than 40 years of age.
- **Pooled Income Fund**—a fund that operates much like a mutual fund. Administrative fees shall be paid from the income earned on the pooled income fund. No income beneficiary in the fund shall be younger than 55 years of age. No more than two income beneficiaries may be named. The minimum initial contribution to the fund shall be $10,000. Additional gifts may be added for amounts beginning at $1,000.
- **Charitable Trusts**—a trust of which the XYZ Organization does not act as trustee. The administration of these trusts should be performed by a bank trust department or other trustee selected by the donor.
- **Charitable Remainder Unitrust**—an individual trust providing for annual income to a donor and/or named beneficiaries that can increase or decrease year to year, depending on annual valuation of the trust's assets. A unitrust is well suited to a donor seeking income growth, though with some downside risk. A net income only unitrust is well suited to donors of real estate.
- **Charitable Remainder Annuity Trust**—a trust offering the assurance of a fixed dollar income. The donor and/or beneficiary receive annually an amount of dollars fixed irrevocably at the time the gift is established and stated in the trust agreement. The minimum gift is $100,000.
- **Lead Trust (Income to Charity for a Term Certain)**—a trust whose income or "lead" interest is given to the XYZ Organization and the remainder interest is given to one or more non-charitable beneficiaries, which can be the donor or his or her family. This gift option offers current income to the XYZ Organization and is a method where assets can be retained by the donor or passed to heirs at a later time, often at considerable tax savings.
- **Bequest**—a gift bequeathed to the XYZ Organization in a donor's will. Unless its use is specified by the donor, the XYZ Organization will direct this gift to the organization's endowment fund.

Source: AFP's Ready Reference Series, *Developing Fundraising Policies and Procedures*, Association of Fundraising Professionals (AFP), 2007, Arlington, Virginia.

Exhibit 3–3 Sample Acknowledgment Policy and Procedure

1. Acknowledge all gifts within three business days using appropriate thank you letters based on level of gift.
2. Gifts of $249 or less will be acknowledged with the appropriate thank you letter or pre-printed card signed by the executive director.
3. Gifts of more than $250 will be acknowledged with the appropriate thank you letter signed by the executive director and including the required IRS language. If no goods or services were received in exchange for the gift, insert "No goods or services were received in exchange for your gift. Therefore, the full amount of your contribution is tax deductible as allowed by law." If a good or service was received, the organization must inform the donor of its fair market value in order for the donor to know the tax-deductible portion of the contribution. "In exchange for your contribution of $500, you received a book with an estimated fair market value of $75, which means $425 is your tax-deductible contribution."
4. The board chair will send an additional thank you letter to donors of gifts of $500 or more.
5. The director of development will call donors of $500–$999 to thank them personally.
6. The executive director will call donors of $1,000 or more to thank them personally.
7. Members of the board of directors will be assigned five thank you calls at each board meeting.

Source: AFP's Ready Reference Series, *Developing Fundraising Policies and Procedures,* Association of Fundraising Professionals (AFP), 2007, Arlington, Virginia.

For other sample policies and procedures, see AFP's Ready Reference booklet, *Developing Fundraising Policies and Procedures: Best Practices for Accountability and Transparency.*

Computer

A development office will need to have at least one desktop computer that is compatible and linked with the organization's other computer equipment, networks, and software. Whether the operating environment is Windows- or Mac-based depends upon what is currently operational within the organization. If the organization is so new that no computer system has been selected, then an IBM PC compatible personal computer system is recommended, because most of the software packages used in fundraising and financial management are based on the Windows operating systems. Again, if the organization and development operation are so new that acquiring capital expenditures is not feasible, it is possible to lease computer equipment with the option to purchase once enough money has been raised. A number of organizations across the country work with nonprofits to help them acquire used computers. See Appendix 3–C at the end of this chapter for a list of such organizations. It is important for maximum efficiency to accept donated computers that are not more than three years old; have at least a Pentium 3 processor running at 1GHz or more; 20GB hard disk; and 256MB or more of RAM. Larger development offices within a university system or large-membership organizations most likely will have a mainframe system or use an outside vendor who maintains their member or alumni lists for them. Usually, the reason to link with this system is to have access to the membership or alumni data, which can then be downloaded into the development office computer system for manipulation.

The basic hardware needed to operate a development office includes the following:

- CPU. The central processing unit (CPU) is the "heart" of the computer. When selecting a computer, refer to the requirements of the software that you will be using and make sure that the computer is capable of running all of the software at speeds necessary to perform the job. Get all of the power and memory that you need in the beginning. Don't "pinch pennies" at this stage. Make sure that the system is capable of being upgraded, as technology changes nearly daily. Again, because of the rapid changes in technology, it may be wise to lease equipment instead of purchasing or budget for hardware upgrades every two to three years. Be aware that if there is more than one staff person, the office computers need to be able to "talk" with one another or be "networked."
- Monitor. Select a monitor with a screen at least 17 inches diagonally or larger, especially if the office will be responsible for designing brochures and using graphics and drawing software packages.
- Keyboard. There are many types of keyboards available today. Find one that is comfortable to use and compatible with your equipment.
- High-speed Internet. Connection is either through DSL or a high-speed cable connection.
- Printer. A laser printer is necessary because the work that is produced by the development staff needs to be of superior quality. If you are considering an inkjet printer, use it as a back-up printer or for color printing only. Consider it for purchase after you have bought a top-quality laser printer.
- Surge Protector. This is a device that protects both hardware and software from being damaged by a surge in power through the electrical or phone wires. Some will even maintain a power supply for up to 30 minutes.
- Back-up System. It is vital that you have an external back-up system to maintain copies of your computer files. The files should be saved or backed up on a daily or weekly basis. Services are available for a small monthly fee that will remotely back-up your system. Otherwise, you should purchase an external back-up system for your office.
- Virus Protection. Make sure that appropriate virus protection software is purchased and installed.

- Service Contract. One of the most important items to remember when purchasing equipment is the service contract. Make sure that it is as broad as possible and covers both parts and labor.

The basic software needed to operate a development office includes the following:

- Word Processing. Word processing software, such as WordPerfect or Word is a necessity in the operation of a development office. Almost all written communication will be created using the word processing program.
- Spreadsheet. Spreadsheet software such as Excel is useful when creating budgets, tracking data, or developing reports that compute totals and percentages, etc.
- Relational Database. There are many software programs available that have been designed specifically for fundraising. A sampling of companies that offer software designed for this purpose can be found in Appendix 4–B. Some organizations initially use Microsoft Access to develop their database before purchasing a commercial product.
- Association Management System. There are special software programs that help associations and nonprofits manage other departments, such as conferences, meetings, and publications.

Before selecting a computer software system to aid with fundraising, evaluate your needs and the services that each system provides. Consider the following when making your decision to purchase software: (1) Is it flexible and easy to use? (2) Is there training available to the customer and what is its cost? (3) What type of technical support is provided and at what cost?

Chapter 4, "Your Fundraising Database—A Tool for Success," provides more information regarding fundraising database management systems.

Copier

One of the most important pieces of equipment required in the development operation is a high-quality copier. The organization should have a high-speed copier that can run multiple copies, enlarge and reduce copy, collate and staple, and use various sizes of paper. If the cost of this type of copier is beyond the scope of the organization, then find the nearest copy center that has 24-hour service (or extended service hours, including weekends) and make arrangements to open an account. Although reproductions of everyday correspondence can be made on small, slow, single-function copiers, there often will be a need to run multiple copies of proposal documentation and exhibits.

Postage Machine

A U.S. Postal Service survey reports that you could save up to 20 percent in postage costs using the right meter system. A postage meter will print the exact amount of postage needed. There are

"THERE. I THINK I'VE UNJAMMED IT. YOUR PROPOSAL WAS CAUGHT ON A TECHNICALITY."

Source: Copyright © Mark Litzler.

no trips to the post office because you are out of the exact denomination of stamps. Also, a meter prevents stamps from being available for personal use or theft.

In addition, accurate accounting of postage can be kept using a meter machine. Plus, staff members can use the meter to print postage right in the office, thus saving energy and trips to the post office for overnight delivery packages. By metering envelopes, time also is saved on mail delivery because metered envelopes don't have to be cancelled and postmarked at a postal station (the meter has taken care of these two steps).

The smallest to the largest organizations can develop their own identity by having a "slug" designed to carry a tagline or message promoting the organization. A slug is printed to the left of the postage each time an envelope is put through the postage machine. This message can be changed to reflect different slogans, campaigns, anniversaries, centennials, etc. The small organization can be more efficient with the use of a postage meter and look more official with the use of a slug.

A postage meter is also a timesaver. Envelopes can be sealed and stamped in one step. There is no more "licking" of envelopes and stamps or "sticky" fingers when working on a mailing. When considering large mailings, it is definitely wiser to contract with a direct-mail house for these services. Most small offices will not have the space available to organize such a mailing, nor the staff to handle a project of this size.

File Cabinet

It is important to first consider the storage needs of the office—what is needed immediately and what will be needed in the near future and in the long range. In addition to establishing files, there undoubtedly will be a need for storing printed materials and office supplies. A storage cabinet may be required, or a lateral file cabinet with drawers whose fronts lift up and slide back may be used for storage of paper, supplies, etc.

Every development office needs to have at least one file cabinet with a lock. Any check that cannot be deposited in the bank on the day it arrives in the office needs to be kept in a locked and secure place. There also will be confidential documentation that requires a locked file.

Lateral file cabinets cost more but save space in an office. The tops of these two-drawer files can be topped with wood or laminate to look more like a piece of furniture. These can be used to assemble documents or hold printers, postage machines, or other office equipment. Whatever type of file cabinet is selected, be sure to purchase one of good quality. Look for drawers that open smoothly and easily and that will not drag or tip if fully loaded. It is wiser to spend a little more and buy file cabinets that will last for many years under heavy use. Do not be afraid to purchase secondhand, used, or previously owned cabinets. Someone else may be upgrading, and it could save much of your office's budget. Also, these can be electrostatically painted to present a uniform look in the office.

Calculator and Adding Machine

An adding machine or calculator with a tape is essential to balance the daily intake of money, run a tape of accounts, or accurately track the statistical breakdown of donations.

To make quick calculations, a small handheld calculator may be easier to use than the adding machine. These are inexpensive and should be considered a "must" for a development office. Also, the computer can be used as a calculator.

Telephones

There are many types of telephones and telephone systems available today as well as telephone companies to provide service to fundraising operations. It is important to understand what your immediate needs are and what your future needs will be. If the organization is extremely small and has only one office space, then a single phone line with a "call-waiting" feature may be sufficient. Most likely, if the organization has been in existence for awhile, it will have several departments and many offices, and the phones will be interconnected, with many lines and options. If not, be careful in your planning and determine what your specific needs are today and what they may be in the future. It is best not to use a cellular phone as your only phone. Although popular with many for their personal phones, the reception is not always clear. Keep in mind that this may be your prospective donors' first impression of you and your organization.

The development office should have a telephone number of its own and should list this number in its publications so when phones are being answered, the receptionist can respond by identifying the development office as opposed to just stating the foundation or organization's name. Just be sure to price and compare various systems. Is it necessary to have a series of sequential telephone numbers that roll over to the next when one is busy? Is an intercom system vital to the operation? Will a multi-line phone with teleconferencing capabilities make it easier to communicate with fundraising volunteers? Make sure that all options are considered and priced before installing phones and a phone system.

Voice Mail Service

A voice mail system or telephone answering service is required for times when the staff is speaking on one of the phone lines or when the office is closed or unoccupied. This service can be provided either through the phone company or through private management companies. Whatever type of service is selected, make sure that the message recorded or read is clear, concise, grammatically correct, and professional. This is not the place to be "cute" or to wish people "a nice day." The message might sound something like this:

> This is the ABC Development Office. We are currently unable to answer your call. Please leave your name, telephone number, date and time of call, and a brief message, and we will return your call as soon as possible. Thank you for calling the ABC Development Office.

E-mail

E-mail has made communicating even more simple. No longer does one need to call during business hours or send a letter or fax. It can be used 24 hours a day, and documents and photos can be sent as attachments. Whatever provider service is selected, e-mail is the number one means of communicating within the development office and between the office and board members, volunteers, and even donors and prospects.

Supplies

There are many office–supply companies available, many of which offer large discounts to their members and nonprofit organizations. These companies will deliver directly to your door. You may also wish to use the "warehouse" office supply centers, such as Costco, Staples, or Office Depot, for lower prices.

Office Space

If the opportunity exists to select the offices for the development operations, keep in mind that the space will need to be large enough for the following.

One-Person Office

The single office space will include a full-size desk with ample drawer space; one or more file cabinets, at least one with a lock; a computer, monitor, and keyboard; adequate workspace for mailings (either a table or the tops of lateral file cabinets); three chairs (one comfortable staff chair with good lumbar support and two guest chairs); printer; adequate lighting (both overhead and desk lamps); and other standard items necessary to run an office.

Many small shops rent available space from larger organizations or elect to rent an office in an "office suite," which provides reception/telephone coverage and meeting space.

Two- or Three-Person Office

Office space for two or three persons should include two or three rooms with desks, computers with a server to connect them, and chairs for the staff and guests. File cabinets and office equipment usually will be kept in a work room or outer office, where the workspace for the support staff will also likely be located. The director's office should be large enough to hold meetings or there should be access to other rooms within the organization in which to hold meetings—small or large conference rooms will do. Again, adequate lighting is a necessity.

Multi-Person Office

With more than three persons in an office, it is time to look for space that includes a reception area. In this area, one person will welcome guests, manage the phones, keep the files, as well as serve as administrative support for one or more other staff members. If possible, it is best to have a separate area away from the public's view for the office equipment and for such activities as collating, stuffing, copying, etc. Also, the director should have a quiet space away from the staff for confidential meetings, planning, etc. Plus, it is imperative to have a place for volunteer help and meetings. This may be part of the development office space or be located elsewhere within the organization's complex.

Any development operation should be close to the president or executive director's office because he or she is frequently consulted or needed. Plus, placement of the office near conference, supply, and production rooms allows these rooms to be used for meetings, storage, and work and avoids the need to pay for extra space out of the development operation's budget.

Staff

Many development offices consist of only one staff person, the director. In a typical case, specific funds are set aside for the director's salary for a single year, and the director is expected to raise funds to cover his or her own salary and the expenses of the office. Additional staff will be added only if the money is raised in advance. Most institutions will not risk funding a two- to three-person office until adequate funds have been raised.

> *Most institutions will not risk funding a two- to three-person office until adequate funds have been raised.*

If enough money has been raised or budgeted for additional staff, the first person to be hired should be a highly qualified administrative support person. This person needs to be completely familiar with the software system used in the office as well as have an understanding of relational databases. He or she must also have a good command of the English language and be a good speller and an excellent grammarian. In addition, he or she must be discreet—able to maintain confidentiality. This person often will be the first person met by someone contacting the development office. Thus, good phone skills and impeccable personal grooming are essential.

In addition, this person must be able to operate the printing and copying equipment as well as understand filing systems. Look for a person who fits the personality of the office and organization.

When adding a third person to the office, the type of skills a person should have often depends upon the activities of the fundraising operation. If there are many special events held, then hire someone to focus on events. If the office is operating a capital campaign, then a staff person to manage the campaign (do research or work with volunteer solicitors) may be needed. Whatever the need, the third person is usually a junior professional brought on to support the activities of the director. The administrative work is usually performed by the administrative assistant, with back-up support from the junior professional.

Office structures beyond the three-person staff will vary widely depending upon the activities of the development operations. There may be a large annual appeal direct-mail operation requiring many staff persons, or a capital campaign large enough to command several—10 or more—staff persons. It is difficult to suggest any pattern of hiring after the third staff person has been added. The position descriptions developed for hiring staff will reflect the direction that the development operations are taking. Some common job titles include

- Manager, Annual Giving
- Manager, Foundation Relations

- Major Gift Officer
- Director, Corporate and Foundation Relations
- Manager, Sponsorships

THE DEVELOPMENT OFFICE BUDGET

The size of the budget will vary, but the elements will remain the same for small, medium, and large development operations. An example of a budget for a development office is presented in Exhibit 3–4.

VARIOUS MODELS FOR A DEVELOPMENT OFFICE

One-Person Office—Director of Development

The director of development must be a strong manager of people, time, and money. The individual who manages a one-person office must be exceedingly well organized and capable of handling multiple tasks, including the following: volunteer training and development; office budgeting, financial planning, and fiscal management; direct mail production; proposal writing; donor solicitation, acknowledgment, and recognition; data entry and updating; purchasing and monitoring of supplies; research; all telephone calls and other communications; and special events and receptions.

Whatever the size of the development staff, the director must report to the most senior person in the organization—the chief executive officer (CEO), the president, or the executive director. The development director also must have access to the board of the organization. Be wary of an organization in which the CEO wants all access to the board to come first through him or her. The development director must develop a relationship with the board to build a good fundraising program. The board chair should alert the director of development of potential problems that the CEO may not want to admit. Anyone considering accepting the position of development director should always ask to meet with the board chair before accepting the position. Make sure that as director of development you will have the authority to make changes if and when needed. See sample Director of Development job description in Exhibit 3–5.

> *Whatever the size of the development staff, the director must report to the most senior person in the organization.*

Office with Both Professional and Administrative Staff

The office that has grown to include administrative staff will finally free the development executive of the clerical and administrative tasks that can be so time-consuming. Tasks that can be delegated to a secretary or administrative assistant include the following: ordering and monitoring supplies; opening and distributing mail; reception and phone duties; gift processing, monitoring donor records, and pledge monitoring; research and file controls; database maintenance; report generation; Web site updating; and other administrative duties. The executive's duties can then expand to include additional prospect cultivation and solicitation, proposal writing, volunteer management and training, and strategic planning. See sample job description for a development associate that includes both administrative and fundraising duties in Exhibit 3–6.

Integrated with Other Departments In the Organization

A more complex and highly structured development office will be found in large-membership associations, cultural organizations, and institutions of higher education. Within a university setting, there will be several development operations in the various colleges or departments as well as a central office. Within this structure, there may be a vice president of institutional advancement along with directors of the following: the annual fund, the capital campaign, corporate fundraising, foundation relations, planned giving, research and records, public relations, alumni relations, etc. All of these directors report to the vice president. In association fundraising, a similar structure may exist, with the addition of directors of direct mail and membership, who also report to the vice president. Usually these offices will be connected through weekly meetings of their senior staff and electronically via a networked computer system. Communication is as vital to organizations of this size as it is to smaller offices. Here, there is more to coordinate, more diverse personalities to manage, and more money to raise.

Formal education is essential to the development of fundraising staff of all levels. Training should occur both on the job and through continuing education. Classes in management, leadership, computer literacy, financial planning, tax laws, human relations, interpersonal skills, etc., should be included in the planning and budgeting process. Any professional staff member who does not have a baccalaureate degree should be encouraged to obtain one. Those having undergraduate degrees should be encouraged to obtain certification (CFRE, ACFRE, CAE, CMP), a master's degree, or a doctorate.

> *Formal education is essential to the development of fundraising staff of all levels.*

The size of the development operation is not the most important factor determining the operation's success. A small, well-managed operation can raise as much money as a large, mismanaged development office. In a small or large operation, the development director must get to know the board immediately. Board members must have confidence in the talent and personality of the development staff. If they don't, success will be difficult to achieve. Also, be sure to know the organization's mission and programs. It is impossible to present the cause effec-

Exhibit 3–4 Development Office Budget

Development Salaries	Previous Fiscal Year	Current Fiscal Year	Estimated Next Fiscal Year
Director of Development	$ _____	$ _____	$ _____
Associate Director	$ _____	$ _____	$ _____
Assistant Director	$ _____	$ _____	$ _____
Research Assistant	$ _____	$ _____	$ _____
Special Events Coordinator	$ _____	$ _____	$ _____
Development Associate	$ _____	$ _____	$ _____
Administrative Assistant	$ _____	$ _____	$ _____
Receptionist/Office Manager	$ _____	$ _____	$ _____
Temporary Employees	$ _____	$ _____	$ _____
Student Employees	$ _____	$ _____	$ _____
Subtotal	$ _____	$ _____	$ _____
Fringe Benefits (%)	$ _____	$ _____	$ _____
Projected Pay Increases (%)	$ _____	$ _____	$ _____
Development Operations	$ _____	$ _____	$ _____
Office Rental	$ _____	$ _____	$ _____
Equipment Fees	$ _____	$ _____	$ _____
Purchases	$ _____	$ _____	$ _____
Rentals/Leases	$ _____	$ _____	$ _____
Maintenance	$ _____	$ _____	$ _____
Postage	$ _____	$ _____	$ _____
US Mail	$ _____	$ _____	$ _____
FED EX	$ _____	$ _____	$ _____
UPS	$ _____	$ _____	$ _____
Printing	$ _____	$ _____	$ _____
Telephone	$ _____	$ _____	$ _____
Local	$ _____	$ _____	$ _____
Long Distance	$ _____	$ _____	$ _____
Travel	$ _____	$ _____	$ _____
Local	$ _____	$ _____	$ _____
Out of Town	$ _____	$ _____	$ _____
Meals	$ _____	$ _____	$ _____
Tips/Gratuities	$ _____	$ _____	$ _____
Dues/Memberships	$ _____	$ _____	$ _____
Conferences	$ _____	$ _____	$ _____
Consulting Fees	$ _____	$ _____	$ _____
Vendor Fees	$ _____	$ _____	$ _____
Web Site Design and Hosting Fees	$ _____	$ _____	$ _____
Supplies	$ _____	$ _____	$ _____
Entertainment	$ _____	$ _____	$ _____
Volunteer Committee Expenses	$ _____	$ _____	$ _____
Board Expenses	$ _____	$ _____	$ _____
List Rentals	$ _____	$ _____	$ _____
Mailing House Fees	$ _____	$ _____	$ _____
Books, Magazines, Periodicals	$ _____	$ _____	$ _____
Photography/Art/Design	$ _____	$ _____	$ _____
Awards/Plaques/Gifts	$ _____	$ _____	$ _____
Professional Development	$ _____	$ _____	$ _____
Insurance	$ _____	$ _____	$ _____
Subtotal	$ _____	$ _____	$ _____
GRAND TOTAL	$ _____	$ _____	$ _____

tively to a potential donor if your homework hasn't been done or if your board and other volunteers have not been trained to solicit donors.

If the organization is large, meet with the heads of all departments. Also, visit similar organizations within the community to see how their development operations are run. Pattern your operations after those that are successful. Carefully review your organization board, fundraising history, and donor profile. How well do they fit the community? Are community leaders on your board? Are they and others giving fully of their means? Have all

Exhibit 3–5 Director of Development Position

The Director of Development is responsible for developing and coordinating the XYZ Organization's comprehensive development program. The director plans, organizes, implements, and promotes the organization's development goals. The director is responsible for raising unrestricted, restricted, and capital campaign funds to meet the needs of the organization.

Reporting Relationship

The Director of Development reports directly to the President/CEO or the Vice President of Development.

Roles and Responsibilities

- To communicate the mission of XYZ and the possibilities for support enthusiastically and articulately as required to individuals, corporations, foundations, and other organizations.
- To develop fundraising-related goals and strategies with the President/CEO, Board, Development Committee, and other volunteers.
- To maintain a development office and organize all development activities, including supervision of staff and volunteers and maintenance of donor database. Responsible for implementing development policies and procedures.
- To plan, organize, and conduct a fundraising program that utilizes a variety of appropriate methods including direct mail, special events, telephone and personal solicitation to raise unrestricted, restricted, and capital campaign funds to meet XYZ's needs. Working with the President/CEO, Board of Directors, and senior staff to determine programs that are priorities for funding.
- To prepare, submit, and monitor, in conjunction with the Chief Financial Officer, an approved budget for the development program.
- Responsible for providing President/CEO, Board, and Development Committee with regular reports on fundraising progress.
- To prepare and monitor a timeline for year's development activities.
- To oversee, guide, and assist the Development Committee and subcommittees with the help of the Development Committee co-chairs and subcommittee chairs.
- To train and manage volunteers involved in special event fundraising for XYZ.
- To conduct research on prospective corporate, foundation, and government funders. Draft proposals with input from program staff.
- To be responsible for ongoing cultivation and solicitation of current and prospective major donors.
- To prepare regular communications for donors, prospects, and the wider community, i.e., newsletter, informational mailings, etc., or to use XYZ Organization materials and publications whenever appropriate for cultivation and stewardship purposes.
- To develop appropriate printed and written materials to be used in all fundraising activities.
- To prepare, in conjunction with the Chief Financial Officer, and distribute an annual report of development activities, including a listing of donors.
- To be responsible for keeping current with issues and trends in the development field in order to make recommendations for their implementation to the appropriate leadership.

Experience and Skills Required

- Bachelor's Degree
- A minimum of seven years increasing experience with demonstrated success
- Development experience with similar organization highly desirable
- CFRE required
- Strong verbal and written communication skills
- Excellent organizational and people skills
- Strong computer skills
- The ability to work under pressure and meet deadlines
- Must be creative, able to generate ideas, and a self-starter
- The ability to maintain accountability and to work independently and creatively, while functioning as part of a cooperative and coordinated team
- Must be responsible, dependable, and display the highest level of integrity

giving opportunities been explored or has the organization been using only one or two methods? Why do the current donors support the organization? What is the profile of the average donor? Having a clear understanding of why people support the organization will help in the development of plans to expand support.

The development director also should become an active member of the nonprofit professional world. By joining the Association of Fundraising Professionals, which focuses on general fundraising; the Council for Advancement and Support of Education (CASE), which focuses on educational fundraising; the Associa-

tion for Healthcare Philanthropy (AHP), which focuses on raising funds for hospitals; the Association Foundation Group (AFG), which focuses on Associations and their supporting foundations that fundraise; and the American Association of Homes and Services for the Aging (AAHSA), which focuses on raising funds for retirement communities and other facilities for seniors, you will find colleagues who have experienced the same successes and plights. These colleagues may help you in your current position and can certainly open doors for you when seeking other positions in the development field. By sharing knowledge with and learning from your colleagues, you can better understand what

Exhibit 3–6 Development Associate Position Description

The Development Associate assists the Director of Development in conducting the XYZ Organization's comprehensive development program. This person is responsible for the daily operations of the development department, including managing the donor database, entering gifts, preparing acknowledgment letters, creating progress reports, working with volunteers, and communicating with donors.

Reports to: Director of Development

Responsibilities include, but are not limited to, the following:

- provide support to Director of Development and Development Committee of the Board of Directors
- manage administrative aspects of fundraising campaigns such as arranging meetings, producing mailings, Board and committee follow-up, and scheduling appointments, if appropriate
- handle donor database management, preparation of thank you letters, fundraising reports, etc. Update database on a regular basis of major gift prospect contacts, meetings held, and solicitations completed
- draft fundraising-related materials, as needed
- coordinate communications to donors and wider communities on development-related matters
- coordinate and provide support for grant applications and foundation proposals
- other duties as assigned

Desired qualifications:

- bachelor's degree
- knowledge of nonprofit organizations
- word processing and database management skills
- strong written and oral communication skills
- strong organizational and time management skills
- detail-oriented, with strong attention to follow-through
- ability to work collaboratively with others
- must be responsible, dependable, and display the highest level of integrity

makes a good development director and operation. Exhibit 3–7 lists the duties of a development officer and Exhibit 3–8 lists questions to consider for a successful development program.

KNOWING WHEN TO MOVE FROM THE ONE-PERSON SHOP TO A LARGER OPERATION

When the director of development has raised enough money to support more than one person and the tasks at hand require more than one full-time staff person, then it is time to hire a second person in the development office. If the program has been running successfully with two people, then it is time to consider

Exhibit 3–7 The Duties of a Development Officer

1. Serve the administration and board through fundraising assignments.
2. Develop a plan that includes specific schedules and goals for obtaining funds from each public.
3. Promote loyalty, interest, and support between your institution and its publics.
4. Enlist, train, and raise effectiveness of volunteers making calls for donations.
5. Cultivate donors and prospects, and ask for donations.
6. Understand why donors give.
7. Be a partner with the Dean/President/Executive Director.
8. Be able to communicate.
9. Live up to a schedule.
10. Accept responsibility.

the next step. This could be hiring a person to concentrate fully on grantwriting—the researching and writing of proposals to support the many activities and programs of the organization. This is a time-consuming, full-time job that requires someone with excellent writing, research, and communication skills. If this proves successful after a year or two, then additional staff can be added when more money is raised to support them. This also may be the time when the board decides to embark upon a major fundraising effort that will require additional personnel. These new staff members may be hired as consultants or permanently. If the decision is made to hire permanent staff, make sure that this decision fits with the long-range goals and budget of the department.

The final step in the expansion of a development operation is the creation of a planned giving program. First, make sure that all other fundraising programs are running well, then introduce planned giving into the picture. This move can start small just by including in newsletters and other regular mailings information on how donors can remember the organization in their wills. Seminars can be held for the board and major donors to introduce them to the many options of planned giving/estate planning. At this point, a planned giving consultant could be brought on for advice, for direction, to organize and run the seminars, and to write articles. You may wish to work closely with a planned giving company to develop a limited program or contract

> *The final step in the expansion of a development operation is the creation of a planned giving program.*

Exhibit 3–8 A Readiness Checklist for a Successful Development Program

1. Is the mission relevant? Does the mission describe why the organization exists?
2. Does the organization have a vision for its future?
3. Is there an overall plan that identifies programs and services that the organization offers, their income potential, and cost to support?
4. Does the organization have a budget?
5. Does the organization have a strategic plan for the next three to five years?
6. Does the organization have a Board of Directors who governs the organization by planning, setting policies, and acquiring resources for the organization?
7. Does the Board participate in fundraising? How long do board members serve? Are there term limits for board members?
8. Are there opportunities for others to volunteer?
9. Does the organization have a written case for support? Do they refer to the case for support regularly to see if it needs updating?
10. Is there a professional staff? How many and for what departments? Is there sufficient staff to perform the duties necessary to advance the organization's mission?
11. Are there identified markets for fundraising, such as individuals, corporations, foundations, government support, other types of organizations? What does each constituent group need? How is research conducted on prospective donors?
12. Does the organization involve board members, nonboard volunteers, and staff in identifying, engaging, and soliciting potential contributors from potential sources?
13. Is the organization using a variety of fundraising activities to raise funds based on different purposes for different prospects? What types of activities do they use? Which are the most successful? Which have not been as successful?
14. Is the management style of the organization a team-approach or do people work independently based on their department and responsibilities?

with a planned giving vendor who offers a Web-based program. See Chapter 15, "Planned Giving," for more information.

EXPECTATIONS FOR THE DEVELOPMENT OFFICE

Any future expectations for the development office are established based upon the past performance of the operation. They also should be based upon successful completion of a development plan. The development office should complete a strategic development plan that is consistent with the strategic plan for the entire institution. Achievable goals and objectives should be set

based on this plan, and the development staff should be held accountable for meeting only the goals and objectives listed in the master plan. It is easy to have high expectations for a development operation, yet if proper planning is not done, the fundraising operation may fall short of its goals and expectations.

Proper planning makes it possible for the development staff to reach their goals. Improper planning can create a situation in which the staff may never be able to recover. Expectations may be set too high and be totally unrealistic. Establish a plan with a detailed timetable that is approved and accepted by the board or senior management. Define the role of the staff and the volunteers who will execute the plan and clearly state what support is needed from the board or other institutional departments to make the plan succeed. Only after clearly written goals and objectives have been accepted by all can the departmental staff be held accountable. See Chapter 5, "Developing and Evaluating Your Fundraising Plan," for more information.

Suggested Publications for the Development Office Library

A development office is not complete without a library of professional resource materials. In addition to a dictionary, thesaurus, and manual of style, all development offices should have fundraising resources available online, in the office, or at a nearby library or office resource center. These could include the following:

- *Advancing Philanthropy*, Association of Fundraising Professionals, Arlington, VA
- *Contributions*, Medfield, MA
- *Fundraising Success*, Skokie, IL
- Jones and Bartlett's nonprofit management and fundraising books, Jones and Bartlett, Sudbury, MA
- *Successful Fund Raising*, Stevenson Consultants, Sioux City, IA
- *The Chronicle of Philanthropy*, Washington, DC
- *The Corporate Fund Raising Directory*, Public Service Materials
- *The Foundation Directory*, The Foundation Center
- *The Leadership Library—Corporate Yellow Book, Federal Yellow Book*, Leadership Directories, Inc.
- *The Nonprofit Times*, Cedar Knolls, NJ
- *The Special Events Report*, International Events Group, Chicago, IL

Additional resources can be found in the bibliography.

Sample Gift Acknowledgment Letter

June 21, XXXX

Name
Address
City, State Zip

Dear Mr. Last Name:

On behalf of the ASCE Foundation, please let me extend our thanks for your gift of $100.00 received on June 13, XXXX, to the Foundation's XXXX *Annual Appeal*. This gift, along with your previous gift of $100.00 received on December 8, XXXX, brings your total contribution to the XXXX *Annual Appeal* to $200.00. We will be pleased to recognize your gifts at the Patron Level in the next issue of the ASCE Foundation News.

The IRS requires that the ASCE Foundation, a 501(c)(3) organization, provide contemporaneous acknowledgment of all gifts and include the fact that the Foundation provided no goods or services in exchange for these contributions. This letter serves not only to acknowledge this gift, but also to notify you that no goods or services were given by the ASCE Foundation in return for your gift of $100.00. This is your official tax receipt. Please retain it for tax-filing purposes.

Please know that your generosity serves as an important example to other ASCE Members, their colleagues, and friends, and helps to establish a strong base of support for the Foundation and civil engineering philanthropy.

Again, thank you for your gift.

Sincerely yours,

Jeanne G. Jacob, CAE, CFRE
Executive Vice President
ASCE Foundation

Sample Sponsor Acknowledgment Letter

April 24, XXXX

Name
Title
Firm
Street
City, State Zip

Dear Mr./Ms. Last Name:

On behalf of the ASCE Foundation and the Society it serves, please let me extend our thanks to FIRM NAME for its gift of $20,000.00, received on March 13, XXXX. This completes payment on your pledge for sponsorship at the Diamond Circle for the American Society of Civil Engineering's OPAL Awards Dinner, being held at the Ronald Reagan Building and International Trade Center, Washington, D.C., on April 25, XXXX.

The IRS requires that the ASCE Foundation, a 501(c)(3) organization, provide contemporaneous acknowledgment of all gifts and include whether or not the Foundation provided goods or services in exchange for these contributions. This letter serves not only to acknowledge this gift, but also to notify FIRM NAME that it will receive 16 tickets at $275.00 per ticket, of which $115.00 is taxable, for a total of $1,840.00 in goods or services in return for its gift of $20,000.00. This document is your official tax receipt. Please retain it for tax-filing purposes.

The OPAL Awards recognize the best of civil engineering. We are delighted that you will be joining us for the presentation of these most prestigious awards.

Again, thank you to FIRM NAME for sponsoring ASCE's OPAL Awards Dinner.

Sincerely yours,

Jeanne G. Jacob, CAE, CFRE
Executive Vice President
ASCE Foundation

Organizations That Help Provide Used Computers to Charities

For nonprofits that are just starting out and do not have the budget to purchase new computers, there are organizations that help provide used computers to charities. Following is a sampling of some organizations. Also, check in your local areas for other organizations that could assist your organization.

However, keep in mind that donated computers must be fairly new so that you can use the various software products you need to run your development operation. An older computer may not be as useful as you would like.

Alameda County Computer Resource Center
1501 Eastshore Highway
Berkeley, CA 94710
Phone: 510-528-4052
E-mail: info@accrc.org

Computer Bank Charity
P.O. Box 55441
Shoreline, WA 98155
Phone: 206-214-7779
E-mail: compbank@hotmail.com

Computer Reclamation, Inc.
10759 Tucker Street
Beltsville, MD 20705
Phone: 301-595-0995

East-West Education Development Foundation
55 Temple Place
Boston, MA 02111
Phone: 617-542-1234
E-mail: Alex@donate.org

Gifts in Kind International
333 North Fairfax Street
Alexandria, VA 22314
Phone: 703-836-2121
E-mail: info@giftsinkind.org

Marin Computer Resource Center
60 Leveroni Court, Suite 200B
Novato, CA 94949
Phone: 415-883-1428
E-mail: info@mcrc.org

National Cristina Foundation
500 West Putnam Avenue
Greenwich, CT 06830
Phone: 203-863-9100
E-mail: ncf@cristina.org

Non-Profit Computing, Inc.
125 East 63rd Street
New York, NY 10021
Phone: 212-759-2368
E-mail: npc@igc.org

Your Fundraising Database—A Tool for Success

KEY VOCABULARY

- Application Service Provider (ASP)
- Back-up
- Computer Virus
- Database
- LAN
- Technology Consultant

NEED FOR DATA MANAGEMENT

In these times of fierce competition for charitable contributions, nonprofit organizations must maximize their fundraising potential. Fundraising needs to be more efficient and more productive. By doing so, a nonprofit organization can implement programs that serve the public good and meet the needs of its donors. Everything you read or hear today reinforces the belief that donors are increasingly more concerned that their contributions are used effectively. Because of the competition in the nonprofit sector, an organization must value its donors to retain their continued support. You will learn later in this book that it is much less expensive to renew a donor than to acquire a new one. In the current environment, donor information, the technology on which it depends, and its proper use will be the determining factors for an organization's success in fundraising.

> *In the current environment, donor information, the technology on which it depends, and its proper use will be the determining factors for an organization's success in fundraising.*

There are often obstacles that must be overcome so that an organization can use technology effectively. These may include the following:

- A donor database may not be current, may have many errors, or may be difficult to extract information.
- Generating necessary reports may be difficult.
- It may take too long to get counts, segments, and data from the system, and only one or two people may even know how to do it.
- Computer systems may be inadequate, overloaded, and/or used inefficiently.
- Donor database information may not integrate with accounting, special events fundraising, membership, and other types of data.
- Organizations using computer systems with old hardware or software technology may view changes to these systems as too complex, too disruptive, and too expensive.

These examples illustrate why a nonprofit organization may be dissatisfied with its current computers, hardware, and software. Most lack sources of useful advice and support, fail to do adequate planning, are unable to invest in the systems they really need, and lack the knowledge to apply computing power to their complex needs.

Today, there are many resources available to organizations. Nonprofit support groups are forming across the country to provide technical assistance, training, and exposure to a variety of software and hardware products.

Organizations that provide technical assistance include the following:

- NPower—www.npower.org
  - NPower affiliates including Phoenix, Arizona; Los Angeles, California; Denver, Colorado; Greater Washington, DC, area; Atlanta, Georgia; Indianapolis, Indiana; Greater New York City metro region; Charlotte, North Carolina; Portland, Oregon; and Seattle, Washington provide a suite of technology assistance services to their communities
  - National projects that promote the use of technology in the nonprofit community
- N-TEN—www.nten.org
  - Nonprofit Technology Enterprise Network (N-TEN) of nonprofits, technical support organizations, consultants, for-profit technology companies, and funders
  - Nonprofit Technology Conference (NTC): annual event
  - Regional conferences
  - 501 Tech Clubs that meet informally in 12 cities in the United States
  - TechFinder: an online directory of tech service providers for nonprofits; a service of N-TEN in partnership with TechSoup.org
- CompuMentor—www.compumentor.org
  - One of the nation's oldest and largest nonprofit technology assistance agencies
  - Collaborates with local and regional partners to provide technology implementation and support to San Francisco Bay area nonprofits, including its mentor-matching program
  - Hosts and participates in numerous educational conferences and events
- TechSoup—www.techsoup.org (a CompuMentor program)
  - One-stop resource for technology needs by providing free information, resources, and support
  - TechSoup Stock: a philanthropy service for donated and discounted technology products

For many organizations, the move to technology is hindered not only by a lack of expertise but also by finances. Today, a growing number of foundations make capacity-building grants that support technology: companies such as IBM donate computer equipment, and software companies such as Microsoft offer some software products free to organizations and through TechSoup. Appendix 3–C lists some organizations in the United States that help provide used computers to charities. However, keep in mind that donated computers are often older models that are inadequate to operate today's software products. Another resource is a consultant like Robert Weiner, who specializes in computer technology needs for nonprofit organizations and is not a specific vendor of any particular software or hardware application. See Appendix 4–A for Weiner's *Ten Common Mistakes in Selecting Donor Databases.*

THE NEED FOR A TECHNOLOGY PLAN

Using technology such as computers and software requires an investment not only measured in dollars but measured in staff resources as well. Many organizations budget only for the purchase of such equipment and not for the necessary training and support services that staff persons will need to be able to use the technology efficiently. Whether the purchase is small, like a PC to do word processing, or major, like the purchase of a fundraising software package, an organization wants to be sure it gets a solid return on its investment. This is achieved by making the correct choices and putting these new tools to their most effective use.

An organization can ensure getting the best return on its investment by developing a technology plan that establishes organizational goals and objectives. Not having a plan can lead to the purchase of hardware and software products that are not compatible or cannot easily exchange information. This could cause an organization to lose critical information or files for which there is no back-up.

> *An organization can ensure getting the best return on its investment by developing a technology plan that establishes organizational goals and objectives.*

ASSESSING YOUR NEEDS

The best way to determine your technology requirements is to do a needs assessment. This is a written analysis of your organization's current data management system and what the organization will need from a future system. To be able to plan effectively, an organization needs to look beyond the current day-to-day operations. Questions that need to be addressed include the following:

- Where is the organization now and where does it want to be in three to five years?
- What challenges will be encountered when implementing a strategic plan?
- What information will be needed to run the organization more effectively?
- What information is needed to better serve the organization's members or clients?
- How can effective communication and information sharing both within the organization and with resources outside the organization advance the mission?

To begin, involve all appropriate staff in reviewing the current word processing and data management systems. Staff persons should prepare lists of their particular department's needs and recommendations to use in discussions with other departments as the needs assessment process continues. A final needs assessment document should include the conclusions and recommendations resulting from this series of meetings. Exhibit 4–1 lists ways a needs assessment helps an organization.

After conducting a needs assessment, an organization must prioritize its technology goals and determine the most critical areas for improvement. For some organizations, the need for hardware and software standards becomes critical. What type of machine? How much memory? Is it time to install a local area network (LAN) that would connect all staff, thereby enhancing communications and information sharing? Software standards are equally important. Are all staff using the same word processing and spreadsheet software? Is there a procedure for training new staff on software? Has the software been upgraded and should the organization change?

Security, virus protection, and data back-up procedures protect an organization's investment. The importance of creating back-up copies of critical information cannot be overemphasized, and procedures should be practiced to ensure that it is accomplished. A data back-up policy should include who is responsible for creating the back-ups, what information will be backed up, when the back-ups will be made, where the back-up files will be stored, and how long back-ups will be kept.

If you have confidential information on your computer, and most development offices do, protect it by installing password protection and permitting only certain staff persons to have access. When looking at a particular software package, examine the security features it offers. Also, take steps to protect against computer viruses. You can install virus protection software on the machines. These programs are relatively inexpensive and can prevent serious damage to the computers.

As mentioned earlier, technology is an investment for an organization. It is not a one-time cost. Costs for technology should be planned for on a continuing basis. Staff training is essential to ensure that these new tools are used effectively. It is not enough to budget the purchase without budgeting training for staff. There are a number of for-profit and nonprofit organizations that offer training on different kinds of software fairly inexpensively. In addition to training, technical support and trouble-shooting assistance will be required. Does the software vendor offer technical support? Is there a fee for such support?

Does the organization have an in-house technology expert? Can technology consultants provide the support needed?

Keep in mind that technology is constantly changing. An organization will need to periodically upgrade its software and hardware. One also must consider that an organization and its needs will change. For these reasons, an organization will need to periodically review and modify its technology plan.

A COMPREHENSIVE FUNDRAISING DATA MANAGEMENT SYSTEM

Keep in mind what a computer can and cannot do. Computers track, sort, compile, and calculate. These functions are essential for a fundraising program because they enable the computer to do the following:

- store and retrieve biographical and gift information
- track prospects
- produce lists and mailing labels
- prepare financial reports
- create acknowledgment letters, receipts, and pledge reminders
- create personalized appeal letters
- track and record solicitations
- track contacts with donors and prospects

There will be different computer needs depending on the types of fundraising programs being conducted by an organization. When determining technology needs, it is important to consider any new fundraising programs that will be initiated within the next three to five years. Exhibit 4–2 lists major components of a development program. Exhibit 4–3 helps an organization chart

---

Exhibit 4–1 Five Ways a Needs Assessment Helps an Organization

A needs assessment:
1. Defines in advance the organization's basic data management requirements.
2. Creates a consensus of what is needed and expected from the new system among key groups of staff who use the information, who use the system, and who will help with maintenance and computer problems.
3. Justifies the need for a new system.
4. Establishes a timetable for the purchase of a new system.
5. Serves as a guide to help vendors know an organization's needs before their first meeting and also weeds out those systems that do not fulfill an organization's requirements.

Exhibit 4–2 Analyzing Your Fundraising Program Needs

Listed below are the various components of a development program. Determine if each is a C = current need, F = future need, or NA = not applicable for the organization.

1. annual giving _____
2. corporate support _____
3. foundation grants _____
4. capital campaign _____
5. endowment campaign _____
6. donor research _____
7. honor and memorial gifts _____
8. major donor cultivation _____
9. volunteer and staff solicitors _____
10. planned giving _____
11. special events _____
12. volunteer coordination _____
13. alumni tracking _____
14. parents/students tracking _____
15. membership _____
16. other _____

_____ _____
_____ _____

Exhibit 4–3 Rating Your Current System

Rate your current fundraising data management system on whether you are able to accomplish the following tasks and with what level of ease (1 = easy; 2 = somewhat easy; 3 = somewhat difficult; 4 = difficult; 5 = cannot do).

Annual Giving

- Segmentation is available by:
  constituencies _____
  past giving history _____
  amount of gift _____
  recency of gift _____
  renewing donors and members _____
  current donors _____
  LYBUNT (last year but unfortunately not this year) _____
  SYBUNT (some year but unfortunately not this year) _____
  first-time donors _____
  prospects _____
  size of gift _____
  giving to special funds, campaigns, or appeals _____
- Allows for inclusion of information mentioned previously to individualize appeal and acknowledgment letters _____
- Mail merges acknowledgment letters for appropriate level of gift _____
- Tracks donor recognition and gift clubs _____
- Upgrades donors by specific dollar amounts or range _____
- For phonathon/telemarketing, the system can:
  customize scripts _____
  print forms _____
  include last gift _____
  include solicitor _____
  include the targeted gift amount to be solicited and outcome _____
  verify address _____
  send reminders _____
- Ability to report on any and all of the previous _____

Corporation and Foundation Tracking

- Ability to track multiple contacts at a corporation or foundation _____
- Ability to track matching gifts with both "hard" and "soft" credit _____
- Ability to track board members, employees, and officers of a foundation or corporation _____
- Ability to track grant requests and proposal status _____
- Linkage between corporation or foundation records and individual records _____

Capital/Endowment Campaigns

- Ability to assign and track volunteer solicitations _____
- Ability to evaluate and rate donors and prospects _____
- Ability to track moves or action steps _____
- Ability to track prospect status during the campaign _____
- Ability to track and report on campaign structure and divisions at any level _____
- Ability to service pledges _____

Prospect Research

- The following biographical information is available to track:
  first, middle, last name _____
  maiden name _____
  family linkages _____

company name for institutions and foundations _____
contact and position with the company _____
salutations _____
titles _____
source (alumni, parent, friend, patient) _____
group source (corporation, individual, foundation) _____
occupation _____
sex _____
activity code (such as donor or prospect) _____
special codes _____
membership levels and dates _____
social security number _____
nickname _____
date of birth _____
marital status _____
spouse information _____
children's names and information _____
affiliations (political, religious, clubs) _____
giving level or net worth _____
employer name _____
multiple addresses _____
position or title at work _____
profession (specialty) _____
employer information for spouse _____
hobbies, interests, avocations _____
organizations and clubs _____
colleges or universities attended _____
major and minor areas of study at college _____
degree(s) earned from college or university _____
graduation date from college or university _____
- Ability to import electronic screening information _____
- Allows for unlimited notes and comments _____

Management of Major Donor Cultivation

- Ability to evaluate and rate major donors and prospects _____
- Ability to track the next moves related to major donor cultivation _____
- Possesses tickler system by date and subject matter _____
- Allows for unlimited notes and comments _____
- Allows for assignment of staff, volunteer, primary, and secondary contacts _____
- Ability to track all correspondence history _____

Honor/Memorial/Tributes

- Ability to track:
  memorial and honor gifts _____
  bereaved family members _____
  relationship of bereaved family members to deceased _____
- Allows for personalized follow-up letter based on relationship of donor or bereaved family to deceased or honoree _____
- Ability to select which bereaved family members need to be acknowledged _____
- Ability to restrict memorial or honor gift to a specific fund _____
- Ability to split gifts to multiple memorials _____

continues

Exhibit 4–3 Rating Your Current System (continued)

- Ability to print memorial lists for newsletters and reports _____

Planned Giving

- Ability to evaluate and rate planned giving prospects _____
- Ability to track biographical and personal data and information _____
- Ability to track seminars attended and information requested from planned giving mailings _____
- Allows for follow-up tracking and tickler system _____
- Allows for unlimited notes and comments _____

Special Events

- Provides for invitation and event list tracking _____
- Ability to track invitation and event responses _____
- Provides event specifics (seating, registration fees, foursomes) _____
- Ability to link with other development software _____
- Provides reports for flexible event reporting _____

Volunteer Coordination

- Can track volunteers by:
  - interest areas _____
  - service areas _____

   times available _____
   awards and recognition _____
   limitations _____
   hours _____
   attendance _____
- Ability to report on any and all of the previous _____

Other

Alumni Tracking

- Ability to track class year _____
- Provides linkage with alumni spouses _____
- Ability to track and bill dues _____
- Ability to track alumni by chapter _____
- Ability to track and manage class reunions _____
- Ability to link to other development software _____
- Ability to report on any or all of the previous _____

Membership

- Ability to track effective and expiration dates _____
- Ability to track category and renewal level _____
- Ability to track gift memberships _____
- Ability to process membership renewals and cards _____
- Provides linkage to other development software _____
- Ability to report on any or all of the previous _____

Source: Copyright Systems Support Services/Donor 2, Charlotte, North Carolina. Reprinted by permission.

the types of current fundraising activities and which activities will be added in the future.

Once the strengths and weaknesses of the current system are identified, the next step will be to prioritize which programs have the greatest need for new or upgraded technology. Exhibit 4–2 can be used again to rank these programs from 1 through 10 with 1 being the highest priority for enhanced technology.

EVALUATING FUNDRAISING SOFTWARE

Today, there are two types of fundraising software available. One type is run internally on an organization's server and desktop computers (in-house), and the other type is run externally by a vendor known as an application service provider (ASP; outsourced). There are a number of factors to consider when evaluating fundraising software. First-time buyers are most often influenced by price, the level of ease to implement, and equipment needed. However, experience shows that a second-time buyer chooses to purchase a particular software package for very different reasons. Their selection is based on the level of technical support available, the reputation of the vendor, and the training provided. Important considerations, besides possible budget constraints, should be the quality of the product, training and installation, and ongoing tech-

> *Experience shows that a second-time buyer chooses to purchase a particular software package for very different reasons.*

nical support. Costs associated with software purchases alone can range from several hundred dollars to tens of thousands of dollars.

The following is a list of where to find information about the various software products available to nonprofit organizations:

- "National Technology Buyer's Guide" published annually by *Contributions*
- *Chronicle of Philanthropy*'s Technology Guide, published annually
- "Technology Guide" published annually by the *NonProfit Times*
- AFP's special *Advancing Philanthropy* Fundraising Technology section published each spring
- exhibitors at annual conferences and national meetings hosted by AFP, Association for Healthcare Philanthropy (AHP), and Council for the Advancement and Support of Education (CASE)
- general advertisements in publications previously listed
- referrals from nonprofit organizations using different software packages
- Internet listservs and other online sources like Idealware that provides candid consumer-reports-style reviews and articles about software of interest to nonprofits. Through product comparisons, recommendations, case studies, and software news, Idealware allows nonprofits to make the software decisions that will help them be more effective

A sampling of some of the current fundraising software products are listed in Appendix 4–B.

After gathering information on various software products, contact vendors to get basic information on their product and to request written information. You will need to provide the vendor with some information about your current system and needs. Be prepared to tell the vendor how many records are on your current system, what your future needs will be, the type of hardware currently in use, how many current users there are, and any serious limitation of the current system.

Questions to ask the vendor include the following:

1. How long has the company been in existence? How many clients currently use the software? When was the last upgrade?
2. What is the cost of fundraising software? Are there other modules to add? Is there an interface with accounting or membership software?
3. Which word processors are recommended?
4. What hardware is required? What other equipment such as printers are needed?
5. What are the storage requirements?
6. What is the import capability for file conversion? Will the vendor do the conversion? What is the cost?
7. Can data be exported electronically to a mailing house or telemarketing vendor?
8. Where will training take place? What are the on-site costs? What are the vendor's headquarter costs?
9. What technical support is available? Is there an 800 number to call? What is the charge?
10. Can I talk to current users in the local area?

Each company contacted should send a trial version or interactive CD along with a brochure. Be sure to ask if sample screens and reports are included in the materials, because it is often simpler to review these than the trial version. Review this information as it relates to the needs determined by using the analysis worksheet in Exhibit 4–3. Come up with a list of no more than three companies and request that they do a demonstration of their product either online or in person so that you can determine how each product does what your organization needs.

Each vendor will furnish a list of clients who are currently using their product. Call those clients whose fundraising programs would be most similar to those of your organization. There is no better way to learn if a product and vendor are all that they are purported to be than by speaking to those individuals who use that product and vendor. Ask specific questions such as the following:

- How long ago did you start using your database system?
- What kind of hardware, operating system, accounting, and word processing do you use?
- Does your organization have an information systems department or computer support person?
- How did you convert your old files? What was the cost?
- Do you find the system instruction manual helpful?

- How was the training conducted? On-site? At vendor? How many staff persons were trained? Would you make any changes in how the training was conducted?
- How responsive is the vendor when you call the technical support number?
- How long does it take a staff person to enter 50 names and gifts?
- How long does it take to generate mailing labels?
- How many staff persons currently use the system? Are they comfortable with it?
- Are you able to interface with your accounting and/or membership software?
- How do you back up files? How often is it done and how long does it take?
- Would you select this same system again? What would you do differently?
- Do you have any suggestions for my organization in this process?

If a current user is in your area, visit the organization and see the system in use. Some database systems, like Blackbaud's Raiser's Edge, have local user groups, which can be most helpful.

By following these steps, an organization should be able to select the fundraising software that best suits its needs.

USING AN APPLICATION SERVICE PROVIDER

ASPs are vendors that manage and distribute software-based services from a central data center to customers across a wide area network. For many nonprofit organizations, it is a way to outsource some or all of their information technology needs.

Using an ASP that provides access over the Internet has distinct advantages:

- Users can access data from any location that has Internet access.
- New users can be connected to the system immediately without complex setup procedures.
- It is easy to link the user to other Web site information.

Many ASPs provide additional technologies that enable the following:

- e-messaging (e-mailing newsletters, requests for volunteers, and fundraising appeals at a small fraction of the cost of direct mail)
- links from your organization's Web site to a donation screen that feeds directly to the database
- a Web site that allows members or Internet surfers to build a community of people (i.e., alumni or people with similar interests) who can contact each other, leave information about themselves, buy a product, or put information on or retrieve information from a bulletin board.

The technology needs assessment covered earlier in this chapter will be very helpful in determining whether or not an ASP is the right data management solution for an organization. Some of the reasons organizations choose an ASP are as follows:

- system is typically offered on a subscription basis so there may be a lesser up-front expense
- handles all hardware and software problems, which can be a great help to those organizations that do not have information technology (IT) staff
- conducts file maintenance, production output, and system back-ups on a regular basis

An ASP may be the answer for many nonprofit organizations; however, it must be understood that an organization's database is then no longer directly in its own hands but primarily in the hands of an outside vendor. If an organization should choose to pursue using an ASP, it is recommended that the organization follow similar steps when evaluating the work of ASPs as those we covered in the section on evaluating software providers and their products.

THE TRUE COSTS OF IMPLEMENTING A NEW SYSTEM

You will need to consider the total cost of implementing this new system, not just the purchase price of the fundraising database system. Other costs include hardware, software, ongoing maintenance, training, customization, conversion of current data, implementation, staff downtime during conversion, and technical difficulties. As mentioned earlier, it is important that you evaluate your current computer hardware to be certain you can use your new software to its fullest.

One of the costs that is often overlooked is that of staff time. Select staff must dedicate considerable time working closely with the vendor to convert data properly and implement the new system in the following steps:

1. Cleaning the data
   Existing data must be prepared to move into the new software. This involves mapping old fields to new, deleting redundant and unnecessary data, and testing the data in the new system. This step should not be postponed or done lightly as you will import many of your old problems into the new system. Clean data will also reduce conversion costs, which are typically billed on an hourly basis.
2. Making the switch
   At one point, staff will stop entering data into the old system and begin using the new system. Be certain you have built in some flexibility to this step to allow for unforeseen circumstances. Avoid scheduling the switch at a critical time in your fundraising program.
3. Implementing the system
   Assign a staff person to be responsible for data quality, creating new reports, and defining security. A database manager should be appointed who can add new users, perform

back-ups, and add new categories. Staff roles and responsibilities should be determined and documented.
4. Training
   As soon as the software is selected, staff should start becoming familiar with the new system. This will be especially helpful in properly mapping existing data into the new system. Schedule online training or in-person training as early as possible. Create a manual for how the organization works with donor data to be certain that all users are entering data and extracting data correctly. This manual will be an excellent resource for new staff. It is important to provide ongoing training opportunities for staff, not just at the start of using the new system. This will allow staff to be able to use additional features of the system when needed.

AN INVESTMENT, NOT AN EXPENSE, FOR YOUR ORGANIZATION

A challenge development staff often encounter when seeking funds to purchase a fundraising database system or even to upgrade from current software is making the case to staff and volunteer leadership that such a purchase can help maximize the organization's fundraising success. The purchase should be viewed as an investment for the organization and not just a budgetary expense. Tony Ciconte, Senior Vice President, Technical Services for Donor Strategies, Inc.'s *MissionAssist*, developed the talking points in Exhibit 4–4 to help potential clients make that case.

WORKING WITH A TECHNOLOGY CONSULTANT

The technology explosion in the nonprofit sector has produced another type of consultant—the technology consultant, whose role is to help organizations choose the best solutions for their technology needs. There are a number of situations in which a technology consultant could be helpful, such as

- an old system needs to be upgraded or replaced
- new initiatives or significant changes are to be undertaken that will affect the system
- a change in fundraising, accounting, or membership management software is needed
- new communications expertise is needed
- current technical support or vendor is inadequate or nonresponsive
- existing staff do not have the expertise needed

Good technology consultants are

- concerned about finding the right products and services for your organization, *not* with fitting your requirements to certain products and services
- eager to explain technical items in sufficient detail to give you a clear understanding (so *do not* hesitate to ask questions)

Exhibit 4–4 Make the Case It's an Investment—Suggested Talking Points for Executive Director and Board of Directors

Point \$1: Having a fundraising database system that is easy to use and easy to learn will enable us to dedicate more time to getting to know our donors and volunteers, thereby building the relationships we need to sustain our future.

Point \$2: It will allow us to be more efficient, to cut mailing costs, and to identify new opportunities for raising more funds from our current donors which is easier and less expensive than to acquire new donors.

Point \$3: Since it is simpler to learn and use, it will save time needed for data entry and will automatically generate thank you letters, thus, allowing staff to do other necessary donor-related tasks and projects. It will also make staff turnover less traumatic.

Point \$4: Fewer errors in entering data ensures that the database has the latest, most accurate information on donors including addresses, giving history, interests, etc. which allows us to communicate more effectively with our donors, members, and prospects by telephone, mail or e-mail.

Point \$5: New features allow us to do all tasks involved in special events and meetings (registration, attendee/non-attendee lists, nametags, seating) through the database. We do not have to generate word or excel documents and then enter data into the database.

Point \$6: The ability to easily track donor/member interests and giving histories (date, size, and purpose of gift) allows us to solicit donors for a specific increased gift at the proper time of year for a program or project they care about, thus increasing success in fundraising.

Point \$7: We will be able to segment our donor base using a variety of criteria that will allow us to identify the best donors and prospects for particular projects, therefore, increasing our fundraising results.

Point \$8: Targeting specific groups of donors and prospects for cultivation mailings, solicitations, and general communications will substantially reduce our mailing costs.

Point \$9: The new system allows us to record and manage all contacts we have with donors, members, and prospects. It has a tickler system to remind us when a letter, proposal, call, or visit is needed.

Point \$10: Being able to easily prepare numerous types of standard and ad hoc reports will allow the staff to respond to senior staff and board requests for information more quickly.

Point \$11: The ability to prepare special reports will enable us to measure the effectiveness of specific appeals, campaigns, or events. This will assist us in evaluating our current development program for future planning.

With increased fundraising success, the return on investment will be far greater than the initial purchase price.

Source: Tony Ciconte, Senior Vice President, Technical Services, Donor Strategies, Inc., Chevy Chase, Maryland.

- concerned about your expectations
- willing and able to train your in-house staff in a professional and nonintimidating manner
- sensitive to your budget constraints and are willing to offer options based on spending limits

When looking for a technology consultant, an organization should look for someone who has experience with the needs of nonprofit organizations, broad experience in the technology arena, vendor independence, flexible pricing, guarantees and warranties, post-project support, and at least three references that can be contacted. Exhibit 4–5 provides questions to ask prospective technology consultants, and Exhibit 4–6 provides questions a technology consultant can answer for your organization.

Exhibit 4–5 Questions to Ask Prospective Technology Consultants

1. Are you affiliated with any specific hardware or software vendors? If so, do you work on commission?
2. How much experience do you have in the area(s) related to our particular needs?
3. Are you users of the products you recommend?
4. How will you support our organization after your recommendations are implemented?
5. What effect will your recommendations have on the office hardware and software systems?
6. Will you provide a detailed cost accounting for all services?
7. Can you recommend other specialists if necessary?

Exhibit 4–6 Questions a Technology Consultant Can Answer for Your Organization

1. What equipment can or should be retained or upgraded?
2. What equipment should be replaced?
3. What software products make the most sense for our specific requirements?
4. How do we best convert from one system or software product to another?
5. How do we best customize products for a particular organization?
6. What equipment and software should we purchase, lease, or upgrade?
7. Where and from whom should we acquire equipment and software products?
8. What types of maintenance agreements make the most sense?

TIPS FOR BUILDING YOUR DATABASE

No matter what database system you use, it is critical that you use your system as a fundraising tool and not just to build mailing lists. Below are 10 tips for how to build your database into the effective tool you need for successful fundraising.

1. Determine what basic information should be collected on each donor or prospect.
   - name, home address, telephone number, office address, telephone number, e-mail address
   - spouse name, other family members' names (dependent on the type of organization)

- gift and pledge information (date and amount of gift or pledge, payment schedule)
- source of gift (specific mail appeal, special event, personal solicitation, online)
- purpose of gift (unrestricted, program gift, capital campaign gift, scholarship gift)
- attendance at events
- newsletters, invitations, and other organizational communications received
- board and committee assignments
- board member or volunteer assigned to donor (major gifts and capital campaigns)

2. Limit the number of staff and/or volunteers who enter data to ensure consistency and accuracy of data.
3. Prepare a database procedures manual to train staff in proper procedures of data entry. This is critical for reports, mail merges, labels, and envelopes.
4. Have one or more mechanisms to capture the basic contact information you need such as on the reply card and/or envelope and required fields for making a gift online.
5. Code reply cards and/or envelopes so that you can easily track the source of the gift.
6. Provide opportunities on reply cards and online for donors to let you know what specific programs and areas are of greatest interest to them, such as a listing with boxes to check for more information or to direct their gift to assist in developing future fundraising strategies for the donor.
7. Train staff to carefully review response devices for additional information to record or update in addition to entering a gift.
8. Be certain you keep a record of all communications a donor or prospect receives (newsletters, brochure mailings, appeal letters, special event invitations, etc.).
9. Review your donors' patterns of giving for developing fundraising strategies and plans.
   - single or multiple gifts
   - time of year gift is usually made
   - types of programs and projects supported
   - fundraising method they respond to (mail, event, online, personal solicitation)
10. Focus on gathering and tracking information on major donors and prospects that you plan to use in developing personalized cultivation and solicitation strategies.
    - reports of meetings and telephone calls
    - attendance at events
    - board members and senior staff they know
    - their interests and activities with other organizations

© 2005 Donor Strategies, Inc. All rights reserved.

THE CHRONICLE OF PHILANTHROPY   MARK LITZLER

"If they had real wealth, wouldn't the art museum have spotted them by now?"

Source: Copyright © Mark Litzler.

Ten Common Mistakes in Selecting Donor Databases (and How to Avoid Them)

by Robert Weiner

How do you choose a donor database that will support successful fundraising? The software is only half the story. Fundraising technology strategist Robert Weiner addresses ten common mistakes that can prevent you from selecting the right database and managing it effectively.

Picture, if you will, two nonprofits. The first has a donor database that is full of bad data. Donors are getting the wrong receipts or no receipts at all. The organization cannot use the database to plan their fundraising strategies or track their effectiveness. The few reports they can get are useless. Staff members complain that no one trained them, and they get no technical support. For obvious reasons, they hate the system. The second organization loves its database. Their data is clean, their donors get timely, accurate mailings, the organization has a good handle on its fundraising activities, and staff get the reports they want. New personnel are trained on the database before they ever log on, and someone on staff helps them resolve any problems and questions that arise.

Both nonprofits are using the same software package.

How can this be? Perhaps the first organization has outgrown its old system. But it is quite likely that the organization never had the right software to begin with, and then proceeded to use it incorrectly. They made a series of bad decisions and have been struggling with them ever since.

How do you avoid this fate? Selecting and managing a donor database is never easy, but if you avoid the mistakes on this list, you can start out on the right foot.

1) Letting Techies Make the Decision

In the early days of computing, programmers created all donor databases. Their role was to turn fundraising concepts into software programs. But since most fundraisers did not (and still do not) want to be involved in the detailed decisions and testing required to design a database, programmers usually drove the project.

Although the market for donor databases has changed significantly over the past three decades, techies still make many of the purchasing decisions. However, few techies have experience with fundraising. This makes it critical to get input from the people who will actually use the database. You don't need to include every staff member, but you should get input from all levels of the organization (management, departments, end users), fundraisers from all areas of Development (direct mail, grants, major gifts, corporate relations, and planned giving—if you have all of these), and other staff who may be impacted by a new system (administrative and data entry, those who create and run reports, other departments that provide input or use fundraising data). The techies should be there to advise on whether a system will fit into your organization's technology strategy and be supportable in the long term, but they should not make the final decision.

2) Wishful Budgeting

Before you go shopping for a database, you need to know what you can spend. And before you sign a contract, you need to make sure you can afford to pay the bill, now and in the future. Over a five-year period, software could be as little as one-fifth of your total cost. You might need new computers and printers, network upgrades, help in moving your data to the new system, extra end-user training, help developing new processes and policies, and perhaps even new staff to manage the system. This effect is magnified as the software price rises—more complex software requires more staff training, stronger policies, and better business processes. You also need to plan for the annual software maintenance fee, which is usually about twenty-five percent of the software's retail price. The bottom line: if you cannot afford to train your staff and pay the annual maintenance fee, do not buy the software.

3) Prioritizing Price above Everything Else

Buy the product that meets your top needs, fits your resources, *and* offers the best price. Think in terms of Return on Investment. Software that allows you to have better control over your fundraising programs, manage your solicitations, track your results, and analyze your effectiveness is a good investment that will pay dividends for many years.

Accept a donation (whether of software or services) only if it fits your selection criteria. Feel free to accept input from board members, donors, volunteers, or the boss, but in the end, make an educated, strategic decision.

4) Randomly Looking at Demos

Yogi Berra is supposed to have said, "You've got to be very careful if you don't know where you're going, because you might not get there." And if you do not know what you want from your donor database, you might get to the wrong "there." Randomly looking at software demonstrations is not likely to produce a good result.

Your first step should be to convene a selection team that will help you make the decision. Make sure they understand their role—is it their decision, or are they advising management? Will the decisions be made based on majority-rule or consensus?

The team should start by understanding the current system (what works? what doesn't? what codes and reports do you actually use?). Next, develop a list of needs. These can be general, like "ad-hoc report writer," or specific, like the ability to track a 15-character appeal code or analyze membership upgrades, downgrades, and renewals. Don't forget to consider future needs, especially if major organizational changes are anticipated. Then the team should identify the mandatory items on the list. "Mandatory" means that if the system cannot provide that one single feature you will have to reject the database, no matter what else it can do. Everything that is not mandatory goes on the "wish list," which should be ranked roughly in priority order (e.g., A, B, C). Consider what worked at your last job only if the needs, budgets, and staffing are similar.

Next, identify a pool of possible vendors. Links to several vendor listings are posted at http://www.rlweiner.com/resources. html#donors. In addition, you can ask for suggestions from your professional network, or on email forums for nonprofit professionals. Be sure to get references from comparable organizations (e.g., type of nonprofit, number of staff, budget size, fundraising volume, number of locations, etc.). There is no point in finding out which database the Red Cross headquarters uses if your organization's annual budget is $250,000.

You might wish, or be required, to use a Request for Proposals (RFP). If you do, be sure that the questions you ask can be answered unambiguously, and will help you narrow the vendor pool. Think ahead to how you will use and rate the responses. Keep in mind that not all vendors will respond to an RFP, particularly a lengthy one.

When you look at software demos, make sure the vendors address your mandatory and top priority requirements. You can help ensure this by providing a list of your requirements, or a script that the vendors must follow. Make sure each vendor follows the same process: If you use a script for the demos, every vendor will need to follow the same script. If one vendor gets four hours for a demo, the rest should as well. Give each vendor the same information about your needs. If you answer a substantive question for one vendor, give the same information to the others. Follow up the information that vendors provide by checking references carefully and spending time testing a demo version of the software.

5) Falling in Love with Cool Features

Your donor database has to meet your needs and provide room for growth. But the vendor is also a critical factor. The right vendor will keep up with changing technologies, provide good training and support, and supply usable documentation. Remember, if the vendor disappears you will have to do this all over again. Reference checks will help you check the vendor's track record. If the company's stock is publicly traded, you can find detailed financial information. You can also get some financial information from Dun and Bradstreet. If the company seems risky, you might want to visit their office and see how they run their operation.

6) Falling in Love with the Salesperson

You are not buying the salesperson. In fact, in most cases you will never hear from the salesperson after you sign the contract, so don't worry about hurting his or her feelings. Try to look past who has the best personality or the nicest suit and judge the software on its own merits.

7) Buying More Than You Need

Don't buy a Ferrari if you only need (or can afford, or can maintain) a Honda Civic. It's great to be able to track every detail about every prospect and donor, but will your staff have time to use those features? Plan for the future, but make sure you can use it now. With some systems, you may be able to start small and buy additional modules as needed (although you will have to be prepared to pay for additional training and annual support along with the new modules). One often-overlooked option is improving what you have—it isn't reasonable to compare a five-year-old version of your current software to the most recent versions of other software.

8) Confusing Highly Functional Software with Highly Trained Staff

Complex software requires your staff to have more computer skills, not less. Under-trained staff, poor communication, dysfunctional business processes, and poor management will not be solved by new software. Usually, the problems will get worse.

It's also important to look at your staffing and procedures as part of the project. Beware of management and "people" problems masquerading as technology problems. For instance, if you are having problems getting accurate reports, are the problems being caused by the database software, sloppy data entry, lack of communication between fundraisers and techies, poor training, or bad programming logic in the reports? If it takes two weeks to produce a receipt, does the problem lie with the database or with your business practices?

9) Hoping That the Database Will Install Itself

Although it accounts for eight of the ten topics in this article, buying software is usually the easiest part of the project. Next comes the hard part: the conversion project. Conversions usually have many components: mapping the fields, codes and reports in the old database to the new one; cleaning up your current data (manually or through programs); figuring out what to do with data that does not fit easily into the new database; defining new codes and reports; testing the converted data; setting up business rules (how various tasks will be accomplished); defining system security (who can log in and what can they view, add, change or delete); setting up system parameters (code types and values, user-defined fields); building interfaces to other systems; defining and documenting your procedures; creating a data entry style guide; and writing training materials.

Someone is going to need to oversee that work. This project manager will need to understand your fundraising programs and learn how the software works. He or she probably has a full time job that may be derailed by this project, and his/her manager will need to understand this before the project starts. The project manager is also likely to need help from your fundraisers and administrative staff, each of whom have their own jobs to do. Some organizations get through conversions by reassigning staff or hiring temporary staff to support the staff working on the project. Complex software must also be properly configured, which may require help from the vendor or a consultant.

If you have a hard deadline (like the end of the fiscal year), you need to make sure everyone knows this. You also need to consider the implications of missing it and have contingency plans in place.

Finally, you should try to build some flexibility into your budget, in case unexpected costs arise. They say that time is money, but the reverse is also true. More money can pay for temporary staff, overtime, and more help from the vendor or consultants.

10) Leaving the Database to Fend for Itself

At long last, your new system is live, your data is clean, all processes and data entry standards are documented, you have a training manual, and your staff are fully trained. (Well, you can dream.) The second law of thermodynamics says, more or less, that if you do not continue to put energy into maintaining the system it will degrade. How can you keep entropy at bay?

First, someone should "own" the database and be responsible for quality control. This role is sometimes called the "data manager" (as opposed to a technical "database administrator.") This person must make sure that your data entry procedures are documented and followed, and run periodic audit reports to identify problems.

Someone will also need to make sure that staff are trained on new features and procedures, and that new staff are trained before they start entering data.

New systems often change the way work gets done. You will need to make sure that job duties and descriptions still match reality. You might also need to spend time thinking through how data and paperwork move through your organization.

Finally, you will need to budget for ongoing hardware and software upgrades, annual software maintenance fees, and ongoing training from the vendor—including attendance at annual Users Group conferences.

In Conclusion

How do you end up like the contented nonprofit mentioned above, with clean data, solid reports, and happy staff? The software tool itself is only half the story—the other half lies in understanding what you need, and then following through. Sophisticated fundraising combines a realistic development plan with appropriate staffing and the financial and technical resources needed to achieve the plan. With a solid selection process, proper attention during the conversion, and good staff training and support, you can choose software that supports your organization's long-term goals.

Source: This article was adapted from a workshop created with Dawn Trygstad Rubin for CompassPoint's Silicon Valley Conference on Nonprofits and Technology. Many thanks to Tim Mills-Groninger and Dawn Trygstad Rubin for their advice. Copyright © Robert Weiner 2006.

A Sampling of Companies That Provide Software for Fundraising

Compass CRM
Compass Technology
Phone: (888) 239-8515
www.compass.net

The DataBank
Thedatabank
Phone: (877) 603-0296
www.thedatabank.com

D-B Cultivator
Oaktree Systems
Phone: (800) 726-8163
www.oaktreesys.com

DonationDirector
Cascade Data Solutions
Phone: (800) 280-2090
www.donationdirector.com

Donor 2, Donor2 Enterprise
Donor2/Systems Support Services
Phone: (800) 548-6708
www.donor2.com

Donor Perfect
Softerware
Phone: (800) 220-8111
www.donorperfect.com

DonorPro
Towercare Technologies
Phone: (866) 935-8281
www.towercare.com

Donor Records; Donor Records/Nonprofit Starter Kit
Executive Data Systems
Phone: (800) 272-3374
www.execdata.com

eTapestry
eTapestry
Phone: (888) 739-3827
www.etapestry.com

Exceed! Basic; Exceed! Premier
Telosa Software
Phone: (800) 676-5831
www.telosa.com

FastFund
Araize
Phone: (800) 745-4037
www.araize.com

Fundraising Management Systems
CMDI
Phone: (703) 790-8676
www.cmdi.net

Gift Works
Mission Research
Phone: (888) 323-8766
www.missionresearch.com

iMIS
Advanced Solutions
Phone: (800) 727-8682
www.advsol.com

Kintera Sphere
Kintera
Phone: (866) 546-8371
www.kintera.com

Lifeline Nonprofit Management System
Straight Forward Software
Phone: (802) 865-0480
www.straightforwardsoftwareinc.com

Matchmaker
Heritage Designs
Phone: (800) 752-3100
www.matchmakerfrs.com

Matchmaker, Enterprise
Access International
Phone: (617) 494-0066
www.accessint.com

MissionAssist; MissionAssist Essentials;
MissionAssist for Grantmakers
Donor Strategies
Phone: (888) 722-2033
www.donorstrategies.com

Pledgemaker
Softrek
Phone: (800) 442-9211
www.pledgemaker.com

Portfolio
Amergent
Phone: (800) 370-7500
www.amergent.com

Results Plus!
Metafile Information Systems
Phone: (800) 638-2445
www.resultsplussoftware.com

Sage Fundraising 50; Millenium
Sage Software
Phone: (800) 811-0961
www.sagesoftware.com

Saturn Corporation
Phone: (800) 872-0090
www.saturncorp.com

Serenic Navigator for Not-for-Profits
Serenic Software
Phone: (877) 737-3642
www.serenic.com

Team Approach
Target Software
Phone: (888) 876-2275
www.targetsite.com

The Raiser's Edge
Blackbaud
Phone: (800) 443-9441
www.blackbaud.com

Total Info
Easy-Ware Corporation
Phone: (866) 739-3827
www.easy-ware.com

Chapter 5

Developing and Evaluating Your Fundraising Plan

CHAPTER OUTLINE

- The Critical Need for Planning
- Role of Strategic Planning in Fundraising
- The Development Audit
- Setting Realistic Goals for Your Fundraising Program
- Involving Board Members and Volunteers
- Preparing a Budget

- Stages of a Development Program
- Steps to Develop Your Fundraising Plan
- How Your Return on Investment Is Important to Planning
- The Evaluation Process

KEY VOCABULARY

- Analyzing
- Cost-Benefit Guidelines
- Cost per Dollar
- Development Audit
- Evaluation
- Fundraising Goals
- Planning
- Return on Investment
- Strategic Planning

THE CRITICAL NEED FOR PLANNING

The need for strategic planning within the nonprofit sector has never been greater. Competition for charitable contributions has caused current and prospective donors to want more information about how organizations are managed, how their programs are serving the public good, and how investments in the organizations are being used. Through the planning process, organizations assess where they are, decide where they want to go, and determine how and when they will get there.

The truth is, however, that few organizations conduct effective planning. Among the barriers that get in the way, foremost is the lack of time. How often have you heard someone say or said yourself, "I have too much to do now to take time to plan." However, you and your organization need to adopt the philosophy that planning does not take time, it saves time. Planning is not an easy task. Trying to forecast the future can be difficult,

but planning is necessary and can pay great dividends to your organization. Planning

- builds a spirit of ownership within the organization's leadership
- provides a structure, a framework, that will serve as a guide for day-to-day decisions
- focuses attention in a certain direction, thereby increasing the chance of success
- sets goals and objectives that promote the organization's growth

Tools needed for successful planning include the following:

- written case for support
- printed materials
- list of donors and accurate giving information
- report of past fundraising results
- identified prospects for giving

ROLE OF STRATEGIC PLANNING IN FUNDRAISING

Strategic planning plays a critical role in establishing fundraising goals because it defines what the organization is today, identifies what it wants to become or do that will enhance its program in the future, and determines what programs or services should be provided to achieve new or continuing objectives. One of the key elements of the strategic planning process is to examine the external environment as it impacts the organization. Consideration should be given to competition from other nonprofit organizations, trends in giving, the current economy, the political climate, and state and federal regulations. The purpose of reviewing external factors is to identify opportunities and threats that the organization might encounter in the next three to five years. A second key element is to analyze the organization's internal environment including staff and volunteer leadership, physical facilities, staffing capabilities, program development, budget, and current revenue sources. Look at current strengths and weaknesses that need to be factored into the equation for success.

Once the organization has sets its future course, it must determine the costs related to implementing the strategic plan. Securing funds for priorities outlined in the strategic plan serves as the basis for establishing fundraising goals and creating an accompanying development plan. The fact that your organization has a strategic plan is also very important to major donors and funders who are interested in knowing the long-range goals, objectives, and financial health of nonprofit organizations they support. Today's donors want to be certain that their gifts are making an impact on the organization's ability to deliver services, offer programs, and aid those who are directly being served.

> *Securing funds for priorities outlined in the strategic plan serves as the basis for establishing fundraising goals and creating an accompanying development plan.*

THE DEVELOPMENT AUDIT

A very effective planning tool used by nonprofit organizations is the development audit. The Resource Development Assessment, created by Robert F. Semple, founder of Semple-Bixel Associates in Nutley, New Jersey, is designed to provide an organization with a quick, graphic profile of its potential to compete for charitable dollars (Exhibit 5–1). It is not meant to be a substitute for an in-depth analysis of an organization's capacity to raise funds. Administered by professional counsel and completed by an organization's staff members and volunteer leaders, it will suggest where strengths and weaknesses lie within the overall resource development process. The 10 key result areas are as follows:

1. planning
2. leadership
3. volunteers
4. resource development staff
5. financial resources
6. donor research
7. fundraising aids
8. fundraising techniques
9. public relations
10. fundraising environment

Exhibit 5–1 The Resource Development Assessment (Abbreviated Version)

Introduction

This abbreviated version of our Resource Development Assessment questionnaire is designed to provide an organization with a quick, graphic profile of its potential to actively compete in the philanthropic marketplace. It is *not meant to be a substitute* for an in-depth analysis of an organization's capacity to raise money. Normally, an expanded version is administered by professional counsel to a study group composed of the CEO, development staff, select board members, and key volunteers. However, in its current format, it will *suggest* where strengths and deficiencies lie within your resource development program.

Ten key areas have been selected for this brief investigation. These are areas known to have considerable impact on the success or failure of fundraising programs. Please wait for the introduction to each section before selecting your answer. There are no right or wrong answers, only your *judgment* as to conditions that currently exist within your organization.

Each of the numbered statements is to be rated either as *Below Standard, Standard*, or *Above Standard*. These conditions correspond to a numerical scale of 1, 2, or 3 respectively. After you have made your assessment, place the numerical value in the grid adjacent to each statement.

After completion of each section, add the sub-totals to derive a cumulative score. Then transfer the cumulative score from each key area to the Resource Development Assessment Profile (attached).

Instructions

Assign a numerical rating to each item: 3 = Above Average; 2 = About Average (Standard); 1 = Below Average.

After completing each section, add the sub-totals to derive a cumulative score. Then transfer the cumulative score from each grid to the Resource Development Assessment Profile.

A word of caution: Because every development effort responds to a unique set of circumstances, e.g., popularity of cause, staff expertise, budget, etc., some of these questions may not apply to you. If so, for purposes of this exercise, substitute another question you believe to be relevant.

continues

Exhibit 5–1 The Resource Development Assessment (Abbreviated Version) (continued)

Fundraising Environment

	Below (1)	Std (2)	Above (3)
1. External: capacity to compete with other nonprofit organizations performing similar services within your service area			
2. External: corporate gift *potential* within your geographic locale			
3. Internal: the board and volunteer leadership support for the resource development program			
4. Internal: office space and equipment to conduct business (e.g., FAX, computers)			

Donor Research

	Below (1)	Std (2)	Above (3)
5. Availability of reference materials including on-line capacity to conduct donor prospect research			
6. Prospect gift evaluation procedure			
7. Ability to retrieve donor gift data			
8. Frequency of gift analysis reporting			

Fundraising Techniques

	Below (1)	Std (2)	Above (3)
9. Effectiveness of board and volunteers in conducting face-to-face solicitation			
10. Dollars raised by special events			
11. Phonathon			
12. Direct mail program			

Fundraising Aids

	Below (1)	Std (2)	Above (3)
13. A case statement for support is available (do not have one = 1; in the works = 2; complete = 3)			
14. Caliber of written proposals to solicit contributions			
15. Capability of software packages in preparing proposals, acknowledgments, and statistical reports			
16. Availability of training materials to assist volunteers participating in fundraising program			

continues

Exhibit 5–1 The Resource Development Assessment (Abbreviated Version) (continued)

Leadership

	Below (1)	Std (2)	Above (3)
17. The access board members have to funding sources			
18. The board's understanding of the resource development process			
19. The board's participation in soliciting gifts			
20. The board's percentage of gift participation in reaching annual goal (Below = less than 25% participate; Standard = 25 to 75%; Above = more than 75% participate)			

Volunteers (non-board members)

	Below (1)	Std (2)	Above (3)
21. Availability of volunteers to help solicit gifts			
22. Effectiveness of the volunteer orientation and training program			
23. Volunteer's percentage of gift participation in reaching annual goal (Below = less than 25% participate; Standard = 25 to 75%; Above = more than 75% participate)			
24. The recognition program for volunteers contributing their services			

Staff

	Below (1)	Std (2)	Above (3)
25. Development staff experience at designing and conducting fundraising programs			
26. Chief development officer reports directly to the organization's chief executive officer (No = 1; Sometimes = 2; Yes = 3)			
27. Chief development officer has access to the board regarding resource development matters (Never = 1; Seldom = 2; Frequently = 3)			
28. Extent of development officer's opportunity to enhance fundraising skills through workshops, seminars, and conferences			

Public Relations

	Below (1)	Std (2)	Above (3)
29. The access your organization has to the communications media			
30. The procedures to release information to the local newspapers, periodicals, and electronic media			
31. Name recognition organization has in the community			
32. Your organization's "image in the community (Poor = 1; Good = 2; Excellent = 3)			

continues

Exhibit 5–1 The Resource Development Assessment (Abbreviated Version) (continued)

Planning

	Below (1)	Std (2)	Above (3)
33. Frequency of reviewing fundraising plan to determine its effectiveness			
34. Involvement of key leadership in planning (CEO, development staff, selected board members, and key volunteers)			
35. The budget allocation to support the plan			
36. The effectiveness of your current fundraising plan			

Resource Attraction

	Below (1)	Std (2)	Above (3)
37. The overall ability of your organization to attract gifts from individuals			
38. The overall ability of your organization to attract corporate gifts			
39. The overall ability of your organization to attract gifts-in-kind			
40. The overall ability of your organization to attract gifts from private foundations			

Resource Development Assessment Profile

Source: Courtesy of Robert F. Semple, Semple Bixel Associates, Inc., Nutley, New Jersey.

"How do you keep a straight face when you say our priorities aren't based on what local corporations and foundations will support?"

Source: Copyright © Mark Litzler.

SETTING REALISTIC GOALS FOR YOUR FUNDRAISING PROGRAM

There are many ways to establish fundraising goals, and, all too frequently, development staff are not part of that process but rather are assigned a dollar goal based on the organization's operating budget. The following is a common scenario for establishing a fundraising goal:

1. The organization's leaders look at only the previous year's fundraising results.
2. They then look at next year's operating budget, including additional programs, new staff, etc.
3. They project a reasonable increase, usually 10–20 percent.
4. They establish a goal through some compromise between the operating budget and the 20-percent factor, a goal that is almost never less than the previous year's.

A better approach to setting a realistic goal would be to gather and analyze data collected during a three- to five-year period. This means that the organization must keep accurate records and be able to generate a variety of analytical reports. With the increased use of technology in fundraising (see Chapter 4), this type of analysis is now easier to do. Many of the most popular donor database systems have features that enable users to analyze their data in a variety of ways. New or smaller nonprofit organizations that may not currently use such sophisticated systems can still see which types of fundraising have increased, decreased, or remained stable during this multi-year period as long as they have accurate records of past fundraising results.

Look for the following when reviewing the data on the different types of fundraising:

- Which type generates the largest share?
- Which are the most reliable sources of income?
- Which are the least reliable sources of income?
- Which have the greatest potential for growth?

Once you have analyzed the results of your current fundraising program, the next step in developing your fundraising plan is to ask yourself the following questions:

- To which areas should you allocate more time?
- Are there any areas you should eliminate?
- Where should you involve more volunteers?
- Given a larger budget, in which areas would you invest more?

Keep in mind that different organizations will see varying results using the same methods of fundraising. For example, special events may be highly successful and appropriate for chapters of the American Heart Association but may fail to raise significant funds for public radio stations. Annual campaigns can have differing levels of success from year to year depending on the campaign committee's leadership and composition. It is very important that volunteers remain motivated and enthusiastic about their tasks. A true-to-life example would be the following: Jane Smith, a board member, chaired the annual campaign committee last year, personally recruited 25 volunteers, who in turn each solicited 10 prospects and raised $25,000 for the organization. This year, Jim White, a well-known community leader, agreed to chair the committee, personally recruited 10 volunteers, who in turn each solicited 5 prospects and raised only $11,000.

An excellent tool to use when analyzing your fundraising data and establishing your fundraising goals is the form presented as Exhibit 5–2.

When using this or any other type of form to analyze fundraising results, it is important to note any special circumstances that affected this year's results (Exhibit 5–3). Examples might include the receipt of a sizable bequest or major gift that will not be repeated the following year. When developing the upcoming year's goals, the organization must plan how it will raise those funds through other means. For example, if a $10,000 gift was received, is there a new major gift prospect who will give at that level? Are there 10 new prospective donors who will each contribute $1,000? Can you encourage 20 donors who gave $500 last year to increase their giving to $1,000 this year? Or will you look to other fundraising techniques to make up the difference, such as special events, foundation grants, or corporate support?

INVOLVING BOARD MEMBERS AND VOLUNTEERS

An organization's leaders and volunteers need to understand that fundraising goals are targets, not fixed figures. Involving leaders and volunteers in the goal-setting process is an excellent way to educate them. Having them participate in an assessment of the institution's capacity to raise money (e.g., using the Resource Development Assessment instrument) will give them a sense of ownership in the development effort. It also helps volunteer leaders better understand the role of the development office and what their role should be.

It is believed that each annual giving method requires three to four years to reach the level of maturity at which predictable levels

Exhibit 5–2 How to Plan Accurately for Next Year's Annual Fund

Do your board, CEO, and chief financial officer want you to accurately project fundraising results for the coming year? If so, it *can* be done. And you can reach your goals.

There are two basic sets of figures that must be generated and compared to plan and project accurately. First, you need to determine what you are *likely* to accomplish—the amount of money that you are *likely* to raise next year based on past results. These figures will be logical extensions (increases or decreases), category by category, of what has happened during these past three years.

Sections one and two of this instrument will help you to measure three years' growth, category by category, and to use these growth figures to project what next year's figures are likely to be.

If where you are *likely* to be is where you *want* to be, then give yourself a gold star and pat on the back. Photocopy the completed Sections one and two for your board, CEO, and chief financial officer and continue raising funds in the same manner as you have been. However, you may want to re-examine your institutional needs to determine what your fundraising goals *should* be.

In Sections three and four (columns O, P, Q) you will need to itemize specific fundraising objectives, category by category. These will add up to be your goal as it should be to meet all financial needs. Here's how to arrive at these objectives:

First, work with your CEO and department heads to determine what your fundraising needs will be for next year. Discuss program growth, new equipment needs, new staff, and increases in numbers of people to be served. (Or, in some cases, reductions in these areas.)

Working with your financial officer, carefully estimate the costs of these changes. Add or subtract these costs from last year's department budget and allow for inflation.

Total all program or department budgets. Don't forget to add administrative costs. From the total, subtract assured income (fees for services, yields on investments, government contracts, continuing grants—all sources of income not related to next year's fundraising efforts).

Now you have a net fundraising goal. Estimate fundraising costs by determining how much you are spending this year to raise your current income. Apply the same percent to your next year's goal. Add fundraising costs to net fundraising needs to determine your total development goal.

Using past experience as your guideline, break this total development goal down into fundraising methods or categories in Section three and four (lines 1–18, columns O, P, Q).

Finally, in columns R, S, and T, enter the differences between where you are likely to be (columns L, M, N) and where you want to be (O, P, Q).

continues

Exhibit 5–2 How to Plan Accurately for Next Year's Annual Fund (continued)

Section 1

	A	B	C	D	E	F
		TWO YEARS AGO			LAST YEAR	
	No. of Gifts	Total $ Raised	Average Gift	No. of Gifts	Total $ Raised	Average Gift
1. New Donor Acquisition Program	_____	$_____	$_____	_____	$_____	$_____
2. Reinstatement of Lapsed Donors	_____	_____	_____	_____	_____	_____
3. Renewal of First-Time Donors	_____	_____	_____	_____	_____	_____
4. Renewal of Ongoing Small Gift Donors	_____	_____	_____	_____	_____	_____
5. _____ (large gift club)	_____	_____	_____	_____	_____	_____
6. _____ (large gift club)	_____	_____	_____	_____	_____	_____
7. _____ (large gift club)	_____	_____	_____	_____	_____	_____
8. Board's Personal Call Program	_____	_____	_____	_____	_____	_____
9. Corporate Solicitation	_____	_____	_____	_____	_____	_____
10. Foundation Grants	_____	_____	_____	_____	_____	_____
11. Government Grants	_____	_____	_____	_____	_____	_____
12. Commemorative Giving Program	_____	_____	_____	_____	_____	_____
13. Yields on Planned Giving	_____	_____	_____	_____	_____	_____
14. Yields on Endowments	_____	_____	_____	_____	_____	_____
15. Telemarketing	_____	_____	_____	_____	_____	_____
16. _____ (special event)	_____	_____	_____	_____	_____	_____
17. _____ (special event)	_____	_____	_____	_____	_____	_____
18. Other Fundraising Income	_____	_____	_____	_____	_____	_____
19. TOTAL GIFTS	_____			_____		
20. TOTAL DOLLARS RAISED		$_____			$_____	
21. AVERAGE GIFT			$_____			$_____

Examine the fundraising methods (1–18) and circle the number of each method used. For each method you use, fill in columns A, B, and C with accurate figures to show how well you did two years ago. Then, complete columns D, E, and F to reflect last year's results. To complete G, H, and I, take this year's results and project to year end.

continues

Exhibit 5–2 How to Plan Accurately for Next Year's Annual Fund (continued)

Section 2

G	H	I	J	K	L	M	N
	THIS YEAR'S PROJECTIONS		Average Three-Year % Growth No. Gifts	Average Three-Year % Growth Total $	NEXT YEAR'S PROJECTIONS BASED ON THREE-YEAR TRENDS		
No. of Gifts	Total $ Raised	Average Gift			No. of Gifts	Total $ Raised	Average Gift
_____	$_____	$_____	_____%	_____%	_____	$_____	$_____
_____	_____	_____	_____%	_____%	_____	_____	_____
_____	_____	_____	_____%	_____%	_____	_____	_____
_____	_____	_____	_____%	_____%	_____	_____	_____
_____	_____	_____	_____%	_____%	_____	_____	_____
_____	_____	_____	_____%	_____%	_____	_____	_____
_____	_____	_____	_____%	_____%	_____	_____	_____
_____	_____	_____	_____%	_____%	_____	_____	_____
_____	_____	_____	_____%	_____%	_____	_____	_____
_____	_____	_____	_____%	_____%	_____	_____	_____
_____	_____	_____	_____%	_____%	_____	_____	_____
_____	_____	_____	_____%	_____%	_____	_____	_____
_____	_____	_____	_____%	_____%	_____	_____	_____
_____	_____	_____	_____%	_____%	_____	_____	_____
_____	_____	_____	_____%	_____%	_____	_____	_____
_____	_____	_____	_____%	_____%	_____	_____	_____
_____	_____	_____	_____%	_____%	_____	_____	_____
_____	_____	_____	_____%	_____%	_____	_____	_____
	$_____					$_____	
		$_____					$_____

Take the increases (category by category) from year one to year two and add those to the increases from year two to year three. Divide by two to get an average. Divide the average increase by this year's results to determine average % growth (J and K). G + J = L; H + K = M. Do this for each of the methods you use in fundraising (1–18). Now, add L and M vertically. You have the *likely* number of gifts and *likely* dollars you'll raise if you continue development methods and procedures as you have in the past three years. Turn to page four.

continues

Exhibit 5–2 How to Plan Accurately for Next Year's Annual Fund (continued)

Section 3	O	P	Q	R	S	T
		OBJECTIVES FOR NEXT YEAR			DIFFERENCES BETWEEN O, P, Q AND L, M, N	
	No. of Gifts	Total $ Raised	Average Gift	No. of Gifts	Total $ Raised	Average Gift
1. New Donor Acquisition Program	_____	$_____	$_____	_____	$_____	$_____
2. Reinstatement of Lapsed Donors	_____	_____	_____	_____	_____	_____
3. Renewal of First-Time Donors	_____	_____	_____	_____	_____	_____
4. Renewal of Ongoing Small Gift Donors	_____	_____	_____	_____	_____	_____
5. _____ (large gift club)	_____	_____	_____	_____	_____	_____
6. _____ (large gift club)	_____	_____	_____	_____	_____	_____
7. _____ (large gift club)	_____	_____	_____	_____	_____	_____
8. Board's Personal Call Program	_____	_____	_____	_____	_____	_____
9. Corporate Solicitation	_____	_____	_____	_____	_____	_____
10. Foundation Grants	_____	_____	_____	_____	_____	_____
11. Government Grants	_____	_____	_____	_____	_____	_____
12. Commemorative Giving Program	_____	_____	_____	_____	_____	_____
13. Yields on Planned Giving	_____	_____	_____	_____	_____	_____
14. Yields on Endowments	_____	_____	_____	_____	_____	_____

Section 4	O	P	Q	R	S	T
		OBJECTIVES FOR NEXT YEAR			DIFFERENCES BETWEEN O, P, Q AND L, M, N	
	No. of Gifts	Total $ Raised	Average Gift	No. of Gifts	Total $ Raised	Average Gift
15. Telemarketing	_____	_____	_____	_____	_____	_____
16. _____ (special event)	_____	_____	_____	_____	_____	_____
17. _____ (special event)	_____	_____	_____	_____	_____	_____
18. Other Fundraising Income	_____	_____	_____	_____	_____	_____
19. TOTAL GIFTS	_____			_____		
20. TOTAL DOLLARS RAISED		$_____			$_____	
21. AVERAGE GIFT			$_____			$_____

Columns L, M, N tell you the numbers of gifts and dollars you are *likely* to raise if you continue using the same methods and procedures. Columns O, P, and Q, above, show what you should or want to raise. Line by line, subtract L, M, and N from O, P, and Q and enter the difference on the corresponding lines in columns R, S, and T. Method by method, procedure by procedure, what are you going to have to do *differently* to reach your objectives for next year? Develop a separate, detailed plan for each fundraising method to be used.

Source: Courtesy of W. David Barnes, Barnes Associates Inc., Modesto, California.

Exhibit 5–3 Year-to-Date Analysis

	YEAR A	%	YEAR B	%	YEAR C	THREE-YEAR AVERAGE
Direct Mail	$100,000	18.0	$118,000	23.0	$145,000	$121,000
Special Events	75,000	33.0	100,000	25.0	125,000	100,000
Major Gifts	175,000	14.2	200,000	12.5	225,000	200,000
Foundations	300,000	0.0	300,000	−25.0	225,000	275,000
Corporations	150,000	16.6	175,000	0.9	190,000	171,666
TOTAL	$800,000		$893,000		$910,000	$867,666
		+11.6		+0.2		

Note the following:

- Income has increased each year but at a declining rate of growth.
- Further research is needed as to why the foundations and corporations programs are not growing.
- How did volunteers, staff, and the external environment influence the direction and success of the program during this three-year period?

of annual support can be projected. For an organization just beginning to build an annual giving program, it is important to maintain a positive environment for volunteers and staff. Successful programs build volunteers' confidence in their ability to perform and in the methods used. One positive outcome is that volunteers will continue to serve the next year, perhaps taking on a leadership role. Their continuing involvement increases the potential for even greater levels of commitment from volunteers and donors.

PREPARING A BUDGET

It is common for nonprofit organizations starting new development operations to choose to make a major investment in personnel alone. Believing that all the organization needs to raise funds is a development staff person is a critical error. The staff person is only one part of the investment. Funds to produce materials, do mailings, travel, set up recordkeeping systems, hire secretarial support, and contribute toward other items are also required.

Believing that all the organization needs to raise funds is a development staff person is a critical error.

Note that in the early stages of a development program, the costs of fundraising eat up a large percentage of the funds raised. It is usually a "break even" proposition at best. But as a fundraising program matures, the costs will total a smaller percentage of the funds raised. The percentage will vary depending on the size of the organization.

In constructing a fundraising plan, items to consider (in addition to personnel costs) include the following:

- design and printing
- postage and mail services
- supplies
- telephone
- photocopying
- travel
- food and entertaining

- professional services (e.g., photographer, entertainment for special events, consultants)
- membership dues for professional organizations
- conference and workshop attendance
- computer needs (hardware, software, annual maintenance agreements)
- Internet usage
- public relations

STAGES OF A DEVELOPMENT PROGRAM

As mentioned previously in this chapter, planning is a developmental process. So, too, is an organization's development program. It is unwise for an organization to attempt to include every fundraising method in the early years of its development program. It is best to begin expanding and enhancing those individual programs that have produced successful results for the organization. The development program illustrated in Exhibit 5–4 shows how a program advances through a number of stages. Note that the length of time an organization's fundraising program remains at a specific stage will vary depending on the organization.

STEPS TO DEVELOP YOUR FUNDRAISING PLAN
Step One

Determine your fundraising goal, number of gifts needed, and time line. Review your current strengths in sources of funding. Assess the likelihood of continuing and/or increased support from your current sources. Evaluate other sources of funding such as lapsed donors, current donors, and special event attendees. See Exhibit 5–5 for a sample gift-range chart to raise $1 million.

Step Two

Diversify your fundraising program by including appropriate fundraising methods for your organization. It is best not to become

Exhibit 5–4 Stages of a Fundraising Program

Stage 1

1. Direct Mail
   - two to four appeals
2. Annual Giving Volunteer Committee
   - conducts personal solicitations
3. Special Gifts
   - mailing to board members
   - mailing to key volunteers and prospects
4. Special Events
   - general ticketed event
   - smaller events hosted by CEO or board chairperson
5. Foundations, Corporations, Government
   - conduct research on prospective funders
   - gather guidelines and other pertinent information
   - prepare letters of inquiries
   - develop proposals for key funders
   - institute a reporting procedure for funders

Stage 2

1. Direct Mail
   - renewal mailings to current donors
   - donor acquisition mailings
   - special mailings to lapsed donors
2. Introduce Mail/Phone program
3. Annual Giving Volunteer Committee
   - increase number of personal solicitations
4. Special Gifts
   - do special cultivation/informational mailings to current donors
   - introduce gift clubs
   - continue personalized mailings and increase number of personal solicitations
5. Special Events
   - expand successful general ticketed event to increase revenue by instituting a sponsor/patron structure
   - continue smaller events hosted by CEO, board chairperson, or major donor

6. Foundations, Corporations, Government
   - continue research on possible funders
   - set up meetings with current funders
   - target new group of prospects preparing letters of inquiries
   - prepare written proposals and continue reporting procedure
7. Planned Giving
   - introduce concept of wills and bequests in communications and newsletters
   - begin drafting gift policies for board approval
8. Memorial Giving
   - introduce concept in communications and newsletter

Stage 3

1. Direct Mail
   - renewal mailings to current donors
   - increase donor acquisition mailings
   - continue mailing special appeals to lapsed donors
2. Mail/Phone Program
   - continue program doing more donor segmentation
3. Annual Giving Committee
   - increase activity of committee
4. Special Gifts
   - continue cultivation/information mailings from CEO
   - expand number of gift clubs
   - identify prospects for special attention
   - continue personalized mailings and personal solicitations
5. Special Events
   - maintain current program with some enhancements
6. Foundations, Corporations, Government
   - maintain current program
7. Planned Giving
   - establish a bequest society
   - prepare special marketing materials on planned giving
   - do special mailings to selected prospects
8. Memorial Giving
   - continue to include information in communications/newsletter

Exhibit 5–5 Annual Development Plan Gift-Range Chart

Goal: $1,000,000

Gift Range	Gifts	Prospects	Subtotal	Cumulative
$100,000	1	4	100,000	100,000
$ 50,000	2	8	100,000	200,000
$ 25,000	4	16	100,000	300,000
$ 10,000	10	40	100,000	400,000
$ 5,000	20	80	100,000	500,000
$ 2,500	25	100	62,500	562,500
$ 1,000	100	400	100,000	662,500
$ 500	200	800	100,000	762,500
$ 250	500	2000	125,000	887,500
$ 100	500	2000	50,000	937,500
Less than $100	many	many	62,500	1,000,000

Top 152 gifts produce $662,000 (66% of goal).
Next 700 gifts produce $225,000 (23% of goal).
Last 500+ gifts produce $112,500 (11 % of goal).

too dependent on any one or two sources of funding. Among the methods from which to choose are the following:

- individuals
  - annual giving through
    - personal solicitation
    - direct mail
    - telephone programs
    - special events
    - online/e-mail programs
  - major giving
  - planned giving
- private foundations
- corporate support
- organizations
- government grants/contracts

See Appendices 5–A, 5–B, and 5–C for different types of planning formats.

Step Three

Identify potential donors, especially major donors and funders among individuals, foundations, corporations, and government sources through prospect research. Determine who among board members, staff, volunteers, current donors, and community leaders can help you reach out to these potential donors

Step Four

Develop strategies for each major gift prospect including the following:

- best person(s) to reach out
- cultivation activities for relationship building
- approach (letter, telephone call, visit)
- case for support message to use
- ask level
- timing
- follow-up

Assign a staff member or volunteer to take the lead in managing the major gift prospect's cultivation and solicitation process.

Step Five

Plan a 12-month calendar of donor cultivation activities using printed materials, events, and communications from the executive director and board chair.

Step Six

Review current organizational materials such as brochures, annual appeal materials, newsletters, and Web site to see what needs to be updated or revised. Determine if any new print materials are needed.

Step Seven

Develop policies for acknowledging gifts, including who signs thank you letters based on the level of gift, and what level gift warrants a personal call by a staff or board member.

Step Eight

Create a plan for recognizing donors at public events, in print materials, and in special ways based on level of gifts.

HOW YOUR RETURN ON INVESTMENT IS IMPORTANT TO PLANNING

There is growing attention on an organization's Return on Investment, or ROI, which relates the costs of fundraising to the actual dollars raised. According to the Association of Fundraising Professionals (AFP), fundraising professionals always have been asked, "How much money have you raised?" But now, there are additional questions such as: "How much did it cost? Is that cost reasonable? How do your costs compare with others? What are the standards to measure performance? Can you estimate next year's results?" AFP has developed some guidelines outlined in Exhibit 5–6 for evaluating fundraising costs that can assist fundraising professionals in responding to these questions.

Over the years, there has been considerable interest in having industry-wide guidelines and standards. James M. Greenfield, CFRE, FAHP, author of several books on fundraising, was one of the first development professionals to conduct research in this area in the 1990s. In his 1996 book, *Fund-Raising Cost Effectiveness: A Self Assessment Workbook* (John Wiley and Sons), he

> *It is important that you focus staff, board, and volunteer time and effort on those types of fundraising programs that have a higher return on investment for your organization.*

developed a performance index for organizations to use in evaluating their fundraising programs and a listing of reasonable cost guidelines for solicitation activities. Greenfield believes that there is more to performance management than "bottom-line" analysis. To measure fundraising performance, one must begin with individual fundraising program assessments.

Although many development professionals believe Greenfield's original guidelines are still fairly true today, recent research reveals some fundamental reasons why it is not yet possible to have industry-wide standards:

- Nonprofit organizations do not conduct fundraising in the same ways.
- Different types of fundraising programs perform differently depending on the organization's mission, age, and geographic location, etc.

Exhibit 5–6 Guidelines Useful for Evaluating Fundraising Costs

Fundraising is a process that has many components, and investments must be made to complete the process. Individual components of the fundraising process should be evaluated as part of a total development program, and boards of directors of nonprofit organizations should determine a reasonable rate of return on investment for their own organization based on prior results.

If only three to five percent of the donations from a particular campaign actually go to the cause, donors may want to look elsewhere. On the other hand, it may not be reasonable to expect that 90 percent of the contributions go directly to the cause. Just like for-profit entities, charities have operating expenses.

Consider the following factors when evaluating an organization's fundraising costs and returns.

- Age of the organization. A well-established organization will likely have a greater return on investment than a newly established nonprofit.
- Age of the fundraising department. A mature, professionally run development program will be expected to produce a higher return on investment than a newly formed department.
- Source of funds. Nonprofits that rely heavily on small gifts from individual donors will have higher fundraising costs. In contrast, organizations that receive support from the federal government, corporations, foundations, or large gifts from wealthy donors, tend to have lower costs.
- Different methods used in the fundraising process will produce different returns. For example:
  - A donor acquisition mailing will have a much lower return on investment than a donor renewal mailing.

- A capital campaign will produce a much higher return on investment than an annual fundraising program.
- A new planned giving program may have zero return on investment for the first few years.
- The return on investment for a special event will be lower than that for a major gifts program.
- Size of an organization. The return on investment may be affected by the size of the organization.
- Profile of the constituency. The economic and geographic profile of the constituency being solicited will affect fundraising costs and return on investment.
- Location of the organization. An organization located in an affluent region should expect a higher return on investment than one located in a less affluent area.
- Popularity of the cause. The cause and its level of community acceptance will affect the return on investment.
- Competition for funds. Within the community or constituency that the organization is appealing to for support, competition by other organizations may lower the return on investment.
- Sometimes, a fundraising campaign may lose money in the short term, but generate significant returns in the long run. The cost of direct mail acquisition (mail solicitations sent to potential new donors) may range from $1.00 to $1.25 per dollar raised. However, once new donors have been identified, a second mailing to that group may cost only $0.20 per dollar raised. Thus, while the first mailing may not bring in much money, the second mailing should bring in a substantial number of contributions. These newly identified donors may ultimately donate even larger gifts to the nonprofit (e.g., land, stocks, charitable bequests).

Source: Courtesy of the Association of Fundraising Professionals (AFP), Arlington, Virginia.

"When charities measure their success only in terms of 'lives changed,' it's a sign that they didn't meet their fund-raising goals."

Source: Copyright © Mark Litzler.

And most importantly, throughout the nonprofit sector, there are inconsistencies in how nonprofit organizations track and report expenses related to fundraising.

In developing your fundraising plan and time line, it is important that you focus staff, board, and volunteer time and effort on those types of fundraising programs that have a higher return on investment for your organization. According to Greenfield's guidelines, programs that solicit larger gifts such as corporate and foundation programs, capital campaigns, and individual major and planned gifts are found to incur a $.10 to $.30 cost to raise a $1.00 while special events often incur a $.50 to $1.00 cost to raise a $1.00 due to the significant costs associated with producing a special event. Direct mail acquisition programs often lose money, meaning the incurred cost is more than $1.00 to raise $1.00, because an organization is mailing to people who have never before given to that organization. Since acquisition programs are important to the growth of an organization's donor base, they are viewed as investment programs because the cost of renewing a donor averages only $.25 to raise $1.00.

THE EVALUATION PROCESS

Nonprofit organizations need to view the evaluation of their development program as a continuous process. During the year, refinements and revisions often will be made as events and circumstances dictate. If you developed your fundraising plan by analyzing past results and their cost-effectiveness, you already have begun.

The evaluation process does not conclude by viewing the bottom line only. There are a number of other factors that affect the level of success of your development program. As you proceed in your evaluation, here are some possible questions to pose:

- What was the performance level of the board, staff, and volunteers? Was new leadership revealed?
- Was the budget sufficient in all areas? Are changes needed?
- Is funding more or less diversified than before?
- Are the computer technology support systems adequate?
- Are the gift-processing, acknowledgment, and tracking systems running efficiently?
- How well did the prospect research effort function?
- How well did the printed materials for fundraising and public relations perform?
- How effective were the cultivation activities?

In many ways, the evaluation process is a continuing audit of the organization's capability to raise funds successfully and effectively. Once completed, the evaluation becomes the basis for the next year's planning process.

Sample Action Plan Calendar

Months/Programs	Jan.	Feb.	March	April	May	June	July	Aug.	Sept.	Oct.	Nov.	Dec.
Direct Mail			Appeal Mailing			Appeal Mailing			Appeal Mailing			Appeal Mailing
Mail/Phone				Calling						Calling		
Annual Giving Committee						Recruit Committee			First Meeting		Personal Solicitations of Identified Prospects	End of Campaign
Special Gifts			Target Group Mailing						Invite to CEO or Board Chair Event	Special Follow-up to Attendees		Continue Special Follow-up
Special Events					Event					CEO or Board Chair Event		
Foundations Corporations Government	Research and Contact Potential Funders		Proposal Due			Proposal Due				Proposal Due		Report to Funders
Planned Giving	Newsletter Mailing				Newsletter Mailing				Newsletter Mailing			

Fund Development Plan: Fiscal Year 2007 Goals

GRANT FUNDING

FY06 Anticipated:
FY07 Goal:

Strategies Planned FY07:
- Renew (and increase where possible and appropriate) current grant funding sources.
- Obtain $40,000 in new grants, including seeking out funding for CASA expansion and grants specific to Public Education efforts.
- *Board members can help by alerting Development Director about any personal connections to local foundations.*

INDIVIDUAL GIVING

FY06 Anticipated:
FY07 Goal:

Strategies Planned FY07:
- Support United Way campaign efforts and seek to maintain level designation donations.
- Organize and implement one mail solicitation in August.
- Organize and implement Child Abuse Prevention Month/ Mother's & Father's Day card solicitation campaign to be mailed in late March.
- Include "Giving Highlights" in both newsletters (one on planned giving opportunities) and a donation envelope in each newsletter.
- Include donation/support opportunities in each monthly e-newsletter with links back to relevant pages on SCAN website.
- Cultivate additional media exposure for SCAN "success stories."
- *Board members can help by providing new prospects to add to SCAN's current mailing list of 2,400; personalizing solicitations to key contacts; making individual thank you calls to donors over $100.*

CORPORATE GIVING

FY06 Anticipated:
and/or FY07 Goal:

Strategies Planned FY07:
- Continue to cultivate companies regarding the Allies Award Event in April, and obtain at least $20,000 in sponsorships linked to that event.
- Research employers of current volunteers and send annual report and letter in honor of the employee's volunteer work with request for contributions.
- Look for opportunities for cause marketing partnerships to underwrite specific publications public education give-away items.
- Solicit grocers and restaurants to underwrite Allies Coalition lunches and parent education meals.
- *Board members can help by calling prospect contacts with whom you have a relationship to initiate meetings; attending meetings with corporate prospects with staff; making thank you calls to corporations who make contributions over $1,000.*

UNITED WAY/CIVIC/FAITH

FY06 Anticipated:
FY07 Goal:

Strategies Planned FY07:
- Cultivate current United Way relationships; maintain grants.
- Cultivate connections with Alexandria Women's Giving Circle.
- Send annual report with request letters to faith and civic groups with whom SCAN has a link.
- *Board members can help by alerting staff about your own memberships in faith-based and civic groups; adding personal notes to the solicitation to those groups; alerting staff when your company, or a company with whom you have a connection, will be running United Way or other workplace campaign; serving as spokesperson for SCAN.*

SPECIAL EVENTS

FY06 Anticipated:
FY07 Goal:

Strategies Planned FY07:
- Organize a fall Toast to Hope with sponsorship opportunities and silent auction, with particular appeal to individual supporters and small businesses or those not interested in golf.
- Cultivate returning and new golf sponsor prospects with a save the date postcard in the fall, brochure mailing in January, e-blast in February, and follow up contacts in spring.
- Organize and publicize quarterly restaurant nights during the year, focusing on restaurants in Arlington and Alexandria who will donate at least 20–25% of all food proceeds.
- Cultivate partnerships with HiBall Events and other benefit organizers, including a Fashion Luncheon in DC in the fall.
- *Board members can help by assisting in identification and solicitation of sponsors for Toast, Golf, or Allies Event; assisting in promotion (ticket sales) for fall fundraiser and promoting participation of new individuals in restaurant nights.*

Source: Courtesy of SCAN of Northern Virginia, Alexandria, Virginia.

Sample Fundraising Plan Template

STRATEGY	ACTION STEPS	WHO/WHEN	COST	FUNDS RAISED AS OF:
1. New Donor Acquisition Goals: 50 new donors $7,500	1. Launch two direct mail campaigns to XXXX prospects each. 2. Each board member recruits one donor per quarter. 3. Event attendees make a gift later in the year.	Staff —May/Sept. Board—Quarterly Staff—Fall	$ no cost $	
2. Renewals Goals:				
3. Special Appeals Goals:				
4. Special Events Goals:				
5. Major Donors Goals:				
6. Businesses/Corporations Goals:				
7. Foundations Goals:				
8. On-line Giving Goals:				
9. Workplace Giving Goals: (Funds will come in next year)				
10. Planned Giving Goals: (Income cannot be predicted)				
			TOTAL COST: $	TOTAL INCOME: $

Chapter 6

Building Relationships for Your Organization Through Annual Giving

KEY VOCABULARY

- Acknowledgment
- Annual Giving
- Brochure
- Case Statement
- Challenge Gift
- Constituency
- Donor
- Donor Pyramid
- Gift Clubs
- Matching Gift
- Personal Solicitation
- Reunion or Anniversary Giving
- Solicitor's Kit
- Steering Committee
- Unrestricted Funds

THE ROLE OF ANNUAL GIVING

An annual giving program uses the greatest variety of fundraising techniques to introduce an organization's programs, services, and needs to the widest audience. Often considered the "front lines" or "trenches" of fundraising, an annual giving program seeks funds on an annual or recurring basis from the same constituency, or a broadening one, to be used for operating budget support. In the "pyramid of giving" shown in Figure 6–1, annual giving forms the base of the pyramid because its purpose is to identify the largest number of donors and provide them with information about the organization.

The annual giving program provides the first in a series of contacts with a donor that the organization hopes will develop into a long-term relationship and lead to a major gift and/or estate or planned giving. The program recruits new donors and brings back previous donors and tries to persuade previous donors to increase the size of their gifts. It offers opportunities for donors to be involved as volunteers in special events and annual campaign committees. One very important purpose of an annual giving program is to identify potential leaders and prospective major donors. Throughout an annual giving program, you are friend raising as well as fundraising—building relationships that will be important for your organization's future.

Key elements of a successful annual giving program include the following:

- compelling case for support
- careful planning
- trained volunteers
- assigned staff
- clear delineation of volunteer and staff tasks
- donor communications and appropriate recognition
- time line and benchmarks for success

Figure 6–1 The Pyramid of Giving

THE NEED FOR DONOR-CENTERED FUNDRAISING

The term donor-centered fundraising was used in the past to help organizations focus more on meeting the needs of the donor rather than only the needs of the organization. However, due to the groundbreaking research on how donor relations can influence retention and generosity, conducted by Penelope Burk, President of Cygnus Applied Research, we now have data to support that a donor-centered fundraising approach will result in increased contributions and donor loyalty. Her book, *Donor-Centered Fundraising*™, is based on five years of research and testing with over 600 North American charities and donors. It is a comprehensive study of donor communication, recognition, and donor relations that describes what motivates today's donors and the type of relationship they are seeking with the charities they support.

Penelope Burk shared the following key highlights of these findings at the Association of Fundraising Professionals (AFP) 2007 International Conference (Burk, 2003):

- Donors want prompt, personal gift acknowledgement but say they get prompt but impersonal gift acknowledgement.
- Donors want confirmation that their gifts have been set to work as intended and measurable results but say they get general appeals with few measurable results.
- More than 94% of study donors said they never or rarely get a call or are ever visited unless it is a solicitation.
- 46% of study donors stop giving for reasons related to a "failure to communicate."
- 28% of individual donors and 79% of corporate donors say recognition gifts are always inappropriate.

More importantly, Penelope Burk learned what donors would do if communication was improved:

- 85% of study donors would definitely or probably support the charity again if they had received a personal telephone call from a board member to say thanks; 86% of this group would definitely or probably make a larger gift.

- 93% of study donors would definitely or probably give again to a charity that provided a prompt and personal thank you and followed up later with a meaningful report on their gift at work; 64% of this group would definitely or probably give more; and 74% of this group would definitely or probably continue to give indefinitely as long as they continued to receive these things.

Thanks to Penelope Burk's research, staff and volunteers raising funds for nonprofit organizations now know what they need to do to develop a donor-centered fundraising program for their organizations. They must first satisfy donors' needs for meaningful information including measurable results on how their gifts were put to use; then enhance donor communications through more personal contact; and finally, design a recognition program that uniquely reflects the culture of the individual nonprofit organization. Visit http://www.cygresearch.com for more information about *Donor-Centered Fundraising*™ and Penelope Burk.

DEFINING THE CASE FOR SUPPORT—YOUR COMPETITIVE EDGE

Before an organization can develop a successful annual giving program, it needs to identify its needs and priorities. Additional funds are always needed to expand operations. However, keep in mind that the organization's mission statement sets the direction for specific programs and services that will benefit the public and meet the needs of the community being served.

The case for support, or the "case statement," informs your donors and prospects who you are, what you are trying to do, and why. It presents the organization's objectives and needs as persuasively as possible so that a person will see the benefits of investing in the organization. The case for support tells donors and prospects the following:

- your purpose and importance
- specific approaches and strategies your organization employs to address an issue or solve a problem
- short- and long-term goals

- major accomplishments and successes
- how your organization plans to have a future impact on the cause or issue

Given the tremendous competition for donors that exists in the nonprofit sector today, you must make a strong case for support. People will not give to an organization only because it says it requires funds. People view their gifts as investments that will help organizations accomplish their objectives. That is why a well-written compelling case for support is your competitive edge.

Because the purpose of annual giving usually is to raise unrestricted funds for operating costs, it is sometimes difficult to develop a compelling case for support. However, by focusing on the organization's mission and describing its programs or services, a case may be made for providing general support and not restricted to a specific program or service. Exhibit 6–1 lists tips for preparing the case statement.

Because an organization appeals to several different constituencies—current donors, prospects, individuals receiving services, community members—you may need more than one case statement. A good test to use is to ask two key questions about each group: "What does this constituency know about my organization?" and "How much does this constituency care about my organization?" How your donors and prospects relate to these questions will communicate to you whether to have one case statement or several versions and how to focus the case for each. Investing a reasonable amount of time in writing the case statement is extremely important.

> *Because an organization appeals to several different constituencies, you may need more than one case statement.*

For those who believe they do not have the time to prepare a written case, keep in mind that material from the case can and should be used in a variety of ways—appeal letters, foundation proposals, brochures, and talking points for personal solicitations. By developing the case, you will indeed save time in preparing other development-related materials.

Exhibit 6–1 Tips for Preparing the Case Statement

1. Involve key staff, board members, donors, and volunteers.
2. Have only one writer.
3. The case statement does not need to be long.
4. Use simple, brief language that people can understand.
5. Be convincing and optimistic.
6. Present a positive image.
7. Base it on organization's strengths, not needs.
8. Project the future, not the past.
9. Tell the story with pictures and charts.
10. Make the case from the prospect's point of interest; be donor oriented.
11. Demonstrate the capacity to solve problems that are important to donors.
12. Show that the organization's needs and wants are a good investment.

Exhibit 6–2 Ways to Strengthen Your Competitive Edge

- Staff and board should review annually the written case for support.
- Have staff and board members use key messages from the case for support in their "elevator speeches"—a brief description about your organization.
- Ask your current donors why they support your organization.
- Incorporate pertinent data from recent studies and reports to keep the case updated and vital.
- Have major donors and prospects review the case and solicit their comments as a cultivation activity.

SOLICITATION METHODS USED IN ANNUAL GIVING

There are four ways to ask people for money: by mail, by telephone, online, or, the most successful way, in person. Creatively combining these methods makes for a successful annual giving program. The following are most commonly used in annual giving programs:

- personal solicitation
- gift clubs
- telephone campaigns, telethons, telemarketing
- direct mail
- online solicitation

This chapter focuses primarily on using volunteers to do personal solicitations for an annual giving campaign. Information is included on how volunteers can use gift club membership to solicit increased gifts and new gifts. Chapter 9 also covers personal solicitation and how it can be used to secure major gifts for a nonprofit organization. More information on direct mail, telephone campaigns, and online giving is found in Chapter 7.

RECRUITING VOLUNTEER LEADERS

Volunteers are vital to a nonprofit organization. As board members, they govern and establish policies; as program volunteers, they help the organization offer its services; and, most important, as volunteer solicitors, they enable the organization to achieve its goals. To keep an active core of volunteers, an organization must maintain the volunteers' confidence, use their time and talents effectively, and thank them regularly for the many contributions they make to the organization. (See Chapter 2 for more in-depth information.)

The first step in recruiting volunteer leaders is to decide on the basic campaign structure. There are a number of ways you might structure a campaign. The simplest is to have an annual giving chairperson and committee. Search diligently for the best person possible for this position. The following are some qualifications to consider when looking. The chairperson should

- be a generous donor to the organization
- be capable of making a large gift and soliciting other large gifts
- have a strong commitment to the organization and its mission

- be experienced as a volunteer and as a fundraiser and enjoy challenges
- be inspired by the organization and be capable of helping recruit and inspire other key volunteers
- be a successful business executive or community leader who is widely known and admired in the community

It is a good idea to go over the list of possible chairpersons with your organization's chief executive officer (CEO) and the board chair, if appropriate, before contacting any of them. Because the person chosen will serve as a spokesperson for your organization with donors and prospective donors, it is important to select the right person. When the job is offered to a candidate, it is best that the CEO and/or chairperson of the board make the offer in person. They can answer any questions and discuss any reservations the person may have in accepting the position. This is not the time, though, to do any "arm twisting" or minimize the duties involved. Serving as the annual giving chairperson takes effort, money, and commitment. You are not looking for a "letterhead" leader but an active leader.

WORKING WITH THE STEERING COMMITTEE

Once the annual giving chairperson position is filled, you should immediately set up a meeting with him or her and set the plans for the campaign. The chairperson should be involved in planning each step of the drive. It is important that the chairperson have sufficient information about the organization's past fundraising efforts so he or she can help set goals for the current campaign. Recruiting members for the steering committee is one of the first tasks. If you have developed a plan to solicit different groups within your organization and community such as board members, gift club donors, business executives, community leaders, and clients, it is important to have a volunteer chairperson from each group or constituency. As you think about possible candidates for these positions, you are again looking for people who are available, willing to take part in the program, and have good contacts with potential donors and important groups. Once these chairpersons are recruited, they can begin recruiting other volunteers for their area of responsibility, thus increasing the number of volunteer solicitors. When determining how many volunteers are needed to complete the organizational structure, keep in mind that you should ask a volunteer to contact no more than five or six prospects. If you require more than this from your volunteer, the chances are that he or she will not complete the assignment.

The steering committee, chaired by the annual giving chairperson, helps to set the goals, recommend policies, and then assumes responsibility for the success of the campaign. The CEO of the organization must be an active member of the steering committee. The development officer is the staff liaison. Setting goals and deadlines, approving strategies, and assigning major prospects make the committee feel involved and needed, thereby ensuring motivation and success for the program. Exhibit 6–3 shows the structure for a steering committee.

Exhibit 6–3 Steering Committee Structure

- Annual Giving Chairperson
- Annual Giving Steering Committee Comprised of the Following Subcommittee Chairpersons:
  - Board
  - Gift Club #1 (Highest Giving Club)
  - Gift Club #2 (Next Highest Giving Club)
  - Business Community
  - Clients
  - Community
  - Volunteers

TRAINING AND MANAGING VOLUNTEERS

With the committee structure set, the next step is to train the volunteers. Do not simply assign tasks. Offer training so that you can build the volunteers' confidence and inspire them to do a better job. Training sessions also will help identify potential leaders for future campaigns.

In planning volunteer training, consider the following:

- how much money you need to raise
- the complexity of your fundraising plan
- the number of volunteers involved and their knowledge of and experience with your organization
- the volunteers' fundraising experience
- the amount of time committed by the volunteers

Because many of today's volunteers are employed outside the home, you will need to design training sessions that use their time effectively. Depending on your group of volunteers, you may need to schedule a series of training sessions to be held on evenings and weekends. Do not present your sessions as lectures. Your volunteers will learn best by being active participants, so allow for open discussion and opportunities to practice the skills they need to be effective fundraisers.

Provide opportunities during your training sessions for the volunteers to do the following:

- meet, get to know one another, and begin forming a successful team
- hear the executive director or chief executive officer and others discuss the "state of the institution"—its purposes, policies, and programs
- understand completely the case for support—the goals, plans, and procedures—and to understand the strengths of the organization and its particular needs at this time
- learn and understand the methods and techniques to be used in soliciting gifts
- review the campaign's timetable, reporting dates, deadlines, and procedures
- review the solicitation materials included in their kit (Exhibit 6–4)

The first objective of training is to provide volunteers with the necessary information and materials for them to be successful in

Exhibit 6–4 What to Include in a Volunteer Solicitor's Kit

1. General organizational brochures
2. Copies of the case for support
3. Lists of donors and prospects
4. Fact sheet of answers to questions most often asked
5. Information about making a gift and tax deductibility
6. Pledge cards and envelopes

their fundraising. While accomplishing this objective, you are showing your workers that you and your staff are behind them all the way, and are readily available for advice and help.

The development staff play an important role in both managing and supporting the volunteers. The following are keys to managing volunteers effectively:

- Keep in regular contact with your volunteers.
- Set up a schedule for progress reports.
- Call meetings only when needed, so as not to waste their time.
- If a volunteer can no longer fulfill his or her responsibility on the committee, accept the volunteer's resignation graciously and look for a replacement.
- If a volunteer is not "pulling his or her weight" on the committee, consult with the team captain and the annual giving chairperson about approaching the member. It is best if the volunteer leaders have a friendly but frank conversation with the member. He or she will either resign or agree to fulfill his or her commitment. The purpose of this meeting is to "clear the air."
- Always make your volunteers feel they are an important part of the effort because they are.

You have identified, recruited, trained, and provided tools and assistance to your annual giving campaign volunteers. Your volunteer program is now established. To ensure that it continues to be a success, there is one basic key you must remember—to say thank you. Like all of us, volunteers need to be thanked for the job they do. Even if they are not successful, they still need words of appreciation and encouragement.

In Chapter 2, we covered a number of ways to provide recognition to volunteers. Depending on your organization, there are almost limitless ways to say thank you to your volunteers. At the very least, a word of thanks from you, as the development officer, and a letter from the executive director or board chairperson are appropriate. A certificate or memento from the organization also shows appreciation. Whatever you choose, the volunteers will know the organization appreciated their efforts and will be more likely to serve on the annual giving committee again next year.

USING GIFT CLUBS TO MOTIVATE INCREASED GIVING

One of the most successful ways for an organization to solicit larger annual gifts is to establish gift clubs. Gift clubs are created at those giving levels that produce the most funds in annual campaigns. Usually, the top category encompasses gifts of $1,000 and above, and the next covers gifts of $500 to $999. Experience shows that most individuals who can give $500 a year will instead contribute $1,000 to be a member of the most prestigious gift club; therefore, fewer people donate $500. The next range is $250 to $499, with most of the donors contributing at the $250 level. The lowest category is $100 to $249, with the majority of members giving at the $100 level.

These gift levels, or whatever other levels fit an organization's constituency, form the basis for gift clubs. The name for each gift club could have special meaning for the organization. Using names of persons or places that played an important role in the history of the organization helps establish the importance of membership in these groups. For example, at American University, the gift clubs have had names such as the following:

- The President's Circle ($1,000 and above)
- The Hurst Society ($500–$999), named for the university's founder, John Fletcher Hurst
- The Mary Graydon Associates ($250–$499), named for the first dormitory, now a student center
- The American Club ($100–$249)

"Dear Dean Vande Clyde: I was flattered by your invitation to join this year's Leaders Circle until it occurred to me that you were talking about my giving money."

Source: Copyright © Mark Litzler.

When looking at the methods used in annual giving described earlier in this chapter, keep in mind that personal solicitation is reserved for the top gift clubs whereas direct mail, telephone fundraising, and online approaches are used at all levels. (A further discussion of gift clubs is found in Chapter 7.) As shown in Exhibit 6–3, the two top gift clubs each have a chairperson who serves on the annual campaign steering committee. Keep in mind that it is best for volunteers to solicit individuals for gift club membership at the level they themselves can expect to contribute. No volunteer solicitor should make a call until his or her own contribution is made. The volunteer will then know

> *No volunteer solicitor should make a call until his or her own contribution is made.*

what is expected of him or her and will be comfortable working with prospects in his or her giving range. He or she can tell prospects about the events they attend and communications they receive, which makes them feel more involved in the organization. Frequently using the names of the gift clubs in oral and written communications also shows the importance of these clubs to the organization.

The gift club structure increases the total of annual gifts and is also the best method to raise the giving levels of donors. Each year donors should be encouraged to "move up" to the next gift club category. Experience shows that few people are offended by being asked for too much, and, by the same token, few donors suggest that the solicitor did not ask for enough.

RECOGNIZING ANNUAL DONORS

Donor recognition is an important component of stewarding continued support from your donors. In Exhibit 6–5, you see the types of recognition or "benefits" provided by the American Health Information Management Association's FORE Foundation to donors at various levels of giving. When designing your gift clubs and corresponding benefits, be certain that the benefits can be fulfilled easily and do not require significant staff time and money to offer. Exhibit 6–6 shows how the Franklin Square Hospital Center Foundation promotes its donor giving society on the hospital's Web site.

THE ANNUAL CAMPAIGN CALENDAR

Because your annual campaign has a specific duration, it is important to set targets and deadlines for staff and volunteers. As illustrated in Exhibit 6–7, the annual campaign actually has three phases: planning, solicitation, and recognition. Depending on your organization's needs, this calendar could be used to develop a 6-, 9-, or 12-month annual campaign. Attempting to do an annual campaign in less than 6 months will leave insufficient time for the critical planning phase.

Exhibit 6–5 Example of Donor Recognition Opportunities

—Individual Donor Recognition—

FORE Donor (up to $100)
- Name listed in appropriate category in the FORE Annual Report ($50 or higher)
- FORE donor designation on ribbon for name badge at the National Convention

FORE Bronze Donor ($100–$249)

All of the above plus:
- Name listed in Honor Roll of donors on AHIMA/FORE Web site
- Bronze donor lapel pin

FORE Silver Donor ($250–$499)

All of the above plus:
- Name listed on Honor Roll of Donors at the FORE Booth at the National Convention
- Silver donor lapel pin

FORE Gold Donor ($500–$999)

All of the above plus:
- Name published in AHIMA Journal
- Gold donor lapel pin

FORE Platinum Donor ($1,000–$2,499)

All of the above plus:
- Invitation to Donor Reception in President's Suite at the National Convention
- Recognition on the Honor Roll of Donors scrolled at a Convention General Session
- Platinum donor lapel pin

FORE Diamond Donor ($2,500–$4,999)

All of the above plus:
- Access to VIP Lounge at National Convention
- Diamond donor lapel pin

Gifts and pledges of $5,000 or more will be recognized as major gifts, with a separate set of recognition guidelines.

Source: Courtesy of Eileen M. Murray, MM, CAE, CFRE, VP and Executive Director, FORE Foundation, American Health Information Management Association, Chicago, Illinois.

EFFECTIVE TECHNIQUES TO INCREASE YOUR ANNUAL CAMPAIGN

Matching Gift Programs

In the past, these programs benefited only educational institutions. Today, they benefit a wide variety of nonprofit organizations, including hospitals and retirement communities, arts organizations, cultural organizations, and social service agencies. A corporation with a matching gift program will match the contributions of its employees dollar for dollar up to a set figure. Some companies will match more than dollar for dollar and will match retired employees and employee spouse gifts. A matching gift program is a terrific source of additional funds for all eligible organizations.

Exhibit 6–6 Example of a Donor Recognition Society Promoted on a Web Site

A leader is one who follows his heart and sees with his soul and in every leader there lies a vision.

Dr. D. Thomas Crawford Giving Society

The Dr. D. Thomas Crawford Giving Society provides an opportunity to recognize and honor our dedicated donors and demonstrate our gratitude to those who support us through charitable gifts and believe in the hospital, its mission, and most importantly, its patients.

The Franklin Square Hospital Center Donor Giving Society is named in memory of Dr. D. Thomas Crawford; one individual who exemplified the very definition of a leader. Dr. Crawford's commitment to Franklin Square Hospital Center dates back to the hospital's original location in downtown Baltimore. His vision and passion for healthcare was instrumental in bringing the new hospital to life and making it what it is today.

As Director of Medical Education, Dr. Crawford made it his mission to raise funds to support medical education and provide opportunity to his residents and physicians. He believed that as the world of healthcare constantly evolved, the progression of technology and advanced medical treatments should and must be available to the community that Franklin Square serves. As a result, Franklin Square Hospital Center offers patients today excellent medical treatment, personalized patient care, and the latest technology in advanced healthcare.

The Dr. D. Thomas Crawford Giving Society provides an opportunity for you to make the same kind of meaningful contribution. Please accept our invitation to make a difference!

As a member of the Dr. D. Thomas Crawford Giving Society, you belong to a distinctive family of generous and compassionate friends of the medical community. Donors will be recognized in the Foundation's annual report, invited to attend the annual recognition event, and will receive a subscription to the Foundation's newsletter. You'll be kept informed of the special programs and services provided by Franklin Square Hospital Center and how they impact lives in the community. Your gift adds meaning to what we do.

$100–$149	Supporter
$150–$249	Friend
$250–$499	Associate
$500–$999	Champion
$1,000+	Visionary*

*Donors will also receive an invitation to enjoy an Evening with the President.

Donors become members by contributing a minimum of $100 annually to the Foundation in a calendar year. These gifts include direct mail and those made in tribute of other individuals. Gifts are considered cumulative on an annual basis. Members will be asked to renew their gift each year.

$25–$99	Partnership Fund**

**These donors are not members of the society, but are still recognized as a donor to the Partnership Fund.

Franklin Square Hospital Center Foundation invites you to partner with us to support the advancement of healthcare and patient care. Your name will be recognized in our Partnership Fund Commemorative Album displayed in the main lobby of the hospital.

For more information, please contact the Franklin Square Hospital Foundation at 443-777-7454.

Source: Courtesy of Kristi Rasmussen, Director of Annual Fund Programs, Franklin Square Hospital Center Foundation, Baltimore, Maryland.

Exhibit 6–7 Annual Campaign Calendar

Phase One—Planning
- Recruit campaign chairperson and leaders.
- Prepare case for support, solicitation, and acknowledgment materials.
- Assemble steering committee.
- Set goals, make assignments, and evaluate prospects.
- Approve campaign schedule of tasks and events.
- Steering committee and staff recruit general volunteers.

Phase Two—Solicitation
- Solicit gifts from steering committee.
- Solicit gifts of $1,000 and more through personal solicitation and President's Circle special events.
- Solicit gifts of $500 to $999 through volunteer solicitation and Hurst Society events.
- Solicit lower giving categories using direct mail or telemarketing programs.

- Arrange public announcement of campaign—goal, gifts received to date—at an event and in organization's publications.
- Continue direct mail, telemarketing, and online programs for all levels of gifts.

Phase Three—Recognition
- Acknowledge gifts and pledges promptly. Develop and implement a pledge reminder system.
- Announce successful completion of campaign—total dollars raised—in organization's publications.
- Hold special celebration dinner recognizing chairperson and steering committee members.
- Plan for honor roll listing of gift club members and donors in upcoming publications.

Challenge Gifts

A challenge gift can come from a donor or funder. It can be issued in several different ways—dollar for dollar, double the dollar, or whatever appeals to the challenger. Based on advice from the development staff, sometimes the challenge donor will match only new or increased gifts. Experience teaches that the best time to issue a challenge is when your annual giving has reached a plateau or is declining.

Gift Clubs

As stated previously, establishing gift clubs is an excellent way to engage donors and motivate increased giving. Common levels for such clubs are $100–$249, $250–$499, $500–$999, and $1,000 or more. Through a variety of solicitation methods, donors should be encouraged each year to move up to the next gift club category.

Reunion or Anniversary Giving

Used primarily by educational institutions, a reunion celebration is an excellent device for soliciting new or increased gifts. The same model can also be used by organizations and institutions celebrating a special anniversary of their founding. Reunions and special anniversaries are excellent public relations activities for the organizations. Structured as mini-campaigns, they can follow the annual giving campaign model and can incorporate other fundraising approaches such as special events, direct mail, telephone campaigns, and online giving.

Reunion and anniversary giving campaigns must have a compelling case for support that focuses on the organization's future plans and not just on the celebration events. To be successful in raising funds, the case must explain how donors' support will have an impact on the organization's ability to implement these plans.

EVALUATING THE CAMPAIGN

As one annual campaign comes to a close, another begins. It is very important that staff and volunteers schedule a meeting to evaluate the past year's program and to make recommendations for the coming year. Those who should attend are the development staff, the CEO of the organization, the campaign chairperson, the steering committee, and representatives of the board of directors. Every aspect of the campaign is reviewed. To assist in evaluating the annual campaign, follow the checklist in Exhibit 6–8.

All sizes and types of nonprofit organizations engage in annual giving using some or all of the methods discussed here and in related chapters. These methods by and large have proven to be productive and profitable. The challenge for organizations and their development staff is to evaluate and refine these methods continually in order to increase their productivity and profitability. For additional information on annual giving, see *Donor Focused Strategies for Annual Giving* by Karla Williams, another book published by Jones and Bartlett.

ANNUAL GIVING AND CAPITAL CAMPAIGNS

Nonprofit organizations are often concerned that a capital campaign will negatively impact the annual giving program, even

---

Exhibit 6–8 Checklist for Evaluating an Annual Campaign

BUDGET
1. Were expense projections accurate? Under? Over?
2. Were there any specific problem area(s)?
3. Were there any unexpected changes, situations, etc.?
4. Were there areas to cut for next year?

CAMPAIGN MATERIALS
1. Was the case for support well received?
2. Were the brochures effective?
3. Were supplemental materials—pledge cards, envelopes—easy to use?
4. Did volunteers find solicitation materials helpful? Did they suggest any changes?

CALENDAR
1. Was the schedule manageable?
2. Were any tasks omitted?
3. Did any areas need more time? Less time?

PUBLICITY
1. Was the campaign well publicized to internal publics? External publics?
2. What helped to get more publicity-campaign chairperson, event hosts, key volunteers?

3. What would you continue to do?
4. What would you change for next year's campaign?

CAMPAIGN LEADERSHIP, VOLUNTEERS, AND STAFF
1. Was the steering committee active in the campaign?
2. Were you able to recruit the number of volunteers needed?
3. Was the volunteer training effective? Well attended? Helpful?
4. Who should or should not be asked to serve again?
5. Was staff support available? Was it effective?

DIRECT MAIL/TELEMARKETING PROGRAMS
1. How did each direct mail letter do? Which were most effective?
2. Was the telephone follow-up effective?
3. What changes should be made for next year's campaign?

ANALYSIS OF GIFTS AND DONORS
1. How many new donors did you recruit? To which method did they respond?
2. How many donors were renewed?
3. How many increased gifts did you receive?
4. How many lapsed donors made a gift? To which method did they respond?

before the capital campaign begins. In reality, this is not the case. It is more common for the annual giving program to be more successful during a campaign due to the increase in the organization's visibility and prospect cultivation activities.

Andrea Kihlstedt tells us there are two general approaches to handling the relationship between the capital campaign and annual giving (Kihlstedt, 2002).

Fold the Annual Campaign into the Capital Campaign

Because it might be confusing and a burden to both staff and donors to ask for two types of contributions during the same period, the annual appeal campaign is included in the capital campaign. The campaign goal is increased to include the funds normally included in the annual campaign for the duration of the campaign pledge period. The organization designates a specified amount from campaign revenues to cover annual operating expenses during the campaign period, which is usually three years.

During the first year, when capital campaign funds are being solicited, the organization does not conduct a separate annual appeal. Once the campaign solicitations have been completed, the organization then reinstates the annual solicitation. Those who have made three-year pledges are not resolicited for an annual gift during the following campaign pledge years, but those who have not given to the capital campaign are solicited for an annual gift following the completion of campaign solicitations.

Maintain the Annual Giving Program During the Capital Campaign

This approach works best when the capital campaign will fund a project that is clearly distinct from the organization's ongoing operations and programs. When the campaign's goals are separate from operational expenses, many donors will understand the need to make a special campaign pledge to boost the organization to a new level, while continuing their support for the operations by maintaining or even increasing their gift to the annual campaign.

One common strategy, according to Kihlstedt, is the "double mention, double ask." With this approach, donors are solicited separately for the annual and capital campaigns. The campaigns are timed to provide breathing room between the solicitations, but each solicitation mentions the other campaign. By doing this, donors are not surprised when they are asked to give again at a later time, and people who have given as a result of the earlier solicitation are acknowledged for that gift while being solicited again.

ANNUAL GIVING FOR ASSOCIATIONS

It is relatively easy for an association foundation to start an annual giving or annual appeal program, as there is already a membership base from which to solicit annual gifts. There is no need to gather names of potential donors or rent lists for a direct

"Shipwrecked or not, I never miss sending out my annual contributions."

Source: Copyright © Joseph A. Brown.

mail appeal; prospecting for donors can be done with the organization's membership base. The key to starting an annual giving program is to know how to start, to whom to send the first solicitation, and what budget is available for the expenses of the first-time appeal. Chapter 16 discusses the overall fundraising relationship between associations and their foundations, including the annual appeal. In particular, Exhibit 16–2 lists the questions to be asked when developing a budget for an association foundation annual appeal.

Most annual giving programs conducted by an association foundation will be staff driven and not volunteer driven, in contrast to annual giving programs at a college or university. Also, it is unlikely that there will be prospecting outside of the association's membership, in contrast to the normal strategy of advocacy or issue-driven organizations that routinely rent lists for prospecting purposes. Thus, the association foundation can reduce its initial annual appeal costs substantially by making use of its built-in constituency. After a few years of success with the annual appeal, prospecting can be done outside the association's membership, but it is then focused on the association's vendors and advertisers.

Although annual giving programs conducted by an association foundation may be structured somewhat differently than those conducted by other nonprofit organizations, it is critical that the association foundation develop programs that build relationships using some of the methods described earlier in this chapter so that members will choose to become donors to the organization as well.

REFERENCES

Burk, P. 2003. *Donor-Centered Fundraising,* Chicago, IL: Cygnus Applied Research.

Kihlstedt, A. 2002. *Capital Campaigns-Strategies That Work, Second Edition,* Sudbury, MA: Jones and Bartlett Publishers.

Chapter 7

Using Direct Mail, Telemarketing, and the Internet to Build a Donor Base

KEY VOCABULARY

- Business Reply Envelope
- Closed-Face Envelope
- Constituency
- Donor Acquisition
- Lapsed Donor
- Mail/Phone Program
- Reinstated Donor
- Teaser Copy
- Telemarketing
- Wallet Flap
- Window Envelope

USING DIRECT MAIL

There are entire books devoted to the subject of direct mail fundraising, some just on how to write the best direct mail appeal letters. A number of these books are listed in the bibliography. This chapter presents an overview of the important elements and provides tips on how to establish a direct mail fundraising program.

Direct mail, an integral part of a fundraising program, can be used to reach thousands of people. It can be used not only to raise funds for the organization but also to educate the public about the organization and its cause. Organizations of all sizes use direct mail to recruit new donors, renew current donors, and reinstate support from lapsed donors. Direct mail helps build an organization's donor base by

- attracting new donors
- keeping donors informed of the organization's mission and programs
- nurturing long-term relationships between donors and the organization
- renewing donor support
- upgrading donors for increased gifts

Keep in mind that direct mail is only one of several techniques used to raise funds. Given the increasing costs of paper, printing, and postage, it remains an expensive way to raise funds. The appeal must be carefully thought out, and the budget must reflect the risk factor of any direct mail appeal. The appeal may fail miserably, thereby incurring large expenses with no hope of recouping losses; it may barely break even; or it may be a wonderful success.

There are two factors that are of major concern when raising funds through direct mail. One is the intense competition for the philanthropic dollar today. The second is the ease with which the receiver can ignore the appeal by depositing the envelope unopened in the wastebasket. In view of these two factors, it is important that an organization view its direct mail program as the method to use to begin building relationships with current and prospective donors.

To raise funds more successfully using direct mail, an organization should

- plan the number and content of mailings for the coming year (case, timing, and format) instead of working completely separately on each mailing
- send out thank you letters as quickly as possible so that donors know their support is appreciated
- be certain each appeal consists of a letter, separate response device, and return envelope (Exhibit 7–1)
- segment the donor base based on level of gifts, number of gifts, and identified interests in order to increase the use of personalization
- send out newsletters and informational mailings, not just solicitation letters, to report to donors on how their gifts made a difference

Writing Effective Direct Mail

Basic rules to follow when writing your direct mail appeal letter include the following:

- Pretend you are writing to one person. Write from the prospective donor's viewpoint. What concerns the donor most? What does he or she feel strongly about? What does he or she want? Use current events to make your appeal timely. Let the donors know that their past gifts made a difference and that future gifts will make a difference.
- Be clear about your basic proposition. Let the donors know on whose behalf you are addressing them. Tell them what you want them to do and why they will want to do that. State when you want them to do it and how they should go about making a contribution.
- Have the letter look like a personal letter as much as possible. To do this, do not typeset the letter. Create it using a computer-generated prototype. Use a font style and size that make the print easy to read. Include a date line. Indent paragraphs and vary their lengths. If possible, use a personal salutation. If you cannot, at least use "Dear Friend of the XYZ Organization." Know that a P.S. will be read, so be sure you make good use of it.

Exhibit 7–1 Elements of a Direct Mail Package

1. Carrier envelope (window or closed, live stamp or postage metered)
2. Appeal letter (length determined by case for support)
3. Response card (reply device)
4. Reply envelope (business reply envelope, no stamp or stamp)

To write an effective direct mail appeal, you need to plan your strategy. In the prewriting phase, decisions need to be made regarding the following:

- Who will sign the letter?
- What are the issues to stress?
- What focus will produce the best results?
- Who will be the audience?

With your strategy outlined, you can now "put pen to paper." The tone used may vary from informal and friendly to serious, depending on the appeal. You need to capture and hold the reader's attention. This means that the opening is the most important part of the letter. Begin with an attention grabber! Write with emotion and back it up with facts. People do not give because an organization needs money. They give because something in the letter aroused an emotion—concern, sadness, or anger. Write about the people the organization serves. Give the people names—use real people and stories if possible. Do not wait until the last page to mention money.

Develop a persuasive argument clearly, concisely, and vividly. Use simple words, not jargon. Use words that are active, concrete, and colorful. Sentence length gives rhythm to a letter. By varying sentence length, a rhythm is set that creates interest. The use of emphasis affects rhythm and interest. Call attention to pertinent phrases or paragraphs by using bullets, check marks, quotation marks, color, and photographs. Use underlining, but not too much. Almost as important as the opening is the closing—the request for action. Kay Partney Lautman, CFRE, a well-known direct mail consultant and author of *Direct Marketing for Nonprofits: Essential Techniques for the New Era,* another book published by Jones and Bartlett, says "Rework the opening and closing paragraphs until they 'sing.'"

But just how long should the appeal letter be? As mentioned earlier in this chapter, there is some debate on this matter. Keep in mind your audience. A four-page letter could be better if you are mailing to people who may not know the organization, whereas a two-page letter may be sufficient for those who already know it. The rule, once again, is make the appeal letter as long as is necessary to make a strong case for support.

> *Make the appeal letter as long as is necessary to make a strong case for support.*

Designing the Direct Mail Piece

For a direct mail appeal to be effective, it must be opened! For that reason, the design of the direct mail package is important. This subject is covered in greater detail in books on direct mail fundraising. The following is a checklist of items to be considered when designing a direct mail appeal.

- ink color
  1. sets the mood

2. can be used in attention-getting devices
3. affects readability
- illustrations or photographs
- type and design of paper used
- envelope (important to get opened)
  1. size
  2. window or closed-face
  3. plain, with "teaser" copy, or with photographs
- reply envelope
  1. preprinted address
  2. postage paid (business reply envelope [BRE]) or not
  3. plain or wallet flap
- signer
- use of personalization
  1. inside address and salutation
  2. reference to past gift
  3. reference to time of last gift
  4. reference to programs and campaigns that addressees responded to in the past
- enclosures
  1. survey
  2. request for names to add to mailing list

Once the appeal is written and designed, have more than one person proofread the appeal and review the package before it is either sent to the printer or reproduced for mailing. You will also need to decide how the appeal will be mailed. Options include first class (using a stamp, preprinted indicia, or a metering machine) or nonprofit rate (using preprinted indicia, a metering machine, or a live nonprofit stamp). If you are using a BRE, you must first establish a business reply account at the post office, check to see if there are specific printing regulations, secure the permit required, and be sure to have funds in the account to pay for the return postage. Many organizations encourage donors to use their own stamps to save themselves mailing costs.

THE DONOR ACQUISITION PROGRAM— AN INVESTMENT FOR THE FUTURE

There are three types of direct mail programs—renewal, upgrading, and acquisition. Renewal programs solicit previous donors to "renew" their support by continuing to contribute to the organization. This type of program serves as the foundation for an annual direct mail program. Upgrading programs are designed not only to renew donors but also to have the donors increase their gift over last year's amount. However, no organization is assured that every past donor will give again or give a larger gift. That is why regularly acquiring new donors is so important to an organization's future. Acquisition programs are indeed developmental programs and are key to continuing to build a donor base.

Knowing how important acquisition programs are to an organization's future, one might ask why there is such difficulty in convincing the leaders of organizations to embark upon them. The primary reason is that acquiring new donors through direct mail can be the most expensive type of fundraising. Because these programs are developmental, an organization may not see any profit for up to three years. First-year acquisition programs will not raise any additional funds. The best scenario is a "break-even" one. During the second year, a small net profit may be seen. In year three, however, the organization will see increased net profits from the original pool of new donors acquired in the first year. More important than the income is the number of new donors you have added to your donor base. (See Appendix 7–A for a sample donor acquisition letter.)

Exhibit 7–2 provides an example of how a donor acquisition program works.

An organization invests in its future when it conducts an acquisition program. But before developing such programs, an organization should analyze its constituency, because constituents are people, and people are prospects for support. The constituency can be identified as those who are currently involved with the organization, those who have been involved in the past, and those with the potential for some level of involvement in the future. These people hold a value for fundraising because they can be identified as current and active donors, past donors who no longer give, or suspects and prospects who could contribute in the future.

But how does an organization get lists of people who may be interested in supporting it? Organizations can either rent donor lists from or exchange lists with other organizations whose donors may be likely prospects. For a fee, list management companies are available to assist nonprofit organizations in renting new lists and marketing their own lists for exchange. Renting lists is a major cost of an acquisition program. Arranging to exchange your list with another organization that has a list with an equal number of names is less costly. These costs are among the reasons why acquisition programs are so expensive. List management firms can be found in many of the fundraising trade publications.

Although there are a number of risk factors associated with developing an acquisition program, we emphasize the importance of including such programs in the organization's overall fundraising plan to continue building the donor base.

Exhibit 7–2 An Example of How a Donor Acquisition Program Works

	Income	Cost
Year 1	$17,600	$17,600*
Year 2	10,788	1,280
Year 3	10,498	1,344
Year 4	10,716	1,408
Year 5	11,050	1,536
TOTAL	**$60,652**	**$23,168**

Minimum 5-year net $37,484

*Renting or purchasing mailing lists is a major expense during year 1.

TESTING AND ANALYZING DIRECT MAIL PACKAGES

An essential step in developing a successful direct mail program is testing different packages. Possible elements to test include

- the message
- the envelope size and color
- the stationery size and color
- the postage
- reply devices
- the length of the letter
- the letter signer
- the form of personalization
- any additional brochure
- special enclosures

When testing, test only one thing at a time or test the entire package against a control package (one you have used successfully before). You will need to mail a large enough quantity to get a good sampling, but quantities will vary depending on the organization. Tests of direct mail packages are not appropriate for every organization. Experience doing tests of varying sample sizes will help an organization design future tests more efficiently.

A critical part of testing is the analysis of the results. Make sure you code each test package so that the results can be interpreted accurately and easily. Mail the test and control packages at the same time in the same place. Keep to a minimum any outside factors that might affect the test. Before changing the control package, you may want to test this same package with people from other lists. Review your results daily and weekly, charting the peak of returns and the drop-off from the mailing. Consider the long-term results of the test by tracking continued donor giving during the next two years.

Analyzing the success of each type of direct mail appeal is very important for an organization's direct mail fundraising program. Your fundraising database management system can generate reports tracking the results of the different appeals (Exhibit 7–3).

Exhibit 7–3 What to Track in a Direct Mail Fundraising Program

1. Date sent
2. Number sent
3. Number returned
4. Average gift
5. Percentage return
6. Cumulative statistics (total received, response to date)
7. Comparison with previous year
8. Cost per mailing
9. Comparison of test results
10. Results versus expected return

TYPES OF DIRECT MAIL DONORS

When you analyze your organization's donor base, you should be able to identify five types of donors.

1. First-time donor. Acquired through a direct mail donor acquisition program.
2. First-year renewal donor. Needs special treatment to create an ongoing relationship so that the gift will be repeated.
3. Ongoing renewal donor. Has given two or more years and should be asked to increase or upgrade his or her gift.
4. Special gift donor. Has been an ongoing renewal donor and, because of high level of confidence in organization, should be asked to do something special—bequest in will, planned gift, or a large one-time gift.
5. Lapsed donor. Needs special attention because he or she has not given in one or more years. Donor needs to be convinced that past gifts were appreciated and important to the mission of the organization. Common terms used to describe lapsed donors are *LYBUNT* (last year but unfortunately not this year) and *SYBUNT* (some year but unfortunately not this year).

DONOR RENEWAL PROGRAMS

An organization works hard to build its donor base. Renewing donor support is crucial to an organization's ongoing financial stability. A basic renewal system gives people more than one opportunity to renew their support.

> *Renewing donor support is crucial to an organization's ongoing financial stability.*

Through a planned series of mailings, donors are asked to renew their support during the year. All mailings should be sent according to a timetable so that donors will have enough time to respond to one mailing before receiving the next. When developing your renewal appeal, follow the recommendations made above pertaining to designing a direct mail appeal.

A suggested timetable for mailing renewals might resemble the following:

- First renewal mailing: January 11
- Second renewal mailing: March 7
- Third renewal mailing: May 3
- Final renewal mailing: October 11

Even when using this formula, second and third renewal mailings may occasionally overlap with a donor's renewal check. Donors, like the rest of us, do not like to be reminded about a bill they have paid already. Therefore, it is very important that second and third renewal letters acknowledge that they might be crossing in the mail with a renewal check. The postscript is a good place to put this thought: "P.S. If you already have sent in your contribution, thank you. Your gift and our letter have probably crossed in the mail."

The plan outlined in Exhibit 7–4 describes a strategy for first-time donors. Of the utmost importance is the ability to upgrade their giving in future years.

UPGRADING DONORS

In Chapter 6, you read about the donor pyramid-the simple graphic that illustrates a nonprofit organization's overall donor-base. The bottom of the pyramid represents the bulk of an organization's members. Here is where you use direct mail. The middle levels depict decreasing numbers of increasingly generous donors. At the peak are the organization's most generous supporters.

The donor pyramid shows the tremendous potential represented by the pyramid's base. That potential can be realized only if the organization has a consistent strategy for moving its donors up through the levels of the pyramid. In building relationships with prospective donors, organizations move through a process known as the Seven I's—identify, invite, inform, interest, involve, invest, and inspire. As donors move up the pyramid, their interests, needs, and desires grow. At the same time, the organization is informing the donors about its mission and programs and involving them in the programs. As the donors' commitment grows, usually evidenced by larger gifts, so does the organization's attention in building and sustaining relationships with them.

Strategic elements in relationship building:

- Educate donors about the mission and programs of the organization and the importance of ongoing donor support.
- Acknowledge donor support.
- Remind donors of their level of support to help them identify with that level and then encourage them to move up the pyramid.
- Create incentives and clear goals for upgrading support.
- Show donors how their gifts are effectively used to meet organizational needs and achieve organizational goals.

Exhibit 7–4 A Three-Year Plan for First-Time Donors

Year 1:
Acquire first-time gifts through general, restricted, and membership appeals. Develop strategies that will generate new gifts.

Year 2:
Focus on retaining first-time donors. Develop strategies aimed at renewing the gifts at the same level. Do not be concerned with increasing gifts. The goal is to develop a "habit" of support. It is estimated that 40 to 60 percent of first-time donors will renew.

Year 3:
Begin to upgrade the donor. At this time, it is appropriate to try to upgrade the donor's level of giving. Develop strategies to increase support, including sending more than one appeal during the year or asking for an unrestricted gift early in the year followed by a request for a specific program gift. Fifty to 60 percent of donors will make multiple gifts in a year.

Steps in an Upgrade Program

The first step in an upgrade program is to review your donor file to identify a core group of donors. This group will be made up of donors who have consistently supported the organization because they care about its work. Look for the amounts of the gifts, the recency of the gifts, and the sources of the gifts. By keeping track of the sources, you will know to which appeals the donors responded.

For example, suppose a donor last contributed $150 to the year-end appeal but also gave $100 in the spring for a new van to transport senior citizens and $75 in the summer to expand the homebound seniors meal program. Because last year's gifts totaled $325, we call this type of donor a multigiver. Multigivers are excellent candidates for an upgrade program or as a sustainer (monthly donor) prospect. Keep in mind if you are not storing information and tracking the sources of gifts, you would miss this individual when targeting prospects for similar campaigns.

A person's ability to give more can be identified by the following:

- the donor's maximum single gift in the previous 24 to 26 months
- the donor's cumulative annual gift from the previous year
- the life-time total contributions of the donor
- the size of the donor's average gift
- the length of the donor's membership or support

Different Types of Upgrade Programs

To motivate donors to give more than their customary $25 contribution or to respond to more than one appeal each year, you must create a structure for giving and make it easy to give by offering a credit card option. Programs that encourage donors to upgrade their giving include the following.

Monthly Giving Programs—Sustainers

Establish a club for individuals who choose to make a monthly gift. You will find that many of your donors will consider giving $10 to $15 a month, which equals an annual gift of $120 to $180—a gift many of them would not consider giving at one time.

To encourage more donors to become monthly givers, many organizations set up programs with banks or a vendor like EFT Corporation (http://www.etransfer.com; 800-338-2435) to manage the monthly processing of credit card charges or debits from checking or savings accounts.

Gift Clubs

Creating gift clubs is a popular and successful way to encourage higher annual gifts. By using the file analysis to identify your file segments, you can set suggested club tiers that are within reach of each segment of upgradable donors. Usually the minimum donation for the lowest gift club level is $100. Be careful when creating gift clubs—do not offer excessive benefits or services because IRS regulations mandate that the value of goods or services received be deducted from the donor's charitable deduction. For the organization, it can also cut into the effective use of the contributions.

Cumulative Giving Programs

This type of program is more commonly used by institutions and organizations that have alumni. Specific levels are established to recognize lifetime giving. Once an alumnus reaches one level, the next level is waiting for him or her. Moving toward the next highest level is used in each appeal.

Matching Gift or Challenge Gift Programs

There are two types of matching gift programs. Many companies across the country offer corporate matching gift programs to encourage their employees to give. Companies will set formulas, such as one-to-one or two-to-one matching of employee gifts. This is an excellent source of funds for many schools, universities, colleges, and a growing number of other types of nonprofit organizations.

A second type of matching gift is the challenge gift. Challenge gift funds are often used to increase giving levels by matching dollar for dollar all new, returning, or increased gifts. When donors know that a challenge gift fund will double the value of donations, the incentive to increase the size of the gifts is also doubled. Challenge gift funds can be established through a foundation grant, a major gift from an individual, board member giving, gifts from key donors, or the organization itself.

Using Personalization in Your Appeal

By making a gift, each donor already has formed a special relationship with your organization. By requesting an upgrade, you are attempting to strengthen that relationship. The more powerfully you can remind donors of their past involvement and what it has accomplished, the more likely it is that they will be committed to increasing their support.

We know that with computer technology we can use names, addresses, and personal salutations in our appeal letters. This is only the first step in personalization. Depending on what information you have in each donor record, you might include the donor's length of continuous support, the specific dates of donations, the appeals the donor responded to, and offices the donor held in the organization. Always try to mention a donor's giving level with a suggestion to move to a new level or become a member of a specific gift club. State how far the donor is from a cumulative giving goal if you have a cumulative giving program.

Personalization also allows the organization to relate the appeal to a donor's needs and his or her local community and to explain how family and friends have been helped and will be helped in the future. Donors have a certain image of your organization and of how they fit into it. Fulfilling this image successfully is essential to their continued and increased support. Exhibit 7–5 lists how to move your donors up the giving ladder.

Exhibit 7–5 How to Move Donors Up the Giving Ladder

1. Identify and target a group of donors.
2. Establish a system of giving levels (i.e., gift clubs).
3. Ask for a specific gift that would move them to the next level.
4. Make a compelling case for support; show how past gifts made a difference.
5. Use personalization in the letter (i.e., salutation, past support, and specific program that benefited).
6. Send appropriate thank you letter for level of gift.

REINSTATING LAPSED DONORS

When setting fundraising goals, you must also include objectives related to reinstating lapsed donors. A lapsed donor is defined as someone who has given to your organization in the past but not during the last calendar or fiscal year, nor during the current calendar or fiscal year. Even if your goal is to raise as

> *When setting fundraising goals, you must also include objectives related to reinstating lapsed donors.*

much money as you did last year, you will need to reinstate lapsed donors or acquire new donors. However, if your organization is like most, you will want to increase the number of gifts and the dollar income over the past year. To do this you will need to reinstate lapsed donors and acquire new donors as well as upgrade the giving of those who renew.

Following are four major reasons why a donor lapses:

1. The donor feels unappreciated.
2. The donor is asked to give too much too soon.
3. The donor is asked to give too often.
4. The donor did not respond to a particular appeal.

Keep in mind that of the donors who have given to your organization for the past two or more years consecutively, 10 percent to 20 percent will not give next year no matter how hard or how often you try to renew their support. However, to have fewer lapsed donors, you need to do the following:

- nurture lapsed donors
- listen to them
- act on their demands and complaints
- praise them for their past support
- let them know that you miss them

Exhibit 7–6 lists steps you can take to reinstate lapsed donors.

SAYING THANK YOU

The "care and feeding" of donors has three phases:

- Inform. Educate donors about the organization, its needs, and how their support will make a difference.
- Involve. Encourage donors to make contributions to or become volunteers for the organization.

Exhibit 7–6 Steps to Reinstate Lapsed Donors

M. Sue Woodward, CFRE, President, Woodward Associates, Inc., Potomac, Maryland, a consultancy that provides integrated direct response fundraising programs for organizations, offers some simple steps to reinstating lapsed donors:

1. To ensure you have the most up-to-date donor information, continuously clean your files by updating addresses, and purge or archive donors who cannot be located or are deceased.
2. Run your file through the National Change of Address (NCOA) database (including lapsed donors) at a minimum two times annually.
3. Treat the lapsed donors as a separate, special group. Create a letter or series of letters, stressing how much the donors' ongoing support and involvement mean to the organization and what their past gifts have helped to accomplish.
4. Once they renew, immediately put them back into your direct mail series that includes appeals, newsletters, updates, and cultivation pieces.
5. Donors who do not reinstate by mail should be contacted by a well-thought-out telemarketing campaign. (Note: With the correct approach, 10 to 15 percent on average reinstate.)
6. If the donors are still not responsive, include them in your next acquisition mailing to reintroduce them to the organization.

*Remember: It is more cost-effective to continue to try and reinstate lapsed donors than to acquire new donors.

- Recognize. Thank donors in a timely manner and acknowledge their support publicly through the organization's publications.

Many organizations put much effort in the first two phases and then make the mistake of exerting less effort in the recognition phase. As you have read in the section on reinstating lapsed donors, a donor who does not feel appreciated is less likely to renew his or her support than one who feels adequately recognized. Therefore, it is extremely important for organizations to continue the same high level of effort throughout all phases of the care and feeding of its donors. Exhibit 7–7 lists ways to say thank you.

You would not use all these techniques for all your donors. Each organization sets minimum levels of gifts that warrant special attention from the chief executive officer (CEO) or board president. The important thing is to put an acknowledgement

Exhibit 7–7 Ways to Say Thank You

1. Personalized letter from CEO or board chair
2. Telephone call
3. Letters from others (president, volunteers, senior staff)
4. Personal visit (reserved for larger gifts)
5. Token-of-appreciation memento
6. Listing in honor roll of donors
7. Invite to special events

system in place so that thank you letters will be mailed within a short period—one rule of thumb is to get the letters out within 24–48 hours. Preprinted cards and receipts are sufficient for gifts less than $100. In the $100 to $249 range, the preprinted card and receipt can be followed several weeks later by a personal letter from the president or CEO thanking the donor on behalf of the organization and briefly mentioning how the donor's support makes a difference. For gifts of $250 to $499, the same procedure can be used, with the addition of a personal telephone call from the chief development officer after the letter from the president or CEO, a call that again emphasizes how much the contribution meant to the organization. In some organizations, a larger than usual contribution (e.g., a gift of $500 or more) is first acknowledged by a preprinted card, then by a personal call from the "top" person, then by a brief personal letter from the person who made the call.

An acknowledgement procedure is a must in any fundraising program. People like to be thanked for their support, even though they may tell you differently. Remember that a timely and professionally executed thank you tells your donor that you know what you are doing, that you appreciate his or her willingness to support your organization, and that you look forward to a continuing relationship. Acknowledgement efforts are cultivation efforts. You are establishing a link without asking for another contribution, but you are also getting your donor ready for a future upgrade request. See sample policy in Chapter 3, Exhibit 3–3.

TRENDS IN DIRECT MAIL FUNDRAISING

Experts in the direct response field predict that a number of factors, indicated in the list below, will affect the way nonprofit organizations use direct mail fundraising in the future:

- There will be ever-increasing competition for donors.
- Fundraising costs will rise due to increased postage, printing, and list rental fees.
- Organizations will shift their attention to keeping current donors.
- More information is available on donors that can be used to develop highly personalized approaches.
- Stronger enforcement of state and federal regulations related to direct mail fundraising will occur.
- Middle-aged donors (baby boomers) are more sophisticated, more demanding, and more skeptical of nonprofit organizations.
- Donors will increasingly place a premium on known and trusted organizations.
- Donors will demand effective programs offered by nonprofit organizations of all sizes.
- Organizations will need to ensure that donors can communicate and donate through a variety of vehicles including mail, phone, and online.
- Organizations will need to develop strategies to attract and retain donors and volunteers from the fast-growing ethnic minorities.

USING TELEMARKETING IN FUNDRAISING

Telemarketing is an effective way for nonprofit organizations to solicit annual contributions from donors and prospective donors because, unlike direct mail, it is more similar to a personal solicitation. Although we hear that many people do not like receiving these calls at home in the evening, telemarketing remains a very effective way to raise money for nonprofit organizations. In recent years, some organizations have seen significant results when using telemarketing to solicit mid-level and larger gifts during a capital campaign. Exhibit 7–8 explains why telemarketing is effective in fundraising.

Establishing a Telemarketing Program

An organization needs to evaluate what resources it has at hand when developing a telemarketing program.

- Does it have the facilities and equipment for phoning?
- Does it have a core group of volunteers who will call?
- Does it have staff who can train and monitor callers?
- Does it have technology that can generate the different types of materials needed for telemarketing?

If an organization can answer yes to these questions, it has the ability to establish its own program using a volunteer caller program. Likewise, if an organization must answer no to any of these questions, it should consider using one of the professional telemarketing companies working with nonprofit organizations, schools, and universities today. How to work with this type vendor is discussed later in this chapter. Exhibit 7–9 lists the steps involved in developing a telemarketing program.

What You Need To Get Started

Data and Materials

Before embarking on a telemarketing program, you must ensure that your records are accurate. Your results will be affected

---

Exhibit 7–8 Why Telemarketing Is Effective in Fundraising

- It can be used to personally reach large numbers of donors and prospective donors.
- It helps donors better appreciate how their gifts are used, resulting in increased gifts to the organization.
- It increases donor involvement by giving them an opportunity to speak to an organization's representative.
- It gathers important donor information about reasons for giving as well as data for keeping records accurate and current.
- It allows better communication with donors in times of calm and crisis.
- It allows the organization to express its gratitude in person!
- It is an excellent way for volunteer callers to become more involved with the organization, see the organization's needs more clearly, and become better donors themselves.

Exhibit 7–9 Steps Involved in Developing a Telemarketing Program

- Identify prospects to call.
- Enlist callers.
- Find site.
- Produce pledge cards.
- Produce support materials such as scripts and fact sheets.
- Segment pledge cards based on giving history or special affiliations.
- Train callers.
- Call prospects and ask.
- Create fulfillment pieces for immediate mailing and a reminder series.
- Give appropriate thanks.
- Report results.

---

if you are unable to reach a large number of your prospects. The data a caller needs include the donor's name, address, telephone number, previous giving history, and special affiliations (e.g., gift club membership) as well as other pertinent information, such as class year, parents' names, and special interests.

Location

The site for phoning must have multiple phone lines and enough space and be convenient and safe for your callers. Few organizations besides educational institutions have designated phone center space. Usually, callers are assigned to desks throughout the office. If the organization's office space is not suitable, contact educational institutions to see if they rent space to other organizations or contact board members and donors whose offices would be more suitable. Regardless of whether the space you are using is your own or rented, remind callers to take their materials with them, keep the space clean, and leave a brief thank you note for the deskholder.

Follow-up Procedure

All pledges must be recorded clearly and accurately on the pledge confirmation form. See Exhibit 7–10 for an example. The bottom part of the form is sent to the donor the following morning, and the top part of the form is used to record the pledge and any updated donor information on the system. Using a tally sheet each evening is a convenient way to double-check totals. For all large pledges and for any questionable pledges, have someone else re-call the donor immediately to thank him or her for the specific pledge amount. Check all pledges and responses six weeks later.

Establish a reminder system that will mail reminders every 30, 60, and 90 days to people who have not yet fulfilled their pledges. Some systems send reminders more frequently, using a 4-, 8-, and 12-week schedule. Either schedule will significantly increase your fulfillment rate by 30 to 50 percent. Use each reminder to once again thank the donor and include a reply card and envelope.

Exhibit 7–10 Pledge Confirmation Form

Jane Smith, '91
555 Oak Drive
Milton, MD

Home (301) 555-8963
Work (202) 555-4972

GIVING HISTORY

Date	Amount	Fund	Type
11/01/95	$25.00	Annual	Cash
11/05/97	$100.00	Annual	Pledge Pay
02/27/99	$100.00	Annual	Cash
01/08/00	$100.00	Annual	Pledge Pay
10/20/06	$500.00	Bldg	Cash
11/06/08	$500.00	Bldg	Cash

Total Given: $1,325.00

Largest Gift: $500.00

Latest Gift: $500.00

NEW ADDRESS ❏ HOME ❏ BUSINESS

_____

_____

_____

Telephone _____

❏ Pledge $ _____ Matching Gift $ _____
❏ New Donor/Increased
❏ Will give (Unspecified)
❏ Undecided
❏ Refused/Reason _____
❏ Do Not Call
❏ Sent Gift Earlier
❏ Send Information

❏ Mastercard   ❏ Visa   ❏ Discover
_____ / _____ / _____ / _____

Exp. Date _____ / _____

CALL RECORD

Caller	Date/Time	Comments

OFFICE USE ONLY

Entered on _____ By _____

Mailed on _____ By _____

Washington College of Law
The American University
4400 Massachusetts Avenue, NW
Washington, DC 20016-8084
202-885-2609

Thank you for your pledge of $ _____ to the Annual Appeal made on _____.

Your participation and your support are greatly appreciated. _____
                                                                        (Caller)

My employer will match my gift. The matching gift form ❏ is enclosed ❏ will be sent later.

Please send your check payable to the Washington College of Law by April 30.

❏ Mastercard   ❏ Visa   ❏ Discover

_____ / _____ / _____ / _____

Exp. Date _____

Contributions are deductible for income tax purposes to the extent provided by law.

Source: Courtesy of the American University, Washington College of Law, Washington, DC.

Setting Goals

As with any fundraising program, you must establish goals for your telemarketing program. In doing so, understand the need and urgency for funds, review past successes of the program, and note any special circumstances that will affect results, such as a challenge grant, a new organizational leader, or a special opportunity. Look at each donor segment individually and build each segment's goal separately—current donors, lapsed donors, nondonors.

How many calls must you make? Some rules of thumb to consider are the following:

- An effective caller will dial 50 numbers during each two-hour session.
- An effective caller will reach 25 to 30 prospects each session.
- One staff member can manage 20 callers each session.

Establishing a Budget

Included in your budget should be the following:

- computer data conversion costs for forms and letters
- printing costs for forms, letterhead, envelopes, etc.
- telephone costs
- costs for food and amenities for volunteers
- salaries for paid callers
- postage

Recording Results

Statistics are critical when evaluating the success of your telemarketing program. First, you must track the individual results of each of your callers. See Exhibit 7–11 for a checklist of items you need to include on the nightly tally sheet for individual callers and to total in order to see the night's results. Also, keep a record each year of the number of calling nights held and the program totals from each category. That way you will be able to set realistic and attainable goals for the next year's program.

> *Statistics are critical when evaluating the success of your telemarketing program.*

Exhibit 7–11 Statistics Checklist

1. Name of caller
2. Number of calls made
3. Number of pledges received
4. Number of dollars pledged
5. Number of unspecified pledges made
6. Number of refusals
7. Number of noncontacts (bad addresses and telephone numbers)
8. Average gift
9. Number of increased and decreased gifts
10. Number of new gift club members
11. Number of new gifts pledged

Using Volunteer or Paid Callers

The length of time your telemarketing program will run will largely determine whether you should use volunteer or paid callers. Programs that use volunteer callers are usually shorter in duration (on average, two weeks) because it is more difficult to get long-term commitments from the callers. Programs that run four to six weeks are best staffed by paid callers or contracted out to a telemarketing firm.

The Volunteer Caller Program

Your first task will be to find volunteers who agree to participate in the telemarketing program. If you know of volunteers who have done this before, be sure to ask them again. You may even need to hold a "recruitment phonathon" to get more callers. As was discussed in previous chapters, it is very important to give your volunteers the proper recognition and appreciation they deserve. Giving them the tools to be successful is also extremely important.

Once you have commitments from your volunteers, schedule training sessions that provide opportunities for them to practice making calls using the prepared script. A training session can be held either before the start of the telemarketing program or at the start of each night's calling. The training should include the following:

- the case for support
- the reason for the call
- specific procedures regarding how someone can make a gift
- ways to request a specific amount
- ways to overcome objections
- steps to increase last year's gift

Match up new callers with more experienced callers. Start new callers off with current donors whom you are calling to renew their support. Remember, soliciting gifts is a difficult task even for the most experienced caller, so you need to provide reinforcement by praising good performance immediately. Also, mix the cards so that no one gets all the nondonors, ring a bell for each pledge of $100 or more, create team rivalry, and offer special prizes. When the program is completed, be sure to send thank you letters, including a report of the results, to the volunteers. List their names in publications.

Like many volunteer programs, this type of program can be demanding on staff, because they will need to contact volunteers to confirm their attendance, conduct continuing volunteer training, and be constant cheerleaders and motivators to keep the enthusiasm of the volunteers at the highest level.

Paid Callers

As in the case of volunteers, you will need to interview and hire paid callers. Seek individuals who have experience in telemarketing or who are eager to participate. Require a minimum of hours or nights per week. These callers will be paid to attend a training session, one that is more intense than the volunteer session.

Evaluation and feedback are key to successful programs. Staff or hired calling supervisors need to monitor calls regularly. Callers should be critiqued with constructive comments to help them be more successful. Like with the volunteers, reward good performance. Those callers who are performing poorly should be retrained. However, those callers who consistently underperform should be terminated.

The Most Important Tool for Callers—The Script

The training session should focus on the best ways to use the prepared script to have a dialogue with donors and prospective donors. Instruct the callers that this is a tool, one that gives them the information they need to encourage prospective donors to contribute. Callers should structure each call as a conversation by seeking the input of the person called and using as conversational a tone of voice as possible. Encourage callers to underline and asterisk those key areas of the script they need to remember when making a call. Exhibit 7–12 provides a basic script format.

Overcoming Objections

Even though callers have a prepared script with which to work, they will be more successful if they are good listeners. We hope each contact will be a two-way conversation so that the caller can gather important opinions and beliefs expressed by the donor that explain why he or she gives.

Being able to overcome objections is critical to success. Callers must be able to handle an objection in a professional, empathetic, and genuine manner while still representing the organization and its needs. Twenty years ago, telemarketing programs were able to reach 80 percent to 95 percent of the population that were called. Today, such programs are lucky to reach 50% of the nondonor population. Because of this, keeping the connection once made with the person called is very important!

Kathleen E. Pavelka, CFRE, Founder and President, Telecomp, Inc., a company in Rochester, New York, that provides client-specific telephone outreach programs to nonprofit organizations across the country recommends the following formula to successfully overcome objections a caller may hear: (See Appendix 7–B for a case study of one of their clients.)

- Acknowledge—Let the donors/prospects know that you heard them by repeating a portion of the objection in the acknowledgement or by using a simple statement such as "I understand."
- Address—Let the donors/prospects know that you are listening and care about what they have to say.
- Build Case—Rebuild your case by reminding the donor/prospect why giving is important and what impact it will have.
- Ask—Solicit another gift at a lower level, which allows the donor/prospect to respond to a specific request with a yes/no answer.

Exhibit 7–12 Basic Script Format

Opening

Introduce yourself (full name), the name of the organization, and the reason for your call (do not open by asking if this is a convenient time, as many people will say no).

Acknowledge their past support and what it helped accomplish.

Verify receipt of lead letter.

Establishing Rapport

Ask open-ended questions.

Provide opportunity for feedback.

Establish a relationship with the donor/prospect (particularly powerful for volunteers who can establish a truly peer relationship with the donor/prospect).

Case for Support

Make one to two key points regarding the case for giving (in keeping with engaging in a dialogue, limit time on case and, instead, build the case throughout the asking structure).

Emphasize how donor support makes a difference.

First Ask

Ask for largest target gift and give an example of why their support is important.

If not successful, move to "second ask."

Second Ask

Ask for next target gift level (less than "first ask") and give another example of why donor support is so important.

If not successful, move to "third ask."

Third Ask

Target a small increase over last year's gift and again give an example of how gift will make a difference.

Fourth Ask

If the response is negative to the first three asks, then ask if you can count on them to make a gift in the same amount as last year.

Closing

If solicitation is not successful, thank individual for his or her time. If they have been a donor, once again thank them for their past support.

If solicitation is successful, thank them, take down pertinent information, and verify current address.

" ... SORRY. WE GAVE IN THE CAR. "

Source: Copyright © Mark Litzler.

Here are some examples of objections and responses that Kathleen Pavelka recommends:

Objection: "I really can't do anything right now."

Response: "M_____, you have been such a wonderful part of our family in the past. Have we done something to lose your support?"

This allows the caller to determine what the issue is—we tend to assume this statement is a financial issue, but you don't really know unless you ask. This response will usually result in the donors/prospects sharing more about their particular situations, thus providing an opportunity for the caller to address the situations in a manner most appropriate and more comfortable for the donors.

Objection: "I'm busy and I can't talk to you now."

Response: (First, this is why the introduction is so important. For instance, if you begin the entire call by saying "I'm so glad that I've reached you, M_____," chances are less that the person will say this to begin with.)

"M_____, I know how crazy everyone's lives are getting that is why I'm so glad that I've reached you. I promise I will be as brief as possible. You're such a wonderful friend of (organization name). Would you allow me a few moments?"

Objection: "I have a daughter in college, and I can't afford to give now."

Response: "Well, that's wonderful. Where does she go to school? You must be very proud, M_____." (Pause for response)

"It sounds like this isn't the greatest time, especially for a leadership gift. Your support is so critical to us. This year, just as one example, we are hoping to (goal and impact of accomplishing it), so, perhaps, a more modest gift of $___ is more comfortable for you this year. Can we count on you for a gift of $___ this year, M_____?"

Objection: "I just sent something in."

Response: "Oh, that's terrific. On behalf of (organization's name), thank you very much for your gift. It will help us reach our goal to . . ."

In all cases, the caller should thank each person who had an objection for spending time speaking with him or her. Often, all a person wants is some extra attention. The telemarketing program presents an excellent opportunity to provide it to him or her.

DIRECT MAIL AND TELEMARKETING— A WINNING COMBINATION

In this chapter, we discussed the individual benefits of including direct mail and telemarketing in your fundraising program. Each program can produce successful results. However, combining these two techniques in a mail/phone program will significantly increase those results. This program involves a lead letter followed by a telephone call within three to five days of receipt of letter.

The Lead Letter

The "lead letter" serves three purposes: (1) introduces the call, (2) makes the case for support, and (3) suggests a number of giving levels for consideration. If the organization has giving clubs, the gift levels should be presented in the letter and mirror the "Ask" levels that are utilized in the call.

Since we know peer-to-peer solicitation is the most effective approach for major gift solicitations, it is best that the "lead letter" come from a peer of the audience included rather than a staff member, such as the executive director. For instance, an alumnus writes to alumni; a parent of a patient writes to other parents of patients; a member writes to other members, etc. The advantages of a peer-to-peer solicitation, a donor-centered approach, are as follows:

- allows the signer to share his/her story and reason why he/she supports the organization
- asks donor/prospect to "join him/her" with a gift
- provides an opportunity to brag about the organization, including the staff leadership, without sounding self-serving

The case for support can then focus on the impact of the gift rather than on what the funds will actually purchase. For instance, alumni can write to other alumni and talk about how

Exhibit 7–13 Delineation of Staff and Vendor Roles

TASK	STAFF	TELEMARKETING COMPANY
Develop scope of program	X	X
Provide projected results		X
Provide data on donors	X	
Analyze data and put them in usable form		X
Provide publications and materials about organization	X	
Draft pre-call letters		X
Approve pre-call letters	X	
Provide samples of letterhead and envelopes	X	
Print letterhead, envelopes, and forms		X
Produce, sign, and mail pre-call letters		X
Draft scripts for callers		X
Approve scripts	X	
Train callers		X
Monitor and critique callers	X	X
Prepare daily and weekly reports		X
Send out pledge confirmations		X
Send out reminders	X	
Prepare final report of results		X

they were able to attend due to the generosity of other alumni, what this has allowed them to accomplish in their lives as a result, and how they are now giving to the institution that made that possible. For health care institutions, it is far more powerful for patients to tell their story of their situation and the care received that saved their lives or the lives of their children than the hospital CEO extolling the virtues of the institution. Community-based organizations recruit letter signers from among their donors and volunteers.

Because a peer is writing to a peer, the "lead letter" is frequently sent out on the signer's letterhead rather than the organization's letterhead. This has been found to increase the chances that the letter will be opened and read, particularly if it is sent with a live first-class stamp. Remember, the objective is for the recipient to identify with the signer and make a gift as the signer has.

Making the Call

It is believed that a prospect will make his or her decision to give during the first 12 seconds. Therefore, the caller should link the call to the lead letter already received by highlighting only one or two items. The caller will then follow a script similar to that described above. The caller should describe the highest giving club and ask the prospect to join. If that level is too high, the caller should try to negotiate an increase over past gifts. After getting a confirmed gift and payment date, the caller thanks the donor.

> *It is believed that a prospect will make his or her decision to give during the first 12 seconds.*

Selecting and Working with a Telemarketing Company

For those organizations who want to do telemarketing but do not have the space to create their own phone centers, the answer is to work with an outside telemarketing company. The telemarketing company will provide many services usually handled by the organization's staff. Even with this high level of support, a staff person needs to act as a coordinator and liaison to monitor the telemarketing program.

When choosing a telemarketing firm, look for the following:

- experience with your type of organization
- results of efforts with similar organizations (to discern viability of projected results)
- history of meeting projected results by checking references
- a current client list and do your own checking
- a site visit to the call center
- who owns the data
- compliance with state registrations, bonding requirements, and federal law

Exhibit 7–13 provides a list of services typically offered by telemarketing companies and the associated responsibilities of the organization's staff.

USING THE INTERNET FOR FUNDRAISING

Studies show that online giving to nonprofits continues to increase. We saw most definitely it was the giving vehicle of choice for people who wished to respond quickly to such tragedies as September 11, 2001, or natural disasters like the Asian tsunami or Hurricanes Katrina and Rita in the United States. Stories describing the online giving successes of a variety of nonprofit organizations are now common in such publications as the *Chronicle of Philanthropy*, *The NonProfit Times*, and *Fundraising Success* magazine. The Internet has certainly opened up new and exciting ways to communicate with donors and the general public, but admittedly online donations still amount to a relatively small percentage of total giving today. According to *Giving USA*, online donations were only about one percent of total giving in 2007. However, trends point to a not-too-distant time when the Internet will play a key role in charitable transactions because the public uses the Internet as a key source of information on nonprofits and their missions and has become more comfortable in making financial transactions online.

Why Fundraise Online

Nonprofit organizations recognize that there are several advantages to online fundraising. First and foremost, it is more cost-effective for communicating more frequently and maintaining ongoing relationships with donors than the two methods covered earlier in this chapter—direct mail and telemarketing. Integrating e-mail communications with direct mail and telemarketing efforts has proven to be key in improving both online and off-line fundraising results. A second advantage is the ability to execute a fundraising campaign and to respond to timely issues in a much shorter time period than drafting, designing, printing, and sending a direct mail piece. In the same manner, e-mail appeals produce quick results both in response time and receipt of funds immediately and automatically when given online.

It does not matter what type of fundraising method is employed; the goal is to get to know your donors' interests and giving behaviors. By tracking how many people click on both e-mails and links within e-mails to your Web site, you can quickly analyze the effectiveness of the fundraising campaign, determine donor motivations, and evaluate donor behavior and giving trends that will help to improve future campaigns. Through Internet communications, you can encourage constituents to participate in online surveys and polls that help to identify their interests. Use that information to segment your list and target groups for communications and appeals. This will ensure that each communication is relevant and valuable to each constituent and will more likely inspire him or her to respond.

Every online fundraising program should have the following basic goals:

- make people aware of the organization
- get people to care about the organization
- encourage people to support the organization
- keep people connected to the organization

Developing an Internet Plan

In Chapter 5, you learned that effective development programs need annual plans with fundraising goals that are implemented and evaluated. Successful online development programs need a communication and solicitation plan, too. Consider the following when creating an Internet plan:

- Fundraising goal and time frame
  - How much compared to other fundraising methods?
- Available budget
  - How much is budgeted for Web site updating and maintenance?
  - How much is budgeted for training on online fundraising?
  - How much is budgeted for new staff, if needed?
  - How much is budgeted for outside vendor and/or consultant?
- Staffing
  - Is there staff to update the Web site and online fundraising pages?
  - Is there staff to respond to inquiries and requests for information?
  - Do we need to hire staff, and if so, should they have online fundraising experience?
  - What is the process for hiring vendor/consultant, if needed?
  - Who will monitor the Internet plan?
- Current activities
  - Donate Now page on Web site
  - special event registration
  - subscribe to e-newsletter
  - survey or poll for advocacy
  - how to volunteer
  - send e-newsletter
- New activities to add
  - capital campaign
  - planned giving
  - honor and memorial giving
  - auction
  - online community

Evaluate the annual Internet plan regularly in order to be able to modify it based on fundraising results and donor behaviors. Technology companies that specialize in online constituent relationships management include Convio, Kintera, and Blackbaud. Those that specialize in collecting online contributions include Network for Good, Click & Pledge, firstgiving, and Entango. Check out *Chronicle of Philanthropy*, *The NonProfit Times*, *Fundraising Success*, AFP's *Advancing Philanthropy*, and other trade publications for other vendors assisting nonprofit organizations in online fundraising.

How Online Donors Are Like Off-Line Donors

Organizations both large and small have found that simply putting online giving systems in place is no guarantee of continued donations. Just like donors who give through traditional mail and telemarketing vehicles, online donors must be cultivated and stewarded to win their ongoing support after they make their first donation online.

Sue Woodward, CFRE, reminds development professionals that whether you are looking to create a more enhanced online experience for your existing donors or starting from scratch to create your "donor experience," you must keep the following fundraising basics in mind:

1. The donor is more important to you than you are to the donor.
2. Fundraising is all about relationship building.
3. Successful fundraising focuses on an organization's mission and values.
4. Donors want to know that their gifts are making a positive impact.

5. Know your donors—who they are, to what they respond, and when they give.
6. Make sure your current donors feel appreciated, informed, and involved.

WAYS TO BUILD YOUR DONOR BASE

Nonprofit organizations building significant online membership and donor bases, according to Woodward, are investing in tools and strategies that utilize these basics to recruit, renew, cultivate, and steward their donors. Many of the tactics currently used in the online medium are similar to those in direct mail. Outbound e-mail appeals, renewals, and e-newsletter campaigns are used in even the most basic online programs.

Spam laws are strict, and donors feel more violated by receiving unsolicited e-mails rather than pieces of mail landing in their mail boxes; purchasing e-mail lists, unlike mailing lists, is not a viable option for acquiring donors. So, how can an organization bring donors to their file? How can you grow a file if you can't go directly to a potential donor?

There are a variety of strategies that are working effectively, including Workplace Giving Campaigns and Customer Donation Programs. Strategic placement of Web site or donation micropage addresses on all print and multimedia materials is a vital component of any campaign. Organizations need to review their existing Web site to assure careful positioning of "Join Us," "Donate Now," and "Donor Forum" buttons. "Tell a Friend" links also need to be prominent on your Web site, for effective viral marketing.

A number of companies such as Care2 will send your message to a mixture of online subscribers to assist you in building your house contact file. (See Appendix 7–C for a case study.) Additionally, many online consultants are suggesting that organizations invest in search engine marketing to drive more donors to their Web sites, hopefully to opt into receiving updates and information. Many organizations are using those first initial contacts with an online subscriber as strictly cultivation, to build the relationship before asking them to take an action or to make a gift. Additional strategies include media buys for banner placement on sites visited by potential donors that might be interested in your issue or organizational mission.

Strategies and tactics for online recruiting, interaction, and engagement to build your donor base are changing. Organizations are finding that effective fundraising requires more than just investing in an online tool. They must continuously test a variety of approaches to bring donors to the file, begin to build a relationship, and retain their support. See Exhibit 7–14 for ten tips to remember for success.

TIPS FOR WRITING E-MAIL SOLICITATIONS

There are two key components of an e-mail solicitation: the subject line and the body of the message. Madeline Stanionis, CEO

Exhibit 7–14 Ten Tips to Remember for Success

1. Gather e-mail addresses at events and on your Web site.
2. Keep your audience—age, technology comfort-level, and Internet connection—in mind when designing your Web site.
3. Your online identity and message should be the same as your off-line identity and message. Maintain your brand with a consistent look and message.
4. Keep your Web site updated and fresh.
5. Make it easy to give by posting the "Donate Now" button clearly and prominently on each page.
6. Be clear and be brief. You only have a few moments to capture the visitor's attention. Your Web site should not look like your printed brochure.
7. Personalize e-mail messages. Each online interaction is an opportunity to learn more about the visitors' interests, which you can then use to personalize communications.
8. Be interactive. Give people the opportunity to sign up to volunteer, to tell you what information they would like to receive, and to post messages.
9. Track responses to e-mails and test different messages.
10. Stay flexible and adapt to what your donors want. Offer an array of easy-to-use options: give by check, charge over the telephone, give online. Be ready to modify your online fundraising program to meet your constituents' needs.

and co-founder of Watershed, a consulting and services firm that specializes in online relationship building, and author of *The Mercifully Brief, Real World Guide to Raising Thousands (If Not Tens of Thousands) of Dollars with E-mail*, tells us that to get a constituent's attention, you have a second or two to convince them to read your message. To do that, be careful that your subject line is not too long. Because e-mail programs vary as to how many characters your reader will see at first, keep your subject line to no more than 50 characters. Avoid using words such as free or sale or shouting symbols like $ or ! that will land your e-mail in the spam filter. Stanionis believes the subject line should tell, tease, and ask readers to take action.

The following are several of her examples:

- A relief agency lets donors know how they help a crisis overseas: "Send a blanket to Bamgarian flood victims."
- A reminder to users: "Order Your Gala tickets now" or "Your membership expires soon – renew today."
- A tease subject line must be quick, easy to scan, and clever: "It's beginning to look a lot like justice…" sent just before the Christmas holidays by Earthjustice.

The best "'take action" e-mails are specific, well-timed as the topic is in the news, and local, if possible: "Tell Big Tobacco to stop selling to Boston children."

Like all other writing for fundraising, it is important that you tell your story well, offer a compelling reason to give, and use clear and persuasive language. Experts in the field, like Woodward and Stanionis, remind us of this with the following tips:

1. Use short sentences, short paragraphs, numerous links to the donation Web page, graphic inserts telling your reader

what to do, bullets, and selective use of bold and italics (reserve underlining for hyperlinks only) that create a persuasive message that can be scanned in a few seconds to tell the reader what to do.

2. Unlike a direct mail letter that allows you to develop your story, your e-mail message should be short and to the point. In order to do this, present only one or two key points, using as few words as possible to state the case, and avoid detailing the history of the appeal.

3. Since e-mail tends to be more casual than print, a message should be more personal and less formal. Use more relaxed salutations like "Hello Sue" rather than "Dear Mrs. Woodward." E-mail uses more colloquial terms such as "Wow! You overwhelmed us (and that's hard to do)!" rather than the direct mail message of "We were truly overwhelmed by the generous response to our request." And finally, e-mail uses an up-to-the minute style of writing—"I'm writing this at midnight, just getting home after the anniversary party. Whew! What a night!" instead of the direct mail phrase—"It was lovely to celebrate our anniversary with you last month."

Writing e-mail is different from other forms of writing; however, good writing is good writing—specific, clear, forceful, and grammatically correct. Keep that in mind for effective e-mail solicitations.

WORKING WITH CONSULTANTS AND VENDORS

Depending on the size of the organization and its budget, the organization may seek professional advice on its direct mail, telemarketing, and Internet fundraising programs. For information on vendors and consultants, refer to the *Chronicle of Philanthropy*, *The NonProfit Times*, *Fundraising Success*, and *Advancing Philanthropy*; visit their exhibit booths at conferences; or participate in online seminars they offer.

To identify the best vendor and/or consultant for your organization, call other nonprofits to find out which companies they have used. Interview several firms to learn how each one provides services to its clients and their respective fee structure. As with all contracts, have your legal representative review the contract between the organization and the consultant/vendor before signing it.

REFERENCES

Lautman, K.P. 2001. *Direct marketing for nonprofits: Essential techniques for the new era.* Sudbury, MA: Jones and Bartlett Publishers.

Stanionis, M. 2006. *The mercifully brief real world guide to raising thousands (if not tens of thousands) of dollars with e-mail.* Medfield, MA: Emerson and Church Publishers.

Case Study: Direct Mail Acquisition
Community Council for the Homeless

This acquisition package to enlist first-time donors was created pro-bono by Lautman Maska Neill & Company, an award-winning direct marketing firm in Washington, DC.

The package was created for Community Council for the Homeless at Friendship Place (CCH/FP), which is a small local organization in the District of Columbia. It tripled the organization's donor file in five years by mailing to postal zip codes in the vicinity as well as to "similar" organizations willing to exchange lists on a test basis.

The letter is easy to read, friendly, and personal. It creates immediate interest, beginning with a "Johnson box," which sets the tone for a neighborly message. The lead states the problem on page one in a unique way and immediately offers a solution. The letter includes a story about a man who overcame his problem—a must for all organizations doing "hands on" work.

The entire package is a simple, two-color piece, and includes a four-page letter and a contribution form bearing the donor's name and address. The form (which the donor will return) offers a range of 4 gifts beginning with the minimum amount sought of $35, and ascending to a high request of $250. A second panel was recently added to the contribution form, illustrating what gifts from $35 to $250 could accomplish, ranging from feeding a homeless person to life-saving medical care. The two-panel card was tested against the original one-panel card, and was declared the winner as it brought in far more gifts.

The letter uses a P.S., which is arguably as important as the lead. This P.S. restates the case, asks for the gift, and directs the reader to the contribution form. Facts are included in the letter (and updated for each mailing), but it is a human interest package rather than an institutional package—more about the people who are homeless (there is a case history in the letter) than about CCH/FP.

Source: Courtesy of Lautman Maska Neill & Company, Washington, DC.

COMMUNITY COUNCIL FOR THE HOMELESS AT FRIENDSHIP PLACE
4713 Wisconsin Avenue NW ◆ Washington DC 20016 ◆ Telephone 202-364-1419 ◆ Fax 202-364-8767
cchfp@cchfp.org ◆ www.cchfp.org

BOARD OF DIRECTORS

COMMUNITY REPRESENTATIVES
Lisa Adams
Andrew Aning
John Arata
Claudia Coonrod Barnett
George Bohlinger
Marshall Bykofsky
Lee Carty
David Cohen
Ed Cowan
Jean Duff
Peter Espenschied
Edmund Frost
Deborah House
Ernestine James
Helen Kenney
Amy Kossoff, M.D.
June Kress
Kay Partney Lautman
Lynn Mehaffy
Jim Nathanson
Glenn Piercy
Nan Roman
Elizabeth Siegel
Mark Tannenbaum
Debbie Weil

BUSINESS REPRESENTATIVE
David DeSantis

CONGREGATION REPRESENTATIVES
Seth Rosenthal
Adas Israel Congregation
Anna Tyng
All Saints Episcopal Church
Vacant
Chevy Chase Presbyterian Church
Vacant
Chevy Chase United Methodist Church
Patricia Frohman
Church of the Annunciation
Pat Goeldner
Church of the Pilgrims
Dick Jorgensen
Cleveland Park Congregational Church
Janet Murdock
Community of Christ Church
Ken Jacques
Holy Trinity Church
Dick Schleicher
Metropolitan Memorial United Methodist Church
John Haltiwanger
National Presbyterian Church and Center
Phi Fostvedt
Our Lady of Victory Catholic Church
Mary Gorman
Shrine of the Most Blessed Sacrament
Sally Craig
St. Alban's Episcopal Church
Ted Hirt
St. Ann's Roman Catholic Church
Nan Hildebrand
St. Columba's Episcopal Church
Vacant
St. Luke's United Methodist Church
Joan Janshego
St. Paul's Lutheran Church
Martha Adler
Temple Micah
Richard Jerome
Temple Sinai
Jane Stein
Washington Hebrew Congregation
Rev. Whit Hutchinson
Wesley United Methodist Church

I'm writing to you today as your neighbor in Northwest Washington to share an exciting opportunity…an innovative way to help other neighbors who happen to be <u>homeless but who are neighbors nonetheless</u>.

February 2006

Dear Friend and Neighbor,

Haven't you sometimes wondered about the sad, homeless people you see on the street – how did they come to this? Where do they go when it rains or snows? To bathe or dress? To fix a toothache? To treat or recover from the flu? To just find a friendly person to talk to?

For years, I wondered too, especially when I'd walk to the Tenleytown Metro station on Albemarle Street and Wisconsin Avenue. Back then, I'd literally step over the many homeless people as I made my way through those huddled by the Metro entrance.

I gave quarters and dollar bills to destitute people I didn't know how else to help. Surprisingly, there were as many women as men – and many of them were elderly. As I later learned, some had degrees from our country's finest schools.

"There, but for the Grace of God," I realized, "go I."

But then some 14 years ago, a group of volunteers fixed up and opened a house on Wisconsin Avenue. A house that was not a shelter…not a soup kitchen…not a group home. Rather it is a resource center to help our homeless neighbors get into real housing and back into society. It's called Community Council for the Homeless at Friendship Place (CCH/FP).

Some 70% of the homeless we serve are struggling to cope with a treatable mental illness. Almost as many have alcohol or drug addiction as a result of having to self-medicate while on the street. <u>Sadly, there are no mental health services for the homeless on the streets of Ward 3 other than those provided by CCH/FP.</u>

Few of our homeless neighbors have family ties or personal relationships. Most have tried unsuccessfully to work within conventional

(over, please)

social and treatment systems but, because of bad experiences, almost all homeless men and women mistrust attempts to help. Only a very few seek it out voluntarily.

But CCH/FP's mission is not to sit and wait for these people to come to us. Instead, our mission is to reach out to our homeless neighbors…to build trusting relationships…and provide or refer them to appropriate services.

For example, even though the long-range goal for a client may be to attend an alcohol detox program, get employment or permanent housing, CCH/FP staff meanwhile encourages him or her to come to Friendship Place to just get acquainted. And for those who cannot – or will not – come in, our staff and volunteers reach out with van runs bringing sandwiches, water, blankets and other necessities, as well as a friendly voice to the men and women who huddle alone in the dark.

Our small, energetic staff provides medical and psychiatric care, financial counseling, job readiness and life skills training, transitional and permanent housing, referrals to addictions counseling and most important, ongoing support and the secure knowledge that no matter what happens, there is someone who cares and somewhere to go. Over 250 neighborhood volunteers provide that real sense of community connection to the 430 clients we served last year.

We have a wonderful house on MacArthur Boulevard – for five formerly homeless women with severe mental illness. And, we operate another home on Western Avenue – for five formerly homeless men with mental illness. There are three apartments on Wisconsin Avenue and two on Connecticut Avenue where people are able to live independently with our support. In partnership with St. Columba's Church, we operate a comfortable home for five homeless women in need of temporary shelter. We provide services at four local congregation-based shelters, as well as for residents of apartments owned or leased by neighborhood congregations for formerly homeless individuals with mental illness.

<u>We have been able to do all this because people in our community – people like you – have refused to turn their backs on their less fortunate neighbors</u>. Individuals, business owners, congregations and community groups have rallied to make our work possible.

Earlier I mentioned how many needy, homeless individuals I noticed before CCH/FP came to be. I don't mean to imply that we have completely solved the problem. We haven't! But we've made an enormous dent, which is why we no longer see so many homeless huddled at the Tenleytown/AU metro. <u>Let me tell you about one man named Andrew</u>.

Several years ago, when Andrew lost his job as an insurance adjuster, he started drinking, lost his home, and ended up sleeping in abandoned houses and similar places. When he first arrived at our clinic at Friendship Place, he literally crawled up the steps to the front door. Because of a spinal injury, he could barely walk.

Our professional staff got him the immediate care he needed – food and a place to sleep – and surgery to correct his spinal problem. We provided emotional support as he learned to walk again – and to live without alcohol. Eventually he learned how to design web pages through a work program, and he's now taking courses to update his knowledge in the insurance field, so that he can return to work as an adjuster.

(next page, please)

Last year, Andrew was able to move out of a CCH/FP-supported group home and into his own apartment. After working hard to rebuild his life, he'd finally reached the end of a three-year journey of recovery, and regained his independence and dignity.

<u>I only thank God that CCH/FP was there for him.</u>

Like most of the cases we take on, this outcome was not quick or easy. Happy endings require dedication and patience – and most of all, they require money.

<u>And that, my friend, is where you come in.</u>

Will you be there for others like Andrew…who have lost their way, but whom we can help, if you will help us?

- A gift of $35 could provide dinner for five formerly homeless men with disabling mental illness in our group home;
- A gift of $50 could provide one month of transportation to job training, medical appointments or work for a formerly homeless person;
- A gift of $100 could provide life-saving medical or psychiatric care for someone with a serious untreated illness;
- A gift of $250 could provide one month of breakfasts for the women at our transitional shelter;
- A gift of $650 could provide one month of rent for a formerly homeless person.

As I said earlier, I used to give money to virtually every sympathetic-looking street person I saw – especially during the cold winter months. But that was only instant gratification for me. Today I give my money to the Community Council for the Homeless at Friendship Place.

<u>Believe me, the money I give goes a lot further, and it's tax-deductible, too.</u>

Please join me in reaching out to a homeless neighbor by sending a contribution of $35 or more if you can. If you can't send that much right now, send a smaller amount to be a part of this important work. Your gift today will help us do so much for our homeless neighbors. On behalf of our entire "family" of staff and volunteers, thank you for being one who cares.

Sincerely,

Kay P. Lautman

Kay P. Lautman
Board Member

P.S.   Every day we are trying to make a real difference in the lives of our homeless neighbors. Won't you help? The enclosed contribution form shows approximately what gifts of varying amounts will do.

COMMUNITY COUNCIL
FOR THE HOMELESS
AT FRIENDSHIP PLACE
4713 Wisconsin Avenue NW
Washington DC 20016

CONTRIBUTION FORM

❑ **Yes!** I would like to help more homeless people rebuild their lives and regain their independence by providing food, housing, health care and other critical services. I have checked off one of the boxes below and have returned this entire from with my gift.

❑ $35   ❑ $50   ❑ $100   ❑ $250   ❑ Other $_____

Kay Lautman
Lautman & Company
Ste. 301
1730 Rhode Island Ave., NW
Washington, DC 20036

A262XMB

For information about our street outreach, housing program, advocacy and educational activities, please call 202-364-1419.

Please return the entire form with your check made payable to **Community Council for the Homeless at Friendship Place** or **CCH/FP**. All gifts are 100% tax deductible. Thank you!

$35   FOOD

could provide dinner for the residents of our group home for formerly homeless men with disabling mental illness.

$100   HEALTH

could provide life-saving medical or psychiatric care for someone with a serious untreated illness.

$50   TRANSPORTATION

could provide one month of transportation to job training, medical appointments, or work for a formerly homeless person.

$250   FOOD

could provide one month of breakfasts for the women in our transitional shelter.

$70   OUTREACH

could provide one month of gas for our Outreach Van so we can take sandwiches and blankets to people too afraid to come in for services.

COMMUNITY COUNCIL
FOR THE HOMELESS
AT FRIENDSHIP PLACE

Case Study: Telemarketing Campaign

THE NEED

Morristown Memorial Hospital (MMH), in Morristown, New Jersey, had addressed the healthcare needs of a growing community by undertaking a major capital initiative that resulted in the Carol G. Simon Cancer Center, which opened in 1998. Since then it had developed an exceptional reputation, treating more than 98 percent of the patients first diagnosed there.

Clearly, Morristown Memorial saw and met a vital need. But that need was growing. The number of people diagnosed or treated for cancer at Morristown Memorial had increased 37 percent annually since 1997. Almost as soon as it opened, the Carol G. Simon Cancer Center was at capacity and it soon became clear that an expansion would be necessary if Morristown Memorial was to continue to offer extraordinary care to the entire community.

The *Campaign for Encompassing Care* was launched to add two floors to the existing facility and a third linear accelerator for radiation treatments. An $18 million effort towards a $20 million project, Morristown needed just $400,000 to reach their goal when they received a challenge grant for $150,000.

The Morristown Memorial Health Foundation, a progressive and successful development program under the leadership of James F. Quinn, CFRE, Chief Development Officer, believed a telephone outreach program to engage new donors as well as raise the required dollars would be a winning strategy to successfully meet the challenge opportunity.

Telecomp, Inc., based in Rochester, New York, had successfully served Morristown with a telephone outreach program during the original capital campaign to build the Carol G. Simon Cancer Center in 1997, generating over $1.2 million in pledged income, and uncovering several donors of $25,000 and above, while engaging a broad cross-section of the community.

PROGRAM OBJECTIVES

The original campaign reached out to both prior and current donors and former patients discharged/seen in up to an 18 month period. With only $400,000 remaining in the Campaign's goal, *The Campaign for Encompassing Care* did not require as great an outreach effort and only included those who had made a gift to the Foundation within the last three years.

This effort was expected to generate $366,000 in pledged income and matching corporate gifts from 750 donors.

At the same time the program was designed to generate information and longer-term benefits by:

- **providing** a well-designed opportunity for each individual selected to **participate** in this significant effort.
- **obtaining** capital gifts above and beyond annual fund giving, thus increasing donors' total giving to the Foundation.
- **serving** as a public relations effort, heightening awareness of the Campaign and the Hospital's plans for the future to a broader constituency.
- **updating and enhancing** donor records.
- **identifying,** for future cultivation and solicitation, potential donors of major gifts.
- **contributing** to a successful long-term plan for development growth.

PROGRAM OPERATION

The program was guided by a very deliberate and comprehensive action plan that included:

File Accuracy and Program Outreach

A two-step process in order to verify and secure accurate telephone numbers, including computer matching services and directory assistance calls was conducted. Up to 25 attempts were made to reach each individual as well as scheduling call-backs when requested.

The Pre-Call Lead Letter Series

The system for this Campaign included two distinct and sequentially mailed pre-call Lead Letters and a "Mini-Case Statement" brochure, followed by a carefully structured telephone call and immediate written acknowledgement series to each individual who made a pledge or wished to consider a pledge.

Caller Representatives

Telecomp used a three-step process to ensure high-caliber telephone representatives for the Foundation, recruiting articulate and qualified individuals who best represented Morristown Memorial and its needs and undergoing extensive training for the Cancer Center Campaign. Staff members of the Foundation were encouraged to participate in the initial caller training sequence as well as listen to calls, which could be accessed from any location.

Script and Supporting Materials

A critical element to any solicitation program is its content. The Foundation's team of callers worked from a carefully crafted calling outline written specifically for *The Campaign for Encompassing Care*; establishing rapport, building the Case for Support and moving through a series of "asks" to find the gift level most comfortable for each donor. Supporting materials provided responses to the most frequently asked questions and any sensitive areas that came up in the conversation.

Pledge Follow-up

Each individual who made a pledge—either of a specified or unspecified amount—was sent two follow-up communications to ensure immediate pledge acknowledgment, stewardship and timely fulfillment. This series mirrored the Pre-Call Lead Letter series and included a hand-written letter on Campaign letterhead.

Reporting

MMH received a record of each and every completed solicitation call. This included the result of the call, any biographic updates including business information and detailed accounts of any comments. Results were compiled daily. At the conclusion of the program, a prospect inventory was provided which fully accounted for each individual assigned to the program.

For those who pledged, or wished to consider a pledge, Telecomp attempted to obtain each individual's employer's name and to determine whether or not it is a matching gift company. This generated additional income for the program. The Foundation then had the opportunity to record this information on its database and to utilize it in subsequent fund raising efforts.

In addition to statistical, biographic and demographic data, this program also provided the kind of information that can be gained only from personally speaking with a substantial portion of the Foundation's most important supporters.

OUTCOME

Telecomp's results for both *The Carol G. Simon Cancer Center Campaign* and *The Campaign for Encompassing Care* were:

	The Carol G. Simon Cancer Center Campaign	The Campaign for Encompassing Care
Number of Individuals Assigned	48,911	10,000
Completed Solicitation Calls	35,081	7,092
Completion Rate	72%	71%
Number of Pledged Donors	2,707	809
Specified Pledge Rate	8%	11%
Average Pledge (3 year payment period)	$437	$483
Pledged Income	$1,184,254	$390,975
Matching Gift Income	$76,056	$29,800
Grand Total Pledged Income	$1,260,310	$420,775
Number of Actual Donors	2,800	1,382
Actual Gift Income	$969,350	Not complete

The utilization of a telephone outreach program also contributed to the identification and acquisition of major gift prospects and donors who have become significantly important to the longer-term growth of the overall development program.

Source: Courtesy of Kathleen F. Pavelka, CFRE, Founder and President, Telecomp, Inc., Rochester, New York, and James F. Quinn, CFRE, Chief Development Officer, Morristown Memorial Health Foundation, Morristown, New Jersey.

Care2 Case Study: Online Recruitment of Donors

THE NEED

The Marine Fish Conservation Network, based in Washington, DC, is a coalition of over 190 organizations dedicated to the conservation of ocean fish in U.S. territorial waters. The Network informs the public, media, and policy makers of threats to the long-term sustainability of ocean fish and works to protect and strengthen the primary law governing fishing in U.S. ocean waters, the Magnuson-Stevens Fishery Conservation and Management Act (MSA).

In 2006, after eight years of operation under a sponsoring fiscal agent the Network became a stand-alone 501(c)(3). This came at the height of an intense effort to convince the U.S. Congress to strengthen MSA, and block efforts from industrial fishing interest to weaken its conservation measures. At the same time, the Network was facing the prospect of diminished interest from foundations once Congress reauthorized the MSA.

Faced with the prospect of a major turning point in its efforts and the potential for foundation money to become even scarcer, the Network recognized the need to both diversify its funding base and identify more online donors to support their work in the future. However, the Network also needed to identify online activists to support their outreach to Congress. These twin needs represented a potential conflict between immediate demand for political support and long-term capacity building.

In 2002, Care2, an online social network that helps nonprofits recruit online supporters based in Redwood City, CA, had helped the Network recruit 4,000 online activists. Letters from these activists helped educate Members of Congress to support important ocean conservation legislation before Congress at that time. Now the Network needed to recruit additional activists that would also become donors and support the Network's efforts moving forward.

PROGRAM OBJECTIVES

With only six weeks left in the regular session of the 110th Congress, the Network needed to quickly inform key Members of Congress that legislation they were about to bring to a vote would allow irreparable harm to ocean fish populations by eliminating key conservation provisions contained in the MSA. In addition, the Network needed to expand its base of potential online donors as part of their funding diversification strategy. The Network retained Care2 to generate support for its policy goals by encouraging its members to send letters to their Members of Congress and recruit subscribers to the Network's e-activist list who would also become donor leads.

This effort was expected to generate more than 20,000 letters from citizens in four key states and recruit more than 10,000 online supporters to join the Network's list.

At the same time the program was designed to generate longer-term benefits by:

- Prescreening subscribers to identify those with genuine interest in ocean conservation
- Guaranteeing that each person recruited for the network would be unique from any previously recruited by Care2
- Providing a complete mailing address for the majority of subscribers

PROGRAM OPERATION

Care2 campaigns follow a very straight forward and efficient process comprised of the following steps:

- Care2 and the Network held a kick-off call to discuss the campaign goals and finalize details regarding the content and timing of the campaign. This was also an opportunity to brainstorm creative approaches.
- The Network provided images and text to help Care2's campaigners develop a campaign customized for their audience.
- The Care2 campaign team drafted materials and solicited the Network's feedback and approval on the creative.
- Care2 launched the campaign and sent a file to the Network every two weeks containing new online subscribers.
- Care2 promoted the campaign until it fulfilled its agreement with the Network and delivered the desired number of subscribers.

OUTCOME

Care2's results for *The Marine Fish Conservation Network* were:

Number of letters to Congress generated	44,000
Number of online supporters recruited	11,000

This online lead generation program fulfilled two critical needs for the Network preventing them from sacrificing either need. It enabled them to communicate with Congress at a critical moment and build its online community substantially with a population that they can communicate with in the future whether asking for advocacy support, sharing information, or donations.

The next steps for converting these supporters into donors involved cultivating the relationship and providing meaningful opportunities for them to help the Network.

Examples of cultivation found to be effective include:

- Telling these supporters about the Network's successful effort (the law was significantly strengthened at the end of the 110th Congress) and ask for donations to support on-going work
- Engaging in telemarketing to call these individuals and ask them to donate
- Sending regular action alerts as opportunities arise
- Adding them to the Network's quarterly e-newsletter
- Sending out donation appeals in conjunction with relevant events such as World Oceans Day (June 8th), National Seafood Month (October), and World Fisheries Day (November 21)

Source: Courtesy of Eric Radin, Care2.com and Marine Fish Conservative Network, Washington, DC.

Chapter 8

Prospect Research

CHAPTER OUTLINE

- Why Research Is Important
- How to Identify Prospects
- The Prospect Profile
- Staffing and Organization of the Research Effort
- Working with Research Consultants
- Sources of Information
- Using Volunteer Screening Committees

- Public Information
- Using the Internet
- Wealth Identification Through Electronic Screening
- The Role of the Development Officer
- Other Benefits of Prospect Research for an Organization
- Ethical Issues and Confidentiality

KEY VOCABULARY

- Briefing Report
- Electronic Screening
- Online Database
- Prospect
- Prospect Profile
- Prospect Research
- Screening and Rating Sessions
- Suspect

WHY RESEARCH IS IMPORTANT

Successful fundraising professionals reveal that only 10 percent of their time is actually spent soliciting major gifts whereas the other 90 percent is spent researching prospects and developing strategies. For that reason, it is extremely important for an organization to allocate resources to establish a prospect research program. The importance of research and knowing something about current and prospective donors was covered earlier in the chapters on annual giving and direct mail. You will see throughout this book that research plays a critical role in every type of fundraising. Methods for researching corporations and foundations are covered in the chapters on how to raise money from these entities.

This chapter focuses on prospect research that helps identify individuals who could make major gifts to an organization.

Prospect research plays a critical role in an organization's continued growth. Identifying individuals who may be interested in an organization leads to greater financial stability and security for the organization. It also offers an excellent opportunity to identify new leaders, supporters, and volunteers. Involving current volunteers in the research process allows them to assist the organization in a meaningful way, too.

Fundraising is a process that involves three simple steps: identification, cultivation, and solicitation. These steps should not be separated but instead viewed as on a continuum. Prospect research itself is a process that uses one name to lead to another or one piece of information to lead to additional pieces of information. The purpose of prospect research, therefore, is to collect data in an organized manner on individuals and organizations who might become significant donors to a specific nonprofit organization.

While conducting research, keep in mind some of the reasons why people contribute to organizations. First and foremost, people give to people, not to organizations. That is why it is important to search for connections or linkages between people. Second, people can give only what they have, not what an organization may think they have. So it is necessary to search for information that will reveal a capability to give. Finally, even if an individual knows someone in the organization and has the ability to give, people give only when they are interested and involved in a cause or organization. Therefore, it is critical to research whether an individual has displayed any interest in the particular issue, cause, or type of organization.

HOW TO IDENTIFY PROSPECTS

There are several ways for an organization to identify prospective donors. The best way is to first use the people and information resources already found within an organization. These resources include board members, staff, volunteers, individual donor files, and special event files. It is also common to use mailing lists of other nonprofit, trade, or professional organizations; civic and city directories; names referred by the board, staff, and donors; and commercial lists rented from national or regional organizations.

In the first phase of the research process, an organization will compile a list of "suspects." Suspects are individuals who with further research may become qualified prospective donors for the organization. The most effective method of identifying new prospects is to consider those individuals who are currently involved or were previously involved with the organization. Look for those groups who make up an organization's "family." Among them would be the following:

- board members (current and past members)
- current gift club members
- current donors
- volunteers
- alumni (graduates, former patients, clients served)
- staff leaders
- affiliated groups (professors, physicians, parents, artists, other related professionals)
- advisory council members
- special event attendees
- those known to believe in the organization's work

Use the "family" groups identified previously to start a list. Segment the list in such a way that those who are or have been most involved, such as current and former board members, are at the top. Another segment would consist of donors who have given over a period of years or who have recently made a significant gift. Many of the names on the list will be identified as suspects. A suspect is defined as someone who may have minimal interest in or involvement with the organization. It is only through careful evaluation that an organization will qualify a number of these suspects as prospects. Further evaluation will result in identifying a reduced number of prospects who merit in-depth research. Exhibit 8–1 is a checklist of questions used when evaluating prospects.

THE PROSPECT PROFILE

When establishing a research system, an organization must develop a prospect research profile that, in a well-organized for-

Exhibit 8–1 Checklist of Questions Used When Evaluating Prospects

1. Does this person have strong ties to the organization?
2. Is this person linked in some way to the organization through family or business?
3. Is this person a donor or volunteer?
4. How often has this person contributed to the organization?
5. What was the largest gift made to date?
6. To which program or service was the largest gift directed?
7. Does this person attend events sponsored by the organization?
8. If not a donor, what is the ability of the person to make a significant gift?
9. To what other organizations is this person a major contributor?
10. How interested is this person in the organization and in what specific area?

mat, lists pertinent information about an individual. Technology plays a critical role in organizing and tracking needed information, especially the organization's donor database system, so that it can be used effectively during the cultivation and solicitation of a prospect. Research should be cumulative and ongoing. A prospect profile should be regularly reviewed and updated, and new information should be shared with volunteers and staff to

> *Research should be cumulative and ongoing.*

whom the prospect is assigned. Exhibit 8–2 lists the types of information you should include in the prospect profile, and Exhibit 8–3 presents a sample prospect file.

Besides the profile, individual research system files should include the following:

- news clippings mentioning the prospect
- articles about prospect from internal and external publications

Exhibit 8–2 Prospect Profile

Basic Information:
- name, address, telephone number
- occupation and work address
- date and place of birth
- marital status and family data
- giving history with organization
- cultivation contacts and organizational events attended

Internal Information:
- gift potential evaluated by peers and professional staff
- solicitation assignments and results

More Comprehensive Information to Include for Selected Prospects:
- income and assets including sources
- insider stock ownership
- directorships (profit and nonprofit)
- family and/or community foundation connections
- social, political, community associations and activities
- club memberships

Exhibit 8–3 Sample Prospect File

CONFIDENTIAL
EMIL J. GAUMONT (BA '78)
416836946

POSITION AND FIRM
President
Signet Communications, Inc.
Five Lanai Boulevard
Palo Alto, CA 94301
(415) 332-1984

RESIDENCE
3672 Grinnell Avenue
Palo Alto, CA 94312
(415) 665-8913

EDUCATION
B.A., Kogod School of Business, American University, 1978

PERSONAL/FAMILY HISTORY
born July 2,1954
married Kathy Gaumont (B.A. Education, American University, 1979)
children Adam Gaumont—16 years old; Ryan Gaumont—13 years old

PROFESSIONAL/FINANCIAL INFORMATION
President, Signet Communications, Inc.
Business: Telecommunications—Internet
Sales: $900 million in 2006 (Dun & Bradstreet)
Employees: 350

NONPROFIT AFFILIATIONS
Chairman of the Board, San Francisco Chapter, American Cancer
   Society
Trustee, Palo Alto Lutheran Church

AMERICAN UNIVERSITY RELATION
Alumnus

AMERICAN UNIVERSITY GIVING
President's Circle Member ($100,000)

AMERICAN UNIVERSITY INTERESTS
Speaker, Kogod Business Roundtable

NOTES:
Visited by Dean Jones, Kogod College, and Development Officer,
   John Sherman — 2/23/08
Expressed interest in getting more involved with AU; agreed to par-
   ticipate in Kogod Business Roundtable program in San Francisco
Prepared by: Diane Pace, 5/1/08

Source: Courtesy of American University Development Office,
Washington, DC.

- copies of all correspondence to and from the prospect
- memos highlighting telephone contacts
- written reports by the development staff on visits with the prospect

A number of these items can also be placed in a prospect's database record if your system has the capacity to store this information. When developing your list of suspects, you will dis-

cover individuals who will be good annual gift prospects at this time and not major gift prospects. The definition of an annual gift prospect versus a major gift prospect will depend on the size and needs of the organization. A donor who contributes $5,000 or $10,000 at one time would probably be considered a major gift donor by a community-based organization but would be viewed as an annual gift donor by a university or hospital. It is important to remember that today's annual donors are good prospects for future major gifts. Keep them on a list to be further researched in the future. Do more in-depth research on the suspects who have the greatest potential now.

STAFFING AND ORGANIZATION OF THE RESEARCH EFFORT

Nonprofit organizations of all sizes need to conduct research so that staff and volunteer efforts can be focused more effectively. Keep in mind that the president, executive director, and/or board chairperson should devote a majority of his or her time to the cultivation and solicitation of major gift prospects identified through research. The challenge of finding time for research is very common in nonprofit organizations. Many believe that unless a staff person can spend a significant amount of time doing research, it is not worth getting started. However, as is often the case, an organization already may be doing research but may not realize it because there is no formal procedure for collecting and compiling data. Many times nonprofit staff will see their donors' names in the newspaper, trade publications, or regional magazines. They may cut out the articles and bring them to the office, but then where should they be filed? How often does a staff member read through a listing of donors and sponsors in a program book to see if he or she comes across familiar names? Without anyone realizing it, the research process is underway!

The question of who is responsible for doing research can be simple or complicated depending on the size of the organization. Certain routine tasks can be assigned to staff (if they have the proper experience) or to volunteers. Training is important to ensure that research is conducted and compiled in a consistent fashion. However, in many nonprofit organizations, the fundraiser is the staff person responsible for conducting research. This is the case because the fundraiser is able to review and evaluate information on specific prospects much better than administrative support staff or volunteers. The fundraiser further plays a critical role by contributing new and updated information to the profile based on meetings and telephone calls with the prospect or individuals who have information about the prospect. (See "The Role of the Development Officer" later in this chapter.) Volunteers also are key to providing information on suspects and prospects (this topic is also covered later).

WORKING WITH RESEARCH CONSULTANTS

If you don't have the staff or research resources to conduct your own prospect research in-house, there are a growing number of consultants who can help you. Typically, consultants will help you analyze your current donor pool to find major donor prospects and to help you prepare profiles designed to understand their giving capabilities and determine their philanthropic interests. In addition, consultants can help find new prospects whether they be individuals, foundations, or corporations.

If you are interested in starting a prospect research component in your own office, consultants will also help train you in how to do this research, discuss ethics and confidentiality of information, and help you choose a database software provider. One such consultant is Maria Semple of the Prospect Finder. She works with nonprofits nationwide to help them uncover their hidden wealth holders and discover new prospects who would be interested in their cause. Semple, a member of the Association of Professional Researchers for Advancement, is a knowledgeable speaker on the topic of prospect research. See Appendix 8–A for a description of how she worked with a client to research and develop strategies for prospective donors. Visit her Web site for additional information at http://www.TheProspectFinder.com.

SOURCES OF INFORMATION

Sources of information that are appropriate for an organization's goals and budget need to be identified and selected. Some sources will be readily available within the organization. As mentioned earlier, these include records and files on current and past board members, current donors, lapsed donors, people who

have attended special events, and participants in the organization's programs. Personal contact by telephone or meetings can offer valuable information, too. Member and alumni surveys are also useful tools in gathering specific information needed.

An organization needs to establish a research budget that includes Internet service, online subscription fees, newspaper and professional publication subscriptions, and various research directories on CD-ROMs or in book form. The first place to start today is the Internet, now the primary source of information we need, replacing such publications as telephone books, zip code directories, and the like. Look to see if you can access newspapers, magazines, and professional-type journals online that are up-to-date sources of information on prospective donors. Depending on your preference for reviewing these types of publications, you might still want to subscribe to newspapers and magazines in order to receive the publication on a regular basis at your office. Other Internet resources helpful to prospect research are covered later in this chapter.

In addition to the Internet, many nonprofit organizations are utilizing online research tools such as Dialog and LexisNexis that charge a monthly subscription fee in order to be able to access databases most relevant to their research efforts. Various directories useful for prospect research are now available on CD-ROM as well as in book form and can be purchased by the organization on an annual basis and added to its research resources.

Another excellent resource is the Foundation Center, an independent national service organization that provides authorita-

"The on-line search didn't turn up any new prospects, but I did find out that two of our current board members are deceased."

Source: Copyright © Carole Cable.

tive information on foundation, corporate, and individual giving. Reference collections operated by the Foundation Center are located in New York; San Francisco; Washington, DC; Cleveland; and Atlanta. (Addresses for these centers are listed in Appendix 8–B.) Cooperating collections located in libraries, community foundations, and other nonprofit agencies across the country provide a core collection of Foundation Center publications and supplementary materials.

The Foundation Center also offers nonprofit organizations membership in its Associates Program, which is a personalized fundraising information service. Staff members supporting the Associates Program have access to all of the significant fundraising research publications, electronic databases, and other resources to be able to help an organization find information on corporate and foundation giving, individual donors, and grant-making public charities. They are experienced researchers who can be viewed as an extension of the organization's staff. The annual membership fee, which is currently $995, includes unlimited on-call research assistance toll-free or through a members-only e-mail connection, exclusive access to a members-only Web site with unique content and information, and customized research reports.

For those seeking information on how to research government funding, see Appendix 8–C.

USING VOLUNTEER SCREENING COMMITTEES

The main purpose of a screening committee is to classify or "rate" prospects according to general giving capabilities. A second purpose is to involve volunteers in a meaningful way that heightens their own level of commitment to the organization. During the initial screening, the primary task is to evaluate an individual's resources or capability to give rather than his or her interest in the organization or ways to involve the individual in the organization.

Screening and rating sessions, as they are called, are conducted by an experienced staff person and should be businesslike and held in a comfortable environment. Refreshments should be served. When recruiting volunteers to participate, it is important to inform them that their anonymity will be respected. At each session, the group as a whole should decide the best way to proceed. Other issues related to screening and rating sessions are covered in Chapter 9. Exhibit 8–4 lists elements of a screening and rating session.

Key to the success of the volunteer screening committee is matching each participant with a specially tailored suspect list to review. Certainly, an organization cannot compile lists of individuals whom each participant is assured to know. However, ways of tailoring lists include segmenting them by

- region, state, city, and community
- occupation or profession

Exhibit 8–4 Elements of a Screening and Rating Session

During the session:

- Participants are provided with suspect lists including pertinent home and business addresses, giving history for donors, and volunteer and board involvement.
- A broad range of giving levels such as $5,000, $15,000, $25,000, $50,000, $100,000, and $250,000 is used to evaluate suspects.
- Each session lasts one to two hours with a follow-up meeting scheduled later.
- Participants evaluate only those suspects they know or of whom they have knowledge.
- Participants may add or delete suspects as desirable.
- Confidentiality of participants' work is respected.

- class year or academic major (for alumni committees)
- parents by grade level and school (for independent school committees)

PUBLIC INFORMATION

For budget-conscious nonprofit organizations, nearby public libraries provide the tools needed to succeed in research efforts. Many county libraries and university libraries have databases that can be searched off-site. With a bar-coded library card, you can gain access to these databases from the convenience of your office, saving your organizations hundreds (if not thousands) of dollars in research databases. These databases may include searchable archives of regional or national newspapers, biographical data, public and private company data, magazine searches, and more. Check with your local reference librarian to see if this cost-efficient alternative will provide you with the information you need.

Library resources (electronic and hard copy) can be divided into the following categories:

- biographical, such as *Who's Who in America, Current Biography,* and the *Dictionary of American Biography*
- professional directories, such as the *Martindale-Hubbell Law Directory* and the *Who's Who* directories (by profession)
- newspapers and periodical indices, such as the *Business Periodicals Index* and the *Reader's Guide to Periodical Literature*

Online Information Services

Online information services are a major resource for development offices across the country. These services bring the information necessary to conduct prospect research right to the staff member's desk. Although a number of these services charge their users a fee, there are many other free services to choose from. Exhibit 8–5 is a sampling of Web sites used by prospect researchers.

Online information services are a major resource for development offices across the country.

Exhibit 8–5 Sampling of Web Sites to Visit

General Search	Private Companies
www.google.com	www.hoovers.com
www.yahoo.com	www.dnbsearch.com
www.altavista.com	**Political Contributors**
Locating People	www.tray.com
www.superpages.com	**Real Estate**
www.argali.com	Indorgs.virginia.edu/portico
Public Companies	**News Sources**
Finance.yahoo.com	www.newsdirectory.com
www.secinfo.com	www.newspapers.com
	www.factiva.com

LexisNexis

Many prospect researchers use online databases to access information in magazines, newspapers, news wires, newsletters, and government and electronic publications. LexisNexis began as LEXIS, which was the first commercial full-text legal information service to help individuals in the legal profession research the law more efficiently. NEXIS is primarily a full-text news and business information service. Because of the cost, it is best to think of NEXIS as an expensive news service that should be used only when other hard-copy and online resources are exhausted. LexisNexis has flexible pricing options including pay-as-you-go, daily, or weekly subscriptions.

Another LexisNexis (http://www.lexis.com) product of interest to fundraising prospect researchers is LexisNexis for Development Professionals, a targeted Web-based solution that brings together key information resources needed for development purposes: news, company, biographical, demographic, public records, and references. Subscriptions for this product are based on a "per seat basis" so that only staff who use the product will be charged.

Dialog

Dialog (http://www.dialog.com) is one of the leading online information retrieval services with more than 900 databases including the top financial, biographical, corporate, and news databases. Although this service might have a relatively high cost, keep in mind that it can help research staff be more efficient and productive in their search efforts.

10K Wizard

This fee-based service dubs itself "SEC Power Search." Indeed, it does provide real-time data from the Securities and Exchange Commission, enabling researchers to pinpoint insider stock holdings and biographical data typically found in proxy statements filed annually by public corporations. Currently, five levels of service are available starting at $199 per year for their Basic service to $2,395 per year for their International Pro service. An organization can customize its package to fit its needs. 10K Wizard can be visited at http://www.10KWizard.com.

USING THE INTERNET

As we mentioned earlier in the chapter, the Internet is an essential tool for conducting prospect research. However, the tremendous amount of information available to us via the Internet can be overwhelming. David Lamb, a leading expert on prospect research, former Director of Prospect Research at the University of Washington, Seattle, and now consultant with Blackbaud, Inc., recommends that researchers do the following:

- focus their search
- limit their search time
- have a plan of attack
- check for relevance and validity
- handle information carefully, especially if they paid for it
- capitalize on the experience and knowledge of others

Because there are too many Web sites to list, following are several sites designed to provide information to prospect researchers on which Internet sites are most helpful.

Prospect Research Page

David Lamb has an excellent Web site that lists Internet sites by topic and includes a brief review. To get there, type http://www.lambresearch.com.

Internet Prospector

This monthly electronic newsletter produced by volunteers offers timely information on corporations and foundations, people, research tools, and news of interest to prospect researchers. People who subscribe to the PRSPCT-L discussion list automatically receive a copy of the newsletter at the start of each month. More information and a sampling of newsletter items are available at a Web site. To get there, type http://www.internet prospector.org/

The Association of Professional Researchers for Advancement (APRA) Web site is also an excellent source of Web resources for advancement research. Their Research Links page lists Web sites built and maintained by researchers or their peers, all employed by nonprofits. These professionals are experts in finding worthwhile Web sites, and each researcher's page consists of a unique set of links to the most current sites and tools researchers are using to identify and qualify prospective donors. Visit http://www.aprahome.org/researchlinks.

WEALTH IDENTIFICATION THROUGH ELECTRONIC SCREENING

With the increased need to establish major gift programs (see Chapter 9), many nonprofit organizations are contracting with firms that specialize in another type of prospect research, wealth identification screening, in order to focus their staff's time and effort for greater success. These firms, found in the *Chronicle of Philanthropy* and *The NonProfit Times*, offer services and products that can help you determine a prospect's ability and propensity to give, attitudes toward various causes, and general interests.

The following are some of the firms that provide these services.

- Blackbaud Analytics (800-443-9441)
  http://www.blackbaud.com
- Grenzebach Glier & Associates' DonorScape (312-372-4040)
  http://www.grenzebachglier.com
- Target America (703-383-6905) http://www.tgtam.com
- WealthEngine (301-215-5980)
  http://www.wealthengine.com

One of the key metrics used to identify the potential to increase donations is the strength of your major gift pipeline in relation to the actual number of all existing donors—big and small. Technology has refined past data mining practices for speed and focus, while the introduction of Internet-based research allows for detailed information on prospects in seconds. Now that research may be done quickly in both large scale prospect review (some large organizations will review hundreds of thousands or even millions of prospects at a time) and one by one through the internet, nonprofits of all sizes can afford prospect research. What once was available only to big nonprofits—national organizations, hospitals, universities, and museums—is now offered a la carte to nonprofits of all sizes and missions. The end result is that more money can be raised, in a more focused and cost-effective manner, through highly sophisticated development campaigns rather than "he-said, she-said" gossip and guessing about a person's giving potential.

Screening Research Methods

There are two basic methods, modeling and fact based, that efficiently segment large constituencies into groups who have major gift potential. The two approaches both involve a batch review of large groups of records and appending information to the constituent record. The differences are related to how the information is identified and what information is appended to the records.

The first approach is often called *modeling* and uses the following information:

- general data about the constituent that has been collected by the nonprofit organization including
  - constituent's name and address
  - business affiliation
  - prior giving
  - details about the relationship with the constituent: whether the constituent is a volunteer or board member, how many years the constituent has been involved with the organization, and whether the constituent has been approached for major gifts in the past
- demographic information related to where the constituent lives, how old they are, and their marital status

Modeling approaches then use this information as inputs to statistical applications that predict charitable potential.

The second method uses the same information the organization has collected about the constituent. Then, instead of demographic information, it uses factual, hard asset data that is publicly available such as the following:

"I'm very confident of the accuracy of the data generated by our new donor-profile software. It put us all in the 'least likely to make a major gift' category."

Source: Copyright © Carole Cable.

- real estate property records
- business affiliations
- luxury ownership (airplane or boats)
- stock holdings
- charitable and/or federal election campaign donations

Using this data, it is easy to identify potential net worth, disposable income, and charitable inclination. This information is used to identify major gift potential and can often verify prior major gift history.

Both methods can identify significant pools of prospects when applied to large constituencies. The main difference is that the modeling approach requires another step to identify the hard asset data used in the second approach because it just scores the prospects or provides a rating. The data mining process involves careful research and evaluation. Prospect research firms like WealthEngine (see Appendix 8–D for a client case study) have helped development efforts by enabling records to be screened against multiple databases for a comprehensive, detailed profile on a prospect. Previously, prospect researchers would spend hours researching an individual through many different databases—real estate, company information, press clippings—and subscribe to multiple data sources. Some of that still exists today but companies like WealthEngine link to multiple data sources so that prospect researchers can reduce research time and cut costs on expensive subscriptions. With Wealth-Engine, a researcher can screen an individual against more than 25 databases in seconds, print that profile for a development officer, and even map directions to the prospects' homes for a development officer's meeting.

Major gift cultivation almost always involves a significant investment of resources including time and money. See Exhibit 8–6 for data to help an organization build a major gift program. The ratings and scores provided as outcomes of the modeling process rarely establish the level of confidence required to make the investment: the hard asset data that is found during the fact-based data process provides this confidence. When a development officer can see that a prospect is an executive of a large business or has multiple real estate properties including a vacation home in a prominent area, they feel considerably more comfortable about approaching the prospect for a major gift.

If an organization does use electronic screening, it must have a plan for how to use the information it receives. For example, it could assign a manageable number of prospects that have received a high rating to development staff so that a personalized cultivation program can be designed for each prospect. Or it could include the top-rated prospects in a special direct mail/telemarketing program to increase annual giving. The critical thing is to do something with these data and not just have the report sit on a shelf! See Appendix 8–D for a case study using electronic screening.

> *If an organization does use electronic screening, it must have a plan for how to use the information it receives.*

Exhibit 8–6 Need for Cultivation of Major Gift Prospects

Recent broad-based analysis of the United States population has identified the number of American households with a net worth in excess of one million dollars to be in the range of five million to eight million individuals. This means that five to eight percent of American households fall within the high-net-worth category. While this is just one attribute that identifies major gift potential, the following table gives several examples of how this looks within nonprofits of various sizes.

Example	Constituency Size	Major Gift Prospects Based on Net Worth
Nonprofit 1	5,000 Donors	500 to 800
Nonprofit 2	25,000 Donors	1,250 to 2,000
Nonprofit 3	100,000 Donors	5,000 to 8,000
Nonprofit 4	1,500,000 Donors	75,000 to 120,000

Based on the table, you can see that there may be potential for major gifts within an organization but donations do not just fly in the door once you have found a prospect. According to Tony Glowacki, CEO, WealthEngine.com, donor cultivation is necessary and as you evaluate the workload and cost for pursuing donors, you should consider the following:

- It takes roughly six calls to get one visit with a prospect.
- Out of every eight prospects that are receptive to a visit, one will actually make a major gift.
- Five hundred prospects will result in roughly eighty visits.
- Eighty visits will equate to roughly twelve major gifts, or one a month.

Of course, there are many other variables that play into a major gift effort. However, if we were to use the above assumptions as an example, then it is critical that the five hundred prospects be good, solid prospects. Applying the above to the number of donors and prospects in Table 1, Glowacki says an organization can quickly identify the number of major gift officers that are needed to cultivate relationships with major gift prospects.

Source: Courtesy of WealthEngine.com, Bethesda, Maryland.

THE ROLE OF THE DEVELOPMENT OFFICER

Prospect research is an interactive process. Although prospect research staff members gather information from a variety of sources (such as those described in this chapter), volunteers, development staff, and chief executive officers need to share additional anecdotal information gathered through contacts with the prospects and/or individuals who may know the prospects. Even the most innocuous bit of information can sometimes be a lead. To ensure that such anecdotal information is not forgotten or lost, it is important to have a procedure for documenting visits and telephone calls. Using a form such as the Individual Prospect Briefing Report (Exhibit 8–7) is extremely important for the prospect research effort. Such reports should be a part of the individual's record in the organization's database. Exhibit 8–8 is a sample request for prospect research, and Exhibit 8–9 is a sample research template.

OTHER BENEFITS OF PROSPECT RESEARCH FOR AN ORGANIZATION

The focus of this chapter is on how prospect research helps the overall fundraising program. However, the prospect research process can bestow a number of added benefits, such as the following:

- identification of potential leadership
- identification of potential organizational volunteers
- identification of potential volunteers and corporate sponsors for special events
- more effective focusing of resources and efforts
- cultivation of current leaders and volunteers (gives them confidence in the organization and in their own abilities to help raise funds)

ETHICAL ISSUES AND CONFIDENTIALITY

Prospect research can lead board members and volunteers to raise a number of questions concerning ethics and confidentiality. As they review the informational files on identified prospects, they may ask if the organization has such files on

> *Prospect research can give rise to a number of questions concerning ethics and confidentiality.*

them and who has access to these files. It is important that the staff members answer truthfully, explaining that files containing information on individuals' involvement with and giving to the organization are important for the organization and that the compilation of these files is part of a researcher's or fundraiser's job. Whether or not they were involved in the research process, explain to them that all information gathered is found in the public domain. At times an organization must convince a concerned individual that prospect research does not constitute an invasion of privacy.

To assure board members and volunteers that prospect research is being conducted professionally, an organization should establish prospect research policies and procedures. The policies and procedures should include the following:

- Filing and database systems should be secure.
  1. Are the file cabinets locked?
  2. Who has access to the files?
  3. Who can view a prospect's database screens?
- Confidential materials should be marked "confidential" and be dated.
  1. Do you have a stamp marked "confidential"?
  2. Do you date materials and mark them "confidential"?
  3. Do you print trip reports and other confidential material on dark-colored paper so copies would be difficult to read?
- A distribution list for information should be set up.
  1. Do you have a set distribution list?
  2. Do you ask individuals to check off whether they have read materials and sent them on to next person on list?
- Any researcher should be granted access to only certain institutional records.
  1. Can the researcher have access to fundraiser files?
  2. Can the researcher contact volunteers directly concerning a prospect?
- Who does the research should be clearly designated.
  1. Are specific staff members assigned to do research?
  2. What role do support staff play?
  3. Are temporary help ever used?

It is important to gather and document only relevant information about a prospect and not report negative comments or personal information learned through a meeting, through a telephone call, or from an individual who knows the prospect that is not necessary for donor cultivation. To ensure that information is relevant and not negative, put your prospect research effort to this simple test. If a board member requested to see his or her file after a recent board meeting, would you feel comfortable having him or her read the file?

An important outcome of the growth that has occurred in the field of prospect research was the creation in 1987 of the APRA, an organization dedicated to serving the prospect research community. APRA, which has regional chapters, holds an annual national conference as well as many regional conferences and meetings hosted by its chapters. APRA developed a code of ethics in 1992 to assist prospect researchers and all fundraising professionals in dealing with the ethical dilemmas that arise in the course of their work. The code, which was revised in 2004, is based upon the belief that everyone has a fundamental right to privacy (see Appendix 8–E). For information about APRA, call 312-321-5196 or write to APRA, 401 N. Michigan Ave., Suite 2200, Chicago, IL 60611; visit their Web site at http://www.aprahome.org; or send an e-mail to info@aprahome.org.

Exhibit 8–7 Individual Prospect Briefing Report

CONFIDENTIAL

STAFF: Ellen Taylor, Director of Development, American University Law School
VOLUNTEER: Paul England, '88

REPORT DATE: 3/15/2008
PREPARED BY: Ellen Taylor

PROSPECT NAME: Mark Evans, '88

BUSINESS ADDRESS: Smith, Powell & Evans
320 S. Charles Street
Suite 1500
Baltimore, MD 21201

BUSINESS TELEPHONE: 301-665-1389

DATE OF MEETING: March 14, 2008

MEETING RECAP

Paul England (Class of 1988, Class Gift Chairman) and I visited with Mark in his office in downtown Baltimore. Paul and Mark were classmates and study group partners while in law school. They had kept in touch since graduation, getting together with their families and referring business to one another. Mark specializes in intellectual property law.

Since Mark and I had not met before, Mark spent a few minutes acquainting me with his background—where he was from, where he had gone to college, why he chose to attend AU's law school. Mark was originally from New York, had grown up on Long Island, and attended Hofstra University there. He decided to go to AU's law school because of its reputation, location in the nation's capital, and two college friends were planning to attend. I told Mark that I had, too, grown up on Long Island and that my brother-in-law had graduated from Hofstra in 1984. We talked about our shared experiences growing up on Long Island. Mark expressed goodwill toward the law school, stating that he had received an excellent education at the law school and remembered several professors he thought were excellent.

Paul explained to Mark that he was serving on the committee planning their class's twentieth reunion. In particular, he was chairing the class gift committee. Mark had received information from the law school regarding the date of the reunion weekend—September 20–21, 2008—and asked about the activities planned. Paul described the weekend's events, which included a program on Law and the Internet for which continuing legal education credits would be awarded to attendees. Mark was glad to hear the law school was sponsoring such a program. He told us he planned to attend the reunion.

Paul and I thanked Mark for his previous support for the law school, which was $500 a year. Paul asked Mark to consider increasing his gift this year to $5,000 in celebration of their twentieth reunion. The goal set for the Class of 1988 gift is $50,000. Mark agreed to do so and also offered to solicit other classmates for the class gift.

He mentioned several other Class of 1988 members:
Aaron Fisch—in New York working for a Wall Street firm
Sheryl Deckert—in Los Angeles in the corporate counsel office for Toyota Corporation
Meredith Janson—in Chicago in the investment area, working at Bear & Stearns
Tom Moran—in Miami in international law practice
Ellen Pace—in Baltimore—not practicing law; has family wealth
Mark agreed to call each one and encourage them to come to reunion weekend and to participate in the class gift campaign. I told him I would provide him with current addresses and telephone numbers and information he could send them about making a contribution.

FOLLOW-UP

1. Ellen will send Mark a note thanking him for meeting with Paul and herself and for his pledge. Include information and materials to be used for contacting classmates mentioned.
2. Add Mark Evans' name to reunion committee roster.
3. Paul to contact Mark in June to see how he is doing on his calls.

PERSONAL OBSERVATIONS

Mark spent over an hour with us. He has warm feelings for the law school. Mark is someone to cultivate and involve with the law school. Speak with faculty he mentioned in the intellectual property area to see if there are opportunities to invite Mark to speak to students. Ask him to become an Office of Career Services mentor.

Source: Courtesy of American University Office of Development, Washington, DC.

Exhibit 8–8 Prospect Research Checklist

Prospect Name

Prospect Address

Organization Resources
- ❏ Research file
- ❏ Database record
- ❏ Vice President for Development
- ❏ Other Development Staff

Telephone and Address Information
- ❏ Telephone directories (printed, Superpages)
- ❏ Real estate assessments
- ❏ Political contributions (Federal Election Commission, Tray)
- ❏ Other _____

Biographical Information
- ❏ Who's Who
- ❏ Standard & Poor's Executives
- ❏ Social Register
- ❏ Other _____

Wealth Indicators
- ❏ 10K Wizard
- ❏ Free Edgar
- ❏ EDGAR People Online
- ❏ Finance.yahoo.com
- ❏ Other _____

Real Estate Holdings
- ❏ Assessor _____
- ❏ Assessor _____
- ❏ Knowx.com _____
- ❏ Other _____

Business and Professional Associations
- ❏ Directory of Corporate Affiliations
- ❏ Dun & Bradstreet
- ❏ Hoover's
- ❏ Martindale Hubbell (lawyers)
- ❏ Standard & Poor's
- ❏ American Medical Association
- ❏ Other _____

Philanthropic Activities
- ❏ GuideStar
- ❏ Foundation Finder
- ❏ Prospect Research Online (PRO) Platinum (if a subscriber)
- ❏ Waltman Associates Donors CD
- ❏ Giving History to Organization _____

continues

General Searches
- ❏ Dialog
- ❏ LexisNexis
- ❏ Google
- ❏ Yahoo
- ❏ Altavista
- ❏ Notes: _____
  _____
  _____
  _____

Exhibit 8–9 Sample Research Template

CONFIDENTIAL

Research Profile Report

Name/Address:

Business Address:

Alternate Address:

Description of Business or Profession:

Salary and Income Information:

Securities:

Real Estate:

Career History:

Corporate Directorships:

Trustees (for Foundation profiles):

Civic and Community Activities:

Nonprofit Affiliations:

Social Affiliations:

Education:

Awards and Honors:

Family Information: (Family members and ages)

Potential Contacts:

Grants (for Foundation profiles):

Contributions:
    Nonprofit Organizations
    Political

Summary of Sources Used:

Listing of Key Articles:

A Case Study: Partnership in Philanthropy

BACKGROUND

Partnership in Philanthropy (PIP) is a nonprofit organization based in Chatham, NJ, with an operating budget of approximately $450,000. Since their inception in 1991, they have helped approximately 130 nonprofit organizations in their capacity-building efforts by providing affordable consultation services focusing on fundraising. Funders and consultants partner to make this happen, with consultants donating a portion of their time pro-bono to each consultancy.

In their tenth year of operation, they received a $25,000 challenge grant from the Hyde and Watson Foundation. One of the grant stipulations stated that they, too, would undergo a consultancy working closely with two development professionals (Maria Semple of The Prospect Finder and John McEwen of the NJ Theatre Alliance) to assess their current state of affairs and chart a course for the future.

THE NEED

Several themes emerged including the need to raise awareness amongst both the potential donors to PIP and the additional outreach to nonprofit organizations who could be helped by PIP's programs and services. Additional Board members would be needed to help with this endeavor and new committee structures would emerge.

A CALL TO ACTION

Maria Semple conducted prospect research of the surrounding communities to determine if there would be new foundations not yet solicited. Numerous family foundations were identified and a cultivation plan was formulated to reach out to these families. With the addition of several new Board members knowledgeable about the community and with ties in both the business and nonprofit world, Maria circulated lists and met with Board members for their input. Her data included the names of all trustees affiliated with family foundations in the community and this crucial step helped to identify networks amongst PIP's Board.

It quickly became apparent that PIP could reach out to more people simply by getting PIP's message out. Board members stepped forward to host small cultivation events at nearby country clubs or their homes. These early morning breakfast meetings enabled PIP to tell their story with words and pictures by incorporating success stories told by the nonprofits that were helped by PIP's services. These events were purely informational and no solicitations took place. Attendees were provided with a packet of information to read more about PIP and the costs associated with running a consultancy. Follow up after the event was done by staff and Board members to answer any additional questions and begin discussions on approaching the family foundation. Each of these family foundations also received an invitation to attend PIP's annual fundraising event, a dinner and theater event held at the New Jersey Performing Arts Center.

SUCCESSFUL OUTCOMES

By providing donors with the opportunity to understand PIP's programs and services and with careful follow-up, contributions to PIP increased after each event. One foundation funder who had been donating at modest levels increased their contribution tenfold. Another new relationship was formed with a funder interested in funding the expansion of PIP's services, in particular, their workshops offered to all nonprofits throughout the state. Without the careful research and concerted effort to form a relationship with these foundations, donations would have remained modest at best. These events also allowed PIP to find new Board members to further champion their cause.

Source: Courtesy of Maria Semple, The Prospect Finder, Bridgewater, New Jersey.

The Foundation Center's Regional Library/Learning Centers

The Foundation Center
79 Fifth Avenue (between 15th and 16th Streets), 2nd Floor
New York, NY 10003-3076
Phone: (212) 620-4230
http://www.foundationcenter.org/newyork

The Foundation Center
312 Sutter Street, Suite 606
San Francisco, CA 94108
Phone: (415) 397-0902
http://www.foundationcenter.org/sanfrancisco

The Foundation Center
1627 K Street, NW
Third Floor
Washington, DC 20036
Phone: (202) 331-1400
http://www.foundationcenter.org/washington

The Foundation Center
1422 Euclid Avenue, Suite 1600
Cleveland, OH 44115
Phone: (216) 861-1934
http://www.foundationcenter.org/cleveland

The Foundation Center
Suite 150, Hurt Building
50 Hurt Plaza
Atlanta, GA 30303-2914
Phone: (404) 880-0094
http://www.foundationcenter.org/atlanta

The Foundation Center's mission is to strengthen the nonprofit sector by advancing knowledge about U.S. philanthropy through its five regional library/learning centers and a national network of more than 275 Cooperating Collections. Established in 1956 and today supported by more than 600 foundations, the Foundation Center is the nation's leading authority on philanthropy, connecting nonprofits and the grantmakers supporting them to tools they can use and information they can trust. The Center maintains the most comprehensive database on U.S. grantmakers and their grants—a robust, accessible knowledge bank for the sector. The Center operates research, education, and training programs designed to advance philanthropy at every level. Its Web site, http://www.foundationcenter.org, offers a wealth of information and resources.

Researching Government Grants

Many nonprofit organizations rely on funding from the federal government to support their services and programs. Government grant support is very restrictive and has extensive reporting and management requirements; however, government grants can provide the largest dollar support for specific programs. Nonprofit organizations that are successful in receiving government grants regularly keep in contact with federal agency staffs to monitor any changes or reductions in federal programs. They continuously educate public officials about the needs that those programs help to meet while observing lobbying restrictions on nonprofit organizations.

Because of substantial cutbacks in government funding in recent years, many organizations that have received government funding now seek funds from private sources such as individuals, foundations, and corporations. However, depending on the type of nonprofit organization and the services it provides, government funding still may be available. Researching current government funding at the national, state, and local levels, therefore, is extremely important. Sources of information about government funding are now primarily available online.

GOVERNMENT RESOURCES FOR NONPROFITS

http://www.nonprofit.gov

This Web site helps to streamline the research process by linking nonprofits directly to FirstGov.gov for Nonprofits, an excellent and comprehensive resource for information about government funding. At this site, visitors will find:

- Agency-Specific Nonprofit Resources—links to every department's nonprofit resources page
- Grants, Loans and Other Assistance—federal, state and local funding directories
- Management and Operations Information for Nonprofits—general nonprofit business resources
- Tax Information for Nonprofits—tax-exempt statistics and IRS forms and publications

http://www.Grants.gov

This Web site allows organizations to electronically find and apply for more than $400 billion in federal grants. Grants.gov is the single access point for over 1,000 grant programs offered by all Federal grantmaking agencies.

Catalog of Federal Domestic Assistance— http://www.cfda.gov

This online catalog gives you access to a database of all Federal programs.

The Federal Register— http://www.gpoaccess.gov/fr

This Web site publicizes rules, proposed rules, and notices of federal agencies and organizations, as well as executive orders and other presidential documents. It is updated daily by 6 a.m. and is published Monday through Friday, except federal holidays.

PUBLICATIONS AND SUBSCRIPTION SERVICES

Guide to Federal Funding for Governments & Nonprofits

Published by Thompson Publishing Group, this guide has information on more than 750 federal grantmaking programs grouped by function, not by agency. Indexes and cross-references help provide information to special opportunities for funding. A one-year subscription priced at $399 includes the Guide, quarterly updates, twice-monthly Federal Grant Deadline calendars, and online access to the Grant Deadline Calendar database. (800-677-3789)

Federal and Foundation Assistance Monitor

Published by CD Publications, this twice a month, 16–18 page report features a comprehensive review of federal funding announcements categorized by subject matter, private grants, and legislative actions affecting community programs. A 12-month online subscription is $427; six-month online subscription is $235. (800-666-6380)

GOVERNMENT GRANT WRITING TIPS

Whether you are writing a letter of intent or a full proposal, think of the process in four phases:

1. Assess the Prospect
2. Create a Template
3. Flesh Out the Proposal
4. Assemble and Submit

Assess the Prospect

- In this phase you are making sure there is a good fit between your organization's mission and the government grant program.
- Research the funding announcements. Grant program summaries and full federal grant announcements can be found on http://www.grants.gov, and you can also place yourself on an e-mail list to receive updates on funding announcements.
- Make sure your organization meets the funder's eligibility requirements to receive a grant.
- Create a 1–2 page Prospect Summary on the funding program with key information:
  1. Brief description: types of projects being solicited by the funder (you can often just cut-and-paste key paragraphs straight from the announcement); make sure to include any stipulations which might be factors in deciding whether or not to proceed (e.g., geographic restrictions, required partnerships, etc.)
  2. Due date: for proposal or letter of intent (indicate if a letter of intent is required prior to submitting a full proposal). Make sure you have enough time to create a quality proposal and indicate when the due date is for the next round of grants if the announcement provides this.
  3. Funding Range: indicate either stated range or research typical range of previous fundings.
  4. Grant Period: indicate either stated range or research the range of previous projects.
  5. Proposed Approach: summarize in a few paragraphs the grant project being proposed by your organization.
- Circulate the Prospect Summary to help with the organizational review that will determine whether or not to proceed with the application.
- IMPORTANT: If you decide to apply for a federal grant, most agencies now require that applications be submitted electronically through the "grants.gov" system unless you obtain a waiver from the funding agency. Your organization must be pre-registered to submit electronically, and

the one-time process is a fairly complex one. To begin, log on to http://www.grants.gov and click on Get Registered. Start this early! It may take a week or two to get registered.

Create a Template

Read the *application instructions and guidelines carefully and follow them closely.* If submitting through the grants.gov system, you can download the application package and instructions following the steps provided on the grants.gov Web site. The first time you do this, you will also be instructed to download software for viewing the application package. All forms required to submit the application will be part of the downloaded package.

- *Create a template of the proposal narrative or letter of intent.* A template is your tool for crafting a proposal that conforms perfectly to the application instructions. To begin, the template should consist of all the main section headings and the sub-section headings *exactly as laid out in the funding announcement.*
- *Format the template* following all page setup requirements for margins or type size stipulated in the announcement. Make sure to number the pages.
- Indicate the *proposal page limitation* in colored font at the top of the first page as a tool that will later be deleted in the final draft.
- Using a colored font, *summarize from the announcement guidelines* the type of information that should be included under each section and sub-section heading (you might even just cut-and-paste these guidelines straight from the announcement). The colored font will keep the guidelines easily distinguishable from your proposal text.
- Be sure to look for any *buzz words and phrases* from the announcement to incorporate into your descriptive text.
- *If the announcement provides rating points for each section,* indicate these as part of each heading (this is important in deciding where to focus your energies when writing and editing the proposal). Delete these rating point notations before submitting the proposal.
- On the last page, *list the attachments* requested by the funding announcements (e.g., forms, timelines, resumes, budget justifications, organizational information). Also check for any materials (such as brochures, CDs) the announcement specifically requests not be sent, and indicate these as well.

Flesh Out the Proposal

- *Begin writing each section responding to the guidelines you have placed in colored font.* (Tip: keep the guidelines in place until you are sure you have provided all the information requested. It is also often helpful to keep these guidelines within drafts circulated for review, so people reviewing the drafts can see why you have organized the proposal and written the various sections the way you have.

- *Whenever possible, save time by cutting-and-pasting boiler-plate text from previous grant proposals* submitted by your organization, such as organizational background or descriptions of key personnel. Be careful to check the text for references to other grant projects. Also, go the extra mile and *modify even this boilerplate text so that it appears to be written expressly for this proposal.*

- *Don't worry too much about page limitations at this time.* When you are done fleshing out the proposal, then you can go back and edit to fit within the page limitations. It's easier when you see the whole proposal before you.

- *If the funding announcement provides rating points* for each section, use these to guide the editing process.

- As you finalize the proposal you can begin to *delete the colored guideline information.* This will give you a better idea of how the proposal is fitting within the page limitations. Government agencies are *notoriously unforgiving on proposals exceeding stated page limits,* and will ignore all pages over the limit. Some agencies will even reject the proposal outright.

- You can also delete from the last page your notes on the attachments required to complete the application package.

Assemble and Submit

- Make sure you are familiar with all the submission requirements and the procedure for providing attachments, especially for federal grants using the grants.gov system. Read this part of the announcement carefully.

- If you are not using the grants.gov system, should you mail, e-mail, overnight or courier your application? Read the funding announcement carefully, it will stipulate exactly how the application package is to be sent.

- Keep electronic and paper copies of proposals. Electronic copies are valuable for providing recyclable text for future proposals.

- If your application is not selected for funding, make sure to request an explanation. Most government agencies will provide such a debriefing, and the procedure is often explained as part of the rejection letter. This debriefing will often provide valuable information for the next time you submit a proposal.

Source: Courtesy of Robert A. Dodd, Consultant, Cape Elizabeth, Maine.

A Case Study: The Cleveland Clinic

This case study will review Cleveland Clinic's use of prospect research within its development department to qualify major gift prospects and support a capital campaign. Cleveland Clinic is located in Cleveland, Ohio, and is a non-profit, multispecialty academic medical center that integrates clinical and hospital care with research and education. The Clinic was founded in 1921 and today is one of the largest and most respected hospitals in the country, having most recently been named one of the top three hospitals in the country by *US News & World Report*. In 2005, Cleveland Clinic responded to more than 2.9 million patient visits.

WealthEngine began working with Cleveland Clinic in 2005 to improve the effectiveness of its comprehensive campaign. One of the key components to increasing the performance of any major gift effort is the effective application of prospect research technology. In the case of Cleveland Clinic, they had already been successful with previous major gift efforts but they knew that they had more potential and that by screening new patients on a regular basis they could boost the number of real prospects and ultimately, major gifts.

Cleveland Clinic currently has 45 major gift officers (MGOs) and 5 prospect researchers on staff. In 2005, each major gift officer had an average of 300 assigned prospects. Cleveland Clinic also had 3 million constituents. Given the number of constituents, Cleveland Clinic had the untapped potential to fill each MGO's pipeline and the capacity to add MGOs and increase the number of major gifts they receive.

Prior to contracting with WealthEngine to assist with the prospect research efforts, Cleveland Clinic had identified this potential and begun planning to increase the production of their major gift program through their comprehensive campaign. They had two target groups—existing donors and new patients. Both groups had a direct connection to the organization but because of the massive size of the donor and patient lists, a screening was the best method to narrow the focus. Think about it this way, if you had three million potential donors, where would you start? For Cleveland Clinic and most other large nonprofits with millions of prospects, unless you use prospect research to qualify lists and define giving potential, it is like finding a needle in a haystack.

Some nonprofits only focus on existing donors and community leaders (local celebrities, politicians, company executives, etc.) when soliciting major gifts. Yet they may be missing an important group of potential donors—their clients. For education groups it's their alumni, for arts groups it's their ticket holders, and for health care organizations, it's their patients. Cleveland Clinic is savvy in their development efforts because they include both existing donors of all sizes (small donors often have the potential to give more), community leaders and new patients.

CLEVELAND CLINIC'S SCREENING PROGRAM

The Cleveland Clinic sought to use the fact-based approach and purchased WealthEngine's FindWealth Screening Service. This method uses the information the organization has collected about the constituent and then seeks factual, hard asset data that is publicly available such as

- Real estate property records
- Business affiliations
- Luxury ownership (airplane or boats)
- Stock holdings
- Charitable and/or federal election campaign donations

Using this data it is easy to identify potential net worth, disposable income, and charitable inclination. This information is used to identify major gift potential and can often verify prior major gift history.

The next step for them was how to implement the process. They identified these components:

- The pool of constituents that would be reviewed
- The size and scope of the effort (how many development officers would be involved and how many prospects each would need)
- The time frame of the effort (when would it start, how long would it last, etc.)
- Criteria for evaluation

After identifying this information, Cleveland Clinic decided on the following FindWealth Screening phases:

Phase 1: Review existing records

- Review 330,000 records in one batch
- Focus on existing donors and patients

Phase 2: Refresh data and review new patient lists

- Review 134,000 records in two batches
  — Refresh data on existing donor records
- Review 2,000 records per week
  — Provide new patient lists

Phase 3: Refine existing data and review new patient lists

- Review 10,000+ records per week
  — Rescreen recurring patients and flag them so they are not rescreened for 36 months. No time was wasted on old patients who have never revisited or donated to the clinic. Those who have regular appointments at the clinic are given priority. Focus on enhancing the prioritization of major gift prospects by adding sorting methods.

In addition to the batch screening, Cleveland Clinic also uses WealthEngine's online WebService Research Center for quick individual review. With the WebService, they can look up an individual, another nonprofit organization, foundation or company at any time, from any location. Often, the online tool is used prior to a donor meeting to see if there is any new hard asset information available. It is also handy when identifying new prospects that may be attending a major event or after a board or staff member has met with someone they think might be of interest. Online research is often bought via an annual subscription (as with WealthEngine) or by the number of look-ups (ex. 500 or 5,000 per contract) rather than on a case-by-case basis.

For Cleveland Clinic, they used the WebService Research Center to manage their research time. The tool helped them validate, verify, and add to their existing knowledge about a prospect. They used the tool to

- Determine how much time to invest in researching a prospect. Either they will do a quick look-up and give the report to the requesting development officer or plan further research on the prospect (known as a full profile)
- Research individuals and companies based on
  — Special event attendance
  — Suggestions from a board member or volunteer (peer screenings)
  — Interest derived from local news coverage

Health care organizations like Cleveland Clinic have the added challenge of conducting research in a manner that respects HIPAA regulations. Prior to HIPAA, smart research

departments would look at where their patients had been seen (i.e., they had heart surgery vs. an emergency room visit) for targeted gift solicitation. Today, prospect research is even more important because it identifies major gift prospects based on who they are regardless of their treatment while complying with all HIPAA requirements for patient privacy.

IMPLEMENTATION

Cleveland Clinic's first phase started in 2005, with the second two initiated in 2006. For the first batch screening, the schedule involved the following tasks:

No.	Task	Time Involved
1	Identify pool of prospects	2 weeks
2	Create file containing constituent information and send to WealthEngine	4 weeks
3	Perform data mining on constituent file	1 day
4	Prepare and deliver results of data mining	2 weeks
5	Schedule and deliver training	Within two weeks of file submission

WealthEngine training covered the following:

- Data mining process
- Data delivery tools
- Use of the tools
- Interpretation of the results
- Strategies for implementing the results

The data mining process involved taking the constituent information and matching it to the hard asset data found in the WealthEngine database. The information found was then appended to the constituent record. Along with this information, significant ratings and scores helped provide for a higher level of interpretation of the results. The results were delivered in a proprietary software application that has extensive sorting, filtering and reporting capabilities. These capabilities were covered in the training which also instructed the prospect researchers on how to look at the new data and use it to determine potential major gift prospects. Finally, using the new data, the researchers were given various options to consider when applying the results to begin major gift cultivation. Prospect researchers can also import the data into their own donor database through an importation procedure.

CONCLUSION

Success is seen in how many new major gift prospects are found through the regular screening and sorting of donors and patients. At print time, phase two and three had identified more than 10,000 strong major gift prospects. From a batch screening of 70,000 records in phase two, more than 1,000 individuals were identified as having the potential to give a major gift of at least $250,000 or more. Cleveland Clinic doesn't think about needles in a haystack. Instead, they focus on using technology and factual, hard asset data to streamline their development efforts and increase major gifts.

Says Kassy Mosier Wyman, Director of Research and Prospect Management at Cleveland Clinic, "Using WealthEngine's data mining services we have the great problem of not having enough researchers or Development Officers for the number of prospects that have been identified. But, more importantly, while we have significant opportunity to increase our development efforts, we're not overwhelmed by possibilities—the end result is that we can narrow our scope and focus on those who have the best potential to give and in a major way. That means we are more efficient in our research and development, and ultimately, more successful in securing major donations to support and expand our goals for patient care, research, and education."

Next steps for Cleveland Clinic include adding more ways to filter the data results, to pinpoint top prospects, and fine tuning the methods for downloading the data to their donor database, to increase access and reporting functions. For them, and those that use data mining for prospect research, the technology has helped them streamline energy and better use resources, which is something every donor can feel good about.

Source: Courtesy of WealthEngine.com and the Cleveland Clinic, Cleveland, Ohio.

Statement of Ethics

APRA Statement of Ethics

Copyright © 2004 APRA
Revised August 2004

Association of Professional Researchers for Advancement (APRA) members shall support and further the individual's fundamental right to privacy and protect the confidential information of their institutions. APRA members are committed to the ethical collection and use of information. Members shall follow all applicable national, state, and local laws, as well as institutional policies, governing the collection, use, maintenance, and dissemination of information in the pursuit of the missions of their institutions.

Code of Ethics

Advancement researchers must balance an individual's right to privacy with the needs of their institutions to collect, analyze, record, maintain, use, and disseminate information. This balance is not always easy to maintain. To guide researchers, the following ethical principles apply:

I. Fundamental Principles

A. Confidentiality

Confidential information about constituents (donors and non-donors), as well as confidential information of the institutions in oral form or on electronic, magnetic, or print media are protected in order to foster a trusting relationship between the constituent and the institution. This means that the information is not available for anyone except development professionals, and their agents, to see.

B. Accuracy

Advancement researchers shall record all data accurately. Such information shall include attribution. Data analyses and their by-products should be without personal prejudices or biases.

C. Relevance

Advancement researchers shall seek and record only information that is relevant to the cultivation, solicitation, and/or stewardship strategy with the prospect.

D. Self-responsibility

Advancement researchers often play a significant role in developing and monitoring advancement department policies on information storage and confidentiality. It is important that advancement researchers lead by example. First, advancement researchers should develop clear policies and procedures for the prospect research department on the collection, storage, and distribution of constituent information and analysis. Second, when possible, advancement researchers should advocate for the development and adoption of institution wide ethics guidelines and privacy policies which are at least as complete as the APRA Statement of Ethics.

E. Honesty

Advancement researchers shall be truthful with regard to their identities and purpose, and the identity of their institutions during the course of their work.

F. Conflict of Interest

Advancement researchers should be careful to avoid conflicts of interest. Prospect research consultants should have explicit policies which outline how they will deal with conflicts of interest between clients. Advancement researchers who are employed full-time for an institution and also perform consulting services should be certain that the consulting services do not represent a conflict of interest with their primary employer.

II. Standards of Practice

A. Collection

1. The collection of information should be done lawfully, respecting applicable laws and institutional policies.

2. Advancement researchers should be experts on the reliability of sources (print, electronic, and otherwise), as well as the sources utilized by third parties to gather information on their behalf.

3. Advancement researchers should not evade or avoid questions about their affiliations or purpose when requesting information in person, over the phone, electronically, or in writing. It is recommended that requests for public information be made on institutional stationery and that these requests clearly identify the requestor.

4. Advancement researchers should use the usual and customary methods of payment or reimbursement for products or services purchased on behalf of their institutions.

5. Advancement researchers who are employed full-time for an institution and also perform consulting services should develop clear understandings with their primary employers about the use of the employers financial and human resources.

B. Recording and Maintenance

1. Advancement researchers shall present information in an objective and factual manner; note attribution, and clearly identify information which is conjecture or analysis. Where there is conflicting information, advancement researchers should objectively present the multiple versions and state any reason for preferring one version over another.

2. Advancement researchers should develop security measures to protect the constituent information to which they have access from access by unauthorized persons. When possible, these measures should include locking offices and/or file cabinets and secure and frequently change passwords to electronic databases. Advancement researchers should also advocate institution-wide policies which promote the careful handling of constituent information so that constituent privacy is protected. The use of constituent databases over a wireless Internet connection is not recommended.

3. Where advancement researchers are also responsible for donor giving records and their maintenance, they should develop security measures to provide very limited access to the giving records of anonymous donors. Access to these records should be limited to only those staff who need the information to successfully cultivate, solicit, or steward said donor.

4. Where there is no existing case law which outlines clearly the rights of a donor in accessing advancement files (paper and/or electronic), advancement researchers should work with their institutions legal counsel to develop an institution specific policy regarding this access. This policy should be put in writing, approved by the President/CEO, and distributed to any advancement professionals who might field a request for such access.

5. When electronic or paper documents pertaining to constituents must be disposed, they should be disposed in a fashion which lessens the danger of a privacy breach. Shredding of paper documents is recommended.

C. Use and Distribution

1. Researchers shall adhere to all applicable laws, as well as to institutional policies, regarding the use and distribution of confidential constituent information. Careful consideration should be given to the use of electronic mail and faxes for the delivery of constituent information.

2. Constituent information is the property of the institution for which it was collected and shall not be given to persons other than those who are involved with the cultivation or solicitation effort or those who need that information in the performance of their duties for that institution.

3. Constituent information for one institution shall not be taken to another institution.

4. Research documents containing constituent information that is to be used outside research offices shall be clearly marked *confidential.*

5. Vendors, consultants, and other external entities shall understand and agree to comply with the institution's confidentiality policies before gaining access to institutional data.

6. Advancement researchers, with the assistance of institutional counsel and the advancement chief officer, should develop policies which address the sharing of directory information on their constituents with other institutions. Constituent requests to withhold directory information should be respected in all cases.

Copyright © 2004 by the Association of Professional Researchers for Advancement.

Source: Courtesy of the Association of Professional Researchers for Advancement, Chicago, Illinois.

Chapter 9

The Use of Personal Solicitation in Major Gift Fundraising

CHAPTER OUTLINE

- What Is a Major Gift?
- The Importance of a Major Gifts Program
- Elements of a Major Gifts Program
- Evaluation of Prospects
- How to Get Started
- Managing the Solicitation Process
- Why Major Donors Give
- Getting Involved—What Motivates Today's New Philanthropists
- An Investment Model of Giving

- An Update on Venture Philanthropy
- Ways to Involve and Cultivate Relationships with Prospects
- The Successful Solicitation—Overcoming the Fear of Asking
- The Successful Solicitation Visit
- How to Say Thank You
- Ways to Recognize Major Donors
- Stewardship—The Practice That Ensures Future Major Gifts

KEY VOCABULARY

- Cultivation
- Development Audit
- Donor-Advised Fund
- Entrepreneurial Philanthropist
- Face-to-Face Solicitation
- Identification
- Research
- Social Entrepreneur
- Stewardship
- Venture Philanthropist
- Venture Philanthropy

WHAT IS A MAJOR GIFT?

What constitutes a major gift varies by size and type of nonprofit organization. For large institutions like universities or hospitals, a major gift may be considered a gift of $100,000 or more. For medium-sized organizations, $25,000 or more is a major gift. And, for smaller, community-based organizations, a gift of $1,000 or more is defined as a major gift. No matter what the definition of a major gift may be, it is a gift that is most commonly secured through the use of personal solicitation.

THE IMPORTANCE OF A MAJOR GIFTS PROGRAM

For an organization to be successful in fundraising, a major gifts program is critically important. At one time, experts believed that 80 percent of an organization's fundraising support came from only 20 percent of its donors. However, results of recent capital campaigns conducted by nonprofit organizations reveal that nearly 90 percent of the campaigns' total goals came from only 5 to 10 percent of the donors. Regardless of whether the amount is 20 percent or 10 percent, it is clear that major gifts play a significant role in an organization's success. These gifts are contributed by individuals, foundations, and corporations. This chapter focuses on major gifts from individuals. Chapters 10 and 11 address corporate and foundation giving.

In the early years of its development program, an organization may not yet be ready to embark on an individual major gifts program. It is important to first establish a broad base of support using mail, the telephone, and special events. These methods enable an organization to educate the public about its mission, program, and services while soliciting support. Enhanced visibility for the organization is an added benefit to the broader-based fundraising activities. To evaluate whether an organization is ready to launch a comprehensive major gifts program, an organization should analyze its current situation including board and staff leadership, fundraising and public relations efforts, and organizational planning and management. The development audit discussed in Chapter 5 is one way to evaluate readiness. If an organization chooses (and it should at the correct time) to launch a major gifts effort, it is important to invest adequate time, resources, and personnel so that programs and strategies that invite major gifts will be in place. See the checklist in Exhibit 9–1 to assess an organization's readiness for a major gifts program.

ELEMENTS OF A MAJOR GIFTS PROGRAM

One cannot stress enough that fundraising is a process. It is a series of steps and actions that hopefully will lead to a contribution for an organization. This is certainly the case in raising major gifts. Therefore, the necessary steps include the following:

- Identification. First identify individuals capable of making a major gift to the organization. Keep in mind that there are major gift prospects among your current donors. Review and analyze current donor data in order to identify length of time giving, how much they have contributed cumulatively over the years, what specific programs they supported, and how they have been involved with the organization. See Exhibit 9–2 for some tips on finding new major gift prospects in your database and in the community.
- Research. Conduct research on an individual's family, background, interests, and financial situation to prioritize capability and inclination of giving. The wealth identification screening process covered in Chapter 8 offers information on current donors that can help to identify major gift prospects.

Exhibit 9–1 Readiness Checklist for a Major Gifts Program

Does the organization have?
- ❑ a strategic plan
- ❑ a compelling case for support
- ❑ a budget describing programs and services that donors can understand
- ❑ major donors on the board
- ❑ influential people from the community involved
- ❑ a development committee focusing on major gifts
- ❑ a system of gift clubs to upgrade donors
- ❑ a program to recognize donors
- ❑ ways to cultivate donors
- ❑ a public relations plan
- ❑ professional looking materials

With a majority of these items already in place and plans to add others as needed, an organization indeed is ready to launch a major gifts program.

Exhibit 9–2 Tips for Finding Major Gift Prospects

1. Find out who is giving major gifts to other organizations by reviewing other organizations' annual reports and development-related materials, as well as reading donor recognition plaques displayed in public spaces.
2. Do regular mailings to professional advisers (estates and trusts attorneys, CPAs, financial planners, stockbrokers) about your organization and its mission that they can share with their clients.
3. See if staff, board, and volunteers know any of the individuals and board members affiliated with those foundations that do not accept unsolicited proposals in order to communicate with them about your organization.
4. Learn who the business leaders are in your area by subscribing to area business journals, joining the Chamber of Commerce, and visiting corporate Web sites to find the names of senior executives.
5. Ask your current major donors to send letters to people they know who might be interested in your organization's mission.
6. Convert those attending your special events into donors and major donors by capturing contact information so that your organization can communicate regularly with them in the future.

- Cultivation. Once identified, develop strategies to involve those individuals in the organization so that they will choose to make a major gift.
- Solicitation. At the appropriate time, a specially selected individual or individuals will invite the donor to make a major investment in the organization.
- Stewardship. Acknowledge, thank, and recognize the donor's generosity. Good stewardship often results in additional future gifts.

Since the first two steps, identification and research, were covered in Chapter 8, we will focus primarily on the remaining steps, cultivation, solicitation, and stewardship in this chapter.

EVALUATION OF PROSPECTS

In Chapter 8, on prospect research, we discussed the methods to use when moving an individual from "suspect" to "prospect" status. One of the methods covered involved screening and rating sessions using key volunteers and staff. The information shared at these sessions is used to evaluate an individual's capacity or current inclination to give to a specific organization. Prospect rating forms are useful tools in this process. These forms range from simple to complex depending on an organization. A common feature of all is the use of a weighting factor to distinguish which criteria are most important when determining ability to give. Exhibit 9–3 is an example of a prospect rating form.

Researching and evaluating prospects is a sensitive task, especially for the first-time volunteer committee member. Questions such as "Isn't this an invasion of privacy?" or comments to the

Exhibit 9–3 Prospect Rating Form

> 1. Rate each prospect 1–5 in each category (5 is highest)
> 2. Multiply by "weight"
> 3. Add totals

Prospect _____

Date _____

Criteria	Score (1–5) ×	Weight	Total
Common Interest		2	
Financial Ability		3	
Commitment to Philanthropy		1	
Commitment to Our Organization		3	
Linkage with Our Organization		1	
Time Window		3	
Personality		1	
Past Solicitation Success		2	
Common Politics/Philosophy		1	

Grand Total
(Highest Score = 85)

Source: Courtesy of Office of University of Advancement, University of Arkansas, Fayetteville, Arkansas.

> *Researching and evaluating prospects is a sensitive task, especially for the first-time volunteer committee member.*

effect that a volunteer is uncomfortable sharing information about people he or she knows must be addressed. In Chapter 8, we discussed the need for organizations to adopt policies and procedures to ensure that issues of confidentiality and ethics are addressed. However, when faced with these types of questions and comments, an organization must be prepared to show how the rating of gifts plays an integral role in the fundraising planning process. Gift rating helps the organization do the following:

- Set a realistic fundraising goal. The process of gift rating will assess how many gifts at various levels can be anticipated and how that relates to the total of gifts needed to reach the fundraising goal. If the representation needed is not demonstrated, an organization will need to re-evaluate its goal.
- Use volunteers more effectively. By doing gift rating, volunteers can make specific requests based on research and information, which enables them to be more successful in their efforts.
- Establish specific donor opportunities for giving. Knowing the range of gifts needed, an organization can establish dif-

ferent opportunities for support to meet the needs and interests of donors as well as those of the organization.
- Reduce the organization's cost of raising money. The more closely the staff and volunteers can come to the most appropriate level for each donor, the more likely they will be successful in soliciting a gift, thereby enabling staff and volunteers to pursue other prospects in accordance with the campaign timetable.

HOW TO GET STARTED

Once an organization has identified a pool of qualified major gift prospects, beginning the solicitation might seem an overwhelming challenge. Chapter 14, which focuses on capital campaigns, describes how the campaign timetable dictates the schedule and program of major gift solicitations. Here we will discuss how a major gift solicitation program fits into an organization's annual development plan.

How many prospects with whom to work, at the start of the major gifts program, depends on the number of staff working in this area (development staff, CEO, and any other organizational staff). A one-person development office or small nonprofit should keep the number of prospects to between 25 and 30 people. A development office with 2 to 4 development professionals and administrative help could handle 100 to 150 prospects. It is best to select a manageable number of prospects for whom specific cultivation and solicitation strategies will be developed. Keep in mind that it could take from 18 to 24 months, even up to 36 months, to successfully close a major gift, depending on the prospective donor and size of gift. Staff should designate specific time on their calendar to work with these prospects and the volunteers involved in the strategy. The volunteers are specially selected because they know the prospects and the organization. They can include board members, the chief executive officer (CEO), or other major donors. Each individual prospect should have a file that contains a copy of a research report and any other materials collected on that prospect. As the solicitation process proceeds this file also should include briefing reports on telephone conversations and meetings. It is very important to record any and all contacts with the prospect and key volunteers in the fundraising database. These contacts also can be referred to as "moves." Many of the donor database systems on the market today have the capability to track contacts (moves), meetings, and follow-up activities as needed. It is critical for success that staff dedicate the time necessary to enter information in the database on prospect and donor contacts regularly. Too often, key donor information is lost due to staff turnover.

As a solicitation strategy is developed, gift objectives will be identified for the organization and prospective donor. Ways to involve a prospect in an organization—the cultivation process—need to be a part of the solicitation plan. Later in this chapter, we will present some suggestions regarding the types of cultivation activities that are available to organizations. Keep track, on a regular basis, the number of moves, their frequency, and by whom they were done. As solicitations are completed, new prospects from the pool can be added following the steps described previously.

MANAGING THE SOLICITATION PROCESS

Significant time and effort on the part of the development professional is spent "managing" the solicitation process. This includes keeping track of contacts and visits by the CEO, board chair, or volunteer; documenting these contacts; ensuring that the appropriate follow-up is completed; and planning the next step in the solicitation strategy. It is recommended that 80 percent of staff and volunteer time be spent on major gift prospects who are or have been donors, with 20 percent of time devoted to new prospects. To keep up with this process, a type of tracking form or report is needed. Exhibits 9–4 and 9–5 present two versions of such a form.

WHY MAJOR DONORS GIVE

To be successful in securing major gifts or gifts at any level, a non-profit organization needs to know why people give and, especially, what motivates certain individuals to make major gifts to hospitals and retirement communities, universities and colleges, schools, social service agencies, arts organizations, or to any other nonprofit organization. An organization may want to collect its own data by surveying its donors regarding why they support that organization.

> To be successful in securing major gifts or gifts at any level, a nonprofit organization needs to know why people give.

A recent study conducted for Bank of America by the Center on Philanthropy at Indiana University examined the giving motivations and habits of individuals with incomes greater than $200 thousand or net worth in excess of $1 million. These "high net-worth" individuals are the wealthiest 3.1 percent of the U.S. population responsible for nearly two-thirds of individual chari-

Exhibit 9–4 A Simple Type of Tracking Form

Sherman L. Lane
365 Mandel Road
Oceanside, NY 11755
516-221-0906 (H)

Date	Plan	Date	Action
1/15	Bob Gates to talk with Sherman Lane's sister about his interest in North Shore Hospital.	1/31	Eleanor Smith (Sherman's sister) told Bob that Sherman is in Florida now. She plans to see him in mid-February when she goes to Florida.
1/31	Bob Gates plans to speak to Dr. Hart, head of the cardiac unit, about his relationship with Sherman Lane.	2/3	Dr. Hart tells Bob he recently saw Sherman for a checkup and had a good conversation with him about the hospital. Knows he is appreciative of the care he got at North Shore.
2/5	Dr. Hart will set up a meeting with Lane and Gates in April when Lane returns from Florida. Meantime, call Eleanor Smith the end of February when she returns from Florida.		

Exhibit 9–5 Solicitation Tracking Report

Prospect
Irma Reckman
3765 Sycamore Place
Chandler, AZ 85224
602-839-2255

Key volunteer
Jane Morgan, Board Chair

Secondaries
Ellen Hayes, Executive Director, YWCA of Maricopa County
Marcia Stone, board member
Alicia Patterson, Y-Teen volunteer

Staff Manager
Susan Gaumont

Gift Objective
$10,000 for Y-Teen leadership program

Plan
Irma is a member of the YWCA Board of Directors; is very interested in youth and the Y-Teen program. Plan is to solicit $10,000 to fund the upcoming Y-Teen leadership conference.

Recent Events
9/3—Jane Morgan and Alicia Patterson met with Irma to discuss future planning for the Y-Teen program. They briefed her on the preliminary plans for the leadership conference and the cost of the conference. Irma expressed interest in helping and asked to see a detailed budget.
9/17—Ellen Hayes and Alicia Patterson met with Irma to go over the budget and solicit ideas for community leaders to invite to participate in the conference. Irma made some suggestions about the budget.

Follow-up
Schedule a meeting the week of 10/4 for Jane Morgan and Ellen Hayes to solicit Irma for her gift.

---

table giving totaling $126 billion in 2005 (Center on Philanthropy, 2007).

Key findings included the following:

- "Giving back" is more important than "leaving a legacy."
- Wealthy donors report that even major tax policy changes would not impact their giving.
- Eighty percent reported being volunteers, while two-thirds had done some kind of active fundraising.
- Entrepreneurs gave on average $232,206 in 2005, more than twice the average amount of $109,745 contributed by people with inherited wealth.
- High net-worth donors are more likely to consult fundraisers and nonprofit personnel than other advisors when making giving decisions.
- Charitable giving increased over the last five years.
- Wealthy donors support a broader array of causes than donors in general.
- Nearly 75 percent of households reported they would give more to charity if organizations spent more on helping constituents and less on overhead.

Another report, *2007 U.S. Trust Survey of Affluent Americans,* recently released by U.S. Trust, a wealth-management company in New York, polled individuals with assets of $5 million or more. It found that nearly 90 percent of the richest Americans say the primary reason they give to charity is that they believe in specific causes and have a desire to give back to society. More than 80 percent of affluent parents hoped to instill in their children social responsibilities associated with the importance of philanthropy and charitable giving. We learned that wealthy Americans also said that accountability and transparency at nonprofits are major factors in deciding whether they would increase their charitable giving. Other findings included 73 percent said it was paramount that they hold the leaders of a charity in high esteem, while 61 percent said they would consider increasing their donations if they had greater access to information about a charity's performance and its use of donations. Nearly 7 in 10 respondents said that they plan to leave some of their assets to charity. These studies and reports help nonprofit organizations understand the motivations and behaviors of major donors; however, there is no substitute for getting to know an individual major gift prospect's own motivations for giving. See Appendix 9–A for the personal story of one family and their major giving.

GETTING INVOLVED—WHAT MOTIVATES TODAY'S NEW PHILANTHROPISTS

While recognition, peer pressure, community responsibility, guilt, immortality, and other traditional motivations are still prevalent today, it is important to understand that the new generation of donors, in which women are playing an increased role, possesses some new motivations that organizations must learn. Thirty-something and forty-something millionaires have been, for the most part, significant creators of the ideas, products, and services that have made them wealthy. They are used to being involved in the start-up phase—creating, implementing, and evaluating. They are results driven and have succeeded by being in control. In some communities, the younger members of wealthy families are directing their money toward programs with higher social impact rather than those with high social recognition. They tend to support grassroots organizations that do not have a natural constituency of support rather than well-established organizations that benefit middle- and upper-class people in their communities.

It is the same motivation—getting involved—that drives many emerging women philanthropists. With the growth in their economic power, women have greater potential for major contributions in their own right. Almost half of the wealth in this country is now controlled by women. Increasing numbers of women are earning more and holding managerial positions. But the most significant factor impacting women's philanthropy is the number of women starting their own companies, three times the rate of men, and the different attitudes women entrepreneurs display regarding happiness, self-fulfillment, achievement, challenge, and helping others. All the studies of women's philanthropy distinguish it from men's philanthropy based on the fact that women get involved first and then give. They are less apt to respond to peer pressure and more likely to follow their heart. The younger generation of donors share some of that same profile and are less apt to give for recognition only. In fact, some choose to do their giving anonymously.

AN INVESTMENT MODEL OF GIVING

In general, we find that more and more donors today look at their gifts as investments in nonprofit organizations. This is certainly true among many people of wealth and affluence, especially those under 40 years of age, who are creating their own foundations with well-defined purposes. They want more hands-on involvement with the organizations they choose to support. These new philanthropists use an investment model for charitable decision making and often seek out organizations they wish to support. The "entrepreneurial philanthropist" believes in grassroots development and helping nonprofit organizations

work toward greater self-sufficiency. Their contributions include more than just dollars, as they contribute their expertise, time, and effort. A nonprofit organization must be prepared to accept gifts made through this investment model, for it positions the donor in a greater "hands-on" role within the organization and brings greater accountability for results and solutions.

AN UPDATE ON VENTURE PHILANTHROPY

It has been more than 10 years since a new approach to philanthropy related to the investment model, *venture philanthropy*, was created. Social Venture Partners (SVP) in Seattle became the leader in the field in 1997 when it raised $2.5 million from 250 donors, most of them young high-tech entrepreneurs in the Seattle area, who also shared their business and professional expertise with social service and educational organizations. Since then, the success of the SVP model has inspired the founding of more than 23 affiliates worldwide in the United States, Canada, Mexico, and Japan.

Many early supporters of venture philanthropy saw it as a new effort to support innovation among charities, to support infrastructure needs, and to demand tangible results from grantees. Since its creation, venture philanthropy has led some traditional foundations, such as the Edna McConnell Clark Foundation, to shift from giving out grants to providing a greater level of support and guidance to a smaller number of organizations.

Venture philanthropy differs from traditional philanthropy in the following ways:

- Provides not only financial resources but also management assistance and other resources that for-profit executives have come to rely upon.
- Features relationships between the grantmaker and nonprofit partner that are more of an active, involved partnership than solely a funding relationship.
- Covers a longer time period than do typical foundation grants.
- Focuses on helping to build and strengthen organizations of its nonprofit partners, not on the development of new programs.
- Helps its nonprofit partners establish and track outcomes and use this information as a basis for assessing the progress of their investments.

Venture Philanthropy Partners (VPP), founded in 2000 to serve children and youth of low-income families in the Greater Washington, DC, National Capital Region, produced a summary report of its first five years (http://www.vppartners.org/impact) that revealed positive results for its investee partners (nonprofit organizations). However, the report also shared what VPP had learned: the insights, adjustments, and lessons gained and made since the beginning. Some of those lessons learned included the following:

- Rather than the original target of investing in younger, entrepreneurial social innovators with workable solutions who wanted to grow their organizations, VPP later shifted its focus to include more established nonprofits—those with the potential for transformational change and the need to sustain, improve, or scale their organizations—because it would have a greater impact on the region.
- Lasting change and growth in the nonprofit sector requires even more capital and more time than envisioned.
- VPP was initially naïve in understanding the time it would take and impediments that needed to be overcome in establishing a trusted advisor relationship with investees. A successful relationship is based on respect, transparency, shared learning, and mutually aligned expectations and accountability.
- VPP came to realize that one of its greatest assets was its regional focus and understanding and ability to navigate the region's formal and informal systems: political, social, economic, regulatory, and educational. VPP was able to circumvent impediments, span boundaries, expand into new areas of the region, form precedent-setting partnerships, and forge cross-sector partnerships and new relationships.
- VPP learned from and compensated for early mistakes, which led to changes in how VPP was built, the seasoned executive-level experience and skill required by its approach, the way it conducted its programs, and a new respect it developed for the accomplishments of those in the nonprofit and philanthropy sectors who came before VPP and laid the groundwork for its approach.

This learning not only makes VPP a better organization, but it will greatly influence what it will do going forward and the kind of impact it can have on the nonprofits, children, the region, and the field. After a period of building its capacity and reflecting on lessons learned, VPP is currently raising a second $50 million for a new fund.

Even though young millionaires, women, venture philanthropists, and social entrepreneurs may approach their philanthropy differently from other groups, the basic tenets of building relationships through research and cultivation (information and involvement) described below still prove true. A nonprofit organization must identify ways to reach these new philanthropists, educate and excite them about the organization and its plans, and involve them in the organization's future.

WAYS TO INVOLVE AND CULTIVATE RELATIONSHIPS WITH PROSPECTS

The cultivation process is one of the most creative pieces in the development of the solicitation strategy. First, an organization should review its annual calendar to see what upcoming events, publications, and programs could be included in a general cultivation program. Next, new opportunities suited for a specific

prospect need to be created. The list that follows contains types of events and publications that are excellent cultivation activities for groups of donors.

- invitations to special events
- open house events for donors to visit the organization's facility
- volunteer opportunities
- participation at seminars, conferences, and programs
- receptions and dinners
- invitations to serve on advisory councils, ad hoc committees, and task forces
- newsletters
- magazines and journals
- annual reports
- news clippings and press releases
- brochures
- Web site

Many of these same events and publications also can be used when developing a specific prospect's solicitation strategy. Use a prospect's specific interests and skills to create other opportunities for involving him or her in the work of the organization. The following is a sampling of the kinds of cultivation activities you can create for a specific prospect. Ask the prospect to do the following:

- volunteer for an advisory council or special committee
- offer advice
- participate on a program panel
- speak at a class, annual meeting, or special program
- host an event in his or her home or office
- join the board
- attend a private dinner with the CEO
- attend a testimonial dinner
- accept a special award given by the organization
- attend a special program or class not open to the public

The nonprofit organization can do the following:

- provide special seating for the prospect at events
- send the prospect special communications, such as birthday and anniversary cards, thank you letters, and congratulatory notes
- feature the prospect in an article or interview in an organization publication, such as a newsletter or magazine
- recognize donors at organizational events

THE SUCCESSFUL SOLICITATION—OVERCOMING THE FEAR OF ASKING

One of the biggest challenges for many development professionals is motivating board members and key volunteers to make personal visits to solicit major gifts. If you have ever served on a board or volunteered for an organization, you have heard people say they prefer calling people on the telephone or writing letters. They are willing to help raise funds but are not comfortable doing it face to face. There are a number of reasons why it is difficult to motivate even the most successful professionals on the board. They, like most people, suffer from fear of being rejected, fear of offending someone, fear of appearing as a beggar, and, most important, fear of failure. Add in the cultural "taboo" against discussing money with people other than family members and you can see why soliciting gifts is uncomfortable for many people.

A proven method for motivating volunteers to make personal solicitations is through training. In Chapter 6, we covered how to train and manage annual campaign volunteers. Some of the elements of the training of those volunteers can be included in the training of volunteers engaged in soliciting major gifts. In addition, training activities to help build the volunteers' confidence in both themselves and the organization will help them bring a more positive attitude to the task at hand. If you are able to help a volunteer approach the task with greater comfort, you are well on your way to creating a successful solicitor for the organization. Make sure the volunteers know they will rarely, if ever, make a visit alone. Usually they will be part of a solicitation team that will include the CEO or director of development or another board member or volunteer. This also helps to make the situation more comfortable for everyone involved.

Volunteer solicitors should do the following:

- Believe in themselves.
- Believe in the project.
- Know the organization and the specific project.
- Be knowledgeable about the prospect they are visiting.
- Tailor the presentation to the donor's needs and interests.
- Be good listeners.
- Be themselves.

Include ample opportunity to role-play major gift solicitations in the training session(s). There is no substitute for having to "think on your feet." It is also important for individuals who will be making solicitation visits together to practice as a team; the preparation will make the flow of the actual meeting go more smoothly.

THE SUCCESSFUL SOLICITATION VISIT

Ample time should be devoted to the earlier stages in a major gift solicitation—identification, research, and, especially, cultivation—to help ensure a positive result. The following scenario illustrates when the time is right to schedule a visit. Suppose an individual was identified as being a possible donor to an organization. Research was conducted by staff, and the individual was rated as a qualified prospect by staff and volunteers. During the past year, the prospect became involved with the organization by serving on the advisory committee, attending events, and meeting several times with the board chair and CEO. At this point a solicitation visit would be in order.

The following are basic steps in conducting a solicitation visit:

- greeting
- questioning
- listening
- presenting the proposal
- overcoming objections
- asking for the gift
- closing

Greeting

Start the meeting by taking a few minutes to catch up with one another. Ask about family members, business activities, mutual interests, acquaintances, etc. This is a continuation of establishing a strong relationship with the prospect. New information may be revealed during this time that could be important to the purpose of the visit. However, do not spend too much time conversing on a variety of issues because you want to be sure you have ample time to present your proposal, discuss any questions or objections, and solicit a positive response. Solicitation visits can last an hour or more depending on the prospect.

Questioning

Use a variety of open-ended questions to broaden the conversation and encourage discussion. It is important that the prospect think his or her advice is important to the organization. Some sample open-ended questions are the following:

- How do you feel about . . . ?
- What are the advantages and disadvantages of . . . ?
- Some people say . . . What do you think of that?
- If you were in our position, what would be your next step?
- Who else might be interested in this project?

Listening

We believe the most important skill to have in soliciting major gifts is the ability to be a good listener. Do not monopolize the conversation talking about the organization and the specific project. Respond to the prospect's comments and suggestions.

To be a better listener, you should do the following:

- Try to think like a prospect. During the time you have come to know this prospect, you'll begin to anticipate the kinds of questions he or she may ask. Keep the prospect's needs and motivations in mind.
- Limit your own and the solicitation team member's talking. You cannot talk and listen at the same time. This is the advantage of making a solicitation visit with another person: one can be an active listener at all times.
- Concentrate on what is being said. Active listeners lean in toward the speaker, smile, maintain eye contact, take notes (if appropriate), and make comments such as "Yes" and "I see."

- Keep your own emotions under control, even though certain words, phrases, issues, personalities, and behaviors might act as emotional triggers for you. Do not stop listening while you think of a response.
- Often repeat and summarize what you heard. Be sure you have heard what the prospect said. Verify by restating the information or asking for clarification.

Presenting the Proposal

You may have prepared a written proposal, but it is certainly not shared with the prospect during your meeting (see Appendix 9–B for a sample gift proposal). By meeting with the prospect, you have the advantage of bringing your proposal to life in actions and words. The solicitation team needs to present their case in a way that will excite

> *By meeting with the prospect, you have the advantage of bringing your proposal to life in actions and words.*

the prospect. Ways to add excitement to your solicitation include the following:

- Use human interest stories.
- Tell a story.
- Use action words, drama, and humor when appropriate.
- State a problem and show how the donor can be part of the solution by helping the organization.
- Appeal to a prospect's senses and emotions.
- Quote other donors, clients, authorities, and experts on the merits of the program.

Overcoming Objections

There shouldn't be many serious objections to your proposal at the time of the meeting if the prospect has been properly cultivated. Again, listening skills are very important. During earlier contact with the prospect, the solicitation team would have learned if the prospect had serious concerns or questions about a possible project. They then should have addressed those concerns and helped the prospect feel more comfortable about the

Source: Copyright © Mark Litzler.

project if he or she seemed to have a real interest in it. However, if the prospect comes up with some questions or objections at the time of the meeting, the solicitation team must be prepared to deal with them. Because there is no way to truly anticipate what objections a prospect may have, it is best to arm yourself with some techniques to overcome objections (see Exhibit 9–6).

Asking for the Gift

The discussion leads to the moment of asking for the gift. It is extremely important that the solicitation team decide who will be the solicitor before walking in the door. You know the prospect is interested in the organization's programs, so take a positive approach in asking the prospect to make a gift. Let the prospect know the full cost of the project and ask if he or she can fund the entire amount, either as a current gift or through a pledge. As the solicitor, you might say, "David, Mary and I are delighted that you are interested in our arts in the classroom program for area elementary schools. We know that the cost of the program is $50,000. I can provide you with the budget. Will you consider funding this program with a gift of $50,000, either through a current gift or by pledging $10,000 a year over five years?"

Now, be quiet! Wait and listen for the prospect to respond. It is not easy to sit in silence because our first reaction will be to start talking. However, the prospect is the best judge of whether he or she can make a gift of the size you mentioned. By suggesting a multi-year pledge, you leave the door open to discussing

other options for donating the entire amount besides an outright gift of $50,000.

The prospect may or may not choose to fund the full amount of your request. In spite of the research and relationship building that has gone on, there may be a personal or business situation of which you are not aware. Remember, do not take a negative answer personally. If the prospect responds with a lower figure, ask for suggestions as to who might be interested in helping fund this program.

The prospect may ask to have some time to think about the request or to discuss it with a spouse or family member. State that taking time for consideration is fine but be sure to schedule a follow-up meeting while there. See Appendix 9–C for a sample gift proposal covering all details of a meeting and gift request. By setting a date and time to contact the prospect or meet with him or her, you will ensure a decision is made in a timely fashion.

Closing

If the solicitation is successful, offer your own thanks and gratitude immediately as well as those of the organization. Tell the donor that a staff person will contact him or her to confirm the pledge and payment schedule. Or if the prospect has asked for time to consider the request, thank the prospect for his or her time and past support for the organization. Reconfirm the date and time to call or meet.

When summarizing the solicitation meeting, take note of any of the following roadblocks that you might have placed in the way of a successful outcome:

- not asking for the gift
- not asking for a large enough gift
- not listening and talking too much
- talking about the organization and its approach rather than about the clients who benefit from the organization's services
- making your presentation sound like a canned sales pitch
- ignoring honest objections
- forgetting to summarize before moving on to the "ask"
- not having prearranged signals between solicitation members
- asking for the gift too soon
- not being flexible and not having alternatives to offer the prospect
- speaking rather than remaining silent after asking for the gift

HOW TO SAY THANK YOU

Do not confuse saying thank you with recognition of a major gift, especially when a major donor asks for anonymity. Some major donors do not wish to receive public recognition but that does not mean they do not want to know that their gift is appre-

---

Exhibit 9–6 Techniques to Overcome Prospect Objections

1. Be prepared to respond to comments such as "Prove that you will be able to do what you say you will do," and "Prove that your organization is the best one to advance this effort."
2. Prepare answers for objections heard from others in advance.
3. Bring up an objection before the prospect does, treat it as a minor point, and restate the benefits of the project.
4. Never argue with your prospect.
5. Do not inflate an objection by discussing it too much.
6. Never take an objection as a personal attack. Try to understand why the prospect is bringing up this particular objection.
7. Ignore excuses and weak objections.
8. Ask your prospect what he or she would do to solve the problem he or she brings up. Then suggest your organization as a means of doing that.
9. Turn an objection into a question—then answer it.
   "I understand how you feel . . ."
   "You have brought up an important question many people ask . . ."
   Get agreement on the question, then answer it with facts or a dramatic story.
10. Use the very effective technique of using words such as feel, felt, and found.
    "I understand how you feel . . ."
    "Others have felt the same way."
    "They found that . . ."

ciated by the organization and its leadership. It is a *must* to thank all donors, and there needs to be a well-thought-out plan for acknowledging major donors' generosity. By using the term *plan,* we do not mean to suggest delaying the sending of a thank-you in order to develop such a plan. Instead, an organization should have an established process for determining who in the organization acknowledges major gifts. It is believed by many that you cannot thank someone too much. The following example shows how you can acknowledge a donor's support seven different ways.

A donor contributed $50,000 to endow a scholarship fund for a deserving law student. A letter from the president was sent, then a personal letter from the dean, then a handwritten note from the associate dean for institutional advancement, and then an official receipt from the Office of Institutional Advancement. Later in the year, the associate dean sent a letter to the donor informing him or her of this year's recipient and describing the recipient's background and interests. The recipient sent a thank you letter to the donor. The donor received a personal invitation to the scholarship ceremony and reception and was asked if he or she would like to assist the dean in making the scholarship award presentation.

Other ways to say thank you can be of a more personal nature. For example, a thank-you can take into account the donor's interests and activities inside and outside of the organization, such as the giving of a book on a subject of interest to the donor, a video or photo album of a program's activities or project's construction, a personalized gift basket, or a limited edition drawing.

WAYS TO RECOGNIZE MAJOR DONORS

Organizations will want to publicly recognize the significant contributions made by their major donors. First, be sure that the individuals involved are comfortable with public attention by discussing with them the types of recognition an organization is planning. Publicizing major gifts in an organization's publications is an excellent way not only to thank the major donor but also to interest other potential donors in getting involved with the organization. Magazines, newsletters, or annual reports can include an article about the donor and what his or her gift will enable the organization to accomplish. It is important to include some quotations from the donor on why he or she chose to make this gift. Use one or two photographs of the donor with his or her family or organizational leaders.

If an organization has conducted a capital campaign resulting in new facilities or programs, having a major donor's name associated with the facility or program is a wonderful way to recognize the donor. The names we see on university buildings, schools, or hospital centers, for example, are the result of major gifts to those organizations. Within those facilities, specific areas, including rooms, theaters, or wings, can bear the names of other major donors. This type of recognition is seen in lettering and plaques that indicate whose support made the facility possible. If the major gift endowed or created a new program, the donor's name could be associated with the program. The organizational letterhead and all references to the program in publications could bear the donor's name. Be certain your organization has policies for the type of recognition given based on the level of gift so that recognition is consistent and appropriate. Following are two examples:

1. The naming of one of the courtrooms in the law school building at American University. Brass lettering over the door reads, "Kyle P. Gardner [not the donor's real name] Moot Courtroom." Inside the courtroom is a brass plaque measuring 12″ by 18″, which reads, "This Courtroom Is Made Possible Through the Generosity of Kyle P. Gardner, '66." A framed photograph of the donor and his daughter, who graduated from American University in 1995, also hangs in the room.
2. The naming of an international student exchange program. The program is known as the Miriam Ward Fellows program and is referred to by that name in all communications.

There are numerous opportunities and ways to publicly recognize major donors. Organizations also can create an opportunity that will have special meaning to the donor. Listed below are six other common ways to recognize major donors:

1. arrange a testimonial dinner
2. designate the donor as a recipient of a distinguished service award
3. establish an award in the donor's name
4. conduct a special ceremony and event dedicating the facility or program that bears the donor's name
5. prepare a press release and circulate it to print and electronic media in the cities of the organization and the donor
6. send an announcement to professional organizations of which the donor is a member for them to include in their publications

STEWARDSHIP—THE PRACTICE THAT ENSURES FUTURE MAJOR GIFTS

The last phase in a major gift solicitation is stewardship. What is stewardship? It is the process whereby an organization continues to prove it is worthy of a donor's continuing support. It does this through the following:

- acknowledging the donor's gift
- recognizing the donor
- honoring the donor's intent for the gift
- keeping the donor informed
- managing funds wisely
- using funds effectively to forward the organization's mission

The first two steps in the stewardship phase already have been described as standard operating procedures after successfully soliciting a major gift. It is extremely important that the organization honor the donor's intent for the gift. The responsibility of monitoring the use of the gift usually falls to the development professional. An example of this type of monitoring occurs when dealing with scholarship awards. For example, each year the development professional may serve on the scholarship committee for the law school. He or she reads the student applications and helps in selecting those candidates that match the scholarship criteria set up by the donor. Because the development professional is familiar with many of the donors and helped a number of them establish their funds, his or her role on the committee is to ensure that each donor's intent for the scholarship fund be honored. Regarding types of programs that may be more general in purpose, the development professional should periodically check with the appropriate program staff person to get status reports on the program and the ways the gift is being used. For example, the development professional would check to see that the gift is being used for expenses directly related to the program if that was the intent of the donor.

Chapter 11 discusses how important it is to follow a foundation's requirements for reporting how a grant is used. Because few individual major donors require such reporting, it becomes necessary for the organization to impose on itself the duty to keep major donors informed. Reporting is often the weakest area in the stewardship phase. Unfortunately, development staff and volunteers are actively working with new major donor prospects and therefore may not have the time to steward past donors. This is a major mistake, because those individuals who already have given a major gift are the best prospects to make another significant contribution. Keeping donors informed about the organization and how their gifts are being used is yet another way to show them that the organization appreciates their support. Do not worry that donors will feel the organization is in touch too often. It is best to err on the side of too much information than too little. See Penelope Burk's research on donors in Chapter 6 that supports keeping all donors informed on how their gifts are used.

Using the example described previously, it is easy to keep scholarship donors informed. Each year, after the scholarship committee makes its selection, the development professional sends a letter to each donor describing that year's recipient and providing the donor with some information about the student's background and interests. An annual scholarship ceremony and reception held in January provides the opportunity for donors to assist the dean in making the scholarship presentation and to meet the recipients. Good stewardship of the scholarship donors can result in significant additions to established funds and the creation of new funds.

For the climate of an organization to be conducive to major gift fundraising, one must consider again the overall "health" of the organization in view of its leadership and management. Major donors must have confidence in the organization's ability to manage their funds wisely and to use the funds effectively to forward its mission. Therefore, it is critical to keep these donors informed of the organization's plans and status through special communications from the CEO and board chairperson. If serious organizational problems develop, be sure the major donors hear it first from the organization and not through the media. By proactively describing the problems and the solutions planned, the organization can reassure the donors that things are under control.

For additional information on major gift fundraising, see *Developing Major Gifts: Turning Small Donors into Big Contributors*, by Laura Fredricks, another in the Jones and Bartlett library of nonprofit publications.

REFERENCES

Center on Philanthropy at Indiana University. The Bank of America study of high net worth philanthropy. As cited in Affluence and Altruism. *Philanthropy Matters.* 2007, 15(1); 8–9.

New survey shows why wealthy people give. *The Chronicle of Philanthropy,* May 3, 2007, 20.

Venture Philanthropy Partners. Venture Philanthropy Partners (VPP): A summary of our first five years. http://www.vppartners.org.

The Donor's Turn: People who make a difference through generous giving

By Jacklyn P. Boice and Mary Ellen Collins

Carmen and Alcario Castellano: Fulfilling Dreams

Alcario Castellano said he always knew he would win the lottery someday. He just didn't know when. The former farm worker and retired San Jose grocery store clerk had been buying tickets occasionally at his neighborhood liquor store when the jackpot was very high. His conviction became reality on June 23, 2001. He and his wife, Carmen, an administrative assistant and office manager at San Jose City College, won $141 million, the largest single-state lottery jackpot in U.S. history to date.

The Castellanos had a few personal plans for the money, which they took in one lump sum of $70.8 million, or about $41 million after taxes. They talked of traveling the world and paying off their three children's student loans. And they contemplated how their dreams had come true.

Born in New Mexico to migrant farm workers, Al moved to California with his family to pick crops when he was nine years old. He met Carmen, who was from a Mexican-American family in nearby Watsonville, when she was in high school.

After marrying and starting a family, the Castellanos moved to Cambrian Park in suburban San Jose so their children could attend good schools. There, they made a point of telling the local elementary school that it needed to start hiring minority teachers, and that launched a long history of community activism in Latino-related causes.

Carmen continued her student advocacy activities by mentoring many students through San Jose City College's Adelante Program and Evergreen Valley College's Enlace Program. During her 33-year career at San Jose City College, she was a founding member and president of the Latino Education Association, an employee organization that advocates for Latino employees and supports scholarship and leadership development programs for Latino students. She also served on boards for organizations including Los Lupenos, a Mexican folkloric dance group; the Latino Community Foundation; the Quadre Music Group; the Chicana/Latina Foundation; the American GI Forum Scholarship Foundation; and the Latina Leadership Network, a statewide organization of Latina students and employees in California community colleges.

Al, who served in the U.S. Army for two years in the mid-1950s, has been a longtime leader in the San Jose chapter of the American GI Forum and played a pivotal role in adding cultural events at Cinco de Mayo festivals. Attendees at local Latino festivals, parades and fundraisers are accustomed to seeing Al with his video camera, creating a permanent record of the life of his community.

Described by friends and colleagues as solid citizens who are hard-working, generous and caring, it came as no surprise that the Castellanos planned to use some of their winnings to extend their involvement with a variety of Latino causes.

"The community has done a lot for us," Al says. "We have been here [in San Jose] for 40 years. Our children attended public schools, and it has been a wonderful place to raise a family. There are a lot of unmet needs, and we want to give people hope about their future."

After the shock of winning the lottery had worn off, the couple sat down and discussed things before they even told the children about their sudden windfall. "One of the things that came up was setting up a foundation," Al explains. "So we talked with our financial adviser and set some money aside to start it."

"It was natural," Carmen adds. "We had done volunteer work and had board experience. Now we could do more, at a whole different level. I know about nonprofits and how they work. We knew we wanted to run the foundation ourselves and we had the skill set to do it. This was a big factor."

After doing considerable research, talking with people at foundations and getting good advice, the Castellanos used $5 million to endow the Castellano Family Foundation. The foundation is dedicated to the cultivation and enrichment of Latino family values through support of local organizations that promote the arts, Latino culture, Latino leadership and the educational pursuits of Latino students. As of June 30, 2006, they had awarded $1,350,305 to 64 organizations.

Relationship building has played a big part in the Castellano Foundation. "Over the years we have supported many nonprofits, and so it is natural to give them money," Carmen says. "We know them, the board members, and their work. Relationships play a key role and are part of the Latino culture."

Philanthropy also has always been a part of the Castellanos' lives. "I had a wonderful role model in terms of generosity of spirit," Carmen explains. "My father, who had a small trucking business, was a very kind man. It broke his heart to see people who did not have enough to eat or clothes to wear. He would bring them home, feed them and give them clothes. My grandmother raised two children who were not her own. There is an ingrained spirit of generosity in my family."

Al admits that before he had even heard the word philanthropy, he was already doing it. "We observed our parents' helping people, and we picked up on that," he says. "In New Mexico, my dad had a car, and he was constantly taking neighborhood people to see relatives in the area. He helped get them to family. My mother always worked with the church fundraisers. We always have been involved in the community."

In recognition for their leadership in the Latino community, Carmen and Alcario received the Portraits of Success Award from the Hispanic Development Corporation in San Jose in 2002. "People make a point of saying how much they appreciate the work we do," Al says. "This gives Latinos a sense of pride. There are a lot of Latinos who do good work, but they do not get the press. We are role models."

How long will their charity last? "Forever," Carmen says. "The foundation is in our will."

Although they do a lot for their community, in Carmen's opinion, the couple's biggest accomplishments were achieved *before* they won the $141 million jackpot: raising three wonderful children, providing each of them with a college education, and building a closeknit family.

"Our life was beautiful already," she says. "We are Latinos who have achieved the American dream."

Source: Boice, J.P., and Collins, M.E. The donor's turn: People who make a difference through generous giving, *Advancing Philanthropy*, 2007, 39–41.

A Clear Mission

The Castellano Foundation may have started with good luck, but the hard work and dedication of Alcario and Carmen Castellano keep it going.

Q. What are the most important criteria you look for in nonprofit organizations when awarding grants?

A. We look for diversity in the board and the staff. Organizations may do really good work and have programs that help the community, but when we sit down with them we see that the board is not diverse. Even senior staff members are not diverse at all. We may become a member of that organization, but we won't give money until we see changes first. That is a mantra. The community [in and around San Jose] is so diverse, and this needs to be reflected in the boards. We know that if this generates discussion among the board members, we have accomplished something. It's good to hear that they are thinking about this.

Programming is another important criterion. How effective is it? How many are served? This is where having a personal rela-

tionship with the organization helps, because it opens up the channel of communication. They can be open because it is like a personal relationship.

Q. You give funds for operating expenses. Why?

A. This comes from our background and experience working with nonprofits. It is so important to get money that is not tied to programming. If the organization is very credible and well established, we will give to operating expenses.

Q. Has the focus of your philanthropy changed since you started your foundation?

A. One thing that has not changed is our mission. We are committed to the enrichment of Latino family values through education and the arts. When we look at grant applications, we look to see if the organizations fall into that mission or not. In the first year, we gave some large grants. We don't do that now. We give smaller amounts to more organizations and also do some multi-year grants. That is really important. Also, we do some challenge grants that are helpful. We have done three of them, and almost every one has been met. We also have created collaborations among nonprofits. If we see that one organization could work with another, we try to be instrumental in making that happen.

Q. What is the biggest mistake that nonprofits make when they apply for a grant?

A. They do not do the research. If you go to GuideStar, you see where foundations give and how much they give. So, if we get a request for $250,000, they did not do the research. It is clear when organizations do their homework, and that is a plus for them. Also, some applications know what to say to tug at your heart, and you think, "Oh, how could I not fund them!" More people need to know how to do that.

Q. What part of philanthropy gives you most joy?

A. Youth programs are some of the most gratifying. We funded a bus trip to San Francisco for all the fourth graders from the San Antonio Elementary School here in San Jose. For some of the kids it was their first time out of San Jose, their first time in a museum, or the first time they had seen art. We got a thank-you note from each student.

Q. What do you tell your children about philanthropy?

A. They all are involved in their communities. Our oldest daughter, Maria, has been a stay-at-home mom for many years and involved with nonprofits through her kids' schools. She belongs to a group of parents that raised more than $1 million to keep the school system going at a certain level. This was quite an accomplishment given that the community is not large (28,000 people), but they knew how to get people to get that done. Our middle daughter, Carmela, is the CEO of a trade association for community health clinics in California and has served on several boards. Our son, Armando, is a musician and college teacher. He, too, serves on several boards. We have always given back to the community, and they have followed our example.

Sample Gift Proposal—Formal, Illustrative, and Personal

Gift Opportunity for Mr. and Mrs. V
To sponsor Deborah's Visiting Greek Nursing Program

Deborah Heart and Lung Center, in conjunction with AHEPA General Hospital, Thessaloniki, Greece, have developed the Visiting Greek Nursing Program at Deborah. Since 1993, teams of four to five Greek nurses study and observe under the leadership of Deborah's medical professionals, in an effort to improve the patient care services at AHEPA General Hospital.

To date, 75 Greek nurses have been educated at Deborah in the following critical areas:
- Nursing management
- Patient assessment
- Pre- and post-operative care
- Intensive care
- Equipment maintenance
- Hospital administration

To qualify for the program, each nurse must complete an application, undergo an interview, and write an essay about his or her interests and objectives. Only nurses with superior credentials are selected. Those chosen for the program meet regularly with Deborah's Director of Nursing. During their three-month residency, the nurses either rotate their schedules from department to department, which broadens their medical knowledge, or they are assigned to one department, which gives them the opportunity to study specifically within their area of expertise.

The visiting nurses are given a $250 monthly stipend, an apartment on the grounds of Deborah, and access to transportation. On weekends, the visiting nurses have the opportunity to expand their cultural experiences by traveling to neighboring cities, such as New York, Washington, DC, and Baltimore.

Upon their return to Greece, each nurse works closely with other nurses who have participated in the program. Their combined knowledge and newly acquired skills play a major role in the ongoing effort to improve the health care system in Greece.

Deborah has a long and rich history in the Greek community, both here and abroad. For over 75 years, Deborah has stood ready to serve those in need from as close to home as adults and children from your neighborhood and as far away as children in Greece. We come to you now, our loyal Deborah supporters, and ask you to be our proud sponsors of our **Deborah Heart and Lung Center's Visiting Greek Nursing Program.**

It would be our honor and privilege to name you, Mr. and Mrs. V, as our *founding leaders* for this important program. Your commitment to support this project will be instrumental to the success of our shared mission to improve patient care services in Greece.

We ask you to consider making this significant impact by making a $50,000 yearly gift, for the next five years, to sponsor this unique and worthy program. Your first gift can be made anytime by the end of this calendar year. We would like to commemorate your gift with a plaque that would be proudly presented to you in the presence of your family, friends, and colleagues. You may keep the commemorative plaque, or if you prefer, we would gladly display it in the prestigious office of Deborah's President. Attached is some sample language for your plaque. We would be happy to discuss the details of the type and style plaque you prefer to recognize your prospective gift.

With Heartfelt Appreciation to
Mr. and Mrs. V
For Sponsoring Deborah's
Visiting Greek Nursing Program
From Deborah Heart and Lung Center's
Board of Directors,
Administration, Staff, Nurses, and Patients

Source: Courtesy of *Developing Major Gifts: Turning Small Donors into Big Contributors,* by Laura Fredricks, Jones and Bartlett Publishers, 2001.

Sample Gift Proposal—By Letter—Conversational, Covering All the Details

September 27, 2008

Mr. Robert F. Smith
10 South Street
Philadelphia, PA 19107-3818

Dear Mr. Smith:

Thank you for taking the time last week to meet with us. We truly enjoyed getting to know you better and learning more about your family's strong ties with Temple University. It was particularly moving to hear you say that one of the best experiences you had in your distinguished career was teaching seventh and eighth grade students in disadvantaged areas of Philadelphia.

At our last meeting we discussed your interest in supporting our highly successful literacy program, Experience Corps, coordinated by Temple University's Center for Intergenerational Learning. Knowing how much you and your family care about the quality of Philadelphia public education in elementary schools, we thought this would be a great opportunity for you to make a real difference in the reading skills of many deserving Philadelphia children. We are delighted that you have an interest in Experience Corps, and at your request, we are submitting this proposal to you.

Experience Corps began in 1996 as a national pilot program to mobilize teams of older volunteers to work in elementary schools to improve children's reading skills. More than 15 cities were targeted for the project. Here in Philadelphia, three schools participated in the program: Olney, Taylor, and Morrison Elementary Schools. The program was coordinated by Temple University's Center for Intergenerational Learning, in collaboration with the government-funded National Senior Service Corps program. During the 18-month pilot program period, more than 72 trained elder volunteers provided one-to-one tutoring, two to three times a week, for more than 360 Philadelphia children in grades K–2. These students were tested to be most at-risk to fail at reading. The volunteers conducted small group literacy activities with the children and held numerous parent outreach programs, such as parent book club meetings.

The results of the pilot program in Philadelphia were outstanding, and in fact, Philadelphia emerged as one of the most successful of the national programs for three key reasons:

1. The elder volunteers realized an enhanced sense of purpose. By working directly with the children through tutoring and mentoring, they served as leaders in developing new service projects to benefit children and their parents.
2. The children showed marked improvement in academic performance, attendance, classroom behavior, and overall self-confidence.
3. The classroom teachers witnessed improved academic performance in the students' basic literacy and numeracy concepts, reading and math skills, and language development.

At present, there are nine Philadelphia elementary schools participating in Experience Corps that have been funded primarily by public foundations and the U.S. government. While our current funders have committed their support for the existing nine schools, we cannot expand our literacy project to reach even more at-risk children in Philadelphia without the help of private support. Now, we turn to you, Mr. Smith, and ask you and your family to consider a $50,000 gift to Temple University's Center for Intergenerational Learning so we can expand our Experience Corps literacy program in two more North Philadelphia elementary schools.

Your $50,000 investment is needed to cover the costs of screening, training, placing, monitoring, and evaluating volunteers, as well as the costs for the small-group literacy activities and parental outreach programs for two new sites for the program. Your investment would represent your commitment to improve the reading skills for many deserving Philadelphia children and to change the lives of many families in Philadelphia.

Mr. Smith, you shared with us how meaningful and rewarding it was for you during your teaching experience to work with inner-city children. You found the right words and the right teaching style to reach them. They respected you because you believed in them, and in turn, they did learn. In that spirit, we ask you now to help our neediest inner-city children through our Experience Corps program.

Thank you for your consideration and time. Please feel free to contact us if you have any questions about this proposal. We look forward to hearing from you soon.

Sincerely,

Laura Fredricks
Senior Director of Major Gifts

Enclosure

Enclosure to Letter

START-UP BUDGET EXPENSES FOR SCHOOL

A. Volunteer Stipends
   a. 10 volunteers @ $150/mo. × 9 mos. $13,500.00
   b. 1 volunteer @$200/mo. × 9 mos.   1,800.00

B. Staff Expenses
   a. 1 Part-time Coordinator 10–12 hrs/wk × 9 mos.   7,000.00
   b. 1 Part-time Support Staff 2–5 hrs/wk × 9 mos.   700.00

C. Supplies
   a. Photocopies   150.00
   b. Postage   100.00
   c. Curriculum Instruction Manuals   750.00
   d. Books   450.00
   e. Volunteer Uniforms (name badges, shirts)   150.00
   f. Materials for Testing   400.00

    TOTAL COSTS PER SCHOOL $25,000.00
    TOTAL COSTS × 2 SCHOOLS $50,000.00

Source: Courtesy of *Developing Major Gifts: Turning Small Donors into Big Contributors*, by Laura Fredricks, Jones and Bartlett Publishers, 2001.

Corporate Fundraising

KEY VOCABULARY

- Branding
- Cause-Related Marketing
- Charitable Giving
- Coalition Building
- Commercial Giving
- Community Chests
- Company-Sponsored Foundation
- Corporate Annual Report
- Corporate Brochure
- Corporate Foundation
- Corporate Giving Program
- Corporate Philanthropy
- Direct Benefit Giving
- Discretionary Funds
- Employee Matching Gift
- Federated Campaign
- Gifts-in-Kind
- Joint Venture Marketing
- Matching Gift
- Nine Ninety (990)
- Partnerships
- Passion Branding
- Point-of-Purchase Displays
- Proposal
- Query Letter
- Rejection Letter
- Self-Interest
- Social Responsibility Marketing
- Seconded Staff
- Seed Money
- Site Visit
- Strategic Giving
- United Way of America
- Volunteer Points

THE HISTORY OF CORPORATE PHILANTHROPY

Corporate philanthropy has evolved over time based on changes in the economy, tax codes, and attitudes of the public and corporate leaders as well as the introduction and influence of professional staff into the fundraising arena. But why do corporations give? And how much do they give? Will they continue to give as much in the future as they have in the past? Are there any trends in corporate giving? Do corporations give anything besides money? How can corporate support be obtained and maintained? This chapter will focus on these questions and the many others surrounding corporate philanthropy.

The Early Years

Corporate philanthropy in North America began in the late 19th century when the railroads helped to build the YMCA hostels that housed railroad employees as they worked on the rapidly growing rail system in the West. Then, during World War I, the Red Cross began helping the civilians in war-torn Europe. After the United States entered the war in April 1917, corporations were asked to help fund the international war relief efforts of the Red Cross, because the financial burden couldn't be carried by individuals or philanthropic organizations alone. The "Red Cross dividend" was created and enabled companies to request authorization from stockholders for a special dividend, or set amount of money, to be given to the Red Cross.

The IRS Direct Benefit Rule

In 1921, the Internal Revenue Service (IRS) allowed businesses to make donations to charitable, medical, and educational institutions as long as these donations served the needs of their employees. This is termed *direct benefit* giving. Later in the 1920s, Community Chests and United Ways were organized based on the model of the war drives of the Red Cross. Then in the 1930s, Herbert Hoover moved quickly to marshal the resources of business and philanthropic organizations to deal with what he thought would be a short-term emergency but which lasted nearly a decade—the Depression. There was no clear legal status given to corporate giving, however, and corporations were advised by their attorneys that they should put their money into the communities where the workers lived. Again, the principle of direct benefit reigned.

It wasn't until 1936 that a lobbying effort by the Community Chests resulted in amendments to the IRS code that permitted a corporation to contribute to charity if the contribution did not exceed 5 percent of the corporation's net income. There was now a distinct difference between a charitable deduction and a business deduction, and a business could claim one or the other but not both for the same gift. Still, businesses were advised to "play it safe" and contribute only when it was clearly in their self-interest. During World War II, corporate charitable efforts were similar to those during World War I. It wasn't until 1953 that the Supreme Court of New Jersey overturned the direct benefit rule. The new ruling stated that corporations had a larger social responsibility than that of just supporting programs that directly benefited themselves. Unfortunately, guidelines still were not devised to assist corporations with their giving practices (Kane, 1982).

Corporations Create Foundations

Also during the 1950s, corporations began to create foundations to separate the giving process from the direct management of corporate staff. A foundation could set its own guidelines and either fund programs that directly benefited the corporation or those that were of interest and were, perhaps, socially responsible but had no direct benefit. In the 1960s and 1970s, corporate philanthropy took a sharp turn. No longer was it respectable to fund only those programs that would be of benefit to the corporation. Self-interest and direct benefit took on negative connotations. There were the hungry to feed, the environment to save, and peace to bring to the world. Corporate philanthropy reached far beyond its own needs and communities. Corporations discovered the power of doing good,

> *Corporations discovered the power of doing good, and they realized that this power also could be profitable.*

and they realized that this power also could be profitable.

Five-Percent Clubs

When the Minnesota-based Dayton Hudson Corporation established a policy in 1945–1946 to give 5 percent in direct payments to charity, more than 40 other Minneapolis and St. Paul corporations were motivated to follow suit. Kenneth Dayton, who was chair of the executive committee of the Dayton Hudson Corporation at that time, thought that "the purpose of business is to serve society," not to just serve business. The Foundation inspired the Minneapolis Chamber of Commerce in 1976 to establish the Minneapolis 5-Percent Club, which eventually included 23 companies by the 1980s, each donating 5 percent of their respective taxable incomes to charities.

Fifty years after beginning the tradition of giving away 5 percent of their corporate earnings, Dayton Hudson had given out more than $352 million to social and arts-based programs in the greater Minneapolis area, an average of $19,000 per day. Based on its earnings in 1994, the company gave away even more—6.5 percent of its profits or $28 million. Currently, more than 70 corporations in the Greater Minneapolis–St. Paul area are participants in the 5-percent club. In its last year (2000) as the Dayton Hudson Foundation, the Foundation awarded about $7 million of Dayton Hudson's $67.6 million in charitable contributions.

In January of 2000, Dayton Hudson Corporation changed its name to the Target Corporation and the Dayton Hudson Foundation became the Target Foundation. The restructuring was not the result of a merger or acquisition, but rather a result of recognition that the Target Stores comprised more than 75 percent of the company's sales and profits. In 2007, the Target Corporation gave back $3 million dollars to its communities every week!

Cause-Related Marketing Introduced

Corporate philanthropy continued to grow in the 1980s. The first half of the decade was very profitable for corporations, and they responded enthusiastically to the Reagan administration's challenge to pick up the slack when government funding for nonprofit organizations was cut drastically. Also, in the early 1980s, the American Express Corporation introduced "cause-related marketing" to the world of corporate philanthropy and proved that a corporation could make money by directly aligning itself with a charitable cause. (For details, see the section entitled "Cause-Related Marketing—Doing Well by Doing Good.") Finally there was a way to mix direct corporate benefits and social responsibility. In the late 1980s, corporate giving remained steady as companies reviewed their giving policies and their profit levels.

Corporate Mergers

During two years in the 1980s, more than 4,300 companies changed ownership, and national corporate acquisitions increased 27 percent. Some companies merged voluntarily, whereas others were acquired involuntarily. Small and mid-sized local companies were bought by large national and international corporations whose headquarters were elsewhere. These large multinational corporations often did not take the time to learn where corporate gifts had been given in the past and even were accused of assigning too little grant money to outlying plant sites. This trend continued in the 1990s, and many business and philanthropic leaders were concerned about the decrease in corporate support in communities where such mergers had occurred. Often, when two companies with strong corporate giving programs would merge, the giving wouldn't double but would instead usually decrease to the level of one of the two companies prior to the merger. Plus, mergers often meant a loss of jobs within the two corporate communities, because of the elimination of duplicate departments. The first to go was usually one of the corporate contributions departments.

The Recession of the Early 1990s

In 1992, corporate giving to charities decreased for the first time in 20 years. Although it decreased only by 1.3 percent, this drop was indicative of the health of corporate America. Many companies were not doing well financially and were contributing less of their earnings to the nonprofit world. Six major corporations— Aetna Life and Casualty Company, Baxter International, PPG Industries, Texas Instruments, Textron, and Weyerhaeuser Company—gave nothing to their foundations that year. Donations from corporations totaled $5.9 billion, down from $6 billion the year before. This was the fifth consecutive year that donations had not kept up with inflation. Corporations were concerned about the causes their money was supporting and about what they were getting in return for their contributions. Competition for corporate money was becoming more fierce as government funding and grants from other sources were becoming more restricted. Corporate cash donations accounted for 86.6 percent of the $5.9 billion whereas gifts of products accounted for 12.5 percent (AAFRC Trust for Philanthropy, 1994).

Many companies were forced to overhaul their contributions programs because of the economic recession. In 1994, 35 corporations reported in a survey to *The Chronicle of Philanthropy* that "they had redefined their giving priorities during the past year; in most cases, they reduced the number of causes they support" (Dundjerski and Moore, 1994). Of the other companies responding, most had refined comprehensive changes they had adopted just two or three years previous.

Corporate Self-Interest

The companies looked for new ways to direct their corporate giving to the programs that were more closely aligned with their own interests. The following were among the trends that emerged:

- **More international giving.** A growing number of corporations started or expanded contributions programs overseas.
- **A surge in matching employee gifts.** Employees were quick to take advantage of an increase in the number of companies that would match employee gifts to charity. At Eli Lilly and Company, for example, the matching gift programs exploded from $200,000 in 1980, when it began, to more than $5 million in 1996.
- **New opportunities for noncash gifts.** Mergers and layoffs by big corporations produced a surplus of office equipment at some companies. Many decided to donate what they could no longer use to charity. Bank of America, for example, gave away $2 million worth of computers, desks, and other items after it merged with Security Pacific Corporation.
- **More volunteer programs for employees.** General Mills started a new program that offered seven or eight employees near retirement age time off from work to volunteer with nonprofit groups. James River provided information to high school students about jobs that did not require a college degree and helped train students for such positions. The company recruited 50 other companies to help with the program.
- **Renewed attention to education.** IBM announced it would reduce its giving to higher education from half of all donations to about 5 to 10 percent so it could give more to elementary and secondary schools. In 1993, IBM gave away $59.6 million in cash and $27.2 million in computers. Eaton Corporation, an electronics company, began helping first-year engineering students who were members of minority groups by providing each with a $2,500 scholarship, a summer internship at the company, and an employee mentor.
- **More emphasis on evaluation.** Growing pressure to show successes of contributions programs motivated General Electric, General Mills, Campbell Soup, and several other companies to start requiring charities to explain in their

grant applications how a program would be evaluated. Companies like General Electric also have hired outside evaluators to determine the effectiveness of their giving programs and make recommendations for change (Dundjerski and Moore, 1994).

Lack of Interest in Philanthropy

Another concern to appear in the mid-1990s was the apparent lack of interest in philanthropy shown by corporate chief executive officers (CEOs). Corporate foundation giving officers found that they had to justify their donations more frequently to ensure that they would receive the money needed for their budgets. This was found to be true even when the top corporate management had been supportive of the foundation's giving in the past.

In the summer of 1994, ARCO fired the head of its foundation, a 13-year veteran who was highly respected in the field of philanthropy, at the same time it down-sized the foundation by 40 percent. Others involved in corporate philanthropy heeded this as a wake-up call and sensed the urgency of aligning support for their foundations among the top management.

Return to Bottom-Line Thinking

The focus of corporate philanthropy appeared to have come full circle as corporations were again interested in how giving would affect their bottom line. Corporations spent more time looking for ways to use their shrinking pool of money to improve their corporate image, elevate the morale of their employees, and expand their customers' loyalty. Still others sought to give their donations to programs that were more closely tied to their business interests. Included among their strategies were the following:

- forging closer links with the company's marketing, public affairs, and government relations departments
- focusing donations on themes or categories aligned with the company's business goals and directed toward benefiting current and future customers
- ascertaining ways of measuring the impact of contributions on a company's balance sheet
- developing programs to make greater use of company employees as volunteers, including lending executives to charities
- promoting other noncash forms of support, including donations of products, services, and employee expertise
- recycling money by lending it to charities at little or no interest rather than giving it away (Greene, 1995)

Gifts of Products

Corporations can make gifts both in cash and in products. Exhibit 10–1 shows a sample of corporations and their charitable giving both in cash and products in 2005. Pfizer topped the list of the largest corporate donors in the United States when they contributed more than $1.6 billion in cash and products. Wal-Mart continues to be the largest cash contributor. It gave $236 million in 2005. They gave $87 million in cash and products to Hurricane Katrina relief alone.

In 2004, 38 companies gave more than 1 million each for tsunami relief. More than $80 million in cash was raised, and a

Exhibit 10–1 Corporate Charitable Giving in Cash and Products in 2005

Cash and Noncash Gifts	How Much They Donated	What They Produce	Percentage Increase from 2004 to 2005
Albertson's	$ 74,136,620	Beverages, food, consumer products	+7.5%
Alcoa	38,834,833	Metals	+40.0
Bristol-Myers Squibb Company	758,903,506	Pharmaceuticals, consumer products	+13.9
Citigroup	126,071,869	Commercial banks	+15.3
Coca-Cola Enterprises	76,385,868	Beverages, food	+13.1
CVS	8,403,000	Food and drug stores	+197.5
Intel Corporation	110,606,684	Computer products	+47.2
International Business Machines Corporation	148,500,000	Computers and other technology	+3.3
Johnson & Johnson	591,426,000	Pharmaceuticals, consumer products	+12
Merck & Company	1,039,000,000	Pharmaceuticals, vaccines	+6.1
Microsoft Corporation	334,000,000	Computer software	−18.7
Minnesota Mining & Manufacturing Company	39,054,000	Health care and consumer products	−18.7
Pfizer	1,618,100,000	Pharmaceuticals, consumer products	+28.4
Safeway	146,000,000	Beverages, food, consumer products	+7.9
Sara Lee Corporation	59,134,801	Food, clothing	+72.5
Time-Warner	293,772,625	Entertainment	+54.5
Wal-Mart	273,314,036	General merchandise	+20.8

Source: Reprinted with permission of the *The Chronicle of Philanthropy*, August 17, 2006, http://philanthropy.com.

total of nearly $231 million in cash and products. Also, in 2005, $260 million in cash and products were given by 46 companies in response to Hurricane Katrina. Most companies attributed the growth in their generosity to two years of expanding economy and increased earnings.

Outsourcing

Yet even with this leap in earnings, corporations were still trying to reduce the size of their giving staffs. Some companies even looked to outside companies to run all or parts of their philanthropic programs—a practice called *outsourcing*. This practice had been used in other areas of corporate America for years, but this was the first time it affected corporate philanthropy.

One of the most dramatic examples of outsourcing was when the Quaker Oats Foundation asked the Chicago Community Trust to administer all of its giving programs. Other companies that hired out their philanthropic programs tried to keep the arrangements less visible than Quaker by having the contractors use the company's letterhead and forms and answer the phones with the company's name. Most companies, however, were hesitant to try such outsourcing arrangements, for fear of mistakes that could tarnish their reputation and because of a possible lack of understanding by the public—their customers.

Corporate Accountability

Also, in 1996, there was a cry from charities demanding that corporate donors follow standards. The charities claimed that corporations were restricting their gifts only to projects that enhanced their corporate image instead of allowing the charities complete oversight of the money for their needs. They also wanted businesses to decline from mentioning their gifts in advertising and marketing promotions, nor expect charities to give them recognition in their literature. Charities felt that their "hands were being tied" by corporate philanthropy. Corporations found these demands excessive and unacceptable.

In 1997, a bill was introduced in Congress to force corporations to report to their shareholders the amount of money they gave to charities and to which ones. Of the top 20 companies on *Fortune* magazine's list of the largest 500 companies, only two, Chevron and Citicorp, routinely provided this information to shareholders. The goal was to help ensure that corporations would avoid conflicts of interest when making contributions and encourage them to think before making irresponsible or improper gifts.

Electronic Fundraising

In 1998, technology still was not being embraced readily by corporate grantmakers. Very few of the corporate foundations had Web sites, and e-mail was used mostly to communicate with internal staff (only 4.3 percent used e-mail to receive grant applications). Yet charities began to look to technology to increase their giving. The number of Internet addresses assigned

to nonprofit groups increased from 500 in 1992 to 114,000 in 1998. Donors could use the Web to learn more about charities. In 1998, the American Red Cross was considered to be a leader in online fundraising. It received $172,000 of its $543.3 million online. In 1999, it raised $2.5 million online. Plus, nonprofits could "surf the Web" to research corporate and foundation giving. Also, 1998 was a year that saw a large increase in cause-related marketing programs. (See the section entitled "Cause-Related Marketing—Doing Well by Doing Good" for additional information.)

Now, many of the large corporations post all of their giving policies on their Web sites, and many only allow proposals to be submitted online. In fewer than 10 years, corporate America has come to embrace technology in their grantmaking.

Stock Market Surge

In the late 1990s, the stock market surged, corporate profits began to soar, and corporate giving began to increase. Each year from 1996 to 2000, corporate giving budgets saw double-digit growth. In 1999, 97 of the nation's 150 largest companies (as ranked by *Fortune* magazine) reported giving $2.5 billion in cash and $1.1 billion in gifts-in-kind to charities. When both cash and products were counted, three pharmaceutical companies led the list—Merck & Company ($256 million), Johnson & Johnson ($188 million), and Pfizer ($154 million)—with medicine accounting for 70 percent of their total giving. Wal-Mart Stores gave the most in cash ($112 million), with Philip Morris Companies ($98 million), Bank of America ($96 million), Exxon Mobil Corporation ($93 million), and SBC Communications ($87 million) following behind.

The 21st Century

One of the greatest fears of the charities at the end of the 20th century was that corporate mergers would continue at a high rate. Even as corporate giving increased, there were fewer companies to give, and when businesses began to consolidate in the 1980s and continued to consolidate into the 1990s, many plants, offices, and employees moved from locations where they had been for years, taking with them the company's philanthropy. If companies merged and both were headquartered in the same community, philanthropic budgets and staff were more likely to be reduced than if they were in different geographical areas. To assuage the concerns of many local charities, corporations that moved their headquarters due to mergers began to pledge millions of dollars to the organizations they were leaving behind (Charities fear fallout of corporate mergers 1996).

The year 2000 brought even greater giving by corporations, with many new faces entering the arena. When the Goldman Sachs Group took their company public in 1999, they gave $200 million to fund the Goldman Sachs Foundation. This new foundation made more than $40 million in gifts in 2000. Conoco, which spun off from DuPont, decided to look beyond its Houston roots for charities to which to give and focused on increasing its international giving. It was not alone, as more and more corporations in 2000 made significant grants to international organizations. Merck & Company alone gave $224 million (87.5 percent of its total giving) outside of the United States.

The Rise of Technology Companies

The start of the new century brought even more giving by the technology companies, which at that time were the fastest growing segment of the U.S. economy and one of the primary generators of personal wealth in this country. In 2000, the U.S. Trust Corporation in New York surveyed 150 technology executives who were among the wealthiest 1 percent of Americans. They found that 99 percent of those responding had made gifts to charity in 1999. Bankers Trust Private Banking also undertook a study, "Wealth with Responsibility Study/2000," which was conducted among 112 households of which 30 each had a net worth of more than $50 million. Charitable gifts from this group averaged 22 percent of family income—$1.1 million per family (Billitteri, 2000).

Unfortunately, the bubble burst on the "dotcom" companies and eliminated most of the corporate and individual charitable giving that had accompanied this initial surge of this sector's personal and corporate wealth.

World Tragedies

In 2001, after the terrorist attacks on September 11 on the World Trade Center in New York, and on the Pentagon in Arlington, Virginia, the question for fundraisers was how much would this affect their development efforts, in particular, their corporate and individual fundraising. In retrospect, some nonprofit programs were hurt badly when money that was expected to be given to them instead poured in to help those immediately affected by the terrorist attacks. Those nonprofits whose programs were in place that could assist families who lost loved ones in the attacks found that their fundraising increased greatly as people and corporations gave as much as they could to assist in any way possible. Again, after initially left reeling by the terrorist attacks, the corporate community rallied and not only supported the September 11 relief efforts but also continued their commitments to the other charities that they supported in the past.

Then, in 2005, when tragedy struck the world again with the horrible and terrifying tsunami in Thailand and in 2006 with Hurricane Katrina devastating the U.S. Gulf Coast, corporate America again was front and center in the relief efforts. Some of the largest money ever raised from corporations and individuals across America and the world was sent to assist in these two relief efforts. Corporations made gifts outright and matched gifts made by their employees as well. Exhibit 10–2 lists the companies that donated at least $1 million to Hurricane Katrina recovery efforts. Exhibit 10–3 (A and B) show how much Americans gave for disaster relief and where their disaster relief donations went.

During and after Katrina, the American Red Cross (ARC) turned to its corporate partners when it found itself severely short of trained volunteers to provide relief where needed. When its Web site nearly crashed due to overwhelming traffic, the ARC again turned to its corporate partners for help to keep it up and running. Now, the ARC has a disaster training program in place for its corporate partners.

Coalitions and Partnerships

In mid–21st century corporate fundraising, two key words appeared—coalitions and partnerships. Corporations began to demand that nonprofits seeking money from them or their foundations work together with others in their communities who were undertaking similar types of programs. They didn't want to use a "shotgun" approach and spread their grant money around. Instead, they were looking to the "rifle" approach where they gave their money to one entity, which included many nonprofits working together on issues vital to their communities. In the section "Building Coalitions," there is a good example of coalition building among more than 60 groups to work on a national project. Appendix 10–A lists the coalition partners on this project.

Partnerships between nonprofit organizations and corporations are meant to benefit both parties. In the 1980s, this type of relationship was called cause-related marketing; in the mid-2000s, it now has the term of *partnering*. For more information on this type of relationship, see "Cause-Related Marketing— Doing Well by Doing Good" later in this chapter.

As long as the economy remains robust, corporations will continue to give to charities. It is in their public interest to support the endeavors of nonprofits, and as long as corporations are making strong profits, their stockholders will support their philanthropic efforts.

HOW AND WHY CORPORATIONS GIVE

Corporate philanthropy is versatile in its structure. Contributions to nonprofit organizations, including cash gifts and non-cash gifts (often called gifts-in-kind), may be made in several ways, such as through a company foundation or directly by the company. Within the company, giving may be highly centralized or decentralized depending upon its philanthropic culture. Some corporations have large, full-time staff operations spread throughout their divisions and subsidiaries to review proposals and coordinate giving, whereas others run a tight ship by having philanthropic decisions centralized within a small office. Some corporations consider only cash gifts as part of their philanthropic effort, whereas others donate both cash and gifts-in-kind.

Corporations give away money for many reasons. These include the following:

- the desire to build good will and a positive public image
- to increase revenues

Exhibit 10–2 Companies Donating to Hurricane Katrina Recovery

Companies That Donated at Least $1 Million to Katrina Recovery Efforts	Cash donations	Total cash and product donations
Wal-Mart Stores (Bentonville, Ark.)	$32,500,000	$36,000,000
Home Depot (Atlanta)	11,000,000	11,000,000
Exxon Mobil Corporation (Irving, Tex.)	10,000,000	10,902,151
Citigroup (New York)	8,200,000	8,200,000
Chevron (San Ramon, Calif.)	8,000,000	8,000,000
ConocoPhillips (Houston)	7,140,000	7,140,000
Marathon Oil Corporation (Houston)	7,053,000	7,053,000
General Electric Company (Fairfield, Conn.)	6,000,000	14,500,000
Lockheed Martin Corporation (Bethesda, Md.)	5,000,000	5,000,000
Cisco Systems (San Jose, Calif.)	4,700,000	4,700,000
Federated Department Stores (Cincinnati)[1]	3,800,000	3,800,000
Altria Group (New York)	3,738,750	4,675,780
Johnson & Johnson (New Brunswick, N.J.)	3,613,000	8,613,000
Safeway (Pleasanton, Calif.)	3,500,000	3,520,000
Coca-Cola Company (Atlanta)	3,100,000	5,697,500
Walt Disney Company (Burbank, Calif.)[2]	3,000,000	3,000,000
Prudential Financial (Newark, N.J.)	2,712,000	2,712,000
BellSouth Corporation (Atlanta)	2,670,562	14,670,562
Intel Corporation (Santa Clara, Calif.)	2,664,909	5,765,592
Pfizer (New York)	2,600,000	10,600,000
PepsiCo (Purchase, N.Y.)	2,550,000	2,550,000
Wachovia Corporation (Charlotte, N.C.)	2,479,500	2,479,500
General Motors Corporation (Detroit)	2,215,412	2,215,412
Microsoft Corporation (Redmond, Wash.)	2,050,000	8,208,000
Time Warner (New York)	2,004,000	5,884,984
Best Buy (Richfield, Minn.)	2,000,000	10,000,000
AT&T Corporation (San Antonio)[3]	1,902,836	1,902,836
Bank of America Corporation (Charlotte, N.C.)	1,575,000	1,575,000
New York Life Insurance Company (New York)	1,334,030	1,334,030
Merck & Company (Whitehouse Station, N.J.)	1,250,000	13,080,000
Caterpillar (Peoria, Ill.)	1,200,000	1,200,000
Bristol-Myers Squibb (New York)[4]	1,100,000	4,000,000
Countrywide Financial Corporation (Calabasas, Calif.)	1,100,000	1,100,000
Wells Fargo & Company (San Francisco)	1,015,329	1,015,329
Costco Wholesale Corporation (Issaquah, Wash.)	1,010,000	1,389,191
Albertson's (Boise, Idaho)	1,000,000	10,000,000
Boeing (Chicago)	1,000,000	1,000,000
Coca-Cola Enterprises (Atlanta)	1,000,000	1,000,000
Dow Chemical Company (Midland, Mich.)	1,000,000	1,250,000
J.P. Morgan Chase & Co. (New York)	1,000,000	1,000,000
Merrill Lynch & Company (New York)	1,000,000	1,000,000
MetLife (New York)	1,000,000	1,000,000
Motorola (Schaumburg, Ill.)[5]	1,000,000	1,000,000
Northwestern Mutual Life Insurance Company (Milwaukee)	1,000,000	1,000,000
State Farm Mutual Automobile Insurance Company (Bloomington, Ill.)	1,000,000	1,000,000
Sunoco (Philadelphia)	1,000,000	1,000,000

Note: Unless otherwise noted, dollar figures show the fair market value of donated goods. Figures represent all gifts made in 2005, plus donations made so far in 2006.
[1]Figures include Federated Department Stores information only, and do not redirect contributions by May Department Stores, which Federated acquired in August 2005.
[2]Cash figures are solely for donations from the company foundation.
[3]SBC merged with AT&T in November 2005, taking the AT&T name. SBC Foundation is now the AT&T Foundation.
[4]Figure for donated company products is based on their wholesale value.
[5]Figure shows Katrina giving by the company's foundation in 2005.

Source: Reprinted with permission of *The Chronicle of Philanthropy,* August 17, 2006, Page 35, "Companies That Have Donated at Least $1 Million to Katrina Recovery Efforts," http://philanthropy.com.

Exhibit 10–3A and B Disaster Relief Donations

A.   HOW MUCH AMERICANS GAVE FOR DISASTER RELIEF

Individuals last year contributed $5.83 billion to help victims of Hurricane Katrina, the South Asia tsunamis, and the earthquake in Pakistan. Companies provided $1.38 billion to those causes, while foundations provided $160 million.

In billions

Katrina
$4.25

Tsunami
$1.54

Earthquake
$0.04

Total: $5.83 billion

B.   WHERE DISASTER RELIEF DONATIONS WENT

	Dollars donated (in millions)	Percentage of giving
Human services (Gulf Coast hurricanes)	$2,700.17	36%
International aid (tsunamis)	1,001.96	14%
Human services (international)	607.75	8%
Religion	430.81	6%
Public/society benefit	262.82	4%
International groups providing Gulf Coast hurricane relief	140.29	2%
Foundations	51.26	1%
Arts	38.41	1%
Environment	29.27	0%
Education	10.42	0%
Health	9.00	0%
Unknown/other	2,083.002	28%
Total	**$7,365.162**	**100%**

Source: Giving USA Foundation

- to get tax deductions
- to reward employees
- to improve the communities in which they operate
- to continue their tradition of support to certain causes or events—national, regional, or local
- to support certain causes through the commitment of the CEO or board
- to create an environment of community responsibility, which in turn provides an aura of good corporate citizenship that actually helps them to attract new customers.

In many communities, this last reason may make a difference in how local customers perceive a corporation. Is it one that supports the community? Is it one that puts its contributions into the coffers of the organizations supported by those it employs? Does it have a matching gift program? Does it give time off to employees who wish to volunteer for a cause? Does it provide gifts-in-kind to the schools or other nonprofit organizations in the community?

Many national organizations care about the public's perception of them as much as their local or regional counterparts do. For example, because they supported local elementary

> *Many national organizations care about the public's perception of them as much as their local or regional counterparts do.*

schools, Apple Computer was an instant "hit" with educators around the country, and Levi Strauss and Company was giving nearly 3.5 percent to charities across the United States long before other corporations "got on the bandwagon."

Strategic Giving

Recently, the concept of *strategic giving* has become more popular again. Strategic gifts are gifts that align the company's business interests to their philanthropic goals as opposed to *charitable giving*, which is giving that supports the needs of the community whether there is a business benefit or not. Lastly, *commercial giving* is defined as gifts that are given to benefit primarily the corporation, i.e., sponsorships or requests from customers or clients. As companies focus on strategic giving, the number of charitable gifts made by companies may begin to decrease as strategic giving requires more time-intensive involvement on the part of the corporate philanthropic staff.

The 2005 *Giving in Numbers* report by the Committee Encouraging Corporate Philanthropy noted that corporate giving increased by 14 percent (they surveyed more than 100 major companies regarding their giving habits). Of those that completed surveys, 40 were from Fortune 100 companies. Average giving for all of the companies surveyed was $28.95 million, and for the 40 Fortune 100 companies, the average giving was $69.18 million. There were 66 companies which had completed the survey both in 2004 and 2005. Of these 66, their giving increased from $32.9 million in 2004 to $37.7 million in 2005; 77 percent reported their giving increased in 2005.

Cash gifts were the most prevalent (45 percent of all gifts) followed by foundation grants (33 percent), and noncash contributions (22 percent). Areas that were supported included the following:

- health and social services: 34 percent
- community and economic development: 14 percent
- higher education: 13 percent
- K–12 education: 10 percent
- civic and pubic affairs: 6 percent
- culture and arts: 6 percent
- environment: 3 percent
- other: 14 percent

Gifts-in-Kind

In the early 1990s, a corporate trend began of donating in ways other than by giving cash directly. Many gifts-in-kind (noncash gifts) were made. In the past, a request from IBM to underwrite a nonprofit organization's educational program could have meant a sizeable gift of cash. In the mid-1990s, it was giving computer equipment and training instead. Having thought of this idea later than Apple, IBM found that many of today's young adults had been taught as children on Apple computers (Mac-based)—through Apple's early cultivation of elementary schools by giving computers to the classrooms. These children grew up to buy Apple computers and products. IBM decided to provide the same equipment programs as Apple did to schools to ensure future customers.

In 1991, a national nonprofit organization approached IBM with a request of $100,000 to support its educational programs. Instead of receiving cash, the organization received $125,000 worth of computer equipment plus the expertise of the IBM staff to network the computers so staff could communicate with each other at headquarters and with their chapters. The total gift was worth far more than the original amount requested but still left the organization searching for money to support its educational programs.

Other corporations provided their products or even loaned personnel to nonprofit organizations. Often when an organization is embarking upon a capital campaign, the chair of the campaign will be the CEO of a major corporation. That chair will frequently "second," or loan, one or more of the company's staff members to work with the nonprofit organization to organize the campaign and provide assistance to the campaign's leadership team. Thus, the term *seconded executive*.

CORPORATE VOLUNTEERS

Many corporations encourage their staff to volunteer their time to nonprofits and even to track their involvement. Angel Point, a for-profit company in Marin County, California, has developed software used by many large corporations to track employees' volunteer hours. The companies grant recognition and awards based on the level of volunteer involvement. Volunteer support on all levels from the corporate community has drastically increased the amount of work that nonprofits can undertake. Whether sitting on a board, directing one of an association's many committees, leading a charity's fundraising efforts, or working on special events, corporate volunteers are saving nonprofits large amounts of money by enhancing and expanding the work that staff would normally be asked to undertake.

Also, corporations may provide nonprofit organizations with the use of their facilities free of charge. For the organization's annual board of trustees meeting, the corporation may loan one of its conference rooms for the weekend. Some corporations even have provided loans to nonprofit organizations at below-market rates. These types of contributions are indispensable to the welfare of the nonprofit world and often are not included in the giving figures accredited to corporate America. While foundations must contribute 5 percent or more of the foundation's market-value assets, direct corporate giving is less regulated. Information on company-sponsored foundations is available through the IRS and at any of the Foundation Centers. Corporations do not have to give away a specific percentage nor report what they give outside of their foundations, if they have them. Plus, they can deduct on their federal taxes up to 10 percent of pretax income for charitable contributions. Another interesting point is that some corporate foundations have actually given more money to nonprofit organizations than they have received from their parent company. To understand how this is possible, one has to understand that there are two types of corporate foundations. One type is initially established by the parent corporation with a sizable gift and then is in total self-control after that. The other receives cash each year from the corporation based on the earnings of the corporation that year.

CORPORATE–PRIVATE FOUNDATION PARTNERSHIPS

Ever since the Reagan administration began to cut deeply into the government support of the nonprofit world in the 1980s, the corporate community had been taking up more and more of the slack. The big surprise in the mid-to-late 1990s was not that more government cuts were being made (that was expected) but that private foundations were busy courting corporations for support of their programs! Although still the exception, more and more partnerships and alliances were being formed between private foundations and corporations. For example, the Rockefeller Foundation and Bancomer in Mexico joined forces to sponsor a scholarship program. The Markle Foundation and an Oregon-based video games company collaborated to further a cause supported by the foundation—public interest applications of interactive media.

Perhaps one of the largest and most successful partnerships between a private foundation and a corporation was the one between the Robert Wood Johnson Foundation (RWJF), one of the largest foundations in health care, and HBO (Home Box Office), the cable programmer. Together, they worked with the program *Comic Relief* to provide health care to the homeless via RWJF's 22 medical clinics set up across the country to help meet the medical needs of the homeless. *Comic Relief* raised the money through telethons carried on HBO. HBO paid the salaries and expenses of the *Comic Relief* staff, and all of the money raised went to homeless people who were ill instead of paying administrative costs.

All of this potential—the up and down side—was detailed in an article by Smith (1995) in the *Corporate Philanthropy Report.* Smith saw some dangers in these partnerships. He stated, "For non-profits that see the trend on the horizon, the danger isn't hard to detect. Their private foundation allies may decide to break with tradition by working directly with the business world. In other words, most of the nation's nonprofit organizations may be cut out of the loop." He also detected hesitation from the private foundations. "Indeed, true private foundation/corporate partnerships are still rare. The problem is that private foundation grant makers—who rarely admit that their self-interests bias their funding decisions—are loathe to accommodate the self-interests of the very corporations they court."

RESEARCH—SELECTING THE RIGHT CORPORATION FOR SUPPORT

Before writing any proposal, it is imperative that the grantseeker completely understand the reasons for seeking funds from the donor. What is the organization's mission? What are the organization's needs? What are the organization's programs? Why should a corporation support these needs or programs? How will the money be spent? How is the organization spending its money now? A solicitor must be prepared to answer all of these questions and many, many more in simple, direct terms. If there

are any problems with the organization—either programmatically or financially—a solicitor must be ready to respond to questions or even initiate discussion on these topics. There is nothing worse than unpreparedness when being queried by a corporation.

> *Before writing any proposal, it is imperative that the grantseeker completely understand the reasons for seeking funds from the donor.*

In addition to knowing the organization inside and out, a grantseeker needs to know the corporation from which he or she will be soliciting funds. What are their guidelines? To whom have they made grants recently? What has been the size of their grants? Will the organization's mission and programs be of interest to the decision makers? It is important to know not only what the organization needs but the corporation's interests and what it wants for itself. Does it have a specific image in the community, region, nation, or world that it wants to enhance? Does it have a public image. problem that it wants to erase? How can the organization be of benefit to the corporation?

Only when members of the development staff have completely exhausted asking such questions and have satisfactorily outlined responses to all of them are they ready to begin writing a proposal to solicit funds from the organization. A successful proposal cannot be written if the author does not know the mission and needs of the organization or the interests and wants of the corporation. Many proposals are written with passion but do not relay what the nonprofit organization wants. Others are so vague that they leave the potential grantor wondering what is being requested or what the organization is really all about. Ask someone outside of the organization to read the proposal. See if, to them, the proposal makes a "case" for giving. Often, those inside the organization know what they are trying to express but are unable to translate what they do and what they need into language that is understandable to someone outside of the organization.

Another technique to prepare for writing a strong proposal is to ask staff members of other organizations if you can read copies of "winning" proposals they have written. Many organizations are willing to share copies of their successful proposals and even are willing to spend some time explaining why they think the proposals were successful. Of course, this sharing must be reciprocal.

Other options are available to those wishing to learn successful grant writing. One idea is to develop a committee of the organization's staff and board members to suggest ideas, assist in writing the proposal, or review the proposal at various stages in its preparation to ensure that it answers all of the questions mentioned earlier and represents the organization well. Often, grant writers think that the finely crafted proposal is what really sells the donor on the project. Most likely, it is a combination of factors and not just the proposal. No matter how erudite, if a proposal doesn't present the case clearly and succinctly to the potential donor and answer the right questions, the project won't be funded.

In addition, successful corporate fundraising is always a matter of timing and relationship building. It may be several years before some organizations are funded because corporations are

> *Successful corporate fundraising is always a matter of timing and relationship building.*

not aware of their existence. It is not uncommon for an organization to "court" potential donors for years before soliciting money from them. The organization is building relationships and establishing credibility. Then when the organization writes and submits a proposal, it will be received by people who are aware of the organization, its mission, and its needs. In addition, cultivation can lead to many other opportunities for the grantseeker. Corporate staff may attend special events held by the organization or may even provide gifts-in-kind to the organization long before making a cash grant to the organization. Taking time now to get to know a corporation and its world may pave the way for a long-lasting relationship.

It is never too early to begin to compile files about corporations. Go up on the Internet to review their Web sites to see where they give their money. Almost all corporations post their annual reports on their sites. Read the newspapers and business publications to clip articles regarding mergers and acquisitions; earnings and losses; hirings, promotions, and firings; and trends in the business or industry. Develop a profile on each corporation that could be a potential donor for your organization. Read through the corporation's annual reports, either online or in hard copy, and begin to develop a profile of the corporation. Find out what the corporation produces or sells, who its customers are, what its assets and liabilities are, and if it is on a solid financial standing. Then determine who the officers or directors are, who makes the decisions regarding charitable contributions (a committee or an individual), and who is the corporate giving officer (the contact person for proposals). Finally, review the corporation's giving history. What types of organizations are currently receiving grants? Does it support organizations in which its employees are involved? Does it provide seconded executives? Does it encourage volunteerism by its employees? Determine if there are any policies regarding supporting institutions such as yours. See Exhibit 10–4 for an excellent example of a profile form for researching corporate prospects.

Whatever steps are taken to prepare the proposal, never send a blind proposal—one that is mailed to a corporation with no cultivation beforehand. The adage "people give to people" proves true in corporate fundraising as well as in raising funds from individuals. Get to know the staff members who handle the corporate contributions. In a small corporation, these staff members may work in the public affairs office. If the corporation is large, a separate foundation with staff to administer the charitable giving may be located in the city that houses the headquarters or in any community with a large plant. To be success-

ful, it is imperative to nurture personal relationships. Don't be afraid to call corporate contacts to run ideas by them.

In membership associations, it even may be possible to work with members in the corporation to develop the proposal. If high enough in the corporation, most senior corporate staff will have discretionary funds from which they can allocate money to support causes of their choice. In other types of nonprofits, staff can work on developing relations with the corporate community affairs or corporate foundation office staff.

If a good enough relationship has been developed, the corporate staff should be able to share what their interests are during the current funding cycle; what the "ceiling" is for the amount to be requested; if a program can be custom-made for the corporation; and what type of recognition would appeal to the corporation. It also is possible to learn if there is an opportunity to create employee or other tailor-made programs. Don't forget to look for the possibility of developing promotional activities, taking advantage of cause-related marketing opportunities, or creating special market projects. Work with the corporation to clearly define in the proposal how the charity will handle the public relations and media efforts to create as much positive publicity for the corporation as possible. Before you even approach a corporation for a grant, you can learn through open discussion what the corporation needs to obtain final approval on a project. Exhibit 10–5 presents a corporate visit report form.

RESOURCES FOR CORPORATE GRANT INFORMATION

Locating information on corporations requires research. There are more than 15,000 public corporations that file information with the Securities and Exchange Commission. Yet there are at least nine million privately held companies that do not have the same reporting requirements as public companies. It is still possible to find information on these companies. The resources that follow will make the quest easier. See Chapter 8 for additional ideas.

Begin any search by first going up on the Internet to see what is available on the specific corporations in which you are interested. Most will have electronic versions of their annual reports available online. The Internet makes it easy to gather information from almost anywhere. Even book sources that were traditionally used for research are now available on the Internet. Frequently used reference materials either online or in print include the following:

- **Dunn & Bradstreet's North American Million Dollar Database:** Information on approximately 1,600,000 United States and Canadian leading public and private businesses including type of ownership, principal executives, and biographies.
- **Dunn & Bradstreet's International Million Dollar Database:** Information on more than 1,600,000 international companies including total employees, legal status, annual

Exhibit 10–4 Corporate Prospect Profile

COMPANY INFORMATION

COMPANY NAME: _____

ADDRESS: _____

_____

CITY: _____ STATE: _____ ZIP: _____

PHONE: _____ FAX: _____

BRANCH OPERATIONS: _____

_____

_____

PARENT COMPANY: _____

ADDRESS: _____

_____

SUBSIDIARIES: _____

PRODUCTS/SERVICES: _____

_____

_____

_____

CONTACT NAMES

CORPORATE CONTRIBUTIONS DIRECTOR

NAME: _____

TITLE: _____

ADDRESS: _____

_____

CITY: _____ STATE: _____ ZIP: _____

PHONE: _____ FAX: _____

CORPORATE CONTRIBUTIONS COMMITTEE

NAMES: _____

_____

_____

_____

_____

_____

CHARITABLE GIVING

CORPORATE: _____

FOUNDATION: _____

MARKETING DEPARTMENT: _____

PUBLIC RELATIONS DEPARTMENT: _____

DISCRETIONARY FUNDS: _____

DETAILS: _____

_____

_____

_____

_____

continues

Exhibit 10–4 Corporate Prospect Profile (continued)

TYPES OF CHARITABLE SUPPORT GIVEN

_____

_____

_____

_____

_____

_____

CORPORATE LEADERSHIP

CHAIRMAN: _____

CEO: _____

COO: _____

HEAD OF MARKETING: _____

HEAD OF PUBLIC RELATIONS: _____

HEAD OF CORPORATE CONTRIBUTIONS: _____

FINANCIAL DATA

PROSPECT COMPANY

ASSETS:_____

REVENUE: _____

OPERATING INCOME: _____

MARKETING/ADVERTISING COSTS: _____

ANNUAL SALES: _____

PARENT COMPANY

ASSETS:_____

REVENUE: _____

OPERATING INCOME: _____

MARKETING/ADVERTISING COSTS: _____

ANNUAL SALES: _____

SUBSIDIARY

ASSETS:_____

REVENUE: _____

OPERATING INCOME: _____

MARKETING/ADVERTISING COSTS: _____

ANNUAL SALES: _____

SUBSIDIARY

ASSETS:_____

REVENUE: _____

OPERATING INCOME: _____

MARKETING/ADVERTISING COSTS: _____

ANNUAL SALES: _____

SUBSIDIARY

ASSETS:_____

REVENUE: _____

OPERATING INCOME: _____

MARKETING/ADVERTISING COSTS: _____

ANNUAL SALES: _____

continues

Exhibit 10–4 Corporate Prospect Profile (continued)

SUBSIDIARY

ASSETS:_____

REVENUE: _____

OPERATING INCOME: _____

MARKETING/ADVERTISING COSTS: _____

ANNUAL SALES: _____

CORPORATE MARKETING PHILOSOPHY

MARKETING OBJECTIVES:

   LOCAL: _____

   REGIONAL: _____

   NATIONAL: _____

   INTERNATIONAL: _____

PRODUCT FOCUS:

   LOCAL: _____

   REGIONAL: _____

   NATIONAL: _____

   INTERNATIONAL: _____

PRODUCT ADVERTISING:

   LOCAL: _____

   REGIONAL: _____

   NATIONAL: _____

   INTERNATIONAL: _____

CONSUMER DEMOGRAPHICS:

   LOCAL: _____

   REGIONAL: _____

   NATIONAL: _____

   INTERNATIONAL: _____

SOURCES OF INFORMATION

SOURCE: YEAR:

_____

_____

_____

_____

_____

_____

_____

NAME OF RESEARCHER:

DATE:_____

Source: Courtesy of Gerry Frank, President, *INN*dependent Management Group, Alexandria, Virginia.

Exhibit 10–5 Corporate Visit Report Form

CORPORATE NAME:_____

ADDRESS:_____

_____

CITY: _____ STATE: _____ ZIP: _____

PHONE: _____ FAX: _____

E-MAIL:_____

NAME OF PERSON VISITED:_____

TITLE:_____

PHONE: _____ FAX: _____

E-MAIL:_____

ROLE IN CORPORATE CONTRIBUTIONS: _____

_____

_____

NAMES AND TITLES OF OTHERS ATTENDING MEETING: _____

_____

_____

_____

SUMMARY OF DISCUSSION: _____

_____

_____

_____

_____

_____

_____

_____

_____

_____

_____

FOLLOW UP REQUIRED: _____

_____

_____

_____

_____

_____

_____

_____

_____

PERSONS NEEDING TO BE NOTIFIED OF MEETING: _____

_____

_____

_____

_____

_____

_____

_____

_____

NAME AND TITLE:_____

DATE: _____

Source: Courtesy of Gerry Frank, President, *INN*dependent Management Group, Alexandria, Virginia.

U.S. sales dollar equivalent, plus up to four executives on the world's largest entities can be searched and downloaded.

- **Dunn & Bradstreet's Million Dollar Database:** Information on companies throughout the United States and Canada.
- **Ward's Business Directory:** A leading source for quality business information on U.S. private and public companies, including hard-to-find coverage of private companies. About 90 percent of the 112,500 listings in Ward's profile are private companies of all sizes.
- **CorporateAffiliations.com:** Authoritative business intelligence on corporate families that provides current, accurate corporate linkage information and company profiles on nearly 200,000 of the most prominent global public and private parent companies and their affiliates, subsidiaries and divisions—down to the seventh level of corporate linkage. Also, it contains over 700,000 corporate contacts, 110,000 board members, 150,000 brand names, and 140,000 competitors.
- **Hoovers:** More than 16 million private and public companies and their executives and news from 3,000 newspaper, press release, and industry sources with updated coverage throughout the day; wireless access, e-mail alerts, easy-to-use search, list building, and reporting tools.
- **National Directory of Corporate Giving (Foundation Center):** Current information on over 4,400 corporate grant makers, descriptions of more than 3,000 company-sponsored foundations, 1,400 corporate giving programs, and more than 7,500 selected grants: complete profiles feature facts on giving priorities and essential background on each company—business type, locations, and Fortune 1000 ranking—includes vital fundraising information such as program descriptions; fields of interest; annual giving amounts; average size of grants awarded; giving limitations; key contact names; officers, donors, and trustees; and application procedures.
- **Foundation Directory (Foundation Center):** A leading source of information on U.S. grant makers and their grant making activities, it provides descriptions of more than 88,000 independent, operating, company-sponsored, and community foundations as well as corporate giving programs and grant making public charities. The file includes descriptions of active and terminated grant makers.
- **LexisNexis** (division of Reed Elsevier, Inc.): Helps customers access 5 billion searchable documents from more than 32,000 legal, news, and business sources to locate people and assets, authenticate identity, enable commerce, conduct background screening, and support national security initiatives. It is the largest news and business online information service that includes comprehensive company, country, financial, demographic, market research, and industry reports.
- **DataTimes** (newspaper abstract and index): Covers newspapers from all over the United States and the world and includes financial and regional newspapers published outside the United States.
- **Dialog:** Online-based information services that retrieves data from more than 1.4 billion unique records of key information from more than 900 databases. Handles more than 700,000 searches and delivers over 17 million document page views per month. Includes articles and reports from thousands of real-time news feeds, newspapers, broadcast transcripts, and trade publications, plus market research reports and analyst notes providing support for financial decision-making.
- **Business and Industry Index:** An index to important facts, figures, and key events for international public and private companies, industries, products, and markets for manufacturing and service industries. Indexes over 1,300 sources from 1994 to present.
- **Business Dateline** (© UMI): Provides access to full-text articles from more than 530 newspapers, city business magazines, wire services in the United States and Canada. An essential business information tool for monitoring the latest trends in industry, health, environmental issues, education, and much more.
- **Business Week Online:** Selected articles of *Business Week* magazine. Topics include daily briefing, investing, technology, small business, B-schools, and careers.
- **The Yellow Book Leadership Directories:** Provide information to reach leaders of major U.S. business, government, professional, and nonprofit organizations.

Other online and print sources include the following:

- America OnLine
- Bloomberg Financial Markets
- CompuServe
- Contex
- Dellphi
- Dow Jones News/Retrieval
- EyeQ
- FT PROFILE
- Individuals' HeadsUp and First!
- Information Access Company
- NewsBank
- NewsEDGE
- NewsNet
- Prodigy
- Reuter Business Briefing
- Reuter Company Newsyear
- UMI Data Courier

Additional information on these and other sources can be found in Appendix 10–B. In most instances, it is much easier to search online than to use books, especially if you are cross-referencing material on various companies.

In addition to these reference materials, it is easy to access information by reading business journals and magazines. *Forbes, Fortune, Business Week,* and *The Wall Street Journal* all provide information on public and private companies. And there are other alternatives to consider. Reading the business sections of major city newspapers can provide invaluable information. Plus, local chambers of commerce may have business information available. All companies have to provide the secretary of state with specific types of information, and these files are available to the public. If the company is involved in any litigation, court records are available. These usually will include financial disclosures on the corporation and its executives. Plus, don't forget to review the corporation's annual report either online or in hard copy.

WRITING THE CORPORATE PROPOSAL

After completing all of the steps necessary for researching and cultivating a prospective corporate donor, it is time to develop the grant proposal. The process of putting together a good proposal can take several weeks to several months. After identifying a prospective donor and affirming the eligibility of the organization to receive a grant from the corporation, begin making a list of ties or links between the organization and the corporation regarding the project. When writing the proposal, weave these ties throughout to convince the corporation that there are reasons for it to be interested in your organization and this particular project. Again, earlier cultivation should have established these ties or links. The proposal then builds upon this early work.

Find out the guidelines or requirements for the length of proposals acceptable to the corporation and follow them. If there are no guidelines, keep the proposal short. Ten to 20 pages is long enough. If it can't be said in that amount of space, it probably isn't worth saying. All proposals need to have a cover letter that briefly summarizes the project. The cover letter should be signed by the most senior person in the organization, preferably the chair of the board, the president, or the executive director of the organization. The proposal itself should have a cover page with the name of the project; the name of the organization; its address, phone number, and contact person; the date of submission; and the name of the corporation to which it is being presented. An executive summary should follow the cover page; it consists of one or two pages that provide a brief overview of the project, reasons why the corporation should fund the project, and the cost of the project to the corporation. Next comes the organization's background information, including its history, mission, programs, and the audience it serves. Again, this should be no more than one to two pages.

The "guts" of the proposal is included in the narrative: which is the part of the proposal that states the following: the case, the need, the objectives, the activities, the timetable, the reasons that the corporation should support the project, the names of those who will be responsible for the project, the amount of time they will spend on the project, the location of the project if different from the organization's offices, the budget developed for the project, the plan for disseminating any materials developed during the project, how the project will be continued after the initial funding is exhausted, and plans for evaluating the success or failure of the project.

A paragraph or two should provide a conclusion to the proposal and direct the reader to the attachments at the end of the proposal. These attachments should include the following: the organization's tax-exempt charitable status under the IRS code; a copy of its IRS Form 990; an audited financial statement for the previous year; a copy of the current year's operating budget; a list of the names, titles, and affiliations of the board of directors; a list of the names and titles of senior staff; a list of current and relevant past contributors to the organization; an annual report; a development brochure; and any other material that is requested by the corporation or that appears to be necessary to make a case that will persuade this particular corporation to donate funds.

SUBMITTING THE PROPOSAL

Once the proposal is written, re-review the corporation's requirements for submitting a proposal. Carefully follow the directions given, making sure the length of the proposal is within their limit and that all of the required attachments are included. Check to see if the appropriate people signed the document and how many copies of the proposal are required. Are the copies bound in the proper way? Is there a submission deadline? Is there a method of submission that the corporation prefers—mailed, hand-delivered, etc.? Don't forget to ask for a receipt from the company or courier selected to deliver the proposal. Track delivery of the proposal online to ensure that the proposal reached the prospective donor.

Also, don't forget to have all of the in-house organizational approvals completed well before the proposal delivery deadline. The finance department should review all budgets, and the publications department should use its resources to proofread the document for any typographical errors, redundancies, and inaccuracies. Make sure that enough time remains for "sign-off" by any necessary departments, such as the president's office, the grants office, or the department that will be running the project. Once all of these reviews have been completed, the proposal then can be submitted.

REQUESTS TO INTERNATIONAL CORPORATIONS

Requesting funds from international corporations is nearly the same as soliciting funds from U.S.-based companies, but some cultures are different and require a different approach—most notably the Japanese. Patience is crucial when requesting support from Japanese companies. They tend to move slowly and cautiously and consider every angle before making a decision. Also, Japanese companies usually donate only from the profit side of their ledger and often tend to fund high-tech research. In addition, they often consider their public image when supporting requests and typically fund projects from their public relations budgets.

> *Requesting funds from international corporations is almost the same as soliciting funds from U.S.-based companies.*

Japanese companies must be nurtured just like any other company. An excellent example of "courting" Japanese companies is how the development staff at YFU (Youth for Understanding) International Student Exchange in Washington, DC, helped expand a student exchange program. YFU spent several years in the late 1970s and early 1980s discussing with Japanese corporations—Toyota, Nissan, and Kikkoman—the many benefits of sending students from the United States to Japan as exchange students to live with Japanese families for the summer and the many benefits of sending Japanese students to live with families and attend public schools in the United States for a year.

What finally transpired was that the corporations agreed to underwrite the student exchange programs to help increase understanding between the two countries. Toyota sponsored children of employees in both the United States and Japan to participate in the YFU exchange program and paid all of the students' fees. Kikkoman, makers of soy sauce and other soy products, decided to sponsor student members of the Future Homemakers of America and the Future Homemakers of Japan to participate in YFU programs. Kikkoman's reason for this was simple—these students would be the future users of their products. Thousands of students participated in these corporate-sponsored programs over the years, and the program was so popular and successful that the corporations also made other capital gifts to the nonprofit organization. For example, one of YFU's three headquarters buildings was named the Nissan Building after YFU received a large gift from the company, and Toyota also gave automobiles to the organization for its use. YFU was ahead of most other U.S.-based organizations in promoting cooperative efforts with Japanese corporations. Its success was proof that patience and "courting" payoff in soliciting funds from Japanese corporations.

Since then, soliciting international corporations has become much more commonplace as foreign based companies have

LITZLER

"AS WE CONSIDER THE PROPOSALS, LET'S NOT FORGET WHO INCLUDED A GALLON OF ROCKY ROAD AS 'ATTACHMENT B'."

Source: Copyright © Mark Litzler.

become more interested and involved in the United States. In 2007, the American Society of Civil Engineers Foundation began seeking support from major international engineering corporations for a coalition backed program entitled the Global Anti-Corruption Education and Training Program (ACET). The goal of ACET was to develop a DVD and collateral training materials that would be translated into 15 languages and used to help combat corruption in construction and engineering businesses worldwide. More than 20 international corporations were approached to raise nearly $700,000 for the program.

WAITING FOR THE DECISION

After submitting the proposal, follow up the submission within 10 to 15 days to make sure that the corporation has received it and that it is complete and acceptable by its standards. Then, while waiting for the corporation's staff to meet and make their decision regarding the proposal, update them on any progress, new developments, or other grants received to support the proposal. Send copies of any positive publicity surrounding the project. Include a new annual report if a new one has been produced since the proposal was submitted. It is important to use this time to the benefit of the organization. Don't let the corporation receive your proposal and then not hear from you. But don't bombard them with useless information either. Continue the cultivation process during this time in the same way as before. Remember that corporations give to successful organizations just as people do. Both want to be a part of a successful operation. Keep the company informed of any successes during this time.

Also remember that not all proposals can be funded. There is only so much money to give. It is disappointing and discouraging to receive a negative response, but it will happen to everyone who submits proposals for funding. Often it is because the problem hasn't been documented properly or the program's objectives do not match the interest of the corporation. Other reasons that proposals are not funded include the following: the program isn't cost-efficient; the program doesn't interest the company; the budget isn't within the range of the funding available; the program is too ambitious in scope (or isn't ambitious enough); another organization already has created a similar program within the community; the program cannot sustain itself and probably will fold after the funding is expended; the proposal writer didn't follow the corporation's guidelines; and the proposal was poorly written and included grammatical mistakes. Also, one sure way to have a proposal not be funded is to circumvent the staff who make the decisions and try to sell the project to a corporate board member, requesting that he or she tell the staff to fund the project (or, more subtlety, continually promote the project or organization to the staff). Be careful of using senior corporate contacts without cultivating the staff who manage the corporate giving program.

BUILDING COALITIONS

Also, in the 2000s, more corporations encouraged nonprofits to work together to form partnerships or coalitions to undertake projects. Too many programs were being duplicated, and all were seeking support from the same sources. In 2005, a coalition was developed to work on a project of interest to many involved in engineering. More than 50 engineering-based organizations, universities, and corporations came together to launch a project entitled the Extraordinary Women in Engineering Project, which was designed to encourage more math- and science-talented girls to select engineering as a career choice (see the list of coalition partners in Appendix 10–A). In the first year, working together as a coalition, more than $800,000 was raised for Phase I, the production of the book, *Changing Our World: True Stories of Women Engineers*. After being printed, the book was distributed by members of the coalition to school career and guidance offices and libraries. Since then, the coalition continues to work on Phases II and III of the project, which includes developing the messaging for the campaign and producing a television program.

THANKING THE CORPORATE DONOR

A thank you letter always should be written to the corporation, whether or not the organization receives funding from the proposal it submitted. If the response was negative, thank the corporation for considering the proposal and ask if a staff member would be willing to talk with you in person or over the phone to discuss the reasons why they didn't fund the proposal. Also, indicate that you would like to present other proposals for consideration in the future and would thus like to know why this one was viewed as unworthy of support. If the response was positive, make sure that the thank you letter is sent promptly. A 24- to 48-hour turnaround is appropriate. In addition, include the ways the corporation will be recognized for its support.

A corporate donor can be thanked additionally by providing recognition of its gift in the local media—both print and electronic. Its name may be added to a "wall of donors" or to a plaque hung in the organization's headquarters. A plaque or framed photo of the organization's project may be presented to the corporation to hang in a public place in its headquarters or at a local plant. The names of corporate donors can be listed on the organization's Web site and included in the organization's annual report, and the donors can be invited to and honored at special lunches, dinners, or other events sponsored by the organization. In addition, thanking a corporate donor may be as simple as asking for its advice, including its staff members when evaluating the project, asking them to serve on committees of the board or as board members, or sending them copies of letters of satisfied clients. Be creative, and remember, you can never say thank you enough times.

EVALUATING THE PROJECT

Don't wait until the project has ended to evaluate it. Begin by gathering data from the start of the project and continue throughout at assigned intervals. This will help you to remain on track with the project and can help you to magnify the value of the evaluation by providing data to your donors on an ongoing basis. If you find that you are not going to meet your objectives, an ongoing evaluation will give you an opportunity to take corrective action and to prepare your donors for a change of course or results differing from those you anticipated. Also, a timely evaluation may even lead to a better project. A donor even may be willing to pay for the evaluation, especially if it is included in the original budget.

The disadvantage of using staff members to conduct the evaluation is that they may postpone the work until the very end of the project because they are too busy with the day-to-day details.

REPORTING TO CORPORATIONS ON USE OF FUNDS

Nonprofit organizations will be successful in fundraising only when they learn that successful solicitation does not end upon receipt of the gift from the donor but instead continues on as the nonprofit organization reports to the corporate donor on the use of the funds it received. "Corporate giving is a partnership between business and the community," states Burnell Roberts (1990). "Large corporations already are virtually saturated with proposals and funding commitments. Higher fundraising goals in the future will require a broader donor base and more involvement by medium and small companies. Success in fundraising increasingly will go to those who close the loop on accountability and expand the loop on donor relations, and to those who treat the donor like the customer."

Invite donors to a project site and spend time showing them around. Let them see their money at work. Show them the successful programs as well as those that weren't as successful. Keep them "in the loop" and they will be more likely to fund the organization again in the future.

CORPORATE MATCHING GIFTS

In 1954, Philip Reed, chair of the Board of Directors of the General Electric (GE) Corporation, had the brilliant idea of creating a matching gift program for GE employees. He wanted to encourage them to give to their alma maters, and he thought that the company matching the employee's gift would be a great incentive. In the more than 50 years since GE began its matching gift program, its employees have given more than $2 billion to education. Their program was expanded to include other nonprofit groups including community and cultural organizations, hospitals, museums, and zoos. See Exhibit 10–6 for a list of reasons why companies establish matching gift programs.

Today, more than 1,000 corporations and 6,500 subsidiaries offer matching gift programs to their employees. For every dollar given to charity, the corporation will match it either dollar for dollar, two dollars to one dollar, or, in more generous cases, three dollars to each dollar given. It is up to the donor to obtain a matching gift form from his or her company's personnel office. The donor must initiate the process, not the charity.

The Council for the Advancement and Support of Education (CASE) offers a listing of corporations offering matching gift programs. For a copy of this list, contact CASE at matchinggifts@case.org or call 202-478-5678. CASE is located at 1307 New York Avenue, NW, Suite 1000, Washington, DC, 20005-4701, and their Web site for matching gift information is http://www.case.org/matchinggifts. Company profiles, which are updated annually, are compiled both into a book and placed online. Data are cross-referenced for easy use and for easy access to crucial program guidelines.

CASE even provides a leaflet that may be reproduced and used in a nonprofit organization's publications to promote the matching gift concept. See Appendix 10–C for an example of one museum's promotion of the matching gift concept.

CAUSE-RELATED MARKETING—DOING WELL BY DOING GOOD

Launched by American Express

In the early 1980s, the American Express Company coined the term "cause-related marketing" when launching its fundraising efforts to restore the Statue of Liberty. Each time someone used an American Express Card, Travelers Cheque, or Travel Package or received a new AMEX card, American Express contributed one penny to the renovation of the Statue of Liberty. The corporation used extensive marketing and advertising to publicize the benefits of supporting the nonprofit organization that was providing the "facelift" for Lady Liberty. All the community would have to do was use one of the services of American Express. The campaign generated $1.7 million to the restoration project and generated approximately a 28-percent increase in American Express card usage by customers.

American corporations were quick to recognize the success of this marketing program, and since then many more corporations have become involved in business partnerships with nonprofit agencies that can provide increased sales or revenues, raise recognition for both parties, and enhance the corporate image. The practice of cause-related marketing is well captured by the old cliché of "doing well by doing good."

> *The practice of cause-related marketing is well captured by the old cliché of "doing well by doing good."*

Renewed Interest in Cause-Related Marketing

From 2005 to 2007, corporations made a return to an emphasis on cause marketing as more and more partnership arrangements

Exhibit 10–6 Why Do Companies Establish Matching Gift Programs?

1. **A Virtuous Cycle**

   By giving to the institutions that educate their employees, companies "give where they get." Matching gifts are a way for companies to show their appreciation for quality institutions and to ensure that a supply of educated personnel will continue to be available to them. Through a matching gift program, a company is able to advertise its corporate image at a low cost and complement other support programs without conflict.

2. **Corporate Citizenship**

   Companies often want to support educational institutions and nonprofit organizations where their offices and plants are located. Even if matching gift companies do not employ alumni of local colleges, universities, and schools, they may receive indirect benefits from these institutions. They may enjoy the institutions' contributions to the economic or cultural well-being of the community, or the education of family members of their employees.

3. **Employee Relations**

   A matching gift program can be an employee benefit as well as a gesture of appreciation by directors. By respecting and reinforcing the preferences of those who work for it, a company can promote and improve relations among management, employees, and directors. Matching gifts are more effective than regular grants in promoting society's support of education. They encourage a company's employees to give, thus expanding the base of contributions to institutions.

4. **Creating a Challenge**

   Many corporations like the "challenge" aspect of matching gifts. There is little doubt that matching gift programs have been a factor in stimulating educational institutions to make overall improvements in their alumni fund programs. The total benefit to the institutions, then, may be much greater that the number of dollars received in matching gifts.

5. **Broad-Based Philanthropy**

   Gift matching gives companies broad coverage in their contributions. Recipient organizations may be **educational institutions** *(public, private, elementary, secondary, higher ed.)*, **cultural organizations** *(public radio and TV stations, museums, zoos, libraries, botanical gardens)* and **charitable organizations** *(hospitals, health, social service, civic, environmental, United Way).*

6. **Flexible Giving**

   Matching gift programs are flexible. Companies can design them to meet a variety of objectives—to encourage first gifts, larger gifts, continued gifts and so forth—and to fit within almost any budget.

7. **Public Relations**

   Through a matching gift program, a company is able to promote its corporate image at a low cost and complement other support programs without conflict.

Source: Courtesy of the Council for Advancement and Support of Education, Washington, DC. Copyright 2007. All rights reserved. Used with permission.

were made between nonprofit organizations and corporations. In an article by Panepento in the May 2006 issue of *The Chronicle of Philanthropy* titled "To Market, To Market," it was noted that in 2005, St. Jude Children's Research Hospital in Memphis, Tennessee, raised $21 million dollars from corporate marketing deals. "The deals don't happen without a lot of work, however: St. Jude has thirteen employees who have developed alliances with 40 different companies and are seeking out new ones."

In Chicago, United Scrap Metal (a recycling company in Cicero, Illinois) partnered with the Ronald McDonald House Charities of Chicagoland and Northwest Indiana to raise $60,000 for the charities. People were asked to bring the tabs from the tops of aluminum cans to the recycling center where the company paid the charities 25 percent of the going rate for aluminum for each pound of tabs redeemed, which United Scrap Metal then sells.

Another example of both parties benefiting was when the Colorado Chapter of the Salvation Army (Denver) partnered with the Denver Mattress Company. For six years, the company donated $20 for each mattress it sold from Thanksgiving through the month of December and also provided promotional advertising in newspapers and on television during this same time period. Nearly $1 million was raised for the Salvation Army, and the company benefited by being associated with a well-known charity during the crucial holiday sales period.

In 2006, nearly $1.34 billion was raised for charitable organizations using such marketing agreements. This was a 14.5 percent increase from 2005, and 11 times what was spent in 1990—$120 million.

Cause-related marketing not only benefits the nonprofit and the company, but society benefits as well. Often, in addition to providing cash and gifts-in-kind, corporations have encouraged their staff to become volunteers within the community. In fact, many corporations actively encourage volunteerism, track volunteer hours, and credit employees for the time they spend as volunteers. A company in northern California called Angel Points has developed software that tracks the number of hours corporate staff spend volunteering. In addition, the public tends to reward those companies that support charitable causes by greater purchasing from these corporations.

Not only were large charities finding partners with corporations, but smaller ones also benefited from similar marketing agreements. A local brewery in Salt Lake City developed a relationship with a local charity and raised $36,000 to help prevent homeless pets. They donated five cents from each bottle sold to save cats and dogs from euthanasia. Plus, an insert was included with every 6-pack promoting the charity and its mission.

Funds to underwrite a partnership come from the corporation's sales and marketing budget, not from the corporation's foundation. Both the nonprofit organization and the corporation promote the partnership through advertising, point-of-purchase displays, direct mail, and other promotional activities. The corporation hopes that customers will try a new product, thus increasing the corporation's profits. The nonprofit organization hopes for a new stream of revenue. And both hope that the increased publicity will bring a favorable public repsonse for both the organization and the corporation.

Nonprofits need to be concerned about their images as well as the corporations. If partnerships are to be made, they should be made between nonprofits and corporations with like values. The match should appear to be a natural and not leave the public wondering why there would be a connection between the two. Plus, any marketing arrangement should benefit both parties. The goal should be for the long-term benefit of both and not only for a short-term gain.

Cause-related marketing has become the marketing tool of choice for many companies. It links fundraising to the use of a corporation's products and services. Thus, the money to fund these efforts comes from the marketing budget of the company rather than from the company's foundation or community affairs department.

There is a difference between a corporate sponsorship and cause-related marketing. A corporation that underwrites charitable activities such as public television programs, museum exhibitions, theater productions, operas, or special events will receive publicity but not a direct financial return. Cause-related marketing, on the other hand, requires a formal contract between a corporation and a nonprofit for the express purpose of encouraging sales of the corporation's product and bringing publicity to the nonprofit. This contract establishes the amount of the gift to be given to the nonprofit by determining the products sold or the services rendered by the corporation to the public during a set period of time.

JOINT VENTURE MARKETING/PASSION BRANDING

Cause-related marketing is also called "joint venture marketing" and "passion branding." To understand this concept, you have to understand the definition of marketing. Marketing is a process designed to bring about the voluntary exchange of values between an institution and its target markets through careful analysis, planning, and implementation of programs designed to achieve organizational objectives. It is easy to see the parallels between corporate marketing and charity fundraising, and it is clear why corporations would want to form formal alliances with nonprofits.

> *Cause-related marketing is also called "joint venture marketing" and "passion branding."*

People develop strong emotional attachments to certain charities or nonprofit organizations, especially those whose services they have used at some time in their lives. For example, a loved one with a terminal illness may spend her last days in a hospice. The family members may have strong feelings about the disease and the lack of a cure for it or may have strong positive feelings about the hospice's care of their loved one. Then, when these same people see society searching for a cure for the disease or the hospice organization tied to a commercial venture such as the direct sale of a product, they often will increase their interest in that product and may ultimately purchase it. Their support is not so much for the product as it is for the nonprofit organization that helped them in a time of need or that is searching for a cure for the disease.

Through a larger number of sales, the company's income increases. As a result, the company is able to share a portion of its incremental income with the nonprofit organization with which it has formed an alliance. The end result is that both the nonprofit organization and the profit-making corporation benefit from the partnership. And the consumers have a sense of "doing good" by purchasing the product and thus helping the charity.

The National Easter Seal Society took the concept of cause-related marketing to a new dimension—that of "social responsibility marketing" or "social issues marketing," which builds on the potential of cause-related partnerships. The corporations sponsoring Easter Seals extended their support beyond dollars by employing people with disabilities, becoming advocates for the disabled, and encouraging their employees to volunteer. Social responsibility marketing goes beyond cause-related marketing by adding a human dimension, one that will last much longer than any product promotion.

At an AFP annual meeting session, "Cause-Related Marketing: Boon or Bad Idea for Not-for-Profits?" participants thought that cause-related marketing would grow at the expense of corporate philanthropy. During the session, six recommendations were put forth for nonprofit organizations to consider before considering a cause-related marketing arrangement with a corporate sponsor. These six were the following:

1. Consider your image.
2. Carefully select your partner; tell the company how it will benefit.
3. Develop a contract.
4. Select the appropriate format.
5. Maintain good communication.
6. Apply ethical behavior standards.

ADVANCING THE CORPORATE IMAGE

Often, a corporation will seek a nonprofit organization to sponsor as a way of advancing its corporate image. For example, Kinko and Sprint worked together with the Make-A-Wish Foundation to provide free video conferencing for the children at the 82 Make-A-Wish chapters. The two corporations provided the children the opportunity to link with family or friends via one-hour site-to-site or multi-site transmissions at the 130 Kinko's branch offices. Also,

Nestlé Refrigerated Food Company, a division of Nestlé USA, Inc., worked with *Woman's Day* magazine on a campaign to raise awareness about wildlife preservation through an essay contest entitled "Kids Save the Animals." In return for promotion, Nestlé made a donation to the American Zoo and Aquarium Association.

In an article in AFP's former NSFRE Journal (1987), the late Maurice Gurin, a highly respected early leader in the fundraising profession, used the following six questions to suggest the disadvantages, if not the dangers, of cause-related marketing arrangements:

1. Does the corporate offer of financial support qualify as a tax-deductible contribution? If so, it obviously is an acceptable contribution to a voluntary organization.
2. Is it a "no-strings-attached" offer of outright financial support from a corporation's budget for public relations, advertising, or marketing? If so, it is an acceptable contribution.
3. Does the offer provide for a profit for the corporation? If it includes a built-in financial return to the corporation, the offer represents not a contribution but a share of the profits from a business transaction.
4. Could the offer of financial support weaken or debase a voluntary organization's case for public approval and philanthropic support, which is the organization's greatest resource for its continuing financial health?
5. Could the offer of financial support help to blur the public's understanding of the difference between philanthropy and business—a distinction that is essential if philanthropic support of our voluntary organizations is to continue?
6. Could an outright offer of corporate support enhance the public regard for, and increase the sales of, a company marketing a product or service considered harmful to consumers?

CORPORATE SPONSORSHIPS

For more than 10 years, the IRS looked into corporate sponsorships of organizations or their events. In 1993, the IRS proposed that corporate sponsorships would not be subject to Unrelated Business Income Tax (UBIT) unless advertising was suspected, and then the entire amount of money for the sponsorship would be subject to taxation. In 1997, Congress passed the Taxpayer Relief Act, which exempted qualified corporate sponsorships from tax if there was no expectation of a substantial return benefit other than using the sponsor's name, logo, or slogan. Anything else would be considered advertising and would generate UBIT for the tax-exempt organization.

In March 2000, the IRS issued a revised set of proposed regulations regarding corporate sponsorship payments made to nonprofit organizations. They attempt to provide clearer understanding of what differentiates a sponsorship acknowledgment from advertising. For example, using logos and slogans in recognition is acceptable but only if they do not contain qualitative or comparative descriptions of the sponsor's products or services. These proposed regulations would eliminate the strict tainting rule from the 1993 rules. If a tax-exempt organization were to receive monies for sponsorship payments *and* advertising, the entire payment would not be considered subject to UBIT; only that portion to which the standard UBIT analysis would apply would be taxable.

Of course, the IRS left one area controversial—that of exclusivity arrangements. An association or organization can select to have one exclusive sponsor, but this sole sponsor cannot also be designated as the sole sponsor of its products or services in addition to being the sole sponsor of the event. Plus, these new proposed IRS regulations do not apply to trade shows or periodicals. Yet they impose on the nonprofit organization the extra burden of determining the fair market value of any given substantial return benefit. These proposed sponsorship regulations are being opposed by many nonprofit associations, and undoubtedly the controversy between the IRS and the nonprofit community will continue well into the 21st century. See Appendix 10–D—IRS Issues Final Corporate Sponsorship Regulations.

It appears that the controversy began when the IRS decided that the payments from corporations to organizers of college football bowl games were not charitable gifts but taxable unrelated business income that the universities received in exchange for giving the corporations significant advertising exposure at the games.

At the same time, many nonprofit organizations were relieved that putting corporate logos on the organization's materials handed out at special events (such as cups and T-shirts) would not be considered advertising and therefore would not be taxed. Nonprofit organizations look to build ties with corporations that provide for company use of the organizations' names in marketing. These arrangements can be lucrative to the nonprofit organizations. Of course, there is the fear that corporations will try to take advantage of any nonprofit organization's good name, but the nonprofit can benefit greatly from corporate sponsorships, especially if it is careful in constructing its deals.

The Olympic Games of 1996 were a prime example of the opportunities offered to the corporate world to financially sponsor a nonprofit organization's events. The games held in Atlanta, Georgia, cost $1.6 billion to stage. Organizers of the games planned early on to solicit corporate marketing dollars rather than rely upon traditional philanthropy or government grants. In addition to ticket sales, the sale of Olympic paraphernalia and commemorative coins, and fees paid by television stations to broadcast the games, corporate sponsorships were responsible for paying for the games.

According to an article in *The Chronicle of Philanthropy*,

> The Olympic balance sheet is complex. More than $500 million comes from broadcast rights, bought by

NBC and a handful of foreign television networks that will air the Games. Another $500 million comes from corporate sponsorships, which are fees paid by companies for rights to use the Olympic name and logo in advertising. Companies choose from three types of sponsorships:

- Worldwide Sponsors, limited to 10 companies. These were international corporations, such as Coca-Cola and Xerox, that had the right to promote their Olympic sponsorship in any of the 197 countries competing in the Games. Their contracts covered two Olympic seasons, both winter and summer Games.
- Centennial Olympic Games Partners, also limited to 10 companies. These were American companies, such as Home Depot, that didn't have the international market of the Worldwide Sponsors and focused their Olympic promotion in the United States. They could link themselves to two or more Olympic Games depending upon their contract.
- Centennial Olympic Games Sponsors, which were unlimited in number; at least twenty companies signed up. These sponsors had a narrower market than the corporations in the top two categories. They paid lower fees for more limited promotional rights. For example, Georgia Power only promoted its Olympic affiliation in the state, and the "Wheel of Fortune" and "Jeopardy" television game shows promoted their affiliation only to their viewers.

Worldwide Sponsors and Centennial Olympic Games Partners paid up to $40 million each for sponsorship privileges. Centennial Olympic Games sponsors paid less, usually about $23 million each.

However, not all money from sponsorships and broadcast rights ended up in the coffers of the Atlanta Committee for the Olympic Games. A large chunk went to the International Olympic Committee, which owned the rights to the Games, and the United States Olympic Committee, which provided technical assistance to American cities that ran the Games and promoted sports in the United States. In the end, the Atlanta committee received 35 percent of the Worldwide Sponsorship money and 70 percent of the other two sponsorships. Its share of the broadcasting contracts was 60 percent.

Corporate sponsors pay for their promotional rights in cash, in-kind services, or a combination of the two. The IBM Corporation provided an elaborate computer system and personnel to the Atlanta Committee for the Olympic Games to become an Olympic Games Partner, while Home Depot paid $40 million cash for the same right (The Chronicle of Philanthropy, 1996).

Unlike the Olympics or universities with bowl games that attract millions of television viewers and millions of sponsorship dollars, most nonprofit organizations will attract fewer sponsorship dollars for much smaller venues. Also, corporate sponsorships can be relatively simple gifts of cash given to support an event or very complexly structured financial deals between corporations and nonprofits.

In 1999, the American Society of Civil Engineers (ASCE) decided to seek corporate sponsors to underwrite its annual conference and exposition. The conference had been held for years around the United States and always included exhibitors, but never before had sponsorships been solicited. A modest first-time sponsorships goal of $50,000 was set. Events were identified, benefits were assigned to the events, and "prices" were set for the sponsorships of the events. A committee was formed of local, regional, and national ASCE members, along with staff from the ASCE conference/meetings department and the ASCE Foundation. Through a series of weekly conference calls, a list of corporate prospects was developed, the prospects were cultivated and solicited by the committee members, and the $50,000 was secured within four months.

Based on the success of this initial model, the sponsorship program continued to grow at ASCE. In 2002, more than $150,000 was raised for the annual conference at which the Society's 150th anniversary was celebrated. Since beginning its sponsorship program in 1999, the ASCE Foundation has raised more than $3 million through this program to support various ASCE meetings. In 2007, more than $800,000 was raised for ASCE and its affiliates by the ASCE Foundation's sponsorship program.

What was the secret to these successes? The structured weekly meetings of volunteers, the peer-to-peer solicitation methods used, the appropriate pricing of the events, and benefits that interested the corporations being solicited. Committee members asked their business colleagues to support events they knew would benefit their businesses by providing the exposure they needed. In Chapter 16, Appendix 16–F provides an example of a sponsorship package developed by the ASCE Foundation for the 2007 ASCE Conference in Orlando, Florida.

This is an example of corporate sponsorships on a small scale. Large or small, sponsorships are becoming more and more part of the culture of corporate fundraising. Thus, it is important to develop policies regarding sponsorships. First, make sure that sponsorships meet your organization's needs. Then, consider what needs your potential sponsors may have. Define the program so that both your members, the board, the staff, and the vendors understand exactly what is being offered. Identify your entire package in writing and make sure that what it offers fits the image of the organization. Always be conscious of what is and what is not taxable income.

After deciding what you will offer to sponsors, develop your marketing plan. Determine what type of recognition will be given, keeping in mind that recognition is not the same as advertising. Remember, there is a difference between sponsorships and endorsements. Test your marketing by beginning with your own vendors—those close to you. See what works, what attracts them and what doesn't. Consider removing items that are not of great interest and try to expand upon those that are appealing to potential sponsors.

Once your package is tested and set, begin marketing. Once a sponsor agrees to a package, be prepared to send an invoice immediately with the agreed-upon terms. If the corporation is interested in more than the sponsorship package—some agreement that would include some form of advertising—make sure that you provide two contracts or agreements and send separate invoices. This will separate what is nontaxable from what is taxable under IRS rules and regulations. Clearly identify how the sponsor should make out the checks for payment and where to send the payment. If in doubt about anything, consult with your organization's legal counsel.

Endorsements

Endorsements are the opposite of sponsorships. Where sponsorships provide corporate support for the organization or its events, endorsements are provided by the association or organization for the product or services of its vendors. Key here is to remember that your organization's good name is important not only to you but to those who wish to be connected to you through sponsorships, endorsements, or any cause-related marketing program. All you have is your good name, and you do not want to "sell" it without understanding all of the ramifications.

One of the better known examples of an organization providing its name to a product is when the Arthritis Foundation entered into a licensing agreement with McNeil Consumer Products Company, a subsidiary of Johnson & Johnson, to market four over-the-counter analgesic products made by or for McNeil. In return, McNeil agreed to pay the Arthritis Foundation a guaranteed $1 million plus a percentage of royalties if sales reached a certain percentage. Using the Arthritis Foundation's name on the packaging of products and in advertising implied that the medications were made by the Arthritis Foundation. Also, McNeil stated that these products were "especially formulated" when they were no different from other McNeil products. When the attorney generals of 19 states decided to sue for what they determined were false representations of these products, McNeil and the Arthritis Foundation agreed in the settlement that any future advertising would not claim that the products were new, that the Arthritis Foundation helped to create the products, and that they were doctor recommended. Even though it received substantial money from the agreement, the Arthritis Foundation lost its credibility with the public. Their good name was lost for $1 million.

Another example of an endorsement gone awry was the American Medical Association's (AMA's) endorsement of Sunbeam Corporation's home products. Unfortunately, this was undertaken without the buy-in of AMA's membership, and the AMA board was forced to back out of its agreement with Sun-

beam. The company sued, and AMA settled the suit for $10 million. Five of AMA's senior executives lost their jobs due to this unwisely undertaken endorsement agreement.

Endorsing a product essentially communicates to the general public that the nonprofit approves the product, especially when the nonprofit's name is used on the product. If anything were to go wrong with the product, the nonprofit's name could be damaged. Lauren W. Bright, an attorney with Shaw Pittman's Nonprofit Organizations Practice in Washington, DC, notes (Bright and Jacobs, 2004):

> In planning product endorsement programs, consider the following tips to minimize exposure to risk:
>
> - **Protect your intellectual property.** Because any product endorsement program involves the third-party use of an association's name and logo, the structure of the program and the form of the relationship with such third parties are crucial. The potential exists for misuse of intellectual property, which may result in misrepresentation to the consumer or dilution of the value of the association's trademarks.
> - **Consider the market power of your endorsement.** . . . Avoid activities or communications suggesting or requiring the exclusive use of endorsed products by association members. . . . Ensure that the evaluations and process of testing the products are accurate and reliable.
> - **Assess your tort liability.** . . . Courts have ruled that by standing behind a product, the association has a duty to use reasonable care in issuing any statement of approval or endorsement and to assume financial responsibility in the event that the product proves to be harmful or ineffective. An association might also be the subject of a lawsuit based on . . . a claim . . . made by someone who, based on an association's seal of approval, purchases a product that subsequently causes injury.
> - **Consider the tax implications.** The key tax concern for endorsement programs is that revenue generated from the endorsements may be considered unrelated business income and thus subject to the unrelated business income tax. . . . In the event that such revenues are not considered related income, the payments received may fall within a specific exemption for passive income, such as a royalty. . . . Structure the endorsement agreement in a way that does not require the association to take action beyond that required to ensure the quality of the product and protect the interests of consumers.

Legal risks for an association are inherently related to advice or endorsements. Accordingly, endorsement programs must be understood clearly and managed carefully. By taking steps to establish a sound program structure, an association can develop endorsement programs that minimize its exposure to risk.

Exhibit 10–7 provides an example of one organization's policy on endorsements.

Affinity Programs

Often a nonprofit will form an alliance with a corporation offering specific products or services that are of interest or use to the nonprofit's membership. In return for encouraging its members to utilize the services of a particular vendor, the nonprofit receives a portion of the revenue from sales to its members. For example, a membership association might designate a specific bank credit card or car rental agency as its "official" credit card

Exhibit 10–7 American Society of Civil Engineers Endorsement Policy

1. In general, ASCE and ASCE Organizational Entity endorsements, certifications, guarantees, recommendations and warranties of third-party products and services are prohibited. This does not prohibit the use of ASCE's marks for sponsorships of third-party conferences and nonprofit activities related to ASCE's purpose, objective and mission, pursuant to standard terms and conditions, and subject to approval of ASCE's Executive Director or his designee. In the case of an Institute or Affiliated Entity mark, such sponsorships must also be approved by the Board of Governors/Directors of the respective Institute or Affiliated Entity.

2. Individual staff members may give oral opinions or recommendations regarding third-party products and services solely in their individual capacity, so long as they make clear that such opinions are individual and not official opinions of ASCE or its Organizational Entities.

3. Promotional materials, presentations, articles, etc., that identify ASCE or an ASCE Organizational Entity as a customer or client but do not give an opinion concerning the quality of a product or service are permissible. Case studies outlining ASCE's specific activities with a provider of a third-party product or service are also permitted. Such statements and case studies must be accurate, specific and factual and may not express an endorsement or recommendation. Such statements must be authorized in advance by the associated staff Managing Director. An example of a permissible statement is "ASCE is one of Consultant ABC's clients."

4. In cases involving specific vendors formally selected under the affinity program administered by ASCE, use of the ASCE marks may be permitted subject to the terms of a written agreement and ASCE's right to review and approve all uses of such marks in advance. Any such use of ASCE's marks will be restricted to the sale and marketing of the approved affinity programs to members of ASCE and others identified by ASCE, with appropriate protection of the marks and goodwill of ASCE. In addition to use of ASCE marks, other terms of ASCE involvement in affinity programs shall be subject to standard contract terms and conditions.

Source: Courtesy of the American Society of Civil Engineers, Reston, Virginia.

company or car rental agency. In return, members will receive favorable interest rates from the credit card company or lower rental rates when renting a car.

The organization is not stating that one vendor is better than another; rather, it is just saying that if its members use these vendors, it will receive a portion of the profits. This is another form of corporate fundraising. See Appendix 10–E for an example of a policy for a member benefit program developed by the Massachusetts Bar Association.

NONCASH ASSISTANCE FROM CORPORATIONS

More corporate giving officers and staff members of nonprofit organizations are viewing noncash assistance from corporations as a way for the corporations to expand their giving resources at the same time as their actual philanthropic budgets remain the same or even decline. Companies are interested in doing more with less because of corporate downsizing and the continual threat of economic recession. For years, small companies have offered "in-kind" contributions of products, supplies, facilities, services, equipment, seconded (loaned) personnel, below-market loans, and public relations assistance. Now, the larger national and international companies are catching on to this idea and are beginning to understand how to fully integrate noncash gifts with ongoing corporate grant-giving programs. In the beginning, most corporate CEOs considered philanthropy and social responsibility mostly in terms of cash donations. Noncash gifts usually were not listed as part of the corporation's charitable contributions. Often these gifts were made by regional executives without notifying the corporate headquarters or by vice-presidents who took the cost of these gifts out of their budgets. These gifts were counted as the expense of "doing business." Today, this has changed, and corporations are including the cost of noncash "corporate assistance" gifts as part of their total philanthropic dollars. It is estimated that noncash gifts total more than 33 percent of corporate giving.

Nonprofit organizations do not need to spend a lot of time or money persuading corporations to donate their products. They should look at local companies whose products are something they can use. Also, look for companies that are expanding or closing plant operations. Then, contact the company and share with them how their products would help the organization, and tell them the type of recognition they will receive for donating their products. There even are organizations whose sole purpose is to help charities find such donations. A list of some of these organizations is found in Appendix 10–F.

Additional information on the use of noncash gifts to support nonprofit organizations can be found in *Corporate and Foundation Fund Raising: A Complete Guide from the Inside*, by Eugene A. Scanlan, also published by Jones and Bartlett. A comprehensive publication, *Resource Raising: The Role of Non-Cash Assistance in Corporate Philanthropy*, offers information on all of the various types of noncash gifts, brokerage services, and legal and tax aspects of noncash assistance.

OTHER FORMS OF CORPORATE SUPPORT

Corporations may give products, lend executives, share expertise, offer internships, provide office space, or lend equipment in addition to giving cash gifts. In addition, many corporations assist nonprofit fundraising by participating in the local United Way campaign or other federated campaigns. In these campaigns, companies pledge a certain amount of money toward the campaign and then start collecting the money from their employees to meet the pledge. Each year a different employee is asked to chair the campaign for the corporation; goals are set; committees are established; presentations are made; solicitations are conducted; and money is collected. Even special events are held to raise the money necessary to meet the pledge. Also, some companies match the amount of money given by their employees. The collected money is then given to the federated campaign as the corporate contribution to support the community's many charities.

Although there was much criticism in the 1990s and early 2000s of the operations of the national leaders of the United Way of America, local United Way operations represent a long-standing alliance between the corporate world and the nonprofit world. In smaller communities, the alliance remains firm and does much for the health and welfare of local residents.

In the late 1990s, corporations cut back on seeking the involvement of their employees in these campaigns. As campaigns became more hands-off, it was more difficult to maintain the person-to-person relationship, which is what raised the large sums of money in these campaigns.

Some corporations and federated campaigns used electronic campaigns for several years. Ameritech, Federal Express, the Gap, and General Motors used an automated telephone system to collect charity pledges, while IBM used computer kiosks at 75 of its locations. Other companies developed electronic pledge cards that allowed employees to use e-mail to send in their pledges.

In late 2000, even newer technologies were being tested by high-tech businesses hoping to break into office workplace giving by using the Internet. Of course, this challenged all the previous methods of solicitation used by the United Way organizations. Instead of traditional pledge cards, donors were offered the opportunity to give online, essentially eliminating the middleman between the donor and the charity. Obviously, the Internet offered employee givers greater options and flexibility.

The greatest question about the high-tech approaches was what would happen when the human touch was lost. If people give to people and not to machines, would the high-tech campaigns be successful?

Today, people are more comfortable with online giving, and more and more gifts are being made electronically. Overall,

there has been a general decline in giving to the United Way, but the cause is contributed to other issues rather than to a move to electronic giving.

DECLINING CORPORATE SUPPORT BECAUSE OF MERGERS, ACQUISITIONS, AND SCANDALS

Nonprofit organizations are usually the last to hear about mergers or takeovers. They are left in doubt about the continuation or renewal of their grants. It is especially difficult when a foreign corporation acquires a U.S. company, because philanthropy is not likely to be part of the foreign company's culture. For example, when Grand Metropolitan PLC acquired Pillsbury Company in 1988, Minneapolis charities found that, while Grand Met had an impressive giving record in Great Britain ($1 million per year), it paled in comparison with Pillsbury's philanthropic history ($8 million in the year before the merger). Even after a promise by Grand Met's senior U.S. corporate representative to match Pillsbury's previous giving, the corporation never equaled that level of support. Grand Met also proceeded to narrow its giving priorities to focus on families and children, thus leaving out many of the arts organizations who previously were supported by Pillsbury.

Another cause of loss of corporate support is the many scandals affecting corporations in the early 2000s. In Houston, ENRON Corporation was a great supporter of charitable causes. When it collapsed, so did the support for so many nonprofits in the area. Similarly, with the failure of WorldCom, charities in its local communities suddenly were without promised financial support.

Nonprofits again turned to smaller, local companies to pick up the differences. Also, in many cases, small business employees are more generous than their big firm counterparts. For those seeking corporate contributions, it is important to remember the smaller local businesses. Although their giving is small compared to large corporations, their giving is local and is crucial to the local charities.

Even though research showed that larger corporations gave more frequently to the arts, educational, and cultural organizations and that smaller businesses gave more often to international causes, all of those surveyed indicated that the greatest factor in determining where they gave was the organization that asked for their support.

THE FUTURE OF CORPORATE GIVING

Corporations have a long and rich history of supporting nonprofit causes. They should not be considered suspect. It is possible to "do good" and still make a profit. Corporate giving that directly benefits the business does not necessarily alter its charitable nature. All aspects of busi-

> *Corporations should not be considered suspect. It is possible to "do good" and still make a profit.*

ness should be, and can be, carried out while paying attention to social responsibility. It is possible to match the needs of the corporation with the needs of the community. Appendices 10–G and 10-H address the relationship between corporate donors and nonprofit organizations and recognizes that some corporate gifts are seen as investments in, rather than contributions to, the organization. This just emphasizes the need for a well thought out giving program. It also emphasizes the need for frequent contact between nonprofits and corporations. Again, even in corporate philanthropy people give to what and whom they know. In short, people give to people.

REFERENCES

AAFRC Trust for Philanthropy. 1994. *Giving USA: The annual report on philanthropy.* New York: AAFRC Trust for Philanthropy.

Barton, N. 2006. How the chronicle compiled its annual survey of corporate giving. *The Chronicle of Philanthropy* (August 17): 37.

Billitteri, T. 2000. Giving among wealthy detailed in 2 studies. *The Chronicle of Philanthropy* (10 August): 10.

Bright, L.W., and J.A., Jacobs. 2004. Cautions for association product endorsements, *Association Management* (May 1).

Charities fear fallout of corporate mergers. 1996. *The Chronicle of Philanthropy* 8, no. 8 (8 February): 8–10.

Corporate Contributions Up 14 Percent in 2005. Committee Encouraging Corporate Philanthropy (CECP). New York. www.corporatephilanthropy.org/research.

Dundjerski, M., and J. Moore. 1994. A rebound ahead for corporate donations? *The Chronicle of Philanthropy* 6, no. 22 (6 September): 1–18.

Giving In Numbers: 2006 Edition, Corporate Giving Standard, March 2006.

Giving In Numbers. 2007. *Corporate Contributions Up 14 Percent in 2005.* Committee Encouraging Corporate Philanthropy (CECP). (March).

Greene, S.G. 1995. Companies seek to do well from giving. *The Chronicle of Philanthropy* 7 (September 7): 13.

Gurin, M. 1987. Don't rush into cause-related marketing: Disadvantages and dangers. *NSFRE Journal* (spring): 47–53.

Hall, H. 1993. Joint ventures with business: A sour deal? *The Chronicle of Philanthropy* 5 (6 April): 21–22.

Hall, H. 2006. Coming on strong: How much Americans gave for disaster relief and where disaster-relief donations went, *The Chronicle of Philanthropy* (June 29): 25.

Kane, B. 1982. Corporate philanthropy: Historical background. *Corporate Philanthropy,* Council on Foundations: 132–135.

Moore, J., and Williams, G. 1997. Give and tell. *The Chronicle of Philanthropy* (13 November): 9–11.

Murawski, J. 1996. A banner year for giving. *The Chronicle of Philanthropy* 8, no. 16 (30 May): 1–34.

Nobles, M. 2006. Grabbing a cause. *The NonProfit Times* (July): 27.

Olympic fund raising focuses on attracting large corporate sponsors. 1996. *The Chronicle of Philanthropy* 8, no. 6 (11 January): 9–12.

Panepento, P. 2006. To market, to market. *The Chronicle of Philanthropy* (May 18): 20–26.

Roberts, B. 1990. Fund-raising for the 1990s: A changing partnership. *NSFRE Journal* (winter): 14–16.

Smith, C. 1995. Can private foundations woo corporations? *Corporate Philanthropy Report* 10, no. 5: 1, 3–4.

Wilhelm, Ian. 2006. A surge in corporate giving, *The Chronicle of Philanthropy* (August 17): 28–36.

Sample of a Coalition That Successfully Raised Corporate Funds

The Extraordinary Women Engineers Project: *Changing Our World—True Stories of Women Engineers*

Coalition Members

Accreditation Board for Engineering and Technology
Alliance of Technology and Women
American Association for the Advancement of Science
American Association of Engineering Societies
American Council of Engineering Companies
American Institute of Aeronautics and Astronautics
American Institute of Chemical Engineers
American Institute of Constructors
American Institute for Medical and Biological Engineering
American Physical Society
American Public Works Association
American Society of Agricultural and Biological Engineers
American Society of Certified Engineering Technicians
American Society of Civil Engineers—Secretariat
American Society of Heating, Refrigerating and Air Conditioning Engineers
American Society of Mechanical Engineers
American Society of Naval Engineers
American Society of Plumbing Engineers
American Water Works Association
Arizona State University, Ira A. Fulton School of Engineering
AACE International—The Association for the Advancement of Cost Engineering
ASFE
ASM International
ASM Materials Education Foundation
Biomedical Engineering Society
Construction Management Association of America
Colorado School of Mines, Division of Engineering
Illuminating Engineering Society of North America
Institute of Electrical and Electronics Engineers
Institute of Industrial Engineers
Japan Society of Civil Engineers

Junior Engineering Technical Society (JETS)
Kettering University
Key Women in Energy
MentorNet
Mississippi State University, James Worth Bagley College of Engineering
National Academy of Building Inspection Engineers
National Academy of Engineers
National Academy of Forensic Engineers
National Association for College Admission Counseling
National Association of Women in Construction
National Council of Examiners for Engineering and Surveying
National Engineers Week Foundation
National Institute of Ceramic Engineers
National Society of Black Engineers
National Society of Professional Engineers
North Carolina State University, College of Engineering
Purdue University, College of Engineering
Rowan University
Society of American Military Engineers
Society of Automotive Engineers, Women Engineers Committee
Society of Fire Protection Engineers
Society of Hispanic Professional Engineers
Society of Naval Architects and Marine Engineers
Society of Women Engineers
TMS—The Minerals, Metals, and Materials Society
Texas Tech University
University of Delaware, College of Engineering
University of Michigan, College of Engineering
University of Texas, San Antonio College of Engineering
University of Wisconsin—Madison
Women in Engineering Programs and Advocates Network
Women's Transportation Seminar
WGBH

Source: Courtesy of ASCE Foundation, Reston, Virginia.

CHANGING OUR WORLD

True Stories of
Women Engineers

SYBIL E. HATCH

with a Foreword by Dr. Mae C. Jemison

Hollywood Tech Star: A Day in the Life of Wendy Aylsworth

Hollywood produces special effects galore—mostly on computers. But the movies we see are still largely shot the old-fashioned way on celluloid film. It's time movies went digital!

Computer engineer and technical guru Wendy Lynn Aylsworth is leading the charge.

As vice president of technology at Warner Bros. Studios, she oversees the hottest new technology for TV, movies, and Digital Cinema (D-Cinema).

Over time, celluloid film becomes dusty, scratched, and faded, but D-Cinema keeps movies looking as perfect as they did on opening night, even after hundreds of viewings!

Some day soon, you'll see digital movies with more vibrant colors and higher-resolution images on screen for a richer movie-going experience.

WENDY AYLSWORTH IS STANDING IN FRONT OF A SET FROM ER ON THE WARNER BROS. LOT WHERE SHE WORKS ON NEW TECHNOLOGY USED IN TV AND MOVIE PRODUCTION. WENDY'S HELPING TO STANDARDIZE PRODUCTION TECHNOLOGY—GETTING ALL THE BITS AND PARTS TO COMMUNICATE BETWEEN EACH OTHER IN A METHODICAL WAY—SO TV PROGRAMS LIKE ER CAN BE SEEN IN MANY COUNTRIES.

HOW DOES D-CINEMA WORK? IT BEGINS WITH A DIGITAL FILM MASTER THAT'S CREATED USING A DIGITAL CAMERA, COMPUTER-BASED ANIMATION, OR FILM THAT'S BEEN DIGITIZED ON A FILM SCANNER. DIGITAL AUDIO IS THEN ADDED BEFORE THE DIGITIZED FILM IS COMPRESSED AND SENT TO THE MOVIE THEATER VIA DISKS OR SATELLITE. ONCE IT'S RECEIVED AT THE THEATER, DIGITIZED CONTENT IS LOADED INTO A DIGITAL PROJECTOR FOR VIEWING. HERE, WENDY IS CHECKING THE QUALITY OF A DIGITAL MASTER.

When she's not traveling on business, Wendy spends much of her day in meetings figuring out how to put new technology into place behind the scenes. Here, Wendy strolls on the set of the *Gilmore Girls* en route to a planning meeting for a D-Cinema launch, though "we never interrupt during a shoot."

"Troubleshooting technical problems is part of every workday. As technology becomes more complex, problem solving requires different creative approaches." For example, Wendy's team is testing one of the first 4K digital projectors (below) in the world. "We ran a movie on it and suddenly the screen went black for a moment. We had to figure out why the system hiccuped." Warner Bros. has begun a one-year trial of a digital movie system in Japan. The first film to run is Tim Burton's *Corpse Bride*.

Wendy frequently travels abroad to attend conferences on standards for TV and movie technology. In fact, she sits on a United Nations committee for international telecommunications. "When we standardize technology, we can share entertainment all over the world. For example, North American TV programs and movies can be shown in Asia, and vice versa. These trips are exciting and give me a chance to meet interesting people, see other cultures—and do some shopping."

When Wendy's at home, she enjoys watching a softball game with friends and family. Sometimes she even plays on a team. On weekends, she often catches up with her college-age sons. "I recently spent a Saturday painting dorm rooms and moving furniture!"

What's Wendy's other passion? "Making a good education accessible to all kids! A good education teaches you how to get information to make the best decisions. That's a critical skill to have throughout life."

MAE JEMISON WAS THE FIRST AFRICAN-AMERICAN WOMAN IN SPACE. WHILE ABOARD THE SPACE SHUTTLE, SHE CONDUCTED MORE THAN 44 DIFFERENT BIOMEDICAL EXPERIMENTS—INCLUDING HOW FROG EMBRYOS DEVELOPED IN WEIGHTLESSNESS.
CHEMICAL ENGINEER

IN HER SPARE TIME, RUTHIE LYLE ENJOYS TRAINING AND RUNNING IN MARATHONS. SHE'S ALSO STUDYING SPANISH TO HELP DEVELOP A MULTICULTURAL PERSPECTIVE. "I'M ALWAYS LOOKING TO BROADEN MY VIEWS AND EXPAND MY ABILITY TO LEARN BECAUSE THAT'S HOW I WILL FIND NEW WAYS TO HELP THE WORLD COMMUNICATE."
ELECTRICAL ENGINEER

ALBA COLON'S WEEKEND BEGINS ON FRIDAY, A BUSY DAY OF PRACTICE AND QUALIFYING SESSIONS FOR NASCAR. THERE ARE RACE CARS COMING AND GOING FROM THE GARAGE AREA TO THE RACE TRACK. THE CREW'S HOVER OVER THE ENGINES TALKING ABOUT HOW TO GET THE CARS TO GO FASTER.
MECHANICAL ENGINEER

WOMEN DESIGN CARS FOR THEMSELVES AND THEIR FAMILIES! FOR EXAMPLE, THE WINDSTAR WAS THE FIRST VEHICLE TO HAVE "SLEEPING BABY LIGHTS." THE DRIVER CAN OPEN ANY DOOR WITHOUT SHINING OVERHEAD DOME LIGHTS INTO A SLEEPING CHILD'S EYES. THIS FEATURE HAS SINCE BEEN COPIED ON OTHER VEHICLES. OTHER FAMILY-FRIENDLY FEATURES INCLUDE A LARGER GAS TANK TO REDUCE THE NUMBER OF TRIPS TO THE GAS STATION, AND ADDED SAFETY FEATURES THAT GAVE THE WINDSTAR A FIVE-STAR CRASH SAFETY RATING.
WINDSTAR ENGINEERS

EXTRAORDINARY WOMEN ENGINEERS

THE EXTRAORDINARY WOMEN ENGINEERS PROJECT

Changing Our World: True Stories of Women Engineers is the first product of an exciting new venture—the Extraordinary Women Engineers Project (EWEP). This national initiative is a multi-faceted, multi-media project designed to change the way people look at and talk about engineering and to encourage more academically able young women to pursue a career in engineering. The project is led by a coalition of the country's leading engineering associations, universities, and the WGBH Educational Foundation.

There is a disconnect between current messages about engineering and the things that motivate girls' career choices. Plus, teachers and counselors do not feel adequately prepared to guide students toward engineering careers. EWEP seeks to shift the way engineering is portrayed to young women and those who influence them, so they understand more fully the lifestyle and contributions of engineers.

Changing Our Worlds featured stories form the basis of educational and career resources that will be developed in the next phase of the project. Learn more about EWEP and how you can become involved at www.engineeringwomen.org. Order your personal copy of *Changing Our World* for placement in a school or local library, or to give as a gift by calling 800-548-2723 or visiting www.pubs.asce.org.

Funds are still needed to develop the educational materials to accompany the book for distribution to schools. Teacher/user guides will be developed for math/science teachers, guidance counselors, librarians, and volunteer engineers who attend college fairs on behalf of the profession. If you wish to make a gift to help us complete this project, or if you are interested in learning more about the Extraordinary Women Engineers Project, please contact: 703-295-6348 or by e-mail at dmarsh@asce.org.

THE WINDSTAR MOMS

IN 1999, MORE THAN 30 MOMS, 20 WITH CHILDREN UNDER AGE THREE, CELEBRATED THE ARRIVAL OF THE LATEST ADDITION TO THEIR FAMILY—THE FORD WINDSTAR. AS KEY MEMBERS AND ENGINEERS WITH THE PRODUCT DEVELOPMENT TEAM, THESE "WINDSTAR MOMS" WERE INVOLVED IN SAFETY, ERGONOMICS, ELECTRICAL AND FUEL SYSTEMS, PRODUCT DESIGN AND ENGINEERING, AND CLIMATE CONTROL. INTERESTING AND INNOVATIVE THINGS HAPPEN WHEN

JO DA SILVA SPENT MONTHS IN SRI LANKA OVERSEEING THE CONSTRUCTION OF 55,000 SHELTERS TO PROVIDE HOUSING FOR THE HALF-MILLION PEOPLE DISPLACED BY THE DEVASTATING TSUNAMI THAT HIT THE COASTAL REGIONS IN LATE DECEMBER 2004.
CIVIL ENGINEER

JEANNE YU IS WORKING WITH THE FAA AIRLINER CABIN ENVIRONMENT RESEARCH TEAM ON FINDING WAYS TO PROTECT PASSENGERS AGAINST PESTICIDE OR CHEMICAL CONTAMINATION AND TO MONITOR OZONE EXPOSURE.
MECHANICAL ENGINEER

SHALINI GOVIL-PAI WAS TECHNICAL DIRECTOR ON THE BLOCKBUSTER FILMS *TOY STORY* AND *A BUG'S LIFE*. SHE HAS DEVELOPED SEVERAL VIRTUAL REALITY-BASED GAMES AND FLIGHT SIMULATORS. SHE'S ALSO DIRECTED COMMERCIALS FOR MAJOR CLIENTS SUCH AS NABISCO, LEVI STRAUSS & CO., AND MCDONALD'S, AND HAS AUTHORED SEVERAL BOOKS ON COMPUTER GRAPHICS. "ENGINEERING IS THE THE MOST THOUGHT-PROVOKING CAREER THERE IS."
COMPUTER ENGINEER

Resources for Researching Prospective Corporate Donors

Perhaps the easiest method of obtaining general information on corporations is to use the Internet and go directly to the corporate Web sites. Other resource materials include the following:

ANNUAL REPORTS

(Most corporate annual reports are available on the Internet.)

Moody's Investors Service, Inc. (phone: 212-553-0300; Web site: www.moodys.com)

The Gale Group (phone: 800-877-4253; Web site: www.gale.com)

Ward's Business Directory (online)

World Directory of Business Information (Libraries and Information Web sites)

Major Companies of Asia and Australia

The Foundation Center (phone: 212-620-4230; Web site: www .foundation center.org)
  National Directory of Corporate Giving

National Register Publishing (phone: 800-473-7020; Web site: www.natinalregisterpublishing.com)

John Sibblad Associates

Standard & Poor's (phone: 212-438-1000; Web site: www .standardandpoor.com)

Security Dealers of North America

STATE INDUSTRIAL DIRECTORIES

Biz Journal (Web site: www.bizjournals.com; 41 cities)

City Directories (Boston R. L. Polk and Co.; updated frequently)

Rand McNally International Bankers Directory (Chicago: Rand McNally & Co.; semiannual)

CorpTech (Web site: www.corptech.com; 95,000 plus public and private high-tech companies)

Polk's World Bank Directory, North American Edition (Nashville, TN: R. L. Polk & Co.; semiannual)

Directory of American Savings and Loan Associations (Baltimore: T. K. Sanderson Organization; annual)

Directory of Corporate Affiliations (New York: National Register Publishing Co.; annual)

Marketing Economics Key Plants (New York: Marketing Economic Institute; industrial plants with 100 or more employees; biannual)

Thomas Register of American Manufacturers (New York; Thomas Publishing Co.; annual)

The Taft Group (an imprint of the Gale Group; phone: 800-877-4253; Web site: www.gale.com)

Dun & Bradstreet (phone: 800-234-3867; Web site: www.dnb .com; annual)
  Million Dollar Directory (updated every 30 days; businesses are worth over $1 million; online)
  Regional Business Directories
  Dun's Directory of Service Companies
  Dun's Consultants Directory
  Market Identifiers (DMI) (information on all Dun & Bradstreet Company Listings)
  America's Corporate Families

Leadership Directories, Inc. (phone: 212-627-4140; Web site: www.leadershipdirectories.com)
  Financial Yellow Book
  Law Firms Yellow Book
  Corporate Yellow Book
  Foreign Representative Yellow Book

Dorland Healthcare Information (was MLR Biomedical Information Services) (phone: 800-784-2332; Web site: www.dorland health.com)
  Medical and Healthcare Marketplace Guide

CASE (Council for Advancement and Support of Education) (phone: 202-328-2273; Web site: www.case.org)
  Matching Gift Details

THE STANDARD DIRECTORY OF ADVERTISERS

Bix Books, Inc. (phone: 800-486-1513)

Harris Publishing Company (2.2 million company profiles at phone: 800-888-5900; Web site: www.companyreach.com)

Hoover's Online (Web site: www.hoovers.com; database has over 21 million public and private companies)

Securities and Exchange Commission (Web site: www.sec.gov)

EDGAR (Electronic Data Gathering Analysis and Retrieval; Web site: www.sec.gov/edgar.shtml)

EDGAR Online (Web site: www.edgar-online.com)

My Virtual Reference Desk (Web site: www.refdesk.com/paper .html; Associated Press, Reuters, wire-service stories)

Dialog (phone: 800-334-2564; Web site: www.dialog.com)

Factiva (changed from Dow Jones Interactive) (Web site: www .factiva.com; phone: 800-369-0166)

LexisNexis (phone: 800-253-5624; Web site: www.lexisnexis .com)

VENDOR LISTINGS

Prospect Identification

Marts and Lundy (phone: 800-526-9005 or 201-460-1660; Web site: www.martsandlundy.com)
1280 Wall Street West
Lyndhurst, NJ 07071

Prospect Research

Association for Professional Researchers for Advancement (formerly American Prospect Research Association)
401 N. Michigan Avenue
Suite 2200
Chicago, IL 60611
Phone: 312-321-5196

Address Verification

TransUnion (credit report)

Telephone Number Research

TeleMatch
6883 Commercial Drive
Springfield, VA 22159
Phone: 800-523-7346

Sample Notice of Matching Gift Program

Check out your company's

Matching Gift Program

If you work for one of the companies listed on the reverse, your generosity will be matched by an additional corporate gift. All you need is a Matching Gift Form from your company's Public Affairs Department. Complete the section designated for employees and mail the form to us. We'll take care of all the other details and paperwork. Your membership is vital to the future of the MUSEUM OF FINE ARTS, HOUSTON and we appreciate your continued support.

For more information: call the Membership Office at 713/639-7550.

Corporate Matching Funds may not be used to increase your membership category or benefits.

MUSEUM OF FINE ARTS
HOUSTON

Matching Gift Companies

Air Products & Chemicals Inc.
Akzo Nobel Inc.
American Express Financial
American Express Foundation
Ameritech
Amoco Foundation, Inc.
AmGRIP
Apache Corporation
ARCO Chemical Company
ARCO Foundation
AT&T Foundation
Atochem North American Foundation
BankAmerica Foundation
Bankers Trust Foundation
Bank One, Texas, N.A.
Baroid Corporation
Black & Decker Corporation
The Blount Foundation, Inc.
Boeing Company
British Gas Explorations & Productions. Inc.
BP America Inc.
Caterpillar Foundation
Champion International Corporation
Charter Bank Houston
Chase Manhattan Bank
Chevron Corporation
Chubb & Son. Inc.
CIGNA Foundation
Citibank
CITICORP Foundation
Liz Claiborne Foundation
Coca-Cola Company
CogniSeis Development
Compaq Computer Foundation
Computer Associates International
Continental Group Foundation
Cooper Industries Foundation
Cray Research Foundation
Deluxe Corporation Foundation
Digital Equipment Corporation
Dixie Carriers, Inc.
Dresser Industries, Inc.
Dunn, Kacal, Adams, Pappas & Law
Eli Lilly & Company Foundation
Enmar, Inc.
Enron Foundation
Exxon Corporation
Federated Department Stores
Fireman's Fund Insurance
Georgia-Pacific
Glaxo, Inc.
GE Fund
John Hancock Mutual life

Harcourt General Inc.
Hoechst Celanese Foundation Inc.
Houghton Mifflin Company
Houston Endowment Inc.
IBM Corporation
IMCERA Group, Inc.
Johnson & Higgins of Texas Inc.
Johnson & Johnson
JP Morgan
Kemper Securities Group, Inc.
Harris & Eliza Kempner Fund
Lyondell Petrochemical Company
May Stores Foundation. Inc.
Mayor, Brown & Platt
McFall & Sartwelle
McFall, Sherwood & Sheeny, P.C.
McGraw-Hill Foundation, Inc.
Merrill Lynch
The Mitsui USA Foundation
Mobil Foundation, Inc.
Monsanto Fund
MBank Houston
Nalco Chemical Company
The Neiman Marcus Group
The Northern Trust Company
Olin Corporation
Panhandle Eastern Corporation
Pitney Bowes
Pogo Producing Company
RJR Nabisco Foods
RJR Nabisco, Inc.
Santa Fe Pacific Foundation
Sara Lee Foundation
Sedgwick James, Inc.
Shearson Lehman Brothers Inc.
Harold Simmons Foundation
Sonat Foundation
Sun Life Assurance Company Canada
SBC Foundation
Tenneco Inc.
Texas Commerce Bank-Houston
Texas Instruments Foundation
Times Mirror
Transamerica Foundation
Travelers Companies Foundation
Union Pacific Corporation
Union Texas Petroleum
Vastar Resources Inc.
Vista Chemical Company
Wells Design, Inc.
Westinghouse Electric Foundation
WMX Technologies

MUSEUM OF FINE ARTS
HOUSTON

1001 Bissonnet at Main • Houston, Texas 77005
713/639-7300 TDD/TTY 639-7390 *(for the Hearing Impaired)*

Source: Courtesy of the Museum of Fine Arts, Houston, Texas.

IRS Issues Final Corporate Sponsorship Regulations

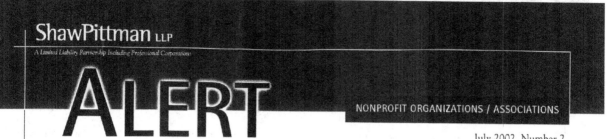

NONPROFIT ORGANIZATIONS / ASSOCIATIONS

July 2002 Number 2

IRS Issues Final Corporate Sponsorship Regulations

On April 25, 2002, the Internal Revenue Service (IRS) issued final regulations to address corporate sponsorship payments to tax-exempt organizations, with several clarifications and one noteworthy change from regulations proposed on March 1, 2000. The IRS first proposed regulations on this issue in 1993, but substantial changes were made in the law as part of the Taxpayer Relief Act of 1997. The final regulations implement Section 513(i) of the Internal Revenue Code (IRC), which determines when a corporate sponsorship payment to an exempt organization will be subject to tax. These regulations include a number of burdensome requirements for tax-exempt organizations that might otherwise expect to avoid tax on legitimate non-dues revenue sources. This Shaw Pittman Alert provides an explanation of the law and final regulations and identifies certain problem areas.

Background

This controversial subject initially arose because of attempts by the IRS in the early 1990s to tax revenues received by the Cotton Bowl (an exempt organization) from Mobil Oil, which was a corporate sponsor of the bowl game. The IRS proposed audit guidelines that were poorly written and soundly criticized. In that effort, the IRS used a "substantial benefits" analysis that had been used for determining whether payments by donors were tax deductible gifts. Following the loud public outcry from the exempt organization community arguing that the "substantial benefits" test was inappropriate, the IRS withdrew the guidelines and instead proposed regulations that were generally more favorable to tax-exempt organizations.

The 1993 proposed regulations focused on the nature of the conduct of the exempt organization rather than on the benefits received by the sponsor. Central to this approach was the IRS definition of sponsor "acknowl-

edgement" as opposed to sponsor "advertising." The 1993 regulations defined a sponsorship acknowledgement as the mere recognition of sponsorship payments or identification of the sponsor rather than promotion of its products, services or facilities. Under this definition, acknowledgement meant use of a sponsor's name, logos or established slogans (as long as they did not contain comparative or qualitative descriptions); listings of sponsor locations and telephone numbers; provision of value-neutral descriptions, including displays or visual depictions; and provision of sponsor brand or trade names and product or service listings. These qualities would indicate that a payment was an acknowledgement of corporate sponsorship rather than advertising. It was provided that qualified sponsorship acknowledgements did not result in unrelated business income tax (UBIT) to the exempt organization.

The 1993 proposed regulations also contained a harsh "tainting" rule. The tainting rule provided that if any portion of a payment did not constitute a qualified sponsorship payment (for example, if part of the payment was for advertising), then no portion of the payment could be considered a tax-exempt sponsorship payment. Under the tainting rule, any activities, messages or programming material constituting advertising made the entire payment to the exempt organization subject to UBIT. In addition, the 1993 proposed regulations expressly did not apply to qualified convention and trade show activities or to the sale of advertising in exempt organization periodicals.

In 1997, with the 1993 proposed regulations still pending (yet not amended, withdrawn or finalized), Congress passed the Taxpayer Relief Act, which amended the IRC by adding Section 513(i) to address corporate sponsorship payments. While the statute reflected much of the 1993 proposed regulations, the legislation differed in some significant ways. Principal among these differences

Washington, DC Northern Virginia New York Los Angeles London   www.shawpittman.com

Source: Courtesy of Jefferson Glassie, Pillsbury Winthrop Shaw Pittman LLP, Washington, DC.

ShawPittman LLP

A Law Partnership Including Professional Corporations

was that the new Section 513(i) returned to the inappropriate "substantial benefits" definition in analyzing the taxable effects. In addition, the new law eliminated the tainting rule and adopted an allocation approach instead. Under Section 513(i), each payment is now analyzed to determine if any portion is a qualified sponsorship payment. Whether a non-qualified part of the transaction between an exempt organization and sponsor would result in UBIT then depends upon application of existing UBIT rules.

On March 1, 2000, the IRS proposed new regulations to address Section 513(i) and indicated that it was officially withdrawing the 1993 proposed regulations. The IRS requested comments and required that they be submitted by May 30, 2000 and a public hearing was held on June 21, 2000. The final regulations on corporate sponsorship payments were recently published and closely resemble the proposed regulations, with one significant departure and several clarifications.

Final Regulations

1.   "Substantial Return Benefits"

Released on April 25, 2002, the final regulations provide guidance for exempt organizations in determining when Section 513(i)'s "safe harbor" will apply to certain corporate sponsorship payments, freeing them from UBIT. Similar to the language of Section 513(i) and substantively the same as in the proposed rules, the final regulations define "qualified sponsorship payments" as *"any payment by any person engaged in a trade or business with respect to which there is no arrangement or expectation that the person will receive any substantial return benefit."* "Payment" includes the payment of money, transfer of property or performance of services. The regulations note that, for purposes of determining whether a payment is a qualified sponsorship payment, it is irrelevant (1) whether the sponsored activity is related to the recipient organization's exempt purpose, or (2) whether the sponsored activity is temporary or permanent.

The final regulations retain the definition of "substantial return benefit" (SRB) created in the proposed regulations, but not provided in the statute itself. An SRB is any return benefit to the sponsor other than (1) a use or acknowledgement of the sponsor's name or logo in connection with the exempt organization's activities, or (2) certain goods or services that have insubstantial value. If a corporate sponsor does receive an SRB for its payment, the safe harbor does not apply and a determination as to whether the payment (or portion thereof) is subject to UBIT depends on existing principles and rules. This analysis is consistent with Section 513(i).

The line between advertising and "use or acknowledgement" is not always clear, but the final regulations provide some examples of situations where the return benefit will not be considered advertising. The regulations state that an exempt organization may display a company's name, logo and slogan, at least to the extent that the slogan is an established part of the sponsoring company's identity. An organization may also display a sponsor's products at the sponsored event and include the sponsor's name in the title of the event. Listing the sponsor's location, telephone number, or Internet address is acceptable as well.

By contrast, qualitative or comparative statements and endorsements of a sponsor's products are treated as advertising and corresponding sponsorship payments may be subject to UBIT up to fair market value of the advertising benefit. Advertising is defined as any message or other programming material which is broadcast or otherwise transmitted, published, displayed or distributed that promotes or markets any trade, business, service, facility or product. However, the mere display or distribution of a product by the corporate sponsor or exempt organization at the sponsored activity is not advertising.

The proposed rules would have required that a return benefit in goods or services have a fair market value of no more than 2% of the sponsorship payment or $79, *whichever is less*, to retain the payment's exemption from

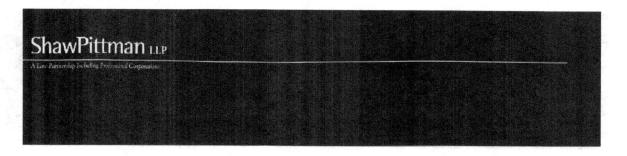

ShawPittman LLP
A Law Partnership Including Professional Corporations

UBIT. This $79 ceiling was widely criticized in public comments and while the final regulations preserve the 2% requirement, the $79 limit was eliminated. To determine whether the 2% threshold has been exceeded in any year, all return benefits in that year (other than use or acknowledgement) must be considered. If the combined fair market value of return benefits is greater than 2% of the sponsorship payment, then the entire fair market value of such benefits, not merely the excess over 2%, is an SRB.

The exempt organization is charged with valuing the SRB on the date the parties enter into a binding, written sponsorship contract or, if no sponsorship contract is entered into, the date on which the return benefit is provided. The final regulations retain the standard for determining a benefit's fair market value as introduced in the proposed regulations, despite complaints from the public that the standard offered insufficient guidance. Specifically, the benefit must be valued at the price at which it would be provided to a willing recipient and a willing provider, neither being under any compulsion to enter into the arrangement and both having reasonable knowledge of relevant facts. So long as the exempt organization makes a reasonable and good faith valuation of the SRB, it will not be set aside for purposes of applying the Section 513(i) safe harbor.

In the comments, several concerns were expressed that a determination of the fair market value of the benefits, a value that would seem to be known only to the sponsor, could be very difficult to make. Some complained that exempt organizations essentially will be forced to analyze another taxpayer's situation. Other commentors were concerned that smaller tax-exempt organizations could be especially hard-hit by this aspect of the final rules. In the final regulations, the IRS responds to these concerns by pointing to current parallel requirements in Section 6115 of the Code, which already requires charitable organizations described in Section 170(c) to make a good faith estimate of benefits provided to donors that exceed $75.

2.   Trade Shows, Periodicals, Internet Links

The final regulations, consistent with the proposed rules, state that the "safe harbor" provided by the law and regulations does *not* apply to payments received in connection with trade shows or periodicals. Qualified trade shows are separately considered exempt from UBIT (further guidance may be found in Section 513(d) and IRS Reg. §1.513-3). With respect to periodicals, income derived from the sale of advertising *or acknowledgements* in exempt organization periodicals is subject to UBIT, pursuant to the rules in IRS Reg. §1.512(a)-1(f). Periodicals are defined as regularly scheduled and printed material published by or on behalf of the exempt organization that is not related to and primarily distributed in connection with a specific event conducted by the exempt organization. The final regulations clarify that material published electronically is included within the term "printed material."

In a new provision not addressed in the proposed regulations, the final rules provide that an exempt organization may acknowledge sponsors by including hyperlinks to their websites that list the names and web addresses of sponsors. However, if the hyperlink includes a promotion or endorsement of the sponsor or links the Internet user to such a statement attributed to the exempt organization on the sponsor's website, it will constitute advertising and an SRB. It is important to note that the IRS stated this guidance on hyperlinks may not apply outside the context of Section 513(i).

3.   Allocation Rule

Like the proposed regulations, the final rules eliminate the strict and ill-conceived "tainting" rule proposed in 1993 and clarify the "allocation" rule adopted by Congress in 1997. As a result, a tax-exempt organization no longer needs to fear that a payment consisting of both qualified sponsorship payments and advertising will automatically be subject to UBIT in its entirety. Regarding the portion of the payment for which the exempt organi-

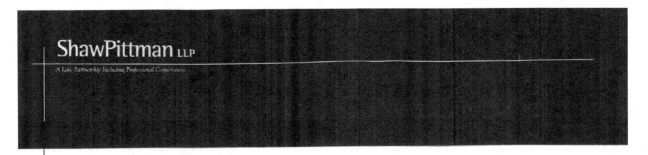

ShawPittman LLP
A Law Partnership Including Professional Corporations

zation provides an SRB, a standard UBIT analysis will apply and the taxability of that portion of the payment must be determined under existing IRS rules.

4.   Exclusivity Arrangements

One of the most criticized aspects of the proposed rules involved exclusivity arrangements. Nevertheless, the final regulations retain language excluding such arrangements from Section 513(i)'s safe harbor. The final rules draw the line at arrangements in which the sole sponsor is designated to be the "exclusive provider" of products or services. Specifically, if the exempt organization agrees, in return for a payment, that products or services that compete with the sponsor's products or services will not be sold or provided in connection with one or more activities of the exempt organization, the portion of the payment attributable to the exclusive provider arrangement is not a qualified sponsorship payment. However, the right to be the sole sponsor of an activity, or the only sponsor representing a particular trade, business or industry, is generally not an SRB. This aspect of the final rules appears to be aimed primarily at universities, colleges and similar academic institutions that often sign exclusivity arrangements with respect to an entire campus or athletic event. Other types of tax-exempt organizations may, nonetheless, be affected.

Some commentators raised concerns that the proposed regulations implied exclusive provider contracts to be automatically subject to UBIT because they fall outside the scope of Section 513(i). In a memorandum published August 14, 2001, the IRS responded that an exempt organization in an exclusive provider relationship, even though the relationship falls outside the safe harbor, would not be subject to UBIT if it did not reach the requisite level of activity to constitute a trade or business under Section 513(a). The IRS contends in the final rules that the level of promotional or marketing efforts taken by the exempt organization pursuant to the exclusive provider contract will be considered in determining whether a payment is subject to UBIT. When an

exempt organization agrees to perform substantial services in connection with the exclusive provider arrangement, the income may be taxable as unrelated to the group's exempt purpose.

Conclusion

The final regulations are effective as of their publication in the *Federal Register* on April 25, 2002 and are applicable for payments solicited or received after December 31, 1997. The final regulations are generally favorable, especially when compared to earlier rules, but there are a number of limitations and provisions that may be potentially difficult for nonprofit organizations and associations to interpret and/or meet. Accordingly, it is important for tax exempt organizations to carefully analyze and evaluate all corporate sponsorship proposals and arrangements and attempt to conform to the provisions set forth by the IRS.

If you have any questions regarding this *Alert* or any other related matter, please contact:

Jerry Jacobs
jerry.jacobs@shawpittman.com   202.663.8011

Jeffery Yablon
jeffery.yablon@shawpittan.com   202.663.8441

Jeff Glassie
jeff.glassie@shawpittman.com   202.663.8036

Tom Arend
tom.arend@shawpittman.com   202.663.8070

Karen Cipriani
karen.cipriani@shawpittman.com   202.663.8069

Lauren Bright
lauren.bright@shawpittmam.com   202.663.8578

Summer Associate Benjamin Chanchkin assisted with the preparation of this *Alert*

Copyright © 2002 by Shaw Pittman LLP. All Rights Reserved. This publication is provided by Shaw Pittman for general information purposes; it is not and should not be used as a substitute for legal advice.

Massachusetts Bar Association Policy for Member Benefit Programs

MBA POLICY FOR MEMBER BENEFIT PROGRAMS

The Massachusetts Bar Association (MBA) may, from time to time, enter into an agreement with a vendor to provide a product or service program (henceforth referred to as a benefit) to MBA members. Any benefit shall be offered to members at a reduced cost not available to the general public and/or must be a unique program, also not available to the general public.

Policy

1. The benefit offered must be of significant interest to a wide range of MBA members.
2. Preference will be given to vendors who have the capacity to offer and service MBA members who reside in all areas of Massachusetts.
3. The proposed benefit must be appropriate for the MBA to undertake and must be related to some aspect of the practice of law and/or the life of an attorney.
4. The benefit program must not conflict with the general purposes of the MBA or any of its established policies.
5. The cost for the benefit must be lower than that available to the general public or the benefit must offer a special service or incentive not available to the general public.
6. The benefit must be of a high quality and the vendor must maintain a reputation for honesty, reliability, and voluntary compliance with the law.
7. The direct and indirect costs related to developing and administering the program shall be assumed by the vendor to the extent possible. In any case, the vendor shall be responsible for all costs related to producing a suitable brochure and/or promotional piece: In addition, the vendor shall assume all costs related to a minimum of one major mailing to the MBA membership promoting the benefit each year. Costs to be assumed by the MBA are

negotiable depending upon the amount of the royalty or service or administrative allowance received by the MBA.

8. The MBA shall have final copy approval on any and all promotional literature prepared by the vendor. No copy may be printed without prior approval of the MBA Executive Director.
9. The MBA benefits are offered to provide special savings or products to its members. The sponsorship of such programs shall in no way imply MBA endorsement of that vendor, products, and/or services over similar products or services offered by other vendors. Such a disclosure must appear on the promotional copy for the benefit.
10. Each proposed benefit will be reviewed by the appropriate MBA staff and must be approved or denied by the Executive Director, who may refer it to the MBA Policy Review Committee as the situation warrants.
11. Once a benefit is approved, all terms of the benefit program must be outlined in a letter of agreement or contract between the MBA and the vendor. This agreement shall include a specific expiration date and options to continue. In addition, the vendor must agree to hold the MBA harmless for any claims arising against vendor.
12. All other considerations being equal, the MBA will approve an in-state vendor over one from out of state and/or give preference to a minority or woman owned business.

Procedure

1. Any vendor seeking to receive MBA sponsorship of a proposed benefit shall receive a copy of this policy from the MBA Membership Development Manager, as well as a deadline date for submitting proposals.
2. The vendor shall then provide a complete written proposal, including:

Source: Courtesy of the Massachusetts Bar Association, Springfield, Massachusetts.

a. a full description of the proposed service(s) or product(s);

b. suggested retail, actual retail, and proposed MBA price(s);

c. proposed marketing and promotional costs to be assumed by vendor;

d. explanation of the marketing plan and sample artwork or brochures, letters, etc., if available;

e. amount and terms of royalty, administrative allowance or service fee to the MBA, if applicable;

f. name of the MBA's contact person at the vendor's office;

g. explanation of the implementation plan and time line for implementation; and

h. information on similar association or group sponsored programs offered by the vendor including names and telephone numbers of administrators at each association or group.

3. The MBA Membership Development Manager must receive this proposal by the date requested during the initial contact. The Membership Development Manager will then submit proposals to the Policy Review Committee for action.

4. The Membership Development Manager shall have the responsibility for the investigation and review of proposed benefits and alternatives and inform the Policy Review Committee of the results of the study.

5. As proposed by the 1985 MBA Special Committee on Membership Services, a special new committee, or subcommittee of the Policy Review Committee, shall be periodically formed to review all current benefits and make recommendations as to possible new benefit programs for the MBA membership. The committee will work directly with the Membership Development Manager.

This policy was approved & adopted by the MBA Policy Review Committee and House of Delegates in 1990.

MBA SALES & MARKETING POLICY TERMS & CONDITIONS JUNE 1995

I. Advertising

Payment. All advertisers are required to pay in advance (payment must accompany insertion order). All rates less 15% recognized agency commission where applicable (no in-house agency discounts given). Publisher reserves the right to hold advertiser and its advertising agency jointly liable for payments due. Advertiser and its advertising agency will be held liable for the total payment for ads cancelled after closing date.

Liability. Advertiser and agencies assume liability and agree to indemnify and hold harmless the publisher for all content of advertisements printed and responsibility for any claims arising therefrom against the publisher. Advertiser acknowledges that it has not relied upon any warranties or representations not incorporated into the agreement.

Restrictions. Advertising space will be sold to vendors, individuals, and/or corporations that provide services and/or sell products which are related to the practice of law and law office management. General consumer goods and services will be considered on an individual basis. Advertisements on the following will not be accepted under any circumstances:

- tobacco;
- alcoholic beverages;
- pornographic material;
- firearms;
- political campaigns (public or bar-related, except as provided by MBA bylaws and election procedures);
- fundraising activities; and
- membership recruitment/solicitations.

MBA Policy

No advertisements will be placed in violation of existing MBA policies. Requests for advertising space are accepted at the discretion of the MBA Executive Director and/or her designee and may be refused if the potential vendor directly competes with an MBA authorized or sponsored program, event or activity.

The MBA Sales Manager and/or the Communications Director will review all potential advertisements for a decision on acceptance. If an advertisement is approved for placement, an Advertising Contract must be completed and returned to the MBA Sales Manager by the date specified. Full payment must be received at the MBA upon approval of the advertisement. No advertisements will run in MBA publications unless full payment has been received. In addition to any legal remedy the publisher may pursue, failure to comply with the terms of the contract will result in the person/vendor being excluded from future advertisements in any MBA publication.

II. Mailing List Rental

Lists/labels rented from the MBA are provided for a one-time use only. Renter and the renter's brokers or agents may not copy, duplicate, record in any manner, or reuse any list/label order. Lists are available in electronic or magnetic media only if the list is provided directly to the renter's mailhouse and, upon completion of the job, is returned directly to the MBA by the mailhouse. In addition to any legal remedy the MBA may pursue, renter agrees to pay $1800 for violation of this provision. Failure to comply with authorized use of the list will result in the person/company being excluded from future rental of MBA lists/labels, as well as other marketing opportunities available through the MBA.

Any person (whether or not an MBA member) and/or company requesting mailing labels must submit a complete sample of the materials to be mailed, along with the completed Mailing Label Agreement. The sample materials and Mailing Label Agreement will be reviewed by the MBA Executive Director or his/her designee and will decide whether or not to provide the mailing labels. If the use of the mailing labels is approved, advance payment, based upon final run estimates, must be received by the MBA before the labels will be released to the renter. A final invoice and/or credit may be issued to the renter after the labels are released, depending upon the final totals.

Mailing lists will be rented to vendors, individuals, and/or corporations that provide services and/or sell products which are related to the practice of law and law office management. General consumer goods and services will be considered on an individual basis. Mailing lists will not be rented for the following under any circumstances:

- tobacco;
- alcoholic beverages;
- pornographic material;
- firearms;
- political campaigns (public or bar-related, except as provided by MBA bylaws and election procedures) ;
- fundraising activities; and
- membership recruitment/solicitations (except as provided by other MBA policies).

No mailing lists will be rented in violation of existing MBA policies. Requests for mailing lists are accepted at the discretion of the MBA Executive Director and/or her designee and may be refused if the potential vendor directly competes with an MBA authorized or sponsored program, event or activity.

Timing of label preparation will depend on MBA seasonal workload. Preparation of MBA-requested lists and labels will take preference over commercially rented labels at all times.

III. Exhibit Space Rental

On-site Services. Exhibitors agree that the exhibit service company assigned by the MBA, to ensure smooth setup, will handle their exhibits. Once the MBA receives the exhibit and advertising contract, with payment, you will receive a package of materials from the exhibit service company detailing their services including electrical and phone installation, identification signs, storage of freight, receiving, and all matters relevant to the operation of the meeting. Exhibitors agree to cooperate with the conditions of the exhibit service company and will not hold the Massachusetts Bar Association or the conference site responsible for providing exhibit services.

Booth Assignments. Exhibit booths are assigned upon receipt of the exhibit contract and full payment. Assignments are made on a first-come, first-served basis. Site determination will be made by the MBA.

Cancellations. Cancellations must be made in writing to receive a 50% refund.

Restrictions.

(1) Exhibitors purchase space solely for their own use and may not allow other vendors to purchase/use space at their booth(s). Exhibitors may display information/literature only at their own

booth. Exhibitors shall only display material that does not conflict with the policies and procedures of the Massachusetts Bar Association, a copy of which will be provided upon request. The MBA reserves the right to remove materials from the exhibition site that conflict with any policy or procedure of the Massachusetts Bar Association. Vendors who have not purchased booth space may not distribute their literature at the meeting.

(2) Exhibit space will be sold to vendors, individuals, and/or corporations that provide services and/or sell products which are related to the practice of law and law office management. General consumer goods and services will be considered on an individual basis. Exhibits of the following will not be accepted under any circumstances:

- tobacco;
- alcoholic beverages;
- pornographic material;
- firearms;
- political campaigns (public or bar-related, except as provided by MBA bylaws and election procedures);
- fundraising activities; and
- membership recruitment/solicitations.

No exhibits which violate existing MBA policies will be accepted. Requests for exhibit space are accepted at the discretion of the MBA Executive Director and/or her designee and may be refused if the potential vendor directly competes with an MBA authorized or sponsored program, event or activity.

IV. Liability

The exhibitor assumes the entire responsibility and liability for losses, damages, expenses and claims arising out of personal injury or damage to the exhibitor's displays, equipment and other property at the exhibit site, and shall indemnify and hold harmless the MBA, its members, employees and agents, from any and all such personal injury, losses, damages, expenses and claims.

EQUAL EMPLOYMENT OPPORTUNITY AND HARASSMENT POLICY

The Massachusetts Bar Association ("MBA"), Massachusetts Bar Institute ("MBI"), Massachusetts Bar Foundation ("MBF"), and the MBA Insurance Agency ("MBAI") affirm their commitment to the full realization of equal employment opportunity in all aspects of their operation, including employment, without regard to race, color, national origin, age, religion, sex, sexual orientation or disability. The MBA, MBI, MBF and MBAI are also committed to take affirmative action to increase representation of minorities, women and people with disabilities in all areas of their workforce.

To demonstrate their commitment to equal opportunity and affirmative action, it is the policy of the MBA, MBI, MBF and MBAI to:

A. Recruit, hire, train and promote persons in all job titles, without regard to race, color, religion, sex, national origin, age, disability or sexual orientation.

B. Base decisions in equal employment so as to further the principle of equal employment opportunity.

C. Ensure that promotion decisions are in accord with principles of equal employment opportunity by imposing only valid requirements for promotional opportunities.

D. Ensure that all personnel actions such as compensation, benefits, transfers, MBA, MBI, MBF and MBAI sponsored activities, education, and social and recreation programs will be administered without regard to race, color, religion, sex, national origin, sexual orientation, age or disability.

Sexual Harassment

Sexual harassment in the workplace is unlawful, and it is unlawful to retaliate against an employee for filing a complaint of sexual harassment or for cooperating in an investigation of a complaint for sexual harassment. The Association, Institute, Foundation and Insurance Agency affirm their commitment to maintain a work environment free of all forms of sexual harassment and discrimination based on race, color, religion, sexual orientation, national origin, age, sex or disability. The Association, Institute, Foundation and Insurance Agency expect all employees to conduct themselves in a professional manner with courtesy and respect for their fellow employees, members and the public. Any harassment on the basis of a person's race, color, religion, sexual orientation, national origin, age, sex or disability will not be tolerated.

This policy defines sexual harassment as any type of sexually oriented conduct, whether intentional or not, that is unwelcome and has the purpose or effect of creating a work environment that is hostile, offensive or coercive to a reasonable person.

In addition, sexual advances, requests for sexual favors, and other verbal or physical conduct of a sexual nature constitute harassment when:

A. Submission to such conduct or communication is made a term or condition either explicitly or implicitly to obtain or maintain employment or services; or

B. Submission to or rejection of such conduct or communication by an individual is used as a factor in decisions affecting such individual's employment or services; or

C. Such conduct or communication had the purpose or effect of substantially interfering with an individual's employment or services or creating an intimidating, hostile or offensive employment or services environment.

The following are some examples of conduct that, depending upon the circumstances, may constitute sexual harassment:

i. unsolicited remarks, gestures or physical contact.
ii. display or circulation of written materials or pictures derogatory to a person's gender or sexual orientation.
iii. unwelcome and unwanted sexual jokes, language or epitaph.
iv. degrading or vulgar words to describe an individual.

Any violations of the policy should be immediately brought to the attention of the Executive Director, General Counselor the Director of Finance and Administration so that a thorough investigation may be conducted and appropriate action taken promptly to deal with your complaint. An investigation of all complaints will be undertaken immediately, and all information will be handled with the highest degree of confidentiality possible under the circumstances and with due regard for the rights and wishes of all parties. Employees may also wish to contact the following agencies:

Massachusetts Commission Against Discrimination
One Ashburton Place, 6th Floor
Boston, Massachusetts 02108
(617) 727-3990

Equal Employment Opportunity Commission
One Congress Street, 10th Floor
Boston, Massachusetts 02114
(617) 565-3200

Any Employee of the Association, Institute, Foundation or Insurance Agency who is found after an investigation to have harassed another in the workplace will be subject to appropriate discipline up to and including termination, depending upon the circumstances of the situation.

USE OF MBA LETTERHEAD

The Massachusetts Bar Association has a policy against distributing MBA letterhead to members for use from their private offices. Any correspondence on MBA letterhead must be prepared at the MBA office and subject to internal review for consistency with MBA policy and compliance with laws and regulations affecting the association. This policy sometimes seems to surprise and even annoy members from time to time.

On Friday, October 11, 1996, at the Legal Section Symposium of the American Society of Association Executives, one of the speakers was Mary Jean Moltenbrey, Chief of the Civil Task Force, Antitrust Division, U.S. Department of Justice. In her presentation, Ms. Moltenbrey stated that the Department has no hostility toward associations, but that the agency has increased resources for enforcement, so they may appear to be more interested in associations than in the past. She also expressed the view that associations are by their nature combinations of competitors, and so any meeting or other form of action creates the possibility of a per se violation of the antitrust laws. Ms. Moltenbrey and her copresenter Art Herold from Webster, Chamberlain and Bean recommended that all associations clearly delineate through policy adopted by the association the authority to speak for the association. They noted that action was taken against the National Automobile Dealers Association based on a speech given by their president at an annual meeting.

Ms. Moltenbrey particularly focused on who can use letterhead and title of office. Actions taken under the apparent authority of the association will create liability for the association. She said that the Department of Justice takes a "strict view of use of association letterhead and titles" and that the department is "unlikely to be swayed by the argument that use of association letterhead was unauthorized."

This presentation supports the MBA policy regarding use of letterhead.

MBA ELECTRONIC CONFERENCE CENTER POLICY

As adopted by the MBA Policy Review Committee on September 30, 1996

The Massachusetts Bar Association is providing electronic communications on the Internet between and among its members, its staff and the public. Before any person may participate in MBA electronic conferences, they must execute and return to the MBA, the following signed Electronic Communications Agreement:

Electronic Communications Agreement

The Massachusetts Bar Association is a private, nonprofit, professional association composed primarily of lawyers and judges. The Electronic Conference Center is provided as a benefit and service of the MBA in furtherance of its nonprofit purpose.

The Electronic Conference Center is intended to provide a forum for interested parties to communicate about common issues in the law and legal practice, as well as the programs and projects of the MBA.

The MBA does not exert editorial control over the materials that are posted by third parties onto this site or materials that are electronically mailed by third parties to any other persons. The MBA is not responsible for any material posted by any third party and the opinions expressed by third parties are theirs alone and do not necessarily reflect the official position of the MBA.

The MBA specifically disclaims any and all liability for any claims posted by third parties, including any expressed or implied warranties of merchantability or fitness for a particular use. In no event shall the MBA be liable for any special, indirect or consequential damages or any damages whatsoever resulting from loss of use, data or profits, arising out of or in connection with the use, performance, or reliance upon any information posted by third parties.

Persons participating in electronic conferences expressly waive all confidentiality of any information or material posted in the Electronic Communications Conference Center.

Persons participating in electronic conferences agree not to post any defamatory, abusive. profane, threatening, offensive or illegal materials.

Persons participating in electronic conferences agree not to post any information or other material protected by copyright without the permission of the copyright owner. By posting material, the posting party warrants and represents that it owns the copyright with respect to such material or has received permission from the copyright owner. In addition, the posting party grants the MBA and users of the Electronic Communications Conference Center the nonexclusive right and license to display, copy, publish, distribute, transmit, print and use such information or other material.

Persons participating in electronic conferences agree not to post information that could encourage or facilitate users in arriving at any agreement which leads to price fixing, a boycott of another's business or other conduct which is intended to illegally restrict free trade.

The MBA does not actively monitor the Electronic Communications Conference Center for inappropriate postings, and does not undertake editorial control of postings. However, in the event that the MBA becomes aware of any inappropriate posting, the MBA will take all appropriate action.

The MBA reserves the right to terminate access to the Electronic Communications Conference Center to any person who violates this agreement.

Signed: _____

Printed Name: _____

Firm Name: _____

Address: _____

Date: _____

Resources for Nonprofit Groups Seeking Donated Products

PUBLICATIONS

Accounting for Gifts-In-Kind
Julia Lafferty and Ted Browning
Publisher: Ernst & Young
1225 Connecticut Avenue, NW
Washington, DC 20036
Phone: 202-327-6000
Available from: Society for Nonprofit Organizations
5820 Canton Center Road, Suite 165
Canton, MI 48187
Phone: 734-451-3582
Available only by special request from SNPO members or on CD-ROM

Discover Total Resources: A Guide for Nonprofits
Publisher: Mellon Bank
Community Affairs Division
One Mellon Financial Center
500 Grant Street, 18th Floor
Pittsburgh, PA 15258
Phone: 412-234-2732
64 pages
Published in 1991
Free

NATIONAL GROUPS

America's Second Harvest
35 East Wacker Drive, #2000
Chicago, IL 60601
Phone: 312-263-2303, 800-771-2303

OR
50 F Street, NW, Suite 600
Washington, DC 20001
Phone: 202-585-1814
Web site: www.secondharvest.org

Brother to Brother International, Inc.
4025 South McClintock Drive, Suite 210
Tempe, AZ 85282
Phone: 602-345-9200
E-mail: BBI@worldvision.org
Web site: www.bbi.org

Gifts In Kind International
333 North Fairfax Street
Alexandria, VA 22314
Phone: 703-836-2121
Web site: www.giftsinkind.org

National Association for the Exchange of Industrial Resources (NAEIR)
560 McClure Street
Galesburg, IL 61401
Phone: 800-562-0955
Web site: www.NAEIR.org

World Vision Gifts International Distribution
210 Overlook Drive
Sewickley, PA 15143
Phone: 412-749-1800
Web site: www.worldvision.org

Source: List updated in 2008 through research based on: "A Sampling of Resources for Non-Profit Groups Seeking Donated Products," *The Chronicle of Philanthropy*, July 12, 1994, p. 41, © 1994, *The Chronicle of Philanthropy*.

REGIONAL GROUPS

The Christian Appalachian Project
P.O. Box 511
Lancaster, KY 40446
Phone: 859-792-3051, 866-270-4227
E-mail: volunteer@chrisapp.org
Web site: www.chrisapp.org

Furniture Bank of Metro Atlanta
538 Permalume Place, NW
Atlanta, GA 30318
Phone: 404-355-8530
Web site: www.furniturebankatlanta.org

Loading Dock
2 North Kresson Street
Baltimore, MD 21224
Phone: 410-558-3625
E-mail: Kirkland@loadingdock.org
Web site: www.loadingdock.org

Massachusetts Coalition for the Homeless
8 Winter Street, Suite 402
Boston, MA 02108
Phone: 781-595-7570
Web site: www.mahomeless.org

Materials for the Arts
33-00 Northern Boulevard, 3rd Floor
Long Island City, NY 11101
Phone: 718-729-3001
E-mail: info@mfta.org
Web site: www.mfta.org

Provider's Resource Clearinghouse
14200 East 35th Place, Unit 105
Aurora, CO 80011
Phone: 303-962-2270
E-mail: prc@prccolorado.org
Web site: www.prccolorado.org

San Francisco Clothing Bank
100 Brannan Street, Suite 206
San Francisco, CA 94103
Phone: 415-621-6100
E-mail: sfcb@dnai.com

Shelter Partnership
523 West Sixth Street, Suite 616
Los Angeles, CA 90014
Phone: 213-688-2188
Web site: www.shelterpartnership.org

Stepping Stone Medical Equipment Bank
515 North Orange Blossom Trail
Orlando, FL 32805
Phone: 407-481-8280

Surplus Exchange
518 Santa Fe
Kansas City, MO 64105
Phone: 816-472-0444
E-mail: rgoring@surplusexchange.org
Web site: www.surplusexchange.org

Volunteer Center of North Texas
(formerly Volunteer Center of Dallas)
2800 Live Oak Street
Dallas, TX 75204
Phone: 214-826-6767
Web site: www.volunteernorthtexas.com

A Case Study: Raising Corporate Dollars

MATHCOUNTS: THE SUCCESS OF ASSESSING AND USING A CORPORATE RELATIONS STRATEGY

This case study relates how a very small nonprofit organization, with a one-person development shop, secured a $1.5M gift from a Fortune 100 company.

MATHCOUNTS, headquartered in Alexandria, Virginia is this country's premiere nationwide coaching, competition, and enrichment program that motivates and rewards middle school students for math achievement. The entire effort is made possible through a unique partnership joining the nonprofit MATH-COUNTS with corporate powerhouses, professional associations, schools and teachers, a huge volunteer force, and families from every walk of life. Recognizing math as "the language of the 21st Century," MATHCOUNTS is preparing America's young people for leadership in tomorrow's workforce and world.

For the first 20 years of existence, MATHCOUNTS relied on one of its founding sponsors to underwrite the $500,000 cost of the annual national event. After 20 years, that sponsor decided that they would no longer support MATHCOUNTS at that level, but would stay on as a $75,000 a year sponsor. They informed MATHCOUNTS of this decision with three-years advanced notice. Like some nonprofits will do, MATHCOUNTS experienced a bit of denial for about two and a half years.

I was hired at the two-year mark during this "denial phase." I came to MATHCOUNTS with 8 years of general fundraising experience but little-to-no-corporate fundraising experience. I knew I had the skill to secure the funding, but the organization had never before secured more than $275,000 for a single sponsorship.

At this time, I was fortunate to attend an educational session taught by Mikel Smith Koon, President of Mosaik Strategies, a leading expert on corporate relations strategies. I found her *Corporate Relations Self-Assessment* worksheet very helpful (see attachment 1). By using some of her key points, I was able to

pull together a better package (proposal and presentation) for approaching my lead prospect in my quest to secure funding for our $500,000 annual event. Keep in mind that I already had a polished PowerPoint presentation that was a very powerful tool. But, I was able to perfect it even more by using the *Corporate Relations Strategy* (see attachment 2).

Koon's *Corporate Relations Strategy* steps follow, and the steps that were important for my case are highlighted in bold type.

- Identifying Benefactors
- Considering Companies Targeting Constituency
- *Understanding the WIIFM Factor (What's In It For Me?)*
- Identifying a Contact
- *Identifying a Champion*
- Make the Connection
- *Follow Up*

As for understanding the WIIFM Factor, I undertook some research on what would be in it for my prospect. Why would this be a great decision for them? How could I show them evidence of that? This prospect was currently a $75,000 donor and had been for 3 years, so I wasn't starting from $0.

I already had a relationship with the corporate and community relation's director at the company—my contact. I now needed to find a champion. It is always important to have both the initial contact person and the champion in place before asking for support. In my case, my contact was my ally through out the process. He strategically chose a champion that would be perfect for our organization. She is a senior vice president with an affinity toward math and furthering students in their educational process to become engineers. With this champion on board, it was time to immerse her into our organization and sell her on MATHCOUNTS. I proceeded with this, while continuing work with my contact in designing a plan of attack.

Once I had the presentation ready to go, I was invited to the company to present our proposal. I secured a meeting with my champion, and some additional executives of the same level. I

Source: Courtesy of Heather C. Gaskins, CFRE, Director of Development, MATHCOUNTS Foundation, Alexandria, Virginia.

had already worked through all of the scenarios with my contact as to what the champion would say and what my response should be. The presentation went perfectly!

Afterward, we continued to meet over the phone for about a month. One day, I received a phone call and was asked to come back to the company for another meeting. At this meeting, they presented me with a letter stating that they would sponsor our event for three years for $1.5 million total. We still were negotiating details throughout the next year, but for us, it was all about flexibility. We could work with whatever they needed and what they thought would make their sponsorship more worth their while.

One year into the sponsorship, I still follow up with the champion. In fact, she has become one of my most active board members and is currently helping me recruit additional $100,000 donors.

After attending Koon's session on *Corporate Relations Strategy,* I was able to assess better the needs of my prospect, articulate our benefits more clearly, and incorporate these into my "pitch" to the company, making it a successful one.

Attachment 1

Corporate Relations Self-Assessment

Corporate Relations Self-Assessment

To have a successful corporate relations program, there are four areas to be considered: planning, value, marketing and quality. If any one of these areas is not thoughtfully considered, your corporate relations program will not be as effective as it can be.

To determine your level of readiness for the implementation of a corporate relations program take the self-assessment below.

Your Name	Date
Organization Name	

PLANNING SCORE

Planning

1. Do you have a comprehensive long-range development plan in place?

	Score
You have a complete development plan in place to include all aspects of fund-raising to cover both long-term and short-term fund-raising goals.	5
You are working from a rough draft or a fluid development plan.	4
You can see the importance of a development plan but you don't know where to begin.	3
You can't see the importance of a development plan but you're willing to try.	2
You can't see the importance of a development plan.	1

© Mosaik™ Strategies, LLC■ Arlington, VA 22210 ■ 703 516 0040■ www.mosaikstrategies.com■Page1 of 7

Source: Courtesy of Mikel Smith Koon, President, Mosaik Strategies, LLC, Arlington, Virginia.

Corporate Relations Self-Assessment

	Score
2. To what level is your board actively involved in your corporate relations program?	
Your Board supports all development efforts and uses their network to connect you with the appropriate champions within potential corporate sponsors.	5
Your Board is aware of your development efforts and has mentioned they may have contacts with potential corporate sponsors.	4
Your Board is aware of your development efforts but the board tends not to be participative when it comes to development efforts.	3
You haven't involved your board in development efforts but you're willing to try.	2
You don't think your Board would be interested in your development efforts.	1

	Score
3. Have you determined whether or not a corporate relations strategy can work for you?	
You have completed a feasibility assessment and are reasonably convinced that a corporate relations strategy could work for you.	5
You have conducted an informal feasibility assessment by conferring with a few corporate representatives who understand your organization well.	4
You know that you need a feasibility assessment and have identified company representatives to help you.	3
You would like to implement a feasibility assessment but have not yet.	2
You've never considered a feasibility assessment and you're not sure how effective it would be if you implemented one.	1

	Score
4. Have you identified a champion who will make your case internally at each prospect company?	
You have researched and identified an enthusiastic champion within each corporate prospect.	5
You have researched and identified an enthusiastic champion within some of your corporate prospects.	4
You know why someone would champion your organization but have not yet identified the appropriate people.	3
You don't know how to go about finding a champion but are willing to try.	2
You don't know why anyone would be willing to champion your cause.	1

Corporate Relations Self-Assessment

	Score
5. Have you identified the best corporate contact person (the decision maker) for each prospect company and have good relationships with them?	
You have identified the best corporate contact person at each company and have good relationships with them.	5
You have identified the best corporate contact person at each company but don't have a relationship with most of them.	4
You understand the value of the contact person but you don't know how to identify that person.	3
Your not sure why there is value in having a contact person and you don't know how to identify the person, but you're open to the idea.	2
You don't know why anyone from each prospect company would agree to being a contact to your organization.	1

VALUE SCORE

Value

	Score
6. Can you clearly define the dollar value of your organization's offerings?	
You have a complete and clear understanding of the value of your organization's offerings.	5
You have a good sense of the value of your offerings.	4
You can identify some of the value a company could want.	3
You're not sure of what value your organization can offer but you're open to the possibility.	2
You don't think a company would find anything your organization could offer valuable.	1

Corporate Relations Self-Assessment

7. Have you matched your mission and goals to the strategic initiatives and goals of your corporate prospect list?	Score
You have matched your organization's mission to the corporate goals and initiatives of all of your prospective corporate sponsors.	5
You have matched your organization's mission to the corporate goals and initiatives of some of your prospective corporate sponsors.	4
You know it is important to find corporate sponsors with goals and initiatives that match your organization's mission but have yet found them.	3
You don't know how to find prospective corporate sponsors who have goals and initiatives that match but you're willing to try.	2
You can't imagine why any corporate sponsors would be interested in your organization's mission.	1

8. How well do you know the market that your organization serves?	Score
You have a clear understanding of the market your organization serves: you maintain statistics and demographic data about the market.	5
You have a vague idea of the market your organization serves but have not yet collected data.	4
You know it's important to collect this data and understand the market your organization serves, but you don't know how to collect or use the data.	3
You hadn't thought to collect this information but you're willing to try.	2
You don't think it's important to know the market.	1

9. Do you use your organization's brand as a benefit?	Score
Your partners and network benefit from being associated with the strong brand of your organization.	5
Your organization has a strong brand that your partners and network value but you've never considered it a benefit for anyone other than your organization.	4
Your brand should be stronger and you would use your brand as a benefit to your partners and network.	3
A strong brand is not important to your organization.	2
Allowing partners to benefit from your brand will hurt your organization's image and negatively impact its mission.	1

© Mosaik™ Strategies, LLC■ Arlington, VA 22210 ■ 703 516 0040■ www.mosaikstrategies.com■ Page4 of 7

Corporate Relations Self-Assessment

Quality

QUALITY SCORE

	Score
10. Do you have a feasible, long-term cultivation process planned for each corporate relationship?	
You have a plan to move corporate relationships from "acquaintance" to "partner" and have assigned all of your corporate prospects to a position somewhere on the scale.	5
You have a plan to move corporate relationships from "acquaintance" to "partner" and have started the process.	4
You have a plan to develop corporate relationships but don't know how.	3
You have no plans to develop corporate relationships but you think it's a great idea and are willing to try.	2
You can't think of any company that would be interested in a relationship with your organization.	1

	Score
11. Do you actively cultivate and manage each corporate relationship?	
You have a contact system set up that allows you to regularly maintain contact with individual corporate representatives and you use it consistently.	5
You have a contact system set up but don't use it to its full potential.	4
You have planned to create a contact system but don't know how to make it work for you.	3
You don't know how to create a contact system but you're willing to try.	2
You don't see the need for a contact system.	1

© Mosaik™ Strategies, LLC■ Arlington, VA 22210 ■ 703 516 0040■ www.mosaikstrategies.com■Page5 of 7

Corporate Relations Self-Assessment

12. Do you leverage the valuable expertise of your network to benefit your corporate partners?	Score
Your corporate partners presently benefit from access to your network of experts and they pay for that access.	5
You are aware of the value of your network but you offer it as a courtesy to your corporate partners.	4
You presently offer your network's valuable expertise to your market and the public and had not thought of it as a benefit to corporate partners.	3
You are not aware of what valuable expertise your network offers but you're willing to evaluate the possibility.	2
Don't think your network has any valuable expertise that a corporate partner would be interested in.	1

MARKETING SCORE

Marketing

13. How strong is your organization's brand?	Score
You have high brand recognition and your mission is strongly identifiable.	5
Your organization is recognized but your mission is not.	4
You want to be recognized and know the steps it takes but have not yet taken them.	3
You think visibility is necessary and are willing to try and gain it.	2
You don't believe that your organization can and/or should be positioned for high visibility and strong brand recognition.	1

14. Have you packaged your value into an attractive offering for potential corporate supporters?	Score
Your benefits package is highly valuable and sought by companies with an interest in your mission.	5
Your benefits package is highly valuable but you have not packaged them into an attractive offering or marketed them yet.	4
You are presently in the process of crafting your benefits package.	3
You don't know how to articulate your benefits and value but are willing to try.	2
You're not willing to package your benefits.	1

Corporate Relations Self-Assessment

15. Have you developed well-tuned messages to educate and interest companies in a relationship with your organization?	Score
You've developed marketing messages to educate corporate partners on your mission and interest them in your benefits.	5
You have marketing messages that neither educate nor interest.	4
You know you need marketing messages but have not yet developed them.	3
You're not sure why you need marketing messages but you are willing to try it.	2
You don't see the value in marketing messages and don't want to use them.	1

TOTAL SCORE

How Ready Are You?

Add the scores from each of the four red focus areas to determine your total score. Evaluate your score according to the scale below.

Assessment Scale	
61 to 75	You have a well-planned development strategy and are ready to infuse your program with an effective corporate relations program.
48 to 60	You're nearly there! You have much in place and can use some help with your strategic planning to prepare for a corporate relations program.
30 to 47	You need to get back to the basics on development. Your planning and/or implementation is not working effectively. Consider re-evaluating your strategic development plan and implementation plan.
29 or below	You are not ready for a corporate relations strategy. You may not understand enough about the value of a corporate relations strategy to determine whether or not it will work for you or a corporate relations strategy might not be right for you.

Attachment 2

Crafting a Corporate Relations Strategy

Resource Guide
Crafting a Corporate Relations Strategy

Definition of Corporate Relations Strategy
A corporate relations strategy is an organization's plan to weave in the support of various businesses to the success of their mission. Through a corporate relations strategy the nonprofit organization can increase their resources toward realizing their mission. This includes increased funding, volunteers and in-kind products and services. In addition, the nonprofit can benefit from increased marketing and visibility through efforts of the companies. This can lead to increased interest and knowledge from the general public about the organization. Support from companies can also lead to enhanced programs as companies offer funding, in-kind products, and volunteer support. Relationships with companies also provide access to senior leaders, offering invaluable guidance.

The WIIFM Question
A corporate relations strategy sounds great, but the question often arises from nonprofit organizations asking what do the companies get out of these relationships? How could they ever match the value we get out of the relationship? That's the WIIFM question. WIIFM = What's in it for me?

What many nonprofit leaders miss is that they offer a great deal of value to companies. Leaders of nonprofit organizations are often experts in a particular field. The relationship provides the company access to field experts that may enhance the productivity of their business or may enhance their community relationships.

Nonprofit missions often meet the needs of community outreach initiatives. Most medium to large size companies have community outreach initiatives as do some small companies. Companies strive to be good corporate citizens by supporting their communities. The missions of many nonprofit organizations fall into the goals of many corporate initiatives. Companies often focus on initiatives that, in the long run, support their own profitability. Community initiatives that improve education, literacy, or health are just a few of the topics that are often supported by companies. Each one of these topics directly impacts the company by enhancing the future recruiting pool and improving the community where their employees work.

Media provides visibility for an enhanced community or diversity image. Companies often announce their relationships with nonprofit organizations in a press release and on their website. This helps enhance community relations and the diversity image if the organization supports a minority or disadvantaged group. The organization benefiting from the relationship might also publish a press release such as the excerpt from an actual press release in illustration 2, which provides visibility for both the organization and for the supporting company.

Good relationships provide limited exposure management. Companies find allies in nonprofit organizations through guidance and advice. Companies may seek out relationships with controversial nonprofit organizations to neutralize a "one-sided" image. See the CVS example below for an illustration.

Resource Guide
Developing a Corporate Relations Strategy
Corporate relationships with nonprofit organizations should be mutually beneficial. Some of the value companies get from the relationship are listed below. The value is much greater than the "it's the right thing to do" philosophy.

Value Companies Get From Relationships with Nonprofit Organizations
- Image enhancement
- Recruiting
- Retention
- Market expansion
- Exposure management
- Productivity
- Profitability

Case Study Exercise
In March 2004, a CVS pharmacist in Texas refused to fill a prescription for birth control pills for a woman because it was against the pharmacist's religious beliefs. The consumer was a married, mother-of-two practicing what she believed was responsible family planning. When the story hit the papers, the pro-choice community was very angry. An informal boycott against CVS was being planned through email and word-of-mouth and the news was spreading very quickly. Major newspapers were picking up the story.

Gloria Feldt, the President of Planned Parenthood Federation of America sent a letter to Tom Ryan, the CEO of CVS demanding his assurance that this would never happen again. He responded assuring that this type of issue, would never happen again. He let her know that the situation was handled. CVS supported the pharmacist's right to her beliefs and did not discipline her. However, they did provide diversity training all of their employees to ensure they respected and understood differences. The training also provided guidance on how to handle this type of situation that might arise.

After communicating with Mr. Ryan, Ms. Feldt issued a statement saying that she was satisfied with CVS' response. Subsequently, the boycott, which was completely independent of PPFA, was called off. CVS has since worked with PPFA on policy issues of concern, such as the bill to make the morning after pill an over-the-counter drug.

Discussion
1. What value did CVS get from the relationship?
2. What value did PPFA get from the relationship?

Illustration 1a

Answer
Both CVS and Planned Parenthood Federation of America benefited greatly from this relationship. A boycott would have been devastating for CVS, especially during this period when CVS was in acquisition talks with the Eckerd drug store chain. Much was at stake. PPFA benefited from the publicity and ultimately with a policy supporter. This situation provides an example of how a company and nonprofit organization provide both entities great value through a mutually beneficial relationship.

Illustration 1b

Creating a Corporate Relations Strategy
Developing a corporate relations strategy should be part of the strategic plan just as marketing and development are. The plan must be well thought out and implemented for the greatest success.

Resource Guide
Developing a Corporate Relations Strategy

Identifying Benefactors
The first step in planning a solid strategy is to identify companies that can benefit from a relationship with your organization. If your organization's mission is related to dealing with medical issues, then companies within the healthcare industry are a great start. Pharmaceutical companies that research illnesses or conditions that affect your constituencies are good prospects. Local companies are good companies to consider as well. Companies often support community organizations in communities where their employees live and work.

Consider Companies Targeting Constituency
Other companies to consider in the prospect list are companies that pursue relationships with your constituencies. These companies would value an opportunity to have their brand in front of your network and the community you serve. In your research, you might find senior leaders in companies that are affected as individuals in your network might be. This could be a reason to add the company to the prospect list.

Understand the WIIFM Factor
Prior to communicating with any potential prospect, make sure you are clear on the value the sponsor would get. Make sure you've thought through every possible benefit. Part of the value is "because it the right thing to do," and marketing value is also a benefit. But hard, quantifiable value can close the deal. The size of your network is quantifiable. It's of great value to a company that wants to reach this community.

Identify a Contact
Company leaders are your best contacts. You need to identify a decision maker at the company who has budget approval and has the right budget. For example, you would not go to the product manager for Propecia (medication for hair loss) if your nonprofit organization supported the public health industry. The manager maintains the wrong budget. S/he would be hard pressed to see the value in a relationship with your organization. However, if your organization was in the public healthcare space, you would consider Merck's Vaccine Division for sponsorship or support.

Identify a Champion
Having the right contact is important. Having a champion is invaluable. If you can find a company representative who can get behind your organization's mission, either from personal experience or from exposure to the organization, it is invaluable. This person can make the introduction for you to the decision maker. As an insider, the champion is more aware of issues or potential concerns, and could advise you accordingly. It is possible to make the connection without a champion, but having a champion is a great asset.

Make the Connection
Whether it's by email, phone call, letter or in person, it starts in making the connection. Without a champion or prior relationship, making the connection almost always takes longer than expected. Be persistent, be realistic and make the connection.

Follow Up
Just as communication is critical in understanding a culture, following up and keeping in touch is critical in maintaining a long term relationship. Many nonprofit organizations have lost

Resource Guide
Developing a Corporate Relations Strategy

supporters by poor follow-up. Companies expect periodic communication and updates. It takes much more work to mend a broken corporate relationship than it does to maintain it through regular communication. An annual "thank you" works well. It does not have to be expensive. It could be a holiday card or it could be a thank you lunch for your supporters. Remember, companies are made up of people who make the decisions. They act on behalf of the company, but they react and respond as individuals.

Summary

A corporate relations strategy is a great way to increase funding, products and services, visibility, volunteer support and senior leader guidance. Your organization can benefit from these offerings just as the company benefits from the relationship with your organization and constituency. Corporate relationships are mutually beneficial.

Excerpt from a Whitman-Walker Clinic Press Release

Washington, DC – Whitman-Walker today announced that Microsoft Corporation has donated more than $380,000 in software to the Clinic. The donation will allow the Clinic to update software on all 12 of its servers and operating software on all 300 PCs Clinic-wide. The donation will also allow the Clinic to enhance its publishing, flowcharting and project management software.

"We are extremely pleased that Microsoft has donated this software to us," said A. Cornelius Baker, Executive Director of Whitman-Walker Clinic. "As a community-based health care provider, it is vital for us to develop partnerships with both the private and public sectors in order to deliver high quality services. Microsoft's generosity will help many people living with HIV/AIDS in the DC metropolitan area and further demonstrates their excellent corporate citizenship."

Illustration 2

Case Study: Raising Corporate Dollars for the First Time

A large national professional association over a hundred years old had continued to grow rapidly but had never undertaken any major fundraising efforts. Membership was on an individual basis, and since most of the members paid their dues individually and paid for other things, such as attendance at the large national conference, there was little incentive to contribute to the association. Besides, the members had never really been asked to give. Also, many maintained that, because of the nature of their profession, they were not wealthy and therefore were not able to give substantial gifts.

A few foundation grants had been received, mostly small grants for project support. Corporate support was almost non-existent; in fact, many in the organization considered all corporate money as "tainted" or "dirty" money.

A consultant was retained by the association to begin to explore how it could start to raise funds and how to best create a development operation. The original intent was to have the consultant do a capital campaign feasibility study focused on meeting the costs of a new headquarters.

The consultant carried out interviews of association leadership and members and also interviewed a limited number of corporate exhibitors at the association's annual conference. The interviews confirmed several things:

- Members generally stated, as was expected, that they themselves could not make major gift commitments because of limited personal means.
- Most members, except a few board members and some key staff, were opposed to seeking corporate support of any kind.
- The limited number of corporate exhibitors interviewed generally felt the association "just wanted their money" for the exhibit booth spaces but wanted no other involvement with them. They felt they were being held "at arms' length" by the association.

- The association generally had not taken a proactive approach to raising money, and in fact many felt it would not be possible to raise significant funds from any sources.

However, the consultant also found a few glimmers of hope for any potential fundraising effort:

- The development assessment process was funded by a six-figure grant from a major national foundation.
- While members said they themselves could not make major gifts, they often cited other members who, because of different circumstances and personal means, could make larger gifts.
- A few members were more open to seeking corporate funds but felt the association needed to first have a clear understanding of parameters and limitations on any possible corporate support.
- The corporate representatives interviewed all wanted to have their companies develop closer relationships, beyond just exhibiting, with the association and said that stronger relationships could result in some possibly significant levels of support. There had already been some very small scale corporate sponsorships of a project and an event at the annual meeting, although these were very controversial within the association.
- Senior staff and a few board members strongly believed that the association should begin to develop a development/fundraising program as soon as possible.

The consultant developed a final report and recommendations focused on undertaking a major campaign effort to raise funds to partially cover the costs of the new headquarters facility. The primary sources of support were seen as some of the members, corporations (especially for underwriting the costs of the first-floor public areas and a possible museum or display area or a technology or communications facility), and some

Source: Courtesy of Eugene A. Scanlan, PhD, CFRE, President, eScanlan Company, Bethesda, Maryland.

foundations. In order to carry out the campaign, the association would have to develop a volunteer infrastructure, begin to explore corporate support through better corporate relationships, and start to change the attitude of its members toward giving to the association.

In order to accomplish these goals, the consultant developed several specific recommendations focused on

- development of a campaign leadership structure headed by one of the association's most prominent members
- development of internal corporate giving policies and guidelines and corporate gift acceptance procedures (these needed to be designed to meet the concerns of members about the types of corporations the association would or would not accept funds from as well as to ensure that the association had some ability to negotiate with a company about the uses of the funds)
- use of the capital campaign effort to begin to change the organizational culture toward becoming more supportive of the work of the association through personal giving
- seeking initial gifts from the board and campaign leadership committee to help set examples for other members
- development of a gift recognition program based upon high visibility for major donors

Soon after the completion of the feasibility study, the association decided to finance its new headquarters through the issuance of tax-exempt bonds. The issue for the association and the consultant then became how to translate the lesson learned and the recommendations of the study into a more general fundraising effort. The association's leadership decided to develop a campaign effort more broadly focused on the critical mission of the association and its programmatic and general needs. Working with the consultant, the board leadership and staff selected a campaign cabinet (a small management group) and a campaign committee. Association volunteer and staff leadership successfully recruited one of the best-known and best-respected members of the profession to head the campaign committee.

The committee met and began to develop a list of key major gift prospects, including its own members and board members as well as others. The board was successfully solicited, and almost all the members participated in the campaign and made major gift commitments. The campaign committee next solicited its own nonboard members and generated additional gifts and pledges of support.

At the same time, the consultant provided the association with sample corporate gift policies and acceptance guidelines and sample gift recognition ideas, which were developed into specific policies. Staff also worked on a revised "case for support" based upon the more general approach for the campaign.

It soon became apparent that the most likely source for significant lead gifts was the corporate sector. The campaign commit-

tee, staff, and the consultant worked together to identify the top four or five most likely sources for such gifts. However, there was also a recognition that the association had a fairly high level connection in only one or two of these companies. One company, which at first did not seem to be a good prospect because of the lack of a high level connection, did have some points in its favor. It had been very interested in and involved with a very small scale project at the association and had underwritten some of the costs of the project in return for some limited recognition. The primary contact had been between the marketing division of the company and the communication and marketing staff of the association.

Using this limited contact as a starting point, the staff, the campaign leadership, and the consultant developed a strategy to discuss with the corporate contact approaching the company management at the highest possible level. The discussion also focused on the reputation of the company as a "good" corporate citizen, which meant there would be the minimum possible objections on the part of the membership if a gift was obtained (although there was also a recognition that some "headcore" members would object to any corporate support whatever).

Staff and leadership originally discussed seeking a gift in the $10,000 to $25,000 range from the company. However, the consultant was able to convince them to "go for broke" and make a $1 million ask, basing the amount on both the health of the company and the potential for partnership between the company and the association. After quite some time and many internal discussions, the senior staff and campaign leadership (including some board members) were able to obtain a meeting with a senior management team of the company, including a senior vice president. The focus of the meeting included educating the company management on the values and mission of the association and offering to work together on areas of mutual interest. Discussions with the company management continued beyond this meeting.

Some time later the company notified the association that it would provide a $1 million gift, of which $250,000 was to be used for "education" programs broadly defined and the remainder was unrestricted funds. The chair of the board of the company, who had been "sold" on the gift by his senior vice president, came to a special association board meeting (which also included campaign committee members and staff) to both present the gift and tell the board why the company had decided to make such a substantial gift. He spoke of the gift not as a gift but as an investment in the association and its important work and said that it represented only the beginning of what he saw as a long-term partnership. He also spoke of how the mission of the association was something the company could identify with strongly and wanted to support. His speech concluded with an emphasis on the close personal relationships that could be developed between the company leadership and the association leadership and on the importance of working together over the long term.

Raising Money from Foundations

KEY VOCABULARY

- Community Foundation
- Conversion Foundation
- Corporate Foundation
- Endowment
- Family Foundation
- Foundation
- General Purpose Foundation
- Grant
- Operating Foundation
- Private Foundation
- Program Officer
- Proposal
- Public Charity
- Special Purpose Foundation

DEFINITION OF A FOUNDATION

Foundations make up another source of funds for nonprofit organizations and institutions. The Foundation Center, an independent national service organization that offers a wide variety of services and comprehensive collections of information on foundations and grants, defines a private foundation as "a nongovernmental, nonprofit organization having a principal fund of its own, managed by its own trustees and directors, and established to maintain or aid

> *Foundations are an excellent source of funds for new approaches to tackling social problems.*

charitable, religious, or other activities serving the public good, primarily by making grants to other nonprofit organizations." Because most foundations have permanent endowments, they do not need to raise funds each year from the general public. They reflect the philosophy and beliefs of the individuals and corporations that establish them. Foundations are an excellent source of funds for new approaches to tackling social problems and often will make multi-year commitments, up to three years, to address community needs.

Giving by the nation's 71,000 grantmaking foundations rose to $40.7 billion in 2006, according to *Foundation Growth and Giving Estimates: Current Outlook* (2007 edition). This estimated 11.7 percent gain followed a 14.3 increase in 2005. U.S. foundations last reported consecutive years of double-digit growth in giving during the period 1996 to 2001. Looking ahead, grantmakers appeared optimistic about continued funding increases in 2007.

Key estimates reported included the following:

- Independent and family foundations, which account for nearly nine out of ten foundations, raised their giving by 10.3 percent in 2006, representing their first double-digit increase since 2001.
- Corporate foundation giving grew a more modest 6 percent in 2006, following a 16.5 percent jump in 2005.
- Community foundations reported the fastest growth in giving, with funding up 13.2 percent in 2006.
- Foundation assets grew by 10 to 12 percent in 2006.
- Nearly 60 percent of surveyed foundations expect their giving to increase in 2007, and overall funding will likely continue to grow at a double-digit pace.

Principal factors driving the growth described were strong gains in the stock market and a higher level of new foundation establishment than was seen in the early 2000s. Other factors contributing to higher levels of giving in recent years include elevated payout rates due to greater numbers of "pass-through" foundations and the establishment of operating foundations by pharmaceutical manufacturers. New analyses show that 12 pharmaceutical foundations established in the 1990s and early 2000s to distribute medications to patients with financial hardships accounted for close to 9 percent of 2005 foundation giving.

Foundations in five states—New York, California, New Jersey, Pennsylvania, and Washington—accounted for nearly half of 2004 foundation giving according to the *Foundation Yearbook, 2006 Edition*. For the first time, the region of the United States that posted the fastest growth in giving was the West, led by foundations in California and Washington; the West also reported the largest increase in terms of actual grant dollars.

Keep in mind that foundation grants totaled 12.5 percent of the billions of dollars contributed to nonprofit organizations, according to the annual report, *Giving USA 2008*, discussed in Chapter 1. Since foundation grants make up a small percentage of the total dollars contributed annually, an organization should first determine if foundations are a potential source of funds for their mission and programs before devoting too much of its staff time and effort to this area. The overall development program should include a variety of programs, such as annual giving, major gifts, planned giving, corporate fundraising, and special events. Nonetheless, foundation fundraising remains an important source of funds for specific programs and activities.

TYPES OF FOUNDATIONS

There are several types of private foundations that distribute money to those who follow their application guidelines and are fortunate enough to be selected. See Exhibit 11–1 for a description of each type of foundation.

PLANNING AN EFFECTIVE FOUNDATION RELATIONS PROGRAM

An effective foundation relations program requires thoughtful planning for long-term development. Developing relationships with foundations that result in support will enhance all other fundraising programs. The following are points to keep in mind:

- Foundations like to be pioneers; they look for innovation.
- People run foundations; they have specific interests and personalities.
- Foundations prefer to fund projects, not organizations.
- Giving criteria and areas of interest change from time to time.
- Foundation staff do not like to think that your financial stability depends almost solely on their funding.
- First approach foundations that have supported you in the past or are familiar with your organization.
- Do not circumvent foundation staff to sell your project to trustees.
- Be careful in using social linkages—it can backfire.

Exhibit 11–1 Types of Foundations

Family Foundation—This is not a legal term but denotes those private foundations whose funds are derived from members of a single family. Generally, family members serve as officers or board members of the foundation and play an influential role in grantmaking decisions.

General-Purpose Foundation—An independent, private foundation that awards grants in many different fields of interest.

Operating Foundation—A private foundation that, rather than making grants, conducts research, promotes social welfare, and engages in programs determined by its governing body or establishment charter.

Private Foundation—As designated by federal law, a foundation whose support is from a single source (usually a person, family, or company) that makes grants to other not-for-profit organizations rather than operating its own programs. Its annual revenues are derived from earnings on investment assets rather than from donations. Private foundations are subject to more restrictive rules than public charities.

Public Charity—As designated by federal law, a foundation that, during its most recent four fiscal periods, has received one-third of its support from donations from individuals, trusts, corporations, government agencies, or other not-for-profit organizations—provided no single donor gives two percent or more of the total support for the period. Normally the charity must receive no more than one-third of its support from investment income. A public charity escapes the stringent rules that apply to a private foundation.

Special-Purpose Foundation—A public foundation that focuses its grantmaking activities on one or a few special areas of interest.

Corporate Foundation (covered in Chapter 10)—A private foundation, funded by a profit-making corporation, whose primary purpose is the distribution of grants according to established guidelines.

Community Foundation—A not-for-profit organization that receives, manages, and distributes funds, including any income from endowed funds, for charitable purposes, typically in a specific geographic area.

Source: Copyright 1996–2003. *AFP Fundraising Dictionary*, Association of Fundraising Professionals (AFP), formerly NSFRE. All rights reserved.

THE SOLICITATION PROCESS

First Step—Know Your Organization

It is extremely important for the staff involved in the solicitation of foundations to have an in-depth understanding of their organization. They should know what current programs and services their organization offers. Are there plans for new initiatives in the future? What are the current needs of the organization and what future needs will there be for the organization to fulfill its mission? One very important piece of information staff should know is the history of past contacts with foundations, including which foundations provided funding and which did not.

Depending on the organization, the development staff may or may not be directly involved in the overall planning for the organization. The advantage of having development staff involved in program planning is twofold. First, staff can make a stronger case for support to potential funders when they have greater knowledge of the organization. Second, when staff members are aware of the current areas of interest within the foundation community, they can take part in helping shape future programs that will both fulfill the organization's mission and appeal to funders' interests. It is very important that an organization does not plan new programs only because they know foundations fund such initiatives, especially if a program does not fit within an organization's mission. Keep in mind that foundation program officers review proposals carefully to see if a new program or service furthers the mission of the organization. If it does not, it will not matter that the program falls within the foundation's giving interests, and the proposal most likely will be rejected.

Researching Foundations

Finding foundations that may fund your organization can be an overwhelming task, especially for the one-person development office. It is best to narrow the focus of the research to only one or two organizational programs. Although there are a variety of approaches to identifying possible funding sources, there are three basic steps to follow.

1. Develop a broad list of prospects. Include foundations that have shown an interest in funding some aspect of your program. Look for foundations that fund organizations similar to yours or are interested in the same causes as your organization. Use subject, geographic area, and type of support as criteria.
2. Refine your list. Eliminate foundations that are unable to fund projects in your subject or geographic area or that do not provide the type of support needed.
3. Investigate thoroughly the foundations remaining. Gather information on staff persons, trustees, current financial status, application procedures, and most recent grantmaking activities. Visit a foundation's Web site to see if they have their guidelines or their latest annual report posted. If

a foundation does not have a Web site, call or write foundations on the final list and ask them to send you their latest annual report, their guidelines, or other materials that outline their giving priorities. Information on many foundations can now be found on the Internet. Visit the foundation Center Web site (at http:\\www.foundation center.org), which has links to many foundation Web sites.

Sources for Researching Foundations

The number of sources available for researching foundations continues to increase, especially online sources. Using technology is key to conducting research today. To start your research effort, you might consider subscribing to one of the growing online research services or purchasing one or more of the published foundation directories. To find out about more recent grants, review the listing of foundation grants in each issue of *The Chronicle of Philanthropy,* published twice a month.

> *Using technology is key to conducting research today.*

For those organizations just beginning a foundation program or with no budget for building a research effort, your public library and the Foundation Center and its affiliated libraries across the country can help you in your research. (See information on public libraries in Chapter 8 and the list of Foundation Center libraries in Appendix 8–A.) The Foundation Center also has copies of the Internal Revenue Service (IRS) Form 990, a form that is completed by foundations and contains financial information and a listing of organizations that received grants during that year. Exhibit 11–2 offers a sampling of the Foundation Center's most popular reference tools. Also, for those doing fundraising in the Greater Washington, DC, area, the office of the Association of Fundraising Professionals (AFP), located in Arlington, Virginia, has an excellent library of books on foundations and grant writing open to members and nonmembers. Information may also be requested from the AFP Resource Center by calling 800-688-FIND.

Other sources include the following:

- **GuideStar**
  GuideStar offers two levels of searching, sorting, and retrieving information from its database, Select and Premium. Its Grant Explorer allows you to access information on 2.5 million grants made by more than 48,000 of the nation's largest foundations. In addition, GuideStar now offers additional research tools and custom solutions for your research needs. Many nonprofits serving a specific geographic region will like GuideStar's advanced search feature enabling you to find family foundations within a specific zip code or within a radius of a specific zip code. For more information and pricing structures for these and other services, visit their Web site at http://www.guidestar.org.

Exhibit 11-2   The Foundation Center's Tools for Identifying Funding Sources

Online Services

- The Foundation Directory Online Subscription Plans
  –updated weekly; subscription plans begin at $19.95 a month
- Corporate Giving Online
  –information on grants, in-kind donations of equipment, products, professional services and volunteers; subscription plans begin at $59.95 a month

Online, Print, and CD-ROM Tools

- FC Search—The Foundation Center's Database on CD-ROM
- Guide to U.S. Foundations, Their Trustees, Officers and Donors (print)
  –covers nearly 70,000 foundations and their leaders
- Grant Guides (print)
  –descriptions of actual foundation grants of $10,000 or more awarded in various subject fields

- The Foundation Directory (print)
  –key facts on the top 10,000 U.S. foundations
- The Foundation Directory Part 2 (print)
  –features the next 10,000 largest U.S. foundations
- The Foundation Directory 1 & 2 on CD-ROM
  –descriptions of the largest 20,000 U.S. foundations
- The Foundation 1000 (print)
  –comprehensive information on the 1,000 largest foundations in the United States
- The Foundation Grants Index (CD-ROM)
  –searchable database of the grants of the largest independent, corporate, and community foundations in the United States
- National Directory of Corporate Giving (print)
  –descriptions of corporate foundations and direct giving programs
- Regional Guides to Grantmaking (print and CD-ROM)

- **FoundationSearch**

  This product launched by Metasoft Systems, Inc., based in Canada, provides you with sophisticated searches of foundation data. You can locate grants by type, value, year, recipient, donor, and other criteria. In addition, they have searchable IRS990PF documents, enabling you to find text embedded in these documents. This can be a powerful tool if you are looking for specific wording on grants funded. For more information and pricing structure, visit their Web site at http://www.foundationsearch.com.

- **Don Griesmann's Grant Opportunities**

  This weekly subscription is edited by Don Griesmann, Esq., and published by CharityChannel LLC. As its title implies, Mr. Griesmann scours the Internet for new grant opportunities that you might not learn about from any other sources in such a timely manner. Headlines, brief descriptions of articles, and links to articles are compiled by him for the benefit of his colleagues. CharityChannel charges a modest subscription fee—$24 for 12 months—to receive any or all of their newsletters. Go to http://charitychannel.com/subscribe to sign up.

- **GrantsDirect.com**

  GrantsDirect, published by Jankowski Associates, Inc., focuses on tracking and profiling more than 4,700 new foundations created nationwide since 1996. Known for its customized foundation and corporate philanthropic research, Jankowski Associates will create a package of current data on new family and regional foundations to meet an organization's needs. Visit their Web site at http://www.GrantsDirect.com.

- **GrantStation**

  GrantStation is an interactive Web site that allows grantseekers to identify potential funding sources for their programs or projects and mentors you through the grantseeking process. It provides access to a searchable database of grantmakers who accept proposals from a variety of organizations, federal grant deadlines updated twice a week, and links to state funding agencies. Quarterly and annual memberships are available. Visit their Web site at http://www.grantstation.com.

There are a number of resources available for researching the larger foundations, but according to the Association of Small Foundations (ASF), about 90 percent of the total number of U.S. foundations are smaller foundations—those led entirely by volunteer boards or operated by just a few staff. These foundations that account for half of the country's total foundation grant dollars are excellent prospects for grants but are often not included in many of the research tools. A way to find out about smaller foundations in your community is to see if you have one of the 32 formally organized, staffed, and full-service regional associations of grantmakers in your area. These organizations represent more than 5,000 philanthropic stakeholders—private and community foundations, corporations, and individuals—interested in strengthening philanthropy in their area. Small foundations will be listed as members of these regional associations with or without links to their Web sites, which is an excellent place to uncover new prospects and begin the research process. To find out if you have a regional grantmaker association, visit the Forum of Regional Associations of Grantmakers at http://www.givingforum.org.

Approaching Foundations

After completing the first phase of research, you should have a list of 10 to 12 foundations to approach in the coming year. Make an initial approach by telephone to request additional materials, such as the foundation's annual report or its guidelines if you have not already found them on the foundation's Web site. If after reading the guidelines and other materials detailing the foundation's interests, you need additional information, call a program officer. For example, suppose your organization has an educational program that looks like it fits nicely within the giving areas of a foundation. You might phone the foundation to find out what specific level of education (e.g., preschool, elementary school, secondary school, or college) it has the most interest in. The call would be an excellent opportunity to establish a relationship with a program officer by seeking his or her advice or help in preparing your proposal. However, you risk alienating the program officer if you ask questions that are covered in the guidelines. You should be prepared to answer specific questions on the goals and costs of the program and explain why the foundation might be interested in your organization or program. You could request a meeting while speaking to the program officer if it seems appropriate. However, be aware that the current volume of proposals received by foundations is making it increasingly difficult to arrange a face-to-face meeting between an organization and a grantmaker.

A number of foundations now request a letter of inquiry rather than a formal proposal. Others are using preliminary letters of inquiry to determine if they have an interest in a project before accepting a full proposal. This letter, usually no longer than three pages, can be signed by the organization's chief executive, the chief development officer, a board member who heads the development committee, or someone from your organization with ties or connections to the foundation. Based on how a foundation wishes to be approached, it can be used to introduce an organization and its programs to the foundation or to request a grant. (See Appendix 11–A for sample letter of inquiry requesting a grant.)

It is useful to develop a checklist or worksheet to help you keep track of the information you are collecting on selected foundations. The data also can be collected and tracked on an organization's computer database. An example of such a worksheet is the Foundation Prospect Profile (Exhibit 11–3).

Meeting with the Foundation

After sending a letter of inquiry to the foundations you placed on your priority list and confirming their interest by telephone, it is time to plan your face-to-face approach. The first task is to decide whom you will take to the meeting. If you are not strongly versed in the organization's program initiatives or if the area is highly technical, make sure that you take a senior level staff member from your organization's program department. If you are confident that you can answer detailed questions regarding the specific program for which you are seeking funding, then consider another source of support. If a member of your staff or board has a contact within the foundation, ask that person to accompany you. It is extremely important that the persons attending the meeting are well prepared. They must know what you expect from them that day, why you are seeking funds from this particular foundation, and what you are asking of the foundation. Meet with whomever is accompanying you to the meeting in advance and practice your solicitation. The meeting should be comfortable, but not casual, with a well-organized presentation that does not appear to be stilted or rehearsed. A team presentation can feel spontaneous but in actuality be well orchestrated.

> *A team presentation can feel spontaneous but in actuality be well orchestrated.*

Exhibit 11–3 Foundation Prospect Profile

Foundation's Name: _____

Address: _____ Telephone Number: _____

President: _____ Contact Person: _____

1. Any previous grants awarded to the organization by the foundation?
2. Are there personal connections to the organization either by board members or CEO?
3. Is there a demonstrated commitment by the foundation to funding in the organization's field?
4. Does the foundation make grants in the organization's geographic area?
5. Is the organization's specific request for funding within the range of the foundation's grants?
6. Is there a foundation policy prohibiting grants for the type of support requested by the organization?
7. Does the foundation usually make grants to cover the full cost of a project/program or does the foundation prefer to be one of several grantmakers supporting a project/program?
8. Over what period of time does the foundation make awards? annual grants? multi-year grants?
9. What types of organizations does the foundation currently support? Who are recent grantees?
10. What are the deadlines for applying for a grant?

Is there an advantage of having a board member from your organization with you? Of course, if you select the right person. The last thing you want is someone who adds nothing to the meeting, who is present only for the reason of name recognition or because they wish to meet the head of the foundation. The foundation officer can read the board member's name on your letterhead. Instead, bring someone who can champion your specific cause, someone who is thoroughly involved with the issues and programs of your organization. This will mean carefully reviewing your board to select the proper individual for a specific foundation approach.

Working with a Program Officer

Foundation program officers come in all shapes and sizes and personalities. If you are fortunate, you will find a program officer who has not only read your letter of inquiry but is interested in your project and wants to meet with you immediately. At the worst, you will find that you have contacted the wrong person in the foundation or that the person is not interested in meeting with you and states the foundation would not be interested in funding your program, despite what the foundation's written guidelines say. Somewhere in between is the reception that most development officers receive. It can be as nebulous as the program officer stating, "Follow the guidelines, submit your application, and you'll hear from us shortly," or as specific and encouraging as, "You fit within our guidelines and we would welcome a proposal from your organization."

If you find an interested, helpful program officer, don't be afraid to ask what you can do to make your proposal more promising. Read through the foundation's guidelines in detail and ask what specifics the decision-making committee looks for that were not included in the guidelines. Some program officers who are interested in funding a potential program or broadening their outreach to new organizations will work with you to develop a "winning document." Program officers have been known to call development officers and suggest that specific items be added or deleted from a proposal to make it stronger from the point of view of the decision-making committee. It is truly good fortune to find a helpful and nurturing program officer.

A word of caution—don't take it personally if a foundation program officer does not return your calls or is not interested in your program even though on paper you appear to be an ideal "fit" for funding by the foundation. It may take several approaches, much nurturing, and several months or years before you are even granted a meeting. Don't give up. Program officers change, foundations expand to include new program initiatives, and you may have fine-tuned your proposal so that it is now just what the foundation wishes to fund. Keep the foundation on your mailing list for appropriate materials from your organization. Let the staff become used to hearing from you and learn the value of your organization to their community.

If you find that your organization falls into several of the foundation's giving categories (e.g., the environmental and the educational), determine in which category your program is most likely to receive funding. Don't hesitate to ask the program officer for guidance. It may be that there is a much larger source of money for funding in one category than the other. Whatever you do, don't try to make your proposal fit both categories. Select one and make the strongest case possible for funding in that category.

One of the greatest challenges a fundraiser encounters is finding the right foundation to fund a specific program. Sometimes you will find that your program falls under the general giving guidelines of a foundation but, upon receiving materials from the foundation, may realize that you do not fit exactly into any of their giving categories. At this point, you must determine how closely your program matches the guidelines in one or more of the foundation's categories and whether you make changes in the program to achieve a good fit without compromising the program's integrity. Minor adjustments are done frequently. Do not rewrite or redefine your program. The danger there is that the program might then be turned down because it is no longer consistent with your organization's mission. Be creative; be cautious; but, foremost, be honest with yourself and with your organization.

Often you will complete your research only to find that the deadline for submitting proposals has passed. At this time, you can do one of two things. First you can proceed as planned, sending a letter of inquiry and then contact the foundation's program officer. Some foundations allow program officers to accept promising proposals after deadlines are past. Others are strict and allow no exceptions to a set deadline. If the foundation is lenient, proceed under the direction of the program officer and meet every extended deadline given to you. This is the time for you to "pull out all stops" because you have been extended a courtesy. If the foundation is strict and you are told that it is indeed too late for this round, then continue to nurture the program officer and submit everything in a timely manner to meet the foundation's next deadline. This is not the time to use influence to bypass the program officer and try to have the date extended by someone else. You will only antagonize the program officer and may preclude your proposal from being accepted at any time.

Another type of program officer you may encounter is the recalcitrant foundation program officer—the one who thinks that the foundation's money is his or hers and is not interested in helping you advance your proposal in any manner. This personality type exists in both large and small foundations. If you are confronted with recalcitrance in a program officer, don't try to fight it; just explicitly follow the foundation guidelines and treat the officer with respect but with an equal amount of distance. Then let the system work for you and respectfully ignore the program officer's recalcitrant behavior.

Grants from foundations may be disbursed over a multi-year period. Often, programs require some fine-tuning or even dras-

Source: Copyright © Mark Litzler.

tic change during the course of the funding. If and when changes are necessary, immediately inform your program officer of the need to make changes and make sure the changes will not adversely affect your funding. This may include extending the deadline for the final product. Often, additional work will need to be done before the final report or product can be delivered. Deadlines can be extended for good reasons. Just keep your program officer informed. Program officers do not like to be surprised because they need to defend your program and funding to their board of directors. The cardinal rule is to keep your program officer apprised—of both your successes and failures. How you manage the grant is as important as having been awarded the grant.

> *The cardinal rule is to keep your program officer apprised—of both your successes and failures. How you manage the grant is as important as having been awarded the grant.*

THE PROPOSAL PROCESS

It can take several months to put together a competitive grant proposal. Those months should be spent cultivating the potential funder and carefully planning, documenting, and internally reviewing the proposals. The following is a suggested timetable for effective proposal development.

One to three months:

- Assess organizational needs.
- Develop ideas for programs and projects that meet the organization's needs and could be funded by foundations.
- Prepare position or concept papers on new programs or projects.
- Research potential foundation funders.
- Approach the selected foundation for additional information.
- Submit a letter of inquiry.

- Develop goals and objectives for the programs or projects and prepare specific plans for implementation.

Three to six months:

- Draft a proposal, circulate it for comment, finalize the document, and receive appropriate approvals.
- Submit the proposal by the application deadline.
- Schedule a face-to-face meeting, if possible.
- Await notice of acceptance or rejection from the foundation.

Preparing the formal proposal is the last step in the process, not the first. Only when a foundation indicates an interest in the program or project based on your initial inquiry should you prepare a formal grant proposal. Follow carefully the instructions the foundation provides in its annual report or giving guidelines. Requirements may include limits on the number of pages, forms to be attached, necessary signatures, appendixes allowed, and the number of copies to be submitted. See Exhibit 11–4 for important points to remember when preparing your proposal.

In an attempt to decrease the amount of paperwork that must be completed by grantseekers, a growing number of regional grantmaker groups have developed common application forms. See the Web site for the Forum of Regional Associations of Grantmakers (http://www.givingforum.org) for information on area grantmakers using common application forms. Appendix 11–B shows the common application form for the Donors Forum of Wisconsin. This form was the first of its kind to be developed and serves as a model for the other regional associa-

tions of grantmakers. On the national level, the National Network of Grantmakers has its own common proposal form tailored for progressive funders.

The Proposal Format

There are several variations of the proper format for a written proposal. Following is a description of the key elements to be included. Keep in mind that you need to follow the specific guidelines of each foundation as to what they want included in a proposal submitted to them. See the sample proposals in Appendix 11–C and Appendix 11–D.

Other sources for samples of grant writing materials include The Grantsmanship Center (TGCI), a national organization that conducts hundreds of workshops each year in grantsmanship (http://www.tgci.com). It also publishes *The Grantsmanship Center Magazine* and its popular *Program Planning and Proposal Writing* guide. TGCI collects the best of funded federal grant proposals annually and makes them available on CD-ROM in its Winning Grant Proposals Online. In addition, Nonprofit Guides (http://www.npguides.org) provides free, Web-based grant writing tools for nonprofit organizations, including grant writing tips, sample letters of inquiry and proposals, and links to other helpful Web sites.

Cover Letter

The cover letter should be one to two pages long and provide a brief summary of the proposal and the specific request. Always begin the letter with a reference to previous contacts such as telephone calls or meetings. Show how the request matches the foundation's purposes and guidelines. Be sure the letter includes a contact name and telephone number and is signed by the chief executive officer or board president.

Cover Page

The cover page includes the name of the program/project, the name of the organization, its address and telephone number, the name and title of contact person, the date of submission, and the name of the foundation to which the proposal is being submitted.

Proposal

The proposal itself should be 5 to 10 pages long if the foundation has no other set guidelines. Always follow the foundation's specific outline. However, if a foundation does not have an outline, use the one that follows.

Summary of the Need. Explain the problem to be addressed and describe the need for the program/project locally, regionally, and nationally.

Background on Organization. Introduce the organization's mission, present its programs and services, and describe its geographic area and constituencies it serves. State the sources of support for the organization.

Exhibit 11–4 Points to Remember When Preparing Your Proposal

1. Be sure your organization is eligible to apply for a grant from the foundation.
2. Explain "who, what, why, when, where, how, and how much" concerning your organization and its program.
3. Present your case in a clear, concise, and logical manner.
4. Use heading and subheading to assist the reader through the proposal.
5. Clearly link your program or project to the foundation's interests.
6. Set realistic goals and objectives for the program or project. Avoid too ambitious plans.
7. Establish a reasonable budget for the program or project.
8. Be certain the program or project has qualified leaders and staff.
9. Describe how the program or project is innovative.
10. Explain how your organization and others have worked to solve the problem addressed by the program or project.
11. If the funder supports only national or regional efforts, illustrate how the program or project can have an impact beyond your geographic area.
12. Be sure the funds you are requesting would be used to enhance a current program or create a new one, not to replace operating funds.
13. If applicable, provide evidence of collaboration with other organizations and outline sources of support.

Planned Programs, Activities, Projects, and Services. Describe in detail the purpose, goals, objectives, and action plan for the specific program for which you are requesting support. Explain how the activity relates to what other organizations are doing to solve the problem but point out how it is different. Include information regarding the management of the program, the staffing, and how it will fit into the overall organization. A timetable for implementation is also needed.

Evaluation. Report on how the program will be evaluated. List how objectives will be evaluated, by whom, and when. The evaluation process will assess the program's progress toward its identified goals at specified and regular intervals.

Fundraising Plans. Explain how the program or service will be funded currently and in future years. List other foundations that are being approached but do not include the amount being requested.

Time Line. Describe the length of time the program or service will be in operation.

Specific Grant Request. State the purpose and amount of the request, including a timeline for a multi-year grant request. List any matching funds you have obtained from foundations or individuals.

Attachments. The following supporting documents could be added as appendixes to the proposal.

1. organization's mission statement
2. proof of tax-exempt status under IRS Section 501(c)(3)
3. financial audit
4. organization's strategic plan or long-range plan
5. organization's operating budget
6. specific budget for described program or service
7. list of other foundation and corporate supporters; proof of matching funds or in-kind contributions
8. list of organization's current board of directors or trustees
9. letters of agreement from other organizations collaborating in program or service
10. letters of support from individuals who have been helped by the organization, program, or service
11. job description of new positions; resumes of staff involved in program or service
12. other collateral material, such as the annual report, brochures, etc.

Submitting the Proposal

If there is a submission deadline, it will be stated in the annual report and/or guidelines. Check to see if this is the date by which the foundation must receive the application or the date by which you should mail it. Foundations seldom extend their deadlines and usually will return late proposals; however, some will hold late submissions for review in the next cycle. Many foundations do not set deadlines. Instead, they may request that you submit a proposal a certain number of weeks before their

next board meeting. Other foundations review applications as they are submitted.

Before a proposal leaves your organization, make sure you have obtained organizational approval in accordance with internal procedures. You may need to have finance staff review the budget and the grants office or officer (if you have one) review the entire proposal. You also may need the approval of your organization's board of directors. Most importantly, be sure to have others proofread the entire proposal to make sure that the proposal does not contain any omissions, inaccuracies, or typographical errors.

Once you are sure the proposal is complete, submit the proposal by certified, return-receipt mail or express delivery so you will have proof that the foundation received it.

After the Proposal Is Submitted

After you submit your proposal, it is important to contact the foundation to make sure it has received it. This is also a good opportunity to once again request a meeting with the program officer if earlier attempts to schedule a meeting failed. Ask the program officer if he or she has any questions about your submission or if there is any additional information he or she needs. Try to get some idea from the program officer regarding the timing and likelihood of funding.

If your organization receives funding from a foundation during the time another foundation is considering your proposal, call the program officer to let him or her know. Also inform the program officer of any other developments, such as a change in senior staff or financial difficulties. If a problem arises for your organization, it is best to let the foundation know of the problem and of your organization's plan or solution.

> *If a problem arises for your organization, it is best to let the foundation know of the problem and of your organization's plan or solution.*

How Foundations Evaluate Proposals

Foundations consider the following when evaluating proposals.

- importance of and need for the program or service
  1. from the foundation's point of view
  2. considering the needs of society
  3. regarding the value of your organization
- effectiveness and soundness of the program's plan
- feasibility of program
- capability of organization to implement program
- cost-efficiency of program
- duplication of services
- continuation of a previous foundation commitment
- interest of the foundation's trustees

THE PROPOSAL IS ACCEPTED

When you learn that your proposal has been accepted and will be funded at the level requested, the first things to do are make a thank you call to the program officer and prepare a thank you letter from the chief executive officer or president of the board to be sent to the foundation.

It is important to know the reporting requirements of the foundation. Do they want a narrative-type report or fiscal reports? How often do they want to receive reports? What other information should you send to the foundation during the year—internal progress reports, newspaper articles? The organization is beginning a new relationship with a funder, so the objective is to maintain a good relationship through proper recognition and reporting. Keep in mind that all activity is in preparation for the next approach to this foundation.

THE PROPOSAL IS REJECTED

Foundations are not able to fund every proposal submitted to them. Therefore, it is not uncommon for an organization to learn that the proposal it submitted was rejected. As the development officer, you need to take advantage of this opportunity and call the program officer to find out why the proposal was rejected. Some reasons why proposals are rejected are listed in Exhibit 11–5. However, it is important for you to learn the specific reasons why your proposal was turned down. Here again, the program officer serves as an adviser and helper. Once you know why the proposal was turned down, ask when you might submit another proposal or ask about other foundations that might be interested in the program.

Exhibit 11–5 Why Proposals Are Rejected

- Format and Composition
  1. The proposal did not follow the foundation's guidelines.
  2. The proposal is poorly written and difficult to understand.
- The proposal was not submitted on time.
- Content
  1. The problem was not documented properly.
  2. The project objectives do not match the objectives of the foundation.
- The problem does not strike the reviewer as significant.
- The project budget is not within the range of available funding.
- The proposed project or program has not been coordinated with other individuals and organizations working in the same area.
- Prospective client groups have not been involved in planning and determining program goals.
- The foundation does not know the capabilities of the organization submitting the proposal.
- The program objectives are too ambitious in scope.
- There is insufficient evidence that the project can sustain itself beyond the life of the grant.
- The evaluation procedure is inadequate.

TRENDS IN FOUNDATION FUNDRAISING

Foundations are joining forces to leverage the power of their grantmaking, set joint agendas, and fund projects that are more national in scope. Because the costs of nonprofit organizations' programs are beyond the ability of a single small foundation to fund adequately, large and small foundations are developing regional associations like the Washington Regional Area Grantmakers and special affinity groups such as Grantmakers in Health. They share information about grantees and programs to disburse their collective grant dollars more effectively. Collaborative funding to deal with timely issues is common today.

Concerned with the potential for duplication of programs and services in the nonprofit sector, foundations expect grantseekers to establish cooperative networks and linkages with other related organizations to address many of society's most pressing problems. To achieve long-term and broad-scale impact, foundations prefer model programs rather than one-shot projects. Directors and program officers like to make grants to programs that address significant problems and those that could reflect well on their foundations. Organizations need to develop programs that simultaneously serve two needy groups, thereby multiplying the effect of foundation funding. To increase a new organization's chances for funding, the organization should involve another trusted community organization in a joint proposal. Some foundations see themselves as catalysts in seeking solutions for today's problems. Increasingly, these foundations no longer accept proposals from organizations. Rather, they approach the individual organizations that are doing innovative programming in these areas to develop joint efforts.

Earlier in this chapter, a new kind of strategic relationship was mentioned, one developing between foundation staff and development officers. Foundations, in an effort to ensure that the grants they make are sound investments, are working with organizations to develop programs and services that help solve many of today's most pressing social problems.

Foundations are now focusing on the longer term sustainability of nonprofit organizations, and a number of them are supporting infrastructure or capacity building. Capacity building grants are made for board development, strategic planning, development program assessments, technology, financial systems, and staffing. Foundations realize that nonprofits cannot create new programs or enhance current programs without infrastructure support. Funders want to see how their grants are affecting positive change through specific outcomes and impacts. They are looking for organizations that are moving to adopt best practices in nonprofit management including planning, branding, and communications.

Community foundations continue to play an important role in grantmaking. According to the Foundation Center's report, *Key Facts on Community Foundations*, estimated giving by the nation's 700 community foundations rose to a record $3.2 billion in 2005. Key findings include the following:

- Community foundation giving rose 10.9 percent—roughly twice as fast as independent and corporate foundations.
- Fifty-nine percent expected to increase their giving in 2006, while 30 percent expected to reduce giving.
- Community foundations in the Center's grants sample gave proportionately more for human services and the arts than did independent and corporate foundations in 2004.

In recent years, a new type of foundation has been created, the conversion foundation, due to the conversion of nonprofit health care institutions to for-profit status. According to a March 2005 report published by Grantmakers in Health, these foundations, which now number more than 170 nationwide, hold assets totaling $18.3 billion. Although some of these foundations have been in existence for decades, many were formed in the mid-1990s or later, bringing new philanthropic resources to the states and communities they serve. While most new health foundations are dedicated to health care, they typically have adopted a broad definition of health and sometimes support wider community needs. There is no one source for information about new health foundations. Those established as private foundations file Form 990-PF with the IRS, and they are included in the Foundation Center's database and directories as information becomes available. The most comprehensive current listing of new health foundations appears in the Grantmakers in Health 2005 report titled "The Business of Giving: Governance and Asset Management in Foundations Formed from Health Care Conversion."

For more information on seeking grants from foundations, see *Corporate and Foundation Fund Raising: A Complete Guide from the Inside,* by Eugene A. Scanlan, another book published by Jones and Bartlett.

REFERENCES

The Foundation Center. 2007. *Foundation Growth and Giving Estimates: Current Outlook, 2007 Edition.* New York: The Foundation Center.

The Foundation Center. 2006. *Foundation Yearbook, 2006 Edition.* New York: The Foundation Center.

The Foundation Center. 2006. *Key Facts on Community Foundations.* New York: The Foundation Center.

Sample Letter of Inquiry to a Foundation

Note: This letter of inquiry was sent to a foundation that focuses on the health of children ages three and younger. The proposal requested $15,000 and was awarded $11,500.

January 23, XXXX

Ms. Ellen Oakley
Executive Director
Generosity Foundation
123 Main Street
Anytown, USA

Dear Ms. Oakley:

The Children's Health Center respectfully requests $15,000 to support developmental assessments and the overall health of children, under the age of three, who live in Wards F and G of Anytown, USA.

The Children's Health Center (CHC) has established a network of community-based pediatric health centers located in medically underserved neighborhoods of Anytown. The centers offer preventive health care services for children, including well-child care, immunizations, tuberculosis screenings, and nutrition counseling, as well as a full range of diagnostic and treatment services for moderately ill or injured children.

The goal of the community pediatric health centers is to meet the health care needs of children in medically underserved areas by positioning health centers in communities where children live. The centers are located in neighborhoods that have the largest concentration of children in the city along with the fewest pediatric health care providers. The federal government has declared these sections of Anytown to be "National Health Professional Shortage Areas." While Ward A, the most affluent ward, has one physician for every 467 children, Ward F has one physician for every 5,209 children (according to the Sachs Market Planner, based on 1997 Census data). The need for accessible medical services in these neighborhoods is hard to overestimate.

These are the most underserved wards in the city, based on statistics from the Annie E. Casey Foundation's Kids Count Fact Book (2002). Citywide, Wards F and G hold the following statistics:

- greatest percentage of children under 18 years old
- greatest number of births to single mothers and teenagers
- lowest percentage of births with adequate prenatal care
- highest numbers of babies with low birthweights
- highest levels of infant mortality
- highest levels of deaths to children
- highest levels of children receiving food stamps
- highest levels of children receiving Medicaid
- highest levels of children in subsidized child care

CHC meets the physical needs of many children in these neighborhoods when they are sick or injured. Our staff would like to make more of an impact on the healthy development of children under three years old, but our efforts have been limited in this area due to lack of funds. This kind of developmental assessment capacity is desperately needed for families in poverty who struggle to meet both their own needs and the needs of their newborns.

The first several years of a child's life are critical to his or her development. When a child is living in poverty with a single parent working multiple jobs to pay the rent and daycare costs, the child may miss out on developmental opportunities that many children take for granted. The parent may not have time to read to the child; the child may not have developmentally appropriate toys; the child may spend most of his time in a car seat to prevent crawling around an apartment overrun with cockroaches. These problems are common in families living in poverty. Children living in these circumstances need access to developmental pediatricians who can evaluate whether the child is developmentally delayed and can inform the parent about changes that will benefit the child.

CHC has partnered with the Anytown branch of Healthy Families America to help parents of newborns get their children off to a healthy start. The program provides home visitation services to new parents, targeting families facing multiple challenges (e.g., elements that would add stressors to any home: single parent status, low income, substance abuse problems, victim of abuse or domestic violence, etc.). Home visitors do the following:

- ensure that families have a medical provider
- share information on children's development processes
- assist families in identifying their baby's needs and accessing other resources
- support families in the home while they respond to their child's and their own needs
- share ideas on caring for babies, toddlers, and young children
- ink families with other resources in the community for assistance with job placement, identification of day care providers, etc.
- help families comply with recommended immunization schedules
- help families feel more empowered

The Healthy Families program in Anytown addresses the needs of families living in Wards F and G. The program offers services to families once a week, focusing on supporting the parent as well as supporting parent-child interaction and child development. Staff is trained to understand, acknowledge, and respect cultural differences among participants. The program connects families to CHC's community health clinic to assure optimal health and development, providing services such as timely immunizations, well-child care, etc. Depending on the family's needs, staff will direct them to additional services such as financial, food, and housing assistance programs; school readiness programs; childcare; job training programs; family support centers; substance abuse treatment programs; and domestic violence shelters.

Home visitors conduct periodic developmental assessments in the child's home, but when the home visitor detects something unusual, often the family and the program do not have the resources to get the child to a developmental specialist. CHC has access to an outstanding pediatric developmental specialist, but his time is funded by the Ward D Council and he currently is not available to see patients who live outside Ward D. Dr. James Smith comes to the community health centers one day a month, evaluating only children from Ward D with developmental problems.

A $15,000 contribution from the Generosity Foundation would allow Dr. Smith to dedicate three half days a month to provide developmental assessments to children living in Wards F and G. He would be able to see between 50 and 75 children during the year, enhancing their chances for appropriate development and reducing the risk that developmental interruptions will turn into significant delays. He will be available to make assessments for families involved in the Healthy Families home visitation program when a home visitor is concerned about a child. He will also be available to children living in Anytown who do not have access to a developmental specialist without overcoming significant barriers in cost and transportation.

In addition to Dr. Smith's time, the grant will allow a social worker to dedicate 5% of his or her time to help families navigate the city's system for early intervention services for those children with identified needs. This individual would also serve as a direct advocate for the child by contacting appropriate agencies, assisting with completion of necessary paperwork, coordinating travel, etc. As part of the Healthy Families program, the staff would also like to provide developmental tool kits to families in the program to increase the children's likelihood of normal development. These kits would be given to each child in the program at the ages of 6 months, 1 year, and 2 years. The kits would include at least one book and at least one age-appropriate play item, which will appropriately stimulate the child's development and promote more effective interaction between parents and their young child.

Developmental challenges and delays affect children living in poverty disproportionately. This funding will promote the development of children who face uphill battles in other areas of their lives, even if they are developmentally on schedule. A contribution from the Generosity Foundation will make a direct impact on the development of children in Wards F and G and strengthen our community as a whole. Thank you for your consideration of our request.

Sincerely,

Henry Coombs

Henry Coombs
Executive Director

Attachment

Attachment

Budget for Children's Health Center
Developmental Assessments for Children in Wards F and G

Developmental Pediatrician, _____% of annual salary + benefits $_____

Social Worker, ____% of annual salary + benefits $_____

Developmental tool kits
$10 per kit, 50 families, each family gets three kits over two $1,500
years at their child's ages of 6 months, 1 year, and 2 years

$15,000

Source: Courtesy of Chris Stacey, Sapphire Consulting, Washington, DC.

Donors Forum of Wisconsin Common Grant Application

WISCONSIN COMMON GRANT APPLICATION FORM
(Revised March 2006)

The Common Grant Application (CGA) can be used for all types of proposals: special projects, capital and general operating support. Please note that there are some differences in the information required, depending upon the type of request.

A list of the funders who have agreed to accept this form is below. Please keep in mind that every funder has different guidelines, priorities, application procedures and timelines. Contact each funder before starting the Common Grant Application Form to ensure that they accept the CGA and that all their requirements will be met.

Information about individual grant programs is available from each funder, and at the Marquette University Funding Information Center at Marquette University Raynor Library: (phone 414/288-1515) or http://www.marquette.edu/library/fic. Additional copies of the CGA may be requested from the Donors Forum of Wisconsin website at http://www.dfwonline.org/page9123.cfm or Marquette's Funding Information Center.

GENERAL INSTRUCTIONS

- The application has three parts. Be sure to complete each part.
- Type all proposals (minimum 10 point).
- Provide all of the information in the order listed.
- All questions relative to the request must be completed fully.
- Submit only one copy with numbered pages; do not bind or staple.
- Do **not** include materials other than those specifically requested at this time.

For specific questions about the Common Grant Application, please call the Donors Forum of Wisconsin at 414-270-1978.

Grantmakers That Accept the Common Grant Application Form
(As of March 2006)

The following funders have agreed to accept the Common Grant Application Form. Other funders, not listed, may also accept the Common Application Form. *Before sending an application to any funder, be sure to check for their specific requirements.*

Ashley Foundation
Assurant Health Foundation
Theodore Batterman Family Fdn.
Elizabeth A. Brinn Foundation
City of Milwaukee
Emory T. Clark Family Charitable Foundation
Patrick & Anna M. Cudahy Fund
Derse Family Foundation
Elizabeth Elser Doolittle Charitable Trusts
Barbara Meyer Elsner Fdn.
Bucyrus-Erie Foundation
Ralph Evinrude Foundation
Forest County Potawatomi Community
    Foundation

Gardner Foundation
Harley-Davidson Foundation
The Dorothy W. Inbusch Foundation
John T. and Suzanne Jacobus Family
    Foundation
Richard G. Jacobus Family Fdn.
Kohler Foundation
Faye McBeath Foundation
Jane Bradley Pettit Foundation
Anthony Petullo Foundation
Roundy's, Inc.
SBC/AT&T
St. Anthony's Foundation

Siebert Lutheran Foundation
Stackner Family Foundation
TCF National Bank
Thrivent Financial for Lutherans
United Performing Arts Fund
United Way in Waukesha Cty.
United Way of Gtr. Milwaukee
Waukesha County Community Fdn.
Wisconsin Energy Corp. Fdn.
The Ziemann Foundation

PART ONE: GRANT AND ORGANIZATION INFORMATION
WISCONSIN COMMON GRANT APPLICATION FORM

Grant Request

Total Amount Requested: $_____

Funder applying to: _____ Date Submitted: _____

Name of Project: _____

Duration of Project: from _____ to _____When are funds needed? _____

Nature of Request: ☐ capital ☐ project ☐ operating ☐ program ☐ endowment

          ☐ other_____
                              please list

In what geographical location will the funds be used? _____

Organization Information

Name:_____

Address:_____

City:_____ State:_____ ZIP:_____

Phone number: _____ TTY:_____ FAX Number:_____

Email:_____ Federal ID #: _____ Date of Incorporation:_____

Chief Staff Officer (Name & Title):_____ Phone number:_____

Contact Person (Name & Title):_____ Phone number:_____

Board Chairperson (Name & Title):_____ Phone number:_____

Dates of Organization's fiscal year:_____

Organization's total operating budget for past year_____and current year_____

Please list the organization's staff composition in numbers:

Paid full-time_____Paid part-time_____Volunteers_____Interns_____Other_____

Total staff (both professional and volunteer)_____

Organization Information (cont.)

Has the governing board approved a policy which states that the organization does not discriminate as to age, race, religion, disability, sexual orientation, sex or national origin? Yes ☐   No ☐

If yes, when was the policy approved?_____

Does the organization have federal tax exempt status? Yes ☐ No ☐   If no, please explain on separate sheet.

Population Served

Please check the **primary** service category of organization (check only one):

❏ Arts/Culture ❏ Health ❏ Human Services ❏ Civil/Economic Development ❏ Education ❏ Environment

❏ Other (specify) _____

Provide percentages and/or descriptions of the populations the organization serves:

African-American _____ Caucasian _____ Native American _____ Asian American _____

Hispanic/Latino _____ Other _____ _____
                                                    please list

Authorization

Has the organization's chief executive officer authorized this request? Yes ☐ No ☐

An officer of the organization's governing body (such as a board member) must sign this application:

You will have to print out this form and sign the application for submission.

The undersigned, an authorized officer of the organization, does hereby certify that the information set forth in this grant application is true and correct, that the Federal tax exemption determination letter attached hereto has not been revoked and the present operation of the organization and its current sources of support are not inconsistent with the organization's continuing tax exempt classification as set forth in such determination letter.

_____   _____   _____
Signature   Print Name/Title   Date

Remember to enclose all required support materials with the application (see Part Three).

PART TWO:
GRANT PROPOSAL NARRATIVE

Please provide the following information in the order presented below. Note that some sections are not required for general operating support. Refer to the glossary of terms (last page) as needed when preparing the narrative. Use no more than five pages; excluding attachments.

Organization Information and Background

- Provide a brief summary of the organization's mission, goals, history, programs, and major accomplishments, success stories and qualifications.
- Show evidence of client & community support.

Project/Program Description (NOT required for general operating requests)

- Abstract: Briefly describe the proposed program, how it relates to the organization's mission, capacity to carry out the program and who will benefit from the program.
- Explain the significance of the program and why the organization is qualified to carry it out.
- Describe the expected outcomes and the indicators of those outcomes.
- Document the size and characteristics of the population to be served by the program.
- Outline the strategy/methodology and timeline to be used in the development and implementation of the program.
- What is the plan to involve the population you intend to serve in the design?
- How does this program enhance the existing services in the community?

Evaluation

- Briefly describe the evaluation process and how the results will be used.
- Explain how the organization will measure the effectiveness of the program.
- Describe the criteria for success.
- Describe the results expected to be achieved by the end of the funding period.

Funding Considerations

- Describe plans for obtaining other funding needed to carry out the project/program or organizational goals, including amounts requested of other funders.
- If the project/program is expected to continue beyond the grant period, describe plans for ensuring continued funding after the grant period.
- List the top five funders of this project (if applying for a program grant) or organization (if applying for general operating support) in the previous fiscal year, the current year, and those pending for the next fiscal year.

PART THREE:
REQUIRED ATTACHMENTS

Submit the following attachments (in the order listed) with the completed proposal:

1) Complete list of the organization's officers and directors.
2) The organization's actual income and expense statement for the **past** fiscal year, identifying the organization's principal sources of support.
3) The organization's projected income and expense budget for the **current** fiscal year, identifying the projected revenue sources.
4) The organization's most recent audited financial statement including notes and IRS Form 990.
5) Copies of the IRS federal tax exemption determination letters.
6) Program Budget (multi-year if applicable). *NOT required for general operating requests.*
7) Grantee Report (if previously funded).

NOTE: This is the end of the Common Grant Application Form. Make sure you have completed **each** section of all **three** (3) parts of the application. A glossary is included on the last page for your reference. Please contact the Donors Forum of Wisconsin if you have any questions about the application form. You must contact funders directly with questions about their guidelines, funding priorities, specific application procedures and deadline.

GLOSSARY OF TERMS

(Please contact the Donors Forum if you have a question about a term not included here.)

Capital Request—A planned undertaking to purchase, build or renovate a space or building, or to acquire equipment.

Community—The people living in the same district, city, state, etc.

Contribution—A tax-deductible gift, cash, property, equipment or services from an individual to a non-profit organization. Most often given annually.

General Operating Support—Funds, both contributions and grants, which support the ongoing services of the organization.

Grants—Generally an allocation from foundations, corporations, or government for special projects or general operating. May be multi-year or annual.

Indicator—The observable, measurable characteristic or change that represents achievement of the outcome.

In-Kind Support—A contribution of equipment/materials, time, and or services that the donor has placed a monetary value on for tax purposes.

Methodology—A sequence of activities needed to accomplish the program objectives.

Outcomes—The changes in (or benefits achieved by) clients due to their participation in program activities. This may include changes to participants' knowledge, skills, values, behavior, or condition of status.

Performance Standard—The number and percent of clients who are expected to achieve the result. Also called target, they should be based on professional judgment, past data, research, or professional standards.

Program—An organized set of services designed to achieve specific outcomes for a specified population that will continue beyond the grant period.

Project—A planned undertaking or organized set of services designed to achieve specific outcomes that begins and ends within the grant period. (A successful project may become an ongoing program.)

Success Story—An example that illustrates your program's effect on a client.

Source: Courtesy of the Donors Forum of Wisconsin, Milwaukee, Wisconsin. (http://www.dfwonline.org)

Sample Proposal

Children's Health Center
Proposal to the Generosity Foundation
April 12, XXXX

Note: This proposal was sent to a foundation dedicated to the health and well being of children in the greater Anytown region. The organization requested $350,000 and was awarded the full amount.

The Pediatric Health Care Center (PHCC) respectfully requests a $350,000 grant from the Generosity Foundation to develop our pediatric palliative care program and continue our oncology patient and family support program.

1. Introduction

PHCC's Gardner Center continues to provide comprehensive state-of-the-art care for children with cancer and blood diseases. Our multi-disciplinary team members include physicians, advanced nurse practitioners, nurses, social workers, a psychologist, a child life specialist, and a chaplain who provide a coordinated and comprehensive approach to caring for children with cancer. Our patient and family support program has been meeting the psychosocial needs of patients and families successfully for many years through support from the Generosity Foundation. We continue to further develop a palliative care program to address the needs of patients and families whose treatment success is unlikely or who need intensive palliation of symptoms during their course of treatment.

2. Specific Aims

The Gardner Center has many programs dedicated to meeting the needs of our patients and families. Our specific aims for this grant request are twofold:

1. Continue providing support to the whole family, psychologically and emotionally, as members adapt to living with a child who has cancer
2. Continue implementing our palliative care program that coordinates care for children with especially difficult symptoms or limited life expectancy

3. Needs Assessment

Despite tremendous progress in the development of new treatments and cures, cancer remains the leading cause of death from disease among children and adolescents, and the incidence of cancer among children continues to increase. PHCC evaluated 200 new cancer patients in XXXX and follows over 750 patients in treatment. PHCC physicians are recognized leaders in this field and attract patients and families because of our expertise, care models and unique therapies.

PHCC strives to meet the psychosocial needs of families in addition to providing the best cancer and blood disease treatment available in the region. This year in addition to continuing our existing work, we plan to address the following unmet needs:

- Assist families in accessing community resources (for basic needs such as food, shelter and medicine during their child's treatment)
- Establish in-hospital learning resources for children with cancer
- Initiate a family services program for families whose children have brain tumors

These needs are more fully explained in the Procedure section.

The cost of quality, multi-disciplinary care is high and when reimbursement is limited, we rely on alternative sources of funding to continue to provide this level of care. The Generosity Foundation has been extremely supportive of these efforts in the past, and survivors of cancer will attest to the effectiveness of the Foundation's investment.

4. Procedure

Patient and Family Support Program

The Patient and Family Support Program offers an array of psychosocial services that support the diagnostic and treatment care provided to children with cancer and blood disorders. The objectives of the program are to help children, adolescents, and their families adapt to devastating diagnoses, cope with the changes that illness brings to every aspect of their lives, and discover their own strengths in order to reach a new point of individual and family equilibrium. To meet these objectives, we have developed a multi-faceted clinical program, which includes patient and family education, counseling, access to hospital and community resources, problem-solving, and diversional activities.

Clinical services remain at the heart of the Patient and Family Support Program. We meet patients and their family members during the diagnostic process and are available to them until they complete their care, transition to an adult care system, or are transferred to a bereavement program. We offer families information about the diagnostic process, treatment regimens, and navigating the hospital system, and we help patients prepare for painful or frightening procedures. We encourage parents to involve their other children in the care of the sick child and offer assistance to parents about explaining frightening information to the patient and siblings.

Families faced with a chronic or life-threatening illness have major new responsibilities added to their already full schedules at home, at work, and with their other children. We identify and access concrete services that offer assistance with:

- The financial burdens of cancer—insurance co-pays, uncovered medical expenses, lost wages, transportation costs, and child care expenses
- Issues raised by employers—juggling work and treatment schedules
- Integrating the student with cancer back into the classroom
- Facilitating homebound tutoring programs for children and adolescents who cannot return to school during treatment

Our psychologist teaches patients active coping skills to manage difficult procedures, nausea and vomiting, and pain, and to offer therapeutic interventions to patients and family members, including siblings, who have emotional problems resulting from the cancer diagnosis. Funding from the Generosity Foundation allows us to continue to provide these services without charge to all patients and their families regardless of income, insurance, or ability to pay.

Assist Families in Accessing Community Resources

This year, we would like to assist families with multiple resource needs to connect with appropriate community agencies to address basic needs such as transportation, food, shelter and medicine. As we see increasing numbers of uninsured and poorly insured children from low-income families, requests for these services continue to multiply. A case aide will supplement the work of social work staff members and allow us to continue to offer both concrete help, as well as educational and counseling services to our families.

Establish In-hospital Learning Resources

We will also develop a pilot educational program for inpatients and those in our outpatient infusion center. Currently only those patients who are absent from school for more than two consecutive weeks are eligible for hospital-based teaching. Even those patients who are eligible rarely receive services, as there are few certified tutors able to come to the hospital. Most patients have no educational services during the time they receive care on-site.

We propose to hire a part-time certified teacher who will utilize curricula developed for parents who "home school" their children. These curricula are recognized by school systems throughout the country and offer patients the chance to receive credit for schoolwork accomplished in the hospital. Individual school systems will be able to modify the curriculum for a particular student as they wish. This critically important service will be available to patients without charge and without requiring their parents to engage in lengthy negotiations with school systems about paying for hospital-based tutoring. This program will reinforce the importance we place on school and education in the lives of our patients and allow patients to maintain their standing in school despite the intensity or frequency of treatment.

Initiate a Family Services Program for Families Whose Children Have Brain Tumors

The neuro-oncology program at PHCC serves 3 to 4 new patients diagnosed with brain tumors per month and follows over 500 active patients. These patients have had minimal access to psychosocial services because they receive most of their treatment as outpatients. Families may not meet a social worker until their child is in the hospital for a life-threatening emergency or end of life care.

We propose to conduct a pilot program to address these issues with families early in the diagnosis and treatment process. Using a needs assessment survey, we will develop a short-term group intervention for families of children recently diagnosed with brain tumors. The group facilitator will teach problem-solving skills so that parents can identify and access resources, advocate within their school system to meet their child's learning needs, and address treatment-related concerns. During group sessions for parents, activities will be planned for patients and siblings to ease parents' concerns about child care issues and to provide age-appropriate learning for the children. This short-term group intervention will facilitate parent networking, introduce patients and families to the psychosocial staff early in treatment, help families and staff identify and develop solutions to problems, and decrease additional family distress.

Palliative Care Program
Although the treatment of childhood cancer has shown remarkable progress, approximately 30% of children with cancer die of the disease or its complications. The pediatric palliative care program within the Gardner Center addresses the physical, psychosocial, and spiritual needs of children and families and serves as a prototype for palliative care services that eventually will be offered throughout PHCC.

Creating a Family-Centered Focus
When a child's cancer no longer responds to standard treatment, parents face a range of decisions, from pursuing investigational treatments to shifting the focus of treatment to support the child's quality of life during the end stages of the disease. Parents and patients need information about the available options, opportunities to ask questions of staff they know and trust, and optimally, the chance to maintain relationships with the team of caregivers they have known from the time of diagnosis. Patients, parents, and other family members, especially brothers and sisters, should be at the center of a circle of professionals who can address the patient's physical needs and also the social, psychological, and spiritual needs of the child or adolescent and his family.

Meeting an Unmet Pediatric Need
In our immediate area, there are neither dedicated pediatric hospice programs nor home hospice programs with staff trained and experienced in meeting the needs of pediatric patients and their families. The palliative care program at PHCC coordinates care for children with limited life expectancy and provides continuity of care in the hospital, into the community and into the home. This program supplements the work of the multi-disciplinary team that has followed the patient from diagnosis, providing direction in the areas of pain relief and management of other symptoms. Staff assist with discussions about limitations of care as the child's illness and symptoms progress.

The program also provides education and consultation for hospital and community staff including physicians, nurses, medical residents and other clinical staff. Palliative Care Project Coordinators are certified ELNEC instructors (End of Life Nursing Education Curriculum) and offer this comprehensive curriculum both to PHCC nurses and nurses at other institutions.

Educating Families about Palliative Care
A range of educational and supportive services are available for parents, patients, and family members, especially brothers and sisters. Staff help with patient and family understanding of diagnosis and prognosis, symptom relief, the availability and side effects of medicines and treatments, resources to address unmet needs, and changes that the family will observe during the dying process. Families and their children have access to the services of a social worker, child life specialist, and chaplain to address emotional, financial, resource, and spiritual concerns. We seek funding for one of the part-time Nurse Project Coordinators to support this comprehensive clinical, educational, and outreach program.

5. Performance Site

PHCC operates the patient and family support and palliative care programs at the main PHCC site, located at 1000 Main Avenue, Anytown, AL, 12345.

6. Consultants/Collaborators/Agreements

The patient and family support program works closely with many organizations in the community, including the Ronald McDonald House, the American Cancer Society, Locks for Love, the Richard Smith Cancer Foundation, StarWars Foundation, Make A Wish, and many others. We were pleased to receive a three-year grant from the Lance Armstrong Foundation to fund the expansion of our palliative care program. We work closely with the Initiative for Pediatric Palliative Care (IPPC) and the End-of-Life Nursing Education Consortium Project (ELNEC). In order to make our educational program successful, we will seek collaboration with the school systems in the area as well as more general educational advocates.

7. Comparison to Similar Organizations

Each of the cancer treatment programs in the area offers some elements of the psychosocial program provided by PHCC's patient and family support program, but none of these programs is able to offer the range of services that we provide with our multi-disciplinary staff. None of these programs has dedicated child psychology staff to provide neurocognitive testing, patient and family psychotherapy, and behavioral interventions. While the leading cancer institutions in the nation have on-site educational resources for children in treatment, no facilities in our region provide that service. Additionally, there are neither hospital-based pediatric palliative care programs nor pediatric hospice programs in our area. The American Cancer Society has recognized our uniqueness, due in large part to the Generosity Foundation, and awarded multiple training grants to our program to support social work education.

Conclusion

The Pediatric Health Care Center deeply appreciates the ongoing commitment of the Generosity Foundation to the Gardner Center for Cancer and Blood Diseases. By renewing your investment, you will ensure the continuation of programs needed to support the children and their families who are facing cancer today. We look forward to a time when these dreaded diseases will be eliminated. Until then, we will continue to meet those needs.

Attachment

Budget for Gardner Center for Cancer and Blood Diseases

Palliative Care Program

Program Coordinator, MSN (X FTE)		$40,000
	Subtotal	**$40,000**

Patient-Family Support Program

M.S.W. Social Workers (X FTE)		$X,000
Ph.D. Psychologist (X FTE)		$X,000
M.A. Group Facilitator (X FTE)		$X,000
B.A. Case Aide (X FTE)		$X,000
Teacher (X FTE)		$X,000
	Subtotal	**$310,000**

Total Request $350,000

Attachments

- List of PHCC Board of Directors
- Copy of most recent grant year-end report
- Most recent Audited Financial Statement
- Evidence of 501(c)(3) status from IRS

Source: Courtesy of Chris Stacey, Sapphire Consulting, Washington, DC.

Brief Proposal Letter

July 21, XXXX

Mr. Bernard Siegel
President
The Harry and Jeanette Weinberg Foundation, Inc.
7 Park Center Court
Owings Mills, Maryland 21117

Dear Bernie:

As a follow up to our recent discussions, I am writing to request The Harry and Jeanette Weinberg Foundation's consideration of a challenge grant of $75,000 for the Maryland Center for Arts and Technology, Inc. (MCAT). The grant will provide support for the relocation of MCAT to a training facility for the next three to five years, allowing us to accommodate our rapid development and growth more efficiently. I appreciate the generous support we received from the Foundation during our initial phases of development. Without it, the expanding scope of MCAT's current program would not be possible.

As you know, MCAT is a non-profit organization that provides customized, employer-focused training to welfare and under-employed adults for technology-oriented industries. Through creative learning strategies, close partnerships with employers and company-sponsored internships, MCAT prepares and trains these adults for full-time employment with family-supporting wages, benefits, and career advancement opportunities. Our training programs focus on building work skills, educational skills, work habits, and life skills in our participants. Through case management support and extensive life skills development, MCAT provides participants with necessary tools to eliminate the barriers to employment.

The vision for MCAT emerged out of a two-year study initiated by the Hoffberger Foundation to identify ways of addressing the skills gap between employers' needs and residents in the City of Baltimore and its surrounding counties. With assistance from two nationally successful training partners—Bidwell Training Center/Manchester Craftsmen's Guild in Pittsburgh, and Wildcat Service Corp. in New York—the Foundation began initial steps in creating a similar center in Baltimore City.

MCAT began its welfare-to-work Financial Services Training Program in March XXXX with Commercial Credit Company (now "CitiFinancial"), a $17.5 billion dollar consumer lending company based in Baltimore and a subsidiary of CitiGroup. In conjunction with CitiFinancial, MCAT developed a 32-week financial services training and employment program: 16 weeks of curriculum and non-paid externship training and, for those successful in training and interviewing, an additional 16 weeks of paid, full-time work experience ("internships") at the employer's offices. The first 16 weeks are focused on implementing a 640-hour curriculum that is comprised of five parts: life and job readiness skills; academic skills (applied Business English and Math); computer and data management skills; workplace-based training specific to the employer; and a paid, work experience activity.

In a similar partnership with Johns Hopkins Health System (JHHS), MCAT offered its first Health Care Administration Training Program in August XXXX. The curricula and paid internships for this program have been developed by MCAT in collaboration with Johns Hopkins staff. The design of this program is similar to MCAT's Financial Services Training Program with the same focus on implementing our 640-hour curriculum as described above.

Source: Courtesy of Ellen Atkinson, Maryland Center for Arts & Technology, Baltimore, Maryland.

To date, MCAT has begun twelve programs and completed the training portion in nine of these: seven Financial Services Training Programs and two Health Care Administration Training Programs. Of the first seven classes, MCAT has placed 87% of the Financial Services graduates in paid internships or full-time positions. In addition, MCAT has placed 92% of its Health Care Administration graduates in paid internships with Johns Hopkins Health System. To date, 66% of our Financial Services interns and 92% of our Health Care interns are continuing in their employment. The average starting salary for these graduates is between $19,300 and $23,000 with comprehensive benefits.

Along with MCAT's achievements come many new challenges. One of the most significant challenges we face is operating in a training facility that does not adequately meet our developing needs. Situated on the Hopkins Bayview campus, our current center includes 2 academic classrooms, 3 computer labs, a conference room, a break/lunch room and office space for 15 full-time staff members.

To support the rapid growth and expansion of MCAT's training programs, we project—by mid-October—needing additional classroom and office space. This projection is based on MCAT's enrollment and employment objectives for FY XXXX, which include starting Financial Services and Health Care Administration Training Programs every eight weeks for our current and new employers in these areas. In addition to these two training programs, we are currently holding discussions with several information technology companies in anticipation of starting a third training program specific to this industry. To successfully achieve our enrollment and employment objectives, our training facility must have a minimum of 7 classrooms (we currently have 5) and office space to accommodate 21 full-time staff members (we currently have 16) as well as 3 part-time staff members. In order to accommodate our anticipated needs, MCAT is in the final stages of negotiating an agreement to occupy the MAP Building, 218 West Saratoga Street. Our efforts in pursuing this space have, in part, been driven by the encouragement we have received from the MAP leadership.

In addition to more efficiently accommodating our programmatic needs, relocating to the MAP building will be beneficial in the following ways:

- place us closer to the center of Baltimore's business district;
- provide greater accessibility, for participants, to major transportation hubs; and
- strengthen our ability to serve as an anchor in this area of the Westside downtown.

Following are the estimated costs and funding support for the relocation of MCAT to the MAP building. The funding support section includes MCAT's contribution of up to $70,000, which will pay for the early termination of our lease to Dome Real Estate.

Estimated Costs		**Sources of Funding**	
Hard Costs of Build-Out	$130,000	Abell Foundation	$75,000
Relocation & Soft Costs	$20,000	Weinberg Foundation	$75,000
Termination Clause on Existing Lease	$70,000	MCAT	(up to) $70,000
Total	**$220,000**	**Total**	**$220,000**

MCAT asks for the support of The Harry and Jeanette Weinberg Foundation of $75,000 to provide funding for our relocation to the MAP Building. If approved, your grant will enable us to request matching funds from the Abell Foundation. This effort will ensure the continued success of MCAT's training programs and strengthen our ability to provide the opportunity for self-sustaining careers, thus building a brighter future for our participants and their communities.

Thank you for your thoughtful consideration of this request.

Sincerely,

LeRoy E. Hoffberger

LeRoy E. Hoffberger
Chairman

Special Events—The Fun in Fundraising

KEY VOCABULARY

- Business Reply Envelope (BRE)
- Corkage Fee
- Gifts-in-Kind
- Graphic Artist
- Mail House
- Outsourcing
- Piggybacking
- Public Service Announcement (PSA)
- Service Bureau/Mailing House
- Sponsorships
- Vendor
- Volunteer

THE FUN IN FUNDRAISING

Special events often are called the "fun" in fundraising. When people think of special events, they often think of the large charity balls or theme events such as chili cook-offs, walk-a-thons, race-for-the-cures, golf outings, or the roasts and toasts that they have attended. Most individuals will attend many special events throughout their lives to honor individuals, create publicity, or raise money for a person or cause. This chapter focuses on the special events that are staged to raise funds to benefit an organization or cause.

Normally, there are four reasons to hold a special event: (1) to highlight the public's awareness of the organization or person,

(2) to raise money to support the interests of the organization or person, (3) to focus attention on the organization's programs or the causes supported by the individual, and (4) to garner attention from and/or for the organization's volunteers.

1. To create public awareness. An event can publicize an organization or cause through coverage in the media by carefully placed public service announcements (PSAs), by direct mailing of invitations to people who ordinarily would not be aware of the organization, and by recruiting volunteers to work on the event who had not been involved previously with the cause or person.
2. To raise money. The obvious way to raise money through a special event is by selling tickets and sponsorships. Yet some events do not always break even, let alone make money. Many events will make money through the selling of sponsorships. In addition to selling tickets and sponsorships, other items may be sold through silent auctions or raffles at the event to raise funds—T-shirts, mugs, cookbooks, posters, luxury trip packages, etc. This is called "piggybacking."
3. To create program awareness. Highlighting the mission and activities of the organization during a special event will create awareness. If someone decides to attend an event honoring a friend or acquaintance and then is exposed to the mission, programs, and activities of the organization, the organization has expanded its audience.

Contact can be made with the community's leadership, those financially able to support the organization, and those who may take an interest in working for the cause.

4. To recognize volunteers. Many events are held just to say thanks to the volunteers who sustain the organization throughout the year. These are not held to raise money, to raise the consciousness of the public, or to introduce new and innovative programs. They are held instead to say thanks to those who have given so unselfishly of their time to the cause. Other goals also can be obtained when honoring volunteers. Well-placed feature articles with photos of key volunteers can garner the recognition that the organization often needs and can attract more volunteers who want to be associated with a "winning cause" and the "right" people.

In capital campaigns, special events can provide an opportunity for continued contact with donors. Groundbreaking ceremonies, donor-recognition dinners, unveilings of donor recognition walls, tours of new facilities, and other special event opportunities associated with a capital campaign (see Chapter 14) are perfect forums for recognizing volunteers and attracting new volunteers and donors to the cause.

The most important questions to ask before planning or holding a special event are these:

- Is it necessary to hold an event?
- What is this event expected to do for the organization—raise funds, raise public awareness, honor volunteers?
- What type of event is best for the organization?
- Will it fit the organization's mission and the community?
- Is there adequate staff and adequate volunteer assistance to stage a successful event?
- Does the organization have the financial resources to undertake a special event and, if so, of what magnitude?
- Will an event bring cohesiveness to the staff and volunteers?
- What is the competition doing? Will this event compete with any events they are holding or are planning?

Once these questions are answered and a decision is made to plan and hold an event, enough time must be allowed to organize it well. At least six months to a year should be allowed for planning and organizing a major event. Although it is possible to plan and execute an event in much less time, it is always wise to allow enough time for thorough planning. Exhibit 12–1 lists questions to help you determine if you are ready to undertake a special event.

In addition, the type of event should be carefully selected. Consider whether this event could be instituted as a yearly event for the organization. Just as the breast cancer organizations have race-for-the-cure 10 kilometer races each year and the National Kidney Foundation has kidney bean chili cook-offs, an organization may have a theme that could be made into an excellent special event. Two good examples of this are the

Exhibit 12–1 Are You Ready to Have a Special Event?

Below are some key points to consider when deciding whether or not your institution should have a special event.

- Will your event be important enough to attract the attention of the groups you want to reach?
- Is the event significant in that it supports some aspect of the organization's overall program, policies, and purposes?
- Can you identify a cadre of volunteers who are willing to do the multitude of tasks necessary to be successful?
- Can your institution justify the time, effort, and cost involved?
- Do you have an idea that is interesting and different that can be presented in an entertaining or dramatic format in order to hold the attention of the audience?
- Will your event create a desire in people to respond in some way—to make a decision, to join or participate, to support through volunteer service, or to make a financial contribution?
- How much publicity will you be able to generate through newspapers, radio, and television?
- Have you attended and observed a variety of special events to assess what is appealing?
- Is there a special occasion that should be commemorated, such as an anniversary, new administrator, new building, new organization name, etc?
- Are similar events already being done by organizations in your community and if so, is there room for another or can you do your event better?
- Is the proposed event appropriate for your institution?

Source: Reprinted with permission from LuAnn Davis, *Start Up: A Fund Raising Guide,* "Are You Ready to Have a Special Event?"

Texas State Society's "Black Tie and Boots" gala and the Illinois State Society's Inaugural Gala, which are held every four years in Washington, DC, to honor the newly elected president and vice president of the United States. More than 12,000 people attend, and enough money is raised to keep the organizations operating for four more years, until the next inaugural galas. Another example is the annual "Black and White" ball held in San Francisco.

After the type of event is decided, careful consideration should be given next to the theme and the location site. Aim for fun and excitement. Is there a recently opened or renovated building that everyone is waiting to see? If so, determine if the event can be held there. Is there a site that is open to the public only during the day that would consider opening its doors in the evening for an event? Museums, zoos, parks, and public buildings such as post offices, banks, historic homes, and historic sites often will open their doors after hours for a fee. This helps them to underwrite their operations as well as pro-

> *People quickly tire of the same old black-tie, sit-down dinner event and long for something creative and exciting.*

vides exciting places for events to be held. Look for something new and different. People quickly tire of the same old black-tie, sit-down dinner event and long for something creative and exciting. In fact, more organizations are emphasizing more informal gatherings rather than black tie.

Establish your budget early. Determine all of the costs of the event, then price the tickets to not only cover the costs but to make a profit. Then consider whether the community and the audience being invited can afford the price of the tickets. If they cannot, then rethink the event and what it offers to those attending. Can less be offered and the event still interest people in purchasing tickets? Perhaps it is best to rethink the event entirely. On the other hand, the ticket price may be too low. After comparing what other organizations have charged for their events, rethink the ticket price. It is better to have conducted this analysis beforehand than to print and mail the invitations and find that no one attended because the tickets were too expensive or find that you are in the "red" because the ticket price did not cover all of the costs of the event.

Sponsorships can be sought to offset the cost of a special event and to keep ticket prices low. Different levels of donor sponsorship also can be established to entice sponsors and to increase the amount of money to be made. For example, a "Silver Circle" sponsor may receive a table for 4 and recognition in the brochure for a cost of $2,500. Those sponsoring at the "Gold Circle" level may receive a table for 8, be given recognition in the brochure, and have one of the honorees seated at their table for a cost of $5,000. "Platinum Circle" donors may receive a table for 10, be given recognition in the brochure, have an honoree seated at their table, plus be included in a before-dinner private reception with all of the honorees. The price for this level of sponsorship could be $10,000. Some donors will be willing to pay more for a higher level of recognition or access to those being honored.

As mentioned above, private prereception gatherings can be held for the highest level sponsors to not only meet with the guests of honor before the event, but also to meet other attendees. Plus, an "after-glow" party can be held affording an opportunity to all of those attending to mix and mingle or to network after the sit-down dinner. This works especially well with events honoring people with awards.

A good example of using both types of receptions is the American Society of Civil Engineers' OPAL Awards Gala, where those receiving OPAL awards meet with VIP guests and the prereception and dinner sponsors and their guests. Later, all attendees are invited to continue the evening at an after-glow reception, again a sponsored event. One of the masters of using an after-glow networking reception is the American Society of Association Executives, which holds this type of sponsored event at their annual conference.

In addition to selling tickets, there are other ways of raising money at an event. For example, if programs are going to be printed for a special dinner, space in the program can be sold for advertisements. Also, if a cash bar is part of the event, a certain amount of the price of a drink can be set aside for the charity. Other merchandise can be sold in support of the cause or to cel-

ebrate the event. At some events, a photographer may be hired to take photos that are then sold to those attending. These photos usually are adorned with a logo or some other indicia to note the event. In addition, raffles or auctions can be held to bring in more revenue. The actual dinner may just break even after expenses, but an event can still make money through these other creative means.

One of the best ways to make money is to save money—by looking for donated goods and services. Seek the vineyard or liquor wholesaler who will donate the wine or alcohol for the event in return for recognition in the program, at the bar, and on the dinner table. Find the printer who works for the organization or other printers who will print invitations for free or at least provide upgraded paper from overstock or special ink colors at no charge. Locate the restaurants, merchants, and other vendors who would like to receive publicity by donating goods or gifts-in-kind to the event. If an item is part of the budget, look for creative ways to obtain it other than paying cash.

THE ROLE OF SPECIAL EVENTS IN FUNDRAISING

Special events are staged to call attention to the organization, cause, or person that they are honoring. Most special events don't raise a lot of money. Indeed, a special event is fortunate if it breaks even. Many are held despite the awareness that they will cost the organization money. Why are these held? Because they bring something else to the organization—publicity. A special event provides the organization with the opportunity to promote its mission and goals to a constituency that may be unfamiliar with its basic tenets of operation. A new "public" may attend that is unfamiliar with the organization. This is the time to capitalize upon this opportunity by providing information about the organization. Have materials that guests can take home with them to learn more about the organization's programs. Don't let those attending leave without providing their name, address, and phone number. If this information isn't obtained when the tickets are sold, then it must be obtained at the event. These are the source of attendees at future events, potential donors, and possible volunteers. Remember, it is imperative to record who attends your events.

> *Remember, it is imperative to record who attends your events.*

Just as publicity is important to an organization, so is a continual source of volunteer help. Special events can help increase the public's awareness of the organization and can attract new volunteers. A special event can be a great opportunity to reach out to the community and recruit new volunteers for the event and for the organization. The excitement and spirit of working on the event can carry over into a desire to work for the organization's other programs and activities. A special event can make it possible for all types of people to volunteer, not just those that an organization would normally see involved with their cause. Special events can draw women and men, the young and the old, the rich and the poor, the working and the nonworking or retired, the highly educated and the not-so-well educated, and they can provide a cross section of the demographics of the area. Enriching the organization's volunteer pool through holding a special event may be as important as the amount of money the event will raise for the organization. Many organizations are expanding their volunteer pool by organizing "junior boards" of young volunteers who identify and plan events that focus on younger people and are priced so they can afford to attend. Those attending these events are then encouraged to become volunteers for the organization. See Appendix 12–A, Reaching the New Kids on the (Philanthropic) Block for examples of events planned by and for younger people.

In addition to all of the previously stated benefits, special events allow the organization to enhance its image within the community through promotion and execution of the event. Securing the best possible volunteer leadership will attract others of comparable position and resources. The event must be first class in every way—this does not necessarily mean that it has to be expensive. The organization should be looking for an event that will not only attract people for the evening but one that will have a lasting effect upon those attending. If an event can be "instituted"—draw people year after year and be associated only with that organization— then it has the potential to increase in popularity each year, draw more and more people, raise more and more money, and enhance the image of the organization within the community.

Organizations should not depend solely on special events for their funds but should have a comprehensive, well-defined development plan and operation that includes special events.

COST VERSUS TIME OF SPECIAL EVENTS

Special events can be costly not only in dollars but in time. The planning of a large event alone can take months. Staff time is taken away from other tasks that normally bring money into the organization. Before deciding to undertake a special event, an organization must decide if this is the wisest method of raising money or creating publicity. It may be the best event ever held in the city with the biggest names in attendance, yet the organization may lose a fortune in staff time and money.

Ask the following questions:

- Is there sufficient available time and staff to plan and execute this event?
- What will this event do for us?
- What could staff members be doing with their time if they were not working on this event?
- Which activity will bring the organization more income and/or publicity?
- Does the organization have the financial ability to hire an event management firm?
- Should the organization spend its money this way?

There are no definitive answers. What may make sense to one organization may not be the answer for another. But whatever the decision, make sure that these questions have been asked and that the many options available are considered.

THE ROLE OF VOLUNTEERS

Most special events run on volunteer energy and expertise. Staff members will usually plan and direct a special event, but typically the volunteer chair and help are the mainstays of most annually held events. Some events are so popular in the community that people vie to be the chair or co-chairs. Volunteers can be used to support events in many different ways. They may loan their homes for parties, house tours, etc.; chair events or committees; use their influence to get underwriting for an event; and cultivate other volunteers for the organization's activities.

> *Most special events run on volunteer energy and expertise.*

Special events give volunteers an opportunity to learn something new and to have fun with people they know and people they would like to get to know. People will come to a special event one year and find that they have had such a good time that they will volunteer the next year to work on the event. They also will share their enthusiasm with their friends. The best way to find new volunteers is to ask the current volunteers to recommend people they know who are interested in the organization's mission, would work hard on a project, and would represent the organization well.

Volunteers can "make or break" a special event. A good volunteer board and a strong chair are no guarantee that an event will be successful, but they certainly can help. A weak volunteer chair and committee almost surely will bring disaster, unless the staff is strong and large enough to rescue the foundering volunteer effort. Make sure that you select volunteers who will get the job done. It is the responsibility of the staff to make sure that volunteers have a clear understanding of all that is required of them and all of the tools with which to accomplish their job. Exhibit 12–2 lists special event committees.

Often, you may find volunteer honorary chairs who lend their name to an event, but who will do nothing more for the event. This is when the name alone will draw interest to the event, but the person doesn't have the time, or perhaps the health to actually work on the event. Having honorary chairs can add instant credibility to new events.

THE ROLE OF STAFF

In an ideal world, staff members are the planners, and volunteers are the workers. In the real world, staff members and volunteers work side by side to produce special events. It is the responsibility of the staff to have the entire event planned in advance down to the smallest detail. Then the staff must train and motivate the volunteers and guide them through the many

Exhibit 12–2 Special Event Committees

- Event Management (Executive Committee)—sets direction, selects theme and date
- Arrangements —plans logistics, contracts for site, selects menus, delegates many details to subcommittees
- Ticket Sales—arranges for distribution and sale of tickets
- Promotion—promotes the organization and all event sponsors, as well as the event
- Publicity—publicizes through press, radio, television, and other media
- Decorations—plans and organizes all decorations around theme
- Finance—controls budget, collects funds, maintains records
- Clean-up—cleans up after the event
- Gifts and Prizes—promotes door prizes and gifts (if there are to be any)
- Entertainment—selects and books entertainment
- Printing—arranges for printing posters, tickets, programs, etc.
- Advertising—arranges to sell advertising for programs; places ads for benefit
- Program—is responsible for editorial content, printing, and distribution of program

Source: Reprinted with permission from Henry Rosso, "The Fund Raising Benefit," *The Fund Raising School Manual.*

stages of the event. Also, the staff must later direct all of the accolades to the volunteers.

There are several points to keep in mind when working with staff and volunteers during the planning and execution of a special event. The following list is just a sample of what should be expected of both:

- Be selective when choosing which staff and volunteers will work the event. Not all people will be good representatives of the organization in a public event. Some people work well behind the scenes but cannot handle stressful situations, make quick judgment calls, or deal with irate individuals.
- Train both the staff and volunteers well ahead of time. It is important for them to have a clear understanding of what will be expected of them during the event. Don't assume that they will have previous special event experience.
- Be cautious of the volunteer who wants to be part of the event because it will be fun. Staff and volunteers will be working at the event, not participating as guests.
- Arrange for a site visit before the event. All workers should be familiar with the general floor plans of the event location—the entrances, emergency exits, restrooms, coat check rooms, security, and so forth.
- Provide volunteers and staff with guidelines on the appropriate dress for the occasion. If it is a black-tie affair, the males may have to rent tuxedos if they don't own them. This may be expensive, so they should have ample time to prepare and budget for this particular event or choose not to volunteer for it. Women should be encouraged to wear low-heeled shoes and clothing that is comfortable yet appropriate to the event.

- Have an adequate number of staff and volunteers assigned to work the event. It is better to have too many than too few. Plan on having several assigned to the chair or co-chairs to act as "runners" and "special needs" persons. The last thing an event chair wants to be concerned about is where are the staff and volunteers?
- No staff or volunteers should be seated before all of the guests are seated. Nor should they have drinks, unless it is appropriate. In fact, staff and volunteers should be instructed to ask the guests of honor if they would like to have their drinks held for them while photos are being taken. In addition, it is suggested that staff or volunteers hold name tags when photos are being taken, as the photos will look much better when printed in newsletters, newspapers, or magazines.
- Staff should have adequate time to prepare for an event. Don't think that staff members can organize a major special event in addition to all of their other responsibilities. If the development director cannot be given the time to plan appropriately, then hire an events management firm and let the development director manage or coordinate the firm's activities.
- Don't depend on promises made by anyone. Plan ahead for all possible contingencies. Staff and volunteers should be empowered to make decisions on the spot. Only well-prepared and well-trained staff and volunteers can make effective immediate decisions.

DONATED SERVICES AND GOODS

A great way to save money on an event is to get as many of the goods and services donated as possible. Examples include the donation of small items, such as the gifts to be given to the guests of honor and the favors to be given to the guests, as well as the donation of more expensive items, such as the printing, the wine, or the food. Use any contacts that the organization has—the contacts of the board members, the committee members, and the staff.

A printing company may be willing to "run" an invitation package at the same time it is printing materials for another client and do the work for cost or even simply in return for the visibility it will receive. The company may be acknowledged in the program, on the back of the invitation, in the organization's newsletter or magazine, etc. See what similar "deals" can be struck with other vendors.

A speaker may be willing to donate his or her honorarium to the organization in return for a tax write-off. Also, don't be afraid to contact celebrities who have an interest in the organization's cause and may be willing to donate their time to help the organization. But be careful in making arrangements with celebrities. They may provide their time for free, but they may want to be reimbursed for their expenses, which could be greater than expected or unreasonable given the organization's budget. Make sure that all agreements are in writing.

Think in terms of who can help and why they would want to be of service to your organization. For example, when planning an awards dinner honoring a top Russian official one year, the American Center for International Leadership (ACIL), based in Denver, Colorado, and associated with the University of Denver, contacted the Russian consulate and asked to borrow a Russian flag to use at the podium along with a flag from the United States. The consulate was pleased to comply, saving ACIL from having to purchase a flag costing approximately $150. For the same event, ACIL asked one of its board members who owned a vineyard to donate wine for the awards dinner. Even though the hotel charged a "corkage fee," it was substantially less than the cost of the wine, thus saving the organization considerable money on the event. Again, an alumna of ACIL who worked for a florist received an invitation to attend the dinner. She replied favorably and asked if ACIL had selected a florist to provide flowers for the evening. As it had not, it worked out an arrangement with the florist that saved it considerable money on the purchase of centerpieces for the tables and gave the florist excellent visibility in the event program.

HOW TO SELECT THE BEST LOCATION

All cities have buildings that are available for special events, and actually some buildings depend upon outside events for their operating budgets. Consider museums, historical homes, or places to which the invited guests normally would not have access. Many times people will want to attend an event to be able to enjoy the location or to be able to say that they have "been there."

> *Consider museums, historical homes, or places to which the invited guests normally would not have access.*

Be concerned about the cost of the site. Many organizations just can't afford to spend $10,000 to $20,000 to rent a museum for an evening event. Be creative in your thinking. In Chicago one of the most successful yearly fundraising events supporting the Boy Scouts is held in downtown Chicago in the "Loop," where the "financial block" of LaSalle Street is closed off for the evening. Tables, bars, bands, etc., are set up right in the middle of this normally very busy thoroughfare. Businesses purchase tables, individual tickets are sold, and the merriment begins immediately after the close of the workday and goes well into the late evening or early morning. Obviously, in Chicago the event is held in the summer!

Thinking "outside the box" can save much money. The Kiwanis in Arlington, Virginia, were seeking a site location for their annual pig/oyster roast. After viewing several locations, one of their active members offered his car dealership for the event. The service bays were steam washed, and rolls of white paper were hung to cover anything unsightly. Ten–foot tables and folding chairs were set up throughout the site and no one cared if anything was spilled. Plus, the event could be held rain or shine.

You will have much more flexibility working with a site other than a hotel. There is room for bargaining at hotels, but not as much as when working with different vendors and caterers at private locations. Remember that caterers can serve food in locations where there are no kitchen facilities. Don't let the lack of a kitchen stop you from selecting a site.

If the location is to be in an urban setting, make sure that there is ample parking or that valet parking has been arranged. Being near a metro or bus stop also is helpful. Alerting taxi companies to the location and ending time of the event is a courtesy to guests. Also, make sure that the site is safe and acceptable to all religious, ethnic, or special interest groups. If the event is being held outside, be sure to plan for inclement weather, insects, and possible noise interference. Whatever site is chosen, be sure to make arrangements with someone with authority who works at the location to be available on the day of and during the event to resolve any unforeseen emergency that may arise.

HOW TO BUDGET FOR A SPECIAL EVENT AND THEN MANAGE IT

Every special event should have a budget. To build a budget for an event, several things must be considered, including the following.

The Facility or Location

The first thing to consider is where the event will be held and how much it will cost to rent the facility. Will furniture be provided or will tables and chairs need to be rented? Is there a public address system and podium? What other audiovisual equipment is available, and is there a cost for its use? Is janitorial service provided both before and after the event and at what cost? Is parking available that is convenient and affordable for the guests? Will there be a need to contract for valet parking? Have local taxi companies been told about the closing time for the event so, when the event ends, cabs will readily be available for guests.

Food, Beverage, Catering, and Decorations

Does the location have food service capabilities and are they of the quality that will be needed for the event? What is the cost of these services compared to outside caterers? Can outside caterers be used? Are the linens of the quality or style that are desired for the event? Can other materials be used? What kind of food and drink should be provided? Will alcohol be served? Will it be an open or cash bar? What prices should be charged for drinks? Will the facility or caterer allow the organization to make money from the sale of drinks? Will they allow food or alcohol to be donated? Consider that outside caterers may be more expensive than using the facility's food service.

Invitations, Programs, and Place Cards

How many people will need to be invited to "break even" or make money on the event? Will the facility being considered hold that many people? What are people in the community accustomed to paying for a special event of the type being planned? Can all of the costs be covered and a profit still be made when charging this amount? What type of invitation should be sent? Will a graphic artist design the invitation? What image should the invitation convey—flashy, conservative, frugal, wealthy, sophisticated, homey, exciting, glamorous, etc.? Will there be a program for the event? Will place cards be used if the event is a sit-down breakfast, luncheon, or dinner? Exhibit 12–3 lists what to include in an invitation for a special event.

Mailing

Is the mailing to be personalized? Should first- or third-class postage be used? How long before the event should the invitations be mailed? Will you send a "hold the date" mailing? Is money budgeted to have a mailing house do this work?

All invitations to small, intimate events should be sent by first-class mail with stamps affixed. Do not use a first-class indicia on the invitations, even though it will save time. Indicia may be used for the "hold the date" mailing. Select a stamp that will coordinate with the invitation package. If it is springtime, for example, select a stamp with flowers. If the event is being held around Christmas, select one of the holiday stamps. If your event is political, then select the American flag or one of the many stamps with an eagle. Consider how the stamp will look with the colors, shape, and size of the envelope. If money is available to spend and has been budgeted for a mailing service, paid staff, or a mailing house can be hired to provide these services. However, a considerable amount of money can be saved by using volunteer help to do the necessary work—stuffing, sealing, and stamping the invitations.

If a large event is being produced, especially if mailing lists will be rented, it is not as necessary to use first-class postage. For example, if the hottest ticket in town is to an inaugural ball or the annual black and white ball, then the recipient usually does not care if the invitation arrived with a first-class stamp or was mailed bulk mail. If the event is that popular, then the organization can afford to skimp on the "look" of the postage. But if the event is new to town and not everyone is vying for an invitation, then mail with a first-class stamp. Also, if there is a short time frame, don't take chances with anything less than first-class mail. An invitation that arrives after the event is held not only is an embarrassment for the organization but obviously will not bring any people or money to the event. Appendix 12–B shows an attractive example of a "save the date" card, which shares with the recipient the excitement of the upcoming event. Hold the date cards serve as a pre-invitation to the event.

> *Hold the date cards serve as a pre-invitation to the event.*

Exhibit 12–3 What to Include in an Invitation to a Special Event

- Name of the event
- Name of the organization holding the event
- Location of the event
- Date and time of the event—include p.m. or a.m.
- Compelling description of the purpose of the event or the cause it supports
- Price of admission—this may include several levels of pricing depending upon what is offered with the event
- RSVP date and phone number so people can inquire about any detail you may have forgotten, a way to contribute to the organization if they cannot attend the event, to volunteer for the organization, or whatever may be of importance to a potential attendee
- Name of organization to which checks should be written
- Date by which checks must be received, tickets purchased, tables reserved, etc.
- Tax status of the organization and exactly how much of the cost is tax-deductible to the attendee
- Name of volunteer chairs and committee members
- Attire expected of attendees—black tie, white tie, country-western, tartan plaid of your clan, etc.

Source: Adapted with permission from M. Guellich and L. Davis, *Fundamentals of Fundraising: A Capital View,* © Association of Fundraising Professionals, Greater Washington, DC, Area Chapter.

Photographers and Video Operators

Is there a plan to have photos taken at the event? Will the photos be used for public relations or media efforts or to make extra money by having photos available for sale after the event? Will the photos be used in future publications of the organization?

Is there a need to have the event videotaped? Can video footage be used in future videos developed for the organization?

If the photos are to be used in publications or on the organization's Web site, be sure that the photographer is taking digital photos.

Speaker's Honorarium

Will there be a speaker or speakers at the event? Will a fee be charged for their services? Will their expenses need to be paid—transportation, food, lodging, etc.? Will gifts be given to the speakers and their spouses? Be careful to select gifts that represent the organization and do not cost too much. Many quality stores have crystal, silver, and pewter gift items that can be personalized for the event or person. Allow enough time for engraving. At high-end stores, engraving can take several weeks, as it is done by hand and not by machine.

Optional Items

What other items are needed to create a spectacular event that will raise money for the organization? Use all of the creative powers of the staff and volunteers to think of ways to make the event special. Then include these expenses in the budget.

PLANNING THE PERFECT EVENT

It is not necessary to invent a new event each year. Most organizations use the same event year after year with great success. Often, though, an organization will want to try something new to create a sense of excitement and anticipation. Appendix 12–C shows an example of an invitation that was designed to use the Valentine's Day holiday as the theme for their event. The reply card and envelope for this event are shown in Appendix 12–D along with examples of other materials used in special events. Appendix 12–E provides a workbook of checklists for events and meetings. Exhibit 12–4 is a list of Seven Tips for Planning Your Next Event. As more and more organizations offer events, it is important to know the organization's constituency to create an event that guests will enjoy not only once, but again and again.

Information or Activities Required for a Successful Event

Time Line

Once a decision is made to hold an event, the most important first step is to develop a time line. Start by working backward from the date of the event and include all the steps that will need

to be taken to complete the event. For each task to be completed, ask questions such as the following:

- When do the invitations need to be received for individuals to RSVP by a particular date?
- When will the invitations need to be mailed?
- How much time is required for the printing, folding, inserting, and stamping process before the invitations can be mailed?
- Will the invitation be the same as last year's or will new artwork need to be designed?
- How much time will a redesign require?

By answering these questions, the amount of "lead time" can be determined and a time line begun for each step of the event. No event should be undertaken without an established time line. Exhibit 12–5 provides a time line for producing a successful special event.

Budget

Once a time line has been developed, the next step is to create a budget based on the needs identified within the time line. Develop the budget by using the concept of "zero-based budgeting"—attach a cost to every item whether it is to be donated or the department already has it. From rental of the site to the food served, the printing of the invitation, the salaries of the staff, the reimbursed expenses of the volunteers, the tape, paper, staples, etc., purchased—all should be included. The budget should reflect the real costs of the event. If items are donated, then this can be shown later as a savings. Also include in the budget other sources of revenue that are planned to be implemented, such as

---

Exhibit 12–4 Seven Tips for Planning Your Next Event

Given that the number of fundraising events continues to grow, events today represent a tremendous range in size, style, purpose, cost, and audience. Here are some tips for you to remember for your next event.

1. One of the greatest enemies of an event is the length of the program. The time to end an event is when your guests still want more. No matter how inspiring or exciting your program, entertainment, and speeches may be, the evening can all be destroyed if it goes on too long. It is both tempting and dangerous to try to include everything in one event.
2. People often measure a fundraising or invitation list by its size. That can often be a misleading measure. A good list of 100 well-thought-out names strongly connected to the event and its leadership can produce more attendees than a more general list of 10,000 names.
3. The ability to create an event that reflects the unique character and personality of the host organization and the cause it represents is an important part of making the event a success and an attraction for the targeted audience.

4. The food at a fundraising event can be simple and not fancy, but it must be delicious. No one likes bad food.
5. The building and management of a good professional team to produce an event is another critical aspect of success. Recruiting the right combination of vendors such as graphic designers, caterers, stage managers, technical firms, and designers helps build a team with mutual respect and trust. This can make all the difference in the product.
6. More and more people say they would rather send a check than attend another event, yet more and more people find themselves attending events. The important goal is to create an event that guests will not only enjoy attending once, but will look forward to attending again and again.
7. In designing an event, it is important to know your audience and first answer the question of what you need to do to get their attention and their attendance. Once you get them to attend, it is important to know exactly with what you want them to walk away and how you plan to achieve that.

Source: Courtesy of Lansdale Associates, Events Consultants, Washington, DC.

Exhibit 12–5 Time Line for Producing a Successful Special Event

EVENT PLANNING CALENDAR FOR A MAJOR HOLIDAY BALL													
ACTIVITY	JAN	FEB	MAR	APR	MAY	JUN	JUL	AUG	SEP	OCT	NOV	DEC	JAN
Present fundraising event idea to board for approval of event, goals, and budget.	■												
Develop, select, and recruit honorary committee and committee chairs. Post on Web site.	■	■	■										
Secure the site and date for the event.	■												
Post "hold the date" on Web site.	■												
Establish dates for monthly committee meetings with tentative, more frequent meeting dates just prior to the event.	■												
Establish theme, type of food and beverage service, and ticket prices for the event.	■	■											
Identify honorees, speakers, or celebrities who are willing to lend their name to the event and solicit. Post on Web site.		■											
Contact honorees, speakers, and celebrities to confirm their attendance.				■	■	■	■						
Solicit sponsors for the event. Post on Web site.						■	■	■					
Meet with the caterer or hotel to arrange for food, beverage, flowers, AV, and other event details.			■						■		■		
Arrange for entertainment.			■	■									
Determine extent of decorations and make arrangements.			■										
Send "hold the date" cards to constituency.							■						
E-mail Hold the Date information to constituency.							■						
Contract with artist to prepare event's printed materials.							■						
Approve artwork and order printing.								■					
Secure purchased or donated magazine space and mail ads.								■					
Recruit and assign volunteers.									■		■		
Collect items donated by sponsors for raffle, silent auction, or door prizes.										■	■		
Mail invitations.											■		
Send e-mail invitations.											■		
Mail press releases to newspapers and PSAs for radio stations.											■		
Send announcement of the event to local magazines.									■		■		

continues

Exhibit 12–5 Time Line for Producing a Successful Special Event (continued)

EVENT PLANNING CALENDAR FOR A MAJOR HOLIDAY BALL													
ACTIVITY	JAN	FEB	MAR	APR	MAY	JUN	JUL	AUG	SEP	OCT	NOV	DEC	JAN
Place announcements of the event in newspapers and on organization's Web site.											▓	▓	
Try to get a feature story about the event or the persons involved in the event in local newspapers and on television.											▓	▓	
Hold final committee meetings.											▓		
Script the event: devise a minute-by-minute event schedule.											▓		
Get attendee list from sponsors.											▓		
Call honorees, speakers, and celebrities to remind them of the event and provide them with event details.											▓		
Call volunteers to inform them of their duties and confirm their attendance.											▓		
Call the honorees, speakers, and celebrities to confirm their itinerary and the event schedule.											▓		
Notify members of the media about the event and inquire about their attendance. Arrange escorts.											▓	▓	
Send out press releases after the event.												▓	
Post photos from the event on organization's Web site.													▓
Hold a thank you party or wrap-up meeting for staff and volunteers.													▓
Send out thank you letters to sponsors, speakers, celebrities, and volunteers.													▓
Hold a "hot-wash" or "post–mortem," including both staff and volunteers to analyze the strengths and weaknesses (opportunities) of the event. Capture these in writing to be used when planning future events.													▓

Source: Courtesy of Gerry Frank, President, *INN*dependent Management Group, Alexandria, Virginia.

the sale of T-shirts, mugs, hats, other trinkets, etc.; the raffling of items in an auction; or other opportunities that will bring in money from sources other than ticket sales. Ticket prices should be determined after the budget is completed. Remember to compare the proposed ticket price with what your competition is charging for their special event, or to other events that are being held in your community. Exhibit 12–6 provides a checklist for budgeting for a special event.

Staffing

Determine the number of professional staff persons needed to successfully plan and execute the event. In addition, plan for the number of volunteer committees that will need to be chaired and staffed by volunteers. Don't forget to include these costs in the budget. It may be possible to determine these numbers based on how the event operated in the past. If the event is new, ask other organizations that have held similar events how they staffed their events. Make calls outside of the immediate area and ask similar agencies what they have done and how their events were staffed. This will be the time to decide whether an events firm should be hired. If it appears that it will cost the organization more in staff time, resources, and money to run the event internally than it would to hire an outside firm to do the work, then the correct decision may be to hire such a firm.

Exhibit 12–6 Checklist for Budgeting for a Special Event

A. The Facility/Location
1. Cost of the facility $ _____
2. Table and chair rental $ _____
3. Public address system and podium $ _____
4. Janitorial and grounds services $ _____
5. Parking and valet services $ _____
6. Tent, awnings, and canopies $ _____
7. Flooring and carpeting $ _____

B. Food, Beverage, Catering, and Decorations
1. Food $ _____
2. Beverages $ _____
3. Linens $ _____
4. Flowers and plants $ _____
5. Signs and posters $ _____
6. Decorations and flags $ _____
7. China and silver $ _____

C. Invitations, Programs, and Place Cards
1. Invitation $ _____
2. Reply card $ _____
3. Carrier envelope $ _____
4. Reply envelope $ _____
5. Postage $ _____
6. Inserts $ _____
7. Program $ _____
8. Place cards $ _____
9. Table numbers and names $ _____

D. Mailing
1. Postage $ _____
2. Service bureau or mailing house $ _____

3. Secretarial support $ _____
4. Food for volunteers coordinating the mailing $ _____
5. Cost of mailing lists $ _____

E. Photographer or Video Operators
1. Photographer $ _____
2. Video operator $ _____
3. Lighting $ _____
4. Staging and backdrops $ _____
5. Staff assigned to work with photographer or video operator $ _____

F. Honorarium for Speaker(s)
1. Fee $ _____
2. Transportation $ _____
3. Lodging $ _____
4. Food $ _____
5. Gifts $ _____

G. Publicity
1. Write PSAs and other press releases $ _____
2. Select photos for promotion $ _____

H. Other/Miscellaneous $ _____

SUBTOTAL OF COSTS $ _____

SUBTRACT COSTS OF ANY ITEMS DONATED − $ _____

GRAND TOTAL OF COSTS FOR THE EVENT $ _____

Source: Courtesy of Gerry Frank, President, *INN*dependent Management Group, Alexandria, Virginia.

Publicity

The success of a special event can depend upon the amount of publicity generated to promote it. To be successful, people need to know about the event and have the desire to attend it. They need to perceive that it is something special and that they want to be a part of it. Publicizing an event is also another way to highlight the involvement of local volunteers. Photos can be taken during dress rehearsals or some other preliminary activity of the event and then sent to the local papers and posted on the organization's Web site with an accompanying article featuring the event and the volunteer help. This can be a motivator for the volunteers, recruit additional interest in volunteering in the community, and further promote the event. The important questions are why the event needs media coverage and who will benefit from it. When these can be answered, there are several ways to publicize a special event.

> *The success of a special event can depend upon the amount of publicity generated to promote it.*

External

1. Radio stations. PSAs should be written and delivered to the local radio stations three to four weeks before the event. These should be 15, 30, 45, and 60 seconds long. They need to cover the Who, What, Where, When, and Why of the event. Attach a fact sheet about the organization in case the station wishes to promote the event beyond what is written in the PSA. The station also may wish to interview some of the celebrities who will be attending or the persons whom the event may be supporting or benefiting. It even may be possible to have the volunteer chair of the event interviewed. Deliver the media package in person to the station manager if possible.

2. Television stations. Contact the local television stations and provide them with the same media kit. Ask if they will be willing to tape a segment promoting the event. This may be possible if the event involves or benefits the entire community.

3. Newspapers. Develop a press release to distribute to all of the local newspapers as well as those in surrounding com-

munities. Don't forget the weekly community newspapers or the monthly "shoppers" papers. If there is a college or university in the area, be sure to include its papers (and radio or TV stations) also. Make sure that the press release is delivered to the correct editor (sports, food, entertainment, home, etc.) and that one is included for the editor of the community calendar.

4. Magazines. More lead time is required for information to be printed in a magazine than in a newspaper. Most magazines for large cities have a monthly calendar of events, and this is probably the best location for an event to be publicized.

5. Local business. Ask the editors of corporate newsletters of local businesses to include an article on your event. This can be particularly successful if volunteers for the event work for one of these companies. The company probably will be pleased to highlight the volunteer activities of its staff. If the company provides services to the local and surrounding communities, it may be possible to have the company highlight the event in the newsletter that accompanies its monthly invoices. For example, the local electric or gas companies may include information on nonprofit events that will benefit their customers. In addition, local companies may be willing to post flyers or posters on their bulletin boards. Don't overlook banks, grocery stores, restaurants, service stations, movie theaters, beauty salons, etc.

Internal

1. Post all details pertinent to the event on the organization's Web site. Begin with a hold the date announcement on the Flashpage and then update weekly as the event unfolds; when honorees are selected, place their photos and bios on the site. When ticket prices are established, indicate when, where, and how they can be purchased.

2. Use all of the organization's media pieces to promote the event. In the newsletters to members, donors, volunteers, the community, etc., place "hold the date" announcements, feature articles, etc. Appendix 12–F shows an example of an invitation sent via postcard that also includes upcoming events on the reverse side of the card. This is an inexpensive, yet attractive way of promoting an event to members while reminding them of upcoming events.

Exhibit 12–7 shows a sample planning calendar for event publicity.

Evaluation

Often it is easy to forget that all events conclude not with the close of the evening's activities but with an evaluation of the overall successes and failures of the event. An evaluation should take place, not the morning after an event, but within two weeks—long enough to allow the staff an opportunity to rest from the stress of producing the event but not so long that details are forgotten. This is also the time to plan for follow up

on the event—how to capitalize on its success or "mend fences" that need mending as a result of its failures. All too often this step is forgotten. It may not take much to keep "the ball rolling" and continue the momentum of the moment. Have thank you notes been sent to the sponsors, volunteers, and those who provided gifts-in-kind? Should telephone calls be made instead of notes being written? Have lists been made of attendees who are new to the organization? How will they be included in future activities? Did this event make money? Could the event have made more money? What should be done to make the event better the next time? Use this opportunity to measure the success of the event and to set the course for the next year—whether it involves this event or some other in its place. Exhibit 12–8 is an example of a special event evaluation form.

Special software programs are designed to help manage all aspects of special events—from invitations, registrations, and attendance to the to-do lists, name badges, seating and group assignments, and "event-day" reports. These programs usually are flexible in design so they can handle all event types, including black-tie dinners, class reunions, annual conferences, walkathons, golf tournaments, etc. They also provide standard and custom reports to assist the development staff in reporting to its board or in analyzing the successes or failures of its events. These programs range in price and usually come packaged with other fundraising or association management software programs.

WHAT MUST BE DONE AFTER THE EVENT IS OVER

Many people think that when the event is over, all of the work has been completed. Unfortunately, this is not so. In addition to the evaluation that must be conducted, everyone who has contributed to the success of the event must be thanked. This includes everyone from the chairs of the event to the sponsors and those who donated gifts-in-kind. All outstanding bills must be paid promptly. If a vendor provided special services, include a thank you letter. It is important to ensure the vendor's participation the next time the event is held. At some point, be in touch with all of those who attended the event. Put them on the list to receive the organization's newsletter. Try to cultivate these people to become annual donors or volunteers for the organization's next event.

CONTRACTING WITH OUTSIDE VENDORS

From caterers to printers, vendors are part of the special event scene. Providing the necessities for the event, vendors can make the event a success or a disaster! It is imperative that the development staff be familiar with the quality of work or goods that a vendor is going to provide. Check references. Attend an event that is featuring the vendors being considered. Listen to the music, sample the food, review printed materials. Call references before signing any contract with a company. It ultimately comes down to "doing your homework." Thoroughly investigate all vendors before agreeing to use them for an event.

Exhibit 12–7 Planning Calendar for Event Publicity

ACTIVITY	6 MONTH	WEEK 12	WEEK 11	WEEK 10	WEEK 9	WEEK 8	WEEK 7	WEEK 6	WEEK 5	WEEK 4	WEEK 3	WEEK 2	WEEK 1 EVENT	POST EVENT WEEK
Send out "hold the date" announcements. Post hold the date on the Web site.	■													
Write PSAs and identify media to which publicity will be sent. Develop a database.		■		■										
Send out press releases announcing the event to the calendar of events editor of area magazines.														
Develop database to whom invitations will be sent.			■											
Prepare labels or write addresses on invitations. Stuff envelopes.				■										
Send out invitations.					■									
Send e-mail blasts to promote event to internal and external constituencies.						■			■	■	■			
Send out PSAs to local and regional radio and TV stations.									■	■				
Send out press releases announcing the event to all local and regional newspapers. Post on Web site.						■					■			
Contact feature story editors of area newspapers and request that a feature story be written on the event.											■	■		
Arrange for the local media to cover the event. Assign personnel to escort each media group.													■	
Send out press releases with photos recapping and publicizing the success of the event.														■
Post photos of the event on your Web site.														■

Source: Courtesy of Gerry Frank, President, INNdependent Management Group, Alexandria, Virginia.

Exhibit 12–8 Special Event Evaluation Form

NAME OF EVENT _____

DATE _____

      SUCCESS OF DATE AND TIME _____

      SUGGESTED DATES AND TIMES _____

NUMBER OF GUESTS ATTENDING _____

NUMBER OF STAFF ATTENDING _____ WORKING _____

SITE LOCATION _____

      SITE APPROPRIATE OR NOT _____

      SUGGESTED SITES FOR FUTURE _____

VOLUNTEER LEADERSHIP _____

      GENERAL CHAIR _____

      COMMITTEE CHAIRS _____

                            _____

                            _____

                            _____

                            _____

      TOTAL VOLUNTEERS INVOLVED _____

      ESTIMATED HOURS OF WORK _____

      SUGGESTED GENERAL CHAIR FOR NEXT YEAR _____

      SUGGESTED COMMITTEES FOR NEXT YEAR _____

                            _____

                            _____

                            _____

                            _____

SUGGESTED COMMITTEE CHAIRS FOR NEXT YEAR _____

                            _____

                            _____

                            _____

                            _____

                            _____

NUMBER OF PROFESSIONAL STAFF WORKING EVENT _____

      EVENT DIRECTOR _____

      STAFF COMMITTEE ASSIGNMENTS   _____

                            _____

                            _____

                            _____

                            _____

ESTIMATED HOURS OF STAFF WORK _____

MONEY RAISED

      TICKET SALES $_____

      OTHER SOURCES $_____

      GROSS $_____

      NET $_____

EXPENSES

      VOLUNTEER $_____

      STAFF $_____

      EVENT COSTS $_____

      TOTAL EXPENSES $_____

TOTAL—INCOME MINUS EXPENSES $_____

continues

Exhibit 12–8 Special Event Evaluation Form (continued)

1. Considering the time invested by staff and volunteers and the total net dollars raised, is the event worth repeating?
   YES _____ NO _____ COMMENTS _____
   _____
   _____

2. What are the benefits to those attending? _____
   _____
   _____

3. What are the drawbacks to holding this event? _____
   _____

4. What problems occurred while planning or executing this event that could be prevented in the future? _____
   _____
   _____

5. What changes should be made before holding the event again? _____
   _____
   _____

6. Why, in your opinion, was this event successful or unsuccessful? _____
   _____
   _____

7. Please comment on the overall performance of the professional staff in executing the event including both positive and negative observations _____
   _____
   _____

8. Comment on the overall performance of the volunteer involvement with the event including both positive and negative observations _____
   _____
   _____

9. Was there enough internal and external publicity to promote the event? _____
   _____
   _____

10. Other remarks pertinent to this event _____
    _____
    _____
    _____
    _____

11. _____ I would be willing to work on this event again.
    _____ I would NOT be willing to work on this event again.

NAME _____
ADDRESS _____
PHONE _____ FAX _____ E-MAIL _____

SIGNATURE _____
DATE _____

Source: Courtesy of Gerry Frank, President, *INN*dependent Management Group, Alexandria, Virginia.

Also, make sure that vendors are adequately insured or that the organization is insured in case someone is injured at the event. Usually, a rider can be purchased to attach to the organization's existing insurance policy. This undoubtedly will not be part of the organization's normal insurance unless conventions, meetings, and special events are a part of the organization's everyday operations. If the event is being planned for out of doors or during the winter months, event cancellation insurance should be considered. In all cases where alcohol is being served, liquor liability should be purchased.

There are many outside vendors who offer software that assists with organizing special events. Appendix 12–G is from the article "Five Tips for Making Fundraising Event Registration More Productive" printed in the *Convio Connection* by Convio, Inc., of Austin, Texas. The article describes their registration software, Convio TeamRaiser, which helps event planners increase and organize registrations for their events, particularly walkathons.

USING AN EVENT MANAGEMENT GROUP

Sometimes it is easier to hire a consultant or an events management group to plan and execute a special event than it is to use existing departmental staff. This is called outsourcing. First, consider the magnitude of the event and whether it has been held before, then consider the commitments, skills, and limitations of the current staff. If this is a "once in a lifetime" opportunity (and these are truly rare), and if the staff has limited expertise in this area, then hire an outside firm to produce the event and use the staff solely to manage the firm's activities.

If this is the direction of choice, be very careful in negotiating the contract with the events firm so it is clear just what is expected from them, what will be managed by the development office, and what the true costs of the event will be. Also, include performance standards, fee structures, and the schedule of payment. Don't overlook hidden costs! If you haven't negotiated a contract before, now is not the time to learn. Ask someone from the legal or financial department to participate. It even may be wise to have a board member who can assist with the negotiations or even to hire an attorney. Whatever is done, don't do it in a "vacuum." Show the contract to the head of finance or the president of the organization before signing anything.

Most event firms are reputable and will do an excellent job. Ask for references and call them! Are the events these firms have organized in the past of the same type the organization wants to hold? Does the image of the event management firm fit with the organization's image? If the organization is promoting gun control and the events firm does the majority of its work for the National Rifle Association, then the organization may not wish to hire this firm even if its credentials are impeccable. Discuss this with the board—do not have any surprises that the board may have to defend.

Events firms also may be able to negotiate better prices with vendors. They work with them every day and continuously steer business their way. Printers, musicians, caterers, florists, etc., are more likely to give a break in prices to those who use them frequently than to those who use them once a year. In addition, outside firms even may have better leverage with the organization's volunteers. If volunteers need to be firmly directed, it may be easier to have the staff of the events firm do the directing rather than the development office staff, who will have to work with the volunteers in the future. Also, board members may perceive the events firm as being "more professional" than the development office when it comes to producing special events because this is what the firm does day in and day out. They may be more willing to trust the expertise of this firm and, as a result, not require as much direction from or hand-holding by the development staff. Be sure to have only one person who is responsible for communicating with the firm managing the event. This is usually the most senior person on the staff of the development office. Don't just sign a contract and walk away. Maintain open communications with the firm and communicate frequently. Meet with staff persons from the firm often to make sure that they are on the right course for the organization.

One of the most overlooked advantages of using an outside firm to produce the organization's special events is that the work is not being done in the development office. The entire project will be organized outside—planning, design, mailings, envelope stuffing, telephone calls, and the management of any crisis will not interfere with the everyday workload of the staff. This alone can make it cost-effective to hire an events firm. In addition, the events firm can bring people to the organization who may be interested in the organization's mission and activities—people who may have never heard of the organization before.

Once again, it is very important to check references. Ask what other organizations similar in size have used the firm before. Determine if the events produced for other organizations are similar in scope and visibility to the one your organization wishes to produce. Call those persons who have worked with the firm and ask detailed questions about reliability, pricing structure, creativity, quality, etc. Request a capability package from each vendor—what they will be able to provide to the organization. Additional information regarding the use of consultants in fundraising may be found in Chapter 17.

IRS REGULATIONS REGARDING SPECIAL EVENTS

Beginning January 1, 1994, the Internal Revenue Service (IRS) required that every charitable organization must provide a written disclosure statement to donors who make a payment described as a "quid pro quo contribution" in excess of $75. This new section of the Internal Revenue Code (§6115) mandates that the charity notify each event participant in writing of what portion of his or her contribution is tax deductible. To determine what portion of the ticket price is tax deductible, total the costs of the food and beverage, printing, postage, etc., and then deduct these from the price of the ticket. If the event includes a theatre ticket, then that also must be deducted at the full box

"They want a receipt for their contribution to the dinner!"

Source: Copyright © Joseph A. Brown

office price charged by the theater, not at the discount price that the organization may have received. For example, if the event includes dinner, wine, and entertainment and costs the organization $85 to hold, and if the ticket price is $125, then the guest's tax-deductible donation is not $125 but $45—the $125 cost of the ticket minus the $85 in goods received.

If a person attends several events sponsored by the same charity during the year but each event is under the $75 threshold, the payments are not aggregated to meet the $75 threshold. However, a donor cannot submit several small checks to cover the costs of one event with a high ticket price to circumvent this ruling. If a donor writes a check to a charity for $100 and receives in return $45 worth of goods or services, the $55 would be deductible, but because the $100 payment, or quid pro quo contribution, exceeds the $75, the charity must provide the disclo-sure statement even though the amount the donor can deduct does not exceed the $75 limit. The safest way for the charity to protect itself after attempting to state the exact amount of the deduction on an invitation is to add "Tax deductible to the fullest extent as provided by law."

Any questions regarding these rules can be answered by read-ing the IRS publication 1771 (07-2005), a copy of which is included in Appendix 12–H. Other resources are available upon request from AFP, ASAE, and Independent Sector.

REFERENCES

Collins, M.E. Save the date: How to ensure a special fundraising event is right for your organization. *Advancing Philanthropy* (July/August 2007): 22–27.

Case Study: How to Involve the Younger Generation in Special Events: Reaching the New Kids on the (Philanthropic) Block

If you want to learn how to develop the younger generation's version of the golf and gala, go straight to the source.

"Many organizations are developing leadership committees or 'junior boards' that plan events like fashion shows and concerts," says Bridget Baughn, senior director of event services for Changing Our World Inc. in New York (http://www.changingourworld .com). "Some of them have been pleasantly surprised that these groups are raising a lot of money and getting exposure for the organization in a group where they hadn't had it before."

Jessica Stannard-Friel, co-editor of the blog Future Leaders in Philanthropy, which is a project of on-Philanthropy (http://flip .onphilanthropy.com), says that young people are price-sensitive and suggest planning events around the kinds of activities that the group already enjoys doing, such as cocktail parties, networking, and playing sports. She also points out an interesting "cart before the horse" trend in this demographic.

"This is the generation that grew up with walk-a-thons and read-a-thons, selling wrapping paper in school, and doing sorority and fraternity fundraisers in college," she says. "Now, a group will decide to do a fundraising event and *then* look for a charity to affiliate with instead of being involved with the organization first."

The Washington, D.C., group SMASHED (http://www .dcsmashed. org) is a perfect example. The Society of Mature Adults Seeking to Help, Entertain, and Donate dreams up wacky events and parties, charges people less then $20 to participate and gives local charities the money it collects. This year's D.C. "Idiotarod," in which costume-clad participants raced grocery carts instead of dog sleds through the streets, raised $4,000 for the Arlington Food Assistance Center. Other SMASHED events have included a Sweet 'Stache ManPageant and an Amazing Race-style scavenger hunt.

Although there seems to be no end to the level of zaniness they enjoy, SMASHED does have some guidelines: it chooses local charities with operating budgets under $5 million, where it feels its donations will have the greatest impact, and it requires the benefiting charity to be present at the event.

"It's not just about raising money," says Ellen Shortill, founder of SMASHED. "It's also about awareness. Last year we did one event that didn't raise that much money, but about 100 people who took part then signed up to participate in the charity's own fundraising walk later on."

For organizations that want to cultivate their up-and-coming generation of donors, Shortill has a few tips. "Accept the value of small donations and value the input of silly ideas," she suggests. "People have serious lives and they look for ways to relax and blow off steam. Create amusing opportunities for friendly interaction. You can raise money wearing black tie, or you can do it in a pirate outfit."

The bottom line? As Shortill says, "Silliness wins."

Source: Courtesy of the Association of Fundraising Professionals (AFP), Advancing Philanthropy, July/August 2007, p. 24, Arlington, Virginia.

Sample Save the Date Card

Chat with friends and neighbors at The Hickman while enjoying an autumn evening of delicious food and an auction...with a twist! The capstone of the evening will be an exciting live auction, sponsored by First National Bank of Chester County, featuring thirteen "Tilt Top Tables" each painted and interpreted by a collected area artist. Beforehand, browse more than sixty enticing silent auction items, packages and unique experiences.

2006 SPONSORS

ARTIST UNDERWRITERS: Peg Anderson & Kathy Head • ACAC Fitness & Wellness • Cannon Hill Farm • 1st National Bank of Chester County • Gawthrop Greenwood • Sue Hartz, Robbe Healey & John Schwab • In Memory of Henry R. Hidell, Jr., by his family • The Hickman Board of Managers • Jane H. Mack, Elizabeth Macy Stratton, Charles Mack & Jane Stratton Mack • National Penn Bank

PRESENTING FRIENDS / PRINTING SPONSOR: Alliance Print Group

OTHER SPONSORS: Knott Capital • Springsteen Hotaling Group at Morgan Stanley
(List incomplete)

The official registration and financial information of The Hickman may be obtained from the Pennsylvania Department of State by calling toll free, within Pennsylvania, 1-800-732-0999. Registration does not imply endorsement.

To view the tables, read about our artists, sponsors and silent auction items please visit www.theartofcaring.org

THE *Hickman*
400 North Walnut Street
West Chester, PA 19380

Non-Profit Org.
U.S. Postage
PAID
West Chester, PA
19380
Permit No. 108

Source: Courtesy of Robbe Healey, MBA, ACFRE, Senior Development Director, The Hickman, West Chester, Pennsylvania.

Example of an Event Planned Around a Holiday Theme

The Animal Welfare League
of Alexandria

presents our 3rd annual

Black Tie & Tails Gala

with Leadership Support from
Your Dog's Best Friends

Saturday, February 10th, 2007
Holiday Inn Hotel & Suites (625 First Street Alexandria, VA)
7:30 pm to 11:00 pm

Join us for an elegant affair with the ones you love. We have planned a unique Valentine's celebration for you and your dog featuring a canine couture fashion show hosted by Carlos Mejias of Olde Towne School for Dogs, a live auction, gourmet dog buffet, signature doggie "cocktails", music by Charlene Cochran & the Fifth Avenue Band, dancing, tempting hors d'oeuvres and desserts and more!

Our thanks to our wonderful sponsors:
Alexandria Animal Hospital
Mrs. James McIlhenny
Belle Haven Animal Medical Centre
Regional Veterinary Referral Center
Crosspointe, Fort Hunt & Hayfield Animal Hospitals

RSVP by February 2, 2007

*Black Tie optional or Elegant Period Dress
(to celebrate our 60 years — 1946 - 2006)*

come dressed in black tie (optional) or elegant period attire from your favorite decade
the forties   the 50's   the sixties   the 70's   the eighties   the 90's   today

Source: Courtesy of the Animal Welfare League of Alexandria, Virginia.

The 3rd Annual
Black Tie
& Tails Gala

a valentine for you and your dog

Animal Welfare League of Alexandria
4101 Eisenhower Ave., Alexandria, VA 22304

The Animal Welfare League of Alexandria is a non-profit 501(c)(3) organization which offers adoption and humane education services, and helps homeless, injured, and abandoned animals. We are contracted to operate the City of Alexandria Vola Lawson Animal Shelter and provide animal control services to City residents.

spend a special evening wtih your sweetheart to help us celebrate 60 years of caring

Samples of Materials Used with Event Invitations

A. **Invitation** (Fulbright Lifetime Achievement Medal Dinner)

B. **Admission Tickets** (Fulbright Medal Dinner and Dalai Lama)

C. **Menu Card** (Fulbright Medal Dinner)

D. **Press Pass** (Faith & Politics Institute's 15th Anniversary Celebration)

E. **Reply Envelope** (Animal Welfare League of Alexandria)

F. **Reply Cards** (Animal Welfare League of Alexandria and the 31st annual Hutch Holiday Gala)

G. **Table Reservation Card** (Fred Hutchinson Cancer Research Center) Faith and Politics Institute 15th Anniversary Celebration)

H. **Table Seating Card** (Faith and Politics Institute's 15th Anniversary Celebration)

I. **Invitation to Pre-Event Reception** (OPAL—ASCE)

A. Invitation

THE FULBRIGHT ASSOCIATION
CORDIALLY INVITES YOU TO ATTEND THE

FULBRIGHT LIFETIME
ACHIEVEMENT MEDAL DINNER

honoring Fulbright alumni

RITA E. HAUSER
JOHN MENDELSOHN
HILDA OCHOA-BRILLEMBOURG

TRIBUTES BY
Harvey V. Fineberg
Senator Kay Bailey Hutchison
Moisés Naím

PERFORMANCE BY
YOUTH ORCHESTRA OF THE AMERICAS STRING QUARTET
FEATURING PIANIST DAVID ROBERT COLEMAN
AND VIOLIST EDMUNDO RAMIREZ

Tuesday, May 17, 2005

Andrew W. Mellon Auditorium
1301 Constitution Avenue, N.W.
Washington, D.C.

7:00 p.m. Cocktails
8:00 p.m. Dinner
Black Tie

RSVP BY MAY 2, 2005
REPLY CARD ENCLOSED

FULBRIGHT
LIFETIME ACHIEVEMENT
MEDAL DINNER
Honoring

RITA E. HAUSER
JOHN MENDELSOHN
HILDA OCHOA-BRILLEMBOURG

Tuesday, May 17, 2005

Andrew W. Mellon Auditorium
1301 Constitution Avenue, N.W.
Washington, D.C.

Source: Courtesy of Lansdale Associates, Events Consultants, Washington, DC.

B. **Admission Tickets**

AN EVENING WITH THE DALAI LAMA

*2003 Human Rights Award
Ceremony & Dialogue*

*hosted by the International League
for Human Rights*

4:00 p.m. Light Refreshments
5:00 p.m. Award Ceremony and Dialogue

Friday, September 19, 2003

Asia Society and Museum
725 Park Avenue at 70th Street
New York, NY

Business attire

ADMIT ONE

Ticket required for admission

FULBRIGHT
LIFETIME ACHIEVEMENT
MEDAL DINNER

Tuesday, May 17, 2005
7:00 p.m. Cocktails
8:00 p.m. Dinner
Black Tie

Andrew W. Mellon Auditorium
1301 Constitution Avenue, NW
Washington, D.C.

Please present ticket.
Complimentary valet parking will be available.

Source: Courtesy of Lansdale Associates, Events Consultants, Washington, DC.

C. Menu Card

Menu

Arctic Char Gravlax
Spring Salad of Pea Pods, Red Lentils & English Peas

2000 Chalk Hill Estate Bottled Chardonnay

∾

Medallions of Spring Lamb
with a Meyer Lemon–Pine Nut Crust
over Baby Spinach & Shallots

New Potato Gallettes

Asparagus & Baby Spring Vegetables

2002 Hogue Cabernet-Merlot

∾

Poached Bartlett Pears
stuffed with Orange Mascarpone
on Hazelnut Cakes

2004 Rockbridge V d'Or

Demitasse

∾

Fulbright Lifetime Achievement Medal Dinner
Andrew W. Mellon Auditorium
Tuesday, May 17, 2005

Source: Courtesy of Lansdale Associates, Events Consultants, Washington, DC.

D. Press Pass

Name _____

Encouraging Reconciliation
INVITING Conscience
COMPASSION Seeking Spiritual Wisdom
ENCOURAGING RECONCILIATION

Deepening Conscience

THE FAITH & POLITICS INSTITUTE'S
15TH **ANNIVERSARY CELEBRATION**

Calling Forth
Courage HEALING OUR WORLD
NATION & OUR WORLD Encouraging Reconciliation

Building Bipartisan Community
Our World CONDUCTING HONEST
onscience CONVERSATIONS ON RACE
Compassion SEEKING SPIRITUAL WISDOM

PRESS

E.   Reply Envelope

3ʳᵈ *Annual Black Tie & Tails*

Animal Welfare League of Alexandria
4101 Eisenhower Ave.
Alexandria, VA 22304

F.   Reply Card

Black Tie and Tails Gala Reply Card

_____ Please reserve _____ tickets at $125 per person (one dog per person).
_____ I cannot attend, but please accept the enclosed donation $_____

Name: _____
Business: _____
Address: _____ Zip_____
Phone: _____ Email: _____
Guest name(s): _____
Dog name(s): _____

Total enclosed: $_____ Payment method: _____ Check (enclosed) _____ Visa/Mastercard/Discover
Card # _____ Exp. _____
Signature _____

Reservations held at the door.
Please RSVP by February 2, 2007.
Space is limited to the first 300 reservations.
Dog registry is limited to the first 100 dogs.
One-half of each ticket is tax-deductible.

For information about additional sponsorship opportunities,
contact Beverly Hoffmann at 703/838-4774 ext. 206.

Source: Courtesy of the Animal Welfare League of Alexandria, Virginia.

F.   Reply Card

31ˢᵗ annual

HUTCH HOLIDAY GALA   *Saturday, December 9, 2006*

Name _____

Address _____

City _____ State _____ Zip _____

Day phone _____ Evening phone _____

E-mail _____

Reserve your seat today by registering online at www.hutchgala.com

☐ Please reserve _____ ticket(s) at $500 per person

☐ Please reserve _____ patron ticket(s) at $1,000 per person

Patron tickets include complimentary valet parking, complimentary delivery (greater Seattle area) of auction purchases and recognition in the auction catalog*

☐ Please reserve one table for 10 ($5,000) in my name with the people whose names appear on the reverse side of this card

☐ I am unable to attend, please accept my tax-deductible contribution of $ _____ to support cancer research*

My gift is in honor/memory of _____

Method of Payment

☐ My check for $ _____ is enclosed, payable to FHCRC Foundation

☐ Please charge my credit card $ _____

   ☐ AmEx   ☐ Discover   ☐ MC   ☐ Visa

Account Number _____

Exp. Date (MM/YY) _____

Signature _____

So that your gift may be matched, please enclose your company's matching gift form with your donation.

The favor of your reply is requested by **November 10, 2006**. Seating is limited. Reservations will be accepted in the order they are received.

* *Contributions will be recognized in the auction catalog if received by October 25, 2006.*

Source: Courtesy of the Fred Hutchinson Cancer Research Center, Seattle, Washington.

G.   **Table Reservation Card**

☐ I wish to reserve a table in my name _____
Tables accommodate 10 – 12 guests. List below the names, addresses and
phone numbers of each guest for catalog mailing and bid assignments.

☐ I will not be a host, but wish to be seated with (list below):

1. _____
2. _____
3. _____
4. _____
5. _____
6. _____
7. _____
8. _____
9. _____
10. _____

You will receive confirmation of your reservation by mail.

FRED **HUTCHINSON**
CANCER RESEARCH **CENTER**
A LIFE OF SCIENCE

Source: Courtesy of the Fred Hutchinson Cancer Research Center, Seattle, Washington.

I.   Invitation to Pre-Event Reception

OPAL

AECOM
and
Clark Construction Group, LLC

Cordially Invite You and a Guest to Attend

a Private Pre-OPAL Reception

to Honor and Meet the 2006

OPAL Lifetime Achievement Recipients
OCEA Finalists
Charles Pankow Award for Innovation Finalists
Henry Michel Award Recipient

Wednesday, April 26, 2006
5:30 pm to 6:15 pm

The Oculus
Ronald Reagan Building and International Trade Center
1300 Pennsylvania Avenue, NW
Washington, District of Columbia

Photo Identification is Required

RSVP Required by April 14, 2006
to Diane Connolly
(703) 295-6159 or dconnolly@asce.org

ASCE
American Society of Civil Engineers

Source: Courtesy of American Society of Civil Engineers (ASCE), Reston, Virginia.

H.   Table Reservation Card

Encouraging
Reconciliation
INVITING
Deepening
Conscience
COMPASSION Seeking Spiritual Wisdom
ENCOURAGING RECONCILIATION

THE FAITH & POLITICS INSTITUTE'S
15TH ANNIVERSARY CELEBRATION

Calling Forth HEALING OUR
Courage NATION & OUR WORLD
Encouraging Reconciliation

Building Bipartisan Community
Our World CONDUCTING HONEST
onscience CONVERSATIONS ON RACE
Compassion SEEKING SPIRITUAL WISDOM

TABLE # ____

Source: Courtesy of Lansdale Associates Events Consultants, Washington, DC.

Checklists for an Event or Meeting

Workbook

Checklists for an event or meeting

DEFINING YOUR EVENT OR MEETING

Name of Event or Meeting _____

Purpose _____

Date(s) _____ to _____

Venue(s) ___Hotel___ Convention Space ___Restaurant(s) __Other

Who is invited (general type) _____
_____

Number of people invited................................. _____
Out of town .... _____
How many require airfare / transportation? ...... _____
Number of sleeping rooms needed .... _____

Format   Plenary ....yes _____ no _____
           Breakout sessions...............yes _____ no _____
           Number of meeting rooms needed _____

Food and drink   In-house catering..............yes _____ no _____
           Outside catering.................yes _____ no _____
           Restaurant dining...............yes _____ no _____
           Receptions ....yes _____ no _____
           Details _____
           _____
           _____

Theme   ....yes _____ no_____
           If yes, description of theme
           _____
           _____
           _____

Guest speakers...........................yes _____ no _____
Outside staff ....yes _____ no _____
Hired entertainment ....yes _____ no _____
Gifts for attendees ....yes _____ no _____
Audiovisual................................yes _____ no _____
Printed Materials (e.g. invitations) ....yes _____ no _____
Budget total _____

VENUE / HOTEL SITE INSPECTION:

Name of venue or hotel _____

Contact person _____

Phone number _____ ext. _____

Fax number _____

E-mail _____

Other contacts _____
_____
_____

Things to make sure you ask:
Adequate parking
Valet ....yes   no _____ Cost
Self ....yes   no _____ Cost

Cancellation policy ....yes _____ no _____

Deposit required ....yes _____ no _____

Banquet facilities ....yes _____ no _____
if yes ask for menus

On-site caterer.........................yes _____ no _____
if yes ask for menus

Group rate for rooms...............................yes _____ no _____
Any construction/renovations planned during your stay
.... yes _____ no _____
Business services (photocopies etc.) ....yes _____ no _____
Audiovisual services ....yes _____ no _____

Results of call or visit _____
_____
_____
_____
_____
_____
_____
_____

Source: Courtesy of *Where* Magazine, Morris Visitor Publications, Augusta, Georgia. 2007.

SAMPLE CONTRACTS

1. Here is a sample contract for booking "sleeping rooms" at a hotel for a group during an event or meeting.

GROUP EVENT AGREEMENT
BETWEEN [HOTEL NAME]
AND [BOOKER'S NAME]

BOOKED BY _____

DATE _____

ACCOUNT NAME: _____

ACCOUNT ADDRESS: _____

Telephone: _____

Fax: _____

This Group Event Agreement and the attached Appendices constitute the entire agreement between [ACCOUNT NAME] and [Hotel] regarding arrangements for the [NAME OF MEETING] to be held over the dates of [DATE ARRIVAL] - [DATE DEPART] inclusive.

In consideration of the mutual obligations of the above parties, respectively referred to as the Hotel and the Client, the parties agree as follows:

1. Guest Room Block. The Hotel agrees to hold a block of guest rooms for the Client for the Event, as set out below, on a tentative first option basis until [DATE].

_____ [NUMBER OF ROOMS]

2. Group Room Rates. Group Room Rates PER NIGHT PER ROOM shall be as follows:

_____ SINGLES

_____ DOUBLES

_____ SUITES

Options

(A) All Group Room Rates are non-commissionable and are subject to applicable occupancy and sales tax, currently 14%.

or

(B) All Group Room Rates are commissionable at 10% per room actually occupied, payable to (Agency of Record) and are subject to applicable occupancy and sales tax, currently 14% (occupancy) and 8.25% (sales). The Client agrees not to change the Agency of Record without notice to the Hotel. Commission payments will only be made to the Agency of Record after receipt in full by the Hotel of all amounts owed to the Hotel by the Client for the Event.

3. Deposit. A deposit of $[AMOUNT] is required on or before [DATE]. In the event that the Deposit is not received by the Hotel on or prior to [DATE], all commitments shall be released. The Deposit will be deducted from the final billed amount.

4. _____ Reservation Method

Options

(A) The Client shall submit an advance rooming list (the List) to the Hotel no later than [DATE] to secure reservations. After this date, any unreserved rooms will be released by the Hotel for general sale. The Hotel will continue to accept reservations after [DATE] only on a space available basis at either A. Agreed upon Group Room Rates; B. National Corporate Rates; C. Rack Rates. The List must be complete with names, arrival/departure dates, smoking preferences and specific payment instructions. Any additions or revisions to the List, subsequent to its initial submission, should be made directly with the Hotel's Conference Services Department.

or

(B) Room reservations will be made directly with the Hotel on an individual basis. Individuals must call the Hotel directly and request the Reservations Department. It is imperative that individuals indicate their group affiliation when making reservations, otherwise the group rate that applies may not be extended. Direct reservations must be made prior to [DATE]. After this date, any unreserved rooms will be released by the Hotel for general sale. The Hotel will continue to accept reservations after [DATE] on a space available basis at A. Agreed upon Group Room Rates; B. National Corporate Rates; C. Rack Rates.)

or

(C) The Hotel will provide (#) reservation reply forms to the Client. The Forms must be returned to the Hotel prior to [DATE] to secure availability. After this date, any unreserved rooms will be released by the Hotel for general sale. The Hotel will continue to accept reservations after [DATE] on a space available basis at A. Agreed upon Group Room Rates; B. National Corporate Rates; C. Rack Rates.
Additional Forms may be purchased for a nominal printing charge. Should you elect to utilize your own reservation form, the Hotel's Conference Services Department reserves the right to review the form, before printing.

or

(D) We understand that reservations will be made through [Local Convention & Visitors Bureau/Meeting Planner]. Reservations for this Event will not be accepted on a direct basis. Reservations must be made prior to [DATE] to secure availability. After this date, any unreserved rooms will be released by the Hotel for general sale. The Hotel will continue to accept reservations after [DATE] on a space available basis at A. Agreed Upon Group Room Rates; B. National Corporate Rates; C. Rack Rates.

All guest rooms will be held for late arrival, if guaranteed. A guarantee on each reservation may be in the form of an advance deposit for the payment of the first night's room and tax, either cash or a major card, or pre-arrangements made with the Hotel's credit department.

5. Changes to the Event. The Client will provide to the Hotel, on a timely basis, any changes to its attendance projections and guestroom and function space requirements for the Event. All changes are subject to availability, and all agreed upon changes will be confirmed by the parties in writing prior to the Event. This agreement has been negotiated based on dates, number of rooms, function space outlined in the contract, any material changes may result in changes in room rates and function space.

6. Full Cancellation of Event and Rooms Blocked. If the Client cancels the Event and Guest Room Block in its entirety, the Hotel shall have suffered damages equivalent to the lost profits that the Hotel would have made from the sales of rooms, food and beverages, incidental purchases, etc., in connection with the Event. The parties acknowledge that it is difficult to quantify such damages and instead have agreed that the Hotel shall assess a fee (The Fee) against the Client as liquidated damages and not as a penalty (such damage amount agreed to be expressed as a percentage of Rooms and food and beverage revenue lost by the Hotel as a result of the said cancellation, as reasonably determined by the Hotel). At such time, the Hotel shall assess the Fee based upon the scale below in Paragraph eight.

7. Partial Cancellation (Attrition). If the Client partially cancels the Event and/or Rooms blocked the Hotel shall have suffered damages (equivalent to the lost profits the Hotel would have made from the sale of Guest Rooms, food and beverages, incidental purchases, etc. in connection with the Event). The parties acknowledge that it is difficult to quantify such damages and instead have agreed that if the Client cancels Rooms or functions committed for the Event that in their totality exceed 10% of the Room block/function commitment as of the Option Date, the Hotel shall assess a fee against the Client as liquidated damages and not as a penalty such damages being agreed to be expressed as a percentage of Rooms and food and beverage revenue exceeding 10% lost by the Hotel as a result of the cancellations, as reasonably determined by the Hotel. At such time, the Hotel shall assess the Fee based upon the scale below in Paragraph eight.

8. _____ Fee Scale for Full and Partial Cancellations.

Number of Days Prior to the Scheduled Commencement Date of the Event Liquidated Damages, Expressed as a percentage of Lost Rooms (Option: Food and Beverage); Revenue

366 days and beyond	15%
365-181 days	25%
180 days-121 days	40%
120 days-91 days	50%
90 days-61 days	67%
60 days-31 days	75%
30 days or less	90%

Notice of any cancellation must be received by the Hotel in writing, and any Fee assessed is payable by the Client no later than thirty (30) days after being invoiced therefore by the Hotel. The Deposit amount will be deducted from any cancellation Fee owed.

9. Check in/Check Out Time. Check-in time is 3:00 p.m. Room assignments prior to this time are subject to availability. Check- out time is 12:00 p.m. If any Room is vacated after this time, the Client will be charged a late charge, as reasonably determined by the Hotel, unless prior arrangements are made with Hotel's management.

10. Porterage/Gratuities. Porterage charges have been established at $[AMOUNT] per bag each way. This charge shall be added to the Client's master account.

11. _____ Payment Procedure.

Options

A) Individual attendees will each be responsible for their Room, tax and incidental charges. A Group master account will be established to include function space, audio-visual, and sched- uled food, beverage, reception function charges for the Event.

or

B) Attendees will be responsible for their incidental charges. A Group master account will be established to include all Guest Room, tax, function space, audio-visual, scheduled food, beverage and reception function charges for the Event.

or

C) A group master account will be established to include Group members' room, tax, inci- dentals, function space, audio- visual and scheduled food, beverage and reception function charges for the Event.

12. Account Settlement. A final invoice (the Invoice) of all outstanding amounts will be prepared at the close of the Event. Final payment is due immediately upon receipt of the Invoice, unless prior billing arrangements have been made with the Hotel's Credit Manager. Any Invoice outstanding for more than thirty (30) days will bear interest at the rate of [RATE]% per month (18% per annum) until paid, unless this rate exceeds the maximum rate permitted by applicable laws, in which event the maximum legal rate shall apply.

13. Damages to Hotel and Indemnity. The Client shall be responsible for all damages, including property damages and/or personal injuries suffered or incurred by the Hotel or any employee or staff member of the Hotel or other guest of the Hotel caused by the negligence or misconduct of the Client or any invitee of or outside contractor hired by the Client. The Client agrees to indemnify and hold harmless the Hotel, the Owner of the Hotel, the Operator of the Hotel, all entities affiliated with each of them and each of their respective officers, direc- tors, employees and agents (the "Indemnities") of and from all actions, costs, claims, losses, expenses and/or damages, including reasonable attorney's fees, arising out of or resulting from the Event or the Client's use of the services and facilities of the Hotel unless the same are due to the gross negligence or willful misconduct of the Indemnities or any one or more of them.

14. Force Majeure. If for any reason beyond the Hotel's or the Client's reasonable control, including but not limited to strikes; labor disputes; acts, regulations or orders of govern- mental authorities; civil disorder; disasters; acts of war; acts of God; fires; flood or other emergency conditions; any delay in necessary and essential repairs of the Hotel; the Hotel or the Client is unable to perform its obligations under this Agreement, such non-performance is excused and such party may terminate this Agreement without further liability of any nature, upon return of the Client's deposit. In no event shall the Hotel or Client be liable for conse- quential damages of any nature for any reason whatsoever.

15. Insurance. Client and Hotel agree to obtain and maintain throughout the term of the Event, insurance of such types and in such amounts as a reasonably prudent company in their respective industries would obtain and, upon request, each agrees to provide the other with evidence of such insurance.

16. Governing Law. This Agreement shall be governed by and construed in accordance with the laws of the State where the Hotel is located.

17. Notices. All notices required or provided for under this Agreement shall be in writing and shall be effective immediately upon receipt by personal delivery, facsimile transmission or registered mail, return receipt requested, addressed to the other party's attention.

18. Non-Waiver of Breach. The Hotel's failure to demand strict and full performance of any of the covenants or agreements on the part of the Client to be observed, kept or performed, while the Client is in default with respect to any such covenant or agreement, shall not be con- strued to be a waiver by the Hotel of any such default or breach of covenant.

19. Authority to Sign. If this Agreement is signed in the name of a corporation, partnership, association, club or society, the person(s) signing represents and warrants to the Hotel that he/she has full authority to sign such contract and that in the event he/she is not so authorized, he/she will be personally liable for the faithful performance of this contract.

20. Entire Agreement. This Agreement contains all of the understandings between the par- ties and may only be modified in writing signed by both parties.

21. Option Date. The block of guest Rooms and function space and services referred to in this Agreement shall be released automatically by the Hotel without notice to the Client, unless a fully executed copy of this Agreement [and] the requisite deposit have been receive by the Hotel on or before [DATE]. In the event that another organization requests the same or similar arrangements on a definite basis on or prior to the Option Date, and the Hotel can- not handle both functions, the Client will be given written notice of such matter and be given seventy-two (72) hours in which to submit an executed copy of this Agreement [and] the req- uisite deposit to confirm the Commitment on a definite basis or space will be released.

IN WITNESS WHEREOF the parties hereto have caused this Agreement to be executed as of the   day of 199 .

("Hotel")
Per: _____
[NAME][TITLE]
Date_____

("Client")

Per: _____
[NAME][TITLE]

Date_____

APPENDIX:
AMERICANS WITH DISABILITIES ACT

1. HOTEL'S RESPONSIBILITIES. [HOTEL] shall be fully responsible for compliance with the Americans with Disabilities Act of 1990, as it may be amended, and all the rules and regulations promulgated under it (the "ADA") with respect to:
a) the [HOTEL'S policies, practices, procedures and eligibility requirements;
b) the provision of auxiliary aids and services in the Hotel, except;
i) in areas designated for the exclusive use or within the control of the Client or other third parties exclusively using areas of the Hotel including, without limitation, tenants, licensees and other groups (collectively "Third Party Users"); and
ii) aids and services required for the specific activities of the Client or other Third Party Users;
c) architectural, communications and transportation barriers in the Hotel, except barriers created by or within the control of the Client; and
d) the availability of wheelchair seating spaces in assembly areas, except to the extent that the Client exercises control or direction over the arrangement of seating in an assembly area.

2. CLIENT'S RESPONSIBILITIES. The Client shall be fully responsible for compliance with the ADA with respect to:
a) the policies, practices, procedures and eligibility criteria employed by:
i) the Client; and
ii) any person(s) other than the Hotel providing goods or services in connection with the Client's use of or activities at the Hotel;
b) the provision of auxiliary aids and services:
i) in areas designated for the exclusive use or within the control of the Client, and
ii) required for the specific activities of the Client (as distinct from the activities of non-Client guests of the Hotel;
c) architectural, communication and transportation barriers created by or within the control of the Client; and
d) any violation of wheelchair seating requirements, to the extent that the Client exercises control or direction over the arrangement of seating in an assembly area.

3. REQUIREMENTS OF THE GROUP. The parties acknowledge that the Hotel's capacity and obligation (under the ADA and paragraph 1 above) to provide auxiliary aids and services and guest Rooms accessible to or otherwise equipped for the benefit of disabled persons are limited in number and kind. The Client, therefore, shall notify the Hotel reasonably prior to the Event, of the number and type of such aids and services or Rooms required by Client members. The Hotel, in turn, promptly will notify the Client of the extent to which such needs exceed the Hotel's ADA obligations and capacity. The Client shall bear the responsibility to provide any aids or services or alternative lodging in excess of the Hotel's ADA obligation and capacity.

4. INDEMNIFICATION. The Hotel and the Client each agree to indemnify, defend, reim- burse and hold the other harmless from and against any and all claims, liabilities, damages, penalties, costs (including reasonable attorney's fees and costs), losses and expenses incurred based upon the failure of the indemnifying party to comply with the ADA with respect to mat- ters for which it bears responsibility under the preceding paragraphs.

GROUP EVENT AGREEMENT

2. The following contract is for an event (in this case a dinner and reception) at a hotel. The covering letter also suggested a range of outside caterers who would be able to provide the food service.

BETWEEN _____
             [HOTEL]

AND _____
       [BOOKER'S NAME]

BOOKED BY _____

DATE _____

ACCOUNT NAME: _____

ACCOUNT ADDRESS: _____

Telephone: _____

Fax: _____

DAY: _____

TIME: _____

EVENT: _____ Reception and dinner

OF GUESTS: _____

ROOM: _____

All reservations for private banquet functions are made upon and subject to the rules and regulations of the [Hotel] and are subject to the following conditions:

1. The menu and all other details of your event(s) are to be finalized a minimum of 3 weeks prior to the date of your event(s) and are subject to the terms and conditions described herein.

2. A deposit in the amount of is required to reserve the above space and will be credited toward the total cost of your event(s). However, this deposit may not be refunded in the event you cancel all or part of your function. Please see paragraph 11 below.

3. For corporations and associations only, direct billing may be requested. The credit application must be completed by the Client and returned, fully completed, to the Hotel with this application. If approved, you will be billed directly with the terms of payment noted on your account. Credit restrictions apply and are not available on all functions.

4. For social or personal events, the estimated outstanding balance is due and payable 8 working days in advance of the function if paying by approved personal check or 48 hours in advance of the function if paying by cash, approved certified or cashiers check or bank draft. A final account will be remitted at the completion of your event and is payable upon receipt.

5. An 19% service charge and an 8.25% sales tax will be added to all food and beverage charges.

6. All details of the food and beverages to be served shall be set forth on a separate menu and arrangements proposal (Event Order) which is made a part hereof.

7. The guaranteed number of attendees must be communicated to the Catering Office at the Hotel not less than 2 full working days (Monday through Friday, excluding holidays), prior to the function. A 5% allowance in food preparation over the guaranteed number will be given on all events. Final charges will be based on the guaranteed number of attendees (or number of persons for which the event was originally booked, if no guaranteed number is provided) or the total number served, whichever is greater.

8. The room(s) designated for your event(s) carries a minimum and a maximum attendance number. If your final guaranteed number is lower or higher than these numbers, the Hotel reserves the right to transfer your party to another function room and/or charge a rental (or and additional rental) to you based on the established Hotel rental schedule.

9. A minimum of 14 persons is required for all food functions. A labor charge of $85.00 will be charged to you should the attendance be less than this minimum. The Hotel reserves the right to charge a service fee for set-up of rooms with extraordinary requirements.

10. No changes to the menu may be made by the Client within the five day period preceding your event.

11. Cancellation Policy: Your advance deposit will not be refunded in the event you cancel your event with the Hotel. In addition, a cancellation fee may be charged to you and payable upon demand in the event of cancellation of all or part of your program after acceptance of this booking by the Hotel. The fee will be based on banquet pricing in effect at the time notification of cancellation is received by the Hotel. These amounts are due as liquidated damages and not as a penalty. The following schedule will apply:

          0-30 days..100%
          30-60 days...50%
          60-90 days...25%

Should another Client rebook the room and date with comparable function after cancellation by the Client, all or a portion of the advance deposit and cancellation fee will be refunded to the Client accordingly.

12. All displays, exhibits and decorations must conform to the city's Building Code and Fire Ordinances and should be free standing without attachment to walls, ceilings or floors. Decorations or centerpieces incorporating candles or any device emitting a flame must be approved by and have a valid permit from the City Fire Department in order to be used for a

given function. This signed permit must be issued for the specific event, and be on file in the hotel's security office prior to the start of the function. If a permit is not obtained, the hotel reserves the right to remove or alter the centerpieces in order to comply with the fire code.

13. The Client shall be responsible for any damages (including property damages and/or personal injuries) suffered or incurred by the Hotel or any employee or staff member of the Hotel arising out of or resulting from the acts or omissions of the Client or any guest of or outside contracted hired by the Client with respect to the Event. The Client further agrees to indemnify and hold harmless the Hotel, the manager of the Hotel, any entities affiliated therewith and their officers, directors and employees (the "Indemnities") from all actions, costs, claims, losses, expenses and/or damages, including attorney's fees, arising out of or resulting from the Client's use of the services and facilities of the Hotel unless the same are due to the negligence or willful misconduct of the Indemnities or any one or more of them.

14. All displays, exhibits, decorations, equipment and musicians must enter and exit the Hotel through the receiving entrance and/or security office. Delivery and pick-up times must be coordinated with the Hotel in advance.

15. All musicians, entertainers contracted by the Client must be approved by the [Hotel]. Amplified music or amplified singing is not allowed in the [following rooms].

16.___No food or beverages of any kind may be brought into the Hotel by the Client without the written permission of the Hotel and are subject to such service and/or labor charges as are deemed necessary by the Hotel.

17-20 [These paragraphs deal with the ADA, and are similar to those in the sleeping room contract, above.]

21. If for any reason beyond its control, including but not limited to strike, labor dispute, accident, act of war, act of God, fire, flood or other emergency condition, the Hotel is unable to perform its obligations under this Agreement, such non-performance is excused and the Hotel may terminate the Agreement without further liability of any nature, upon return of the Client's deposit. In no event shall the Hotel be liable for consequential damages of any nature for any reason whatsoever.

22. Overdue accounts shall bear interest at the rate of 1 1/2% per month (18% per annum) until paid unless such rate exceeds the maximum rate allowed by the applicable laws in which the event the maximum legal rate shall apply.

23. The Hotel reserves the right to inspect and control all private functions. The Hotel cannot assume liability for any personal property or equipment of Client or Client's guests or invitees brought to the Hotel.

Please sign and return both applications along with the requested deposit. If the applications and deposit are not returned to the Hotel by [DATE] the Hotel shall be released from this commitment and free to re-book this space with another Client.

If this agreement is signed in the name of a corporation, partnership, association, club or society, the person signing represents and warrants to the Hotel that he/she has full authority to sign such contract, and in the event he/she is not so authorized, that he/she will be personally liable for the faithful performance of this contract.

Signature by the Hotel shall be regarded as acceptance by the Hotel of the above reservation for the Client's function.

SIGNATURES_____

3. The following, much simpler contract is an example of what a major restaurant might expect.

ACCEPTANCE OF TERMS

The undersigned acknowledges that I have read and understood the [Name of Restaurant] Banquet Information Sheet. I have also read and agree with the arranged information and terms. I understand that the final guest count is due 72 hours prior to any function, and that if no final count is given at that time the last updated guest count will apply., [Restaurant] reserves the right to relocate your group to a more suitable location should the expected attendance change significantly. We also reserve the right to make appropriate substitutions should certain food items or wines not be available. Payment is due on the day of the event, and a signed contract with a deposit is considered a confirmed reservation.

NAME OF CLIENT_____

SIGNATURE_____

NAME OF FUNCTION: _____

DATE OF FUNCTION_____

CREDIT CARD TYPE_____

NAME ON CARD _____

CARD NUMBER_____
I hereby authorize [Name of Restaurant] to charge the above card number in the amount of $ and agree to perform the obligations set forth in the Cardholder's Agreement.

SIGNATURE _____

DATE _____

CHECKLISTS

A CATERING / BANQUET CHECKLIST

	COMPLETED	DATE
Get estimates/proposals		
Set up tastings		
Choose caterer		
Choose menus		
Choose format (formal dinner, reception, informal lunch, etc.)		
Contract signed		
Deposit paid		
Amount		
Finalize menus		
Discuss special needs (vegetarian, low-fat diets etc.)		
Head count		
Confirm menus, seating etc.		
Settle payment method		

A RESTAURANT CHECKLIST

Get estimates/proposals		
Choose menus/beverages		
Set up tastings		
Choose restaurant		
Confirm menus, seating etc		
Settle payment method		
Tell staff who will be paying		
Put down a deposit		
Tips and taxes		
Arrange transportation for guests		
Arrange parking for guests (self/valet)		
Wheelchair accessibility		

      yes   no

Is smoking allowed?

      yes   no

Will you have your own space, or will you share the restaurant with other patrons?

      yes   no

HOTEL CHECKLIST

Rooms blocked		
Rooming list complete		
Verify check-in requirements		
Confirm rates		
Contracts signed		
Check amenities		
Hotel shuttle available		

EQUIPMENT CHECKLIST

Check materials and decorations		
Check technology/audio/ visual requirements		
Check lighting/temperature		
Complete your Planner's Tool Kit		

MISCELLANEOUS

	COMPLETED	DATE
Service personnel (e.g. concierge)		
Parking and parking attendants		
Security staff		
Restroom staff		
Taxes and gratuities rate check		

ENTERTAINMENT AND GUEST SPEAKERS

AN ENTERTAINMENT CHECKLIST

Are speakers booked? _____ Done

Contracts and fees negotiated and signed? _____ Done

Check contingency clauses for bad weather or power outage. ___ Done

Will your venue accommodate your entertainment choice? __ Done

Transportation needs met? _____ Done

Equipment needs discussed and finalized? _____ Done

View demo tapes or live performance? _____ Done

Finalize accommodations _____ Done

Check sound levels _____ Done

Get something to fill in when the band takes a break (taped music, a DJ) _____ Done

Check sight lines to and from stage _____ Done

A PRESENTER'S A.V. CHECKLIST

Presenter's name:_____

Address: _____

City: State: ZIP:_____

Phone: _____ Fax: _____

Presentation title: _____

Presentation date: _____ Presentation time: _____

Do you require a lectern? ....yes   no

Do you require a microphone? ....yes   no

If yes, what type? ....lavaliere   podium

Do you need an overhead projector? ....yes   no

Do you require an LCD panel?........................yes   no

Do you require a slide projector?....................yes   no

Do you need a slide tray?...............................yes   no

Video playback equipment? ....yes   no

If yes, what format? ....yes   no

       VHS   3/4 inch   Betacam

Other: _____

_____

_____

_____

_____

_____

AIRPORT DIAGRAMS

Strange airports can be confusing, and confusion is time-consuming. Help your people through by offering plenty of diagrams and as much information as possible in your welcome kits. "You need to tell people to go down to the baggage claim area and look for a person in a pink shirt who will escort you to awaiting transportation," says Nancy Teper of Caribiner International, a New York Communications firm. Then, at the convention center, post more diagrams so your attendees don't waste any time getting lost.

KEEP DELEGATES IN THE LOOP

The more you can tell attendees the better. "People just want to know what's expected," says Teper. If there are out-of-town guests coming, warn them about the weather. If there are outdoor events planned, tell them to bring warm clothes and comfortable shoes.

A PRESENTER'S CHECKLIST

Professional or experienced speakers, of course, don't need checklists of how to do their job. All they need are some answers to a few basic questions, and to provide you with some basic information. Here are some things you should clarify:

Confirm flight arrangements _____ Done
Confirm transportation needs _____ Done
Confirm AV requirements (see AV Checklist, page 85) ___ Done
Review schedule you have set, and Q&A policies. _____ Done
Inform speaker of rehearsal schedule _____ Done
Is there a "speaker room" (a green room) where speakers can
    wait prior to their appearance? _____ Done

On the other hand, amateurs and first-timers, who can often be nervous and forgetful, need more help. Here's a list of pretty basic questions beginner speakers should ask themselves before presenting a paper, making a speech or leading a seminar. Even some amateurs will be insulted by this, but don't be troubled by that. It's worth it:

In a single sentence, what's the point of my presentation? What do I want to accomplish? How much do they already know? What do I want them to know? _____

_____

How long have I got?_____

Will there be Q&As afterwards, and how much time should I allot?
        yes   no   Minutes: _____

Will someone alert me if I'm running over? If so, who?

_____

What do I do if I finish early? _____

_____

Am I going to ad-lib, or do I need a script?
    If script, is it ready?.................yes   no
If ad-libbing, do I have rough notes on notecards
    in case my mind blanks? ....yes   no
Do I have handouts?.................yes   no
If yes, are they ready? ....yes   no
Who will distribute them? ....yes   no
Are technical people available to
    help me out? ....yes   no

If yes, how do I reach them? _____

Will I use overheads? ....yes   no
Are my overhead transparencies ready?........yes   no
Are they in order? ....yes   no
Will I use a slide projector?.........yes   no
Are the slides in order? ....yes   no
Do I know where the first slide is? ....yes   no
Do I know how to use a slide projector? ....yes   no
Do I have something I can use as
    a pointer?.................yes   no
Do I know where the light switches are, how they work,
    and who will dim lights on cue? ....yes   no
Can I test the sound level ahead of time?......yes   no
Will I need a mike? ....yes   no
If I'm using my computer, have I done run-
    throughs of the presentation?.................yes   no
Are the venue's electronic devices and connectors
    compatible with mine? ....yes   no
Can I field test the equipment
    ahead of time? ....yes   no
If all this fails, can I do the
    presentation verbally? ....yes   no
Is there water handy?.................yes   no

TAKING CARE OF SPEAKERS
Make sure you find out what equipment your speakers need, what they will bring with them, and what you will need to provide. Ask about computer compatibility (both hardware and software).

BADGES AND NAME TAGS
Try not to place a ton of information on badges. Keep them simple with big, legible letters. You don't need the person's company and city. Their name and title is often perfectly adequate. Opt for badges that clip to a suit jacket, not the ones with safety pins. Or provide chains for hanging badges around the neck.

See if you can find a cheap laminator to neaten up badges and name tags

SIGNAGE THAT WORKS
Focus on legibility over cool graphics. Use velcro arrows to help point attendees to the right place for meals, special breakout sessions and the message center. Avoid being cutesy at all costs. In addition, create meeting logo graphics for the podium and stage as well as signs for the airport pick-up spots and hospitality desk.

PERSONALIZE THE MEAL
A restaurant might be persuaded, for instance, to make a stencil of your logo so your company name appears in chocolate on the desserts.

CASH ON HAND
You will need cash for tips, cabs, etc., and for those occasions when credit cards won't be accepted. Who will handle the cash? How much do you need? Where will it be kept?

CREDIT CARDS
Make sure you have a credit card with the right limits on it. Arrange with venues (especially restaurants) ahead of time to discuss what cards will be accepted. Who will be getting the restaurant bill? Let the staff know ahead of time.

WHAT ABOUT SPOUSES?
If there are events for spouses, tell everyone clearly what they are – and what they aren't.

One good rule of thumb on this topic: Don't hold a meeting at a exquisite resort and expect attendees to want to leave spouses behind. If you're choosing a romantic location that will be pleasant for those who want to extend their business trip into a vacation once the meeting is over, you can't tell spouses not to come.

DAILY NEWSLETTERS
If your meeting lasts several days, you might consider putting out a simple daily newsletter with the highlights of the previous day's sessions. This is particularly useful if there are a lot of breakout sessions.

A TYPICAL BUDGET

Here are some typical line items in a function planner's budget. Not all will be applicable to all meetings or events.

	Budgeted cost	Actual cost
VENUE:		
Meeting or event space rental	$_____	$_____
Room setup costs	_____	_____
Equipment rental and setups	_____	_____
Taxes and gratuities	_____	_____
TRANSPORTATION:		
Airfare	_____	_____
Taxis or limos from airport	_____	_____
Parking	_____	_____
Valet parking gratuities	_____	_____
Transportation to and from various venues	_____	_____
ACCOMMODATION:		
Sleeping rooms	_____	_____
State accommodation taxes	_____	_____
Necessary gratuities	_____	_____
Hospitality suite	_____	_____
Incidentals	_____	_____
FOOD AND BEVERAGES:		
Per person food costs	_____	_____
Wine and spirits costs	_____	_____
Break costs	_____	_____
Taxes and gratuities	_____	_____
Transportation and setup costs (for off-site caterers)	_____	_____
Cleanup costs	_____	_____
Staff costs	_____	_____

	Budgeted cost	Actual cost
PRINTING AND MATERIALS:		
Meeting kit production and printing costs	$_____	$_____
Shipping costs	_____	_____
Agendas	_____	_____
Signage	_____	_____
Name tags	_____	_____
Notepads and pens/pencils	_____	_____
Invitations	_____	_____
SPECIAL SERVICES:		
Photographer	_____	_____
Photo developing and printing	_____	_____
Entertainment and speakers fees	_____	_____
Corporate gifts	_____	_____
Shipping	_____	_____
Florals and decorations	_____	_____
Contingencies	_____	_____
AV COSTS:		
Computer rentals	_____	_____
AV equipment	_____	_____
Setup costs	_____	_____
Gratuities	_____	_____
STAFFING:		
Temporary help	_____	_____
Security costs	_____	_____
Gratuities	_____	_____
TOTALS	$_____	$_____

A SAMPLE TIMETABLE

Here is a typical timetable for a business meeting that will involve more than 50 people. This can easily be scaled back for smaller meetings, or for other events such as awards ceremonies, holiday parties, company picnics, etc.

FOUR TO SIX MONTHS AHEAD:

	TARGET DATE	COMPLETION DATE
Confirm # of attendees	__ __ __	__ __ __
Set budget	__ __ __	__ __ __
Site inspections	__ __ __	__ __ __
Book venue	__ __ __	__ __ __
Book entertainment	__ __ __	__ __ __
Book keynote speakers	__ __ __	__ __ __
Set preliminary agenda	__ __ __	__ __ __
Start collecting phone numbers, e-mails and addresses of participants	__ __ __	__ __ __
Decide on theme	__ __ __	__ __ __
Hire a photographer	__ __ __	__ __ __

TWO TO THREE MONTHS AHEAD:

	TARGET DATE	COMPLETION DATE
Put together the meeting or event package (the announcement with registration form, the agenda, the venue and other information that participants will need)	__ __ __	__ __ __
Send out invitations and/ or registration package	__ __ __	__ __ __
Confirm speakers and panelists	__ __ __	__ __ __
Contact caterers	__ __ __	__ __ __
Contact wine & spirits suppliers	__ __ __	__ __ __
Contact florists	__ __ __	__ __ __
Confirm AV requirements	__ __ __	__ __ __
Contact AV and computer specialists	__ __ __	__ __ __
Order the corporate gifts, or other giveaways	__ __ __	__ __ __

ONE TO TWO MONTHS AHEAD:

	TARGET DATE	COMPLETION DATE
Make sure all contracts are signed	__ __ __	__ __ __
Review with legal counsel	__ __ __	__ __ __
Review speakers' assignments	__ __ __	__ __ __
Review all menus, room setups etc.	__ __ __	__ __ __
Review equipment list with participants	__ __ __	__ __ __
Start assembling ideas for the registration kits badges, agendas, vouchers, timetables, leisure activity suggestions	__ __ __	__ __ __
Put a copy of WHERE magazine in each kit	__ __ __	__ __ __
Finalize all menus	__ __ __	__ __ __
Finalize decor and floral arrangements	__ __ __	__ __ __

ONE MONTH AHEAD:

	TARGET DATE	COMPLETION DATE
Rehearse format with the venue, and decide on room setups, podiums, etc.	__ __ __	__ __ __

	TARGET DATE	COMPLETION DATE
Make sure enough electrical outlets are available, as well as the necessary cabling for equipment	__ __ __	__ __ __
If you're using a hotel, decide with hotel management what welcome basket will be in each room, if any	__ __ __	__ __ __
Alert hotel who your VIPs are	__ __ __	__ __ __
Confirm guest list	__ __ __	__ __ __

TEN DAYS AHEAD:

	TARGET DATE	COMPLETION DATE
Do a checklist one more time to make sure nothing has slipped through the cracks	__ __ __	__ __ __
One more time, do an accurate guest list	__ __ __	__ __ __
Prepare seating charts	__ __ __	__ __ __

THREE DAYS AHEAD

	TARGET DATE	COMPLETION DATE
Prepare name tags and badges	__ __ __	__ __ __
Guarantee banquet orders	__ __ __	__ __ __
Confirm all special services (e.g. florals)	__ __ __	__ __ __
Assemble Planner's Tool Kit	__ __ __	__ __ __

THE DAY BEFORE:

Go over your checklist again ....Done
Arrange cash for gratuities, etc. ....Done
Review duties with staff members or hired help ....Done
Make sure signage and directions are completed ....Done
Prepare one-sheet "hot list" of critical phone numbers ....Done
Confirm any outside vendors (e.g. AV specialist) ....Done
Assemble all delegate materials ....Done

ON THE DAY:

Bring your checklists and this publication's Workbook with you. ....Done
Bring your Planner's Tool Kit ....Done
Bring your contact "hot list" ....Done
Have the attendee list, properly alphabetized, ready at the reception table, together with name tags ....Done
Bring extra name tags ....Done
Finalize head count for every event ....Done
Set out table numbers and name tags according to your seating charts ....Done
Solicit business cards from on-site staff, including cell phone numbers ....Done

AFTERWARDS:

Pay the bills...Done
Write thank-yous and send gifts ....Done
Complete your expenditures and match to budget ....Done
Pay gratuities ....Done

Sample of a Postcard Used as an Event Invitation

A. Front of postcard invitation promotes the featured event

The Illinois State Society
Cordially Invites You to Attend

A Reception Honoring

Emily Carlson
The Illinois State Society
2006 Cherry Blossom Princess

Wednesday, April 5, 2005
6:30 to 8:30 p.m.

Rayburn House Office Building
Room B-354
Independence Avenue & South Capitol Street
Washington, DC

RSVP: ISS HOTLINE — 703-461-3610
by Monday, April 3, 2006
Free for ISS members / $15 for non-members

By Metro: Capitol South Metro stop; West on C Street; Right onto South Capitol Street; Enter the Rayburn Building at the "horseshoe" entrance.

By Taxi: Use Independence Avenue entrance.

By Auto: Street parking where available.

Source: Courtesy of the Illinois State Society of Washington, DC.

B. Reverse of postcard invitation is used to promote future events

UPCOMING ISS EVENTS – WINTER/SPRING 2006

The Illinois State Society
of Washington, DC ★ Founded in 1854

3700 Fort Worth Avenue
Alexandria, VA 22304–1707

March 25	**Abraham Lincoln Institute Symposium** National Archives, 8601 Adelphi Road, College Park, MD 9:00 a.m. to 5:00 p.m. For information and required registration visit: http://www.lincoln-institute.org/sym2006
Sunday, April 2	**Opening of Cherry Blossom Festival with Lantern Lighting** The National Mall—Tidal Basin at the Japanese Lantern 2:30 p.m.–No Charge for this Event
Wednesday, April 5	**ISS Cherry Blossom Princess Reception** B-354 Room—Rayburn House Office Building 6:30 p.m. to 8:30 p.m. No charge to ISS Members
Thursday, April 6	**Cherry Blossom Festival Congressional Reception** Caucus Room—Cannon House Office Building 6:00 p.m. to 8:00 p.m. Tickets $50/per person Available through NCSS at Box Office Tickets
Friday, April 7	**Cherry Blossom Festival Grand Ball** Sushi Reception and Dinner The Fairmont Hotel 6:00 p.m. to 12:00 a.m. Tickets $150/per person Available through ISS HOTLINE: 703-461-3610
Saturday, April 8	**Cherry Blossom Festival Parade** Constitution Avenue NW, Washington, DC 9:30 a.m. to 12:00 noon No charge for curb side seating
Wednesday, May 24	**ISS Annual Meeting and Reception** **Illinois & ISS History 1922 – 1972** Former State Senator Mark Q. Rhoads—Speaker Fort McNair Officers' Club, SE, Washington, DC 6:30 p.m. to 9:00 p.m. No charge to ISS Members
Monday, May 29	**General John A. Logan Memorial Day Celebration** Program and Luncheon Logan Circle and the Mary Bethune House—US Park Service 10:00 a.m. to 1:00 p.m. No charge to ISS Members
Saturday, July 23	**Chicago Cubs vs. Washington Nationals** Upper deck, behind home plate, Section 514 • 40 seats total. 1:05pm $23.00 per ticket

For additional information to make reservations, or to join the society, please call the ISS
HOTLINE at 703-461-3610 or visit the ISS website at www.IllinoisStateSociety.org.

Five Tips for Making Fundraising Event Registration More Productive

As the days grow longer, nonprofits everywhere are preparing for spring marathons, walk-a-thons, triathlons, bike-a-thons and just about any kind of a-thon imaginable. Organizations that have planned events in the past know that these events often require a great deal of time and expense—from the registration process through fundraising awards and final accounting.

The following five tips and new capabilities in Convio Team-Raiser (TM) can help any organization make the most of its events by designing a registration process that increases participation, maximizes net proceeds, and provides participants with a painless (and even pleasant) registration experience.

1. Jump start registration

The sooner you get team leaders started on their fundraising activities, and the more resources they can use from previous years, the more time they'll have to meet their fundraising goals for your organization. Begin by sending an email to the previous year's participants inviting them to participate again. For those who cannot participate, provide an option to join as a virtual participant with a donation. Help participants get going quickly using Convio TeamRaiser—participants automatically inherit their past year's Web page, personal address book, and fundraising history, giving them a head start on driving support.

2. Make family registration easy

Event participants often prefer to participate with family members, especially if honoring or memorializing another family member. By reducing the amount of forms to complete and making family registration easy, you can encourage families to participate together, thereby increasing the overall number of registrants. Convio TeamRaiser allows participants to register more than one person in a single transaction, reducing the amount of time they spend entering addresses and credit card numbers and increasing their chances of registering family members.

3. Create more revenue opportunities.

One simple way of increasing revenue for participants is to include options to change the price (up-sells). For example, a runner who wants to see his or her standing in the run might like to rent a timing chip. Additional up-sell possibilities include the opportunity to purchase a branded water bottle or pack of bumper stickers, a brown-bag lunch or event meal plan, XL or XXL T-shirts, shuttle bus tickets, and shipping. Using new capabilities in Convio TeamRaiser, you can provide these optional add-ons to offer value to participants while increasing your revenue-per-participant ration.

4. Help participants drive Web traffic using personalized URLs

To publicize their participation in your event, participants may use many venues, from church newsletters and emails to social networking contacts and parties. No matter how they spread the word, their friends and family will have an easier time supporting them if participants can easily point supporters to their participation page. Using Convio TeamRaiser, a user can define his or her own catchy page address using nicknames abbreviations or other easily remembered phrases. Personalizing a URL for participants can help them be more efficient in their fundraising efforts, yielding more revenue for your organization.

5. Use widgets

Another great way for participants to publicize their registration and raise money is to use a banner or "widget" on their social networking sites and blogs to drive friends and family to your organization's site and encourage them to participate. Convio Widgets allow participants to drive traffic and support from online community sites such as MySpace, from a blog, or anywhere else on the Web where they are posting content. Widgets also allow participants to post meters showing progress toward their goals. Make sure to point this out to participants as part of the registration process to drive even more support.

CONCLUSION

A well thought out registration process is a key part of a successful event. With widgets, personalized URLs, add-on revenue opportunities, single form registration, and an early start, any organization can get more people involved in its events and raise more funds per participant.

Source: Courtesy of *Convio Connection*, Convio Inc., Austin, Texas, 2007.

Internal Revenue Service (IRS) Information—Charitable Contributions—Substantiation and Disclosure Requirements

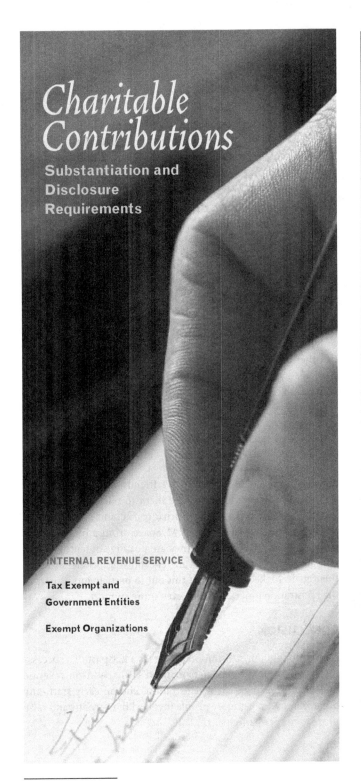

Charitable
Contributions

Substantiation and
Disclosure
Requirements

INTERNAL REVENUE SERVICE

Tax Exempt and
Government Entities

Exempt Organizations

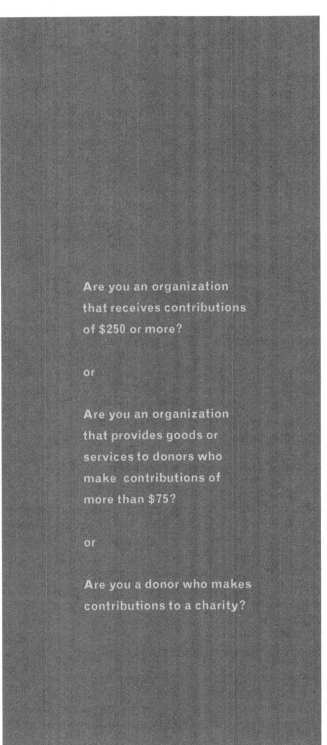

Are you an organization
that receives contributions
of $250 or more?

or

Are you an organization
that provides goods or
services to donors who
make contributions of
more than $75?

or

Are you a donor who makes
contributions to a charity?

Source: Department of Treasury, Internal Revenue Service, Publication 1771 (Rev. 5 2007), Catalog Number 20054Q.

IRS Publication 1771, *Charitable Contributions–Substantiation and Disclosure Requirements,* explains the federal tax law for organizations such as charities and churches that receive tax-deductible charitable contributions and for taxpayers who make contributions.

There are recordkeeping and substantiation rules imposed on donors of charitable contributions and disclosure rules imposed on charities that receive certain *quid pro quo* contributions.

- a donor must have a **bank record** or **written communication** from a charity for any monetary contribution before the donor can claim a charitable contribution on his/her federal income tax return

- a donor is responsible for obtaining a **written acknowledgment** from a charity for any single contribution of $250 or more before the donor can claim a charitable contribution on his/her federal income tax return

- a charitable organization is required to provide a **written disclosure** to a donor who receives goods or services in exchange for a single payment in excess of $75

More on recordkeeping, written acknowledgments and written disclosures is addressed in this publication.

The rules in this publication do not apply to a donated motor vehicle, boat, or airplane if the claimed value exceeds $500. For information on vehicle donations, see IRS Publication 4302, *A Charity's Guide to Vehicle Donations,* and IRS Publication 4303, *A Donor's Guide to Vehicle Donations.*

For information about organizations that are qualified to receive charitable contributions, see IRS Publication 526, *Charitable Contributions.* Publication 526 also describes contributions you can (and cannot) deduct, and it explains deduction limits. For assistance about valuing donated property, see IRS Publication 561, *Determining the Value of Donated Property.*

1

Recordkeeping Rules

Requirement

A donor cannot claim a tax deduction for any contribution of cash, a check or other monetary gift unless the donor maintains a record of the contribution in the form of either a bank record (such as a cancelled check) or a written communication from the charity (such as a receipt or letter) showing the name of the charity, the date of the contribution, and the amount of the contribution.

Payroll Deductions

For charitable contributions made by payroll deduction, the donor may use both of the following documents as written communication from the charity:

- a pay stub, Form W-2, Wage and Tax Statement, or other employer-funished document furnished by the employer that shows the amount withheld and paid to a charitable organization, and

- a pledge card prepared by or at the direction of the charitable organization.

However, if a donor makes **a single contribution of $250 or more by payroll deduction,** see **Payroll Deductions** under **Written Acknowledgment** for what information the pledge card must include.

2

Written Acknowledgment

Requirement

A donor cannot claim a tax deduction for any single contribution of $250 or more unless the donor obtains a contemporaneous, written acknowledgment of the contribution from the recipient organization. An organization that does not acknowledge a contribution incurs no penalty; but, without a written acknowledgment, the donor cannot claim the tax deduction. Although it is a donor's responsibility to obtain a written acknowledgment, an organization can assist a donor by providing a timely, written statement containing the following information:

1. name of organization

2. amount of cash contribution

3. description (but not the value) of non-cash contribution

4. statement that no goods or services were provided by the organization in return for the contribution, if that was the case

5. description and good faith estimate of the value of goods or services, if any, that an organization provided in return for the contribution

6. statement that goods or services, if any, that an organization provided in return for the contribution consisted entirely of intangible religious benefits (described later in this publication), if that was the case

It is not necessary to include either the donor's social security number or tax identification number on the acknowledgment.

A separate acknowledgment may be provided for each single contribution of $250 or more, or one acknowledgment,

such as an annual summary, may be used to substantiate several single contributions of $250 or more. There are no IRS forms for the acknowledgment. Letters, postcards, or computer-generated forms with the above information are acceptable. An organization can provide either a paper copy of the acknowledgment to the donor, or an organization can provide the acknowledgment electronically, such as via an e-mail addressed to the donor. A donor should not attach the acknowledgment to his or her individual income tax return, but must retain it to substantiate the contribution. Separate contributions of less than $250 will not be aggregated. An example of this could be weekly offerings to a donor's church of less than $250 even though the donor's annual total contributions are $250 or more.

Contemporaneous

Recipient organizations typically send written acknowledgments to donors no later than January 31 of the year following the donation. For the written acknowledgment to be considered contemporaneous with the contribution, a donor must receive the acknowledgment by the earlier of: the date on which the donor actually files his or her

3

4

individual federal income tax return for the year of the contribution; or the due date (including extensions) of the return.

Goods and Services

The acknowledgment must describe goods or services an organization provides in exchange for a contribution of $250 or more. It must also provide a good faith estimate of the value of such goods or services because a donor must generally reduce the amount of the contribution deduction by the fair market value of the goods and services provided by the organization. Goods or services include cash, property, services, benefits or privileges. However, there are important exceptions as described below:

Token Exception — Insubstantial goods or services a charitable organization provides in exchange for contributions do not have to be described in the acknowledgment.

Good and services are considered to be insubstantial if the payment occurs in the context of a fund-raising campaign in which a charitable organization informs the donor of the amount of the contribution that is a deductible contribution, and:

1. the fair market value of the benefits received does not exceed the lesser of 2 percent of the payment or $89, or

2. the payment is at least $44.50, the only items provided bear the organization's name or logo (e.g., calendars, mugs, or posters), and the cost of these items is within the limit for "low-cost articles," which is $8.90.

Free, unordered low-cost articles are also considered to be insubstantial.

Example of a token exception: If a charitable organization gives a coffee mug bearing its logo and costing the organization $8.90 or less to a donor who contributes $44.50 or more, the organization may state that no goods or services were provided in return for the $44.50 contribution. The $44.50 is fully deductible.

The dollar amounts are for 2007. Guideline amounts are adjusted for inflation. Contact IRS Exempt Organizations Customer Account Services at (877) 829-5500 for annual inflation adjustment information.

Membership Benefits Exception — An annual membership benefit is also considered to be insubstantial if it is provided in exchange for an annual payment of $75 or less and consists of annual recurring rights or privileges, such as:

1. free or discounted admissions to the charitable organization's facilities or events

2. discounts on purchases from the organization's gift shop

3. free or discounted parking

4. free or discounted admission to member-only events sponsored by an organization, where a per-person cost (not including overhead) is within the "low-cost articles" limits

5

6

Example of a membership benefits exception;
If a charitable organization offers a $75 annual
membership that allows free admission to all of
its weekly events, plus a $20 poster, a written
acknowledgment need only mention the $20
value of the poster, since the free admission
would be considered insubstantial and,
therefore, would be disregarded.

Intangible Religious Benefits Exception — If a religious organization provides only "intangible religious benefits" to a contributor, the acknowledgment does not need to describe or value those benefits. It can simply state that the organization provided intangible religious benefits to the contributor.

What are "intangible religious benefits?" Generally, they are benefits provided by a tax-exempt organization operated exclusively for religious purposes, and are not usually sold in commercial transactions outside a donative (gift) context. Examples include admission to a religious ceremony and a *de minimis* tangible benefit, such as wine used in a religious ceremony. Benefits that are not intangible religious benefits include education leading to a recognized degree, travel services, and consumer goods.

Payroll Deductions

When a donor makes a **single contribution of $250 or more by payroll deduction**, the donor may use both of the following documents as the written acknowledgment obtained form the organization:

- a pay stub, Form W-2, *Wage and Tax Statement*, or other document furnished by the employer that sets forth the amount withheld by the employer and paid to a charitable organization, and
- a pledge card that includes a statement to the effect that the organization does not provide goods or services in consideration for contributions to the organization by payroll deduction.

Each payroll deduction amount of $250 or more is treated as a separate contribution for purposes of the $250 threshold requirement for written acknowledgments.

Unreimbursed Expenses

If a donor makes a single contribution of $250 or more in the form of unreimbursed expenses, e.g., out-of-pocket transportation expenses incurred in order to perform donated services for an organization, then the donor must obtain a written acknowledgment from the organization containing:

- a description of the services provided by the donor
- a statement of whether or not the organization provided goods or services in return for the contribution
- a description and good faith estimate of the value of goods or services, if any, that an organization provided in return for the contribution

- a statement that goods or services, if any, that an organization provided in return for the contribution consisted entirely of intangible religious benefits (described earlier in this publication), if that was the case

In addition, a donor must maintain adequate records of the unreimbursed expenses. See Publication 526, *Charitable Contributions*, for a description of records that will substantiate a donor's contribution deductions.

> Example of an unreimbursed expense: A chosen representative to an annual convention of a charitable organization purchases an airline ticket to travel to the convention. The organization does not reimburse the delegate for the $500 ticket. The representative should keep a record of the expenditure, such as a copy of the ticket. The representative should obtain from the organization a description of the services that the representative provided and a statement that the representative received no goods or services from the organization.

Examples of Written Acknowledgments

- "Thank you for your cash contribution of $300 that (organization's name) received on December 12, 2007. No goods or services were provided in exchange for your contribution."

- "Thank you for your cash contribution of $350 that (organization's name) received on May 6, 2007. In exchange for your contribution, we gave you a cookbook with an estimated fair market value of $60."

- "Thank you for your contribution of a used oak baby crib and matching dresser that (organization's name) received on March 15, 2007. No goods or services were provided in exchange for your contribution."

The following is an example of a written acknowledgment where a charity accepts contributions in the name of one of its activities:

- "Thank you for your contribution of $450 to (organization's name) made in the name of its Special Relief Fund program. No goods or services were provided in exchange for your contribution."

9

10

Written Disclosure

Requirement

A donor may only take a contribution deduction to the extent that his/her contribution exceeds the fair market value of the goods or services the donor receives in return for the contribution; therefore, donors need to know the value of the goods or services. An organization must provide a written disclosure statement to a donor who makes a payment exceeding $75 partly as a contribution and partly for goods and services provided by the organization. A contribution made by a donor in exchange for goods or services is known as a *quid pro quo* contribution.

> Example of a *quid pro quo* contribution: A donor gives a charitable organization $100 in exchange for a concert ticket with a fair market value of $40. In this example, the donor's tax deduction may not exceed $60. Because the donor's payment (*quid pro quo* contribution) exceeds $75, the charitable organization must furnish a disclosure statement to the donor, even though the deductible amount does not exceed $75.

A required written disclosure statement must:

- inform a donor that the amount of the contribution that is deductible for federal income tax purposes is limited to the excess of money (and the fair market value of property other than money) contributed by the donor over the value of goods or services provided by the organization

- provide a donor with a good-faith estimate of the fair market value of the goods or services

An organization must furnish a disclosure statement in connection with either the solicitation or the receipt of the *quid pro quo* contribution. The statement must be in writing and must be made in a manner that is likely to come to the attention of the donor. For example, a disclosure in small print within a larger document might not meet this requirement.

Exception

A written disclosure statement is not required:

- where the goods or services given to a donor meet the "token exception," the "membership benefits exception," or the "intangible religious benefits exception" described earlier

- where there is no donative element involved in a particular transaction, such as in a typical museum gift shop sale

Penalty

A penalty is imposed on charities that do not meet the written disclosure requirement. The penalty is $10 per contribution, not to exceed $5,000 per fundraising event or mailing. An organization may avoid the penalty if it can show that failure to meet the requirements was due to reasonable cause.

11   **12**

Further Information

written acknowledgment — Detailed rules for contemporaneous written acknowledgments are contained in Section 170(f)(8) of the Internal Revenue Code and Section 1.170A-13(f) of the Income Tax Regulations. The "low-cost article" rules are set forth in Section 513(h)(2) of the Code. This information can be found on the IRS Web site at www.irs.gov.

written disclosure — Detailed rules for written disclosure statements are contained in Section 6115 of the Internal Revenue Code and Section 1.6115-1 of the Income Tax Regulation. The penalty rules are contained in Section 6714 of the Code. This information can be found on the IRS Web site at www.irs.gov.

IRS publications — Order publication by calling the IRS at (800) 829-3676. Download IRS publications at www.irs.gov.

IRS customer service — Telephone assistance for general tax information is available by calling IRS customer service toll-free at (800) 829-1040.

EO customer service — Telephone assistance specific to exempt organizations is available by calling IRS Exempt Organizations Customer Account Services toll-free at (877) 829-5500

EO Web site — Visit Exempt Organizations Web site at www.irs.gov/eo.

EO Update — To receive IRS Exempt Organization's EO Update, a regular e-mail newsletter with information for tax-exempt organizations and tax practitioners who represent them, visit www.irs.gov/eo and click on "EO Newsletter."

Stay Exempt (www.stayexempt.org) — An IRS interactive web-based training program covering tax compliance issues confronted by small and mid-sized tax-exempt organizations.

13

IRS
Department of the Treasury
Internal Revenue Service

www.irs.gov

Publication 1771 (Rev. 5 2007)
Catalog Number 20054Q

Chapter 13

Fundraising Communications—Electronic and Print

KEY VOCABULARY

- Bleed
- Blog
- Brand
- Bulk Provider
- Case Statement
- Cascading Style Sheets (CSS)
- Content Management System
- Dots Per Inch (DPI)
- E-marketing
- E-news
- Facebook
- Four Over Zero
- File Transfer Protocol (FTP)
- Home Page
- Internet Providers (IPs)
- Kerning
- Leading
- Pantone Matching System (PMS)
- Podcasts
- Q & A Brochure
- Reply Cards
- Rollover State
- Spam
- Text Messaging
- Throttle
- Thumbnails
- Trim Size
- Virtual Gifting
- Vodcasts
- Web Logs
- Web site

COMMUNICATION METHODS HAVE CHANGED

One of the most rapidly changing areas in fundraising is how fundraisers communicate with prospects and donors. In the past, communication was accomplished either orally or in print, by phone, in person, or by mail. Today, fundraisers still use these tried and true methods, but also in use are all forms of electronic communications. To share the goals, passions, and needs of the organization with the ever expanding community of individuals who may be interested in an organization's cause, fundraisers must use all communication opportunities available to them.

In the past, to share an organization's successes with donors, either a letter was sent or a newsletter printed and mailed. Today, at almost no cost, an e-mail can be sent to highlight a specific accomplishment or an electronic newsletter can be developed to update donors and prospects on a much more frequent and cost-efficient basis. Of course, it is always important to "know your donors," as some individuals will only read printed materials, and others will only respond to electronic communications. The best development offices use a combination of electronic and print materials to communicate. In Exhibit 13–1, you will find the cases made for using either print or electronic format for a newsletter.

Exhibit 13–1 Printed Versus E-mailed News—Make an Informed Decision

It used to be that companies had very few choices when it came to a newsletter: photocopy it or print it. Regardless, it had to go out via U.S. mail. Today, we not only have the choice of electronic distribution, but also Web-based versus e-mail. Which is better? Which is a smarter investment? Let's explore two options.

The case for print.

Did you know that several studies prove that the tactile sensation of holding and touching a newsletter increases retention of the material? Truly, traditional U.S. mail seems more personal nowadays since we see less and less of it. Newsletters delivered via the post office are opened by at least 25–30% of recipients, whereas e-mail newsletters are only opened by about 10%.

Unlike electronic newsletters, printed news involves postage, paper, and printing costs that can be daunting for large mailing lists. To justify this expense, make sure your newsletter will net a good return with great design, appropriate language, and useful and relevant news that your readers can grasp right away.

The case for electronic.

The average Internet user encounters upwards of a dozen or more electronic newsletters every week and immediately deletes most of them . . . so why do companies continue producing them? For many, this provides a cost-effective way to get their name out. Compared to print newsletters, which can cost more than a dollar per unit to print and send, electronic versions literally cost pennies or less.

It may seem like a dream come true, but before you act, here are proven tips to help increase your success:

- Conform to CAN-SPAM laws.
- Use strategic distribution.
- Manage your list constantly.
- Craft a good, catchy subject line, an eye-catching template, and include useful and interesting articles and links.
- Most importantly, DO NOT use the "shotgun blast" approach to distribute your e-newsletter; getting your news out to every e-mail address you can get your hands on will often lead to negative, rather than positive, outcomes. Carefully and regularly cull your list for proper recipients and make sure to build in a feedback component so you can always be improving your content, format, and distribution.

PRINT or ELECTRONIC—Which is better for your needs? To begin, weigh the pros and cons and begin your decision process. This is an opportunity to show customers that you are a leading expert in your field—make it great!

Source: Courtesy of *Mediastudio Quarterly,* Winter 2007, Mediastudio, Inc., Falls Church, Virginia.

COMMUNICATIONS IN DEVELOPMENT

There are basic communication materials that are used by all organizations both large and small in their fundraising efforts. These include the case statement, the annual report, a general information brochure highlighting the organization and/or the fundraising effort, a question-and-answer brochure, newsletters, press releases, pledge cards, and, in some cases, even posters. These communication methods can be included in both electronic and print materials. In addition, fundraising information can be included on the organization's Web site and in its e-mail messages, e-newsletters, and blogs. More and more, electronic communications are being used in fundraising.

ELECTRONIC COMMUNICATIONS

Communicating an organization's fundraising needs by electronic methods rather than in print is effective especially when communicating with younger prospects and donors. Electronic methods include: using the organization's Web site; sending e-mail notices or solicitations; posting electronic fundraising forms or sponsorship opportunities; sharing information through e-newsletters; providing virtual gifts; and social networking through blogs, Facebook, etc. New media are introduced and adapted to development on an ongoing basis. It is important to stay attuned to technological trends and the creative ways they can be used by volunteer and fundraising staff. To be able to communicate better with the technical, creative people on staff as they write, design, and develop the organization's Web site or print materials, it is smart to understand the technical terms they use. Exhibit 13–2 provides a guide to some of the technical terms used.

An Organization's Home Page or Web Site

Today, a major communication tool for an organization is its home page or Web site (these terms are generally used interchangeably). Instead of sending materials or information about an organization's mission, programs, and activities, it is a common occurrence today to direct people to the organization's Web site for the information being sought. Before an organization develops its Web site, it should determine the purpose of the site and how it will be used to further the organization's mission. A commitment of both financial and staff resources needs to be made as producing a Web site initially can cost as much as $10,000 or more. See Exhibit 13–3 for a list of items to include on an organization's Web site.

One of the most difficult challenges facing any organization is how to keep its Web site current. The sheer volume of information included on the site can be overwhelming to maintain and to keep updated. Responsibility for the development and maintenance of the site should be assigned to specific staff or department, and it is important to assign one person in the development office the task of maintaining development-related information on the site. If the organization is small, this also can be accomplished by using a volunteer Web coordinator who works in tandem with the paid staff. The important point is to

Exhibit 13–2 A Quick and Easy Guide to 10 Technical Terms

Here's a handy reference to understand those technical creative people in your midst!

- **CSS**—An increasingly popular approach for design on the Web. Standing for Cascading Style Sheets, this type of code allows web developers to improve content accessibility, provide more flexibility and control of layout characteristics, and reduce complexity and redundancy in structural content. CSS also can allow the same page to be presented in different styles for different rendering methods such as on-screen, in print, by voice, or even on Braille-based tactile device.
- **Rollover state**—A term describing something on the Web that has a different look when your mouse is hovering over it.
- **Trim size**—The final size of a printed document after folding and binding.
- **DPI**—Dots per inch. What is recommended varies whether you are providing illustrations or graphics for the Web or for print.
- **Low res** (pronounced "rez")—short for "low resolution, lingo for what is usually 725 dpi. This is opposed to high res, which is preferred for print.
- **FTP**—File transfer protocol. This is the process where designs, text, or any file are uploaded to the Internet.
- **Kerning and leading**—The terms typographers use to describe the amount of space between lines (leading), and the space between letters (kerning).
- **Bleed**—In this case not blood, but printing ink. Basically, the ink goes right up to the edge of the page with no margins.
- **4/0 or "four over zero"**—Printing terminology for a full-color print job with no printing on the back. If it is full-color on both sides, it is 4/4. At times, the 4 may be a 5, depending on the press, which really adds a layer of complexity.
- **CMS**—Content Management System. Software that allows non-Web developers to update their sites easily.

Source: Courtesy of *Mediastudio Quarterly*, Spring 2006, Mediastudio, Inc., Falls Church, Virginia.

Exhibit 13–3 Items to Include on an Organization's Web Site

1. mission statement, purpose, vision statement
2. staff information—names, titles, how to reach them
3. information on the organization's foundation and a link to its Web site, if it has one
4. listing of the board of directors with professional affiliations
5. current programs, projects, and services
6. information from reports, surveys, and studies conducted
7. how to get involved with the organization—volunteer opportunities
8. how to contribute to the organization
9. recognition of donors—annual appeal, sponsorships, program donors, planned gifts, etc.
10. calendar of upcoming events
11. listing of available resources—publications, videotapes, journals, studies, etc.
12. how to contact the organization—telephone, fax, e-mail address, regular address, etc.
13. links to other Web sites

keep the site "fresh" and focused on issues of importance to donors and prospects. It will need to be updated regularly with new information to keep visitors interested in returning to the site, as the goal is to have repeat visitors. In addition, keeping the Web site's content fresh will encourage other organizations to link to the Web site, which will generate more traffic to the site. Appendix 13–A provides 50 ways an organization can encourage traffic to its Web site.

For the organization's growth, it must have the ability to capture names, addresses, and e-mail addresses of those who visit the site. Many organizations now use a variety of methods to have visitors register on their Web site. Included among these interactive approaches are registering in a guest book, completing a survey or questionnaire, or requesting information. Offering incentives such as a free copy of a recent publication, being placed on the newsletter mailing list, or some token item with the organization's logo on it have been quite effective in registering visitors, which adds names to the organization's mailing list.

The Web site is yet another way to inform visitors as to how they can get involved as volunteers or contributors. The site should include information on how to make gifts to support the organization and its cause or programs. Plus, an organization must be able to accept contributions over the Internet, as well as design its donation page to include all pertinent information on making a gift so an individual can print the form and mail it in with their contribution, if they don't wish to make a gift electronically. A visitor to the Web site should only have to "click" once to be able to make a gift. Whether fundraising is an integral part of the organization itself or if there is a separate foundation fundraising for the organization, the Web site should include how to make gifts and an entrance to the place to make a gift should be only one click off the organization's home page. Appendix 13–B shows an example of an organization's home page with a link to a donation page.

It is vital to make sure that the Web site is secure. People will not make gifts on a site that is not identified as being secure. They must see the "little lock" in the corner of their browser before they will even think of making a gift online. Most gifts made online are to annual appeals, are smaller in size, and are made by younger individuals. This is beginning to change, though, as more organizations drive their donors and prospects to their Web sites to make gifts and as more people find that giving online is easy.

Learn enough about the business "back end" of your Web site to understand how to make using it an easy and pleasant experience for your donors. Too many clicks, confusing graphics or instructions, overt reference to costs of making a donation, and typing in the same information over and over can be turnoffs to potentials donors.

E-mail Communications

Many organizations use e-mail to solicit gifts either for their annual appeal or to solicit support for special causes. When using e-mail to solicit gifts, the message should be short, succinct, and compelling. The subject line can be as important as the message itself as many e-mails won't even be delivered or opened without an appropriate subject line. E-mail solicitations are best when used to follow up a mailed solicitation, as they serve as a reminder to take action. Also, they can be used to introduce a program or opportunity that is being sent by mail. Read Chapter 7 for more tips on writing e-mail solicitations.

Using e-mail to solicit donations does have some pitfalls, though. In order to be successful in raising money, the prospects must be reached. "E-mail software or bulk e-mail service has to send messages from an IP (inbox providers) address to the recipient's inbox provider, who in turn places it in the appropriate mailbox. Nonprofits, hoping for longer-term relationships, can use electronic measures of delivery rates, open rates, click-throughs, and others to gain insights into how effective an electronic campaign is and the overall stability of a particular constituency," states Tim Mills-Groninger in an article in *The NonProfitTimes*, April 2007.

E-mail delivery cannot be guaranteed because it is very easy for e-mail solicitations to be blocked or throttled by IPs. The limit on messages sent can be 1,000 per day or 500 per hour depending upon the ever changing limits set to reduce spam. Large numbers of e-mails going out at the same time can look suspicious. Sending too many at one time can be considered spam and they can be throttled—restricted in number by the IP provider. "Throttling high volumes of e-mail originating from IP addresses that haven't been used previously is one way to reduce spam. Throttled e-mail is not delivered and can be considered deleted," writes Mills-Groninger.

Also, spam filters can throw e-mails into the spam box instead of in the prospects' or donors' files. Most people welcome the filters that provide a separation of the good e-mail from the junk e-mail. Unfortunately, fundraising e-mails can look suspiciously like spam e-mails. When using e-mail to solicit donations, it is best to use an experienced, well-known bulk provider and to maintain their established accounts.

E-Marketing

Another method to generate interest in the organization and to increase gifts to support its cause is to use an electronic service that sends e-mail messages to current and prospective donors. Messages can be customized to drive prospective donors to the organization's Web site. Several vendors provide this service, but one of the first and most sophisticated electronic services is provided by the Stelter Company called iNews. This service sends a monthly e-mail message providing timely planned giving information. The design can be customized to the organization to reflect its brand, the content can be tailored to relate to the mission, and the interactive links to the organization's Web site can be embedded in the copy. Finally, detailed reports are provided to the organization on a monthly basis.

Plus, it isn't necessary to spend a lot of money to market the organization's programs and fundraising needs. Often, it is as simple as giving them something to talk about! Sharing ideas by e-mail or even word of mouth can help promote the organization's services and needs. Each time a communication is sent to the organization's constituency, a tagline can be attached to alert readers to the need that has been identified. "Have you remembered XYZ in your will?" is an example of a tagline that can be used on all marketing materials whether electronic or in print. The key is to educate readers about the organization's needs. By listening to what readers have to say and quickly responding to them, a loyal base of supporters can begin to be built.

If the organization has the resources, it can also use an online e-mail marketing service that can track what is of interest to donors. This information can help in the formulation of new programs and services as well as help in the development of future electronic solicitation materials.

E-Newsletters

Fundraising information can be included in an organization's electronic newsletter. Specially placed articles can provide information on a specific appeal and can provide a link for a prospect or donor to make a gift. Appendix 13–C provides an example of a short article placed in an e-newsletter to encourage planned gifts. Have a specific place in the newsletter with a caption that identifies the development section so that readers come to expect new information with each issue.

To develop a new, fresh, and appealing look for the e-news, have a template designed specifically for the e-newsletter. It should not be the same as the organization's printed newsletter. It is important to use a consistent subject line and to maintain a regular schedule so readers will look forward to receiving it and work to keep the newsletter out of their spam files. It also may be worth working with the Bonded Sender Program (http://www.bondedsender.com) to help keep the newsletter off of the spam blacklists.

Most organizations have found that it is easier to reach donors electronically than in print. If donors are of a certain age, they prefer electronic communication over printed communication. Plus, it also is far less expensive to communicate this way. The quarterly newsletter can become the monthly newsletter. One organization found that each issue of their e-newsletter cost them approximately 50 cents per donor, while their printed newsletter was costing $3.50 per donor. But, remember, it will take more staff time to maintain this increased level of communication, and additional staff may have to be hired.

Blogs (Web Logs)

Even blogs can be used in fundraising. Blogs, officially known as Weblogs, are frequently updated Web pages that are written in an informal (journal or diary) style. Blogs are changing the way many people communicate. They are inexpensive, require little technical assistance, and offer an opportunity to increase interaction with those interested in the organization and what it is doing. Donors especially may be interested in reading blogs created by the development office.

According to Lee Rainie, director of the Pew Internet & American Life Project, there are at least 10 million blogs, with a total readership of more than 35 million Americans (Grobman, 2005). By having someone who is intimately involved in one of the organization's programs write their experiences in a daily blog, donors and prospective donors can relate more closely to the project. Be prepared to have everything shared—warts and all. Make sure that the blog is read by a staff member, though, before being posted.

But, is blogging worth your time? Approximately "one out of every four people, about 35 million, visits a blog regularly . . . this means that they are spending 9% of their working time—40 minutes daily—researching (or not!) this way" (*Mediastudio Quarterly*, 2006). Following are some tips provided by Mediastudio Inc. in their *Mediastudio Quarterly* to make blogs more useful to an organization.

First, a few advantages to blogging:

- **Low-cost and fast.** With the stroke of a keyboard and the press of a button, your thoughts are available for all to see. Blogs are easy and quick to operate, so precious time is not spent on creating them.
- **Involves readers effectively.** Instead of one-sided communication methods, blogs allow readers to take part in forming new ideas.
- **Delivers a human touch.** Unlike text that is written, edited, and put through a number of filters, blogs tend to be prepared differently and can be spirited, highly personal experiences.
- **They breed infectiousness.** Already, blogs are influencing opinions, votes, and even business practices.
- **They are fun.** The "fun factor" of blogs should not be underestimated—that is why so many people are reading them on their own, or on company time.
- **A chance to be an authority.** The nature of the communication tool makes it a great credibility builder.

Second, tips to make blogs profitable:

Due to potential revenue, both businesses and nonprofits have launched blogs to suit their needs. The question is, how can we best make blogs well visited and eventually profitable?

- **Use a view leader.** Here, a group writes its blog using a personality charged to curry favor towards your group in profitable ways.

- **Convince other bloggers to praise your products or services.** The sense of unbiased reporting with blogs can work to build your case in similar ways to using traditional public relations. The upside is that bloggers seem to be more credible at the moment.
- **Advertise on blogs to lead traffic to yours.** Groups or individuals can place advertisements on blogs with complimentary topics, but be aware that the majority of bloggers dismiss the use of traditional ads. To avoid disapproval, blog writers often encourage readers to discuss ads appearing in their blog space.
- **Trade links.** If you mention another blog, use this as an opportunity to have them mention or link to yours.

Podcasting and Vodcasting

An Internet-based broadcast (free to anyone with Web access) is growing popular with organizations who wish to communicate with their donors. It's relatively inexpensive as it takes a computer, a microphone, and some low-budget software to create the most basic podcasts. They are called podcasting because these audio programs can easily be downloaded onto an iPod for listening ease. Also, anyone with a high-speed Internet connection has the ability to download and listen to audio programs. "Several online sites—including Apple's iTunes site, iPodeer, Podcast Alley, and Podcast.net—offer access to podcasts, more of which can be downloaded free," notes Peter Panepento in an article in *The Chronicle of Philanthropy*.

Podcasting first became noticed as early as 2000. In early 2005, UNICEF began using podcasting as a regular way both to raise awareness of its program and its funds. "It's the audio equivalent of the blog," states Blue Chevigny, a freelance radio journalist who has produced most of the pieces for UNICEF. In 2006, UNICEF began to produce video versions of its podcasts—*vodcasts*. These can be played on cell phones and iPods that can play video. UNICEF had more than 3 million downloads during its first year of podcasting. The stories run from 5 to 10 minutes and provide donors and prospective donors with an in-depth look at some of the issues facing the people that the organization helps. Podcasting and vodcasting give nonprofits a high tech way to tell their stories to large numbers of people. UNICEF believes that "every organization has an opportunity today to speak to large numbers of people from the large numbers of platforms that are available." Researchers believe that podcasts will reach as many as 56.8 million people by 2010.

Text Messaging

In 2007, text messaging finally came of age and became a tried and true standard for fundraising when *American Idol* asked donors to use it and telephone calls to raise more than $60 million in one evening to support its domestic and international relief efforts. In that one evening, text messaging set a new record for fundraising. As early as December 2004, the American Red Cross and CARE were using text messaging (SMS; short message service) to raise funds for the survivors of the tsunami. Since then, more and more money is being raised through this electronic means. Currently, there are nearly 200 million wireless subscribers in the United States, and more than 30 billion messages were sent during the first six months of 2005. There even is an association called Cellular Telecommunications & Internet Association (CTIA–the Wireless Association) that decided to team with the Red Cross in a campaign called "Text 2HELP" to raise money for disaster relief. Selected wireless carriers offered their customers the opportunity to make $5 gifts each time they text messaged them (for a limit of $25). The donations were added on to their next bills. The theme selected by Verizon was "It's time to stay connected." One point to remember—even though it's a quick way to connect with donors (and to prospect for others), the carriers receive a large cut of the revenue.

Electronic Forms/Publications

Any forms used in fundraising can be posted on the organization's Web site. If the development office wishes to save on costs of printed materials, they can always refer prospects and donors to materials posted on the organization's Web site. Also, materials can be sent electronically. When seeking sponsors for an event, it is easier and quicker to send sponsorship opportunities and commitment forms electronically than to mail them. Using an e-mail to follow up on a solicitation and including the forms in an attachment can speed up the process by days or weeks. Also, more often than not, organizations are using their Web sites to post electronic versions of their annual reports and saving large sums of money by not printing them.

Virtual Gifting

The social networking site, Facebook, has recently entered the fundraising field by allowing its users to buy virtual gifts (icons) to send to their friends to benefit a charity of their choice. In February of 2007, 28 icons were available for members to give publicly or privately. "Public gifts go in the recipient's Gift Box, and the message sent with the gift goes on the recipient's Wall, i.e., Facebook profile. Private gifts go into the recipient's Gift Box where they can be seen by others but do not reveal the gift giver," stated Abny Santicola in her article, "Virtual Gifting," in *Fundraising Success* magazine.

"More than 7 million gifts were either given away or sold in February, with 50 cents of every icon sold going to Susan G. Komen for the Cure, a network of breast-cancer survivors and activists devoted to eradicating the disease. While the February Gift Shop launch was Facebook's first foray into e-philanthropy, it also was Susan G. Komen for the Cure's first experience with the site," noted Santicola. On the site, a link was provided to the Susan G. Komen for the Cure site so those interested could learn more about the organization. This first joint effort was so successful that the Susan G. Komen for the Cure is planning to expand its presence on Facebook. Plus, Facebook is now planning to expand to include more nonprofit groups.

THE NEED FOR PRINTED PUBLICATIONS

All fundraisers know that "people give to people." They also know that if you don't ask for the gift, it's highly unlikely that a gift will be given. But what most people, including fundraisers, don't understand is how important it is to have the right materials with you when soliciting a gift. By providing a potential donor with information before the visit or leaving materials behind after speaking with the individual or group, you leave a lasting impression not only with your words, but with the images in the brochures—the copy that describes the organization's mission or programs; the photos of the people working tirelessly on the organization's behalf; the numbers, graphs, or charts that relay the financial need of the organization; and the list of reasons why the prospect should make a gift to your organization. The person makes the "ask," the materials provide the reminder of why the potential donors should support you and your cause.

For this reason, all materials (whether printed or electronic) used in development should reflect the style of the organization they represent. They need not be "slick," four-color, bright, or fancy. They must be informative, accurate, fresh, and error-free and have a "feel" that makes the receiver want to read and keep them. All development staff can produce materials that meet these requirements. What kinds and amounts of materials an organization produces will depend upon the type of organization it is, the fundraising effort it is undertaking, and the people whom it will be soliciting.

Remember that there is almost no correlation between the ability of a fundraising brochure to garner accolades and its ability to raise money for the organization. Publications are the "supporting players" in fundraising. The "stars" are the volunteers who solicit the funds face-to-face from their peers. Publications should never take the place of a direct person-to-person solicitation. The only exception to this rule is in direct mail solicitation, where the expected gifts are usually quite small.

> *Publications are the "supporting players" in fundraising.*

Still, there are many communications tools used by fundraisers that work better in a printed format rather than an electronic format, or can be used in either format depending upon the prospect or donor. Following are descriptions of each of these pieces and how they are used in fundraising.

The Case Statement

A case statement is simply the organization's or program's statement of need—an explanation of the needs and opportunities that confront the organization or program. The case statement does not need to be long. It should be concise but comprehensive. All other documents that the organization will use for fundraising—personal letters, brochures, videos, etc.—will be based on the case statement. A case statement that is strong, well thought out, and well written will make it easier for the leadership and volunteers to promote the fundraising effort to prospective donors.

A case statement will relate the history of the organization—why it was founded, what its mission is, how it has helped and served its constituents in the past, etc. It also will present the organization's current position—who does it serve, how its programs affect the public today, and what makes it different from other organizations with similar missions.

A case statement also will present the needs of the organization—why it needs funding, how much money it needs, a plan for how that money can be raised, and how the money will strengthen the organization's programs and change the world that the organization encompasses. It anticipates the questions and provides the answers. It concludes with a succinct wrap-up and leaves the reader with the feeling that the organization makes a difference and is worthy of support. See Chapters 6 and 14 for more information on case statements.

In Exhibit 13–4, Nike B. Whitcomb defines the uses of the case statement and gives suggestions on its design and printing. An example of a well-written, effective case statement developed into a brochure and used in a capital campaign can be found in Appendix 13–D.

Exhibit 13–4 Guidelines for Writing a Case Statement

The case statement is the vehicle used to recruit key volunteer leadership, to secure top gifts, and to open the door to other areas of fundraising. It is a printed document that uses copy, photography, and graphic art to present a first-class image. The case statement varies in size and number of pages based on several criteria, such as the following:

- The cause
- The urgency of the need
- The constituency being approached
- Previous style and type of printed materials

The copy in the case statement has a clearly delineated purpose—to convince the reader of the worth of the project and of the urgent need for a contribution. People give to what they know and understand. Therefore, the case statement must do the following:

- Identify the institution and establish its place in history
- Convey a sense of its value to society
- Give specific information regarding costs involved in solving the problems being addressed in the campaign
- Provide a means of response

Often the basic story can be enhanced through the use of personal "testimonials" from influential members of the community who are already committed to the cause. And, if the cause is to raise funds for a new facility, artists' concepts of the new building, floor plans, and pictures of people who will benefit from the improved services and facilities are helpful.

Generally, the case statement is printed in at least two ink colors to enhance graphic potential. Even agencies without large budgets for printing should consider modest use of four-color artwork in a document like the case statement.

Before beginning the concept, design, and writing of the case statement and all other printed materials, several questions must be asked, such as the following:

- What is the overall budget for printing? What is the specific budget for this piece?
- Is this piece part of a campaign (annual, capital, endowment, etc.)?

- What is the anticipated use of the piece? Recruitment? Solicitation? Short-term cultivation? Long-term awareness? All of the above?
- How does/will the piece fit into the overall image of the institution?
- What is the timetable for creating the piece?
- What materials already exist that will add to the piece (graphs, charts, giving tables, photography, quotes)?
- Who will need to approve the copy? Design?

Costs to produce a case statement include those for writing, photography, design, and printing, and can range from as little as $2 to as much as $25 per copy. The press run will usually be short—1,000 copies is average for most small- to medium-size campaigns. Mutliple pages, use of graphics and photos, multiple ink colors, and quality of paper will add to or subtract from the cost.

To estimate the number of copies needed, look at the potential donor list. All top prospects should get a copy of the statement. All board and staff members should have copies. All campaign workers should have copies. Extra copies also will be useful for distribution to media, to prospects in the middle tier of the potential donor list, and so on.

Once the rough estimate is made, add 10 percent for copies that may not be perfectly produced and for the inevitable "lost" copies that will need to be replaced. This is the number of copies to plan on.

Now is the time to consider the size of the piece. The following are a few things to keep in mind.

- Unless the piece is spiral or perfect bound, binding requirement for the document will be in increments of four pages. Small campaigns ($500,000 goal) may use only four pages—larger campaigns ($30 million plus) may use up to 100 pages.
- The vertical format of 8 1/2" by 11" is the standard size, but not mandatory, and many are using a horizontal format because it is different.
- Ample room for white space, photos, and graphics will enhance the design and readability.
- The type font should be large enough (at least 12 point) and easy enough to read (most find serif faces, such as Times Roman, easiest). Keep in mind that most prospects capable of large gifts are 40 years of age or older.

Source: Nike B. Whitcomb. CFRE, President and CEO, Nike B. Whitcomb Associates, Inc., Chicago, Illinois, 2007.

General Information Brochure

The fundraising brochure is developed from the case statement and is the "professional" presentation of the case statement. It is the polished package that accompanies all letters soliciting funds. It will restate the case, carry a message from the organization's leadership, describe the attributes of the organization, explain the funding needs, describe how to make gifts to the cause, list the gift recognition opportunities (if any), and leave the prospective donor with a sense of immediacy—the feeling that making a gift to the organization is the correct thing to do and it should be done now, not later.

The brochure should look professional but not "slick" or expensive. It should include photos, quotes, graphs, charts, lists,

> *The brochure should look professional but not "slick" or expensive.*

and bulleted phrases. It should be concise and not overly wordy. Four color is preferred, but much can be done creatively with two colors of ink, which is much less expensive. Often the brochure is designed with a pocket either in the front or back into which a fact sheet, question-and-answer brochure, pledge form, or other information can be inserted. The look of these other pieces is modeled after the design of the brochure. They all should be able to stand alone, yet be part of the packaged look.

Fact Sheet

Many times a donor will ask for specific facts and will not want to read an entire brochure. It is easy to provide a donor with a summary of the fundraising need by developing a sheet of all important facts pertinent to the fundraising effort. This piece should be designed to complement the brochure—the colors selected should be one or two of those used in the brochure and the type font should be the same as what was used in the brochure. This fact sheet need not be fancy but should be laid out in a logical, easy-to-follow format.

Question-and-Answer Brochure

Questions that are commonly asked throughout the fundraising effort can be anticipated, presented, and answered in a smaller brochure that accompanies the main fundraising brochure. This can be called the question-and-answer brochure, or the "Q and A" for short. In addition to being used along with the general information brochure, it can also be used separately. This is an inexpensive piece, often considered a "throw-away" piece and can be printed in two color or be "piggybacked" onto the printing of the major brochure and done in four color (if the brochure is being printed in four color). See Appendix 13–E for an example of a question-and-answer brochure.

Annual Report

All organizations should produce an annual report either in a print or an electronic format. It can be used to complement the organization's fundraising materials. The report outlines the

organization's programs and activities during the past year and reports on the financial stability of the organization. Produced annually, it can be used effectively as a supplemental brochure in multi-year fundraising efforts. Posted on the organization's Web site, it can be easily accessed and produced at little cost. Appendix 13–F is an example of a short printed annual report that provides donors with the required basics.

Newsletters

Newsletters are used to communicate both within fundraising campaigns and to the public being solicited for gifts. Written and distributed monthly, bimonthly, or quarterly, a newsletter can provide frequent updates on the fundraising effort by featuring stories on donors, campaign leadership, special events, and other activities of interest to the volunteers, members, potential donors, and others. Material for the newsletters should be planned in advance to set the stage for the fundraising effort, introduce the volunteer leadership, announce key fundraising events, and list the donors as they accumulate over the months. Appendix 13–G provides an example of an article placed in a newsletter to announce endowments established to honor faculty members at American University. Highlighting major gifts made by donors can encourage other donors to make gifts similar in size.

In Exhibit 13–5 Whitcomb addresses the rules that apply to publications other than the case statement developed by the development office.

Exhibit 13–5 Developing Other Publications

The same rules that govern the creation of the case statement play an important role in other adjunct fundraising literature. Newsletters, for example, can reinforce the message about a specific campaign and amplify basic information about the need. For example, institutions providing multiple services can profile each service and its associated personnel in successive issues of the newsletter over a one- or two-year timespan.

The newsletter can also be used to update the constituencies regarding campaign progress. Story ideas include recruitment of volunteer leadership, announcement of early gifts, interview with people who are and will benefit from the services, interview with staff providing services, interviews with key donors, and lists of special needs.

Keep the format simple. For example, consider the following advice:

- Two colors are plenty.
- Stick to 12-point type.
- Stick to one or two type faces for the headline in no more than three sizes, using boldface and italics for variation.
- Use photos that are large enough to have visual impact, but are not overpowering.
- Don't "continue" a story more than once within an issue.
- Four to six pages is enough space to tell the message and still invite the reader to keep reading.

Newsletters are not "newsy" if they are published less often than quarterly, although staff time and budget may dictate less frequency.

Source: Nike B. Whitcomb. CFRE, President and CEO, Nike B. Whitcomb Associates, Inc., Chicago, Illinois, 2007.

Source: Copyright © Mark Litzler.

Press Releases

To inform the public of the organization's fundraising efforts, the staff must write and distribute news releases to announce important happenings such as special events, the receipt of a major gift, the appointment of a campaign chairperson, etc. News releases can be distributed by mail or at a press conference if the news is important enough to get the press to attend. If materials are distributed at a press conference, then a complete press kit should be developed, including the press release, a brochure or fact sheet describing the organization, biographies of any persons involved, and any photographs (black and white) pertinent to the release.

The basic rules of producing a press release are the following: (1) Be sure to use letterhead or "press release" banner head stationery. (2) List a contact name and phone number before beginning the text of the release. (3) Keep the release short—one to two pages at the most. (4) Use quotes, short paragraphs, and include a photo if possible. (5) Put the most important information in the first paragraph. (6) Type "more" on the bottom of the page if continuing to another page. (7) End the release with one of the following sets of marks: ###, -30-, o0o.

Posters

Posters can be effective fundraising tools in many campaigns. Who can forget the March of Dimes poster child or the faces of the animals on the posters of the Society for the Prevention of Cruelty to Animals? A picture says a thousand words, and posters can raise

> *A picture says a thousand words, and posters can raise thousands of dollars.*

thousands of dollars. They also can just be used to raise the public's awareness of the organization and its mission. They do not need to be in four color, but again, if it is in the budget, then use four color, because it is usually more dramatic and appealing.

Pledge Cards

Pledge cards are integral to most campaigns. They allow the donors to convey their intentions—type of gift, size of gift, methods of payment, restrictions or designations, and whether a person or event is being commemorated. Appendix 13–H shows examples of printed pledge forms used in: (A) a capital campaign and (B) an annual appeal. Electronic pledge forms can also be posted on the organization's Web site so they can be submitted electronically or easily downloaded if the printed one is lost. Submitting them electronically most likely will be for smaller gifts, although more and more large gifts are being made electronically.

Reply Cards

Whether a special event or an annual appeal, reply cards and envelopes need to be printed and made available electronically. Basic information needed in most reply cards includes the following:

- personal information: name; title; complete address, including zip or postal codes; telephone number; fax number; e-mail address; a place to write the number and names of those attending the event; and a box to check if seeking volunteer information.
- financial information: the cost of the event; to whom to make payment; where to send payment; payment options available—check, credit card, electronic payment, etc.; and the date by which payment must be received. Appendix 13–I(A) shows an invitation with a reply card, which allows tickets to be purchased electronically.
- gift clubs: list of levels in which the donor would be included if gift clubs are being used. Appendix 13–I(B) shows a sample annual appeal reply/response card that shows gift club levels and is to be returned by using a separate response envelope. Appendix 13–I(C) is an example of a self-mailer response device that lists both the gift clubs for the annual appeal, the organization's planned giving society, and provides giving society benefits. It also allows the organization to charge individuals monthly by debiting their bank accounts on a regular basis. Appendix 13–I(D) is an example of an invitation reply card that lists sponsorship levels and requests names of guests.
- recruitment information: request for names of others to be sent invitations or for volunteers needed by the organization for this event or future events.
- statement requesting any corrections to be made in the files.
- tax information: all tax information required by IRS rules and regulations.

Specialty Brochures

At some time, all organizations will need to produce a brochure for a special project, fundraising program, or occasion. Even though the design could be for a one-time only use, the brochure still should reflect the style (brand) and quality of the organization's other printed and electronic materials. Appendix 13–J is an example of a brochure designed to encourage memorial gifts for an organization.

Special Event Materials

Invitations to special events can be designed, printed, and then mailed, or designed for electronic mailing. To encourage potential guests to hold the date open for a special event, notices can be mailed or printed in other materials that the organization uses to communicate with their prospective guests. In Appendix 13–K is an example of a hold the date notice printed in the organization's magazine.

Special Information Insert Cards

Often, additional information is needed to be supplied to the prospective guests. This could include attire, accommodations, directions to the location, valet or self-parking, registration, credentials needed for entrance into the event, etc. Appendix 13–L shows an example of a card, inserted into the invitation, providing directions to the special event.

PUBLICATIONS REPRESENT THE ORGANIZATION

All publications produced by the organization should be produced in a creative, professional, and cost-effective manner. Also, all printed and electronic materials used in fundraising should present a good image of the organization. For many who read the materials, this will be their first "image" of the organization. If the materials are sloppily conceived, poorly written or designed, or filled with typographical errors they will leave the wrong impression with the potential donor. This may be a lasting impression of the organization, and the potential donor may choose not to give at all.

Publications do not have to be expensive to represent the organization. Simple, neat, well-designed, two-color pieces can be more effective than crowded, complex, four-color pieces. Design the piece to fit the organization and the audience that you wish to reach. Having the image of being able to print expensive brochures may not be what you want to convey to your donors. Be careful not only of what you say but of how it is reproduced and presented in printed or electronic materials.

HOW TO PRODUCE LOW-COST, HIGH-QUALITY PIECES

Desktop publishing is one method to use to design materials to be printed. If there is staff capable of producing design work with one of the many software products available, then consider using desktop publishing, which enables you to produce electronic or camera-ready art directly from your own personal computer without using a designer. Some newsletters, brochures, and invitations are easily designed this way, and using desktop publishing software can save the organization thousands of dollars in design costs. The piece can go straight from the computer to the printer with the right software. Also, material can be designed specifically for electronic use.

An organization that produces many brochures, a monthly newsletter, or other fundraising pieces may wish to consider hiring a person whose sole responsibility is to produce these pieces in-house. With the trend today for organizations to produce most pieces for electronic use, the production of these pieces probably will be one of the first duties to go in that direction.

USE OF CONSULTANTS IN WRITING PUBLICATIONS

Working with a Designer

If an organization does not have in-house design capabilities, then it is imperative that it find a designer who can capture its spirit and mission and deliver these in smartly designed pieces.

Finding the right "fit" between a designer and an organization can take some time and "shopping." Don't worry if you are not interested in the first few you interview. When you find the right person, it will be worth every minute of the search. Having confidence in a designer to produce the right look for a piece, or the right theme for a series of pieces, can ease the pressure from a fundraising executive's already overburdened schedule. It will allow the fundraiser to pursue what needs to be done to bring the money in and to spend less time on the details regarding the fundraising materials—artwork, color, and design.

Selecting a designer for the organization is only half the battle; you also must understand how to work with a designer. The tips listed in Exhibit 13–6 can make working with a designer relatively easy. Do your homework before signing the contract!

When working with a designer, use the form shown in Exhibit 13–7 to help track your projects.

Exhibit 13–6 Seventeen Suggestions for Working with a Design Firm

1. **Find a Firm That Listens.**
Select a firm that listens to you and asks clarifying questions. It is important that they understand your organization and what you are trying to achieve. It is important that you can communicate easily and clearly with them.
2. **Make Them Part of Your Team.**
A good design firm knows how to explore and consider a number of approaches to problem solving. When they understand your project and its context, they can suggest effective ways to reach your audience, maximize the value of their efforts, and stay on budget.
3. **Provide a Clear Budget.**
Indicate what it includes—design only, or some combination of design, copy, printing, photography, illustrations, mailing, etc. This will inform the design firm about your financial expectations.
4. **Allow Enough Time.**
Plan carefully so there is time for the unexpected and so the project can be produced without rushing.
5. **Insist on a Written Proposal.**
Have a signed contract in place before beginning the project. It should include the project description, a production schedule, and rates for out-of-pocket expenses, alterations, and overtime.
6. **Set the Context for the Project.**
Your design firm needs to know about your organization and its current situation. How does it differentiate itself from competing organizations? What attributes do you want to convey? What is your brand?
7. **Define Your Audiences.**
Your design firm needs to know what your audiences expect from you. What do they value about the service that you provide? Why do they give?
8. **Request a Few Design Concepts.**
Suggest comprehensives or less expensive sketches to provide a feel for the design.
9. **Edit Very Carefully.**
If you are providing copy, review and proofread it closely and have it approved before submitting it to the design firm.
10. **Limit the Number of Alterations.**
This is necessary to avoid potentially large charges for alterations. A few changes in a paragraph can require the redesign of an entire page or spread.
11. **Request Color and Paper Samples.**
Color proofs and paper samples will show how the project will look when it is printed.
12. **Buy Printing Directly from the Printer or Through the Design Firm.**
You can buy printing directly from the printer to save the design firm's mark-up, but you will need to manage the printing yourself. If you buy printing directly, some design firms will offer print management and press inspections for a separate fee. If you buy printing through the design firm, they will have the responsibility of quality control and negotiating with the printer if any problems arise with the job.
13. **Make All Alterations Before the Project Goes to the Printer.**
A very small change at the printer can cost hundreds of dollars. More changes can cost much more.
14. **Find Other Uses.**
Can the project be used for other audiences or occasions? It is much more cost-effective to design with several uses in mind than to design several different projects at different times.
15. **Ask for Flexible Solutions.**
Request formats that can be updated easily without having to reprint the entire project.
16. **Print Several Projects on the Same Press Sheet.**
If the specified quantities of each item can fit easily on the same press sheet, this can produce a significant savings.
17. **Coordinate Web and Print Materials.**
Purchase the rights for print design elements for use on the organization's Web site. This will help to build a coordinated brand presence.

Source: Copyright 2006. Chroma Design and Communications, Silver Spring, Maryland.

Exhibit 13–7 Design Specifications Sheet

1. PROJECT TITLE _____

2. CONTACT _____

3. SIZE   FLAT _____   FOLDED _____

4. NUMBER OF PAGES _____   OR PANELS _____
   (Number of pages must be divisible by 4.)

5. COVER   Plus Cover _____   Self Cover _____
            Die Cut Pockets _____   Glued _____

6. COVER INK
   _____
   _____

7. TEXT INK
   _____
   _____

8. COPY PROVIDED
   _____ On disk with hard copy.   _____ Keystroke and proofread from original.

9. CHARTS AND GRAPHS
   _____ Number Note: _____
                             (Simple 2D or more complex 3D)

10. PHOTOS
    Provided (number) _____
    Stock (number) _____
    Photo shoot (number) _____

11. PAPER _____

12. BINDERY _____

13. DEADLINES _____

14. BUDGET _____

NOTE: • "Ownership" of the design is negotiable, but should be established from the start. In large projects, it should be part of a written contract. In small projects, it can be a verbal understanding with the designer. Designers usually want to "own" the design or logo so that other designers don't use it. The organization may want to own the concept so they can use it no matter who is handling the various projects. At the start, it should be clear between the parties what the rules are going to be.
   • The designer will be required to provide the printer with a CD or print-ready electronic files prepared to the printer's specifications.
   • The designer must approve all printer proofs, including digital and match prints.
   • The designer must accompany the project through a press check.

Source: Courtesy of American Society of Civil Engineers, Reston, Virginia.

Working with a Printer

Finding the right printer also is key to producing successful fundraising pieces. Begin by interviewing several printers. If the organization does not have a ready list of printers, ask similar, organizations what printers they use. A different printer may be necessary for each type of piece being developed. A four-color brochure will require a printer with greater capabilities than one who prints stationery and business cards. Some printers have digital color reproduction capabilities that are less expensive and equally effective compared with traditional four-color printing.

This option should be considered for low page count or small run jobs.

When selecting a printer, consider the following issues:

- Reliability. Does the printer complete the job on time and within budget?
- Responsiveness. If a rush job occurs, can the printer handle it?
- Costs. How do the printer's prices compare with the prices of others?
- Quality. Do the materials used as samples of the printer's work reflect the image your organization wants to project?
- Capabilities. Is it a large, small, or mid-sized operation? Does the printer have two- or four-color presses? Does it have a designer on staff? Can you send the materials electronically? Can the printer do the work you need to have done?
- Shipping and storage. Can the printer drop ship your pieces to your mail house, special event site, or office? Or will you need to pick them up and deliver them? Does the printer have room to store your print job until you are ready to use it?

> *Finding the right printer also is key to producing successful fundraising pieces.*

Before selecting a printer, make sure that you meet with representatives personally. In a small shop, you may speak with the owner directly. In larger shops, there may be one or more sales representatives. Ask for a tour of the plant and review samples of the printer's work. Don't just look at brochures or calendars it has printed; look at all sizes and types of materials. Consider the costs, location, and comfort level you have with the staff before making your final selection.

To keep the production of your materials within budget and on time, follow these guidelines:

- Get bids for each piece to be printed, at least two bids although usually three are preferable.
- Have several pieces printed at one time if possible.
- Use standard paper and envelope sizes. Ask if the printer has any paper left over from another print job that could be used at a reduced price.
- Avoid unusual sizes, fancy cuts, die cuts, folds, flaps, pockets, etc.
- Proofread your materials several times before sending to the printer to avoid making expensive last minute changes.
- Avoid overtime charges by getting copy to the printer on time, with no mistakes or changes. Also, be wary of having proofs sent to you by messenger service. The organization, not the printer, will pay for messenger service deliveries.
- Most printers will print 10 percent more than the guaranteed minimum number of items that you wanted printed. Be sure to ask if there will be a charge for this overrun or if the printer provides it free of charge.

- Get all bids in writing. Don't rely upon verbal promises.
- Set deadlines for the production of printed pieces well ahead of the deadlines for use or mailing of the pieces. Allow some delay time.
- Make photocopies of all corrections and directions given to the printer. These may be needed later to verify any claims against work not produced to your satisfaction.

Several steps are associated with the printing process. They include (1) writing the copy; (2) meeting with and selecting a designer and printer; (3) designing and laying out the piece to be printed; (4) selecting the ink colors (PMS) and paper; (5) reviewing the final layout before final proofs; (6) printing the piece; (7) attending a press check with the designer, although this may not be necessary if the proofs are good. Usually only high-end pieces will require a visit by you and the designer; (8) binding, folding, gluing, etc., to finish the piece; and (9) shipping and delivery of the piece to the client.

When producing publications, there are several lessons that usually are learned the hard way. To prevent these, keep in mind the points just highlighted.

When working with the selection of colors for printed pieces, designers and printers often will use the term *PMS*. This stands for Pantone Matching System, a system that allows for specific colors to be used by indicating the Pantone name or number so the correct colors are printed. Colors may look differently when displayed on the computer monitor than in the final printed product. Most colored printing is referred to as a four-color process because it uses three primary ink colors (cyan, magenta, and yellow) plus black. When six-color is used for more vibrant coloring, it is because orange and green are added to the cyan, magenta, and yellow. It helps to create better print materials when staff spends time with a designer or printer to learn more about color applications, because they have a better understanding of the process.

COORDINATED LOOK FOR ELECTRONIC AND PRINT MATERIALS

The development office is not the only department in the organization writing and designing materials for the Web site or having materials printed for use with constituents. If several departments are planning projects that need to be designed and posted on the Web site or printed at the same time, it may be best to bid these projects together to get the best price with the designer and the printer. It is possible to get a break in price for quantity of work. With a designer, this will work only if the pieces don't need to be produced within the same time frame. Remember, a large print shop may be able to handle several print jobs simultaneously, whereas a sole designer has only so many hours in the day.

Branding

"Whether your organization is embarking on a major fundraising campaign or looking to build and sustain operations, a strong brand is good business in today's increasingly competitive and sophisticated fundraising climate," states Sarah Durham in an article on branding in *FundRaising Success* magazine.

A strong brand will create name recognition. This is not done overnight. It takes the involvement of the board and staff and requires a commitment in time and money. All written and printed materials as well as the Web site and other electronic materials also will carry this look or brand. Plus, the organization's logo should be incorporated into all materials. Both visuals and messages are used to create a successful brand. Messages are any taglines used by the organization, the mission statement, and any other materials that are consistently used to present the organization. Selection of colors to use in brochures or on the Web site, type style and sizes, taglines, etc., all are part of the branding process.

All materials, whether electronic or printed, should be designed to carry the organization's brand. See Exhibit 13–8 for the "Big Six" rules of nonprofit branding. Materials should reflect the style and spirit of the organization. This does not mean that all brochures will look alike. Instead, there will be a theme, feel, or look to the pieces that immediately identifies them as belonging to that particular organization and not to another. This is *branding*, the overall look or image for an organization that is distinct from that of other organizations. The appearance of the materials reflects the organization's mission and is recognizable by the public. It's what makes the organization different from its competitors. Use the Brand Preparedness Checklist in Exhibit 13–9 to ensure that you are building your brand.

The brand should be recognizable by everyone, but especially by prospects and donors. It is important that they recognize why your organization is different from others, as it is your story, your experience, your brand. "Your brand story should explain why you do the work you do and how you do it differently. And why we, the potential audience, should care. For it to be effective, everyone in your organization needs to know it, be able to explain it and choose to embody it," notes planned giving specialists, the Stelter Company, in its promotional materials. Appendix 13–M provides a case study on the use of branding in nonprofit organizations.

Once the brand is developed, it should be used as extensively as possible and as long as possible. Over time, it will be difficult to keep staff from wanting to change all or part of the brand, as this is just human nature. Consistency is the key. What may feel old and stagnant to the staff will feel like stability and consistency to the organization's donors.

In most organizations, the communications department will develop basic standards for all printed and electronic materials. The development office should adopt these standards for their fundraising pieces. These standards can include a package of logo sizes, acceptable font styles, colors, etc. If possible, the organization's logo should be incorporated into all materials. Make sure that any designer selected to produce fundraising materials is given this information. Plus, using one designer can assist the organization in maintaining its brand. See Exhibit 13–10, Ten Tips for Fundraising Communications.

Exhibit 13–8 The "Big Six" Rules of Nonprofit Branding

1. **Know Your Audience**
   How well do you know the audience(s) most critical to your success? What are the triggers—emotional and other—that make them most likely to act in the manner you desire? Having a firm grasp on your audience allows you to target your brand for maximum effect. Research and outreach efforts yield big returns if done properly.

2. **Own an Idea**
   When you hear "Volvo," you think "safety." When you hear "Apple," you think "cool, innovative products." The main goal of branding is to own an idea—the simpler the better—in the minds of your audience. What's your unique "promise of value" to your audience(s)?

3. **Sharpen Your Focus**
   If you're seen as a jack-of-all-trades, you're also seen as a master of none. The simpler and more straightforward the scope of your organization, the greater the strength of your brand and your ability to "own the idea." The more you have to say, the less likely anyone will take the time to truly understand.

4. **Pave the Way**
   Nonprofit organizations often have similar missions, particularly as seen by those in the donor community who must choose among a multitude of worthy causes. With so much competition for dollars, it's critical to differentiate your organization through a claim of leadership. Have you pioneered a new approach? Are you the first, most-qualified, largest, or only group that does what you do?

5. **Walk It Like You Talk It**
   So now that you have your brand message together—decided on the idea you want to own, sharpened your focus, defined your leadership—do your actions match your words? Your brand is your promise; every interaction your audience has with your organization—from the way the phone is answered to the way that correspondence is handled—must live up to that promise.

6. **Say It Again . . . and Again**
   Building a brand is like getting a child to follow instructions: you have to say it over and over until the message sinks in. Consistency and persistency are the keys to having your brand message heard above the noise. If asked, would everyone in your organization describe it in the same way? Are you taking advantage of every opportunity to get your message "out there?" And if so, does the message remain the same from week-to-week, month-to-month, year-to-year, employee-to-employee?

Source: Courtesy of Steve Goodwin, Senior Brand Strategist, AXIS Inc., Washington, DC, http://www.axiscomm.com. Reprinted with permission.

Exhibit 13–9 Brand Preparedness Checklist

KNOW YOUR AUDIENCE	Yes	No
1. Have you defined the audience(s) most critical to your success and do you conduct research to learn about their perceptions, priorities, and habits?		
2. Is your audience encouraged to provide feedback on your programs and initiatives and do you incorporate that feedback?		
OWN AN IDEA		
3. Do you know the single, simple idea you want to own in the minds of your audience?		
4. Can you clearly state your unique "promise of value?"		
SHARPEN YOUR FOCUS		
5. Is your mission clear, direct and easily understood by all internal and external audiences? Have you eliminated "clutter?"		
PAVE THE WAY		
6. Have you adequately spoken to—and demonstrated—your leadership position?		
WALK IT LIKE YOU TALK IT		
7. Do your daily operations and the actions of your staff, board, and volunteers live up to the "promise of value" you put forth to all audiences?		
8. Do your public-facing materials (brochures, letters, ads, press releases, reports) accurately, professionally, and consistently support your brand image . . . both in words *and* images?		
SAY IT AGAIN . . . AND AGAIN		
9. Do all internal stakeholders (staff, board, volunteers) tell the same *approved* and accurate story about your organization?		
10. Is your "message" built for the long haul? Does it remain the same from week-to-week, month-to-month, year-to-year . . . employee-to-employee?		

Source: Courtesy of Steve Goodwin, Senior Brand Strategist, AXIS Inc., Washington, DC, http://www.axiscomm.com. Reprinted with permission.

Exhibit 13–10 Ten Tips for Fundraising Communications

1. Manage your message. Every piece of collateral material should look like it came from the same organization. All brochures, the annual report, the Web site, event invitations, stationery, etc. should reflect who you are in a comprehensive design. This is all part of your branding strategy.
2. Get the best quality graphic design you can afford, but don't overdo it. You don't want the donors to think all your money goes to the designer, printer, or Web designer.
3. Graphics drive publications. De-clutter. Strive for good, clean design with an effective use of white space and images that capture readers' attention.
4. Keep a file of design samples. Anytime you receive an impressive invitation or brochure, add it to your sample folder. Bookmark Web sites that are graphically appealing. It also pays to keep samples of things you don't like, so when you're planning new publications and collateral materials, you can easily show examples of the good, bad, and the ugly.
5. Know your audience. Who will be reading your publications? How do they want to hear from you? How often? Important tool: e-newsletter or other regular e-communications. This saves money on multiple mailings and gives people the opportunity to respond quickly.
6. All online communications should be easy to read and easy to navigate. Keep the same de-cluttering and clean design principles used in your printed pieces.
7. Be certain everyone in your organization has a 30-second "elevator speech," that they can easily use when speaking with people who may not know your organization.
8. Remember your publications help tell your story. Craft first-person stories, real life examples that resonate with your stakeholders. It beats the rhetoric every time.
9. Always remember: good communication supports the underpinnings of the entire development effort. Having the right materials helps keep everyone on message, especially those board members who are cultivating major donors!
10. Relationship building is critical. Use communication tools for every aspect of stewardship and keeping in touch with donors, stakeholders, board members, volunteers, and staff, too. Fundraising is friend-raising. A cliché, but true.

Source: Courtesy of Laura Forman Communications, LLC, Silver Spring, Maryland.

REFERENCES

Blogging—worth your time? *Mediastudio Quarterly*, Winter 2006.

Bonney, C. 2005. Ensuring delivery of association e-mails. Marketing. *Association Management*, September: 20.

Durham, S. 2006. Don't rob Peter to pay Paul. *FundRaising Success*, October: 63–67.

Give them something to talk about. Marketing. 2005. *Association Management*, September: 106.

Grobman, G. 2005. Blogging as bonding—A worthy way to reach your constituents. *Contributions*, November–December: 13.

Holt, N. 2005. 50 ways to win Web traffic. *Association Management*, September: 71–74.

Mills-Groninger, T. 2007. Fundraising e-mail faces being blocked/throttled. *The NonProfitTimes*, April.

Nobles, M.E. 2006. Text-messaging connects with donors. *The NonProfit Times*, January 15: 6.

Panepento, P. 2006. Casting call. *The Chronicle of Philanthropy* (January 26): T–10.

Powell, T. 2005. Getting the word out. Technology. *Association Management*, September: 106.

Santicola, A. 2007. Virtual gifting. Facebook's gift shop program lets users give to each other and to charity. *Fundraising Success*, May 12.

What is the biggest challenge you've faced in keeping your Web site current? CEO to CEO. 2005. *Association Management*, September: 110.

What's your brand story? Marketing ideas for planned giving clients and friends. *Stelter Advantage*, Spring 2006.

Watch your Web visits multiply! Marketing ideas for planned giving clients and friends. *Stelter Advantage*, Spring 2006.

Technology
FOCUS

ILLUSTRATION BY MICHAEL MORGENSTERN

50 Ways to Win Web Traffic

Most association Web sites have evolved from simple *brochureware* to powerful member resources. But how do you lure visitors to the treasure trove?

BY NEWTON HOLT

NOT TOO LONG AGO, MANY ASSOCIATION Web sites didn't offer much beyond a mission statement, an overview of the association's products and services, the obligatory "about us" section, and the like. But in most cases, that's changed—dramatically.

Many associations now offer feature-rich Web sites that provide members with critical information and news, while allowing them to interact with other members, access case studies and white papers, purchase products, search for jobs, and much more. The challenge for associations now isn't so much in building a great Web site; it's in getting inundated members to visit the site—and visit it often. Here are 50 practices your organization can implement to do just that.

1. **First, make it worth their time.** Who cares about increasing traffic if your site isn't up to speed? Make sure your content is fresh and relevant, your design appealing, and your site easy to navigate.

2. **Print your Web site address on all outgoing materials.** This is a no-brainer. Press releases, marketing collateral, letters from the CEO, position statements, and anything else that your organization sends out should list the Web site.

3. **Send e-mail news briefs and link back to the Web site for extended coverage.** Send out *teasers* by e-mail—just the bare bones of a story—and include a link in the text that directs readers to the Web site for more comprehensive information. ▶

4. Sponsor smartly. When you sponsor another organization's offerings, make Web visibility a part of the deal. Be sure that your Web site is included with your logo (if your identity standards allow it) on any materials that you sponsor and ask the organization that you're sponsoring to include a link to your Web site on its site.

5. Complement magazine or newsletter articles with online content. Include related content and resources, expanded coverage, and other such offerings online. Not only does this increase Web traffic for you, but it also increases the value of both your publications and your Web site as member resources.

6. Publish online-only content. In addition to including material that complements magazine articles, consider offering online-only articles. Include space each month in the magazine to briefly describe the online-only content to whet readers' appetites.

7. Offer virtual communities. Create chat rooms and other discussion forums where members can interact with one another and discuss common concerns. And, of course, monitor what's going on in these forums to make sure people aren't just using it as a place to hawk their wares.

8. Include your URL in your e-mail signature. Um, is there anyone out there who isn't doing this? Next item…

9. Pay search engine companies for sponsored listings. Many search engines offer *sponsored links* that appear as sidebars alongside search results. Imagine if every time someone searches for information related to the industry or profession you represent, your Web site appears next to (or maybe in) his or her results.

10. Provide postconference material online. After a conference, education session, or other event, provide a roundup of the event online. You can include handouts, PowerPoint presentations, presenter bios, and other relevant content. Attendees will appreciate having this resource, and those who couldn't attend can catch a glimpse of what they missed.

11. Practice trickle-down Webonomics. Ask conference presenters to include a link to your site on their site. This is especially effective if your presenter is well known and is likely to have a lot of traffic on his or her own site.

12. Keep it clean. Broken links and other technical annoyances are a surefire way to alienate people. Even if visitors do value the information your organization provides, there are only so many glitches that even your most avid fans will tolerate before they go elsewhere.

13. Bring in the big dogs. Just as *The Washington Post* and other major papers do, you can host a real-time chat with an expert from your industry. Really want to ramp up the traffic? Make participation free.

14. Be forward-friendly. The "forward-to-a-friend" option is a must. Ensure that every article, white paper, news brief, and the like has a link that allows people to forward the information to friends and colleagues.

15. Prominently announce new site features. When you finally add on that feature that members are screaming for, make sure that you announce it in all of your communication vehicles.

16. Provide a regularly updated feature. Include an item such as a monthly CEO column, a weekly question and answer, or a regular report on the association's advocacy efforts. Send an e-mail to members to let them know when the feature has been updated.

17. Know when it's time for an overhaul. When your design becomes the equivalent of an orange Naugahyde chair circa 1974 (which it eventually will), look at some popular sites and see what you can learn.

18. Trade links with other organizations. This might be tricky to pull off, since so many organizations compete directly with one another, but a great way to increase traffic is to post a link to your site on the Web page of another organization your members might also frequent.

19. Trade banner ads with affiliate organizations. Similar to the preceding example, this is a win for both organizations involved, and it doesn't cost a dime. Plus, it gets your logo out there: a branding bonus.

20. Make sure your site is secure. People are rightfully distrustful when it comes to Internet-based transactions, and if they don't see that little lock in the corner of their browsers, they're likely to lock you out.

> "Include related content and resources, expanded coverage, and other such offerings online. Not only does this increase Web traffic for you, but it also increases the value of both your publications and your Web site as member resources."

21. Perform a search-engine optimization. Maybe you're not getting enough hits because your pages aren't *tagged* correctly and therefore aren't showing up in search results. (For a brief intro to search-engine optimization, visit www.seologic.com/guide.)

22. Let them have it. When people request permission to reprint an article or other resource from your Web site, let them—but make sure they only write up an abstract of what the article or white paper is about and then include a link that takes visitors directly to your site.

23. Archive back issues of your newsletters, magazines, and other communication vehicles. And let readers know in the print edition that they can read back issues online. In current articles, refer to past articles or newsletters that contain further information and provide readers with the URLs of the past articles.

24. Include job listings on your site. On top of being a great member benefit, having an online job bank also is a potential source of revenue for your organization. While you probably don't want to charge job seekers for the service, do charge employers to post open positions.

25. Encourage staff to direct members to the Web site for more information. Staff members receive phone calls and e-mails daily from members who are seeking information. Have staff conclude all of their phone calls with members by directing them to the Web site for more information, and hold regular orientation sessions for staff to familiarize them with the site's features.

26. Call in outside help. Especially in smaller organizations or organizations that don't have a full-fledged IT department, calling in an outside professional might be the ideal solution. There are a number of consultancies that work almost exclusively in increasing Web traffic.

27. Write articles for other Web sites and magazines. Not only does this position you as a leader in the industry; it also presents another opportunity to get your URL out there—especially if your article is written for an online medium, which makes linking back to your organization's site super convenient.

28. Enter the blogosphere. Weblogs, a.k.a. *blogs,* are one of the hottest new media around, and many associations have already begun to exploit the trend. They're the *it* technology of the moment. Use them for all they're worth.

29. Offer podcasts. Podcasts, like blogs, also are a hot technology trend. These prerecorded Webcasts can be downloaded into your members' iPods or other MP3-style devices for listening on the go.

30. Make your site PDA-friendly. With everyone and his brother owning a BlackBerry or some other sort of PDA these days, it's important to make sure that your site translates well to the small screen.

31. Offer a customizable experience. Take a page out of the Amazon.com playbook and give your members the opportunity to customize what they see and how they see it. As associations increasingly realize that one size fits none, many are translating this philosophy into customized member services, including the Web site.

32. Give away free stuff. Hold a drawing or a random prize giveaway on your Web site regularly. The prize doesn't have to be extravagant; something as simple as a 5 percent discount on an education session, a T-shirt, or 30 minutes of one-on-one career counseling will do. Be careful with your e-mail marketing, though: *Free* is a dirty word that many spam filters block.

33. Include polls and other ways to collect feedback. Everyone's got an opinion, as the old adage goes. And most people like to share theirs. If you make polls and informal surveys a regular component of your Web content, people might visit just to see what the question of the week is.

34. ¿Hablas español? Sprechen Sie Deutsch? Offer your Web site content in different languages to meet the needs of your audience. If you're an international trade association, and 8 percent of your site visitors are native German speakers, why are you forcing them to read your content in English, *Dumbkopf?*

35. Include a section for students interested in the trade, profes-

sion, or cause you represent. As students prepare to become members of the workforce, they are hungry for information. Make your site the go-to place for them by providing background information and tips on how to break into the industry.

36. Offer information for industry newbies. Just as students are bewildered by the abundance (or lack thereof) of information on the industry, so, too, are those new to the profession eager for information. Include such items as industry-term glossaries to help them along.

37. Buy an ad (or three). While it's not a guaranteed way to increase Web traffic—and, hey, nothing is foolproof—it never hurts to advertise in trade publications and other media that your constituents might be monitoring.

38. Post to relevant newsgroups and mailing lists. Listservers and other similar media provide a golden opportunity to offer helpful information. Be sure to include your URL in your signature—and don't turn your post into a commercial. No one likes *suitcasers*—virtual or real.

39. Include a comprehensive staff directory. Few like to send an e-mail to a general address. At the very least, include the e-mail addresses of heads of departments. (Beware, though, that this could open you up to directory *harvest attacks,* a method spammers use to collect e-mail addresses from a particular domain.)

40. Develop a resourceful online newsroom. You obviously want to generate good media coverage, so don't annoy reporters by forcing them to call you for organizational history questions, background, or high-resolution photos of your CEO and other key figures.

41. Tag your tchotchkes. Put your Web address on all of the conference kitsch that goes into your attendees' bags at trade shows and other events. Otherwise, you could be wasting money on all those giveaway pens, pads, stress balls, and other toys.

42. Get a spine. Put your Web site address on the spine of all books, magazines, directories, and other bound volumes that your association produces. That way, when your members have them all lined up on the bookshelf, your Web address will be right there, too.

43. Stand on the shoulders of giants. Is your competition ramping up more business than you? To paraphrase the poet T.S. Eliot, amateurs borrow; professionals steal. What is your competition doing with its Web site, and how might you steal—um, apply—some of their concepts?

44. Get organized. Few things are more annoying to visitors than not being able to find what they're looking for. Provide a well-organized site map, so the person looking for information on your advocacy efforts doesn't have to dig through five layers of educational material to get there.

45. Be easily searchable. This goes hand in hand with the preceding example. Especially if your site is multilayered and complex, an intrasite search feature will win you some fans and repeat visitors.

46. Update them on updates. Whenever there is a significant update on your Web site (e.g., a new white paper or article of interest), send out an e-mail to let members know. This works especially well if you use an interest-inventory system and can send targeted updates.

47. Become the CNN of your industry. Stay on top of breaking industry news and be the first to let your members know what's going on. They'll reward you by coming back time and time again.

48. Feature regular member profiles. Any anthropologist will tell you: Just about everyone is a bit self-centered. The human-interest component will be sure to snag at least one visitor—and probably about everyone who knows him or her.

49. Provide tutorials. Your members might be aware of some of your great features but might not know how to use them. Provide step-by-step tutorials.

50. Be in demand. Yes, this is elementary, but if your products and services aren't what the market wants, forget Web traffic. And everything else. It's no accident that the last tip is the most important. Be good at what you do, try some of the tips above, and traffic will come to you. AM

Newton Holt is a contributing editor to ASSOCIATION MANAGEMENT. *E-mail: nholt@asaenet.org.*

Source: Courtesy of Newton Holt, *Association Management*, ASAE, September 2005, Pages 71–74.

Example of an Organization's Home Page with a Link to a Donation Page

Do your part to help the Hearts for Kids Program of Take Heart Association Project (THAP). Our mission is to provide life-saving surgery, support, resources and hope to families of underprivileged children in Kenya and East Africa suffering from heart defects and disease.

Latest News

Dr. Hani Hennein led the first U.S. medical mission team to assist THAP patients in Nairobi, Kenya... **More »**

THAP forms a key partnership with The Mater Hospital in Nairobi, Kenya to perform surgeries and medical treatments for THAP at a much reduced fee... **More »**

In 2006, THAP assisted a record-setting number of children with surgeries and medications... **More »**

A Message from our Chairman »

Meet Our Kids

Cyrus
Successfully operated on at Kenyatta National Hospital in Nairobi, Kenya, in December, 2005. Cyrus, recovered nicely from his surgery, is doing well at home and... **More »**

Mercy
Was one of the children Dr. Hennein and his medical team operated on in October, 2006 at The Mater Hospital... **More »**

Victor
Successfully operated on at Rainbow Babies & Children's Hospital in Cleveland, Ohio, in June, 2005. Victor is recovering nicely from his recent surgery and... **More »**

Faith - Success Story
Successfully operated on at 3 ½ years old at Schneider Children's Hospital in New Hyde Park, New York, in 2002. Faith is now recovered, doing well and playing as a healthy child should... **More »**

Home | Donate Now | About Us | Contact Us
Registered 501(c)(3) in the United States - Offices in Maryland and Kenya
Copyrights © Take Heart Association Project, Inc. All rights reserved.

Source: Courtesy of Take Heart Association Project, Inc. (THAP), Kensington, Maryland.

Example of a Short Article Placed in an E-Newsletter to Encourage Planned Gifts

Helpful Hints For Financial Planning

Do you have questions about estate planning? Planned giving? Your will? Each month, the ASCE Foundation features on its Web site http://www.asce.org/foundation new articles and interactive features that cover such topics.

New This Month . . .

1. Sharpen your pencil and prepare to concentrate. How much do you know about boosting investment income and cutting taxes? Take our new "Q & A" to find out.
2. Welcome to retirement, baby boomers! Retirement allows you to control your time and finances, and this requires careful planning. Discover new opportunities available to you in "Smart Ideas for Retirement Planning."
3. Charitable gifts are as diverse as the donors who make them . . . rate several benefits of philanthropy and discover which planned giving option is right for you in "Your Giving Goals."

Expand your mind. Visit the ASCE Foundation's Web site today!

Source: Courtesy of the American Society of Civil Engineers Foundation, Reston, Virginia.

Sample Case Statement Developed into a Fundraising Brochure

Source: Courtesy of Lisa Williams, Managing Partner—Cincinnati, Skystone Ryan Inc., fundraising consultants for Freestore Foodbank, Cincinnati, Ohio.

337

The Vision of One

In 1971, when Frank Gerson began rescuing useable furniture and household items from the Cincinnati dump, he surely had no concept of the enormous impact he would have on literally hundreds of thousands of lives over the next 35 years.

As he and a handful of dedicated volunteers delivered 428 scavenged items to needy families that year, they were setting the course for an operation that now serves some 160,000 low-income persons throughout twenty counties.

Today, the FreestoreFoodbank has become the region's primary provider of food, personal products and services to help people survive on the road to self-reliance.

As a charter member of America's Second Harvest and a pioneer in hunger management programs, the Freestore Foodbank has built a national reputation for innovative programming to meet the community's most urgent needs.

Now, recognizing the ever-increasing number of citizens struggling with poverty in the Cincinnati area and surrounding region, the FreestoreFoodbank must move to a higher level of proficiency and productivity. To this end, we are launching a capital and endowment campaign that will position the organization to serve the community's burgeoning needs today, and for decades to come.

Frank Gerson, FreestoreFoodbank founder (right, and an
unidentified volunteer), with his old green van in 1971.

first, We Must

Without adequate food, adults cannot work. Children cannot learn. Tragically, the growing number of children and adults living at and below the poverty line is taxing food-delivery systems and support programs in Cincinnati and throughout America. For more than **160,000 individuals** in Greater Cincinnati and the surrounding region who live in poverty, the FreestoreFoodbank and its network of nearly **450 nonprofit member agencies** serve as an irreplaceable safety net.

Hunger in America 2006 reported, "Clients seeking emergency food assistance from America's Second Harvest network are typically

"Nearly one in three Cincinnati children lives in poverty."
– 2004 American Community Survey of the U. S. Census Bureau

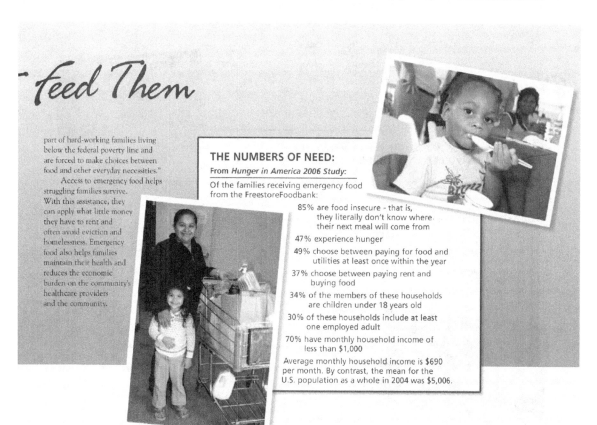

feed Them

part of hard-working families living below the federal poverty line and are forced to make choices between food and other everyday necessities."

Access to emergency food helps struggling families survive. With this assistance, they can apply what little money they have to rent and often avoid eviction and homelessness. Emergency food also helps families maintain their health and reduces the economic burden on the community's healthcare providers and the community.

THE NUMBERS OF NEED:

From *Hunger in America 2006 Study*:

Of the families receiving emergency food from the FreestoreFoodbank:

85% are food insecure - that is, they literally don't know where their next meal will come from

47% experience hunger

49% choose between paying for food and utilities at least once within the year

37% choose between paying rent and buying food

34% of the members of these households are children under 18 years old

30% of these households include at least one employed adult

70% have monthly household income of less than $1,000

Average monthly household income is $690 per month. By contrast, the mean for the U.S. population as a whole in 2004 was $5,006.

Casting Our Safety

The FreestoreFoodbank's Emergency Client Services Center is located on Liberty Street in the heart of Over-the-Rhine, one of Cincinnati's poorest, inner-city neighborhoods. Typically, more than 100 people per day visit the Center seeking some level of assistance. They are Cincinnati citizens in crisis – the homeless, the unemployed, the working poor, and families in turmoil.

Most seek emergency food, and most have nowhere else to turn. In addition to meeting the immediate need – food – the FreestoreFoodbank offers a full range of support services

"At my lowest point, I got thrown in jail and ended up in the hospital from an overdose. When I recovered and applied for housing, Cincinnati Metropolitan Housing Authority recommended I get into the Freestore Foodbank's Direct Rent program. This was the turning point. They taught me that if you're homeless, you can't do anything else. So, the first thing I pay every month is the rent. They made me see I could do something with my life."

– FreestoreFoodbank Direct Rent Program Client

Net

to help those in need begin to rebuild their lives.

Of the neighbors who seek assistance from the Client Services Center, **47% are children.** 33% of households receive food stamps, and less than 15% receive welfare assistance. The need is greatest near the end of the month, when small paychecks are nearly gone, and in the winter, when clients face high utility bills. Few people return to the Client Services Center month after month; **most visit only a few times,** when they have exhausted other options.

FreestoreFoodbank's Liberty Street clients have access to a wide variety of essential services, not just emergency food

- The Food Room – access to emergency food and essential personal care items to sustain them through the immediate crisis or until the next payday

- Food Stamp Outreach Program – connects qualified clients with Food Stamp resources

- Emergency Rent Assistance – connects qualified clients to rent subsidies through the Housing Services Department

- Direct Rent/Utilities Program – helps the working poor budget their limited resources to help keep them stable in the short and long term

- Protective Payee Program – manages the bill-paying process for those who are unable to manage their personal affairs due to mental illness or other disabling circumstances

- Transportation Assistance – bus tokens for those who must travel for doctors' appointments, job interviews, and other essential purposes

- Holiday Food Basket Distribution – distributes over 12,000 holiday meals to families in need

- Homeless Outreach Program – intervention directly with the chronically homeless, helping them navigate the maze of social security benefits and housing application requirements

There Are

At the Mayerson Food Distribution Center in Bond Hill, the Freestore Foodbank receives 10 million pounds annually of donated food and grocery products from 150 corporate donors and hundreds of community food drives. After checking and sorting the food, it is made available to a network of **450 nonprofit member agencies** across 20 counties.

These agencies operate food pantries, shelters, soup kitchens, childcare/eldercare centers, community centers, and residential programs, where food from the FreestoreFoodbank is distributed free of charge to those in need.

"My wife and I stopped at the church one frigid evening, and a young man walked in and asked us for a place to stay. He was homeless after a recent layoff. His brief stay with friends had burdened their low-income household, so he was asked to leave. He said all he had to eat that day was one banana. We gave the man some food from the FreestoreFoodbank. We also got him enough gas to drive to his grandmother's house several counties away."

– From a church pastor in Butler, Kentucky

Hungry People Everywhere

Although hunger and poverty may be more visible in the inner city, statistics show that need is just as great in rural, and even some suburban, areas. Throughout southern Ohio, northern Kentucky and southeastern Indiana, hungry people have access to friendly, local centers equipped to provide emergency assistance, thanks to the support those centers receive from the FreestoreFoodbank.

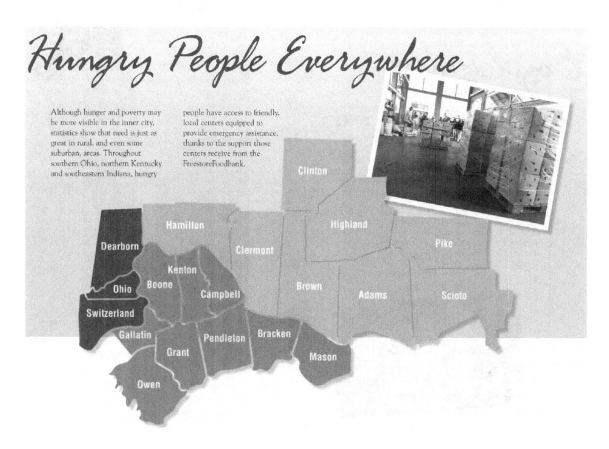

A Step Up to

Cincinnati COOKS!

Cincinnati COOKS! is a free ten-week training program for adults who have serious barriers to employment. Cincinnati COOKS! helps at-risk adults step up and out of poverty by teaching them food-service and life skills. With a new class graduating every five weeks, Cincinnati COOKS! has produced more than 300 graduates since its inception in 2001.

"*Cincinnati COOKS! was an opportunity to do something worthwhile. They had high expectations and gave us serious, realistic training to prepare us for real jobs.*" – a Cincinnati COOKS! graduate, now employed in the kitchen of a women's chemical addiction shelter.

Employment

MEALS FOR HUNGRY KIDS

As a part of their training, Cincinnati COOKS! students learn to prepare balanced, nutritious meals and healthy snacks. Then the meals are served at Kids Cafe sites in low-income neighborhoods where crime rates are high. Volunteers at Kids Cafes provide children with a safe haven for after-school activities.

The Kids Cafe program began locally in 1996 after a nine-year-old girl stole a can of ravioli from the food pantry at Newport Church of God. The site coordinator will never forget: "*After she found the quart-size can of ravioli in the pantry, she took a huge butcher knife from the drawer and used it to punch a hole in the can. We found her in the corner of the Sunday School room, using a plastic fork to dig the ravioli out of the jagged hole in the can. I have kept the knife and the can as a constant reminder of what real hunger looks like.*"

Today **nine Kids Cafes** are operated in Cincinnati, Covington and Newport, and several more are in the planning stages. The program has dished up some 40,000 meals in 2006, a 60% increase over the 25,000 served in 2002.

BUILDING ON OUR STRENGTHS

The FreestoreFoodbank has become one of Cincinnati's most beloved social service organizations. Its unflinching commitment to consistently delivering excellent programs to those in greatest need has situated the revered food bank firmly in the hearts of Cincinnati citizens. The ongoing support of the community for the Freestore Foodbank is unparalleled by any other local organization, with more than 16,000 donors giving to the agency every year.

As we look to the future of the FreestoreFoodbank, the Board of Trustees and administration recognize the importance of developing robust external sources of funding not only to maintain current operations, but also to **expand capacity to meet the ever-growing need**. A multi-year capital/endowment campaign with a goal of $12 million will enable the FreestoreFoodbank to define a new era in social service delivery for families in greater Cincinnati and throughout the region.

Renewing Hope
CAMPAIGN OBJECTIVE

Comprehensive Improvements to Client Services Center on Liberty Street in Over-the-Rhine	$6 million
Improvements to Mayerson Food Distribution Center on Tennessee Avenue	$3.5 million
Endowment	$2.5 million
CAMPAIGN GOAL	**$12 million**

The FreestoreFoodbank operates efficiently and effectively:

94% of annual operating expenses go to programs that feed hungry people and supply area hunger agencies. Only 6% goes to administrative and fundraising costs.

Every $1 received in gifts can provide enough food for 4 meals.

Through its network of 450 agencies in 20 counties, approximately 28,600 people receive food assistance in a given week.

CLIENT SERVICES CENTER ON LIBERTY STREET
IN OVER-THE-RHINE

The largest emergency services provider in Cincinnati, Freestore Foodbank's Emergency Client Services Center serves some 30,000 individuals annually from a conglomeration of 100-year-old buildings in Over-the-Rhine.

The Center's role is essential; however, facilities in disrepair seriously restrict current operations. Human need has always superseded structural improvement, but the **deteriorating, antiquated facilities can no longer be ignored**. Hope is an essential ingredient in our mix of services, and we are committed to delivering that – along with the respect our clients deserve – at every turn.

Over the years, we have channeled every available dollar to our hungry neighbors, but now our aging facilities can no longer be ignored.

– $6 MILLION

To that end, the following challenges illustrate the facility's current inadequacy:

- Waiting rooms are cramped and do not accommodate the client population.
- Counseling areas lack privacy.
- Damaged, cracking walls and floors dampen the spirits of the staff and the clients.
- Dank, deteriorating conditions pose safety and sanitation risks.
- Leaks are so severe that staff members must leave their offices in heavy rains, thus hampering productivity.
- Gloomy, musty surroundings exacerbate feelings of despair.

Despite the limitations of the current facility, however, Liberty Street is the right place for the Emergency Client Services Center to be located, demographically and socioeconomically. With this in mind, following extensive study and analysis, the Board of Trustees has determined that the most cost-effective course of action is to renovate and refurbish the current structure.

ROSENTHAL COMMUNITY KITCHEN

The Rosenthal Community Kitchen, currently housed in a leased facility, hosts the acclaimed Cincinnati COOKS! Program, which prepares and delivers hot meals to Kids Cafe locations throughout Cincinnati and the surrounding region.

Through this campaign, we will increase operating efficiencies by relocating the Rosenthal Community Kitchen. By relinquishing the current leased space, we will no longer be vulnerable to losing the location to the priorities of others, and from a financial perspective, our resources will be better and more responsibly spent in upgrading our own facility.

We are not winning the war on hunger...

The number of clients served at the Liberty Street facility has more than doubled in the past three years, from 1,000 per month in 2002 to 2,225 per month in 2005.

MAYERSON FOOD DISTRIBUTION CENTER
ON TENNESSEE AVENUE –

The FreestoreFoodbank distributes 10 million pounds of food and products annually to 450 nonprofit agencies through the Mayerson Food Distribution Center in Bond Hill. Our long-range plan anticipates an increase to 16 million pounds in five years. Through partnerships with a wide range of nonprofits, including the Salvation Army, the Urban League, and churches of every denomination we are able to leverage our operation to improve the lives of thousands more than we ever could through one facility.

Further, **the needs outside the immediate Cincinnati metropolitan area are growing at an alarming rate**, and options are few for those struggling to survive in the rural areas. We all feel the impact of hunger and its fraying of our social fabric – whether the family is cross-town or across the state.

To accommodate the exploding need, the Center requires upgraded equipment and reconfigured warehousing to maximize capacity and efficiency, as well as expanded cold storage to preserve donated perishable items.

Current warehouse storage and administrative facilities for the entire operation are sorely inadequate. To maintain current service levels and

satisfy increasing demand, we must complete the following as soon as possible:

- Double the amount of warehouse storage through racking
- Increase storage and display space for produce and fresh food
- Create a volunteer space with a meeting/work room and lockers – particularly for those many volunteers needed to help sort the shipments of donated food to prepare for efficient distribution
- Replace 5 aging trucks and 2 forklifts
- Replace roof
- Update administrative offices, including infrastructure priorities such as an inadequate phone system, computer hardware and software, and basic furnishings.

A sophisticated distribution network can get food that would otherwise be wasted into the hands of hungry people throughout our region.

$3.5 MILLION

THE TRAINING CENTER

The Nonprofit Training Program allows the FreestoreFoodbank to empower its member agencies to address hunger in their own communities efficiently and effectively. Representatives from 125 nonprofits each year attend classes and workshops on a variety of nonprofit and hunger-related issues, from food handling to fundraising.

Currently we must hold these trainings off-site. The renovation of the Mayerson Food Distribution Center will include the addition of a spacious, central classroom to help facilitate expanded training options and volunteer meetings.

ENDOWMENT $2.5 MILLION

The long-term stability of any non-profit is enhanced by a healthy endowment. Through this campaign, the FreestoreFoodbank will seek $2.5 million to ensure operating resources well into the future, and enable the organization to serve the hungry in greater Cincinnati throughout this century and beyond.

Renewing Hope

Though the FreestoreFoodbank cherishes its cadre of dedicated donors and stakeholders, we also understand that reaching our goal of $12 million over a multi-year campaign will require the mobilization of a broad constituency of concerned, enlightened philanthropists. A campaign of this magnitude requires many substantial gifts, as this chart indicates:

SCALE OF GIFTS REQUIRED TO RAISE $12,000,000		
1	1,500,000	1,500,000
1	1,000,000	1,000,000
3	500,000	1,500,000
5	200,000	1,000,000
8	100,000	800,000
18	LEADERSHIP GIFTS TOTALLING	$5,800,000
14	75,000	1,050,000
36	50,000	1,800,000
50	PACESETTER GIFTS TOTALLING	$2,850,000
40	25,000	1,000,000
60	10,000	600,000
100	5,000	500,000
200	MAJOR GIFTS TOTALLING	$2,100,000
200	2,500	500,000
2,500	1,000 or below	750,000
2,700	COMMUNITY GIFTS TOTALLING	$1,250,000
	TOTAL	$12,000,000

Since Frank Gerson's first efforts to reach out to our poorest citizens, the FreestoreFoodbank has, with the help of thousands of generous friends, addressed hunger and poverty in Greater Cincinnati and beyond. Sadly, **the need is greater today than ever before**. No longer can we turn our heads or take a different path to avoid confronting the reality of need in our city and our region. In order to serve our neighbors today and be prepared to face the unknown needs our community will face in the years to come, the FreestoreFoodbank must act now to develop facilities commensurate with the magnitude of our mission. **Join us in the fight to Renew Hope!**

MISSION
We provide food and services, create stability and further self-reliance for people in crisis.

1250 Tennessee Ave., Cincinnati, Ohio 45229   •   513-482-4500   •   www.freestorefoodbank.org

Sample Question and Answer Brochure for a Capital Campaign

Source: Courtesy of the American Society of Civil Engineers Foundation, Reston, Virginia.

2002: Building The Future

What is the purpose of the Campaign?
The purpose of *2002: Building The Future* is two-fold.
1) To fund national and community public awareness programs in conjunction with ASCE's 150th anniversary in 2002; and 2) To create an Innovation Fund for ASCE's research affiliate, the Civil Engineering Research Foundation (CERF).

Why support ASCE's 150th anniversary programs?
The 150th anniversary programs are designed to promote and extend the legacy that is our Society, its members, and the profession. Not only will ASCE recognize its own rich heritage, but it will work especially to elevate the public's understanding and appreciation of the entire profession's contributions to the world we know today.

Why create an Innovation Fund for CERF?
It is necessary to ensure that CERF continues to provide leadership, direction, and an organizational structure to expedite the movement of innovation into practice for the civil engineering, construction, and environmental community worldwide.

What is the goal of the Campaign?
The Campaign has a minimum goal of $5 million.

What is the ASCE Foundation?
The ASCE Foundation was established in 1994. Its mission is to generate resources for the civil engineering profession.

Does the Campaign accept pledges?
Yes. Pledges may be paid over a four year period, and payments may be scheduled according to the wishes of the donor.

May a gift or pledge be split between the two Campaign programs?
Yes. At the discretion of the donor, a gift or pledge may be directed to either or both campaign programs. These gifts may be divided using increments of 5%, i.e., 75%-25%, 35%-65%, 60%-40%, 45%-55%, etc.

ASCE Foundation

Will the Campaign accept gifts other than cash?
Yes. Gifts of appreciated securities can be transferred immediately to the Foundation. Other gifts such as real estate, artwork, jewelry, etc., must first be discussed.

How will my gift be recognized by the Campaign?
All gifts of $1,500 or greater will be recognized on a donor wall established at ASCE's World Headquarters in Reston, VA.

Are there different gift recognition levels established by the Campaign?
Yes. The gift recognition levels are as follows:

Titanium	$500,000 and greater
Platinum	$250,000 - 499,999
Gold	$100,000 - 249,999
Silver	$50,000 - 99,999
Copper	$25,000 - 49,999
Bronze	$10,000 - 24,999
Brass	$5,000 - 9,999
Pewter	$1,500 - 4,999

Are gifts to the Campaign tax-deductible?
All gifts are tax-deductible to the fullest extent of the law in the United States as the ASCE Foundation is a 501(c)(3) charitable organization under IRS Code.

How long will the Campaign last?
The Campaign is expected to culminate at the November 2002 ASCE Civil Engineering Conference & Exposition in Washington, D.C. which will mark ASCE's 150th anniversary.

How should gifts be made?
Gifts and pledges should be made payable to the ASCE Foundation and be sent to:
ASCE Foundation
Sixth Floor
1015 15th Street, NW
Washington, DC 20005-2605

If I have any questions about making my gift?
Contact the ASCE Foundation at:
Phone: 202-789-2874
Fax: 202-682-3471
E-mail: ASCEFoundation@asce.org

2002: Building The Future

Gift/Pledge Confirmation Form

My gift to *2002: Building The Future* is:

☐ $1,000,000 ☐ $500,000 ☐ $250,000 ☐ $100,000

☐ $50,000 ☐ $25,000 ☐ $10,000 ☐ $5,000

☐ $1,500 ☐ Other $ _____

My gift will be paid according to the following:

☐ **CASH** Check is enclosed

☐ **STOCK** The Foundation will provide instructions for you regarding transference of stocks/securities.

☐ **PLEDGE** (Check one)

To be paid over ☐ 1 ☐ 2 ☐ 3 ☐ 4 years

With payments to be made at the rate of: $ _____

per: ☐ year ☐ quarter ☐ month beginning in _____, 200__
(month) (year)

☐ **CREDIT CARD** ☐ Visa ☐ MasterCard
☐ Discover ☐ American Express

Account number: _____

Expiration date: _____

Signature: _____

Date: _____

Name: _____

Corporation: _____
(if applicable)

Title: _____
(if applicable)

Address: _____

City/State/Zip: _____

Phone: _____ Fax: _____

E-mail: _____

Please complete reverse side

Gift/Pledge Confirmation Form

☐ This is for a corporate gift. I am authorized to commit to this multi-year pledge.

☐ My corporation/employer has a matching gift program. I will request the appropriate forms, sign them, and send them to the ASCE Foundation office.

This gift should be: ☐ Anonymous ☐ Recognized
If you would like this gift to be recognized, **please print** below the name(s) (personal, foundation, or corporate) you wish to use for donor recognition:

_____

Please check one of the following three boxes:

☐ Use this gift to support the ASCE Foundation's *2002: Building The Future* campaign which encompasses **both** the Civil Engineering Research Foundation's *Innovation Fund* and the American Society of Civil Engineers' *150th Anniversary*. Please divide my gift **equally**.

☐ 100% of this gift should be directed in support of **one program only**: (Check one)

☐ CERF's Innovation Fund ☐ ASCE's 150th Anniversary

☐ This gift is to support both programs, but **not equally**. I wish to divide this gift between *CERF's Innovation Fund* and *ASCE's 150th Anniversary* as follows. (Please use increments of 5%, i.e., 75%-25%, 35%-65%, 60%-40%, 45%-55%, etc.)

_____% to CERF's Innovation Fund _____% to ASCE's 150th Anniversary

Signature: _____

Date: _____

The American Society of Civil Engineers Foundation, Inc. is a 501(c)(3) non-profit organization under the regulations of the Internal Revenue Service. All contributions to the Foundation are tax-deductible to the fullest extent allowable by law.

Mail to:
ASCE Foundation
Sixth Floor
1015 15th Street, NW
Washington, DC 20005-2605

Phone: **202-789-2874**
Fax: **202-682-3471**
E-mail: ASCEFoundation@asce.org

Sample of a Foundation Annual Report in Print Format

ΓΦΒ
Gamma Phi Beta Foundation
Annual Report
August 1, 2005 to July 31, 2006

Source: Courtesy of the Gamma Phi Beta Foundation, Centennial, Colorado.

The Gift of Sisterhood
... making a difference

Total Assets 2002-2006

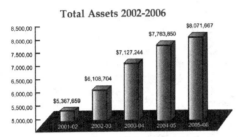

Revenue 2005-2006

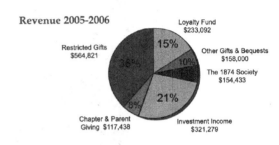

Grants & Expenses 2005-2006

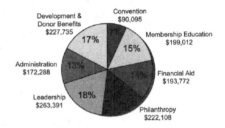

Statement of Net Assets and Changes in Net Assets

	Net Assets as of July 31,	
	2006	2005
Assets:		
Cash and Investments at Market	$7,481,185	$7,190,875
Contributions Receivable	170,807	180,461
Property and Equipment	271,521	292,923
Other Assets	148,154	99,590
Total Assets	$8,071,667	$7,763,849
Liabilities:		
Accounts Payable	$196,426	$67,285
Liability Under Split Interest Agreement	38,393	40,376
Total Liabilities	$234,819	$107,661
Net Assets:		
Permanently Restricted	$4,911,178	$4,576,670
Temporarily Restricted	929,718	884,515
Unrestricted - Board Designated	1,951,660	2,026,831
Unrestricted - Undesignated	44,292	168,172
Total Net Assets	7,836,848	7,656,188
Total Liabilities and Net Assets	$8,071,667	$7,763,849

	Changes in Net Assets For the Year Ended July 31,	
	2006	2005
Support and Revenues:		
Contributions and Support	$1,227,782	$1,206,692
Net Investment (Loss) Income	321,279	736,761
Total Support and Revenue	$1,549,061	$1,943,453
Expenses:		
Program Services	$968,378	$851,709
Supporting	400,023	456,688
Total Expenses	1,368,401	1,308,397
Change in Net Assets	$180,660	$635,056

Looking back over the past ten years, the Gamma Phi Beta Foundation has provided $1,941,130 to support the Sorority's leadership and educational programs, awarded $1,396,301 in financial aid to Gamma Phi undergraduate and graduate students and has granted $985,180 to send young girls to camps across the continent. Gamma Phi Beta has helped to change the lives of young girls, maturing students and thousands of loyal members.

GAMMA PHI BETA *foundation*

The Gift of Sisterhood

Our Vision

The Foundation's vision is to establish philanthropy as an integral part of Gamma Phi Beta membership.

• •

Our Mission:

As an educational funding partner to Gamma Phi Beta Sorority, the Gamma Phi Beta Foundation provides resources for the Sorority's leadership programs, international philanthropy and financial aid to members.

As a Foundation, we:

• Educate Sorority members about our purposes, goals and services.

• Provide support for the Sorority's leadership and educational programs

• Develop heightened philanthropic commitment among Sorority members

• Generate financial aid for members' educational and emergency needs

• Conduct business with the highest ethical and fiscal standards

• •

Board of Trustees and Staff

Foundation Chair
L'Cena Brunskill Rice
(Southern California)
Redondo Beach, CA

International Council Representatives
Linda Daniel Johnson (Vanderbilt)
Houston, TX

Linda Lyons Malony
(Southern California)
Fayetteville, AR

Development Committee Chair
Paula Janis Dean (Memphis)
New York, NY

Finance and Investment Chair
Ginny Harris Hammond
(Colorado-Boulder)
Denver, CO

Grants Committee Chair
Ruth Andrea Seeler, M.D. (Vermont)
Chicago, IL

Governance Committee Chair
Verona Dilbeck Lynam
(Oklahoma City)
Longview, WA

Public Relations and Marketing Chair
Magnes Welsh (Memphis)
Chicago, IL

Foundation Trustees
Mary Ellen Porter Burchfield
(Iowa State) Naperville, IL

Karen Wander Kline (Iowa State)
Houston, TX

Anne Layton (McGill)
Toronto, ON

Cinda Keating Lucas
(Southern California)
Del Mar, CA

Marjory Mills Shupert
(Colorado State)
Sierra Vista, AZ

Barbara Hurt-Simmons
(Nebraska-Kearney)
Chester Springs, PA

Mary Vanier (Kansas State)
Manhattan, KS

Lynn Towsley White
(Colorado-Boulder)
McLean, VA

Sorority Executive Director
Patricia Crowley (Northwestern)
Denver, CO

FOUNDATION STAFF
Executive Director
Bonnie Payne (Denver)
Director of Distinguished Giving
Amy Spikes (Kansas)
Director of Administration
Darla Dakin (Arizona State)
Controller/Administrative Coordinator
Sherry Ochoa-Rounkles (Denver)
Grants Manager/Data Specialist
Ryan Severts
Gamma Phi Beta Museum Curator
Sherry Ochoa-Rounkles (Denver)

Example of an Article Placed in a Newsletter to Announce Endowment Giving

SPA PHILANTHROPY

With the Amos Perlmutter Memorial Lecture and Annual Prize the School of Public Affairs is honoring the memory of one of it most dynamic scholars. In addition to being an expert in comparative politics and foreign affairs, **Amos Perlmutter** published 15 books, was a member of the Israeli Defense Forces, an adviser to the Greek government, a member of the Israeli Atomic Energy Commission, and a columnist for *The Washington Times*. "My husband took an active role in the world," is the modest assessment of his widow, Sharon Perlmutter.

Mrs. Perlmutter was thrilled when she first learned that the School of Public Affairs faculty and staff wanted to honor her late husband, a faculty member from 1972 to 2001, with an endowment.

"Personally, it means a lot to me and is a very suitable way to remember my husband. He gave a lot to the University when he was alive; his work brought prestige to the School. It is important to remember people who have given so much to the education of students and to honor their life's work."

The Perlmutter Endowment will fund an annual award and a memorial lecture. This year the $500 award prize was given to Christine Godowsky, a graduating senior in the School of Public Affairs who excelled in comparative politics. The first Amos Perlmutter Memorial Lecture will be held in 2006.

Two other new endowments were also inspired by outstanding faculty. The Zauderer Key Executive Scholarship Endowment was established in honor of former Professor **Donald G. Zauderer**. The fund will provide scholarships to students participating in the Key Executive Masters

Amos Perlmutter

in Public Administration program, the leading graduate program for government executives.

The **Morley Segal** and **Edith Whitfield Seashore** Fellowship Fund honors the two faculty founders of the AU/NTL master's program for organizational development practitioners. At the time the program was created in 1980, Professor Segal was on the public administration faculty at SPA and Edith Seashore was the president of NTL (National Training Laboratories) Institute for Applied Behavioral Science.

Both the Zauderer Key Executive and the Segal/Seashore endowments will fund an estimated $2,500 in scholarships for the respective programs each year.

> For more information on making a planned or an endowment gift, please contact SPA development director Jenine Rabin at rabin@american.edu or (202) 885-3698

Source: Courtesy of American University, School of Public Affairs, Washington, DC.

Sample Pledge Forms

A. Sample Capital Campaign Pledge Form

ASCE FOUNDATION

American Society
of Civil Engineers
Foundation

2002: Building The Future

Gift/Pledge Form

My gift to **2002: Building The Future** is:

☐ $1,000,000 ☐ $500,000 ☐ $250,000 ☐ $100,000 ☐ $50,000

☐ $25,000 ☐ $10,000 ☐ $5,000 ☐ $1,500 ☐ Other $ _____

My gift will be paid according to the following:

☐ **CASH** Check is enclosed   ☐ **STOCK**

☐ **PLEDGE** (Check one)   ☐ **CREDIT CARD** ☐ Visa   ☐ MasterCard
                                                                     ☐ Discover ☐ American
To be paid over ☐ 1 ☐ 2 ☐ 3 ☐ 4 years   Express
With payments to be made at the rate of: Account #: _____

$ _____ per ☐ year ☐ quarter ☐ month   Expiration date: _____
                                                   Signature: _____
beginning in _____, 200 _____   Date: _____
              (month)   (year)

Name (individual or corporate): _____

Corporation (if applicable): _____

Title (if applicable): _____

Address: _____

City/State/Zip: _____

Phone: _____   Fax: _____

E-mail: _____

☐ This is for a corporate gift. I am authorized to commit to this multi-year pledge.

☐ My corporation/employer has a matching gift program. I will request the appropriate forms, sign them, and
   send them to the ASCE Foundation office.

This gift should be: ☐ Anonymous ☐ Recognized
If you would like this gift to be recognized, please print below the name(s) (personal, foundation, or corporate) you
wish to use for donor recognition:

_____

GIFT RECOGNITION LEVELS

Titanium	$500,000 & greater
Platinum	$250,000 - 499,999
Gold	$100,000 - 249,999
Silver	$50,000 - 99,999
Copper	$25,000 - 49,999
Bronze	$10,000 - 24,999
Brass	$5,000 - 9,999
Pewter	$1,500 - 4,999

Please check one of the following three boxes:

☐ Use this gift to support the ASCE Foundation's **2002: Building The Future** campaign which encompasses
   both the Civil Engineering Research Foundation's *Innovation Fund* and the American Society of Civil Engineers'
   150th Anniversary. Please divide my gift **equally.**

☐ 100% of this gift should be directed in support of **one program only:** (Check one)
            ☐ CERF's Innovation Fund   ☐ ASCE's 150th Anniversary

☐ This gift is to support both programs, but **not equally.** I wish to divide this gift between *CERF's Innovation Fund*
   and *ASCE's 150th Anniversary* as follows. (Please use increments of 5%, i.e., 75%-25%, 35%-65%, 60%-40%,
   20%-80%, etc.)
            _____ % CERF's Innovation Fund   _____ % ASCE's 150th Anniversary

Signature: _____   Date: _____

Print name: _____

The American Society of Civil Engineers
Foundation, Inc. is a 501(c)(3) non-profit
organization under the regulations of the U.S.
Internal Revenue Service. All contributions
to the Foundation are tax-deductible to the
fullest extent allowable by law.

If applicable, make   Mail to: Phone: **202-789-2874**
checks out to: **ASCE Foundation**
American Society   **Sixth Floor**   Fax: **202-682-3471**
of Civil Engineers   **1015 15th Street, NW**   E-mail:
Foundation   **Washington, DC 20005-2605** ASCEFoundation@asce.org

---

Source: Courtesy of the American Society of Civil Engineers Foundation, Reston, Virginia.

B. Sample Annual Appeal Pledge Form

AFP
Foundation for Philanthropy

www.afpnet.org

Name _____   AFP ID _____

Title _____

Organization _____

Address _____

City _____   State _____   ZIP _____

Business Phone _____   Business Fax _____

Home Phone _____   E-mail _____

Chapter to be credited _____

I would like to support AFP Foundation for Philanthropy's Every Member Campaign with a

☐ Gift of $ _____

    ☐ Through my check made payable to AFP Foundation for Philanthropy

    ☐ Through my credit card (VISA, MasterCard, Discover, or American Express)

    Card number _____   Expiration Date _____

    Signature (required) _____   Date _____

☐ Pledge of $ _____   to be paid in _____   payments of $ _____

    Please charge my payments directly to my credit card

    (VISA, MasterCard, Discover, or American Express) according to my payment schedule:

    Payment 1—$ _____   Date _____

    Payment 2—$ _____   Date _____

    Payment 3—$ _____   Date _____

    Payment 4—$ _____   Date _____

    Card number _____   Expiration Date _____

    Signature (required) _____   Date _____

    Please send me reminders during the months checked below.

☐ January	☐ February	☐ March	☐ April	☐ May	☐ June
☐ July	☐ August	☐ September	☐ October	☐ November	☐ December

☐ Continuing Alpha Society monthly gift of $ _____ (minimum of $10). Please sign below.

    ☐ Through my check made payable to AFP Foundation for Philanthropy

    ☐ Through my credit card (VISA, MasterCard, Discover, or American Express)

    Card number _____   Expiration Date _____

    Signature (required) _____   Date _____

    (Should you choose to discontinue your monthly gift and Alpha Society membership, please contact us at 800.666.3863 x410 or in writing to 4300 Wilson Boulevard, Suite 300, Arlington, VA 22203-4168.)

☐ I would like more information on AFP Foundation for Philanthropy's Omega Circle, the planned giving progam.

Thank you for supporting AFP Foundation for Philanthropy. Gifts to the Foundation are tax-deductible to the fullest extent of the law, as no goods or services are provided in consideration of a gift.

Please send your completed pledge form to AFP Foundation for Philanthropy, 4300 Wilson Boulevard, Suite 300, Arlington, VA 22203-4168 or fax it to 703-683-0735. If you'd like to make a gift of securities, or have any questions, please contact us at 800-666-3863 x446.

AFP Foundation for Philanthropy – 2008 Every Member Campaign Pledge Form

Source: Courtesy of Curtis C. Deane, AFP Foundation for Philanthropy, Arlington, Virginia.

Sample Reply Cards

A. Sample of an invitation with a reply card offering opportunity to purchase tickets electronically

Source: Courtesy of the Institute for Policy Studies, Washington, DC.

INSTITUTE FOR POLICY STUDIES

Twenty-Fourth Annual Letelier-Moffitt Human Rights Awards Program

October 16, 2000 • 5:30 pm Reception • 7:00 pm Event • Dinner to follow

▪ I gladly accept the invitation to join IPS, the awardees and special guests at this year's Letelier-Moffitt Memorial Human Rights Awards.

Purchase your tickets on-line today today at http://www.ips-dc.org
or complete the following:

I would like to reserve the following number of tickets _____

▪ **Benefactor** ($2000)
awards ceremony and dinner

▪ **Sponsor** ($500)
awards ceremony and dinner

▪ **Patron** ($1500)
awards ceremony and dinner

▪ **Guest** ($150)
awards ceremony and dinner

▪ **Donor** ($1000)
awards ceremony and dinner

▪ **General** Admission ($35)
awards ceremony only

▪ I/We will not be able to attend, but enclosed is a contribution of $ _____

▪ I am paying by **personal check** made payable to **Institute For Policy Studies**

▪ Please **charge** my ▪ MasterCard   ▪ Visa   ▪ Amex $ _____

Name as it appears on the card: _____

Card Number: _____

Telephone: (Work) _____ (Home) _____

Mailing Address: _____

City/State/Zip: _____

E-mail*: _____

Please print the names of those attending:

_____   _____

_____   _____

_____   _____

For more information on the Letelier-Moffitt event, please call:
Institute for Policy Studies (202) 234-9382 x234

*An e-mail or postcard confirmation will be sent to all RSVP's made before October 6, 2000

RESERVE QUICKLY - TICKETS ARE GOING FAST

B. Sample annual appeal reply card with gift levels to be used with a separate response envelope

ASCE Foundation 2007 Annual Appeal

My gift to support the activities of the
ASCE Foundation is:

☐ $10,000 ☐ $5,000 ☐ $2,500
☐ $1,000 ☐ $500 ☐ $250
☐ $150 ☐ $100 ☐ $75
☐ $50 ☐ Other $_____
☐ Stock Stock name: _____

Number of shares: _____

Please call Jeanne Jacob at 703-295-6346
to learn how to directly transfer stock to
the ASCE Foundation.

Name: _____

Address: _____

City: _____ State: _____ ZIP: _____

Phone: _____ Fax: _____

E-Mail: _____

Please charge my gift to: ☐ Visa ☐ Master Card ☐ Discover ☐ American Express

Account Number: _____ Card Expiration Date: _____

Signature: _____ Date: _____

Make checks payable to: ASCE Foundation

☐ I would like to make a **monthly gift** by credit card to the 2007 Annual Appeal. Please indicate amount to be charged and
automatically deducted each month: $ _____

Please read the reverse side before answering the questions below:

☐ I wish my name to appear in *ASCE Foundation News* and on the Foundation website as follows: _____

☐ I am pleased to make a gift to support the Foundation, but I do not wish to receive the *ASCE Bridges Wall Calendar*.

☐ I prefer to remain anonymous. I do not wish my name listed either in *ASCE Foundation News* or on the website.

ASCE Foundation 2007 Annual Appeal Recognition Categories

	Founder's Circle:	$10,000 or more	
Chairman's Circle:	$5,000 to $9,999	**President's Circle:**	$2,500 to $4,999
Visionary:	$1,000 to $2,499	**Philanthropist:**	$500 to $999
Leader:	$250 to $499	**Patron:**	$150 to $249
Friend:	$75 to $149	**Donor:**	less than $75

For a gift of $250 or greater, you will receive the *ASCE Bridges Wall Calendar*.
All donors will be recognized in the *ASCE Foundation News* and on the Foundation's website
unless requesting to be anonymous.

All contributions are tax-deductible to the fullest extent allowable by law.

ASCE Foundation ■ Third Floor ■ 1801 Alexander Bell Drive ■ Reston, VA 20191-4400 ■ 703-295-6342 ■ ASCEFoundation@asce.org
www.asce.org/foundation

AFFIX
FIRST-CLASS
STAMP

ANNUAL APPEAL
AMERICAN SOCIETY OF CIVIL ENGINEERS FOUNDATION
THIRD FLOOR
1801 ALEXANDER BELL DRIVE
RESTON, VA 20191-9743

Source: Courtesy of the American Society of Civil Engineers Foundation, Reston, Virginia.

C. **Sample reply card that is a self mailer and includes an option to monthly debit a bank account or credit card for payment**

Giving Societies

Annual giving societies recognize unrestricted gifts totaling $250 or more.

Founders Society

$1,000+	Gold Leader
$500+	Silver Member
$250+	Bronze Member

1874 Society

$10,000+	Diamond Member
$5,000+	Sapphire Member
$2,500+	Pearl Member
$1,874+	1874 Member

Giving Society Benefits

	$10,000	$5,000	$2,500	$1,874	$1,000	$500	$250
Charm	•	•	•	•	•	•	•
Newsletter	•	•	•	•	•	•	•
Society Member Reception	•	•	•	•	•	•	•
Special Donor Listing	•	•	•	•	•	•	•
Convention Event	•	•	•	•	•	•	•
Brick (upon request)	•	•	•	•	•	•	•
1874 Pin					•		
Pearl Pin			•				
Sapphire Pin		•					
Diamond Pin	•						

Yes, I want to make a gift to the Gamma Phi Beta Foundation
to ensure that future generations can benefit from all that our Sorority offers.

❏ $10,000   ❏ $1,874   ❏ $500   ❏ $250   ❏ $100   ❏ Other $ _____   FTH-S07

Name _____ Email _____

Home Address _____ City _____ State _____ Zip _____

Chapter _____ Home Phone # (optional) _____

Payment Type: ❏ Check ❏ Visa/Mastercard ❏ AMEX   Acct# _____   Exp. Date ___/___   Security Code _____

❏ Charge $ _____ to my bank account monthly, on the **30th** of the month.
   (Please enclose one of your blank checks, marked "VOID")

❏ Charge $ _____ to my Visa, Mastercard, or AMEX monthly on the **30th**.
   (Please fill in account # and exp. date above)

Signature: _____

Please make your check payable to: ΓΦΒ Foundation. Your contribution is tax deductible to the extent allowed by law. Send Comments to: foundation@gammaphibeta.org

❏ I have remembered the ΓΦΒ Foundation in my will/estate planning

❏ Please send me information on how I can remember the ΓΦΒ Foundation in my will/estate planning

---

Place
Stamp
Here

GAMMA PHI BETA *foundation*
12737 East Euclid Drive
Centennial, CO 80111

Source: Courtesy of Gamma Phi Beta Foundation, Centennial, Colorado.

D. Invitation reply card listing sponsorship levels and requesting guest names

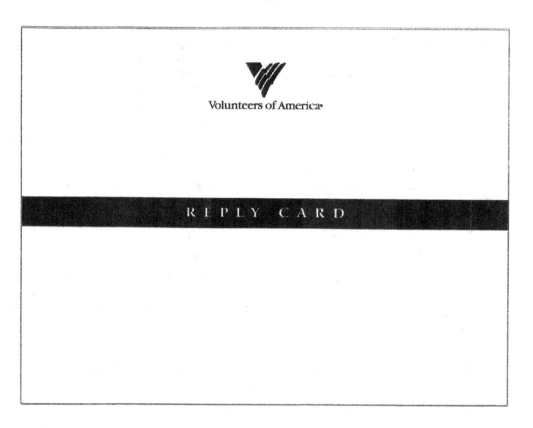

CONTRIBUTION LEVELS:

☐ **DEFENDER** $100,000
Seating at the head table for two
Priority dinner seating for two tables of ten
Premier location for your full page
  acknowledgement in event program
Recognition in Volunteers of America's
  annual report

☐ **BENEFACTOR** $50,000
Priority dinner seating for ten
Priority location for your full page
  acknowledgement in event program
Recognition in Volunteers of America's
  annual report

☐ **CHAMPION** $25,000
Prime dinner seating for ten
Prime location for your half-page
  acknowledgement in event program
Recognition in Volunteers of America's
  annual report

☐ **LEADER** $10,000
Preferential dinner seating for ten
Preferential location for your half-page
  acknowledgement in event program
Recognition in Volunteers of America's
  annual report

☐ **GUARDIAN** $5,000
Dinner seating for ten
Acknowledgement in program and
  annual report

☐ **PACESETTER** $1,000
Dinner seating for four
Acknowledgement in program

☐ **ASSOCIATE** $250
Dinner for one

Contributions are tax deductible less the expense
of $150 per person.

Source: Courtesy of Volunteers of America, Alexandria, Virginia.

Name as it is to appear in program

Name of individual purchasing tickets

Organization

Address

City

State   Zip

Telephone

Fax

E-mail

☐ I/We regret we cannot attend but wish to
enclose a contribution of $_____.

PAYMENT INSTRUCTIONS

By Fax: Complete and fax to 703.341.7001

By Mail: Return and mail payment to:
            Volunteers of America
            1660 Duke Street
            Alexandria, VA 22314

☐ Please reserve _____ individual ticket(s),
$250 each

☐ Please reserve _____ table(s) of ten

  ☐ Check enclosed, payable to
     Volunteers of America, Inc.

  ☐ Charge: ☐ MC ☐ Visa ☐ AmEx

Card Number

Name as it appears on card   Expires

Signature

Billing address of cardholder

Note: If purchasing more than one ticket, please provide names of all guests on back of reply card.
Tickets will be mailed to attendees making reservations by April 18. All others will be held at the door.

THE NAMES OF MY GUESTS ARE:

Volunteers of America National Office • 1660 Duke Street, Alexandria, Virginia 22314 • 703.341.5000

Sample of a Brochure Developed to Encourage Memorial Gifts

SIBLEY MEMORIAL HOSPITAL

Development Department
5255 Loughboro Road, NW
Washington, DC 20016
Telephone 202.537.4362

06/04

Source: Courtesy of Sibley Memorial Hospital, Washington, DC. Design: Harriett Winner, Winner, Inc.

GIFTS MADE IN MEMORY OF A FAMILY MEMBER OR A LOVED ONE are a perfect way to pay tribute and honor their life. Memorial gifts allow you to perpetuate the memory of your loved one, while at the same time helping others.

Gifts in honor of someone special are a meaningful way to commemorate the importance of an individual or group and how they have impacted your life and the lives of others. These gifts are a thoughtful way to express your appreciation and gratitude to a loved one, a physician, a nurse or others. Honor gifts are also a meaningful way to celebrate a birthday, anniversary, graduation or birth.

When an honor or memorial gift is received, a letter of acknowledgement is sent to you and to the person or persons as requested by the donor. Gifts are also gratefully recognized in Sibley's *Honor Roll of Donors*. Gifts of $5,000 or more are recognized with a plaque on the Hospital's *Wall of Honor*.

HOW YOUR SUPPORT MAKES A DIFFERENCE

Sibley Memorial Hospital is a 328-bed community hospital, recognized for the quality of its medical care, compassionate staff, and pleasant surroundings. The Hospital provides inpatient, outpatient and emergency room services for more than 130,000 members of the community annually. Gifts made to Sibley are tax deductible to the fullest extent allowable by law.

Honor and memorial giving is an integral part of funding received by Sibley Memorial Hospital. Your support will help Sibley invest in the latest technology, provide education for staff, and expand and enhance services and facilities.

PLEASE CONSIDER MAKING AN HONOR OR MEMORIAL GIFT. Your gift in honor or in memory of someone is an opportunity to make a gift that benefits others.

Enclosed is my gift of $ _____

Name _____

Address _____

City _____

State/Zip _____

This gift is made:

In honor of _____

In memory of _____

Please send notification of this gift to:

Print Name _____

Address _____

City _____

State/Zip _____

❏ Please send me information on plaques and naming gift opportunities.

Charge Card Information:

Please charge my gift of $ _____ to:

❏ Visa   ❏ MasterCard   ❏ American Express

Card Number _____

Expiration Date _____

Today's Date _____

Signature _____

Print Name _____

Address _____

City _____

State/Zip _____

For more information, please call Sibley Memorial Hospital's Development Office at 202.537.4362.

Sample of a Special Event Save the Date Notice Printed in a Magazine

Save The Date

April 25, 2006

**Heart & Soul Gala—
ASAE & The Center for
Association Leadership's
2006 Partnership
Dinner**

Did you know that heart disease is the #1 killer of both men and women? The Heart and Soul Gala— ASAE & The Center for Association Leadership's 2006 Partnership Dinner, recognizes several associations and foundations for their contributions to The Heart Truth campaign, which raises awareness about this deadly disease.

Mark your calendar now for this exceptional association industry event and check your mailbox for your official invitation.

Date: Tuesday, April 25, 2006
Time: 6:30 p.m.
Place: Marriott Wardman Park Hotel
2660 Woodley Road, NW
Washington, DC 20008

asae & the center
for association leadership

For more information contact
Susan Abbott 202-326-9511 or sabbott@asaecenter.org

Source: Courtesy of ASAE and the Center for Association Leadership, Washington, DC.

Example of a Special Information Card Included with a Special Event Invitation

Map

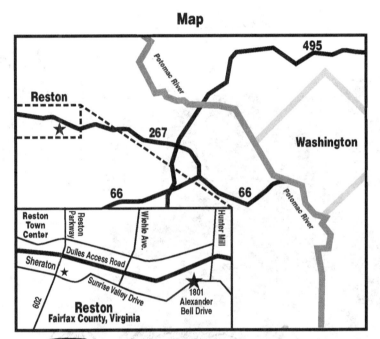

he American Society of Civil Engineers's World Headquarters is located at 1801 Alexander Bell Drive in Reston, Virginia, just off Sunrise Valley Drive, Take either the Hunter Mill Road or Wiehle Avenue exits off the Dulles Toll Road, Route 267, on Sunrise Valley Drive and look for Alexander Bell Drive, for those flying in for the events, Dulles International Airport is closest to ASCE.

If you need overnight accommodations, 50 rooms have been reserved at the **Sheraton Reston Hotel**, 11810 Sunrise Valley Drive, Reston, VA 20191. To make reservations, please call **(703) 262-5929**, ask for the Reservations Manager, and tell her you are with ASCE. Reservations must be made by **Wednesday, November 19, 1997**. Parking is available at the Sheraton and at the ASCE World Headquarters for those who plan to drive. For those staying at the Sheraton, but using other modes of transportation, the hotel's shuttle bus will be available from the hotel to ASCE's Headquarters for the evening's events.

Source: Courtesy of the American Society of Civil Engineers Foundation, Reston, Virginia.

Case Study—The Philanthropic Brand: Lessons for Aging Service Providers

OVERVIEW

Early in 2007, I was invited by the American Association of Homes and Services for the Aging (AAHSA) to give the keynote presentation at the AAHSA Philanthropic Network (APN) Summer Forum in Boston. They asked me to develop a presentation on how senior living providers could learn from such well-known companies as Starbucks, Target, and Ben & Jerry's, each of which embraces social accountability programs as part of its brand. The result was a presentation we called, "The Philanthropic Brand: Lessons for Aging Service Providers."

During the course of researching and compiling the presentation, I had a bit of an "epiphany" that changed the way I thought about branding not for-profit senior living organizations. In this overview of the presentation, my goal is to capture the key ideas from the presentation and how they can help senior service providers. I welcome any questions or comments you may have about these ideas.

What Is a Philanthropic Brand?

There are many definitions of a brand, but most boil down to two basic elements: a claim of distinction, and a promise of performance. In other words, what distinguishes one brand from another are 1) the unique characteristics of each, and 2) the perceived quality of each.

Branding is important because brands with strong positive perceptions can generate greater profitability (or, for not-for-profit senior living communities, greater operating margins), can increase customer loyalty, and can enhance staff morale and performance.

A philanthropic brand is one where social accountability and philanthropy are key elements of the overall brand. Starbucks, Target, and Ben & Jerry's are excellent examples of philanthropic brands. Starbucks promotes sustainable growing practices in third world countries; initiated projects in Indonesia and Ethiopia to provide safe drinking water; makes extensive use of recycled materials and works to reduce its greenhouse gas emis-

sions; and in 2006, Starbucks donated more than $36.1 million in cash and in-kind contributions to charitable organizations.

Ben & Jerry's undertakes a similar number of environmental and socially accountable programs. Target also has many environmentally friendly programs, but its primary social accountability focus is on the arts and education. Each week, Target donates more than $3 million to support arts and education programs in its communities.

While all three companies do these things because they believe they are "the right thing to do," there also is a significant business advantage to their efforts. Not only were Ben & Jerry's and Target ranked #1 and #2, respectively, in the 2006 Golin-Harris Corporate Citizen Rating research project, but both (as well as Starbucks) are among the top financial performers in their business categories.

Branding for Not-for-Profit Organizations

The Starbucks, Target, and Ben & Jerry's stories are compelling, but they are all for-profit companies. The money they donate to charitable organizations comes from their operating income—and thus ultimately from their customers. Can not-for-profit organizations really benefit similarly from socially accountable branding?

To explore this, we looked at several not-for-profit organizations, including the Lance Armstrong Foundation. In 2005 (the most recent data available when we did the presentation), the Lance Armstrong Foundation donated $3.8 million in general awards to nonprofit organizations, awarded more than $1.8 million in community grants, funded 27 research grants totaling more than $5 million, and awarded $2.3 million to four new and four existing LiveStrong Survivorship Centers of Excellence. Where did this money come from?

In 2002 and 2003, the Lance Armstrong Foundation raised $8.3 million and $11.2 million, respectively. But in 2004, the Foundation raised $48.6 million, an increase of more than 300%! What happened? In 2004, they branded and then aggressively marketed the Foundation. (Remember the launch of the yellow LiveStrong wrist bands?) They developed a Website that is full of helpful information and stories of survivors, as well as merchandise to buy. By developing a strong brand, the Lance Armstrong Foundation was able to dramatically enhance the effectiveness of its fundraising, and thus was able to substantially increase its ability to help those facing the many challenges of cancer.

Senior Living Case Study: Westminster Canterbury Richmond

To bring all the elements of the presentation together—branding, philanthropy, and not-for-profit senior living organizations—we told the story of Westminster Canterbury Richmond (WCR), a 30-year-old CCRC in Richmond, Virginia. WCR had always had a positive reputation, but up until about 15 years ago was not especially well known in the Richmond market. At that time, its CEO challenged the organization to "get its light out from under the basket!"

WCR hired a full-time director of public relations to develop strong ties with Richmond media; hired a full-time chaplain to lead outreach to the church community (there's now a pastoral care staff of four); and hired a full-time director of volunteer services (there's now a staff of two).

The cumulative efforts of the community over the years have paid off handsomely on all fronts. WCR has undertaken a broad variety of community outreach activities, including starting a child support center, opening its pool to the public, becoming active members of civic organizations, and sponsoring a variety of activities in its market area.

The results? WCR has grown its foundation to more than $33 million, and in 2006 provided $2.4 million in financial assistance to its residents. Just as impressively, when WCR embarked on a 210-residence expansion in 2002, it reached 70% presales more than six months ahead of schedule—an achievement that was far more due to the presence it had established in its market than to any advertising or direct marketing.

A Different View of Senior Living Branding

When I began this piece, I said that my work on this presentation changed my views on branding not-for-profit senior living organizations. Prior to this, our company would always work hard to determine the distinguishing features of each community or organization, whether they would be its setting (e.g., seaside or mountain view), its philosophy (e.g., wellness), the feel of its community (e.g., close-knit neighborhoods), or a combination of factors.

While factors like those are still quite important, today I believe there is not only an opportunity but also a need to weave in a strong social accountability message as part of a not-for-profit community's brand. Many communities are now coming under attack from local and state authorities to challenge their tax-exempt status. If communities can't clearly demonstrate that the value of their social accountability programs is greater than the value of their tax exemption, they are losing their cases.

By developing a strong, socially accountable brand (a philanthropic brand), senior living organizations can not only defend themselves against tax exemption challenges, they can also position themselves to maintain strong census levels and significantly enhance the success of their fundraising and development efforts. I can even envision a scenario where, by becoming the leading advocate for seniors in its market, an organization's foundation could actually become the centerpiece of its brand.

We welcome your thoughts and comments on these ideas.

Source: Highlights of a Presentation Given to the AAHSA Philanthropic Network (APN) on July 2007. Courtesy of Rob Love, President, Love & Company, Frederick, Maryland, http://www.loveandcompany.com.

Chapter 14

Capital Campaigns

CHAPTER OUTLINE

- What Is a Capital Campaign?
- Rules for Capital Campaigns
- The Relationship Between Capital Campaigns and Annual Campaigns
- Campaign Readiness
- The Feasibility Study
- Developing a Case Statement
- Campaign Structure and Timetable

- Methods of Giving to a Campaign
- Using Commemorative Opportunities to Encourage Gifts and Recognize Donors
- Campaign Materials
- Setting Up Internal Systems
- Maintaining Relationships with Leadership Donors
- What to Do When Campaign Momentum Wanes
- Campaign Evaluation

KEY VOCABULARY

- Active Phase
- Advance Gifts
- Campaign Brochure
- Campaign Chair
- Campaign Director
- Campaign Leadership
- Campaign Management
- Campaign Organization
- Campaign Rules
- Campaign Staff
- Capital Campaign
- Capital Fund Campaign
- Case Statement
- Continuing Care Retirement Community (CCRC)
- Feasibility Study
- Fifty Percent Rule
- Fundraising Counsel
- General Gifts
- Gift Range Table
- Honorary Chair
- Initial Gifts
- Kickoff

- Leadership Gift
- Major Gift
- Pacesetting Gifts
- Pre-Campaign
- Private Phase
- Progress Report
- Public Phase
- Rule of Thirds
- Pyramid of Gifts
- Sequential Giving
- Sequential Solicitation Rule
- Silent Phase
- Special Gifts
- Specific Situation Formula
- Statement of Need
- Table of Gifts
- Yardstick Gifts

WHAT IS A CAPITAL CAMPAIGN?

A capital campaign is an intensive fundraising effort organized to meet a specific financial goal within a specified period of time for one or more major special projects such as the construction of a facility, the purchase of equipment, the expansion of programs, or the acquisition of endowment. At some time in its history, an organization will realize that it needs to conduct a capital campaign. New facilities (bricks and mortar) are needed, equipment must be upgraded, new programs or projects must be started and supported, or endowment must be raised—all reasons to start a capital campaign.

There is never a "perfect time" to start a campaign. Many campaigns just launched should have begun years earlier, but the organization's board was always waiting to find the "perfect" opportunity. Instead of waiting for that time, development staff can create the perfect time through careful planning.

> *There is never a "perfect time" to start a campaign.*

Capital campaigns are not necessarily inclusive. Most of the money raised in a capital campaign will come from a small number of donors. This is the direct opposite of an annual campaign, in which a broad-based appeal is necessary to be successful.

RULES FOR CAPITAL CAMPAIGNS

Anyone thinking of undertaking a capital campaign will either read or be told about the many "rules" of a campaign. These rules include the following:

- The 80/20 rule. This rule applies to the fact that 80 percent of the money raised in capital campaigns comes from 20 percent of the donors. Today, this is even becoming the 90/10 rule.
- The rule of thirds. This second rule describes the formula that has been widely used in constructing gift range tables. The rule of thumb is that about 10 donors account for the first third of funds raised during a capital campaign, about 100 donors provide the next third, and all remaining donors in the constituency furnish the final third. Any failure in achieving the objective of the first third of funds can be compensated for by exceeding the objective of the second third. The last third, however, cannot make up for failure in the first or second thirds.
- The sequential solicitation rule. This third rule is simple—gifts are solicited from largest to smallest. It is a cardinal principle of capital campaign fundraising that gifts should be sought "from the top down," that is, the largest gifts in a gift range table should be sought at the outset of a campaign, followed sequentially by searches for lesser gifts. Thus, the first gifts are called advance gifts, the second are leadership gifts, the third are major gifts, the fourth are special gifts, and the fifth and final gifts are general gifts.
- The 50 percent rule. This fourth rule relates to the concept that a campaign should never be announced to the public until 50 percent of the goal is achieved. Some will argue that a campaign can be publicly launched with only 30 to 40 percent of the gifts received. When in doubt, let the gift dollars accumulate before publicizing.

The success or failure of a capital campaign will rest with the decisions made and activities completed in the initial phases. A fully developed fundraising plan, selection of the proper leadership, the full and complete support of the board and the staff of the organization, and having the proper systems and procedures in place are all necessary for a campaign to be successful. A lack of any of these will have such a negative impact that a campaign, once launched, may never recover.

Before undertaking a capital campaign, any organization should ask itself whether it is ready to embark upon such an endeavor. Are all the variables in place? Has the groundwork been laid? Are the board members, membership, other volunteers, and staff fully supportive and trained to begin? Is the climate right in the community, association, university, etc.? Are there any issues concerning the economy? Eighteen questions to ask yourself before considering a capital campaign can be found in Exhibit 14–1.

If each of these questions has been addressed and can be answered realistically, then the organization can take the next steps toward beginning a capital campaign.

Exhibit 14–1 Capital Campaigns 101

Ask yourself these threshold questions whenever you are considering undertaking a capital campaign:

1. Do you need money?
2. Do you have a convincing case for support, appealing both to the heart and the head?
3. Do you have active and highly visible volunteer leaders?
4. Do you have enough staff to support a campaign?
5. Do you have good access to funding sources?
6. Do you have (or can you get) a system in place for recording and acknowledging gifts and pledges?
7. What is "the competition" up to?
8. It costs money to raise money. Are you willing to make the necessary expenditures?
9. Is there a sense of urgency about your needs?
10. Does your organization have clear priorities?
11. How well have your fundraising efforts worked up until now?
12. Do you have a positive image in the community?
13. Is your organization well known in the community?
14. How well does your organization work from a business perspective?
15. Can you identify five to ten top volunteer leaders?
16. Do you have an idea who your chairperson ought to be? Do you think that person will agree to lead?
17. Can you identify five to ten top prospective donors?
18. Can you identify two to three times the number of donors you will need for each category?

Source: Courtesy of Calder Sinclair, Sinclair, Townes & Company, Atlanta, Georgia, 2007.

THE RELATIONSHIP BETWEEN CAPITAL CAMPAIGNS AND ANNUAL CAMPAIGNS

Often, board members are fearful of embarking upon a capital campaign effort because they think it will impact negatively the organization's successful annual campaign. It is possible for a capital campaign to run concurrently with an organization's annual campaign. Although capital campaigns are a one-time fundraising effort whereas annual campaigns occur year after year, capital campaigns should benefit annual giving by bringing in new donors and creating a higher profile for the organization. As annual campaigns usually support the operational needs of the organization, a capital campaign is held for a specific, single purpose, usually to construct a building (bricks and mortar), to raise money to advance a particular program, or to raise money for endowment. See Exhibit 14–2 for a chart comparing an annual campaign with a capital campaign.

The organization's board of directors will make a greater commitment of time and energy to a capital campaign than to the annual campaign. Board members will need to lead by example. They will be among the first to make their gifts to the campaign. In addition to the board, a special fundraising committee will be developed to focus on the campaign during the period established for the capital campaign. The chairperson of the capital campaign must be a well-known, highly visible individual who has ties with major businesses and the leadership of the community and is respected by almost everyone. Within a university or college setting, the chair may or may not have had a strong leadership role on the board of trustees; it is much more important that he or she have the global recognition, respect, and contacts, particularly with individuals or institutions controlling major financial resources. On the other hand, the chair of the annual campaign must be actively involved with the educational institution. In other organizations, the annual campaign chair may be less well known in the greater public but must have closer ties within the organization itself.

The leadership of a capital campaign—those selected to work with the chair in his or her cabinet—will often include individuals not frequently involved within the organization, those who are called upon only in special circumstances to come forward to "carry the torch" of the organization. These are usually very busy, influential people whose names are well known to everyone who is being targeted for solicitation of a gift. Prestige is the operative word.

CAMPAIGN READINESS

Before embarking on a campaign, the entire organization must be made aware of the importance of the effort and the impact it will have on the lives of those who work there. The president or executive director should meet with the entire staff to relay the big picture and explain why everyone must cooperate for the campaign to succeed.

> *Before embarking on a campaign, the entire organization must be made aware of the importance of the effort.*

If this were a hospital, then the chief administrator and head of the hospital board would share in this responsibility. In a Continuing Care Retirement Community (CCRC), it would be the President and CEO along with the board chair. In a church, it would be the pastor and president of the church council. In a membership association, it should be the voluntary head (board chair) as well as the staff head (CEO or Executive Director).

The success or failure of a fundraising campaign will depend in great part upon the leadership selected and the decisions made early in the planning stages. No details should be overlooked or considered insignificant. Appendix 14–A describes three keys to a successful campaign: (1) a compelling case for

---

Exhibit 14–2 Comparison of a Capital Campaign and an Annual Campaign

Capital Campaign
- Purpose is to raise large amounts of money for a specific goal.
- It is a one-time effort that is intensive and time-limited and it also has a high profile.
- Goals are based on findings of a feasibility study.
- The organization's board members or trustees are directly involved.
- Many volunteers at the highest levels are used for peer-to-peer solicitation to raise large sums of money.
- The campaign chair is well known to the public but is not necessarily active in the organization's activities.
- Prospects will come from a broad base, including more than just members.

Annual Campaign
- Purpose is to raise smaller amounts of money for operating funds.
- It is held yearly and has a lower profile.
- Goals are based on previous year's giving.
- The board members or trustees are indirectly involved; effort is mostly staff driven.
- Fewer volunteers are used (if at all) to solicit smaller amounts of money, and this is usually not peer-to-peer solicitation.
- The campaign chair (if there is one) is active in the organization but may not be well known to the public.
- Prospects most likely will come from the membership, residents, alumni, or the like.

support; (2) 100 percent commitment by the board; and (3) effective volunteer leadership.

Start with a plan and work the plan. Develop the plan from the information gathered during the feasibility study. No campaign should be undertaken without a feasibility study. Just having a need doesn't mean that money can be raised to meet the need.

> *No campaign should be undertaken without a feasibility study.*

Review the calendar of the organization and see what major events can be included in the plan. For example, can the campaign's kick-off be held in conjunction with the organization's annual meeting or the hospital's annual big fundraising special event? Put everything down in writing and divide the plan into measurable segments. Financial goals should not be placed only at the conclusion of the campaign, but should be built into the plan on a quarterly, semi-annually, or yearly basis.

As the plan is being created, leadership gifts should be targeted and cultivated. This part of the campaign proceeds at the same time as the campaign is being developed. In addition, an organization can begin writing the case statement and building the campaign's budget. One piece does not need to wait for the other to be completed.

Staff should divide the prospects into groups to plan the solicitation targeted at them. These groups can be divided according to giving capabilities, geographical distribution, whether internal (board or staff) or external (community leaders or alumni) to the institution, and volunteer potential.

There are several issues that almost always arise during the planning and conducting of a capital campaign. They are

- the readiness of an organization to carry out a capital campaign
- the question of whether to use campaign counsel
- the ability of the current staff to carry out a campaign
- the use of nondevelopment office staff in the campaign
- how much does the association provide as a leadership gift if an association foundation is running the campaign
- the cost of the campaign
- the timing of the campaign's "kick-off" or public announcement
- how to report the capital campaign vis-à-vis the annual campaign
- whether premiums or specific donor acknowledgments should be used to promote giving
- how to recognize donors differently from what is in place for annual or major gifts

Evaluating Resources

Before any organization undertakes a capital campaign, it must evaluate its resources. Does it have enough staff? Does it have the resources? If it is an association, is it willing to make a leadership gift to its foundation's campaign? Does it have the constituents? Is its base broad enough? Is its board strong enough? If an organization can answer positively to all of these, then it can consider a capital campaign. Planning and readiness have a direct effect on the results of a campaign. Appendix 14–B provides a case study of an organization wanting to embark upon a capital campaign and discovering from the results of a feasibility study done by a consulting group that they were not ready.

Often, outside development professionals are hired to conduct both the feasibility study and the actual campaign. Sometimes, they are used only in the feasibility stage. An organization absolutely should not hire outside professionals who work for a percentage of the fee raised. Instead, look for those who work for "fee for service." Although there are many reasons to hire campaign counsel, the most common are the following:

- They have broad capital campaign experience.
- They bring research and resources from other campaigns.
- They have the ability to keep the board and staff focused.
- Board members are more likely to listen to outside counsel than to staff.
- They are objective.

Most organizations don't have development office staff with capital campaign operational experience. Staff members probably have operated in an annual campaign mode, soliciting gifts from within their membership while seeking grants from corporations and foundations. Few have had the opportunity to work on any capital campaign, either large or small. In addition, professional consultants from larger consulting firms can bring many additional resources from other campaigns on which either they or other staff from their firm have worked. Plus, an outside consultant can view the organization objectively and is not placed in the position of having to please the board or senior staff to protect a job. Consultants also can keep the board and staff focused and, if necessary, be more blunt than staff in motivating board members to complete tasks assigned to them.

To be successful, a capital campaign needs the full support and cooperation of the organization's board members and senior staff. Most board members probably will not have participated previously in a capital campaign and will need to be fully briefed, if not trained. This is one of the best uses of a consulting firm—training the board to understand their roles and responsibilities.

The campaign will also look to the board members for a personal contribution as well as leadership and direction in the solicitation of prospective donors. These specific solicitations cannot be done by the staff or by any hired consultants. The board must be behind the campaign and accept full responsibility for as well as ownership of the goal.

The organization's board does not serve as the capital campaign committee. A separate group of individuals needs to be identified, selected, and trained to serve in this role. Some board members, though, may serve on this committee, but only if they meet all of the qualifications necessary.

Calder Sinclair of Sinclair, Townes & Company, an Atlanta based consulting firm specializing in capital campaigns, states, "If a capital campaign is in the offing, there are some key points to cover with the board.

1. The entire board must embrace the objectives of the capital campaign.
2. Each member of the board must be willing to make a financial commitment to the campaign.
3. The board will need to address the annual fund and the potential impact on the organization's cash flow.
4. The board should be involved in the selection of the consulting firm.
5. Board members must realize that this is their campaign."

Strong boards raise strong dollars. Remember the quotation attributed to John Paul Getty: "The meek may inherit the earth, but not its mineral rights!"

Setting a Goal

Before a goal can be established for a capital campaign, a feasibility study should be conducted to discover the amount of money it is possible to raise and from whom. Usually conducted by an outside consulting firm, the feasibility study asks all of the difficult questions, such as the following: How is the organization perceived? Would people want to make a gift to the organization? Is the need to raise money real and necessary? Would this individual make a gift and of how much? Would this person recommend others who would make a gift? How is the leadership (the board) of the organization perceived? If the campaign is being conducted by the organization's foundation, how is the foundation perceived?

After gathering as much information as possible from key individuals in the feasibility study, data are analyzed and categorized, and an attainable goal is set. The goal should be a "stretch" goal—one that will take a concerted effort to reach, yet one that the organization should be able to meet. A goal should never be set before a feasibility study has been conducted, although this is a very common mistake. It is not unusual for a board to think that the need is the same as the goal. A goal could be higher than the need in order to build an endowment or the need could be much higher than the goal if the feasibility study indicated an amount to be raised that was less than the need.

THE FEASIBILITY STUDY

All capital campaigns should begin with a feasibility study to determine if there is a need for a campaign. This is usually conducted by outside counsel, although rarely, it can be conducted by staff. The study should address:

1. the need for a campaign;
2. the strength of the case to be presented;
3. the resources available to use in a campaign—is there an adequate number of staff and volunteers to conduct a campaign?;
4. the number of donors and prospects—are there enough available to successfully reach the goal and complete the campaign?;
5. the plan, budget, and calendar for the campaign;
6. the perception of the organization in the community and among its members, if it is a membership organization;
7. potential leadership for the campaign;
8. potential sources for major leadership and major gifts;
9. the use of the information gleaned from the interviews to develop the campaign plan; and
10. the feasibility of the financial goal suggested for the campaign.

This is also the time to develop an adequate base of public relations for the campaign, both internal and external.

Those approached in a capital campaign should include the leadership of the organization, those who benefit from the organization's services, those who are influential in the community or area served by the organization, and those who have the financial capability to make a contribution to the organization.

How many should be interviewed in a feasibility study? The more interviews conducted, the more potential donors are being cultivated for the organization. This of course assumes that the "right" people are being targeted in the first place. Some feasibility studies are conducted with as few as 20 persons interviewed. Others include more than 100 persons. When developing the list of those to be interviewed, be sure to include leaders within the organization, those who benefit directly from the organization's services, and those capable of making a substantial contribution to the organization. Don't spend too much time and effort interviewing people who belong to constituencies that are not traditionally large givers.

After determining the list of people to be interviewed, a letter outlining the project and requesting a time for an interview is sent to each person on the list. See Appendix 14–C for an example of a letter requesting an interview for a feasibility study. Interviews can be conducted in person or by phone. This depends upon the budget of the organization. All local interviews should be done in person; those far away can be conducted by phone if the budget doesn't allow for travel expenses.

The letter should clearly explain the following: (1) the purpose for the visit, (2) the amount of time required, (3) what results are hoped to be achieved, (4) who will be conducting the interview and their relation to the organization, and (5) that the interview is completely confidential. A copy of the draft of the case statement should be included with the letter, so those being interviewed have an opportunity to understand the reasons the potential campaign will be held. See an example of a case statement turned into a fundraising brochure in Appendix 13–D in Chapter 13.

The person conducting the interview will use a standardized form developed by all those who are conducting the interviews. It will cover the areas indicated by the following questions:

1. How does the person being interviewed view the organization, its mission, its goals, its staff, its volunteer leadership, and its finances?
2. Has this person ever supported the organization either financially or as a volunteer?
3. Does the organization tell its story accurately and effectively?
4. Does this person think that the organization can successfully raise large amounts of money within the community?
5. Does this person know of potential donors and the amounts they may be willing to give?
6. Would the person be willing to support the organization either financially or as a volunteer leader during the campaign?
7. Who else would this person recommend to become involved with the leadership of the campaign?
8. What are some suggestions regarding how high the goal should be set, who should head the campaign, and how long it should run?

It is important that the questions being asked allow the person to expand his or her comments beyond a simple yes or no answer; ask open-ended questions that draw out answers on each issue. Although it is easier to have a questionnaire that is quantifiable, valuable opinions and insight often can be missed if there isn't an opportunity for those being interviewed to expand their answers. Appendix 14–D provides an example of a questionnaire used in a feasibility study interview.

Several guidelines need to be followed when conducting an interview. First of all, be on time! If you are going to arrive later than the scheduled time, call ahead to alert the person being interviewed. This is only common courtesy. Calling the day before the interview to confirm the appointment is also a courtesy. At this time you can ask if the letter and draft case statement have been received and if the person has had time to read them.

Secondly, dress appropriately for the occasion. Professional appearance is a must! You are representing an organization or institution that is seeking advice and financial support from this person.

Third, when interviewing in the home, look for a place to be seated that will afford you good lighting and a writing surface. It is best that you have a portable writing surface such as a clipboard on which you can write the notes during the interview. The goal is to get the questionnaire completed, so the person being interviewed must be comfortable and not anxious for the meeting to end before the task is finished.

The results of a feasibility study should determine whether a campaign can be successful, identify potential leadership, determine what the gift goal (or range) will be, and identify potential gifts to the campaign.

DEVELOPING A CASE STATEMENT

When a business presents itself to its public through a brochure, it usually uses its annual report. If it is trying to generate business, it usually uses a brochure called a *prospectus*. When a nonprofit organization presents itself, it usually uses an annual report or a general information brochure. When the nonprofit organization is trying to raise money and needs to present its fundraising reasoning and strategies, it uses a document called a *case statement*. (See Chapter 6 and Appendix 13–D.) This document outlines the history of the organization, why one should make a gift to the organization, and how the money raised will be used by the organization. It is probably the most important document that an organization will ever write and use. It should be developed through a cooperative effort of both staff and board members, and it requires the commitment and responsibility of both to be effective. In his best-selling fundraising book on preparing a case statement, fundraising consultant Jerold Panas lists nine essentials of a case statement (1995). They are the following:

1. The history of the organization. It is important to include as much as possible about your organization's founding and history, but you also should be as succinct as possible. After all, it is the future that you wish to emphasize, not the past. The past is there to set the stage and should include your mission statement, why you were formed, the leaders of your organization, and any other pertinent information.
2. The problem and the opportunity. Explain the program for which you are raising money. Describe it in compelling terms—the urgency of the need, the people it will help, the lives it will change or help, etc. Don't focus on the institution; focus on the people who have a need and who will benefit from this new program.
3. Proposed solution. How is your institution going to solve the problem outlined previously? Explain why your institution is the best to do this and why it seeks the opportunity to do it.
4. The institution's unique role. Explain why your institution is the best qualified to respond to the challenge and meet the problem or need and why it can do the job better than anyone else. Highlight the successes your organization has had in the past in the community. State how your organization has served its clients better than anyone else could have served them.
5. The goals. Describe the fundraising project at this point, including the reasoning behind the project.
6. The fundraising equation. What will this fundraising effort cost? Who is responsible for raising the money? Where will you find this money? Who will you be asking for this money and how much? Is there a combined effort to raise this money? If so, who will be involved and who will take the lead role? Is there to be a match of the initial gifts?

"WOULD YOU CAMPAIGN-SIZE THAT."

Source: Copyright © Mark Litzler.

7. The fundraising plan. Explain how you will raise the money and why the campaign will be successful. Include any leadership gifts that you have to date—by amount, not by name. Also describe the financial management and operations.

8. How to give. Describe the methods available for making gifts to the campaign. Include the level of giving for which you seek gifts. Also describe opportunities for giving resources other than money, such as time.

9. Leadership. Name those who already have agreed to help in the campaign. This will include your campaign chair, committee members, and other leaders who have agreed to assist with the fundraising effort. This is the group responsible for raising the money and for determining how it will be spent. Explain who these leaders are, how they will function, and what their role is. Also invite your constituents to participate.

The structure of the case statement will vary. You may cover these nine essentials, but you also may include much more.

Case statements will vary in length depending upon the history of the organization and the complexity of the need. Rarely are case statements printed pieces. Usually they are typed documents produced through word processing and some sort of desktop publishing so a more polished (but not slick) appearance is created. They can be bound using any one of several methods—spiraled, drilled, three-hole punched, stapled with a plastic sleeve cover, etc. Whatever method is selected, the document should be easy to read, lay flat when pages are turned, and have plenty of white space for ease in reading and making notes on the pages.

Often, a cover letter signed by the chief volunteer (board chair) will accompany the case statement. Usually, it is not part of the document (it is attached to the cover or left "loose"), but there is a growing trend to bind it at the beginning of the case—after the cover page but before the beginning of the document.

Some question the use of graphs, charts, and statistics in a case statement. If they will help illustrate a point by making it clearer, then use them. If they are being used as "filler," omit them from the document. Graphs can be effective in showing how much money needs to be raised in a specific amount of time. Other statistics can harm the case and deflate the emotional impact you may be trying to make. You can assist the reader by providing visual breaks using headings and subheadings. Quotations from those well known and respected can add impact, also. In addition, a thesaurus can be used to vary words and add impact.

Your case statement will serve as your basic marketing piece to explain to your public *who* your organization is, *what* your organization does, *where* it is located or *what* constituencies it serves, *why* it is raising money, *when* it will begin to raise these funds, and *how* and *when* it will spend them.

Sometimes it is difficult to write a case statement, particularly if you have never written one before. Exhibit 13–4 in Chapter 13 provides guidelines for writing a case statement. Begin by reviewing the materials previously written about your organization. Locate your organization's mission statement. If there is not one, then begin by writing a mission statement and obtain agreement on it from members of the board. Interview board members and senior members of the staff for their ideas on the who, what, where, when, and why of your organization. Ask your colleagues for samples of their organizations' case statements. Don't be afraid to copy ideas; just don't copy the written material! Then begin to write and rewrite. Share the document with staff and board members as you go along. Get input from others who will be making the final decision regarding the document. Have the key leaders of the campaign review the document. Finally, don't be afraid to revise the case statement again and again to gain consensus. Before using the case statement publicly, be sure all senior volunteers and staff members who will be using it "sign off" on the final document.

Don't forget to tailor the case statement to your audience. If your organization has established a brand, follow it. If members of your audience are used to seeing and are comfortable with specific formats, type styles, and color

> *Don't forget to tailor the case statement to your audience.*

combinations, then use these. Don't try to change now—keep a style that is appropriate for your audience. Use correct grammar and have your document free of errors.

Also, according to Panas in his same book, there are six pitfalls to be avoided when preparing your case statement. They are the following:

1. Undefined purpose. If your organization's purpose is not clearly stated, then the persons from whom you are seeking money are not going to understand who you are and what you do. Your mission must be clear and concise.

2. Overstated emotionalism. It is important to appeal to your potential donors, to tug at their heart and purse strings, but it is equally important not to overstate your cause and make claims that may ultimately negatively impact your case.

3. The pleading of needs. Just because your organization has identified a need doesn't mean that someone is going to give you money to satisfy that need. Every organization has needs. You shouldn't dwell on the financial problems but on how your organization will solve those problems.

4. Misunderstanding what motivates a prospect. Keep the case statement succinct. Explain clearly what you need and why. Don't spend too much time on the history of your organization, particularly if your audience is its membership.

5. Vague plans. Know what it is that you want to do. Vague and unclear plans certainly don't inspire or motivate.

6. Unsubstantiated grand claims. It is easy to get carried away and make claims that far surpass what is possible to obtain. Don't be tempted to make the organization sound saintly when it isn't. People can easily ask for or seek substantiation for claims made. Be honest. It is the only right way to raise money.

A professional writer may be hired to develop the case statement, but staff and board members must become involved so that the document represents the organization. An outside writer can gather information and put it down on paper, but if he or she has no fundraising experience, the document most likely will not have the necessary ingredients to effectively "make the case." The "fail-proof" checklist in Exhibit 14–3 should be considered when developing a case statement.

Exhibit 14–3 The Fail-Proof Checklist

- How is the institution positioned in the community and what is its heritage?
    - When was the institution founded?
    - What were the circumstances surrounding the beginning?
    - What are the natural resources in the area?
    - What is the industrial and business concentration?
    - What distinguishes the area from the rest of the county, state, or nation—a capital, a distribution center, a rural area?
    - Describe the population of the service area.
    - Describe the population trends. Is the population increasing or decreasing? Is the population aging?
    - List level of affluence and occupational types of the population.
    - List education level and cultural types of the population.
    - List ethnic origins.
- How does the institution benefit the community and how and whom does it serve?
    - What services does the institution offer?
    - How many people use these services? Have the services been increased or decreased? Why?
    - How much does each of these services cost? Are the services furnished free or subsidized?
    - What services do other organizations in the institution's area offer?
    - Is there any duplication of services or is the organization's niche unique?
    - Does the institution cooperate with other organizations by joining programs or sharing use of facilities?
    - Is there a need for services not currently being met in the community that the institution could fill if the institution had increased funds?
    - How many potential new clients of the institution could you expect to attract if its programs were increased?
- Why is a fundraising program necessary?
- Why does the institution need funds?
    - Is the purpose of the program to gain capital or endowment or both?

- What are the specific components of the campaign and project?
- How will the campaign improve the organization's ability to fulfill its missions?
- How much money does the institution need?
- How will the money be raised?
- Have alternative sources of funding been investigated—government grants, bonds, etc.?
- Is the institution fiscally sound?
    - What is the current operating budget?
    - Is the institution operating "in the black?"
    - Who makes the major contribution to the present operation budget?
    - Does the institution have a membership drive, annual support campaign, admission fee, or subscriptions?
    - Does it have an endowment?
    - What are the financial assets and liabilities of the institution?
    - Are the fees charged (if any) competitive?
    - Does the institution have a planned giving program?
- Does the institution have strong leadership?
    - What is the composition of the board of directors or trustees?
    - How many are on the board?
    - Is the board representative of the varied community interests?
    - Are different ages and both sexes represented?
    - Are commercial interests and those of major businesses represented?
    - Are community minorities or the institution's constituencies represented?
    - Is the staff well qualified?
    - How many persons are on the staff?
    - What are the major strengths and accomplishments of the executive director and other key staff members?
    - Does the institution use volunteers and are they effective?
    - Do the administrative facilities meet the needs?

Source: Adapted with permission from J. Panas, *The No-Nonsense Guide to Help You Prepare a Statement of Your Case,* © 1995, Young & Partners, Inc.

CAMPAIGN STRUCTURE AND TIMETABLE

The long-standing formula for raising money in a capital or major gifts campaign is to divide the amount of the goal into thirds and allocate one-third of the money to come from the top third (leadership gifts), the second third of the money to come from the middle third (major gifts), and the final third of the money to come from the bottom third (small gifts). When placed on a triangle or pyramid, the top tier has a dollar amount equal to the middle and bottom tiers. This approach, called the "rule of thirds," is always discussed as the method to use, but actually it is used less frequently today, because nothing is that simple or predictable.

Although the dollar amounts are divided equally, the numbers of prospective donors are not. The fewest individuals will make up the top third, or "leadership" level, of the donor pyramid, whereas the largest number of donors are in the lowest tier. In other words, very few people will make large, leadership gifts, whereas many people will give small amounts to campaigns. This holds true in most campaigns. See Exhibit 14–4 for an example of the "rule of thirds" donor pyramid.

Pre-Campaign Planning and Preparation

For most campaigns, these phases will last approximately six months to a year. The organization should build consensus within its own ranks during the first three to six months. The feasibility study has indicated that it is possible to conduct a successful campaign for a set amount of dollars; now that information should be shared with, confirmed, and forwarded to the various departments of the institution as well as any volunteers who will be assisting with the campaign. This is the time for issues to be resolved that may affect the campaign and to bring on board all of those who questioned the feasibility of the campaign. It is also the time to identify the volunteer leaders and define their roles as well as those of the staff members. "Advance" and "leadership" gifts can be identified, and a structure for training the board and other volunteers can be initiated. The advance and leadership gifts also may be initially cultivated during this phase of the campaign.

During the next three to six months, the campaign leadership structure should be developed, the leaders identified and recruited, and the board members kept up to date on all activities and trained as much as possible regarding their roles in the campaign. Staff also should be involved in all of these stages and trained whenever necessary. Also, during this time, the case for support should be finalized and tested on various targeted constituencies. Decide what the benefits are for participating and giving to the campaign.

During the "silent phase" of the campaign, use this time to solicit and confirm the advance or leadership gifts to the campaign. "The value of the silent phase is to assemble the leadership gifts that are necessary to give your volunteers and staff confidence that the public phase of the campaign is going to be successful," states Bob Hartsook, Chairman and CEO of Hartsook

Exhibit 14–4 *"Rule of Thirds" Donor Pyramid*

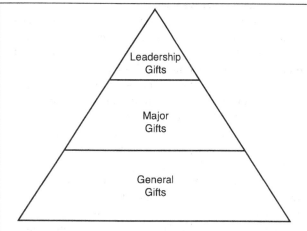

Leadership Gifts

- Smallest number of gifts in this category
- Largest financial gifts made
- Three to four prospects for every donor at this level
- Can be from individuals, corporations, or foundations
- Will be from those who believe most strongly in the organization or case
- Advance or Pacesetter Gifts are included in this category
- Gifts in this level should equal the total of the gifts from Major Donors and General Gifts

Major Gifts

- Large gifts, but not as large as Advance or Leadership gifts
- Usually from corporations or foundations
- At least two prospects for every donor
- The donors often are not known as well as those making leadership gifts

General Gifts

- Largest number of gifts
- Smallest financial gifts in this category
- Usually from individuals

Companies, Inc., Wichita, Kansas (Causer, 2005). Based on these advance gifts, final goals should be set, a calendar developed, and timetables established.

These are the gifts that have been identified in the feasibility study, will be received before the campaign is announced, and are usually the largest given to the campaign. Based on these advance gifts, final goals should be set, a calendar developed, and timetables established. Appendix 14–E provides two examples of the phases of a capital campaign, and Appendix 14–F is an example of a campaign activities timetable.

Recruitment of Volunteer Leadership and the Leadership Gift Phase

Recruiting volunteer leadership is one of the initial steps in organizing a capital campaign. If there is not a wealthy, powerful, or influential board of trustees in place at the organization to make or solicit gifts at the highest leadership level, a volunteer fundraising committee, or campaign cabinet, must be developed immediately to solicit gifts at the highest levels (leadership gifts and major gifts). Everyone's energy must be used to develop this committee quickly. Individuals who know the organization, have an interest in its mission, and are willing to both give of their own personal, corporate, or foundation wealth and to work to raise money for the campaign must be identified. A commitment to serve on this committee is contingent upon the ability to either personally give or to raise large sums of money for the campaign.

Of course, the first step is to find someone to chair the overall fundraising effort. Then, an organization of volunteer leaders will be recruited to form the campaign cabinet, a committee to implement the campaign. The structure may resemble that shown in Exhibit 14–5.

The campaign cabinet is composed of national or local community leaders who will oversee and promote the campaign. The cabinet may be expanded as the campaign grows to ensure representation of all necessary constituencies and to multiply leverage for recruitment and solicitations. Professional counsel may be hired to design the campaign and provide leadership, direction, training, and advice. The following roles are usually associated with the campaign cabinet:

- **Honorary chair.** The honorary chair is an individual of prominence or influence (usually an active or retired chief executive officer [CEO]) who agrees to lend his or her name to a campaign organization with the understanding that he or she will not be expected to assume an active role. Also, serving in this role are celebrities. This is the person whose name recognition is so high among those to be solicited for gifts that the prospects would wonder why he or she was not involved. Note that it is possible for two people to serve as honorary co-chairs.

Exhibit 14–5 Structure of a Capital Campaign

A campaign cabinet may include the following volunteer structure:

- Honorary chair(s)
- General chair (along with campaign counsel and campaign vice chair) is responsible for the leadership gifts
- Vice chair (chair of campaign cabinet)
- Campaign cabinet
  - Individual major donor division chair
  - Capital gifts division chair
  - Special projects division chair
  - Corporate division chair
  - Foundation division chair
  - Member campaign chair, if a membership organization
  - Resident campaign chair, if a continuing care retirement community
  - Alumni campaign chair, usually subdivided by class, if a private school, college, or university

---

- **General campaign chair.** This person, the most visible leader in all phases of the campaign, must command the positive respect of peers so that his or her agreement to help lead the campaign and/or his or her pacesetting gifts will motivate prospects to give to the campaign. The most effective campaign chair is an active CEO.
- **Campaign vice-chair or cabinet chair.** This volunteer works closely with the chair and is actually the "doer." Some campaigns operate without a volunteer at this level, as the general chair assumes this role. If the general chair appoints a vice-chair or cabinet chair, this volunteer is key to the success of the campaign because he or she is the liaison between the trustees and the fundraising committee or campaign cabinet. This person is the working head of the cabinet and works closely with the general campaign chair, the fundraising counsel, the president, committee chairs, as well as the trustees/board members.
- **Divisional chairs/committee chairs.** The divisional chairs/committee chairs will organize committees, recruit divisional leadership as required, and implement the campaign among their respective constituent prospects on a phase-by-phase basis.

Leadership Gifts

The individuals to be solicited for leadership gifts in each division will be solicited by campaign leaders, including the divisional chairs. As the campaign progresses, donors may be asked to join the campaign cabinet to help solicit donations from their peers. Using the old adage that "people give to people," having a recent donor join in the solicitation of funds from another prospect is often a very successful campaign technique. Prospects for the smaller gifts in each division may be approached individually as deemed appropriate or may be contacted by mail with telephone follow up or by telephone with fax or mail back-up.

It is important for the campaign chair and other volunteer leaders to understand the amount of time and effort it takes to raise a gift—large or small—and then decide where that effort is best placed. If it takes the same amount of energy to raise a large gift as it does to raise a small gift, then it is probably wiser to direct this effort toward the highest level—the leadership and major donor levels. If there are no lower level potential donors on which to depend, or very few of them, the campaign will need to focus on leadership gifts and major gifts, allowing small gifts to "fall into" the bottom third, where gifts are not actively sought (see Exhibit 14–4).

> *It is important for volunteer leaders to understand the amount of time and effort it takes to raise a gift.*

When the campaign cabinet is in place and members are trained, approaches then will be made on a wider scale. But as the committee is being developed, solicitations can occur simultaneously for leadership gifts—gifts at the highest level. Potential donors for leadership gifts can be identified by those currently working on the campaign; also, as the chair and committee members are identified and "brought on board," they will be asked to add to this list of potential donors. For each leadership gift needed, three or four prospective donors most likely will need to be identified. Thus, if a $1 million gift is needed, then three or four potential donors must be identified.

Solicitation of gifts from prospects in the middle tier—major donors—will begin once the leadership gifts have been received and the campaign cabinet is in place and actively soliciting gifts. The cabinet members will help to expand the list of prospects in this category. Also, as some individuals, corporations, and foundations are asked for leadership gifts, they will decline to make gifts at that level and will instead make smaller yet substantial gifts that will fall into this middle tier. For each major gift received, approximately two to three prospects will need to be solicited.

The final two stages of the campaign—soliciting special gifts and general gifts—will address the smallest gifts. Again, gifts will be made at this level throughout the campaign when donors wish to give, but the gifts are smaller than what was solicited. Again, approximately two prospects will need to be identified for each donor. The general gifts phase of the campaign may be unnecessary if enough large gifts have been obtained early in the campaign.

At this point in the campaign, a detailed plan and a gift chart or gift table must be in place. This is why a formal feasibility study was conducted. If a feasibility study is not done, the gift chart and accompanying prospect lists are developed without the benefit of this counsel and guidance. For the campaign to be successful, each step must be carefully evaluated to (1) cultivate prospects appropriately, (2) have the "right" person(s) solicit each prospect (so the request is for an appropriate amount and not for too much or too little), and (3) train volunteers to turn an initial no into a yes when soliciting a gift from a prospect.

Finally, the campaign gift chart and the campaign plan are evolving documents that need to be consulted frequently as the campaign progresses. If more money is raised than expected in the leadership phase, then less money will be needed to be raised in the later phases of the campaign. A gift chart is the statistical representation of patterns of giving. The gift chart is used as a planning instrument, as a tool for testing and measuring the availability of donor prospects at the various gift-giving levels, and to raise the giving sights of potential donors. These are flexible documents that need to be revisited frequently during a campaign. A sample gift chart is included in Exhibit 14–6.

Silent, Private, or Quiet Phase of Campaign

The silent, private, or quiet phase includes all the phases of a campaign that take place before the campaign is announced to the public. It is also called by some *the dark phase* and the *prepublic phase*. During this time, all leaders of the campaign are recruited and trained, the case statement is defined, all publications are produced, advance or pacesetter gifts are obtained, leadership gifts are in place, and the focus is now ready to shift to major and general gifts. Gift decisions have been made by the top 100 prospects, all of the board members have made their gifts, and more than half of the goal has been obtained. No shortcuts should be taken to rush to the public phase of the campaign. It is imperative to complete all of the steps. Some fundraisers even propose that 100 percent of the campaign's donors should be identified before going public with a campaign.

Public Phase

"There should be no rush to make that public announcement. Public announcements generally fail to generate the kind of attraction that most people think. Constituents' tolerance for long public phases of campaigns has diminished in the past decade," according to Bob Hartsook (Causer, 2005). Hartsook notes that in smaller communities the public phase of a campaign should not last longer than a year, but larger national and international organizations' campaigns can last up to three years. Campaigns planned for longer periods run the risk of stalling midway through.

Exhibit 14–6 Chart of Gifts or Gift Table

This table illustrates the number of qualified prospects and gifts needed in appropriate categories to conduct a campaign for $12 million for an organization. Gift range tables or charts of gifts are developed for each campaign undertaken and are based on the availability of prospects and their abilities to give.

GIFT LEVEL	# NEEDED	PROSPECTS	TOTAL	CUMULATIVE
$1,000,000	2	6–8	$2,000,000	$2,000,000
$500,000	8	24–32	$4,000,000	$6,000,000
$250,000	10	30–40	$2,500,000	$8,500,000
$100,000	15	30	$1,500,000	$10,000,000
$50,000	10	20	$500,000	$10,500,000
$25,000	25	50	$625,000	$11,125,000
$20,000	20	40	$400,000	$11,525,000
$15,000	15	30	$225,000	$11,750,000
$10,000	15	30	$150,000	$11,900,000
$5,000	15	30	$75,000	$11,975,000
<$1,000	25	50	$25,000	$12,000,000

METHODS OF GIVING TO A CAMPAIGN

Pacesetter, advance, leadership, or major gifts made to capital campaigns can take many forms. Gifts of cash can be given outright or pledged over several years (usually three to five) of the campaign. Most gifts are made with cash, yet some donors making substantial gifts to the organization will use the types of gift vehicles outlined in Chapter 15—trusts, bequests, life insurance, etc. Some donors will make gifts of real property such as real estate, artwork, jewelry, etc., whereas others will make gifts that can be matched by their corporations.

The giving of stock or securities may be of special interest to some donors who have greatly appreciated securities. For the older donor, stock can be used to establish a charitable trust that will generate tax-free income during their retirement years. When the donor dies, the charity will receive whatever money remains in the trust. See Chapter 15 for further information on how to make planned gifts to a charity or other nonprofits.

Giving a gift of appreciated stock is really quite simple. Most brokerage firms will make electronic transfers of stock for their clients at no charge. This precludes the hassles of obtaining stock certificates and paying to have them transferred to the organization. A gift of appreciated stock also affords the donor the opportunity to make a

> *An organization should have systems established to handle different types of gifts.*

substantial gift to the institution and not pay capital gains on the amount of appreciation; the donor also can "write off" the gift as a charitable deduction. It is important for an organization to have a system established to appropriately handle these types of gifts. There is nothing more frustrating for a donor than to want to make a gift of stock to an organization but be unable to because the organization does not know how to handle such a gift. Simple instructions that provide accurate directions for a donor to transfer stock can be developed to be included with a standard letter responding to a donor's inquiry. This information should include the following: the organization federal identification number; the name, address, and telephone number of the brokerage firm handling the organization's account; the electronic transfer code for the brokerage firm; the organization's account number with the brokerage firm; and how to notify the organization when a decision to give a gift of stock has been made. A sample consisting of such a letter and sheet of instructions is presented in Exhibit 14–7.

Also, once a donor has given stock to an institution, he or she is more likely to do so again. Monitor the market to see if the prices of stock have increased or decreased since the last gifts were given. Don't hesitate to encourage these donors to make a second gift of stock. This time the gift may be to the institution's pooled income fund or used to establish a charitable trust. Of course, the organization should be in frequent touch with the donor over the years and ask again only at the appropriate time.

USING COMMEMORATIVE OPPORTUNITIES TO ENCOURAGE GIFTS AND RECOGNIZE DONORS

All capital campaigns should provide opportunities for donors to have their names identified with their gift. It may be as simple as placing their names on a plaque on a wall, or it may be the offering of specific rooms in a building at a set gift level for prospective donors to consider "naming." This is easy if the campaign is raising money for a new building. Most people like to see their names associated with their gifts. Gift clubs can be established and information included in all campaign publications. Some campaign organizers choose to put the gift clubs on the pledge card so donors can view the various club options when deciding upon the size of their gift. Development staff can promote gift clubs or other naming opportunities in newsletters and other publications. Appendix 14–G provides a sample brochure describing donor recognition opportunities.

CAMPAIGN MATERIALS

To promote and conduct a capital campaign, most of the following marketing, communications, and training materials are required: (1) the case statement, (2) a brochure that focuses solely on the campaign, (3) a leadership or major gift prospectus, (4) a pamphlet that presents answers to the most frequently asked questions in the campaign (question-and-answer brochure), (5) an annual report for the organization, (6) pledge cards, (7) a monthly or quarterly newsletter, (8) a theme or slogan for the campaign that is printed on or repeated in all materials, (9) banner paper for press releases, (10) a volunteer guidebook, (11) business cards, and (12) a poster (if appropriate to the campaign).

The Case Statement

A case statement is more than just a listing of the needs of an organization. It also is the basis on which all other campaign materials will be developed. The case statement should put the campaign into perspective with all of the other activities of the organization as well as outline the plans for using the funds raised. Donors will want to know how the money raised will impact the organization's future.

The case statement is also sometimes called the *statement of need*. This piece presents the mission of the institution, the reason for the campaign, and the needs and opportunities—both long and short term—of the organization. The campaign brochure and all other promotional pieces are developed from the case statement.

The development of the case statement should include as many leaders of the institution as possible. If asked to develop the case, the volunteer is more likely to be able to articulate the

Exhibit 14–7 Sample Instruction Letter

February 5, 2008

Mr. John C. Smith
3700 Any Avenue
Anytown, USA 00000

Dear Mr. Smith:

Thank you for your inquiry regarding making a gift through the transfer of stock to the ABCD Foundation's ***Building for the Future*** campaign. The Foundation has opened an account with Charles Schwab & Company, Inc. to facilitate this giving opportunity. The following information describes how to make a gift to the campaign through the transfer of stock. Our hope is to make this transaction convenient for you by providing detailed directions.

As I mentioned in our conversation, Charles Schwab & Company notifies the Foundation on a monthly basis of any account activity, but the report does not include the name of the donor. It would be helpful for me to know when you actually transfer the stock to the Foundation, so I may assign the gift properly. Also, please complete and return the enclosed pledge form. In addition, I have included information on the various vehicles available to make a planned gift to the Foundation. If you have any questions regarding the enclosed information, please call me again at (222) 555-2277.

Again, let me reiterate how pleased I am that you are planning to make a gift to the Foundation's ***Building for the Future*** campaign. We hope you will join us at the ABCD Annual Convention in October in San Diego. The Foundation is planning a special event for donors, as well as a grand celebration of the successful completion of the campaign for all attendees.

Sincerely,

Jane S. Mitchell
Director of Development

Enclosures

cc: Edward Jones, Campaign Chair

TRANSFERRING SECURITIES TO THE ABCD FOUNDATION

1. The Foundation has opened an account with Charles Schwab & Company, Inc. to facilitate this giving opportunity. The **Foundation's account number at Schwab is 1111-1111** and was opened at their **Washington, DC office**.
2. The Foundation's tax identification number is 54-262728.
3. **If you plan to give stock and it is in your name, please complete the attached Third Party Release form [INTER 476-2 (3/91)] and have it notarized** before presenting it to a Schwab broker. Some Schwab offices have notary publics and others do not. If not, most banks and city clerks' offices have notary publics available for your use. When using a notary, you must have some form of photo identification with you.
4. Please call **1-800-435-4000, the toll-free number of Charles Schwab & Company, Inc.,** to determine the Schwab office nearest to you and their hours of availability. At the same time, ask them if they have a notary public available.
5. At this time, you will be asked if the stock certificate is being physically held by you, by Schwab, or by another brokerage firm. **If you are physically holding the stock certificate,** you may either mail the certificate to Schwab with directions that it be transferred to the ABCD Foundation, Inc., whose Schwab account number is 1111-1111, or personally deliver the stock to a broker at the Schwab office nearest to you. In either case, **the back of the stock certificate must be signed by you and must be accompanied by the notarized Third Party Release form. Do not endorse anything on the back of the certificate other than your name** as it appears on the front. Your Schwab broker will complete the remainder of the information for you. All deliveries **MUST** include the Foundation's name and Schwab account number.
6. **If you do not physically hold the stock certificate and it is held by a brokerage firm,** either Schwab or some other firm, they may have the stock transferred electronically (using DTC Clearing 0164, Code 40) directly to Schwab by using the account number 1111-1111 and the complete name of the Foundation's account—The ABCD Foundation, Inc. Again, all deliveries **MUST** include the Foundation's name and Schwab account number.

case clearly and enthusiastically. This is the time to "bring along" potential leadership for the campaign. By involving individuals "up front," it makes their positive involvement with the campaign more likely than not.

The case statement should include a short history of the organization; explain clearly where the organization stands today, what the organization's needs are, and how the campaign will meet those needs; and present a picture of the organization's future if the campaign is successful.

Campaign Brochure

The campaign brochure will be the key sales piece for the fundraising initiative. It can be printed in two color or four color depending upon the budget available. It will convey the case in a concise and compelling way and will be built around the central themes developed in the case statement. Appendix 13–D provides an example of a campaign brochure.

Leadership and Major Gifts Prospectus

The leadership and major gifts prospectus is a special packet consisting of the following:

- campaign brochure
- solicitation letter
- recognition opportunities sheet (if appropriate)
- selected public relations materials
- annual report

Question-and-Answer Brochure

Questions that are commonly asked throughout the fundraising effort can be anticipated, presented, and answered in a smaller brochure that accompanies the main fundraising brochure. This is called the question-and-answer brochure, or the Q and A for short. It can be used along with the general informational fundraising brochure or used separately. It is an inexpensive piece, often considered a "throwaway" piece, and can be printed in two color or "piggybacked" onto the printing of the major brochure and printed in four color (if the brochure is being printed in four color). Appendix 13–E shows an example of a question-and-answer brochure.

Annual Report

As a complement to all fundraising materials, the organization should develop and print an annual report. The brochure outlines the organization's programs and activities during the past year and reports on the financial stability of the organization. Produced annually, it can be used effectively as a supplemental brochure in multi-year fundraising efforts.

Pledge Cards

A pledge card or pledge sheet is the official record of a donor's gift to a fundraising campaign. The following information should be included on the card: the donor's name, address, and phone number; gift or pledge amount; payment schedule; method of paying the gift or pledge; information on what types of payments are available to the donor (check, credit cards, securities, etc.); to whom to write the check and where to send it; the opportunity to indicate how the donor would like to have the gift recognized; a place for the donor's signature; and the date.

Newsletter/E-Newsletter/Web Site

A newsletter from the organization's president, chair of the board, or chair of the campaign can be developed to promote the organization by reporting on new developments within the institution as well as the progress of the campaign. It provides an opportunity to give credit to donors and to recognize the campaign leadership. Any new donors should be highlighted in the next issue. The same materials can be adapted to use on the organization's Web site or any of its electronic communications.

Theme or Slogan

Campaign themes or slogans will vary depending upon the reason for raising the funds. Many campaigns today use the themes of "new millennium," "21st century," and "bridge to the future" in their titles. Use whatever is most fitting to the organization, its mission, and the campaign. Don't try to be cute.

Press Releases

To inform the public of the organization's fundraising efforts, the staff must write and distribute news releases to announce important happenings such as special events, the receipts of a major gift, the appointment of a campaign chair, etc. Press releases can be distributed by mail, electronically, or at a press conference if the news is important enough to get the press to attend. If the information is distributed at a press conference, then a complete press kit should be developed, including the press release, a brochure or fact sheet describing the organization, biographies of any persons involved, and any photographs (black and white or color) pertinent to the release.

Volunteer Guidelines

A handbook of volunteer guidelines should be provided to all volunteers recruited to work on the campaign. It should provide a basic overview of the campaign, including sample letters, scripts, etc.

Source: Copyright © Mark Litzler.

Business Cards

All volunteers as well as staff members should have business cards that are designed specifically for the campaign. The cards should carry the slogan or theme of the campaign and should have all the necessary information on how to reach the campaign headquarters—address, phone number, fax, e-mail, etc.

Posters

A poster may be designed to augment the other campaign materials. Posters can be effective fundraising tools. Who can forget the March of Dimes poster child or the faces of the animals on the posters of the Society for the Prevention of Cruelty to Animals? A picture says a thousand words, and posters can raise thousands of dollars. They also can just be used to raise the public's awareness of the organization and its mission. They do not need to be in four color; but again, if it is in the budget, then use four color, because it is usually more dramatic and appealing.

SETTING UP INTERNAL SYSTEMS

As important as trained volunteers are to the success of a campaign, so too are the systems established within the development office to manage a campaign. From researching a prospect to collecting a gift to thanking the donor, a well-organized development office with systems in place is a must. Both electronic database systems and paper files must have the accurate data maintained, as this is vital to the success of current and future campaigns. Some of the data that should be maintained for analysis for future campaigns include the following: number of

gifts received, amount of cash received, dollar amount of pledges received, dollar amount of deferred or planned gifts received, number of donors, number of prospects contacted, percentage of those contacted who made gifts, average gift size, average advance or pacesetter gifts, average leadership gift, average major gift, average general gift, gifts by range, gifts by category, gifts by size, etc. In most campaigns, this information will be tracked on an ongoing basis and shared with the campaign leadership. The data can help staff manage the campaign and direct the volunteers in areas that need leadership.

Receipt of Gifts

All campaign gifts should be processed through the development office. If gifts are received by other offices, they should be sent immediately to the development office. One person in the development office should oversee the receipt of gifts. This person should make sure that all of the data requested on the pledge card is completely and accurately recorded and that all cash gifts are recorded and deposited on the day they arrive. If this is not possible, then the cash gifts must be kept in a locked file cabinet or another secure place.

Acknowledging Gifts

All gifts should be acknowledged within 48 hours, if possible. If there is such a large number of gifts being made that this cannot be done, then additional staff should be hired temporarily to assist with this process. There is nothing more annoying to a donor than not to be thanked in a timely manner. Acknowledgment letters should be signed by the chair of the campaign or the president or executive director of the organization. If the gift is substantial, more than one thank you letter can be sent from those representing the campaign and the organization. Don't forget to follow all Internal Revenue Service requirements.

Collection of Pledges

If the gifts are made in the form of a pledge, this information must be recorded accurately as a pledge payment schedule—monthly, quarterly, semi-annual, and annual remittances are common. Work with the organization's financial or accounting department to make sure that all requirements are being met for both the donor and the organization. It is important to track pledge payments, because delinquent accounts do not bring cash into the organization. If a donor misses two consecutive payments, a letter or invoice requesting payment should be sent. If this brings no results, then a phone call should be made to determine the problem and arrange for a different payment schedule, if necessary.

MAINTAINING RELATIONSHIPS WITH LEADERSHIP DONORS

Once a gift is made, the organization should never lose touch with the person who gave the gift. In particular, those who have made leadership gifts should be cultivated for future work as campaign volunteers, for board leadership roles, and for other gifts to the organization. Major donors should be invited to all of the organization's major activities, such as receptions, special events, private dinners, etc. Feature donors in the organization's newsletters whenever possible. Once a pledge is completed, solicit the donor for other gifts, including the annual appeal.

WHAT TO DO WHEN CAMPAIGN MOMENTUM WANES

Assessing the Campaign

In almost every capital campaign there will come a time when the campaign appears to be "stalled" and no progress is being made. This is not a time to panic, but a time to assess what has been working well and what has not been successful. Taking the time to analyze the campaign's operations at this point can assist those responsible for its success in making decisions for the direction of the campaign in the remaining time.

Usually the momentum wanes just before the final phase of a campaign. In a three-year campaign, it is usually toward the end of the second year. In a five-year campaign, it is in year four. It is rare when a capital campaign doesn't halt at some point. People just tire of the routine. Also, natural problems occur around the summer months and holiday times such as Thanksgiving, Christmas, Chanukah, Fourth of July, Memorial Day, and Labor Day. Potential donors have other priorities on their minds, and the campaign is usually not high on their list. Also, disasters or national crises can affect campaigns. When the United States was attacked on September 11, 2001, many campaigns came to a halt as times were uncertain. Also, when Hurricane Katrina devastated the Gulf Coast in 2005, many prospective donors were directing their gifts to humanitarian needs. Some capital campaigns came up short on their smaller general gifts, although the larger lead gifts remained stable.

If the campaign plans for these "waning" periods, then the leaders can direct the volunteers through the valleys, and the overall campaign will not be affected. It is better to plan than to deny that a campaign can be stalled. Staff members can build certain "checkpoints" into the campaign plan—a time when the leaders evaluate what has been accomplished, if the campaign is on target, and if the next stages planned for the campaign are still appropriate.

In the mid-1990s, *The Chronicle of Philanthropy* carried an excellent article on "jump-starting" a stalled campaign. More than 10 years later, the advice included in that article is still on target. It stressed that organizations with inexperienced fundraisers can often jump into campaigns not realizing how difficult large goals are to achieve. The organizations then face potential public embarrassment as donations fail to appear as expected. An organization shouldn't publicly announce a campaign until it is certain it can reach its goal. If the best-planned capital campaign appears to be stalled, the following are some ideas to use to get out of those arid stretches:

- Focus attention on the mission of the organization and not on the need to build a new building. Bring emotion back into the campaign.
- Change the volunteer leadership. Bring new people in. Do not embarrass the current volunteers by removing them, but instead add to their numbers. Others suggest removing the nonproducing volunteers totally, as they most likely feel guilty that they haven't done a better job of soliciting funds and would be happy to be "let off the hook." Jerold Panas, a prominent fundraising consultant, says, "You can't let a capital campaign or the welfare of an institution suffer because you're afraid to hurt someone's feelings. You need to take them off the hook and let them get rid of the guilt."
- Solicit challenge grants that must be matched by other sources to lend a sense of urgency to the campaign.
- Hire a new consultant. Sometimes the fundraising consultant or consulting firm is the problem and should be replaced. The match with the volunteers may be wrong, and this may lead to the inability to motivate.
- End the campaign earlier than planned. Sometimes it is best to assess the situation, declare victory, and end the campaign.

Often if a campaign falters or stagnates in the middle of the drive, the leaders may be burned out, the economy may have

> *Evaluate the situation and make plans to either jump-start the campaign or to "declare victory."*

changed, or the goal just may have been set too high. Whatever the reasons, it is important to evaluate the situation and make plans to either jump-start the campaign or to "declare victory" and end the campaign. Either decision is appropriate. What is not appropriate is to allow the campaign to continue to falter by taking no action.

First of all, evaluate why prospects have been slow to make their gifts. Were there enough prospects for each gift level? Does the development staff need to do more research on potential donors? Has the economy in your community changed and affected your prospect base? Has there been a national emergency or crisis that has diverted attention away from the campaign? Is the case still relevant and timely? Were any shortcuts taken in starting the campaign? Were volunteers trained? Were all of the appropriate materials prepared? Were enough leadership gifts obtained before taking the campaign public? Have the donors been kept informed of the status of the campaign? They may be willing to increase their gifts to help you reach your goal. Plus, all donors must be nurtured for them to want to give again.

Options for a Troubled Campaign

To jump-start a faltering campaign, it may be necessary to reconstruct the campaign into smaller units or projects, based on the level of appeal to prospects. It may be that there were just too many programs involved with the campaign, and new priorities have to be set. Then if these priorities become funded, those programs placed aside can be added again. Another, similar approach is to consider the campaign as a series of "mini-campaigns." Aim to complete the goal of the first mini-campaign, then the second, the third, and so forth. It may be easier for donors to relate to a smaller scale campaign. Another option is to broaden the appeal. Review the case statement. Can it be expanded or changed to include new giving options? Consider ways to increase the number of prospects based on the expanded appeal. Also, watch how your money is being spent. Focus on the important tasks first. Organize your tasks by priority and size. Remember that it is possible to achieve victory one step at a time.

CAMPAIGN EVALUATION

Changing Trends

The face of capital campaigns today has changed in many instances. Some people think that campaigns have to bypass the traditional rules to be successful. As the economic environment has shifted, so too has the structure of capital campaigns. It is becoming more and more difficult to find volunteers to work on campaigns. Individuals are becoming more concerned about their time commitments. With the downsizing of corporations,

many persons took early retirement and then went through "retraining" to begin over in another field. Others are working second jobs to maintain their standard of living. Both groups think they no longer have time to volunteer. Others just don't want to have others ask them for favors, so they aren't interested in soliciting gifts in the first place. In addition to downsizing, yet another aspect of the changing world of the capital campaign is the merging of corporations, diminishing the amount of philanthropic dollars available to the nonprofit world. The lack of volunteers and the shortage of available funds have forced some campaigns to take a nontraditional approach to undertaking a capital campaign.

The rules mentioned in the opening of this chapter are being, if not dismissed, at least changed. Although a strong chair is still essential to a successful campaign, development staff are taking on more and more of the work traditionally assigned to the volunteers. With fewer volunteers available to select and train, staff members often are forced to actually solicit gifts—this once being the domain of the volunteers alone.

Again, the rules have changed so that campaigns are being launched without large advance gifts and without reaching 50 percent of the goal, although this is not recommended. Some campaigns are launched with only 30 percent of the goal obtained, and instead of several leadership gifts, only one or two lead gifts are included with a group of several smaller major gifts being added to reach the "launch" numbers. This really isn't advisable, as what this does is use gifts needed later in the campaign to reach the goal established by the feasibility study. Finally, sometimes the lead gift will come much later in the campaign, often as a closing gift or a gift to "top off" the campaign total. If this happens, it should just be considered a blessing and not part of any campaign plan.

Donors are expanding the number of charities that they support, giving less initially and then "adding to" their initial gifts if they are pleased with how their initial gift is being used, and they are not contributing at the levels they once were, nor at the levels research suggests donors might contribute. Many are making challenge gifts or pooling their gifts with other members of their families to give less but still donate a substantial amount. Yet others are making their gifts through planned giving vehicles instead of donating outright gifts of cash, in which case the charity does not receive the cash for many years. All this underscores the great need today in the nonprofit world for professional development officers who are well trained to handle the realities of capital campaign fundraising.

Capital campaigns also are the time to seek professional assistance from consultants. These are the individuals or firms who specialize in running capital campaigns and can provide the leadership necessary for success.

As more and more organizations are undertaking capital campaigns, the goals are becoming larger. This is especially true with university campaigns. It used to be common for their campaigns to seek millions of dollars. Now, the goals are in the billions. Some question whether the general public will continue to tolerate campaigns of this size, especially when a university may already have billions in its endowment. Certainly, it doesn't help when campaign goals seem to be determined by competition and not by the true needs of the institution or organization. But, the trend seems to be toward larger campaigns, both in dollars and scope. One hopes that the donors are asking the questions that the organizations may not be: what are the organizations' priorities and is the money truly needed to help the organizations fulfill their missions?

When to Start the Next Campaign

Some universities view capital campaigns as a source of "big money" with no ending. They ask donors for the next check as they thank them for the most recent. Donor burnout is happening more often, and the nonprofit world should beware. With several major fundraising scandals in the 1990s (The United Way of America and the New Era Foundation) and early 2000s (American Red Cross after September 11 and Hurricane Katrina), it is no wonder that many people are skeptical about giving again to an organization to which they have just donated a large sum of money. So when is the right time to start the next campaign? Ask your membership and your constituents through a feasibility study. Listen carefully, because they will be honest and direct. It may be that the organization's prospects perceive the new programs or buildings to be unnecessary. If this is the case, it will be nearly impossible to raise the money being sought. The supporters and donors need to think that there is a need and that they are not giving to an organization just caught up in a numbers game.

There have been attempts to regulate capital campaigns, especially among universities. Some have wanted capital campaigns to last no longer than seven years, oral pledges not to count in campaign totals, government dollars not to be counted in totals, and the full value of deferred gifts not to be counted, only the reduced value based on actuarial tables or other data to determine how much the gift is actually worth at the time it is made. Others have wanted a separation between outright gifts, pledges, and deferred gifts, making it easier to determine how much money would be available for immediate use. The fairness of these issues will continue to be debated. Whatever is done, it should not deter donors from making gifts to campaigns, and a firm belief should be instilled in donors that supporting organizations' and institutions' capital campaigns is the proper thing to do with their disposable cash or property.

For more information about capital campaigns, see *Capital Campaigns: Strategies That Work, Third Edition*, by Andrea Kihlstedt, another book published by Jones and Bartlett.

REFERENCES

Capital ideas: Highlighting capital campaigns, planned giving, and ethics. 1996. *Digest of Southern Giving* 10, no. 6: 5–6.

Causer, C. 2005. Shhh! Be very, very silent . . . we're hunting for capital. *The NonProfit Times*, October 1; 24–26.

Lipman, H. 2006. Money for capital needs is often scarce, study finds. *The Chronicle of Philanthropy*, May 4; 39.

Nobles, M. 2007. Capital campaigns are changing both in method and in donors. *The NonProfit Times*, October 1; 16–19.

Panas, J. 1995. *The no-nonsense guide to help you prepare a statement of your case*. Young & Partners, Inc.

Panas, J. 2003. *Making The Case—The No-Nonsense Guide to Writing the Perfect Case Statement*. Institutions Press.

Turning a campaign around—What fund raisers can do to jump-start a stalled campaign. 1996. *The Chronicle of Philanthropy*.

Three Keys to a Successful Capital Campaign

There are three keys to a successful capital campaign and organizations that have learned the importance of these critical ingredients are always more successful than those who do not understand the wisdom of following the tried and true principles of campaigning.

These critical requirements are:

- A Compelling Case for Support
- 100 Percent Board Commitment
- Effective Volunteer Leadership

One organization that learned the importance of following these time-tested principles was a volunteer firefighters association, starting their first ever capital campaign. After talking to key community leaders, they followed the advice of these business professionals and engaged a consultant to guide them through the process. The consultant helped them see the importance of developing these three key ingredients of successful capital campaigns.

A COMPELLING CASE FOR SUPPORT

One of the first things the consultant did was to help them develop a case statement for the campaign. Their case was certainly a compelling one. The organization's members included firefighters from over a hundred volunteer fire departments who pooled their resources to build a firefighting training center to train firefighters, not only from their county but from several surrounding counties and several other states. When the center was built more than fifteen years prior to the campaign, it was a state of the art. However, as one could well imagine, years of setting a building on fire in order to train firefighters in how to safely extinguish these fires, left its mark on the facility. The campaign was to upgrade and repair this much needed facility at a cost of $1.5 million.

The organization had already approached the county commissioners to help with this project and, after hearing the campaign plan, agreed to contribute half the amount that was needed. This commitment helped solidify the case, showing that the project would be a private/public partnership. The case outlined the renovations that were needed, the project budget, and a brief history of the center. It showed the number of firefighters that were trained there annually, and listed the geographic areas that were served by the center. It also contained some dramatic pictures of firefighters in action at the training center. And, as an important selling point to potential donors, it showed the opportunities for participation that included a number of named giving opportunities. The case was both emotional, appealing to anyone who has ever been a victim of a fire or knew someone who had been; and rational, showing clear costs and benefits to the community.

The case was then translated into a number of campaign materials including a leadership case statement, a brochure for the community appeal, pledge cards, and response envelopes that would be used during the various approaches to businesses and individuals in the community and grant proposals for foundations.

100 PERCENT BOARD COMMITMENT

As one would well imagine, an organization of this nature typically does not have a board comprised of the community's "movers and shakers." In fact, its board of thirty three members were all volunteer firefighters from a variety of backgrounds, mostly blue collar workers who cared enough about their community to devote a great deal of their time away from work to serve as volunteer firefighters.

When the consultant stressed the importance of 100 percent board commitment, she knew that the total amount raised from this board would not be a significant percentage of the campaign goal. And further, she recognized that there would likely be no major gifts received from board members. She stressed to the board that it was not the size of their individual gifts that was the

Source: Courtesy of Linda Lysakowski, ACFRE, President, Capital Venture, Las Vegas, Nevada.

critical factor, but that 100 percent commitment from the board would be an important sign to the community that this was a vital project for the organization and for the community. She suggested that if each board member would contribute $100 a year for three years, together they would raise nearly $10,000, a small percentage of the $750,000 that was their campaign goal, but an amount that showed the good faith and commitment of these hard working board members.

Board commitment also included at least four board members who would serve on the Campaign Cabinet and a commitment that each board member would promote the campaign in their individual fire companies and in their community. The board agreed to this step without hesitation.

When the board appeal was conducted, most pledged the suggested $300 and a few gave more. This amount, when reported to community leaders who were being recruited to serve on the Campaign Cabinet, made an impression on these volunteers who were amazed at the commitment of the board. In fact, they were impressed enough to step up to the plate and ensure that the last of the three critical ingredients would be successful.

EFFECTIVE VOLUNTEER LEADERSHIP

The consultant advised the board that the first person to recruit was the Capital Campaign Chair. There were two key community leaders identified by the board as being the ideal campaign chairs. An appointment was arranged with the head of the community's largest business to invite him to serve as honorary chair of the campaign, believing that his agreement would lead to the ability to recruit a top notch Campaign Cabinet.

A recruitment packet was prepared which contained the case for support, the campaign timeline and budget, the position description for the Honorary Chair as well as information about the organization and the project. After reviewing the packet and listening carefully to the reasons why this campaign was important to the community, the volunteer prospect had just one question—what would be the expected donation from his company towards the campaign goal? The recruitment team—the board chair, vice chair, and campaign consultant—explained that they would like the Honorary Chair to make the lead gift to the campaign. The prospective Honorary Chair not only agreed to serve as Campaign Chair but to attend monthly meetings, make the lead gift, assist in recruiting other Campaign Cabinet members, and solicit a select group of prospective donors. This volunteer agreed because the case and plan had been laid out, his duties and expectations of the organization were clearly defined and the people asking him to volunteer were able to clearly articulate the compelling case for support, and were fully committed board members.

Once the Chair was in place, a Vice Chair was easily recruited and together they signed a prepared letter inviting the community's "movers and shakers" to join the Campaign Cabinet. Almost every prospective cabinet member invited agreed to serve on the cabinet. The Chair was an effective leader, inspiring the team to success by his own commitment of time, money, and enthusiasm for the campaign.

This campaign reached its goal because the organization heeded the advice of a consultant in following the time-tested triduum of successful campaigns—a compelling case for support, 100% board commitment, and effective volunteer leadership.

Case Study: Getting Ready When You Are Not Ready

A small, local social service agency retained counsel to do a feasibility study for a $3 million capital campaign for a new building. The agency had been a part of the community for almost 100 years and provided educational, social, and recreational programs in one of the poorest parts of the city. Its present facility, while constructed in the early 1960s, was rapidly deteriorating due to heavy usage about 12–15 hours every day.

The agency was heavily funded by the United Way and received some small donations from community members but had no major donors. Its budget was relatively small, with limited flexibility. The board consisted of several local business people and professionals.

Counsel initially reviewed background information on the agency, including historical and financial records, leadership information, funding sources, plans for the new building, solicitation materials, and other items. Working with a small special committee established to help oversee the study process, the consultants prepared a list of interviewees, including several key corporate, civic, and philanthropic leaders. The interviews were carried out over a period of several weeks.

When the consultants started their analysis of the information collected from the interviews, there was one very obvious fact: almost none of those interviewed beyond the board and staff of the agency knew anything about it or what it did. Many did not even recognize the name of the agency.

This posed a very real problem for the agency and for counsel. If the key decision makers and donor prospects (especially the corporate and foundation leadership, who would be the primary prospects for the major gifts needed for a successful campaign) did not even know the agency or what it did, how could the agency launch a successful campaign?

The initial recommendation in the consultant's final report would have to be that the agency should not proceed with a campaign. This conclusion was due to the lack of recognition in the community, the lack of involvement of volunteer leadership able to access large gifts, and the small and limited donor base that already existed, thus indicating almost no prospects for major gifts.

But what should be done? The consultants felt that there needed to be an action plan to help the agency deal with this difficult issue so that it could get ready for a future campaign, hopefully in a relatively short time. But how could the agency quickly achieve recognition among the key community leadership and how could it build sufficient awareness and credibility to achieve its campaign goals?

After again reviewing all of the information collected, the consultants reached the conclusion that the problem and the solution were interconnected. Those people interviewed—especially the corporate, community, and philanthropic leadership—might be willing to give the agency help and advice on how to achieve greater recognition. The consultants saw there were a few keys to getting them involved in helping the agency:

- First, since they were all already active in the community, they needed a time-limited and task-focused way to become involved.
- Second, if they were to be recruited to help, it would take someone who was seen as a peer, and there wasn't anyone already involved with the agency who would probably fall into this category.
- Third, strategically it would be important to involve some people who might become volunteer leaders for the future campaign.
- And finally, it would be important to structure their activities so they would also learn more about the agency.

The consultants proposed to the agency that they establish a task force on image and awareness. The task force would only meet two times, and its role was to develop recommendations on how the agency could gain greater recognition and awareness in the city. The consultants worked with the staff and board of

Source: Courtesy of Eugene A. Scanlan, PhD, CFRE, President, eScanlan Company, Bethesda, Maryland.

the agency to determine any possible connections, even very limited, with individuals who might effectively recruit the task force members. It turned out that the executive director had grown up with a person who presently headed a major redevelopment organization and also was the head of the state senate. They had not kept in touch over the years, but it was decided to make the contact. After a few meetings with staff, some board members, and the consultants, the individual agreed to recruit and head the task force. One of the factors that probably convinced him to help was having him come to the agency to see some of its programs and meet the children, teenagers, and adults it served.

The consultants had identified six to ten key prospects for the task force based upon people interviewed, including the editor of the local newspaper, the retired head of the local university, and several corporate and other leaders. The chair of the task force also identified some additional people, including a prominent individual who had helped fund the startup of at least two major national companies headquartered in the city. The recruitment strategy included explaining that the consultants had recommended the formation of the task force to deal with the image/awareness problem rather than proceeding with a capital campaign, that the task force would only meet twice, and that people were only being asked for their help and advice.

Part of the strategy suggested by the consultant was to have the meetings of the task force at the agency, rather than in an office or club, so that the members could see the facilities. Members were taken on tours, and the physical plant needs were pointed out to them. Also, at the beginning of the first meeting the executive director gave a brief orientation to the agency, including its history, programs, and services, the nature of the area it served, and the needs it met.

The task force accomplished its tasks and developed a series of key recommendations to help raise the profile of the agency in the community, which were successfully implemented. But, also many members of the task force offered to help the agency in other ways. And finally, the prominent investment person was successfully recruited to head the capital campaign effort by the task force chair and some board members. When he had first walked in the door of the agency for the initial task force meeting, he had known nothing about it—he only knew he had been asked to help by a friend.

Campaign Planning: Sample Letter of Invitation for Feasibility Study Interview

January 14, 2008

Name
Address
City, State, Zip

Dear _____:

ABC organization would like your help and advice. We are carrying out an extensive planning process and are seeking the opinions of people like you who are concerned about the issues facing our area.

Specifically, we are inviting you to be interviewed by one of our consultants from Donor Strategies, Inc.—Barbara Ciconte, CFRE or Gene Scanlan, PhD, CFRE. These interviews, which will take about 45 minutes to one hour, are an important part of ABC's planning process. Your advice and suggestions will be of considerable value to us as we look to our future.

The interviews will be carried out in confidence by the consultants. They will not be asking for anything other than your views of ABC, the greater community it serves, and the human service needs of the area. No preparation is necessary. If possible, the consultants would prefer to conduct your interview in person at a time and location convenient for you.

A member of ABC staff will be contacting you to see if you will agree to be interviewed. If you agree, Barbara or Gene will contact you directly to arrange a time. We have enclosed a brief (brochure) (Case Statement) for your information. If you have any questions or need additional information, please call _____ at _____.

We will greatly appreciate your help with this important project.

Sincerely,

Board Chair name
Board Chair title

Example of a Feasibility Study Interview Questionnaire

AMERICAN SOCIETY OF CIVIL ENGINEERS FOUNDATION 2002:
BUILDING THE FUTURE

FEASIBILITY STUDY QUESTIONS

SECTION ONE—GENERAL QUESTIONS

N/A = No Answer

1. Have you read the Case Statement sent to you previously?

   Yes   No   N/A

2. Do you have changes to recommend to the Case Statement?

   Yes   No   N/A

   If yes, please explain.

   Comments:

3. Describe your relationship to the civil engineering profession?

   Comments:

4. How long have you been a member of ASCE?
   Circle # years:
   1–9 yrs
   10–19 yrs
   20–29 yrs
   30–39 yrs
   40–49 yrs
   50 plus
   Not a member

   Comments:

Source: Courtesy of the American Society of Civil Engineers Foundation, Reston, Virginia.

5. Are you familiar with ASCE's mission and programs?

   Yes　　　　　**No**　　　　　**N/A**

   Comments:

6. Are you familiar with CERF's mission and programs?

   Yes　　　　　**No**　　　　　**N/A**

   Comments:

7. Are you familiar with ASCE National's scholarship program?

   Yes　　　　　**No**　　　　　**N/A**

   Comments:

SECTION TWO—ASCE SCHOLARSHIPS

1. ASCE National awards approximately 30 scholarships. Do you think there are too many or too few scholarships given out?

   Too many　　　**Too few**　　　**Unsure**　　　　**N/A**

   Comments:

2. The average award is approximately $2,000. Do you think that this is adequate?

   Yes　　　　　**No**　　　　　**Unsure**　　　　**N/A**

   Comments:

3. If not, what do you think the awards should be?　　Circle one.
   $1
   $2K
   $3K
   $4K
   $5K
   $6K
   $7K
   $8K
   $10K
   $15K
   Full tuition scholarship

   Comments:

4. Do you think that the ASCE scholarship funds are well managed?

   Yes　　　　　**No**　　　　　**Unsure**　　　　**N/A**

   Comments:

5. Do you think a fund raising drive to secure more funds for scholarships would be successful?

    Yes   **No**   **Maybe**   **N/A**

    Comments:

6. Would you give money to support the current scholarship endowments?

    Yes   **No**   **Maybe**   **N/A**

    Comments:

SECTION THREE—CIVIL ENGINEERING RESEARCH FOUNDATION (CERF)

1a. Are you familiar with CERF?

    Yes   **No**   **N/A**

    Comments:

1b. If yes, how long have you been aware of it?

    1–5 years   **5–10 years**   **10+ years**   **N/A**

    Comments:

2. How familiar are you with CERF's mission and programs?

    Very Familiar   **Generally Familiar**   **Not Familiar**   **N/A**

3. Do you think CERF fills a valuable or unique niche in the design and construction industry?

    Yes   **No**   **Unsure**   **N/A**

    Comments:

4. CERF's mission statement has 3 components. I'm going to read each one to you and I want you to rate each as a high, medium or low priority. (Each ranking is independent of the other. They can all be 1's, 2's, or 3's.)

    1—High priority   **2—Medium priority**   **3—Low priority**

		1	2	3	No Answer
a.	To facilitate and coordinate greater cooperation between government, industry, and academia with respect to research and development				
b.	Leveraging limited research dollars and resources to maximize return on investment				
c.	Streamlining evaluation processes and assisting in overcoming barriers to moving innovation and new technologies into the marketplace				

    Comments:

5. What are the most useful and significant services or programs CERF offers you or your company?

6. What do you consider to be the most compelling aspects of CERF? What themes or projects should be highlighted as we present CERF's case for support?

7. Do you believe a major fundraising campaign solely for CERF would be supported by ASCE's members?

   Yes   **No**   **Unsure**   **N/A**

   Comments:

8. How high a priority would you rank a campaign for CERF compared to other campaigns or activities individual ASCE members are asked to be involved?

   High   **Medium**   **Low**   **N/A**

   Comments:

9. Can you think of any potential conflicts, or possible impediments, to raising funds for CERF?

10. Do you agree that there is a need to fund additional research and development efforts for this civil engineering?

    Yes   **No**   **N/A**

    Comments:

SECTION FOUR—PROMOTING PUBLIC AWARENESS OF CIVIL ENGINEERING
Please rate the importance of each according to the following:

High Priority   **Medium Priority**   **Low Priority**   **N/A**

1. **Postage Stamp**
   Lobby for issuance of a United States postage stamp honoring 150 years of civil engineering progress. (Approximate Cost: To be determined)

   High Priority   **Medium Priority**   **Low Priority**   **N/A**

   Comments:

2. **Broadcast Teleproduction**
   Create a "high-end" television program dealing with an appropriate aspect of civil engineering to be broadcast on: The History Channel, The Discovery Channel, and/or PBS. (Approximate Cost: $350,000 to $500,000)

   High Priority   **Medium Priority**   **Low Priority**   **N/A**

   Comments:

3. **Public Service Outreach**
   Partner with a recognized philanthropic organization (such as Habitat for Humanity) in the area of community service to take advantage of the skills and knowledge of professional engineers. A well-orchestrated community service outreach, perhaps more

so than any other program, will communicate our key messages by demonstrating the leadership of civil engineers as people-serving and problem-solving. (Approximate Cost: $50,000 for planning and administration)

High Priority   Medium Priority   Low Priority   N/A

Comments:

4. **Education Initiative**

ASCE needs to educate America's youth about the role of civil engineers in society. This is an investment in the future of our profession. The future leaders of our profession are represented in today's classrooms. They will become tomorrow's community and opinion leaders, influencing future public infrastructure projects. There is a need for a significant educational outreach component. (Approximate Cost: To be determined)

High Priority   Medium Priority   Low Priority   N/A

Comments:

5. **Museum-Based Efforts**

Hold discussions with the National Building Museum (NBM) to identify various collaborative projects that would support the objectives of both the Society and the Museum, such as the Civil Engineering Hall of Fame. (Approximate Cost: To be determined)

High Priority   Medium Priority   Low Priority   N/A

Comments:

6. **Smithsonian Exhibit**

Work with the Smithsonian Institution to enhance its existing civil engineering exhibition. (Since the Smithsonian has curtailed its efforts to add to its engineering collection, this would be a far less ambitious effort than that at the NBM.) (Approximate Cost: $70,000)

High Priority   Medium Priority   Low Priority   N/A

Comments:

7. **Gallery Exhibition**

A gallery exhibition at a special museum (such as the National Building Museum) as a joint effort of ASCE and NBM. To extend the reach of the exhibit, it could be designed for use as a touring exhibit offered to science and technology museums in the years following the anniversary. (Approximate Cost: $500,000 for NBM efforts)

High Priority   Medium Priority   Low Priority   N/A

Comments:

8. **Traveling Exhibition**

Develop a traveling exhibition to bring this visual history of the profession to audiences nationwide with key components taken from the permanent collection. The exhibits are intended to be displayed at meeting of a wide range of organizations representing our target audiences, such as the National Governors Association, the National Conference of Mayors, or Founders Society meetings, or at local venues such as public libraries, state capitals, or even shopping malls. (Approximate Cost: $250,000)

High Priority   Medium Priority   Low Priority   N/A

Comments:

9. Do you think that ASCE should conduct a fundraising campaign to support public awareness of civil engineering?

Yes   **No**   **Unsure**   **N/A**

Comments:

10. Would you make a gift to support such a campaign?

Yes   **No**   **Unsure**   **N/A**

Comments:

SECTION FIVE—A UNIFIED CAMPAIGN

1. Do you think that a unified campaign for these three (3) areas (Scholarships, CERF, and Public Awareness of Civil Engineering) would be successful?

Yes   **No**   **Maybe**   **N/A**

Comments:

2. What amount would you recommend to be considered as a goal for such a unified campaign?
$1–2 million
$2–4 million
$3–5 million
$5–6 million
$7–8 million
$9–10 million
$10–15 million
$20–40 million
$25 million
No answer

Comments:

3. Do you think this campaign, if publicly launched in October 1999, would be following too closely to the recent **Building for the 21st Century** Campaign?

Yes   **No**   **Maybe**   **N/A**

Comments:

4a. Do you think reaching a $5 million goal is feasible within one year?

Yes   **No**   **Maybe**   **N/A**

Comments:

4b. Do you think this is feasible within two years?

Yes   No   Maybe   N/A

Comments:

4c. Do you think this is feasible within three years?

Yes   No   Maybe   N/A

Comments:

5. Do you think the money raised should be shared equally by all three interests?

Yes   No   Maybe   N/A

Comments:

6. Should the money raised be divided according to pre-determined percentages?

Yes   No   Maybe   N/A

Comments:

7. Should donors be able to designate to where they their gift would be assigned?

Yes   No   Maybe   N/A

Comments:

8. Which ones would you designate? (You can designate more than one.)
    Scholarship
    CERF
    Public Awareness
    No Answer

Comments:

9. Would the amount of your gift change if you were able to designate your gift to a specific area?

Yes   No   Maybe   N/A

Comments:

10. Leadership gifts of $10,000 or higher will play a major role in the success of this campaign; 80% of the goal should be received at this level. Would you be willing to make a leadership gift?

Yes   No   Maybe   N/A

Comments:

11. On the page I am handing you are ranges of gifts. Where in this range do you think your gift will fall?
    A = $100,000 and above
    B = $50,000 to $99,999
    C = $25,000 to $49,999
    D = $10,000 to $24,999
    E = $5,000 to $9,999
    F = $1,000 to $4,999
    G = Below $1,000
    N/A

    Comments:

12. Would you be more likely to give, if you could pledge your gift over two, three, four, or five years?

Yes	2 years	3 years	4 years	5 years
No	Unsure	N/A		

    Comments:

13. Are there ASCE members or friends of ASCE you would consider to be top prospects for giving at the leadership level above $10,000?

Yes	No	Maybe	N/A

14. Would you share their names?

15. Would your company or employer make a gift?

Yes	No	Maybe	N/A

    Comments:

16. Would recognition play a part in your being willing to make a gift? For example, if your name were to be included on a plaque in the ASCE World Headquarters, would this be an influence in your giving?

Yes	No	Maybe	N/A

    Comments:

17. What kind of recognition do you think is appropriate for contributing? Circle one.

    Plaque

    Name published in monthly ASCE periodical

    Invitation to special event at ASCE annual meeting

    Ribbon/badge recognition at ASCE annual meeting

    Other (Please describe):

18. Would recognition make a difference in the amount of your gift?

   Yes   No   Maybe   N/A

   Comments:

19. Do you see any obstacles to a unified campaign?

   Yes   No   Maybe   No Comment

   Comments:

20. Would you recommend that ASCE conduct this unified campaign?

   Yes   No   Unsure   N/A

   Comments:

21. Would you make visits or telephone calls on behalf of the campaign?

   Yes   No   Maybe   N/A

   Comments:

22. Are there any firms, foundations, individuals, etc. that you would recommend we contact during this feasibility stage?

23. When do you think that this unified campaign should begin?

24. Most fundraising campaigns have an overall theme or a name. For example, the campaign to raise money for the new ASCE World Headquarters was called the *Building for the 21st Century* Campaign. What would you recommend that this new joint effort campaign be called?

25. A campaign depends upon volunteer leadership. Are there any persons you would recommend to chair this campaign?

Interviewer Notes & Comments

Capital Campaign Phases

A. GENERIC CAMPAIGN PHASES

The campaign will be conducted in five phases beginning in January 2008 through December 2011. Each phase will have a number of specific objectives.

PHASE I—ORGANIZATIONAL

January 2008–August 2008
- Complete planning phase.
- Complete campaign brochure.
- Establish campaign calendar.
- Employ campaign counsel and support staff.
- Hold preliminary planning meetings.
- Recruit campaign volunteer leadership.
- Develop list of leadership gift prospects.
- Develop gift chart and rationale.
- Develop campaign materials: stationery, business cards, *Volunteer Handbook*.
- Request annual reports from corporations and foundations to be solicited.

PHASE II—LEADERSHIP GIFT SOLICITATION

September 2008–May 2009
- Solicit prospects to obtain 35 leadership gifts totaling $8,500,000.
- Complete recruitment of campaign cabinet (volunteer committee).
- Identify additional leadership gift prospects.
- Complete campaign materials: brochures, pledge cards, prospect lists, letterhead, solicitation guides, *Volunteer Handbook,* etc.
- Identify major gift prospects.
- Recruit major gift volunteers (expand campaign cabinet) for various constituencies.
- Complete leadership gifts ($230,000 to $1 million).
- Develop pledge and gift-tracking and collection procedures.
- Thank donors and enter into database.
- Send newsletter and annual report to donors.
- Develop donor recognition opportunities.

PHASE III—MAJOR GIFTS

June 2009–February 2010
- Announce publicly the campaign, goal, leadership, and leadership gifts totaling $8,500,000.
- Solicit major gifts from more than 100 prospects to raise $2,625,000.
- Expand volunteer organization for solicitation of special and general gifts.
- Identify special and general gift prospects.
- Train special and general gift volunteers.
- Initiate intensive publicity campaign.
- Monitor pledges.
- Thank new donors and enter into database.
- Send newsletter to donors.

PHASE IV—SPECIAL GIFTS—EXPANSION OF CAMPAIGN

March 2010–December 2010
- Complete major gifts.
- Conduct solicitation of special gifts from 100 prospects to raise $775,000.
- Finalize general gift prospect list.
- Monitor pledges.
- Thank new donors and enter into database.
- Send newsletter to donors.
- Train new volunteers.

PHASE V—GENERAL GIFTS, CLOSURE, AND VICTORY CELEBRATION

January 2011–December 2011
- Complete special gifts phase.
- Solicit general gifts from more than 55 remaining prospects to raise $100,000 for a general campaign totaling $12 million.
- Thank new donors and enter onto the database.
- Hold victory celebration-ribbon cutting or ground breaking with dinner for significant donors.

B. EIGHT CAMPAIGN PHASES—*2002: BUILDING THE FUTURE*

PHASE ONE

Phase One will require six months (March–August 1999) and focus on the following:

1. Execute Memorandums of Understanding with ASCE and CERF.
2. Research and identifying possible volunteers for the honorary chairs, campaign chairs, and other top leadership.
3. Secure leadership gifts from ASCE and CERF.
4. ASCE and CERF will address and act upon recommendations.
5. Develop a detailed campaign plan, public relations program, and timetable.
6. Establish a campaign office and arrange support staff.
7. Write and design the plan for total marketing package including the case statement, brochures, any audio-visuals, and a gift recognition/giving club plan.
8. Prepare a leadership gift prospectus.
9. Develop all campaign operational materials including pledge forms and volunteer training manuals.
10. Prepare comprehensive prospect lists.

PHASE TWO

Phase Two will require seven months (September 1999–March 2000) and will focus on the following:

1. Recruit all of the campaign leadership and cabinet.
2. Solicit at least $1,000,000 in leadership gifts, in addition to soliciting a gift of $2.5 million from ASCE.
3. Solicit the ASCE and CERF Boards and Past Presidents.
4. Plan the public announcement of the campaign at: April 2000 ASCE Board meeting; the CERF International Symposium and Trade Show in August 2000; and the ASCE Convention in October (with at least $3 million committed).

PHASE THREE

Phase Three will require seven months (April 2000–October 2000) and will focus on the following:

1. Conduct public launches of campaign in April, August, and October.
2. Begin the public relations program.
3. Continue to solicit leadership gifts.
4. Launch major gift solicitation from prospects that are capable of gifts of $20,000 or higher.
5. Launch the public relations program.
6. Solicit an additional $500,000 to bring the total to $3.5 million.

PHASE FOUR

Phase Four will require seven months (November 2000–May 2001) and will focus on the following:

1. Complete all leadership and major gift solicitations.
2. Expand public relations efforts.
3. Solicit an additional $500,000 to achieve a total solicitation of at least $4 million.

PHASE FIVE

Phase Five will require seven months (July 2001–December 2001).

1. Launch an Every Member Campaign to engage the general ASCE membership.
2. Emphasize solicitation of all ASCE members for support at the general recognition level of $1,500 or greater.
3. Launch the solicitation of funds from all ASCE members emphasizing giving $1,500 for the 150th anniversary.
4. Solicit an additional $500,000 to reach $4,500,000.

PHASE SIX

Phase Six will require eight months (January 2002–August 2002).

1. Coordinate special fundraising efforts with 150th Anniversary events as they occur across the country.
2. Solicit $500,000 to reach $5,000,000.
3. Plan the celebration of reaching the goal of $5,000,000 at the ASCE 2002 Convention.
4. Celebrate the campaign's success at ASCE's Convention in July or August of 2002.
5. End campaign on January 31, 2003.

PHASE SEVEN

Phase Seven will require five months (September 2002–January 2003).

1. Complete all planned solicitations.
2. Continue to coordinate special fundraising efforts.
3. End campaign on January 31, 2003.

PHASE EIGHT

1. Design and coordinate installation of donor wall (Monument to American Civil Engineering) with ASCE and CERF.

Campaign Activities Timetable

2008 CAMPAIGN ACTIVITIES FLOW CHART
Month-to-Month Timetable

Activity	Jan.	Feb.	Mar.	Apr.	May	June	July	Aug.	Sept.	Oct.	Nov.	Dec.
ORGANIZATION/RECRUITMENT												
Campaign Cabinet/ Divisional Chairs												
Train Volunteers												
SOLICITATION												
Leadership Gifts $250K to $1M												
Major Gifts $25,000 to $249,999												
Identify Gift Prospects												
Write Planned Giving Handbook												
PUBLIC RELATIONS/CAMPAIGN MATERIALS												
Announce Campaign												
Foundation/Newsletter												
Annual Report												
FOLLOW UP												
Acknowledgments to Prospects/Donors												
Collection of Gifts and Pledges												

2009 CAMPAIGN ACTIVITIES FLOW CHART

Month-to-Month Timetable

Activity	Jan.	Feb.	Mar.	Apr.	May	June	July	Aug.	Sept.	Oct.	Nov.	Dec.
SOLICITATION												
Major Gifts $25,000 to $249,999												
Special Gifts $10,000 to $24,999												
Identify Prospects for General Gifts												
PUBLIC RELATIONS/CAMPAIGN MATERIALS												
Newsletter												
Annual Report												
FOLLOW UP												
Acknowledgments to Prospects/Donors												
Collection of Gifts and Pledges												

2010 CAMPAIGN ACTIVITIES FLOW CHART

Month-to-Month Timetable

Activity	Jan.	Feb.	Mar.	Apr.	May	June	July	Aug.	Sept.	Oct.	Nov.	Dec.
SOLICITATION												
General Gifts, < $1,000 to $9,999												
PUBLIC RELATIONS												
Newsletter												
Campaign Celebration												
Annual Report												
FOLLOW UP												
Acknowledgments to Prospects/Donors												
Collection of Gifts and Pledges												

Donor Gift Recognition Opportunities Guide

Source: Courtesy of the American Society of Civil Engineers Foundation, Reston, Virginia.

Donor Gift Recognition

We are delighted that you are considering making a gift to the ASCE Foundation's *2002: Building The Future* campaign. At whatever level you decide to make your gift, you can be assured that it will be much appreciated.

To make gift giving easier, please note that you can pledge your gifts over several years and make your payments in installments by check or credit card, and you can even use appreciated stock. We have included instructions on how to transfer appreciated stocks to the Foundation.

The Gift Recognition Levels for *2002: Building The Future* are as follows:

■	Titanium	$500,000 and greater
■	Platinum	$250,000 - 499,999
■	Gold	$100,000 - 249,999
■	Silver	$ 50,000 - 99,999
■	Copper	$ 25,000 - 49,999
■	Bronze	$ 10,000 - 24,999
■	Brass	$ 5,000 - 9,999
■	Pewter	$ 1,500 - 4,999

Please read the following pages. After reviewing them, if you have any questions regarding how to make a gift or what recognition you will receive for your gift, please contact:

Campaign Manager
2002: Building The Future
Sixth Floor
ASCE Foundation
1015 15th Street, NW
Washington, DC 20005-2605
Phone: 202-789-2874
Fax: 202-682-3471
E-mail: ASCEFoundation@asce.org

Transferring Securities to the ASCE Foundation

1 The Foundation has opened an account with Charles Schwab & Company, Inc. to facilitate this giving opportunity. The **Foundation's account number at Schwab is 1121-6843** and was opened at Schwab's **Washington, DC office**. The Foundation's **Tax ID number is: 52-1891243**.

2 **Please call 1-800-435-4000, Charles Schwab & Company, Inc.'s toll free number**, to determine the Schwab office nearest you and their hours of availability. At the same time, ask them if they have a notary public available.

3 If the stock you plan to give is in your name, please complete a **Third Party Release form [INTER 476-2 (3/91)] and have it notarized** before presenting it to a Schwab broker. Some Schwab offices have notary publics and others do not. If not, most banks and city clerk's offices have notary publics available for your use. When using a notary, you must have some sort of photo identification with you.

4 You will be asked if the stock certificate is being physically held by you, by Schwab, or by another brokerage firm. **If you are physically holding the stock certificate**, you may either mail the certificate to Schwab with directions that it be transferred to the American Society of Civil Engineers Foundation, Inc. whose Schwab account number is **1121-6843**; or personally deliver the stock to a broker at the Schwab office nearest you. In either case, **the back of the stock certificate must be signed by you and must be accompanied by the notarized Third Party Release form. Do not endorse anything on the back of the certificate other than your name** as it appears on the front. Your Schwab broker will complete the remainder of the information for you. All deliveries **must** include the Foundation's name and Schwab account number.

5 If you do not physically hold the stock certificate and it is held by a brokerage firm, either Schwab or some other firm, they may have the stock **transferred electronically (using DTC Clearing 0164, Code 40)** directly to Schwab by using the account number 1121-6843 and the complete name of the Foundation's account - The American Society of Civil Engineers Foundation, Inc. Again, all deliveries **must** include the Foundation's name and Schwab account number.

Thank you for considering a gift of securities to support civil engineering and The American Society of Civil Engineers Foundation, Inc.

TITANIUM - $500,000 or greater

- Name on donor wall at TITANIUM level in ASCE World Headquarters

- Naming opportunity for CERF's Main Conference Room

- Name as sponsor of major civil engineering exhibit in the National Building Museum, Washington, DC

- Opportunity to publicize name as sponsor of ASCE's 150th anniversary celebration

- Additionally receive:

  ▶ Special listing in CERF's research reports disseminated worldwide

  ▶ Recognition in ASCE's "Advertorial" in major national newspapers/magazines

  ▶ Name on "traveling" civil engineering exhibit that will circulate across the country

  ▶ Name listed as a sponsor of the Congressional Reception honoring ASCE's 150th anniversary

  ▶ *The American Civil Engineer* (Wisely) - Complimentary leather bound copy of the 150th anniversary edition with your name printed in the book

  ▶ Name listed in *ASCE News* and *ASCE Foundation News*

  ▶ Invitation to an exclusive, festive event celebrating close of campaign

PLATINUM - $250,000 to $499,999

- Name on donor wall at PLATINUM level in ASCE World Headquarters

- Name as exclusive supporter of **one** of CERF's two Clearinghouses, if appropriate:
  - HITEC Information Clearinghouse
  - EvTEC Information Clearinghouse

  or

  Name as major supporter of **one** of CERF's seven major programs which are:
  - Materials Program (CONMAT)
  - Information Technology Program
  - Benchmarking Program
  - Sustainable Development Program
  - Infrastructure Program (PAIR)
  - Energy Efficiency Program
  - Buildings Program

- Major recognition in an ASCE "Advertorial" and acknowledgment as a supporter in ASCE 150th anniversary promotional materials in the print media

- Opportunity to publicize name as sponsor of ASCE's 150th anniversary celebration

- Additionally receive:

  ▶ Special listing in CERF's research reports disseminated worldwide

  ▶ Name on "traveling" civil engineering exhibit that will circulate across the country

  ▶ Name listed as a sponsor of the Congressional Reception honoring ASCE's 150th anniversary

  ▶ *The American Civil Engineer* (Wisely) - Complimentary leather bound copy of the 150th anniversary edition with your name printed in the book

  ▶ Name listed in *ASCE News* and *ASCE Foundation News*

  ▶ Invitation to an exclusive, festive event celebrating close of campaign

2002: Building The

GOLD - $100,000 to $249,999

Name on donor wall at GOLD level in ASCE World Head-quarters

Naming opportunity for **one** of CERF's key office facilities:
- President's Office
- Executive Conference Room
- Innovation Awards Lobby

Name as sponsor on "traveling" civil engineering exhibit

Opportunity to publicize name as sponsor of ASCE's 150th anniversary celebration

Additionally receive:

▶ Name listed as a sponsor of the Congressional Reception honoring ASCE's 150th anniversary

▶ The American Civil Engineer (Wisely) - Complimentary leather bound copy of the 150th anniversary edition with your name printed in the book

▶ Invitation to one of CERF's corporate gatherings to hear and discuss the latest innovative technologies and processes

▶ Special listing in a select CERF research report dissemi-nated worldwide

▶ Name listed in ASCE News and ASCE Foundation News

▶ Invitation to an exclusive, festive event celebrating close of campaign

SILVER - $50,000 to $99,999

Name on donor wall at SILVER level in ASCE World Headquarters

Name as sponsor of the keynote speaker at CERF's Corpo-rate Advisory Board dinner in 2002
or
Naming opportunity as a supporter of **one** of the following CERF sabbatical or intern positions in the year in which they are offered:
- Sabbatical/intern position in Buildings
- Sabbatical/intern position in Information Technology
- Sabbatical/intern position in Environment
- Sabbatical/intern position in Materials
- Sabbatical/intern position in Energy Efficiency
- Sabbatical/intern position in Transportation

Opportunity to publicize name as sponsor of ASCE's 150th anniversary celebration

Additionally receive:

▶ Name listed as a sponsor of the Congressional Reception honoring ASCE's 150th anniversary

▶ Invitation to one of CERF's corporate gatherings to hear and discuss the latest innovative technologies and processes

▶ Special listing in a select CERF research report dissemi-nated worldwide

▶ The American Civil Engineer (Wisely) - Complimentary copy of the 150th anniversary edition with your name printed in the book

▶ Name listed in ASCE News and ASCE Foundation News

▶ Invitation to an exclusive, festive event celebrating close of campaign

Future

BRONZE - $10,000 to $24,999

- Name on donor wall at BRONZE level in ASCE World Headquarters

- Name listed as a major supporter in a CERF research report presented to Members of Congress and disseminated worldwide

- Opportunity to publicize name as sponsor of ASCE's 150th anniversary celebration

- Additionally receive:

  ▶ Invitation to one of CERF's corporate gatherings to hear and discuss the latest innovative technologies and processes

  ▶ *The American Civil Engineer* (Wisely) - Complimentary copy of the 150th anniversary edition with your name printed in the book

  ▶ Name listed in *ASCE News* and *ASCE Foundation News*

  ▶ Invitation to an exclusive, festive event celebrating close of campaign

BRASS - $5,000 to $9,999

- Name on donor wall at BRASS level in ASCE World Headquarters

- Name listed as a supporter at one of CERF's corporate meetings focusing on innovation and collaboration with key industry executives and government officials

- Additionally receive:

  ▶ Invitation to one of CERF's corporate gatherings to hear and discuss the latest innovative technologies and processes

  ▶ *The American Civil Engineer* (Wisely) - Complimentary copy of the 150th anniversary edition with your name printed in the book

  ▶ Name listed in *ASCE News* and *ASCE Foundation News*

  ▶ Invitation to an exclusive, festive event celebrating close of campaign

PEWTER - $1,500 to $4,999

- Name on donor wall at PEWTER level in ASCE World Headquarters

- Recognition in ASCE 150th anniversary newsletter

- Additionally receive:

  ▶ *The American Civil Engineer* (Wisely) - Your name printed in the 150th anniversary edition

  ▶ Name listed in *ASCE News* and *ASCE Foundation News*

  ▶ Invitation to an exclusive, festive event celebrating close of campaign

Example of an Ask Letter for a Leadership Gift

November 7, 2000

Mr. John Q. Smith, P.E., M.ASCE
President and CEO
ABCDEF Corporation
Suite 1000
8000 Michigan Avenue
Chicago, Illinois 60000

Dear John:

As you know from our recent visit and discussion with you, the American Society of Civil Engineers (ASCE) Foundation is embarking upon a major capital campaign to support ASCE's 150th Anniversary Programs and to grow CERF's Innovation Fund. Entitled, *2002: Building The Future*, this campaign will help to build a financial foundation for the advancement of the art and science of civil engineering in the 21st century.

The early support of the leadership of ASCE will be crucial to the success of this endeavor. Accordingly, we seek your financial support by asking you to make a commitment of $500,000 to the Campaign which may be paid over several years. A gift at this level would mean a great deal to the Society and to our entire engineering and construction community. We ask that you give most serious consideration to our request for a leadership gift to support the *2002: Building The Future* campaign.

In return, the ASCE Foundation would be honored to offer commemoration of your gift in the ASCE World Headquarters Building. The *Monument to Civil Engineering* will be permanent recognition of those whose leadership to the campaign contributed so much to our success. Materials describing gift recognition opportunities are enclosed.

On behalf of Honorary Chairs Stephen D. Bechtel, Jr. and Charles J. Pankow, we look forward to having you join us in making a gift to this important Campaign. With your support, we will continue to create exciting momentum for *2002: Building The Future*.

Sincerely yours,

Robert W. Bein, P.E., L.S., F.ASCE   Stephen C. Mitchell, P.E., F.ASCE
Co-Chair   Co-Chair
2002: Building The Future   *2002: Building The Future*

Enclosures

cc: S.D. Bechtel
     C.J. Pankow
     J.G. Jacob

Source: Courtesy of the American Society of Civil Engineers Foundation, Reston, Virginia.

Letter Requesting a Meeting to Seek a Major Gift for a Campaign—but Not a Leadership Gift

August 13, 2001

Mr. John Q. Smith, P.E., M.ASCE
President and CEO
ABCDEF Corporation
Suite 1000
2000 Michigan Avenue
Chicago, Illinois 60000

Dear John:

As you may know, the American Society of Civil Engineers (ASCE) Foundation is embarking upon an exciting capital campaign to support ASCE's 150th Anniversary Programs and to grow CERF's Innovation Fund. Entitled *2002: Building The Future*, this campaign is both historic and future focused.

The monies raised by the campaign will be used in a number of ways including: honoring the successes of civil engineering, increasing the public's awareness of the profession, and helping to ensure the industry's future value and competitiveness.

With the help of many friends and current supporters of ASCE and CERF, *2002: Building The Future* has achieved outstanding success to date—we have surpassed half of our campaign goal, raising more than $3.6 million! However, the support of all ASCE's and CERF's top leadership, such as you, will be crucial to the success of this endeavor, and we want to explore your interest in supporting the campaign.

Within the next few days, our campaign manager Mary Jones will contact your office to inquire if it is possible for you to meet with us sometime next month in Chicago. Our meeting will require approximately 30 minutes of your time.

In the meantime, please let us thank you in advance for your cooperation in scheduling an appointment. We look forward to visiting with you in September and telling you more about *2002: Building The Future*.

Sincerely yours,

Robert W. Bein, P.E., L.S., F.ASCE   Stephen C. Mitchell, P.E., F.ASC
Co-Chair   Co-Chair
2002: Building The Future   *2002: Building The Future*

cc: S.D. Bechtel
     C.J. Pankow
     J.G. Jacob

Source: Courtesy of the American Society of Civil Engineers Foundation, Reston, Virginia.

Letter to Campaign Chairs to Update Progress of Campaign After a Major National Catastrophe

November 1, 2001

Mr. John Q. Smith, Hon. M.ASCE
Chairman Emeritus
XYZ Corporation
9000 Main Street, Suite 1000
San Francisco, CA 94000

Dear John:

I want to take the opportunity to address the impact of the September 11th terrorist attacks on the ASCE Foundation's *2002: Building The Future* campaign.

The horrific events of September 11th have had an enormous impact on all of us individually and, in particular, on civil engineers and our profession. In the wake of the terrorist attacks, safeguarding our nation's infrastructure and securing the public's safety has been at the heart of national dialogue. During the past six weeks, ASCE has been rallying its members and their expertise in support of the Society's Disaster Response efforts. The outpouring of support from ASCE's membership has been phenomenal.

In addition to providing our support for these efforts, the ASCE Foundation is moving forward with its campaign to help ASCE and CERF continue with their work by building strong financial foundations for the advancement of civil engineering in the 21st century. By continuing with the campaign, we hope to bring to the public's attention the role of civil engineering in strengthening our infrastructure, as well as ensuring the industry's future value and competitiveness.

On an encouraging note, the Foundation continues to receive positive responses to its solicitations for support of the *2002: Building The Future* campaign. Needless to say, with the public's attention and philanthropy focused on the disaster response efforts, as well as the weakening economy, the Foundation faces quite a challenge in meeting its campaign goal of $6 million; however, we do not think this is an insurmountable goal.

As you probably are aware, ASCE launched its 150th Anniversary Year programs this October in Houston, Texas during the Society's annual conference. We expect the anniversary year to create great momentum for the campaign and its programs.

If you have any questions or concerns regarding *2002: Building The Future* in light of September 11th, please contact me at (703) 295-6346.

With my very best personal regards.

Sincerely yours,

Jeanne G. Jacob, CAE, CFRE
Executive Vice President

Source: Courtesy of the American Society of Civil Engineers Foundation, Reston, Virginia.

Chapter 15

The Basics of Planned Giving

CHAPTER OUTLINE

- Definition of Planned Giving
- The Steps to Establish a Successful Planned Giving Program
- Identifying the Best Prospects
- Marketing Your Planned Giving Program
- The Role of Volunteers
- The Bequest Society: The Simplest Way to Begin
- How Planned Giving Fits into a Major Gifts Program

KEY VOCABULARY

- Annuities
- Bequests
- Bequest Society
- Estates
- Gift Policies
- Gift Vehicles
- Life Income Gifts
- Planned Giving
- Planned Giving Committee
- Trusts
- Wills

DEFINITION OF PLANNED GIVING

Planned giving is also known as deferred giving, future giving, and gift planning. Also, for those new to the area of planned giving, there is a simple way to understand the difference between planned giving and major gift fundraising. Major gifts are defined as outright gifts from one's income (cash or securities) while planned giving primarily deals with gifts of assets such as real estate, works of art, life insurance policies, tangible property, and securities. The vast majority of these gifts are given after the donor has died and the arrangements for planned gifts have been made in a donor's will or estate planning. Planned giving opportunities also allow a donor to make a contribution and receive income back, after a certain age, from gift vehicles such as annu-

ities or various charitable trusts. Exhibit 15–1 lists reasons why planned giving is important to nonprofit organizations.

This type of fundraising, with its own jargon, is by far the most technical in the development field. The best way for development officers to promote this type of giving is not to focus on the technical aspect but, instead, to focus on the donor perspective and what planned giving can do for the donor. What are the donor's philanthropic goals? Who are the people for whom the donor needs to provide, such as a spouse, children, and/or grandchildren? What type of assets (cash, stocks, bonds, insurance, independent retirement account, real estate, art, antiques, family business) does the donor have? Are the donor's financial objectives to avoid capital gains tax or to increase income? In addition to family, does the donor have other interests for which he or she would like to make a planned gift—his or her university, prep school, professional society, etc?

Exhibit 15–1 Why Planned Giving Is Important to Nonprofit Organizations

- Planned gifts generally tend to be large gifts.
- Because many planned gifts are irrevocable, they allow organizations to do better planning for their future.
- Publicizing gifts can help generate interest among other prospective donors.
- Planned gift donors, when properly cultivated, are likely prospects for annual gifts and subsequent larger gifts, including an additional planned gift.

Cultivating donors or building long-term relationships with donors is the beginning of a planned giving program. Very few people will make a planned gift without a strong commitment to an organization or institution. The connections can be made by the president of the organization, a key well-respected volunteer, or the head of the development office. The people may change over the years, but what is important is the ongoing contact that builds relationships with the institution. These are not short-term relationships that result in quick gifts. Instead, these are relationships built over the years that require an investment of time and money by the organization. The institution's leadership must understand that this is a long-term process—an investment in the organization's future. Planned gifts received will be larger than those that are received through annual giving.

THE STEPS TO ESTABLISH A SUCCESSFUL PLANNED GIVING PROGRAM

More and more organizations of all sizes and types are initiating planned giving programs due to the dazzling estimates of wealth that will be transferred in the next 50 years. The often-cited figure of $10 trillion established by Cornell University researchers has been challenged by Paul G. Schervish, Director of the Boston College Center on Wealth and Philanthropy (CWP) and Associate Director John J. Havens. Their report estimates that the forthcoming transfer of wealth (from all adults alive today to heirs, charities, taxes, and other recipients) for the period from 1998 to 2052 will be between $41 trillion and $136 trillion. Schervish and Havens further estimate that charitable bequests over the 55-year period will range from $6 trillion to $25 trillion after estate taxes. Inheritance and other fees are taken into consideration. However, it is important to realize that some organizations are better suited for planned giving programs than others. The following factors are important to that success:

- a track record of accomplishments
- stability and a plan for the organization's future
- a strong constituency of older donors
- a strong and mature annual fund program
- a group of long-term, consistent donors
- the ability of the organization to afford upfront costs now, with benefits not realized for several years
- the presence in the organization of someone who is responsible for planned giving and is trustworthy, is able to deal with older people, believes in the organization, and is able to understand the financial and technical aspects of the program

If an organization has these factors, it is suited to launch a planned giving program. Then, one of the first things to do is to contact several organizations similar in mission and size that have planned giving programs underway. Important questions to ask include the following:

- When did they start their program?
- With how many staff members did they start?

- What were their first responsibilities?
- Who made the first gift? A board member? A staff member? Was it an unsolicited gift?
- How long did it take to secure the first gift from outside the board and staff?
- How long before the organization can use the gift income?
- What is the current number and worth of the organization's planned gifts?

Having done this research, it will be clearer to see just what is needed to establish a successful program. The information gathered will help develop the case for starting such a program, which will need to be presented to the board and chief executive officer (CEO). A basic requirement for all involved is patience. The board and CEO must understand that when launching a planned giving program, an organization is investing in future stability. It is an ongoing, long-term effort. As in the other methods of fundraising, there is a series of steps involved, from identifying prospects, completing research, cultivating prospects, making personal visits, soliciting gifts, and finally working with the donors' tax and legal experts to secure the gifts. Each step takes time. But when you are talking about gifts of tens of thousands, hundreds of thousands, or millions of dollars, the investment of time will prove worthwhile. See Appendix 15–A for a case study of the development of a planned giving program.

Step 1: Commitment from Organization's Staff and Board Leadership

First and foremost, to launch a successful program, you must have the support of the organization's CEO. With his or her help, you need to get a commitment from your board chair or development committee chair to pursue this effort. These three individuals, the CEO, board chair, and development committee chair, now have the task of securing the support of the entire board. The board should feel a sense of ownership of the program and be well informed about the operation of the program and the benefits the organization will reap in the long run. The board should pass a resolution to recognize the importance of planned giving and instruct the staff to start the program. Before you begin soliciting planned gifts, the board should approve a set of administrative policies, including guidelines for which types of gift vehicles will be offered, procedures for accepting such gifts, and marketing strategies to promote these gift vehicles. See Appendix 15–B for sample gift policies.

Step 2: Increase Knowledge of Planned Giving

It is extremely important for the staff involved in the program to have knowledge of planned giving. See Appendix 15–C for a list of "34 Planned Giving Dos

It is extremely important for the staff involved in the program to have knowledge of planned giving.

and Don'ts" developed by Calder Sinclair of Sinclair, Townes & Company, planned giving specialists in Atlanta, Georgia.

There are a number of resources available to you to increase your personal knowledge. They include seminars and conferences sponsored by the National Committee on Planned Giving; the Association of Fundraising Professionals; the Council for Advancement and Support of Education; the Association for Healthcare Philanthropy; and many planned giving consulting firms. Begin building a resource library with publications such as *Planned Giving—A Board Member's Perspective* by Grant Thornton, LLP; *Raising Money Through Bequests*, published by Emerson and Church; and *Planned Giving: Management, Marketing, and Law, Third Edition*, published by Wiley Publishers.

Step 3: Set Realistic Goals and Priorities

Because this is only one of the many fundraising programs going on each year, it is important to set clear and realistic goals and priorities. When setting planned giving objectives, make sure they are achievable given the time and money allocated to the program in the organizational budget. Once goals are established, performance objectives and detailed operational plans can be prepared.

Step 4: Decide on the Scope of the Program

Closely related to goal setting is determining the scope of the organization's planned giving program. It is important to analyze the requirements for marketing and supporting the various types of gift vehicles to determine which gift vehicles can be included in a program. For example, although almost any organization can encourage donors to include planned giving in their wills, the organization may not have the staff or expertise to encourage charitable trusts or to support gift annuities. Most development professionals would recommend beginning by establishing a selective or partial planned giving program. As mentioned earlier, promoting bequests is by far the easiest way to begin. Depending on the type and size of the organization, there are varying opinions about which gift vehicles to include next. Exhibit 15–2 lists the different types of planned gift vehicles an organization can choose to include in its planned giving program. Today, it is possible to offer a very comprehensive planned giving program simply by using the services proved by vendors. Some can offer a completely seamless planned giving program by linking the organization's site to the vendor's Web site. By designing a Web home page with the look of the organization's, visitors to the organization's Web site click on the planned giving page and are linked to the vendor's site with all of its specialized planned giving materials.

Step 5: Prepare an Adequate Budget

No fundraising program can be effective without adequate funding. In previous chapters, we listed many budget items necessary for running annual giving, direct mail, telemarketing, and major gift fundraising programs. Planned giving programs are no different in that it takes money to raise money. Some additional items not found in the other program budgets but necessary for planned giving include the following:

- legal fees
- bank administration fees
- consultant or vendor fees
- special subscriptions and publications
- additional professional memberships

Step 6: Develop a Well-Conceived Marketing Plan

Keep in mind the ways the organization communicates with its donors and prospective donors. When developing a marketing plan for planned giving, include regular newsletters and publications, direct mail, personal mail, telephone cultivation, Web site, e-mail, and personal visits.

Step 7: Involve Volunteers

Volunteers can be recruited to serve on a variety of committees—the board of directors; the board's development committee; the planned giving committee, which is covered later in the chapter; and special technical committees needed for planned giving.

IDENTIFYING THE BEST PROSPECTS

After establishing a planned giving program, it is time now to identify those individuals and donors who are the best prospects for making a planned gift. To determine who the best prospects are, it is important to understand what is most important to them—financial security. The donor may need to feel secure now and in the future or may be more concerned about the financial security of a spouse and heirs. Remember, planned giving is based on providing benefits to the donor, such as tax advantages, income or net worth growth, or preservation of assets, that are consistent with charitable giving.

> *To determine who your best prospects are, it is important to understand what is most important to them—financial security.*

To be successful in discussing planned giving with a prospect, you will need to learn the prospect's priorities relative to the benefits previously listed. Is there a spouse who needs special care? Are there grandchildren with future educational needs? Understanding the prospect's personal financial needs is your first responsibility. Then the gift vehicles that best suit the donor's needs can be presented. Exhibit 15–3 lists possible criteria to use when analyzing your donor base for the best planned giving prospects, and Exhibit 15–4 is an evaluation form that can be used to gather more information on selected prospects. Once

Exhibit 15–2 Eleven Types of Planned Gifts

There are eleven types of planned gifts with which development staff should be familiar. They are presented in priority order for implementation. The first four can help you to ease into planned giving with minimum complications. Numbers five, six, and seven can be incorporated once you begin to grow comfortable in your knowledge of planned giving. You can implement number eight in a few years when you feel confident in securing more than a few participants. Numbers nine and ten most likely will require special licensing through your state department of insurance. Number eleven is designed for that extremely wealthy prospect down the road. Numbers five through eleven now require an extensive disclosure statement presented to and signed by the donor(s) before the vehicle's legal documents are signed.

1. **Bequest**—One of the most common planned gifts. A nonprofit organization is bequeathed a gift in the donor's will. The gift may be designated as (1) percentage of the donor's estate, (2) specific dollar amount or description of property, (3) residual of the donor's estate, or (4) contingent upon a certain event happening. Estate taxes are reduced by the value of the gift to the nonprofit organization.
2. **Outright gift**—Cash, securities, real estate, personal property, etc., the title of which is legally transferred to a qualified nonprofit organization. In most cases, an income tax deduction is allowed for the full market value and capital gains taxes are avoided, reducing the cost of the gift to the donor.
3. **Life insurance policies**—A relatively inexpensive way for a donor to leave a significant gift to a nonprofit organization. A new policy may be taken out on the life of a younger donor to "create" a major, deferred gift to a charity with the cost of the premium being a small fraction of the face value of the policy. Donors also may have existing policies that are no longer needed for their original purposes (to ensure a child's education). With a change of policy ownership and beneficiary to the nonprofit organization, the donor can contribute the premium amount to the charity and the policy's face value can be maintained, or, if the donor chooses not to continue payments, the face value or "paid up insurance" value can be significant. Donors' tax deductions are equal to their cash/replacement value or premiums paid, depending on the type of policy.
4. **IRAs and other IRD Retirement Plans**—IRD (income in respect to descendent) retirement plan distributions are taxed for both estate and income tax purposes (often 75% to 80%) when passed from the descendent to someone other than the descendent's spouse. Since 100% of the IRD plan can be gifted to a qualified charity without tax, it has become a prime estate planning gift, leaving other estate assets (which are not taxed for income) to go to loved ones. Gifts of IRD plans must be gifted directly to the charity by completing the retirement plan's distribution form.
5. **Charitable remainder unitrust**—The donor receives a variable income from the gift for the rest of his or her life. The income to the donor is based on a specified percent of the trust principal, revalued each year, reflecting any increases in the value of the trust's assets. More than one person may receive income. The trust assets become the property of the nonprofit group upon the donor's death or in a pre-established time frame. Additional contributions may be made to the trust. Income tax deductions for the donor are based on the current value of the remainder interest going to the nonprofit organization.
6. **Charitable remainder annuity trust**—Similar to the unitrust, except that (1) the donor receives a fixed income from the gift for the rest of his or her life, (2) the income amount is based on the original value of trust's assets, and (3) additional contributions cannot be made.
7. **Life estate**—A donor deeds his or her personal residential property to a nonprofit organization. While the donor is still living, he or she has legal interest in the life estate with full rights to live there, or to rent or sell those rights. The donor receives an immediate income deduction for the remainder interest value of the estate.
8. **Pooled life income fund**—Contributions from several donors are placed in a common trust fund for investment and management. Each donor has a pro rata share interest of the pooled fund and receives his or her share of the total net ordinary income earned. When the donor dies, his or her share becomes the nonprofit organization's property. Income tax deduction is based on the current value of the remainder interest going to the nonprofit organization.
9. **Charitable gift annuity**—A donor's gift is not placed in trust but immediately becomes the property of the nonprofit organization. In exchange, the nonprofit organization promises to pay a fixed income to the donor for the rest of his or her life. A portion of the income is not taxable, but considered a return of principal. An income tax deduction is allowed for the difference between the gift value and the amount required to fund the annuity (actuarial value). There is a maximum of two income beneficiaries.
10. **Deferred gift annuity**—A donor makes a gift now and receives an immediate tax deduction. The donor begins receiving income at a later date—usually at retirement. Because the principal compounds between the date of the gift and the first date when the donor receives income, the amount of income can be significant and increase at a greater rate than that of the standard charitable gift annuity.
11. **Charitable lead trust**—A nonprofit organization receives income payments from the trust for a given number of years. At the end of the trust term, the assets of the trust are returned to the owner or his or her designee. This allows the transfer of assets to children while greatly reducing gift taxes.

Source: Courtesy of W. David Barnes, CFRE, Barnes Associates, Inc., Modesto, California, 2008.

Source: Copyright © Mark Litzler.

Exhibit 15–3 Characteristics of Planned Giving Prospects

- Long-term consistent donors
- Board members and former board members
- People who are unmarried or married without children and couples whose adult children are financially secure
- People with a long-term relationship and commitment to your organization's mission
- People who have received services from your organization or been involved in its programs
- Donors aged 55 and older
- Volunteers
- Women in all of the above categories

the best prospects are identified, be sure to record each prospect's key information in your fundraising database system so that you can track and monitor future communications and contacts with them.

MARKETING YOUR PLANNED GIVING PROGRAM

When marketing your program to donors, remember to stress the theme covered in this chapter—benefits to the donor! The best way to do this is to use real-life stories as well as fictional scenarios that illustrate how planned giving can help prospective donors address their needs and support the organization at the same time. To keep program costs down, use publications and communications regularly sent to donors and members.

Print Publications

Use the organization's newsletters and publications such as magazines and annual reports to create awareness and promote the benefits of planned giving. Develop a series of articles or advertisements that cover a variety of planned gifts. Run the articles on a planned schedule, so readers will find information in each issue of the publication. Exhibit 15–5 depicts two ads ("Give and Take: The Sibley Charitable Gift Annuity" and "All I Have Left Are My Memories") used in Sibley Memorial Hospital's newsletter, the *Sibley Senior*, a quarterly publication of the Sibley Senior Association. Another example from Sibley is shown in Appendix 15–D. It combines a request for planned gifts with outright direct gifts. This piece can be used as a "drop-in" with any letters of communication being sent to donors or prospects. Also, included in Appendix 15–E are samples of generic planned giving brochures that can be purchased from a vendor and used as printed without customization. In Appendix 15–F is a sample of a planned giving brochure that is customized for the organization.

Exhibit 15–4 Planned Giving Prospect Evaluation Form

_____	_____
date	last name

Title and full name of prospect: _____

Prefers to be known as: _____

Home address: _____

City, State, ZIP code: _____

Home telephone number: ( )_____-_____

Work telephone number: ( )_____-_____

E-mail address: _____

Salutation on correspondence: Dear: _____

Birth date: _____
month   day   year

Spouse's title and full name: _____

Spouse prefers to be known as: _____

Salutation on correspondence: Dear: _____

Prefix on correspondence: _____

Suffix on correspondence: _____

Birth date: _____
month   day   year

Names and ages of children: _____

Names of our board members or administrators who are personally acquainted with prospect and/or spouse: _____

Name of firm for which prospect works: _____

Position or title with this firm: _____

If no children, who are likely heirs: _____

Financial data: Estimated net worth: $ _____ Estimated annual income: $ _____

Prospect's attorney and phone number: _____ ( )_____-_____

Prospect's CPA or CFP and phone number: _____ ( )_____-_____

Source: Courtesy of W. David Barnes, CFRE, Barnes Associates Inc., Modesto, California, 2008.

Some institutions also provide planned giving newsletters for donors who have made planned gifts and become members of their "legacy societies." Others provide it to alumni and prospective donors; however such pieces are used, newsletters provide an opportunity to educate constituents about estate planning. A sample of Cornell University's newsletter, *2006 Financial Planner*, is included in Appendix 15–G.

Electronic Publications and Planned Giving Web Sites

An inexpensive way to provide a full-service planned giving program is to enlist the assistance of a vendor who provides planned giving materials for Web sites. The American Society of Civil Engineers (ASCE) Foundation in Reston, Virginia, was spending large sums of money on direct mail to send planned giving materials to their members aged 55 and older. By teaming with the Stelter Company, planned giving specialists in Des Moines, Iowa, the ASCE Foundation was able to reduce its planned giving direct mail expenses by driving members to the foundation's planned giving Web site. Instead of mailing brochures, the foundation used their publications (print and electronic) to direct their association's members to the foundation's Web site, where they could find up-to-date articles to read and a gift calculator for their use. Appendix 15–H shows two pages from brochures produced by the Stel-

Exhibit 15–5A Give and Take: The Sibley Charitable Gift Annuity

Plan Wisely

Give and Take:
The Sibley Charitable Gift Annuity

Tired of rolling over your CD's for lower and lower rates? Tired of worrying about declining returns on your stocks or money market accounts? This may be a good time to consider a gift of cash or appreciated securities to Sibley Memorial Hospital, in exchange for a Charitable Gift Annuity.

Charitable Gift Annuities offer an opportunity to make a gift to Sibley, while potentially increasing income from low-yielding assets. Benefits include:

- Fixed, guaranteed income (fixed rates) for life for you and/or a spouse;
- Immediate income tax deduction;
- Removal of assets from your taxable estate;
- Receipt of a portion of the annuity payments tax free or at more favorable capital gains tax rates;
- Making a meaningful gift to Sibley.

For a **FREE** brochure on Sibley's Charitable Gift Annuity Program, please call Fern Stone or Anna Tate at 202.537.457.

SAMPLE GIFT ANNUITY RATE CHART*

One Life		Two Lives	
Age	Rate	Ages	Rate
65	6.0%	65/65	5.6%
70	6.5%	70/70	5.9%
75	7.1%	75/75	6.3%
80	8.0%	80/80	6.9%
85	9.5%	85/85	7.9%

Source: Courtesy of Sibley Memorial Hospital, Washington, DC; Design: Harriet Winner, Winner, Inc.

ter Company describing their Web-based planned giving products.

Stelter provided a comprehensive planned giving package that was seamlessly linked to the ASCE Foundation's Web site. Stelter describes it as "take your look and wrap it around the most comprehensive planned giving Web package available." When members visited the ASCE Foundation's site, they could not tell they had been linked to an outside vendor's site because the home page of the planned giving site was designed exactly the same as the other ASCE Foundation and Society pages. Yet, visitors were being linked to a site that was being updated and maintained by a company whose sole purpose is planned giving.

More than 250 articles are available for viewers, tax and legal accuracy is monitored daily, and ASCE's members can request brochures that address 17 estate planning topics. In addition, they can easily access the gift calculator as it is embedded in more than 100 articles throughout the site, allowing the reader quick access to make personal calculations.

The cost was minimal compared to what the ASCE Foundation was spending previously, and the content was up-to-date and required no maintenance by the development staff. In the

Exhibit 15–5B All I Have Left Are My Memories

| Plan Wisely | 9. |

All I Have Left Are My Memories

A retired teacher reminisced one day, "All I have left are my memories." And though our first temptation might be to view this as in a "glass-half-empty" mind-set, the truth is that she was attempting to communicate a valuable lesson: *memories are the fabric from which legacies are created.*

Building memories is a lifetime endeavor—not just a senior thing. When a grandchild crawls into grandpa's lap, he's doing more than bringing a smile to grandpa's face. He's building memories that will deliver returns again and again in the years to come.

A group of seniors over the age of 90 were asked once if they had life to live over again what they would do differently. First, they said they would take more risks—walk barefoot in the sand, eat more ice cream and fewer yogurts, enjoy the small things in life. Second, they would work more on personal relationships, building more beautiful memories. And finally, they would create a living legacy by which they would be remembered after they were gone.

Creating a Legacy
Last year, a donor to Sibley did just that, creating an endowed nursing scholarship in memory of her husband.

The fund provides annual income to support Sibley's nurses who are continuing their schoolwork or pursuing advanced certification. This donor and her husband will be remembered forever by those who benefit from her generosity and foresight. This is the type of living legacy you can create—a memory with meaning, benefiting generations to come.

To learn how to create a living legacy, a memorial to a loved one, now or in the future, call Fern Stone at 202. 537.4257 or complete and mail the coupon below.

sketch by Max Winkler

Dear Friends at Sibley:

❏ Please send me information about how to create a living legacy at Sibley.
❏ Please contact me. I have a specific question. My number is _____.
❏ I have provided for Sibley in my will or trust arrangement, so please send me information on the Lucy Webb Hayes Founders Circle.

Name _____

Address_____ City_____State_____

Phone (   ) _____

Please mail this form to: Fern Stone, Development Office, Sibley Memorial Hospital, 5255 Loughboro Road, NW, Washington, DC 20016.

Source: Courtesy of Sibley Memorial Hospital, Washington, DC; Design: Harriet Winner, Winner, Inc.

first full year of use, more than 2,000 visits were being made per month, and the ASCE Foundation received more inquiries regarding planned giving brochures and opportunities than they had when using direct mail to reach prospects.

Seminars

Depending on the size and type of the organization, seminars can be a useful tool in providing an overview of the estate planning process to donors and the general public. These seminars can increase an organization's visibility in the community, but only if the presentations are of the highest quality. Be sure that the seminars are accurate, educational, and polished enough to represent your organization. Presenting seminars may not be the best way to market your program, because in many major cities there is much competition among organizations and companies offering free seminars on estate planning. These seminars are given by many nonprofit organizations, banks and securities houses, and financial planning professionals.

For membership associations, estate and financial planning seminars can be held in conjunction with national or regional annual meetings, conferences, meetings, or workshops. Using local bank trust officers or other estate planning specialists, these presentations provide a service to the association's members and their families. For 11 years, the American Society of Civil Engineers Foundation has offered an estate/financial planning seminar at its annual conference where members are encouraged not only to plan for their family's future but also for their profession.

Direct Mail

Using regular or special publications does not prevent using direct mail as well. One easy way to use direct mail is to print a small box on all fundraising business reply envelopes for donors to check if they would like information about wills and other planned gifts (see Exhibit 15–6). Focus each mailing on a specific area of planned giving and include a brochure. Remember to use

> *Remember to use real-life scenarios as often as you can to further educate your donors.*

real-life scenarios as often as you can to further educate your donors. Include a reply card that donors can return if they are interested in additional information. Those individuals inquiring about this type of giving should receive information as soon as possible, along with a follow-up call from you. To do timely follow-up, it is best to plan several smaller mailings rather than one large mailing so that time is available to follow up on each inquiry.

There are many outside planned giving vendors who can provide development staff with preprinted planned giving brochures to be included with direct mail appeals (see Appendix 15–E). There is no reason for staff to write this type of material, especially in small offices where there is not enough staff to devote solely to marketing and cultivating planned gifts. Sample brochure titles may include: Leaving a Legacy; Create a Legacy; Questions and Answers About Gift Annuities; Gifts Made Through Wills; How to Use IRAs to Make Gifts; Charitable Remainder Trusts; Estate Planning for Women; How to Make Gifts with Securities; and Securing Your Future. See Appendix 15–E for samples of generic preprinted planned giving brochures written by planned giving specialists that can be included with cover letters and mailed or given to prospective

donors. Appendix 15–F provides examples of planned giving brochures that have been customized to an organization. Almost all planned giving vendors will customize their products for a fee.

Telephone Follow-up

Personal outreach is very important in planned giving. To determine a prospective donor's needs and priorities you need to speak to them. Exhibit 15–7 describes a follow-up call to a

Exhibit 15–7 Sample Follow-up Call

Staff:	Good morning, Mrs. Hansen. This is Jane Smith with XYZ. How are you this morning?
Mrs. H:	Quite well, thank you.
Staff:	Mrs. Hansen, I'm calling you this morning for two reasons. First, I want to thank you for your generous support of XYZ. Because of you we are able to continue . . . (give an example of how gift will be used). We want you to know how much we appreciate it.
Mrs. H:	Well I'm just glad I can do it.
Staff:	May I ask, Mrs. Hansen, how you became interested in XYZ? What prompted you to make your gift? (Commonly asked by nonprofit organizations that are not schools, membership organizations, or perhaps hospitals.)
Mrs. H:	I've always been interested in . . . and heard about the work you're doing in that area.
Staff:	That leads me, Mrs. Hansen, to the second reason for my call. You said you are interested in the work we do, and your request for our recent publication on wills tells me you are interested in that as well. Would you mind telling me if there is anything in particular that prompted you to request that information?
Mrs. H:	Well, you hear so much these days about wills, trusts, and estate planning, I thought I'd better do a little reading on my own.
Staff:	That is a wise decision Mrs. Hansen, and I'd like to help you, if I may. The information we sent was very general in nature. I would be happy to send you more specific information on the subject of estate planning or even stop by for a visit. Sometimes these matters are better discussed in person rather than over the phone.
Mrs. H:	Oh, a visit won't be necessary. Just send me something in the mail on trusts. You hear so much about them these days.
Staff:	I'll be happy to do that. I'll call you shortly to answer any questions you may have or please feel free to call me if I don't get back to you soon enough. Thank you again, Mrs. Hansen. I look forward to speaking with you soon.

Other fact-finding questions that could be included are the following:

- Have you always lived in (city)?
- When was the last time you were in (location of XYZ)?
- If you plan to be in the area again, please give me a call or stop by for a visit. I'd enjoy meeting you and showing you some of the things your gifts have made possible.
- Does your family live in the area?

Exhibit 15–6 Business Reply Envelope Sample Text

Founded Upon a Rock....

❏ I have remembered the ΓΦβ Foundation in my will/estate planning.
❏ Please send me information on how I can remember the ΓΦβ Foundation in my will/estate planning.
❏ I am interested in joining the Tau Epsilon Pi Society by making a planned gift to the ΓΦβ Foundation. Please send me more information.

Source: Courtesy of Gamma Phi Beta Foundation, Centennial, Colorado.

prospective donor (fictionally named Mrs. Hansen) 10 days after she was sent a booklet on wills that she requested after receiving a planned giving mailing.

There will always be a number of objections when you make your follow-up calls. Remember, do not take these objections personally. The best offense is to have several responses prepared to deal with the most common objections. For example, if the objection is, "I received the booklet I requested but I haven't read it yet," your response could be, "It would be most helpful to me if when you read the booklet you note how it's written. Do you like the style? Are the examples clear? Do you have any suggestions on how we might improve it?"

Usually the donor will agree to do that, which allows you to set up a future time to call back. If the objection is, "I just asked for the booklet because I like to stay current on these matters," your response could be, "That's a good idea with all the changes taking place. We will keep you on our mailing list and I will check in with you from time to time to see if some of the ideas might relate to you."

The most delicate type of objection to overcome is the one expressed by the donor who has spoken to his or her attorney about the gift and has been advised against it. Offer to speak to the attorney to clarify any issues he or she may have, but be careful not to put the attorney in a negative light, as the donor trusts his or her counsel.

Personal Visit

As was covered in Chapter 9 on major gift fundraising, relationships are established with donors through a combination of telephone calls and personal visits over a period of time. Meeting with prospective donors will help you continue gathering information about their specific needs and priorities. Once a donor has expressed an interest in pursuing some type of planned gift, it is important to learn more about his or her personal circumstances. Always assure the donor that any personal information will remain confidential and is needed only to assist in selecting the type of gift that best suits his or her needs.

One way to start this discussion would be to say, "I'm not trying to pry, Mr. X, but there is some information I'll need that will help me in suggesting some of the best ways to make your gift." The information you will need includes date of birth and, depending on the type and size of gift you are discussing, tax bracket, types of assets to be used in making the gift, income tax deduction needed, whether gift will be outright or life income, and name and age of beneficiary. More specific questions will follow as a natural outgrowth of the conversation.

It is natural for those who have donated to your organization to be interested in continuing to support it. Staff's role is to help them do it in a way that benefits them and the organization.

Exhibit 15–8 lists types of specific information that should be gathered for each planned giving prospect to assist in the individual's solicitation. Exhibit 15–9 is a form for recording contacts

Exhibit 15–8 Prospect Information Checklist

The prospect:
- ❏ Has a will
- ❏ Does not have a will
- ❏ Owns primary residence
- ❏ Owns land or other residences
- ❏ Owns stock
- ❏ Owns closely held stock
- ❏ Owns life insurance
- ❏ Is retired or close to retirement
- ❏ Is living on fixed income
- ❏ Has independent income
- ❏ Inherited family wealth
- ❏ Has provided for children
- ❏ Has art or antiques
- ❏ Has obligation to grandchildren

Other:

with a prospect. The information gathered about each prospect needs to be entered in his or her record in the fundraising database for future reference to help plan a successful solicitation.

THE ROLE OF VOLUNTEERS

Just as in the other types of fundraising covered in this book, there is a role for volunteers in planned giving. The planned giving committee may consist of members of the board or the development committee or could include key volunteers and professionals from the community who would help strengthen the planned giving program. The committee chair probably should be a board member. However, consider the following list of individuals who could serve on this committee:

- attorneys (estate planning practitioners)
- trust officers
- certified public accountants
- certified financial planners
- certified life underwriters
- real estate brokers
- stockbrokers
- major donors
- corporate executives

Each member of the committee needs to have a basic understanding of and commitment to planned giving.

Earlier in the chapter, the steps involved in establishing a planned giving program were outlined. A planned giving committee will play an active role in helping the organization through these steps. One of the first tasks is to develop a policy paper establishing the planned giving program guidelines. Subject to board approval, the paper will outline the scope of the program by prioritizing which gift vehicles will be implemented,

Exhibit 15–9 Planned Giving Prospect Contact Record

<table>
<tr><td>_____
date</td><td></td><td>_____
last name</td></tr>
</table>

Prospect Contact Information:

Name: _____

Address: _____

City, State, Zip: _____

Telephone (H) _____ (O) _____

E-mail: _____

_____ bequest
_____ charitable remainder unitrust
_____ life estate
_____ charitable gift annuity
_____ charitable lead trust
_____ life insurance
_____ charitable remainder annuity
_____ pooled income
_____ deferred gift annuity
_____ outright gift of: _____
_____
_____
_____ other: _____

	Month Date Year	Notes/Results
How was first contact made:	____ ____ ____	_____
What was follow-up to first contact?	____ ____ ____	_____
Follow-up:	____ ____ ____	_____
Follow-up:	____ ____ ____	_____
Follow-up:	____ ____ ____	_____

Source: Courtesy of W. David Barnes, CFRE, Barnes Associates Inc., Modesto, California, 2008.

> *A planned giving program can be implemented in stages, beginning with simply asking donors to include the organization in their wills and estates.*

define the processing procedure, and review the approval process for accepting such gifts. Input from this committee will help develop the multi-year marketing plan.

The planned giving committee should meet regularly to help accomplish the following:

- provide names of individuals for the prospect list who should be cultivated
- discuss and plan strategy for selected prospects
- help provide personal and financial data on prospects without violating the prospects' confidence or any code of ethics
- help prepare individualized proposals for selected prospects
- review proposed gifts for acceptability
- periodically review program's results and compare them against goals and objectives

THE BEQUEST SOCIETY: THE SIMPLEST WAY TO BEGIN

Many people think that planned giving is just too technical an area for their organization to pursue. Remember, a planned giving program can be implemented in stages, beginning with simply asking donors to include the organization in their wills and estates. Statistics show that 80 percent of the money raised through planned giving comes from bequests. The best way to solicit bequests is to invite donors to join a special recognition group or society. Many organizations are surprised when they receive a bequest because they never knew it existed. By honoring those donors who have included the organization in their wills now, the organization can show its appreciation to the donors during their lifetime. Many benefits beyond the bequest can be realized by the organization through creating a bequest or legacy society today.

When creating a bequest society, do not spend too much time determining a name. Often there is an individual or family who has made a significant contribution to your organization whom you would like to honor in this way. At the Washington College of Law, American University, the Mooers Society is named after a much loved and respected alumnus and teacher, Dr. Edwin A. Mooers, class of 1914, whose involvement with the school spanned more than 50 years and was carried on by his son, Edwin A. Mooers, Jr., class of 1941, also a former faculty member, until his death. If no individual or family comes to mind, commonly used names such as "Heritage Society" or "Founder's Club" can be just as successful in promoting planned giving.

The Gamma Phi Beta Sorority, whose international headquarters is in Centennial, Colorado, created a bequest society to honor all sorority members and friends who make gifts to Gamma Phi Beta's future through planned gifts. This special recognition society, the Tau Epsilon Pi Society, takes its name from the sorority's Greek open motto, *Tethemeliemenae Epi Petran*—Founded Upon a Rock. The sorority promotes its planned giving program by promoting this name. They declare that planned gifts are vital to the future of the sorority and to maintaining its tradition of excellence—the future of the sorority can truly be "Founded Upon a Rock."

Once established, a bequest society provides an excellent opportunity to communicate regularly with this special group of donors. These donors should receive regular publications and information about the organization. Sending special mailings about planned giving and tax issues is also important. Remember to keep this group of donors updated on the mission of the organization and how their continued support makes a difference. This will be key to the organization remaining in their will.

Membership in the bequest society should be as inclusive as possible. Include all donors who have informed the organization that it is in their will or estate plans as well as individuals who have made one of the other types of planned gifts. Request copies of their wills or those portions that pertain to the organization for your files. Most of these gifts are revocable, which means the donor can change his or her mind in the future. List the members of this group as you would those of any of your other gift clubs.

Develop a special newsletter for the group if your budget allows. Use this as a marketing piece for other prospective members. Use regular publications such as the newsletter, annual report, or magazine to highlight society members and the activities of the group. In appropriate publications, provide a sample of the language the donor should use when including the organization in his or her will (see Exhibit 15–10).

Exhibit 15–10 Sample of Language to Use in a Will

Outright Bequests

I give, devise, and bequeath to XYZ (legal name should be provided), a tax-exempt organization, located at _____, the sum of $_____ or percentage of (cash, real or property herein described) to be used for the general purpose of XYZ at the discretion of its board of directors.

Bequests for a Specific Purpose

I give, devise, and bequeath to XYZ (legal name should be provided), a tax-exempt organization, located at _____, the sum of $_____ or percentage of (cash, real or personal property herein described) for the purpose of _____.

Annual events such as luncheons, receptions, and other special events sponsored by the society are desirable benefits of bequest society membership in addition to providing opportunities for donor recognition. The type and number of events will depend on the size of the organization. An annual luncheon or other special event is a wonderful way to show your appreciation to this group and keep them updated on the activities of the organization. Remember to invite bequest society members to other organization-wide events throughout the year so they can continue to see what the organization is doing and so others can meet the donors who are ensuring the organization's future. Your bequest society is the key to a regular planned giving awareness program. Bequests will be the most common gifts donated, but other planned gift vehicles also can be incorporated over time.

HOW PLANNED GIVING FITS INTO A MAJOR GIFTS PROGRAM

In the past, organizations of varying sizes and types have maintained separate efforts for major and planned gifts. This often creates an adversarial relationship between major gift officers and planned giving officers. The fundraising climate today is more competitive than ever. As a result, some organizations are rethinking the division between these two areas and are developing a "gift planning" philosophy that brings major gift and planned giving staff together as a team.

In this new relationship, the major gift officer becomes familiar with the concepts of planned giving so that this information can be shared during meetings with donors who are unable to make outright gifts. He or she then involves the planned giving officer in developing a strategy that allows for the information gathering necessary to determine which gift vehicle meets the donor's needs. The planned giving officer will assist in preparing gift proposals for use in solicitations or accompanies the major gift officer on visits.

In turn, the planned giving officer must prioritize the tasks usually performed to allow for time to work with the major gift officer. One way is to develop better stewardship methods for

"*Mighty challenging stuff in your sermon! I had no idea how versatile a charitable remainder unitrust could be in estate planning.*"

Source: Copyright © Mark Litzler.

the donors who give small, life income gifts, which will result in more free time for the planned giving officer. Another way is to streamline the procedures used to follow up general inquiries so that the planned giving officer is not spending as much time with people whose gift potential is in the $5,000 to $10,000 range. In general, the planned giving officer needs to spend more time with those individuals who are identified as major gift prospects.

With the large amount of wealth to be transferred over the next 50 years, it is imperative that the planned giving officer and the major gifts officer work together closely. In addition, as the baby boomer generation ages, they will be making both major gifts and planned gifts to support the causes they embrace. If the two persons/departments cannot be combined, the head of the development office needs to ensure that the staffs of the departments communicate effectively with each other to ensure that those who wish to make major or planned gifts to the institution are cultivated and stewarded appropriately.

For more information about planned giving, see Appendix 15–I for a list of national companies that provide planned giving materials and services. Finally, Appendix 15–J is a list of planned giving terms.

REFERENCES

Golden Prospects. 2000. *Philanthropy Matters,* 10(1): 3–5.

The 20-Year Commitment, Marketing your bequest program for long-term value. The *NonProfit Times*, May 1, 2006; 18–19.

Case Study: The Development of a Planned Giving Program

This is how a real organization, let's call it "Worthy Conservation," got started in planned giving.

Worthy, established 50 years ago, has a membership of 15,000 individuals interested in the protection of the many species and habitats of the world's oceans. Many of the individuals are older than 55. Although Worthy Conservation has received cash donations from its membership over the years, the principal funding of its programs has been through foundation grants. Occasionally, Worthy has been the beneficiary of bequests, even though they were not solicited.

Worthy's board, concerned about its dependence on foundation grants, decided to establish a planned giving program to tap the transfer of the trillions of dollars that will pass from one generation to the next over the next several decades. Not wishing to incur the expense of adding a planned giving professional to its staff at this point, Worthy retained the services of a planned giving specialist who, working at an hourly rate, would help it get started on a cost-effective basis.

The recommendations of the planned giving specialist addressed

- the members and their potential for planned gifts
- how they can be reached most effectively with planned giving information
- which planned gift options to offer and when
- how the gifts should be screened to avoid accepting those that may be more expensive than they are worth
- how gifts of stock, life income plans, and insurance policies could be handled
- guidelines for the establishment and prudent management of Worthy's endowment:
  1. what gifts should go into it
  2. how it could be effectively invested
  3. what monies could be withdrawn for use by Worthy's programs
- the coaching of board members, staff, and volunteers to show how each of them can contribute to the success of the major/planned giving program
- the establishment of a legacy society to recognize and honor those who have committed to make planned gifts to further Worthy's mission

Following the plan, Worthy Conservation

- added planned giving promotional material to its existing newsletter and Web site at minimum incremental expense and immediately began receiving expressions of interest from its members
- answered inquiries with brief information booklets about the requested gift plan
- made follow-up phone calls to get the donors' thoughts about the information they had requested

During the conversation with a donor, if the staff person was asked detailed questions, a further conference call was arranged to include the planned giving specialist. As a result of the conference call, the specialist would develop a written illustration of the gift for the staff person to send to the donor to share with his or her advisor. In this manner, the gift process was moved toward fruition.

The results for Worthy Conservation included the following:

- Within several months of commencing the promotion, Worthy began to receive outright gifts of appreciated stock, offers of gifts of real estate, inquiries about life income options (charitable gift annuities, charitable remainder trusts), and requests from donors who had included Worthy in their estate plans to be added to Worthy's legacy society.
- After 18 months, Worthy could justify the addition of a planned giving officer to its staff, as the increasing volume of committed gift plans indicated a strong future flow of gift income from matured gifts.
- Within three years, Worthy began to receive the cash from realized bequests and matured life income plans. This is not surprising, as people tend to revisit their estate plans in the event of failing health. In this case, Worthy stood in a much better position to be included in those plans because of their repeated planned giving promotion.

Because of the addition of planned gift options to their major gift program, Worthy Conservation not only feels more comfortable with its broader sources of funding, but its donors have found new ways to help Worthy carry out its mission by utilizing the win-win opportunities offered by planned gifts.

Source: Copyright 2000 Richard D. Barrett, Barrett Planned Giving, Inc. This material appears in the publication *Planned Giving Essentials: A Step-by-Step Guide to Success, 2nd Edition,* © 2001, Jones and Bartlett Publishers.

Sample Gift Acceptance Policies and Procedures

GOODWIN HOUSE FOUNDATION

November 7, 2007

PURPOSE

The purpose of this Gift Acceptance Policy is to:

- ensure that the best interests of donors and Goodwin House Foundation (GHF) are served;
- encourage funding of programs GHF supports without encumbering GHF with gifts that may prove to generate more cost than benefit or which are restricted in a manner not in keeping with the goals of GHF.

This policy includes both current and deferred gifts and is intended as a guide to allow flexibility on a case-by-case basis.

CRITERIA FOR ACCEPTING GIFTS

GHF will evaluate gifts on several criteria. Gifts that are accepted will:

- promote and be consistent with GHF's mission which is:
  to strengthen the mission of Goodwin House Incorporated by providing it with financial support. It seeks to provide financial security to residents who live in or are seeking admission to Goodwin House communities through a confidential financial assistance program. Also, it brings attention to the needs and issues facing the elderly and grants funding for other activities that are consistent with the mission of Goodwin House Incorporated. The Foundation conducts fundraising activities and holds Endowment Funds.
- conform to GHF's code of ethical business practices;
- fulfill the donor's intention for charitable giving;
- support funds/programs approved by the Board of Directors. Currently these funds/programs are: The Fellowship Program; The Clinical Pastoral Education (CPE) Program; Continuing Education Funds; The Hospice Fund; Alice Story Biache Fund; the All Staff Education Fund; The Claude Moore Charitable Foundation Scholarship Fund; and The Endowment Fund.

GHF will not accept a gift from any donor who lacks sufficient title to the asset(s) or is not mentally competent legally to transfer funds as a gift to Goodwin House Foundation.

GHF retains the right to refuse any gift.

Ethical Considerations

GHF follows all applicable federal, state, and local laws and regulations pertaining to charitable giving. Finder's fees are not paid for directing potential gifts to the organization.

GHF will not share its mailing list(s).

Payment of Fees

GHF's preference is to have costs associated with gifts of personal or real property, such as an appraisal, environmental inspection, market evaluation, or preparation of a deed to be paid by the donor. Should the donor refuse to pay for an appraisal, GHF will have an appraisal done at its expense to protect its interest(s). Fees shall be reasonable and directly related to the completion of a gift. They shall be limited to:

- appraisal fees by persons who are competent and qualified to appraise the property involved and who have no conflict of interest;
- legal fees for the preparation of documents;
- accounting fees associated with the transaction;
- fees of "fee for service" financial planners.

Financial planners must affirm in writing that they are compensated only through fees for services rendered and that they are not compensated for the sale of products to clients. This distinction is vital in avoiding the payment of commissions, which could be construed as triggering securities regulations.

Restrictions

GHF will not honor any restrictions on how gifts may be used without prior approval or if they are in violation of tax exempt statutes. If GHF receives a gift by bequest that contains restrictions it has not previously approved, GHF will honor those restrictions, if legally possible, only after review and approval and will inform the donor's estate.

Protection of Donor's Rights and Interests

No program, agreement, trust contract, or commitment shall be urged upon any donor or prospective donor that would benefit GHF at the expense of the donor's interest(s). No agreement shall be made between GHF and any agency, person, company, or organization on any matter—whether it be investment, management, sale, or other interest that would knowingly jeopardize or compromise the donor's interest.

It shall be the policy of GHF, its Directors, staff, and volunteers, to inform, serve, guide, or otherwise assist in fulfilling the donor's philanthropic wishes, but never under any circumstance to pressure or unduly persuade. All will exercise extreme caution against the use of high pressure sales techniques when dealing with prospective donors.

Authority to Invest

Investment policies are established by GHF Board of Directors and reviewed annually. All gifted securities will be sold upon receipt. It is essential that the investment policy be clearly stated and rigorously followed. *(All investments shall be managed by the Investment Committee of Goodwin House Incorporated. Further, the Investment Committee will make all investment recommendations to GHF's Board of Directors. Language must be made consistent with the by-laws.)*

Confidentiality

All information obtained from or about donors or prospects shall be held in the strictest confidence by GHF.

Review of Gifts

Each gift arrangement shall be reviewed from the perspective of its potential benefit to GHF's mission. While the interests of the donor are paramount, no gift shall be accepted if its benefit to GHF is so remote as to be negligible. GHF retains the right to refuse gifts in any form that are deemed inappropriate to its purpose.

If a proposed gift poses issues beyond the scope of this policy, the Chair of Goodwin House Foundation will appoint an ad hoc Gift Acceptance Committee to provide additional review of the merits of the gift and evaluate implications it may have for GHF. After the Gift Acceptance Committee has evaluated the proposed gift, it will make a recommendation to the Chair for final decision by the Goodwin House Foundation Board of Directors.

GHF will review this policy on an annual basis to ensure GHF remains in compliance with all federal laws and regulations and with the ethical guidelines established by the Association of Fundraising Professionals and the National Committee on Planned Giving.

TYPES OF GIFTS

Cash

GHF accepts gifts in the form of cash and check. Checks shall be made payable to Goodwin House Foundation. In no event shall a check be made payable to an employee, agent, or volunteer for credit to GHF.

Publicly Traded Securities

GHF accepts securities (including mutual funds) traded on a recognized stock exchange and other readily marketable securities. For gift crediting and accounting purposes, the value of the gift of securities is the average of the high and low prices on the date of the gift according to IRS regulation. For gift acknowledgement to the donor, the high, low, and average of the securities on the date the gift was received will be reported to the donor for tax purposes. All gifted securities will be sold upon receipt. In no event shall an employee or volunteer working on behalf of GHF commit to a donor that a security will be held by GHF.

Closely Held Securities

GHF may accept non-publicly traded securities after consulting with the Gift Acceptance Committee. Prior to acceptance, the committee will explore methods and timing of liquidation of the securities through redemption or sale. The committee will determine:

- an estimate of fair market value;
- any restrictions on transfer;
- whether and when an initial public offering might be anticipated.

No commitment shall be made by staff or volunteers working on behalf of GHF for the repurchase of such securities prior to the completion of a gift of the closely held securities.

Other Securities

GHF accepts gifts of bonds that require a "holding" period. They will be cashed when the holding period has expired.

GHF will not accept the following securities as gifts:

- securities that are assessable or that in any way could create a liability to GHF;
- securities that, by their nature, may not be assigned (such as Series "E" Savings Bonds);
- securities that, on investigation, have no apparent value.

Real Estate

All gifts of real estate will be taken to the GHF Gift Acceptance Committee for approval for recommendation to the Board in the case of non-residential property. GHF will work with donors and the appropriate professionals, such as real estate brokers, attorneys, and others to prepare documents for gifting property to GHF.

Prior to acceptance, any gift of real estate must be appraised by at least one recognized appraisal firm, totally independent of GHF, or by the appraisal department of a major bank or S&L to establish fair market value. This appraisal will perform three (3) functions:

- establish the donor's tax deduction;
- give GHF auditors a reasonable value at which to carry the asset on GHF's books;
- establish the asking price for the property.

Normally, the donor will be asked to pay for this appraisal because it is tax deductible. If the donor wishes to provide his/her own appraisal, GHF will carry the gift on its books at $1.00 and the donor will be so informed. GHF will then list the property at whatever it deems to be fair market value.

In general, residential real estate located within the continental United States, with a value estimated by the donor or others at $100,000 or greater will be accepted, unless the Board of Directors determines the property is not suitable for acceptance as a gift, or if the Board chooses to make an exception in a specific case.

In general, GHF will not accept residential real estate located outside the continental United States.

The property will be listed for sale with a broker or brokers in the area in which the property is located at an amount consistent with the fair market value established by the appraisal. The property may be held for a reasonable amount of time. Reasonable is defined as one year.

If GHF is unwilling to hold the property for a reasonable period and/or is forced to cash-out as quickly as possible, the prospective donor will be informed.

Due diligence concerning environmental concerns shall be considered before accepting any gift of real estate. This may involve conducting an environmental audit of the property.

GHF will review all proposed gifts of real estate with mortgages on a case-by-case basis.

GHF will evaluate gifts of commercial properties and businesses taking into consideration:

- GHF may have to pay tax on unrelated business income;
- GHF as a non-profit organization receives no benefit from depreciation.

The property must be conveyed to GHF prior to any formal offer or contract for resale is made.

Tangible Personal Property

GHF staff have the authority to work with donors on all gifts of personal property. No personal property shall be accepted that obligates GHF to ownership in perpetuity.

Gifts of Works of Art

GHF accepts appropriate gifts of works of art both self-created and purchased. However, gifts of art will be placed on GHF books at $1.00 unless a valid independent appraisal is supplied at the donor's expense, as the cost of the appraisal is deductible to him/her. GHF will make no commitment to keep a work of art in perpetuity.

Gifts of Furniture

GHF accepts gifts of furniture if the furniture is useable or can be quickly sold. GHF may elect to keep furniture, but will make no commitment to keep furniture in perpetuity.

Gifts of Miscellaneous Personal Property

GHF accepts other items of personal property if they are usable or are easily saleable. The donor is responsible for establishing the value of the item(s). GHF will evaluate gifts of personal property taking into consideration costs of: transportation, storage, sales, maintenance, and repair.

GHF will not accept gifts of automobiles and/or other vehicles.

GHF maintains a list of charities that accept gifts of furniture, automobiles, and other personal property for donors whose personal property cannot be used by GHF.

PLANNED GIVING PROGRAM

The purpose of Goodwin House Foundation's Planned Giving Program is to encourage, solicit and recognize charitable bequests, gifts of life insurance, and gifts created by life income agreements for all purposes consistent with the objectives of GHF. This program is designed to supplement and enhance the funds and programs GHF supports by encouraging estate planning and preparation of wills that can:

- offer donors the opportunity for life-income gifts that will enable them to retain income from their capital;
- offer donors the opportunity to make a larger gift during their lifetime than they otherwise could make without losing income;
- offer donors the opportunity to provide for life income of a survivor;
- provide for outright bequests and additions to agreements and trusts which qualify for deduction of exemption under existing tax laws.

General Policies

GHF's Planned Giving Program offers donors an opportunity to make gifts in the following forms:

- gifts by will and bequest;
- gifts of remainder interest, including: charitable remainder trusts, charitable gift annuities, and the gifts of one's personal residence or farm with retained life interest;
- other gifts including: life insurance policies, eligible retirement plans, charitable lead trusts, and gifts of an undivided interest in property.

When donors are provided planned gift illustrations or sample documents, these will be provided free of charge. For any planned-gift-related documents, materials, illustrations, letters, or other correspondence, a disclaimer should be included, such as:

This information in no way constitutes legal advice. We strongly urge you to consult with your attorney, financial and/or tax advisor to review and approve the information GHF has provided without charge or obligation. We will gladly work with your independent advisors to assist in any way.

GHF Board of Directors shall establish specific guidelines and conditions for various types of gifts and will review the policies and guidelines annually.

Confidentiality

All information obtained from or about donors or prospects shall be held in the strictest confidence by GHF. Neither the name, the amount, nor the conditions of any gift shall be published without approval of the donor and/or the beneficiary.

Review of Agreements

GHF may seek advice of legal counsel in all matters pertaining to its Planned Giving Program, (and shall execute no agreement, contract, trust, or other legal document with any donor without the advice of legal counsel). Likewise, the prospective donor shall be advised to seek counsel of his or her choice in any and all aspects relating to the proposed gift, whether by bequest, trust agreement, contract, or other. The donor shall particularly be advised to consult his or her tax advisor on matters related to the tax implications of a gift and matters related to planning of the donor's personal estate.

GHF will review each gift arrangement from the perspective of its potential benefit to the Foundation's mission. While the interests of the donor are paramount, GHF will not accept any gift if its benefit to GHF is so remote as to be negligible. GHF retains the right to refuse gifts in any form deemed inappropriate to its purpose.

PLANNED GIFTS

Bequests

Bequests are gifts made to GHF as part of a donor's will and are received after the donor's death. Bequests can take various forms:

- general bequests—gifts of a specified dollar amount;
- specific bequests—gifts of specific pieces of property;
- residuary bequests—gifts of the donor's property after all debts, taxes, expenses, and other bequests have been paid;
- percentage bequests—gifts expressed as a percentage of the estate or the residuary estate;
- restricted bequests—gifts designated for a specific purpose.

GHF recognizes bequests only when they become irrevocable and have been determined as to amount.

GHF reserves the right to decline any gift that does not further its mission or goals. GHF may decline any gift that would create an administrative burden or cause GHF to incur excessive expenses. GHF shall expeditiously communicate the decision to decline a gift to the legal representatives of the estate. If there is any indication that the representatives of the estate or any family member of the deceased is dissatisfied with the decision, this fact shall be communicated to GHF staff or to the Gift Acceptance Committee and/or GHF Board of Directors as quickly as possible.

GHF shall attempt to discover bequest expectancies wherever possible. Where possible, intended bequests of property other than cash or marketable securities should be brought to the attention of the staff who will inform the Chair of the Board of Directors. Every attempt should be made to encourage the donor to conform his or her plans to GHF policy.

GHF shall not act as an executor (personal representative) for a donor's estate.

Life Insurance Policies

Life insurance policies are contracts issued by a life insurance company to an individual.

A donor can name GHF as the primary or final beneficiary, or she/he can transfer ownership of an existing policy. If GHF is named the beneficiary of the policy, the funds will not be included as a contribution until they are received. However, if GHF is both the owner and the beneficiary of the policy, the cash surrender value will be included as a contribution at the time the policy is transferred.

Charitable Remainder Trusts

Charitable Remainder Trusts (CRTs) are income trusts created by transferring property irrevocably to a trustee under a trust agreement that provides the donor and/or designated beneficiary with income for life. The minimum payout rate is fixed by law. After the deaths of the income beneficiaries, the remainder is paid to the charitable beneficiary and the institution may use the gift for charitable purposes. CRTs were created under the Tax Reform Act of 1969. (By law the trustee may be the charitable institution receiving the gift. However, administering a trust is extremely complex and GHF does not believe it is prudent to act as a trustee.)

There are two primary types of charitable remainder trusts: Annuity Trusts and Unitrusts.

Charitable Remainder Annuity Trust: a CRT that provides a fixed payout that must equal a sum certain of not less than 5% of the initial fair market value of the gift in trust. Whatever remains in the trust becomes the property of the beneficiary (GHF) at the time of his or her death. Annuity trusts do not permit additional contributions.

Charitable Remainder Unitrust: a CRT that provides an income that is a fixed percentage of the net fair market value of the trust assets. The trust assets are re-valued annually. This percentage must be at least 5%. The income payments of a unitrust will vary from year to year as the trust's value changes. The unitrust may be set up for the lives of the beneficiaries or for a term not to exceed 20 years. The governing instrument may include a provision to permit additional contributions.

Two variations of the unitrust are the *income only unitrust* and the nimcrut. Under an income only unitrust, the unitrust provides for distribution to the beneficiary of either the net income of the trust or the fixed percentage specified in the agreement, whichever is less. If the unitrust's annual earnings are deficient in any given year, the corpus (principal) need not be invaded to bring up the pay-out. Instead, payments may equal the trust's earnings for that year, and the shortfall can be made up during the years when the yield is higher.

> Deficiency is defined as the difference between the stated percentage of the trust assets at the time the trust agreement was established or valued and the net income.
>
> For example: If a trust with a 5% payout were established with $300,000, the "stated percentage" would be $15,000. Any year in which the trust income was less than $15,000 would be a year in which the pay out was deficient. Any year in which the trust income exceeded $15,000 would produce an excess that could be distributed to "make up" the deficiency in a prior year.

The nimcrut is a hybrid. This agreement permits a donor to create an income-only unitrust and, at some later date, to switch to a straight unitrust upon occurrence of a permissible triggering event such as, a specific date—beneficiary reaches a certain age, or a specific event—marriage, divorce, death or birth.

The trust agreement shall provide that an appropriate independent fiscal agent, including a bank or financial institution, serve as trustee. GHF will retain the right to change the trustee. Other provisions:

- no trust shall be established for less than 5% payout or more than 10% payout;
- the recommended minimum funding for a Charitable Remainder Trust is $100,000;
- agreements are limited to two beneficiaries;
- cash, publicly traded stock, bonds, and appreciated properties may be used to establish charitable trusts.

Charitable Lead Trusts

A Charitable Lead Trust (annuity or unit) provides payments to a designated charity for a term of years of any duration, after which the assets in the trust either revert to the donor or pass to a non-charitable beneficiary designated by the donor. Charitable lead trusts enable an individual to benefit a charity and pass principal to family members with little or no tax penalty.

To create a lead trust, the donor transfers assets to a trust and the trust provides payments to the charity. At the end of the term, the trust principal goes to the donor's designated beneficiaries.

The recommended minimum funding for a Charitable Lead Trust is $50,000.

GHF may provide sample charitable lead trust proposals to the donor and the donor's advisors for preliminary discussion and review. Any proposals and tax calculations prepared by GHF are for illustrative purposes only. The final trust document must be prepared and approved by an attorney representing the donor. GHF may ask counsel to review and approve a trust document before it is signed.

Charitable Gift Annuities

The Charitable Gift Annuity (CGA) generates cash payments to a donor or other(s) for life in exchange for a transfer of cash, marketable securities, or property. Gift annuities may be immediate or deferred. The difference between an immediate and a deferred gift annuity is that a deferred annuity starts to pay out at a date in the future. GHF policies specify that all gift annuities:

- will offer rates that generally conform to the gift annuity rates set by the American Council on Gift Annuities.
- will only be offered to Virginia residents.
- will not be promoted as investment vehicles or compared to any investment alternatives.
- may not be written for less than $5,000.

A CGA agreement funded with non-liquid assets must be approved by the GHF Board of Directors. If the asset is determined not to be appropriate, GHF will inform the donor. If the donor is willing to consider other options and is able to give other assets such as cash, securities, or bonds in lieu of the intended property, GHF will discuss other gift options at this time. Tangible personal property is generally unsuitable.

A disclosure statement, as required under federal law, should be provided to the donor with the initial gift proposal or illustration, and must be provided prior to execution of the gift annuity agreement.

CGA gift assets are invested according to investment policies set by GHF Board of Directors.

The Gift Annuity Agreement provides funding for the Fellowship Program unless the donor designates another GHF Fund to receive the gift assets when the annuity payment terminates.

Summary: Gift Amounts and Limitations

Annuity trusts, unitrusts, and gift annuities are not feasible below specific sizes. GHF Board of Directors has established the following minimum amounts for charitable gifts and annuities:

Charitable Gift Annuity	$5,000
Deferred Gift Annuity	$10,000
Charitable Remainder Annuity Trust	$100,000
Charitable Remainder Unitrust	$100,000
Charitable Lead Trust	$50,000

As required by law, GHF may only accept life income gifts for one or two lives, and also a term of years. In some circumstances, payments may extend to additional lives or a combination of one or two lives plus a term of years. The usual minimum age for acceptance of the donor/first life income beneficiary is sixty-five (65). The exception to the above would be the deferred gift annuity. The usual minimum age for acceptance of the second life income beneficiary is fifty-five (55).

Source: Goodwin House Foundation, Alexandria, VA.

Thirty-Four Planned Giving Do's and Don'ts

1. **Do** have a planned giving program; don't defer it.

2. **Don't** believe you can limit your fundraising to foundations, corporations, capital campaigns, and annual giving programs. Planned giving will likely be 20 percent to 40 percent of your total dollars raised.

3. **Do** believe your program will be cost effective. A study completed by one firm found that for every $1 spent on a planned giving program it will bring in $72.43. The study was done using only those organizations in operation from 50 to 100 years and having had a planned giving program in place for at least seven years.

4. **Don't** think your program has to be an expensive one to succeed. For example, planned giving brochures cost 23 cents and setting up a Web site costs virtually nothing after the initial set-up. To fund the publication, a nonprofit would approach local bank trust departments, accounting firms, and others for financial support. (Calder Sinclair noted that this also will further the relationship between the nonprofit and these key financial and estate planning advisors.)

5. **Don't** think that you will have to wait seven to eight years to show results. Some donors create charitable gift annuities upon creation of their planned giving program. And, some people die prematurely. In fact, a charitable gift annuity is the most important program a nonprofit should have in place. If the donor argues that the stock market will bring a better return, then push the charitable intent.

6. **Don't** expect too much too soon.

7. **Do** get board approval and participation. Use the three A's: advocacy, advice, and action. In other words, ask, ask, and ask. The Board should make its own annual, capital, and planned gift. The organization should first approach its development committee and then the Board.

8. **Do** decide what types of gifts you will accept and promote them. Develop guidelines for planned gifts.

9. **Do** have legal counsel. The right legal counsel will help an organization close more gifts by helping work through a donor's expectation and showing how it can be done. Hire specialized attorneys who know charitable estate planning.

10. **Do** consider having a planned giving consultant.

11. **Do** educate donors on financial and estate planning. Many affluent board members and friends don't have wills, or their wills are dated. Also, some donors aren't aware that their planned gift can cost nothing. For example, if a board member is asked to create a $100,000 planned gift but argues that he'd rather leave that money to surviving family, advise him that he can purchase an insurance policy (for $100,000 to make up for the $100,000 planned gift he gave to the nonprofit) and tell him that he can pay for the policy with the money he receives from the gift.

12. **Do** ask for the planned gift.

13. **Don't** make the mistake of asking for a smaller outright gift when you could get a larger gift. For example, some donors make $10,000 annual gifts. Endow that gift with a $200,000 or more planned gift.

14. **Don't** make the mistake of learning all the technical aspects of planned gifts, but forget to ask for the major outright gifts.

15. **Do** have staff ask for the planned gifts as well as volunteers.

16. **Don't** think a planned giving program should be run the same way as a capital campaign or an annual fund. Generally, the cultivation/solicitation process takes longer for planned giving.

17. **Do** "piggyback" planned giving with your annual giving and capital campaign. If you're not serious about planned giving as part of your capital/endowment campaign, you're leaving big dollars on the table.

18. **Don't** be too selective with your identification of prospective donors. Everyone should have a will. There is a true story of a janitor at a nonprofit organization who was passed over for a planned gift ask. The janitor had major real estate holdings and was worth millions. Remember your staff.

19. **Do** spend more time on prospects who are single or married without children.

20. **Do** follow-up on prospects. This is essential.

21. **Don't** be too timid in asking prospective donors to make gifts.

22. **Do** have a good volunteer network to help you. Planned giving donors tend to easily "sell" others on the concept by just talking about their own planned gift.

23. **Do** cultivate a relationship with estate planning professionals, but don't expect too much. Attend meetings, visit accounting offices, help with or offer continuing education credits. This could result in referrals of affluent prospects. Certified public accountants are generally the best resources.

24. **Don't** team up with just one life insurance company or agent. Let life insurance people identify prospects for you. Approach a company or agent and ask if they've thought about setting up a committee for life insurance professionals. Of course they'd need to make their own $100,000 or more life insurance gifts first.

25. **Do** have periodic mailings on planned giving. A survey completed by the National Committee on Planned Giving found that planned giving publications are the number one reason donors give for considering planned giving.

26. **Do** host seminars on estate planning and planned giving. Why? They bring the prospect to you. Hold the seminars in the morning.

27. **Do** maintain a good file/record keeping system. Consider a geographic file as well. And, follow-up, follow-up, follow-up!

28. **Don't** give out erroneous advice on planned giving. Make sure you have an expert assist you.

29. **Don't** always try to represent both the nonprofit and the donor. Make sure the donor is represented by outside counsel to avoid any conflicts of interest.

30. **Don't** get "roped-in" to giving unrealistic projections on what the planned giving program will produce each year.

31. **Don't** get "roped-in" to giving unrealistic estimates of bequest expectations.

32. **Don't** try to run your planned giving program just like someone else's. Circumstances and geography, among other things, should be considered.

33. **Do** expect the unexpected.

34. **Do** expect substantial results from your planned giving program. Planned giving is where the big money is.

Source: Courtesy of Calder Sinclair, Sinclair, Townes & Company, Atlanta, Georgia.

Sample of a Brochure That Combines a Request for Planned Gifts with Outright Direct Gifts

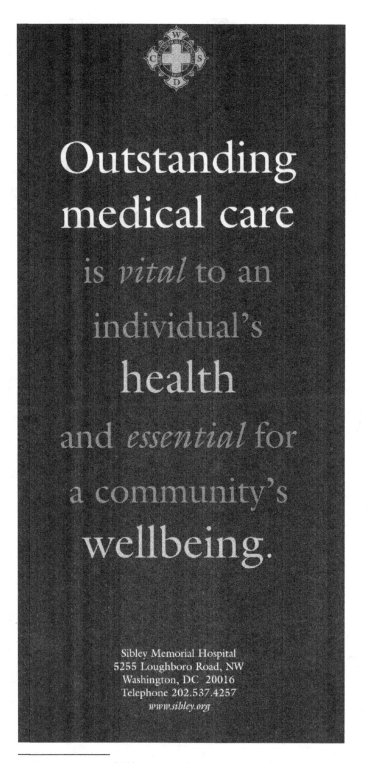

Please consider
Sibley Memorial Hospital
as one of the organizations you
choose to support.

A gift to Sibley may be made in memory of a loved one, to honor someone special, or in appreciation of care given. Sibley is a tax-exempt 501(c)(3) nonprofit organization, so your charitable contribution is tax deductible to the fullest extent allowable by law.

Gifts of Cash
Gifts made by cash, check or credit card are the simplest way to give.

Gifts of Stocks, Bonds or Mutual Funds
Gifts of appreciated stock can provide substantial support to Sibley and have a long-term impact on the hospital. You may benefit from a gift of appreciated assets by deducting the full fair market value of long-term appreciated assets and avoiding tax on the capital gain.

Life Income Gifts
Charitable gift annuities, charitable remainder trusts, pooled income funds, charitable lead trusts, and gifts of remainder interest in homes and other real estate can make it possible for donors to make gifts of a lifetime, while maintaining or enhancing their personal financial situation.

Bequests
A gift in your will is an effective way to make a meaningful contribution to Sibley, while also providing estate tax savings for your heirs. Gifts through wills, revocable living trusts, retirement and savings accounts, life insurance, and similar plans are an important component in the support Sibley receives and can be structured to benefit you, your family, and Sibley.

For more information, please contact:

Sibley Memorial Hospital
Development Office
5255 Loughboro Road, NW
Washington, DC 20016
202.537.4257
www.sibley.org

Combined Federal Campaign #7359

Source: Courtesy of Sibley Memorial Hospital, Washington, DC.

Samples of Generic Planned Giving Brochures

Questions & Answers
About Gift Annuities

Questions & Answers
About Estate Planning for Women

Questions & Answers
About Giving Securities

Source: Courtesy of The Sharpe Company, Memphis, Tennessee, 2008 (www.sharpenet.com).

Sample of a Customized Planned Giving Brochure

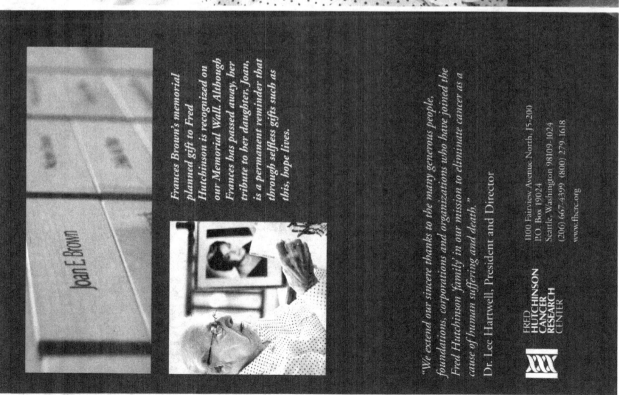

Source: Courtesy of the Fred Hutchinson Cancer Research Center, Seattle, Washington.

FRANCES BROWN

At age 90, Frances Brown became her daughter Joan's caregiver, supporting the Julliard-trained pianist through rounds of chemotherapy, radiation treatment and surgery. After her only child's death, Frances chose to honor Joan's life by naming Fred Hutchinson as a beneficiary in her will through charitable remainder trusts. Frances' deepest wish was for a future in which someone else's child, spouse or friend might live, free from cancer. "I think there is a good chance for this. The people at Fred Hutchinson are very knowledgeable," she said. "You have to have hope." And—like Frances—the heart to help.

DID YOU KNOW YOU CAN MAKE YOUR BEQUEST OR OTHER PLANNED GIFT IN MEMORY OF A LOVED ONE?

Perhaps you are considering or have already included a gift to Fred Hutchinson Cancer Research Center in your estate plans. Your gift can become even more meaningful when made in memory of a loved one.

Through a memorial planned gift, you accomplish two things: You establish a legacy that invests in life-saving research and you make a lasting tribute to a loved one. As the donor, your name can be permanently recognized on our Lifetime Giving Wall while your loved one can be permanently recognized on our Memorial Wall.

You can make a memorial planned gift to Fred Hutchinson through:

Once received, a gift of $5,000 or more will memorialize your loved one's life on the Center's Memorial Wall.

Bequests

Name the Center as a beneficiary of your will or living trust. You can give tangible property (stocks, real estate, bonds), a specific dollar amount or a percentage of your estate.

Life-income plans

Name the Center as a beneficiary of your charitable remainder trust, charitable lead trust or create an immediate or deferred charitable gift annuity.

Retirement assets

Name the Center as first, second or last beneficiary of all or part of your pension plan or Individual Retirement Account (IRA).

Life insurance policies

Make a gift of an existing fully paid policy; establish a new whole life policy and name the Center as owner and beneficiary; or add the Center as a joint or first, second or last beneficiary of your policy.

Other assets

Real estate, CDs, bonds and commercial annuities can be given by naming the Center as a beneficiary.

Researchers at Fred Hutchinson are making boundless advances in the prevention, early detection and treatment of cancer.

With a memorial planned gift to Fred Hutchinson Cancer Research Center, you join us as a Partner in Research with the assurance that your support will continue to save lives in the memory of your loved one.

Learn more about making a memorial planned gift to Fred Hutchinson. Contact Fred Hutchinson's Planned Giving Office at (206) 667-3396 or toll-free at (800) 279-1618. You can also e-mail planned giving staff at plannedgiving@fhcrc.org.

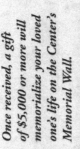

Planned Giving Newsletters

2006
Financial Planner

Gift planning ideas for alumni and friends of Cornell   *Spring 2006*

THE CAYUGA SOCIETY
Now Over 3,000 Members

Celebrating Our Baby Boomers Reaching Retirement Age: Philanthropic Retirement Planning

Robert H. Foote, MS
'47, PhD '50

Flexible Trust Funds Retirement

Robert H. Foote, MS '47, PhD '50, the Jacob Gould Schurman Professor Emeritus of Animal Science, has a deep commitment to Cornell University. He began teaching at Cornell in 1950; and although he retired in 1993, he still works five days a week helping graduate students, writing papers, and responding to requests on cloning and stem cells. In 2005 he was the featured speaker at three Cayuga Society events in Florida.

Professor Foote has been giving back to Cornell throughout his career. He and his wife, Barbara, established the Robert H. Foote Cornell Tradition Fellowship.

In 1997, Professor Foote used appreciated stock to establish a **net income with make-up charitable remainder unitrust (NIMCRUT)**. "This type of trust is very flexible," Professor Foote explains. "I chose it because it will grow tax-deferred."

At the moment, his trust pays only modest income so that the principal can grow. When he needs more income, Cornell will shift his investments to emphasize current income. The "make up" provision allows the trust to pay him any income in excess of the set percentage to make up for the period that he was receiving a lower yield. He benefits from Cornell's expert management of the trust and the resultant growth.

continued inside

NIMCRUT: An Attractive Retirement Plan Alternative

- Charitable income tax deductions during high-income years
- No capital gains tax on the initial transfer of highly appreciated securities
- No contribution limits
- No distribution requirements
- No early age withdrawal penalty
- No mandatory age when you must begin taking distributions
- Trust assets bypass your estate, probate, and income and estate taxes
- Expert asset management without fees
- After your lifetime, a significant gift to Cornell

INSIDE

How a Charitable Trust Can Help You Save More for Retirement

How Can You Reduce or Eliminate Taxes on Your Retirement Plan Assets

Retirement Planning: Important Things You May Not Have Considered

Can we be of assistance? Please send for our new booklet, *Planning for Post-Retirement Years.*

Source: Courtesy of Office of Trusts, Estates, and Gift Planning, Cornell University, Ithaca, New York, and Pentera Inc., Indianapolis, Indiana.

Flexible Trust *continued*

When Professor Foote and his wife are no longer living, the trust's principal passes to Cornell to support University programs they have selected, including Mann Library and the Herbert F. Johnson Museum of Art—particularly its art appreciation programs. But their favorite is the Cornell Tradition Fellowship. "I hope that students will have some of the same opportunity and appreciation that I have had and later can contribute back their time and talent," he says. Confident of Cornell's ability to manage his money despite stock market volatility, he says that the trust provides financial security. "I'll have future income if I need it, but I want most of the money to go to the students. Rising costs make it difficult for families to underwrite a first-class education." Foote points out that "A penny saved is a dollar earned." He adds, "The tax benefits of using appreciated stock allowed us to put more into the trust than we could have if we'd sold the stock and used the proceeds. We see this as an investment, and the return is something money can't buy."

His advice to others considering a planned gift: "Do it as soon as possible. You won't know until you do it how good you'll feel. It's a great relief knowing these things are taken care of. Do it today. Don't wait. It's really a good feeling—great peace of mind."

Tax-Deferred Retirement Growth: How a NIMCRUT Works

Jane and Jim Redfield are a hypothetical Cornell couple. They are both 55, and they plan to retire at the age of 65. They have maxed out their retirement plan contributions and need to accumulate additional assets for retirement, but they are also interested in supporting Cornell. They have decided to use the flexible charitable alternative called the net income with make-up charitable remainder unitrust, (NIMCRUT). They established a 5% NIMCRUT with Cornell to which they will contribute $25,000 annually for 10 years, for a total of $250,000.

During the 10-year accumulation phase, Cornell will invest the assets for growth. Each year the trust is valued, and the lesser of the net income and 5% of the market value of the trust is paid out to the Redfields. If the amount paid out is less than 5% of the market value of the trust, an "I.O.U." is created for the difference. Because the trust has been invested for growth, the amount paid out is minimized and the "I.O.U." balance increases each year.

When the Redfields reach retirement at the age of 65, Cornell will shift investments to emphasize current income. The trust will begin to pay them income for life to supplement their retirement income. If in any taxable year the actual net income for the unitrust exceeds 5% of the market value of the trust, then the payout to the Redfields will include such excess income, to the extent there is an accumulated balance in the "I.O.U." account.

The Redfields will realize a total of $71,725 in charitable income tax deductions during the period that they pay into the trust. If the trust has a total investment return of 8% during the 10-year build-up and yields a net income of 6% in later years, the Redfields will receive total income of approximately $477,979 over their projected life expectancy. After their deaths, the assets that remain in the NIMCRUT—approximately $372,103—will transfer to Cornell for the purposes they have designated.

Retiring Soon?

Now is the time to update your will and review your financial plan. Here are some ideas to consider:

Avoid Undesirable Tax Consequences with Thoughtful Estate Planning

Let us show you how you can. . .

- Reduce estate and income taxes
- Increase your income
- Provide a significant gift to Cornell

Retirement Plans Face Double Taxation

An increasingly important element in estate planning is the retirement accounts that you have been accumulating tax-free in order to supplement your retirement income. It's natural to want to name your children, niece, cousin, friend, or others as the beneficiaries of the account. However, did you know that if an individual other than your spouse is named, whatever is left in your account could be taxed twice? Unlike other property that passes to your heirs and is subject only to estate tax, the balance of your retirement account (except in the case of the new Roth IRA) is subject to income tax as well. And it is your heirs who will have to pay it when they receive the funds.

Taxation of Retirement Account
(based on maximum tax rates)

IRA	$750,000
Less 46% estate tax*	(345,000)
	405,000
Less 35% income tax	(141,750)
Net to heirs	263,250
Total tax as a %	65%

* For estates larger than $2,000,000

Use Your Retirement Plans to Fund a Charitable Remainder Trust (CRT)

Have the balance of IRAs or retirement plans transferred at your death to a Cornell-managed charitable remainder trust. The trust will pay income to a surviving spouse or other heirs for their lifetimes or for a period of years. If your spouse is the bene- ficiary, no estate tax is due on the funds. If others are beneficiaries, the charitable deduction will reduce the estate tax. In either case, the transfer of assets will not trigger income tax. Because of the tax savings, the income beneficiaries could receive more using the charitable remainder trust than if they had received the retirement assets outright. Here's an example:

Mrs. Ezra is a widow with two sons, aged 57 and 53. She establishes a 6% charitable remainder unitrust (CRUT) in her will, and she names Cornell as the beneficiary of her $500,000 retirement fund. She dies with a total estate of approximately $3,000,000. Her $500,000 of retirement assets would be taxed at a rate of 65% if she left it outright to her sons. Using the charitable remainder unitrust (CRUT), the retirement assets avoid some of the tax and the $500,000 is invested to provide $893,342 of income to her sons over the next twenty years.

New Tax Law May Allow More Retirees to Convert IRAs to Roth IRAs

A recent change in the tax law has opened up an opportunity for some retirees over the age of 70 ¹/₂ to convert traditional IRAs to Roth IRAs. Contact us to show you how this could be part of your charitable gift planning.

Consider a Deferred Gift Annuity

June is 70 years old. She will be required to take $20,000 out of her IRA next year. She will use this amount to fund one deferred gift annuity with Cornell that will pay her 12.9% in quarterly installments for her lifetime starting at the age of 80. (For additional income, she could establish several deferred gift annuities.) Upon her death, the remainder will go to Cornell University.

June receives the following benefits:

- *A fixed income of $2,580 each year starting at the age of 80*
- *$668 of the annuity amount is tax-free for nine years*
- *An immediate income tax deduction of $13,718, leaving only $6,282 of her minimum withdrawal subject to tax*
- *The opportunity to support Cornell University*

If you choose this option, the income you receive will depend on the amount you contribute, the length of the deferral period, and your age at the time payments begin. You will know in advance exactly how much you will receive, and your payments will be backed by the full resources of Cornell University.

Reduce Tax on Your Required Minimum Distribution

Once you reach the age of 70 ¹/₂, you must begin taking minimum distributions out of your IRA or retirement plan. The amount you must take out is determined according to your age and the IRS's uniform table.

TIP: Income tax on minimum distributions can be offset by a deduction for charitable gifts. Consider using your minimum distribution to make an outright gift or life-income gift to Cornell that generates an offsetting charitable deduction. Better yet, use appreciated securities of an equal amount and avoid the capital gains tax. Then, use your distribution to repurchase the stock.

Uncover Hidden Value in Life Insurance Policies

If you have reviewed your current needs and believe that you no longer need a group, individual, or business life insurance policy, STOP! Before you drop it or cash it in, find out what it is really worth.

Depending on your computed life expectancy, a life settlement company may purchase your policy for as much as 25% of the face value, even if it has little or no cash value. The proceeds can be used for any purpose, including a charitable gift annuity, which can give you an immediate charitable tax deduction, an additional lifetime retirement income stream, and the satisfaction of leaving a legacy to Cornell. All this with no out-of-pocket cost!

Thinking of Downsizing, but Worried About Long-Term Capital Gains Tax?

If the recent surge in the real estate market has left you facing the prospect of a large capital gains tax, transferring your home to a charitable remainder trust at Cornell may be a solution. First, however, make sure to take advantage of your combined $500,000 exemption on capital gains from the sale of your primary residence. How? Keep an undivided portion of your home equal to $500,000 in value and transfer the remaining undivided portion to a charitable remainder trust that will pay you an income for life. When the home sells, you receive $500,000 of the sale proceeds free of capital gains tax. The balance of the sale proceeds goes to the tax-exempt charitable trust tax-free. So the full proceeds are available to provide you with additional retirement income. You'll also receive a charitable income tax deduction for the present value of Cornell's interest in the trust and the joy that comes with knowing you are helping to build the future of Cornell.

Check Those Beneficiaries!

Retirement accounts, IRAs, life insurance, annuities, and trusts all pass to beneficiaries outside of your will and outside of probate. If you have not reviewed these in a while, you may be surprised at what you find! Find out why failing to name both primary and secondary beneficiaries can be a very costly mistake. Give us a call to learn how using retirement assets for your Cornell legacy can allow you to give more by reducing income and estate taxes.

HOW TO REACH US:
Office of Trusts, Estates and Gift Planning
130 East Seneca Street, Suite 400
Ithaca, NY 14850-4353
(800) 481-1865
E-mail: gift_planning@cornell.edu

 Please visit our Web site at:
http://www.alumni.cornell.edu/gift_planning

You should consult your attorney about the applicability to your own situation of the legal principles contained herein.

 Cornell University

Nonprofit Org.
U.S. Postage
PAID
Cornell
University

OFFICE OF TRUSTS, ESTATES AND GIFT PLANNING
130 East Seneca Street, Suite 400
Ithaca, NY 14850-4353

T55 P424 ***AUTO**SCH 3-DIGIT 220
Mr. Richard G. Frank
3700 Fort Worth Ave
Alexandria VA 22304-1707

Cornell University

Name
_____

Class year   (please print)
_____

Address
_____

City
_____

State/ZIP
_____

Home phone
_____

Business phone
_____

E-mail
_____

☐ Please send me a free copy of your new booklet, *Planning for Post-Retirement Years.*

☐ I am interested in knowing more about different types of gift options at Cornell.

☐ I have made provisions in my estate plans that include a bequest for Cornell University.

  • The value of my bequest is $ _____

☐ I am interested in naming Cornell University in my will or trust. Please send me information, along with suggested language.

☐ Please send me a personalized life-income illustration:

  Amount of gift _____

  ☐ Cash ☐ Securities—original cost $ _____

My date of birth _____

Spouse's/heir's date(s) of birth _____

_____

(Please fold and tape closed before mailing.)

Dragon Day, March 17, 2006

NO POSTAGE
NECESSARY IF
MAILED IN THE
UNITED STATES

BUSINESS REPLY MAIL

FIRST-CLASS MAIL   PERMIT NO. 104   ITHACA, NY

POSTAGE WILL BE PAID BY ADDRESSEE

CORNELL UNIVERSITY
OFFICE OF TRUSTS, ESTATES AND GIFT PLANNING
130 EAST SENECA STREET, SUITE 400
ITHACA, NY 14850-9944

Example of How to Market Planned Giving Programs Through the Web

4 Simple Ways
To Encourage More Gifts

Effectively inform, communicate and build relationships

with donors and professional advisors through...

1. iNews™
Informative e-mails sent to your audience that will boost Web traffic with little cost

2. iAdvise™
Electronic communication that will connect you with professional advisors

3. iDream™
Custom e-mail messages built to your unique specifications

4. iAutopilot™
A customized, automated e-mail conversation between you and your prospects

Drive Traffic To Your Site.

We help donors find you and your Web site. With more than 40 years of marketing experience, we can supply proven strategies and ideas to piggyback on your current e-marketing efforts, or we can create targeted planned giving e-mails for your best prospects. Call us for a personal consultation.

Find Security

Visit our estate and planned giving Web site to discover how making a gift today secures your dreams for tomorrow.

ACCESS a wealth of information, allowing you to make educated decisions regarding your estate plans.

DISCOVER charitable donations can provide payments for yourself and your loved ones.

MAXIMIZE your giving capacity with our online gift calculator.

LEARN how new tax laws will change the way your IRA pays you and your beneficiaries.

❶ Go to www.organizationname.org
❷ Click on "Link."
❸ Then click on "Link."

FOR MORE INFORMATION PLEASE CONTACT:

Joe Planner
Development Officer
jplanner@your.org
(555) 555-1212

Envelope Enclosures. Whether sent with your printed Stelter publication or any other mailing from your organization, our envelope enclosures contain step-by-step directions on how to reach and explore your planned giving site.

Source: Courtesy of the Stelter Company, Des Moines, Iowa, 2008.

National Companies Providing Planned Giving Materials and Services

Caswell Zachry Grizzard
8226 Douglas Avenue
Suite 655
Dallas, TX 75225-5946
Phone: 800-972-3187
Fax: 214-528-8456
Web site: http://www.czg.net

Estes Associates
41 Spoke Drive
Woodbridge, CT 06525
Phone: 203-393-3159
Fax: 203-292-3857
Web site: http://www.ellenestes.com

The Sharpe Group
6410 Poplar Avenue
Suite 700
Memphis, TN 38119
Phone: 800-238-3253
Fax: 901-761-4268
E-mail: seminars@sharpenet.com
Web site: http://www.sharpenet.com

Sinclair, Townes & Company
670 Village Trace
Building 19
Atlanta, GA 30067
Phone: 770-988-8111
Fax: 770-988-8665
E-mail: info@sinclairtownes.com
Web site: http://www.sinclairtownes.com

The Stelter Company
10435 New York Avenue
Des Moines, IA 50322
Phone: 800-331-6881
Web site: http://www.stelter.com

Planned Giving Computer Software
Crescendo Pro/Plus/Presents
Crescendo Interactive
110 Camino Ruiz
Camarillo, CA 93012
Phone: 800-858-9154
E-mail: crescendo@cresmail.com
Web site: http://www.crescendointeractive.com

PG Calc
PG Calc Incorporated
129 Mount Auburn Street
Cambridge, MA 02138
Phone: 888-497-4970
E-mail: info@pgcalc.com
Web site: http://www.pgcalc.com

Glossary of Planned Giving Terms

Administrator
The person appointed by the court to manage one's estate when he or she dies without leaving a will. Administrators have the same duties as executors.

Annuity
A sum of money payable yearly or at other regular intervals.

Appreciated Property
Property, such as real estate or stock, which has increased in value.

Beneficiary
An individual designated to receive benefits or funds under a will or other contract, such as an insurance policy, trust, or retirement plan.

Bequest
A gift or legacy left by will, typically personal property or assets.

Charitable Gift Annuity
Typically an agreement in which you transfer cash or other assets to a charitable organization in exchange for its promise to pay you an annuity for life.

Charitable Trust
A trust having a charitable organization as a beneficiary.

Codicil
A legal instrument made to modify an earlier will.

Corporate Fiduciary
An institution that acts for the benefit of another. One example is a bank acting as trustee.

Cost Basis
The original value of an asset, such as stock, before its appreciation or depreciation.

Durable Power of Attorney
A written legal document that lets an individual designate another person to act on his or her behalf, even in the event the individual becomes disabled or incapacitated.

Estate Tax
A tax imposed at one's death on the transfer of most types of property.

Executor (or Personal Representative)
The person named in a will to manage the estate. This person will collect the property, pay any debt, and distribute your property or assets according to the will.

Fiduciary
A person or institution legally responsible for the management, investment, and distributions of funds. Examples include trustees, executors, and administrators.

Gift Tax
Tax on gifts generally paid by the person making the gift, rather than the recipient.

Gift-Tax Annual Exclusion
The provision in the tax law that exempts the first $12,000 (as adjusted for inflation) in present-interest gifts a person gives to each recipient during a year from federal gift taxes.

Grantor
The person who transfers assets into a trust for the benefit of him/herself or others.

Gross Estate
The total property or assets held by an individual as defined for federal estate tax purposes.

Guardian
An individual legally appointed to manage the rights and/or property of a person incapable of taking care of his or her own affairs.

Inter vivos Trust
A type of trust created during one's lifetime to hold property for the benefit of him/herself or another person.

Interest
Any right or ownership in property.

Intestate

The term applied when an individual dies without a will.

Joint Ownership

The ownership of property by two or more people, usually with the right of survivorship.

Life Insurance Trust

A trust that has an individual's life insurance policy as its principal asset.

Living Trust (Revocable)

A revocable trust established by a grantor during his or her lifetime in which the grantor transfers some or all of his or her property into the trust.

Living Will

A legal document directing that the maker's or signer's life is not to be artificially supported in the event of a terminal illness or accident.

Marital Deduction

A deduction allowing for the unlimited transfer of any or all property from one spouse to the other generally free of estate and gift tax.

Power of Attorney

A written legal document that gives an individual the authority to act for another.

Powers of Appointment

A right given to another in a written instrument, such as a will or trust that allows the other to decide how to distribute the property. The power of appointment is "general" if it places no restrictions on whom the distributees may be. A power is "limited" or "special" if it limits who the eventual distributees can be.

Probate

The court process for determining the validity of a deceased person's will.

Testamentary Trust

A trust that is created upon death by the terms of a person's will or living trust.

Testator

An individual who dies leaving a will or testament in force.

Trust

A written legal instrument created by a grantor for the benefit of him/herself (during life) or others (during life or at death).

Trustee

The individual or institution entrusted with the duty of managing property placed in the trust. A "co-trustee" serves with another. A "contingent trustee" becomes trustee upon the occurrence of a specified future event.

Unified Credit

A federal tax credit that offsets gift tax and estate tax liability. For gift tax purposes, the unified credit remains at $345,800 through 2009, which is equivalent to an applicable exclusion amount of $1 million. For estate tax purposes, the unified credit is $780,800 in 2006 through 2008, and $1,455,800 in 2009, which is equivalent to an applicable exclusion amount of $2 million in 2006 through 2008 and $3.5 million in 2009.

Will

A legally executed document that directs how and to whom a person's property is to be distributed after death.

Source: Courtesy of the Association of Fundraising Professionals (AFP), Arlington, Virginia 2007.

Association Foundation Fundraising

KEY VOCABULARY

- 501(c)(3)
- 501(c)(4)
- 501(c)(6)
- American Society of Association Executives (ASAE)
- Associations
- Association Foundation
- Association Foundation Group (AFG)
- Branding
- CAE
- Chapters, Affiliates, Sections, Branches
- Dues Checkoff
- Foundation Board
- Gift Clubs
- Independent Sector
- Matching Gifts
- Memorandum of Understanding (MOU)
- Parent Association
- Pension Protection Act of 2006
- Planned Giving
- Premiums
- Query
- Sister Association
- Sponsorships
- Type 3 Supporting Foundation
- UBIT (Unrelated Business Income Tax)

OVERVIEW OF ASSOCIATION AND FOUNDATION STRUCTURES

At some time, most of our lives are affected by nonprofit organizations. Whether we give or receive blood, walk or run in a charity event, belong to an association that services our career choice, attend a play, visit a museum, or take children to the zoo, all are services provided by some type of nonprofit organization. The number of nonprofit organizations has increased dramatically in the past 25 years. There are nearly 1.5 million nonprofits, and if religious organizations and mutual assistance groups are included, there are more than 2 million. The most recent statistics show that the number of nonprofit employees has doubled in the last 25 years. Nonprofits have 9.5 percent of the total work force in the United States with total employees numbering 12.5 million. In the independent sector (501(c)(3) or (c)(4) organizations, employment is 11.7 million—9 percent of total employment. Of these, 42 percent of all workers are employed in health services and 22 percent in education. In Washington, DC, nonprofits are the second largest employer behind the federal government.

When most people think of nonprofits, they think of those that provide charity work or the museums, zoos, and theaters. What they do not realize is how much nonprofits have an effect on our daily lives. Those that readily come to mind include: Salvation Army, American Diabetes Association, American Cancer Society, American Red Cross, American Heart Association, International Institute for Highway Safety, Susan G. Komen Breast Cancer Foundation, National Kidney Foundation, Nature Conservancy, National Leukemia & Lymphoma Society, Boys and Girls Clubs of America, Girl Scouts of America, Campfire Girls, and the Boy Scouts of America, among numerous others.

One of the most overlooked and least understood subdivisions within the nonprofit community consists of membership associations. These are organizations or associations formed to serve the members of a particular constituency (people who work in a specific field of endeavor), such as the American Bankers Association, American Society of Civil Engineers (ASCE), National Association of Social Workers, American College of Nurse Midwives, International Association of Fire Chiefs, International Association of Meat Processors, etc.

These associations are often founded as 501(c)(4) social welfare membership associations or 501(c)(6) professional or trade associations or business leagues, which can lobby, and not as 501(c)(3) charitable organizations. However, many of these have 501(c)(3) foundations that are separate from but "attached" to or support their associations and thus are able to receive tax-deductible donations from members and others.

Often these foundations were started long after the "parent" associations. It also is possible to find associations that are themselves 501(c)(3) charitable organizations launching foundations to undertake projects that fall outside the mission of the association. For example, ASCE is a 501(c)(3) organization, but it had at one time, two separate foundations, the Civil Engineering Research Foundation (CERF) and the American Society of Civil Engineers Foundation, Inc. (ASCE Foundation). The association's purpose is not only to serve its members but "to advance professional knowledge and improve the practice of civil engineering." CERF's purpose was "to provide leadership, direction, and an organizational structure to foster research for the civil engineering profession at large." And the ASCE Foundation's mission is "to generate resources for the civil engineering profession." The purposes of the three organizations differ from each other, yet each is vital to the industry.

> *The foundation is the philanthropic arm of the membership association.*

More association foundations are being started each year, and the primary purpose is usually to fundraise for the industry or profession represented by the association and to provide a vehicle for receiving charitable gifts. As foundations are in an earlier stage of development, they are less encumbered by the rules and regulations of governance that the associations have established over the years and thus must follow. Because they have fewer rules encumbering them and usually a smaller board from which to seek permission, foundations can move more quickly to undertake projects, especially fundraising efforts.

THE FOUNDATION'S RELATIONSHIP WITH ITS "PARENT" ASSOCIATION

The relationship between an association and a foundation can be similar to that between a parent and child or between siblings. The same type of interaction that one would find in a human relationship also can be found in an association-foundation relationship—competition, envy, greed, rivalry, friendship, closeness, arguments over money, etc. An association sometimes tries to control the foundation it has launched even though there must be an "arm's-length" relationship between the two organizations. A level of trust between the two must be developed as quickly as possible so they can develop a strong, mutually respectful relationship.

There have been very few studies done on the relationships between associations and their foundations, most likely because these relationships are young and still developing. The Association Foundation Group (AFG), a 17-year-old organization in the greater Washington, DC, area dedicated to the association foundation executive, undertook a survey of its membership in 2003 to obtain a better understanding of the complex relationships between associations and foundations. AFG found in its 2003 Membership Survey that 70 percent of its foundation members had parent organizations that were 501(c)(6) organizations; 27 percent were 501(c)(3) organizations, and 3 percent were 501(c)(4) organizations. Of the parent organizations,

- 54 percent have individual professionals as members
- 27 percent have corporate members
- 42 percent have memberships of 25,000 or more
- 45 percent have annual revenues greater than $10 million
- 64 percent make financial contributions to their foundations
- 21 percent require a management fee from their foundations
- 59 percent are using e-commerce to take payments for dues and other purchases
- 4 percent of association and foundation boards are completely separate
- 50 percent of associations view their foundations as independent entities
- 23 percent view the foundation as a supporting organization reporting to the association CEO

Of the foundations,

- 82 percent have annual revenues below $2.5 million
- 45 percent have two or fewer staff members running them
- 85 percent have annual giving programs
- 60 percent use special events to raise money
- 78 percent have sponsorship programs
- 44 percent have planned giving programs
- 55 percent with annual giving programs use a dues check-off option

- 27 percent find corporate grants most productive in raising money
- 25 percent find annual giving the most productive
- 63 percent have their own Web pages
- 90 percent have links to their parent society's Web pages
- 47 percent can accept donations electronically

In the same survey, AFG also found that

- 1919 was the mean date for the founding of the parent organizations
- 1923 was the median date for the founding of the parent organizations
- 1977 was the mean date for the founding of the foundations
- 1978 was the median date for the founding of the foundations

The complete 2003 Membership Survey can be found in Appendix 16–A, by visiting the AFG Web site, or by e-mailing AFG at afghqtrs@afgnet.org. Membership in AFG is open to anyone involved with an association foundation, although there are many members who work for other types of supporting foundations. Members actively use the AFG Listserv to network and to seek input on issues affecting their work.

TRENDS IN ACCOUNTABILITY

Associations and their foundations are an active part of the larger nonprofit world. Issues that affect most nonprofits also have a profound effect on associations and their fundraising operations. In the early 2000s, the Independent Sector—a national coalition of more than 700 voluntary organizations, foundations, and corporate giving programs headquartered in Washington, DC—brought together six major organizations, including the Council of Nonprofit Associations, to address the issue of "accountability in the sector." In this first meeting of the six, participants reported that the environment in which nonprofits operate is changing rapidly and dramatically, and a number of trends are emerging regarding accountability. "These trends include:

- The growing use of the Internet for both fundraising and disclosure
- The start of a massive transfer of wealth through inheritance
- Tremendous growth in foundation assets
- A rise in the number of young philanthropists
- An increase in the number of small family foundations
- The "blending of sectors," meaning that nonprofits are increasingly carrying out quasi-public functions normally reserved for government agencies
- The growth in corporate philanthropy
- The increased use of nonprofits for political purposes
- The growth of commercialism within the sector
- Increasing dependence on the media to serve as watchdog over the sector

- A growing number of people calling for greater government oversight of the sector, including those lobbying for a national commission
- The public's increasing confusion over the overwhelming choices and level of information already out there and its clamor for someone to tell them who they can trust to give their money
- Increased anxiety and insecurity on the part of nonprofit board members about what's expected of them in terms of accountability
- A growing interest in accountability coming from "small and local charitable organizations"

It is interesting to note that most of these trends are still relevant today, have a direct relation to fundraising, and provide the development staff of nonprofit associations with many challenges. With increased fundraising being done on the Internet, development staff must not only determine how to work within this rapidly changing environment, but also be able to reach those who still desire to give the old-fashioned way through personal contact.

Today, it is common for charitable gifts to be made online to association foundations, especially by younger members. In 2005, more than 26 million individuals made gifts online, 10 million more than five years earlier. People are willing to make larger donations online if they know the site is secure. Also, Internet donors are described as being more skeptical and demanding than donors who give by more traditional means.

Although historically online gifts have accounted for a very small percentage of overall fundraising, recent surveys show a marked increase in their significance to organizations. This is especially true after a major catastrophe such as a tsunami, hurricane, or terrorist attack. In the Association of Fundraising Professionals' State of Fundraising 2006 report, 87.7 percent of respondents indicated raising more funds online than in 2005. In 2006, 70.0 percent of respondents said that online gifts accounted for 20 to 30 percent of their annual fundraising, and no respondents said online gifts accounted for less than 20 percent. In contrast, the 2004 and 2005 reports showed that most respondents said online fundraising accounted for less than one percent of their annual fundraising. In 2005, just 6.7 percent of participants said online gifts accounted for more than 10 percent of their annual fundraising, the highest percentage category.

Internet donors are more inclined to request information about the charities they support and demand accountability regarding how their money is being spent by the charities. As associations created Web sites to give their members easier access to the services and products available to them as dues-paying members, it became easier for the members to make instant demands on the associations and foundations. No letter had to be written and sent; instead, an e-mail instantly reached its intended audience.

Plus, with the wealth of many members increasing so rapidly, either due to inheritance or to stock market gains, many small family foundations were established. It is difficult for fundraisers to know how to approach these individuals properly for gifts to support their organizations, as these foundations often do not have guidelines that are established, published, or followed. Perhaps a further use of technology can help both sides. If all nonprofits and foundations—old and new—developed Web sites, they could provide accurate information on goals, objectives, policies, and procedures for all to review and use.

BOARD INTEGRATION

Foundations are separate corporations governed by their own boards of directors. Yet an association foundation's board membership may overlap somewhat with the board membership of the parent, "brother," or "sister" association. One model of association foundation leadership is to have all or a subset of the association's board serve as the foundation's board. (Of course, separate meetings must be held and separate minutes must be kept of the foundation and association board meetings.) This structure provides the most control for the association but can be a significant burden on the volunteers. A second model calls for some of the officers of the association to serve as officers or trustees of the foundation. The highest volunteer leader (i.e., the president) in an association may also be on the board as well as others, including the chief staff officer of the parent association. This model provides for control by the association while allowing additional volunteers to become involved. A third option is to have the foundation board completely separate from the association board. This provides the most autonomy and the most opportunity for volunteer involvement but can lead to a separation between the two organizations that ultimately could be unhealthy. It is wise not to have too many members on the foundation's board so that decision making is easier and expenses are less.

FOUNDATION STAFFING

When a foundation is started, its staff will often be provided by the association and will be paid by the association until the foundation becomes financially stable. As with any enterprise, the more staff time available for work on the foundation's business, the more the foundation will be able to do. Thus, if the foundation or association can afford full-time, dedicated staff, the programs are more likely to be successful. However, it is not uncommon in the association environment for staff members to spend a portion of their time working within the association and the remainder of their time with the foundation. The foundation can choose to hire its own staff or to have the association hire staff and charge the foundation an administrative fee. Having staff provided by the association often enables the foundation to provide benefits and pay at a lower cost than if the foundation were to provide them on its own. Among other questions to

consider, will foundation employees be eligible for the same benefits package as the association employees and will they have the same personnel policies?

CORE FUNDING FOR THE FOUNDATION

It is not uncommon for an association to fund a new foundation for the first few years until the foundation can raise enough money to support itself. Start-up costs usually include staff salaries; rent; utility fees; and the purchase of furniture, computers, a copy machine, etc. Often the association will share necessary items or provide them at a subsidized cost to the foundation even after the foundation is on its own financially. But, by law, it cannot charge the foundation more than cost for these items.

OVERVIEW OF FINANCIAL RESOURCES

There are many revenue streams for associations, but the highest producing is still dues income. Also, convention, conference, and meeting fees; vendor exhibit fees; continuing education programs; and the sale of publications account for an average of nearly 26 percent of total association revenue. This large pool of unrestricted income allows the association to cover its overhead and operate its general programs and services. Smaller organizations depend more upon dues income, while larger organizations have many more sources of income upon which to rely. Yet, trade associations that have corporations as members, find themselves heavily reliant on membership dues. There seems to be a growing trend, however, toward declining dues income in associations.

Associations also rely more and more on their foundations to expand their funding resources beyond their dues, publications, conferences, specialty meetings, vendor exhibit fees, educational programs fees, etc. Because of this, association foundations have taken on a greater role in helping to advance the missions of the associations.

Foundations have traditionally sought funding from members, industry suppliers, and corporate and private foundations as well as from government agencies (for specific program-restricted money). Foundations also receive unrestricted income through corporate sponsorships. Where at one time associations sought additional money for their conferences and meetings only by charging fees to exhibitors, they are now, often through their foundations, encouraging corporations to sponsor various conferences and auxiliary events to raise additional unrestricted funds. Even vendors committed to exhibiting are being asked to become sponsors to broaden their visibility to conference attendees. Plus, corporations are being asked to underwrite events at more than one conference or meeting during the year.

In addition, both associations and foundations have begun to look beyond their normal scope of fundraising activities, and some associations have entered a completely different arena, that of starting for-profit subsidiaries and partnerships to raise money. When the amount of income generated by affinity

"*Twentieth floor—director's office, public affairs, resource development. Mind your wallet.*"

Source: Copyright © Mark Litzler.

programs—credit card and insurance programs—or selling/renting mailing lists is at an amount that will affect the organization's nonprofit status, many will decide to establish for-profit subsidiaries and pay taxes on this income that is unrelated to the charge of the organization.

Unrelated business income is defined as revenue derived from activities that are deemed essentially unrelated to the original purpose for which the organization was granted exemption from taxes. Thus, this income is subject to unrelated business income tax (UBIT). If the association or foundation pursues this unrestricted type of fundraising, it is important that a separate organization be established to manage this fundraising so as not to affect the tax status of the foundation. With good planning and organization, there is no reason that the for-profit subsidiary cannot operate alongside the foundation as it undertakes its fundraising efforts as well as alongside the association as it generates funds through dues, publications, and conferences.

FUNDRAISING INTEGRATION WITH THE ASSOCIATION

As fundraising is usually the main reason for an association to start a foundation, there is bound to be a point at which it can cause friction between the two. Should the foundation be allowed to raise money from the association's membership? Will

this conflict with the membership department's collection of dues? Should the foundation be able to solicit money from the advertisers in the association's publications? Will solicitations from the PAC and the foundation confuse members? Can conference exhibitors be asked to make annual or capital gifts to the foundation? Should the association be able to fundraise as well as the foundation?

If these questions haven't been addressed, they must be. If not dealt with early in the foundation's life cycle, they can become major stumbling blocks obstructing the future growth of the foundation. The question of who will solicit which prospects for what purpose and when must be the focus of an ongoing dialogue between the association and foundation leadership. See Appendix 16–B for a case study of whether an association's dues increase should take precedence over the foundation's annual appeal.

First, the foundation's mission should be established. It can be as simple as "to raise money for the ABC profession." The mission will be the driving force for all fundraising efforts. How does its mission relate to the association's mission and thus benefit the members? The foundation needs to have an identity of its own, yet it needs to be in concert with the association to be successful, particularly because many potential donors to the foundation will contribute as a result of their relationship with the association. Also, many donors will contribute only if there is a separate foundation, as they view making gifts to the association as seeing their money going into a "black hole" and being absorbed for operating shortfalls.

The scope of the foundation should be determined next. Will it just raise funds or will it carry out programs? Will these programs support the association's current endeavors or will they be in addition to them? All of this can be decided in a strategic planning session that should include both the foundation's board and selected association board members. There is no reason that the foundation's mission and scope cannot be larger and broader than the association's, but it doesn't need to be. Also, it is wise to have members of the foundation board who are not association members. Not all board seats need to be filled immediately. The strategic plan can call for deliberate long-term growth of the board so it can increase in size as the foundation matures. The foundation will need to find strong leaders who are also strong fundraisers (either capable of making gifts or soliciting them) to serve on the board. To do this, it may have to look outside of the association and its membership. Also, if it is not desirable to increase the size of the board by adding new members, a development committee of key leaders can be organized to fundraise.

TYPES OF FUNDRAISING AVAILABLE TO ASSOCIATION FOUNDATIONS

Dues Checkoff Option

One of the responses of association members when solicited for support by the foundation or association is, "I already pay dues. Why should I do more?" There are many answers, but the simplest is, "Dues income only covers a portion of what the organization hopes to accomplish. Thus, more money is needed to have a healthy, active organization." Another point of view is that people pay dues to help themselves; they make charitable gifts to help others.

> *I already pay dues. Why should I do more?*

Many association foundations will use their membership dues notices as an opportunity to raise funds for the foundation in addition to renewing membership within the association. On the dues notice, one of the many lines will be a voluntary automatic or nonautomatic "checkoff" for the foundation. Appendix 16–C shows a sample of an association's dues notice with a specific request to support the education and research foundation with a voluntary gift. An automatic checkoff indicates a specific amount of donation the association would like to have the member give. Sometimes, this is shown as a separate line on the dues statement and added to the total amount due. This is usually the most successful return, but it is still a voluntary contribution, since the member has the option of striking it out and

just paying the dues amount. A nonautomatic form allows the member to decide how much he or she would like to contribute, which ensures that the potential donor is making a conscious decision to support the organization. Exhibit 16–1 presents two samples of dues notices, one with an optional contribution with a specific amount indicated as a checkoff (A), and the other with an optional, nonspecific contribution amount as a checkoff (B).

Often a request for a dues checkoff meets with resistance, either because there are so many association departments competing for space or because the membership staff is concerned that the "high" amount will discourage membership renewals. Also, the dues checkoff alone will not provide enough annual resources. The most common method of obtaining additional annual funding is to conduct a traditional annual appeal campaign. Many foundations provide a dues checkoff option and conduct a traditional campaign.

The Annual Appeal Campaign

It is relatively easy for an association foundation to start an annual appeal program, as there is already a membership base to which to send solicitations for annual gifts. There is no need to rent lists for a direct mail appeal; prospecting for donors can be done from the organization's membership base.

The key is knowing how to start, to whom to send the first solicitations, how to solicit funds (i.e., mail only, a combination of mail and personal appeals, and/or an e-mail solicitation component), and how much is to be budgeted for the expenses of this first-time appeal. Exhibit 16–2 lists the questions that should be asked when developing a budget for an annual appeal.

If there are current donors who are not completing pledges, then add these donors to your mailing list. If there are no current donors and you are truly beginning from scratch, then select a number of your members who have some relationship with the association. Even if your organization is a trade association with corporate members, you must write to an individual who is capable of making a gift decision. Use the data available from the association to identify those who have volunteered for the organization or have obtained professional certification, attended conferences, or purchased publications, especially if those products or conferences are tied to the foundation's mission. Also, you might want to include a selection of members from various age groups or budget sizes (if you have this information available) to add to your first "test" group. Let's assume that you have 15,000 members but do not have the budget to mail to all 15,000. Instead, you have enough money to send 3,000 prospects a solicitation packet that takes first-class postage.

How do you determine to whom to send the packet? Instead of selecting all 3,000 prospects from the same group, select a sample number from a variety of different age groups. For example, divide your membership into age brackets and select the same number from each bracket. Then, as gifts are received,

Exhibit 16–1A and B Sample Dues Notices

A. Example of dues notice with voluntary checkoff that indicates a specific amount to be given to the Foundation.

Directions: Please indicate which dues and/or voluntary contributions you would like to add/renew by checking the appropriate "New/Renew" box. Only Dues are mandatory. Section Dues and International Air Service Option are voluntary but their amounts may not be changed.

Dues and Voluntary Contributions	Write-in Amount	New/ Amount	Do Not Renew	Renew	Code
2000 Dues Balance	140.00	■		■	PY
2001 Dues	170.00	■			ND
Life Member Service Fee (if applicable)					LM
2001 Section Dues	17.00				SD
ASCE 150th Anniversary	30.00				ANV
Public Image Fund	10.00				PUB
Diversity and Career Guidance	10.00				DCG
Voluntary Fund					VOL
Section Voluntary Fund	25.00				SV
Civil Engineering Research Foundation (CERF)					CRF
International Air Service Option ($57.00) (Receive *Civil Engineering* magazine and *ASCE News* via air delivery service.)		■			ISL
Dues and Voluntary Contributions** SUBTOTAL:	**$ 432.00**				

Renewal Date	Renewal Number
09/20/00	2970131

Member Number	Life Year	Member Grade
36070001	2021	Affiliate

PAYMENTS ARE DUE BY JANUARY 1, 2001

Check must be made payable to ASCE in U.S. dollars drawn on a U.S. bank or appropriate credit card. Federal ID No. 13-1635293

PLEASE REMIT TO: ASCE/Membership
P.O. BOX 79084
BALTIMORE, MD 21279-0084

**See your copy for more information on all items listed

$36.00 of your dues payment represents the value of *ASCE News & Civil Engineering* Magazine. The balance of your dues and all voluntary contributions may be deductible as a charitable contribution. Your approximate tax deduction is $343.00 *Alternatively, you may qualify to deduct the full amount of your dues as an ordinary and necesssary business expense. We recommend that you consult your tax advisor.

*These calculations assume you pay the Grand Total listed in Step 4. Contact the Section to determine what portion of their dues is deductible (see your copy).

Source: Courtesy of the American Society of Civil Engineers Foundation, Reston, Virginia.

B. Example of a dues notice with an optional nonspecific contribution checkoff.

Membership Renewal

Please renew my NRTA membership for:

❋❑ 3 yrs/$20   ❑ 1 yr/$8

❋ *Renew for 3 years and save!*

❑ My payment includes a tax-deductible contribution of $ _____ for the AARP Andrus Foundation.

Total Enclosed $ _____
ACCOUNT 999999999 3

Please return this form with your check or money order (no cash) payable to AARP. Do not staple payment to form.

EXPIRES Dec 9999

‖‖₁‖‖‖‖‖₁‖‖‖‖‖‖‖₁‖‖‖‖‖‖₁‖‖‖₁‖‖₁‖‖₁‖‖‖‖‖₁₁‖‖‖‖₁₁‖‖

Joe Sample
9999 Anyst St
Cypress CA 99999-9999

R6ZN6TXA
RN00206

Y0000000000000000000000000000000

Source: Courtesy of the AARP Foundation, Washington, DC.

Exhibit 16–2 Developing an Annual Appeal Budget

- How much can I afford to spend on soliciting donors?
- Are there current or past donors?
- Is there a donor base with up-to-date addresses?
- If there are current donors, are they paying on pledges?
- Are there current donors whose pledges have been completed?

you can compare the results of the test groups. If you find that you receive a larger number of gifts from one group than the others, a second mailing can then be undertaken in which you send packets to a larger number of prospects from the more successful group. This type of segmentation also can be done around geographics. You may find that your largest group of donors is aged 65 to 75 years and living in Florida and Arizona. In this example, your next test group would include more members of this age group living in these two states. Analyzing your data is the key to success.

Most annual appeals conducted by an association foundation are driven by the staff and not by volunteers, unlike annual appeals conducted by colleges and universities. Encouraging volunteers to make some of the solicitations, however, ensures a peer-to-peer approach and may help reduce some of the foundation's costs. Also, there probably will not be prospecting outside of the membership, as one would find in annual appeals conducted by cause-related nonprofits, who routinely rent lists for prospecting purposes. Thus, the association foundation can reduce its initial annual appeal costs substantially by concentrating on its built-in constituency. After a few years of success with the annual appeal, prospecting could be done outside the membership if that is appropriate. But, if solicitation is done outside of the membership, the foundation must register with state authorities.

Gift Clubs/Circles

As described in Chapter 6, gift clubs or gift circles can be used to motivate and increase giving among donors. What are gift clubs/circles? They are predetermined levels of giving, each with a specific name and specific recognition components. The names may have some meaning or may just be used to describe levels of value. Exhibit 16–3 depicts a gift club with circle names selected only for their level of value.

In Exhibit 16–3A, the top level is named after the most expensive gem, while the bottom level is named after one of the least expensive. In Exhibit 16–3B, this example has expanded as the gift levels have increased. Club names that have a special connection to the association (if there are any) are likely to have special meaning for its members. Exhibit 16–4 lists the gift club names used by the AIST Foundation in Warrendale, Pennsylvania, in their annual appeal, "Forging the Future." The names not only hold meaning for the membership but are recognized easily by anyone as having a connection to the iron and steel industry.

Exhibit 16–3A and B Annual Campaign Gift Circles

A.

Emerald Circle	$1,000 or greater
Diamond Circle	$500 to $999
Ruby Circle	$250 to $499
Sapphire Circle	$100 to $249
Topaz Circle	$99 or less

B.

Expanded as Gift Sizes Increased

Founder's Circle	$10,000 or greater
Chairman's Circle	$5,000 to $9,999
President's Circle	$2,500 to $4,999
Visionary	$1,000 to $2,499
Philanthropist	$500 to $999
Builder	$250 to $499
Patron	$150 to $249
Friend	$75 to $149
Donor	Less than $75

Source: Courtesy of the American Society of Civil Engineers Foundation, Reston, Virginia.

Each year, donors can be encouraged to "move up" the ladder of giving by increasing their donations to the next higher club/circle level. If possible, recognition of the size of a donor's gift from the previous year should be made in the solicitation letter, and the donor should be asked to give at the next higher level in this appeal year.

More and more, donors are paying for their gifts by charging them to their credit cards. It may be the sign of the times, but one of the best "premiums" a foundation can offer its donors is the ability to use their credit cards to make their annual gifts. Why? For the frequent flyer miles, bonus point plans, or money-back programs that their credit card companies offer. Not only do they receive the tax-deductible advantages of making a gift to charity, but they also receive whatever benefits their credit card company offers. It is not unusual to see $5,000 to $25,000 gifts to charities made by credit card. Because of this, a credit card payment option also should be part of any annual appeal. Appendix 16–D shows the brochure used by the AIST Foundation in its

Exhibit 16–4 AIST Foundation Gift Clubs for Their Annual Appeal

Carnegie Circle	$25,000+
Frick Society	$10,000–$24,999
Oliver Council	$5,000–$9,999
Schwab Associates	$1,000–$4,999
Morgan Guild	$250–$999
Bessemer Club	$1–$249

Source: Courtesy of the AIST Foundation, Warrendale, Pennsylvania.

annual appeal, which includes the opportunity to use a credit card to make a gift.

Premiums

Donors can be offered small token gifts in return for their contributions to the annual appeal. It is doubtful that anybody makes a donation just to receive one of these small gifts, but they can be used by the foundation as a marketing device. By giving a calendar or a desk-size cube of Post-it Notes with the name of the foundation or association on it, others will be able to view the gift and perhaps be reminded also to make a donation. These small gifts are called *premiums*—goods or services, or both, offered as an inducement to a prospective donor to make a donation.

Examples of premiums include calendars, key chains, bookmarks, tote bags, coffee cups, umbrellas, desk writing pads, pens, etc. Make sure that the value of the premium does not negate the value of the charitable contribution being made by the donor. For example, if a contribution is made in response to an annual appeal that offers a premium, the donor must deduct the fair market value of the premium from the contribution when applying the gift amount as a charitable deduction. Who determines the fair market value? According to the IRS, if the contribution exceeds $75, the charity must provide a "good faith estimate of the fair market value" of the benefit in writing to the donor.

Not every premium received will reduce the amount or tax value of the contribution. If a premium is considered "insubstantial," the amount of the gift that can be deducted is not reduced by the value of the premium. For example, token gifts bearing the foundation's name or logo and costing less than $8.60 do not have to be deducted if received as a premium for a contribution made to the charity of at least $43.00. Benefits of which the total fair market is less than 2 percent of the value of the gift, up to a maximum of $86 do not have to be deducted. For a clear understanding of what is and what is not tax-deductible each year, refer to the guidelines provided by the IRS. Also, reference materials are available from the Independent Sector at 202-223-8100 or via their Web site at http://www.indepsector.org.

Matching Gifts

Some gifts to the annual appeal can be doubled or even tripled by being "matched" by a gift from a corporation that has a matching gifts program. A "matched gift" is defined as (1) a gift contributed on the condition that it be matched, often within a certain period of time, in accordance with a specified formula, or (2) a gift by a corporation matching a gift contributed by one or more of its employees. Not all corporations offer this type of benefit to their employees, but many more are doing so. Foundations should always remind their donors that these programs are available and ask the donors to check with their employers to see if a matching gift program is available. Most corporations will match a gift one for one, some will match two for one, and a very few will offer a three-for-one match for any gift an employee makes. Appendix 10–C shows one nonprofit's brochure, which lists corporations with matching gift programs. In Appendix 16–D the annual appeal brochure also directs donors to ask their employers if they have a matching gift form.

Designing the Annual Appeal Mall Package

Chapter 7 provides guidance on how to develop the best package for an annual appeal, from writing an effective direct mail piece to designing the package. Association foundation appeals will use the same step-by-step processes described therein.

The Planned Giving Program

Creating a Planned Giving Program

Beginning a planned giving program for an association foundation can be even easier than beginning an annual giving program. Each time a mailing is sent to the membership, a phrase can be added such as "Have you remembered the ASCE Foundation in your will?" or "Leave a legacy to support the future of civil engineering. Remember the ASCE Foundation in your will." These phrases either can be added as postscripts or can be printed on the foundation's stationery. To expand planned giving efforts is relatively simple for foundations connected with individual membership organizations. Again, depending upon your budget, it is only a matter of selecting prospects from your membership base to whom to mail estate planning information.

Begin your planned giving program by understanding the investment required to launch such a program. Present your case to your board and explain that they would most likely see no results from a planned giving program for five to seven years. They need to recognize this and also realize that money will be spent for the cultivation of donors who might or might not make planned gifts but who might in either case contribute to the annual appeal or to a capital campaign. In other words, not only will the program reap planned gifts, but annual gifts and major gifts will also come from the prospects being cultivated.

Using the Web Site to Create Awareness

There are several vendors that have planned giving materials available for use for organizations' Web sites. For example, the Stelter Company, based in Des Moines, Iowa, is one of the leading sources for online gift planning marketing. They were the first to offer organizations a program of online gift planning. Visitors access content through a planned giving home page on the organization's existing site and linked to the Stelter site.

As the largest planned giving publisher in the business, Stelter has loaded its Web link with nearly 250 articles. They monitor the copy daily for tax and legal accuracy and update the site with new articles every month. Content throughout the entire site is automatically personalized with your organization's name and contact information where appropriate. At key points throughout the site, visitors can request customized informational e-brochures that cover 17 estate planning and planned giving topics in greater depth.

Visitors can instantly calculate the benefits of any planned gift they are considering by using an online gift calculator customized to meet the organization's specific gift criteria. In addition, links to the gift calculator are embedded in articles throughout the site, allowing visitors quick access to specific calculations.

Reports done by WebTrends are e-mailed monthly and provide traffic analysis that includes the number of visitors and visits, stay time, and top pages.

With a staff of 75 individuals, Stelter serves more than 1,800 clients nationally and provides all of the traditional materials that are associated with planned giving programs such as the following:

- a complete line of direct mail gift planning programs (custom designed newsletters, targeted newsletters, brochures, postcards);
- the Relationship Building Workshop®, which provides major gift training for development professionals;
- the Essentials for Gift Planning Success seminar, which provides training on how to launch a gift planning program and basic technical instruction for anyone in gift planning;
- a seven-person field staff that conducts face-to-face, on-site marketing consultations with clients and prospects;
- gift planning assessment and strategic plan;
- donor research;
- testimonial writing;
- on-site printing and mail processing facility;
- free phone access for clients to an on-staff gift planning attorney to answer technical questions.

Using Direct Mail to Inform Prospects

Define what age range you think would be most likely to make a planned gift to your organization. Ask your membership department to "run a query" on the membership database to determine how many members are in these age ranges (e.g., 50–55, 56–65, 66–75, 76–85, and 85 and older). The largest number of prospects most likely will come from the 60–75 age range. In addition, past chairs, board members, and other industry and association leaders should be considered.

Determine the numbers of prospects to which you wish to mail. Will it be 1,000 members, 5,000 members, 10,000 members, or some other number? Assume that your budget allows you to mail to approximately 5,000 members. Count the members you have between the ages of 60 and 75 to see if there are 5,000 in this group. If so, use the list of these members for your first mailing of estate planning materials.

Next, determine what you will send to this group. Ask yourselves several questions:

- Will this be a one-time mailing or will you mail several times over the year?
- What type of materials will you send?
- What will you say in these materials?
- By what means will the prospects respond?
- What will you send to prospects who do respond to the mailing?
- Should you have some sort of club or society that they can join if they decide to make a planned gift to your foundation?
- Are there other types of recognition that you could give them in return for making a *future* gift?
- Are there other ways to reach this group of prospects that would be less costly?

Once these questions are addressed and answered, you can begin. If your foundation is related to a trade association with corporate members, you may or may not have information in your database about individuals at those corporations. If you don't have this information, begin gathering demographic data (date of birth, home addresses, etc.) as soon as possible.

Recognition Clubs, Circles, or Societies for Planned Gifts

To recognize those donors who care enough about the association and its mission to make a "future" gift via estate planning, the foundation should establish some sort of club, circle, or society. When donors notify the foundation of their decision to make a planned future gift to support the organization, the foundation can then include them in this special group. Chapter 15, which contains a more detailed description of how to begin a bequest society, presents two examples of such societies, The Mooers Society at American University and the Tau Epsilon Pi Society of Gamma Phi Beta Sorority.

What level of verifying information is required before including donors in the club is up to the foundation. For example, some may require only a written and signed document stating that the donors have made such provisions. Others may require a copy of the actual legal document to be sent to them and to remain on file. It would be nice to have the latter, as it would give you documentation of the legal work completed for the foundation's files, but if a donor hesitates, it is probably not necessary to require it. After all, it is important to cultivate and keep the donor happy, and the more donors included in the society or club, the more likely others will be attracted to join. Plus, the purpose of the club is to be inclusive, not exclusionary. Exhibit 16–5 provides examples of names for planned gifts societies or clubs used by selected nonprofits.

Exhibit 16–5 Examples of Planned Giving Society or Club Names

- The Cayuga Society—Cornell University
- The Civil Engineering Legacy Society—The American Society of Civil Engineers Foundation
- The Mooers Society—American University, Washington College of Law
- Tau Epsilon Pi—Gamma Phi Beta Sorority
- The 1847 Society—The University of Iowa
- Ballington and Maud Booth Legacy Society—Volunteers of America
- The Atherton Society—Pennsylvania State University
- Omega Circle—Association of Fundraising Professionals
- Mary Lyon Society—Mount Holyoke College
- The Matthew Miegs Society—The Hill School
- Old Main Society—Knox College
- The Burnett Society—University of Nebraska
- The Heritage Club—Boys and Girls Clubs of America

Capital Campaigns

At some point, to support a special cause or program, an association or its foundation may have an extraordinary need for income beyond what can be derived from dues, publications, conferences, and normal fundraising. If a new building or a new wing of an existing building needs to be constructed or a special program is to be started, the foundation may decide on its own, or at the request of the association, to undertake a capital campaign to underwrite the expenses. The question then becomes whether the foundation should conduct the campaign itself, from feasibility study to completion, or hire an outside consulting firm to undertake all or part of the effort. If the foundation staff is familiar with the processes of conducting a capital campaign, then it may wish to take on the entire task itself. If the staff is lacking in capital campaign experience, or if the foundation is not in a position to increase the staff size required to undertake a campaign, as necessary, then it is imperative to bring in outside counsel.

Campaigns Operated In-House

If the decision is to keep the campaign in-house, then the foundation's board must realize that it will need to add staff to manage the campaign and not just expect the existing staff to take on more responsibilities. Usually at least two staff members should be added, a manager and an administrative assistant, but if the campaign is large and complex, then more staff may be required.

The first step in any capital campaign is to undertake a feasibility study to determine if the campaign can be successful and how much money it can expect to raise. This is the time to test the case statement to see if the message is clearly stated, strongly made, and resonates with the prospect base. Chapter 14 provides detailed information on planning and undertaking capital campaigns.

Campaigns Operated with Outside Counsel

If there are no staff members with capital campaign expertise, then the foundation must select to work with outside counsel. This means not outsourcing the campaign, but working with a qualified fundraising consulting firm that will provide both guidance and on-site staffing.

How does one select a firm? Begin by speaking with other associations that have foundations to see if they have conducted successful capital campaigns. Look for ones similar in membership, staffing, and budget size and whose campaign was similar in size to the one you wish to undertake. Ask what firms assisted them in their campaigns, what the firms' fees were, were they pleased with the counsel the firms provided, were their members pleased with the manner in which the campaigns were conducted, were the firms completely professional and ethical, etc.

Spend time interviewing several consulting firms before selecting one. It is important that the firms understand the culture of your organization (and, indeed, the culture of associations in general), for not all nonprofits are alike. In particular, the culture of a membership association directly reflects the industry of its members. Lawyers, doctors, civil engineers, human resource managers, airline pilots, food distributors, etc., have different corporate cultures, and the fundraising approach used with each group would be unique. Chapter 18 provides more information on how to select the right consultant or consulting firm for your fundraising efforts.

Sponsorships

Sponsorships often are solicited to support association activities. Which group coordinates these efforts—the association or foundation—depends upon the arrangements made between the two organizations. (If both solicit sponsorships, careful coordination is needed.) But whichever group does the soliciting, there is a natural base of prospects—the association's vendors. What better prospects could there be than those who rely upon the association's members for their business success? The companies who sell or market credit cards, car rentals, insurance, computer software programs, etc., to the association's members are all prime targets for sponsorship solicitation as well as for exhibiting at conferences and specialty meetings.

Others to be considered as prospects include specialty groups who seek to influence the membership, companies who employ large numbers of the association's members, and users of the products and services of the association's members.

If the foundation is designated to conduct all fundraising for the association, it should also coordinate the sponsor solicitations as well. Appendix 16–E provides an example of a Memorandum of Understanding (MOU) that defines how sponsorship fundraising will be done by the association's foundation for the association's annual conference. Foundation staff will need to work with the association membership, conference, meetings, and publications departments to develop a list of vendor prospects. All those who sell to the association or advertise in the association's publications should be considered as prospects for sponsorships. Any company that exhibits at any of the association's conferences or meetings should be asked to become a sponsor. A sponsorship will provide the opportunity for a company to have its name even more visible to the association's membership.

Sponsorship Opportunities Packages

A carefully organized sponsorship package should be developed. See Appendix 16–F for an example of an overview of the sponsorship packages developed by the American Society of Civil Engineers Foundation to raise money for the 2007 ASCE Annual Conference in Orlando, Florida, in November 2007. Sponsorship opportunities ranged from $1,000 to $20,000 and covered most everything to be offered at the conference, from lunches and coffee breaks to student programs and the closing banquet. Any program or opportunity that would provide visibility for those being solicited was selected.

It is important to remember that sponsorship fees are in no way related to the cost of the event or venue being sponsored. The cost of the sponsorship for a banquet may be only $25,000, but the cost of this event could be well over $100,000. Event packages should be priced according to what the sponsors will likely be willing to pay, not necessarily what they cost. For example, conference tote bags may cost less than $5,000, but the visibility afforded a company from having its name placed in front of the association's members could allow this sponsorship opportunity to be sold for $10,000. When beginning a sponsorship program, start with modest pricing to make sure you can obtain the necessary sponsors. Prices can be adjusted upward in the second year, especially if the first year is sold out and there were few or no complaints about the pricing.

Fundraising with Chapters or Affiliates

Most associations have chapters. Although they may be called many things other than chapters (sections, branches, clubs, etc.), these entities provide service and support to the association's membership. They have been referred to as the "heart and soul" of organizations. Some use their chapters to raise funds for the parent association/organization, and others use their national offices to raise the funding to support their chapters. Chapter 17, Fundraising with Chapters and Affiliates, provides a more in depth look at how organizations with chapters or affiliates raise money.

PROMOTION AND MARKETING

A typical association has spent years cultivating its image and has a public relations or communications department to market its programs and itself as a whole. When an association creates a foundation, a decision has to be made as to how closely the image of the foundation—the logo and promotional materials—will resemble the association's image.

Branding

Will the foundation adopt the total brand look of the association, will it create a look that is related to but differs slightly from the association's look, or will it have a completely separate look? It is important for the association and the foundation leadership to discuss this issue and come to a decision together, then share the decision with the staff of both organizations, as the staff may be more parochial in their thinking than the boards. Often, communication is lacking between the association staff and the foundation staff, and the role of the foundation is often not understood by the association staff.

The foundation should have a logo of its own and should use it on all of its materials. The foundation can use the association's public relations or communications department to develop its materials, or it may undertake this effort itself.

Annual Reports

The foundation's annual report can be printed separately or included as a section of the association's annual report. In its early years, the foundation may not be able to afford to print its own annual report and may wish the report to be included in the association's annual report or newsletter or other printed material. It is important to complete an annual report so the public views the foundation as a stable, separate entity and is apprised of the donors' investments.

Web Sites

The foundation's Web site can stand alone and be linked to the association's Web site or it can be part of the association's site. In larger associations, the maintenance of the Web site may be the responsibility of a staff Web master. It may make sense for the foundation's Web pages or Web site to be created and maintained by the association, as long as any fees charged are equal to or less than those charged by outside vendors. Having the same designer can maintain the "branding" created for the association and foundation.

FORGING A FUTURE TOGETHER

The tension created between associations and foundations over fundraising is healthy. As a foundation grows, its broadened sphere of influence, productivity, and fundraising can only enhance the association with which it is related. The two organizations can function on parallel, with each having its own board, mission, programs, and financial resources. Yet their relationship can be symbiotic. The foundation is in a position to help the association further its goals by undertaking fundraising that the association may not be able to do on its own. Also, it may conduct philanthropic programs on behalf of the industry or help prepare industry professionals for the future through leadership, development, scholarship, or other programs. The association can help the foundation keep its expenses low by providing services, products, and office space at or below cost (e.g., it can loan the foundation office equipment it is not currently using).

As the two continue to exist side by side, the association may have the foundation undertake all of the fundraising for the association that it may have undertaken itself or outsourced previously, including sponsorships, capital campaigns, annual appeals, and special events. Also, some programs may be transferred to the foundation from the association if they are more closely aligned with the foundation's activities.

Foundations, on the other hand, can also be grantmaking/giving institutions, and a foundation may actually make grants to support its parent association, depending upon how their relationship was initially established. But whether the foundation is to be an "arm" of the association or an independent, stand-alone entity not subject to the association's board, their relationship will continue to evolve as the foundation grows in years, maturity, and financial wealth.

The key to forging a healthy future together is communication. Open lines of communication can dispel any fears the foundation might have that it will be overly controlled and any fears that the association might have that the foundation will be overly independent. If the two boards have representatives on each other's boards and maintain open, healthy communications, then trust and cooperation will be established and the staffs of both entities will be more likely to work together cooperatively. A commitment to open communication and cooperation should be made at the top level so that both organizations may experience productive growth.

Appendix 16–G, "The Seven Habits of Highly Successful Foundations," provides a checklist for foundations by which they can measure themselves. Appendix 16–H is an example of a model affiliation agreement between an association and its related foundation and can be used as a basis on which to develop a formal agreement between the two if one does not currently exist. Appendix 16–I addresses the questions that are frequently asked by association members when asked to make charitable gifts to support the association's foundation.

The Pension Protection Act of 2006

The Pension Protection Act of 2006 (the Act) caused many problems for supporting foundations in the association and health care communities. Many of these foundations were established as Type 3 supporting foundations as this was the quickest and least expensive path to follow for many attorneys at the time. The Act, in trying to regulate the actions of some Type 3 supporting foundations, created chaos when the legislation enacted created an umbrella effect—applying its regulations to all Type 3 foundations, both the good and the bad and not just the bad ones that they were trying to regulate.

More issues were created when the IRS provided no directions on how to handle the problem situations created by the Act. For example, many charitable trusts and community trusts were no longer able to make gifts to foundations which they had been supporting for years because they were established as Type 3 foundations. In order for the trusts to make gifts as directed by their donors, the trusts required additional clarification regarding the status of the foundations. For foundations, responding to these requests required additional legal and staff work as well as additional expense.

Appendix 16–J addresses the problems caused by the Pension Protection Act of 2006 for one association's supporting foundation even though the foundation wasn't meant to be affected by the legislation. Hopefully, the IRS and U.S. Congress will address and correct these issues in the future. As of the close of 2008, nothing had been done to change the legislation. Thus, it is important that foundations affected by the Pension Protection Act of 2006 work closely with attorneys who are familiar with the Act and its issues to ensure that they are able to receive funds from donors made through community and charitable trusts and designated for them. Also, it is important to understand the Act, so these particular foundations do not incur additional problems in the future because of this legislation, and so they can successfully lobby to have some of the Act's regulations changed.

REFERENCES

Association Foundation Group. 2003. *2003 Membership Survey*. Washington, DC: Association Foundation Group.

Association of Fundraising Professionals. 2006. *AFP State of Fundraising 2006 Final Report*. Association of Fundraising Professionals.

Levine, M. 2000. Are chapters still viable. *Association Management*, June, 81–90.

Association Foundation Group 2003 Issues Survey

Compiled April–May, 2003

The Association Foundation Group gratefully acknowledges the support of CTE Associates in preparing this survey and tabulating the results.

Members of the Association Foundation Group and attendees at the first National Conference on Association Foundations & Fundraising are entitled to a complimentary copy of the survey. Others may purchase a copy for $25.00. Contact assnfoundationgroup@yahoo.com for details.

The survey instrument was sent to 300 executives of association foundations or philanthropic membership organizations; 54 surveys were returned by the response date—a response rate of 16%. Following is a profile of those who participated and a summary of their responses:

RESPONDENT PROFILE

Job Titles

General/Executive	70%
Development (exclusively)	13%
Shared Positions/Other	17%

Experience: Length in the Association Foundation field (in years)

0–3 years	23%
4–6 years	25%
7–10 years	27%
More than 10 years	25%

Primary Role in the Association Foundation

Board liaison	48%
Fundraising	74%
Programs	46%

Professional Experience

Fundraising only	25%
Association management	31%
Both equally	36%
Other	8%

Other Professional Memberships

ASAE	67%
AFP	52%
GWSAE	23%
Other	2%

Does the senior executive of the foundation also hold a management position in the association?

Yes   55%   No   45%

Source: Courtesy of Association Foundation Group, (AFG), Washington, DC, http://www.afgnet.org.

ORGANIZATIONAL PROFILE

Founding Dates

Associations:	mean: 1919 (84 years)	median: 1923 (80 years)
Foundations:	mean: 1977 (26 years)	median: 1978 (25 years)

Foundation's Tax Status: 100% are 501(c)(3) organizations

Parent Association's Tax Status

501(c)6	70%
501(c)4	3%
501(c)3	27%

Foundation's Employees (FTEs)

	2003	*1999*	*Increase (Decrease)*
1 or fewer	25%	31%	(6%)
2	20%	21%	(1%)
3–4	29%	25%	4%
5–6	18%	17%	1%
7 or more	8%	6%	2%

Parent Association's Employees (Full-Time)

5 or fewer	5%
6–10	7%
11–20	11%
21–40	13%
40–75	21%
76+	43%

Association's Primary Membership

Corporate	27%
Individual professionals	54%
Individuals	17%
Other	2%

Association's Membership Size

Less than 1,000	19%
1,001–5,000	16%
5,001–10,000	10%
10,001–25,000	13%
25,001–50,000	10%
50,001–100,000	13%
Greater than 100,001	19%

Foundation Annual Revenue

		% with endowment
less than $500,000	33%	94%
$500,001–$1,000,000	31%	100%
$1,000,001–$2,500,000	18%	100%
$2,500,001–$5,000,000	12%	100%
$5,000,001–$10,000,000	4%	100%
$10,000,001 or greater	2%	100%
Revenue, $1 million or less	63%	97%
Revenue, greater than $1 million	37%	100%

Foundation's Endowment

No Endowment	2%
Less than $500,000	20%
$500,001–$1,000,000	16%
$1,000,001–$2,500,000	18%
$2,500,001–$5,000,000	18%
$5,000,001–$10,000,000	22%
$10,000,001 or greater	4%

Parent Association's Annual Revenue

Less than $1,000,000	10%
$1,000,001–$5,000,000	29%
$5,000,001–$10,000,000	16%
$10,000,001–$20,000,000	16%
$20,000,000–$50,000,000	10%
$50,000,001 or greater	19%

Parent Association's Endowment

No Endowment	3%
Less than $1,000,000	10%
$1,000,001–$2,500,000	10%
$2,500,001–$5,000,000	17%
$5,000,001–$10,000,000	15%
$10,000,001–$25,000,000	22%
$25,000,001 or greater	22%

FOUNDATION PROGRAMS

Types of programs funded or offered by the Foundation

Industry or practitioner-based research	54%
Scholarships for students in the field	52%
Public education	46%
Achievement or service awards	46%
Professional education	44%
Grants to the association	37%
Scholarships for members to attend association meetings	22%
Internships	17%
Technical assistance (expertise) as public service	16%
Community service	11%

Programming plans for next five years?

Expanding existing/new programs	42%
Opening programs/funding access to new groups	21%
Expanding geographic coverage (international)	21%
Maintaining current program areas only	16%

Percentage of the foundation's program work accomplished by outside contractors

	% Respondents
100%	10%
80%	10%
50%	10%
30%	17%
0%	53%

FOUNDATION-ASSOCIATION RELATIONSHIP

How is the foundation viewed by the related association?

As an independent entity	50%
As a supporting organization reporting to the association CEO	23%
As a department reporting to the association CEO	21%
As a department reporting to another association executive	6%

How does your parent association interact financially with your foundation?

	Mean Score	The Provided Services are:				
		Free	Subsidized	At Cost	Cost-Plus	Total
Office space	1.86	52%	10%	38%	0%	100%
Office equipment/tech.	1.96	40%	24%	36%	0%	100%
G&A/overhead	2.30	38%	15%	45%	3%	100%
Accounting services	2.00	41%	22%	37%	0%	100%
Audit services	2.53	19%	11%	67%	3%	100%
Legal	2.30	28%	15%	58%	0%	100%
As an employer	2.09	40%	11%	49%	0%	100%

Does the association make a financial contribution to its respective foundation?

Yes:	64%
No:	36%

Does the parent association require a management fee for services?

Yes:	21%
No:	79%

Overlap between the association and foundation Boards of Directors

All foundation board members are also association board members	8%
Some foundation board members are association board members	44%
Some association board members are foundation board members	44%
Foundation and association boards are completely separate	4%

Appointment of Foundation Board Members

All directors are appointed/elected by the association board	26%
All directors are appointed/elected by the foundation board	26%
Some directors are association-elected, some are foundation-elected	26%
Other	23%
Appointed by association president	33%
Elected by membership	33%

Is a slate of candidates presented for elections?

Yes:	66%
No:	34%

FOUNDATION FUNDRAISING ACTIVITIES

Fundraising Methods Used

Annual Giving	85%
Special Events	60%
Corporate Grants	58%
Gifts-in-Kind	50%

Foundation Grants	44%
Planned Giving	44%
Sponsorship from non-member firms (e.g., vendors)	42%
Capital/Endowment Campaigns	40%
Sponsorship from member companies	36%
Government Grants	28%

Which method has been *most* productive (most net revenue on a consistent basis)?

Corporate Grants	27%
Annual Giving	25%
Capital Campaigns	18%

Which method has been *least* productive (least net revenue on a consistent basis)?

Special Events	33%
Planned Giving	21%
Gifts-in-Kind	18%

Do you have an annual giving program?

Yes	85%
No	15%

Participation by Association Members in Annual Giving

Less than 5%	46%
5%–9%	17%
10%–24%	17%
25%–49%	17%
50% or more	2%

Average Size of Annual Gift: $107.60

Use a contribution check-off option on the association's dues renewal invoice:

Yes	55%
No	45%

How is the dues check-off represented on the invoice?

Suggested but not included in the total invoice	36%
Left blank for the donor to specify	36%
Specified and included in the total invoice	16%
A variety of amounts are suggested	12%

What percentage of your members contributes via dues check-off?

Less than 5%	54%
5%–9%	14%
10%–24%	14%
25%–49%	14%
50% or greater	4%

Average Dues Check-Off Gift Size: $53.61

In which fundraising programs are association foundations investing their time and money?

	Time Allocations	Expense Allocations
Annual Giving	29%	32%
Planned Giving	7%	7%
Capital Giving	14%	12%
Grant Giving	13%	12%
Sponsorships	13%	10%
Special Events	18%	21%
Other	6%	6%

To which program would you like to devote more resources?

Planned Giving	30%
Annual Giving	26%

Describe your foundation's electronic presence:

	Yes	No
My foundation has its own Web page	63%	37%
A link to my foundation appears on my association's home page	90%	5%
My association can accept payments (orders, dues) electronically	59%	33%
My foundation can accept donations electronically	47%	41%

How concerned are you about the following issues or trends that may affect your work?

("1" Being very concerned, and "5" being not at all concerned)

MORE CONCERNED:

Ability to measure foundation impact and importance	2.12	53%	(1 and 2)
Keeping the mission of my foundation meaningful to members	2.24	66%	(1 and 2)
Financial challenges in our industry leading to reduced contributions	2.36	60%	(1 and 2)
Keeping my volunteers engaged and motivated	2.46	54%	(1 and 2)
Attracting new volunteers into the foundation	2.69	47%	(1 and 2)
Straddling the association/foundation relationship	2.91	37%	(1 and 2)

LESS CONCERNED:

Technology overwhelming my association	4.08	84%	(4 and 5)
Competition from for-profits	3.94	71%	(4 and 5)
Business continuity planning and disaster recovery	3.82	69%	(4 and 5)
Technology overwhelming my association members	3.78	61%	(4 and 5)
Competition from outside non-profits	3.14	45%	(4 and 5)
Consolidation in the field reducing our members (donors)	3.26	45%	(4 and 5)
Reductions in association membership	3.08	38%	(4 and 5)

What future trend do you fear the most for your association foundation?

Economy

Keeping volunteers engaged

Member expectations for program outcomes

Case Study: Should an Association's Dues Increase Take Precedence over the Foundation's Annual Appeal?

A foundation affiliated with a national trade association has just completed a very successful capital campaign. It was its first ever. The leadership and staff are moving forward to initiate an annual giving campaign and are fully committed. However, the association's leaders have just recently come to the foundation's leaders to explain that the association is going to increase dues next year and that they do not think it is in the foundation's best interest to institute a request for funds at the same time the association is increasing dues. Further, some of the leaders in both the association and the foundation are raising questions about issues such as "protecting" donors who have already given and how the foundation can justify starting an annual appeal so close to the conclusion of the capital campaign.

The Association Question

Managing the relationship between an association and an affiliated foundation is one of the major challenges of the executives of each organization. The relationship is complicated by each organization having a separate leadership that comes from the same leadership group. Determining who "goes after the money" is just one of the many issues in managing this relationship.

The perspective taken by the association in this case is the one often assumed by associations with affiliated foundations. Yet if a deeper exploration of the issues were undertaken, the result would be—*the enlightened perspective.*

The foundation and the association should agree that the competition for available funds is not between the two related organizations but between the two organizations and all other organizations in the world. If the association chooses to limit or restrict the ability of the foundation to seek these funds, it will in essence be making these funds available to other organizations soliciting funds. This could include similar foundations within the same industry, other associations, or all charitable organizations. The question is not how to divide the available "pie" between the association and the foundation but rather how to make the "pie" larger to accommodate both the association and foundation and to make sure the donors have the opportunity to consider all the options when "slicing the pie."

This enlightened perspective also looks at the source of funds. Typically, dues for the trade association and funds for capital campaigns come from businesses' operations budgets, although gifts to capital campaigns can also come from corporations' foundations. (Businesses gain tax advantages from allocating funds to their foundations, which can then use them for charitable purposes.) Funds for annual giving campaigns are usually gifts from individuals who are making personal charitable contributions. The annual appeal's emphasis can be on *"giving back to the industry from which you have benefited"* and/or *"consider the foundation in your year-end charitable giving."* This stresses individual gifts and does not create competition for capital gifts or dues that come from the business operations. The "member" paying dues joins from one source of funds, and the "donor" making a gift contributes from another source of funds.

The enlightened perspective considers the concept that *success breeds success.* The association and the foundation will *both* succeed if they cast a shining light on each other. For instance, if the reason to support a national trade association is that it is offering a comprehensive set of programs to address industry needs, the members will feel good about their dues, and a dues increase becomes more viable, not less viable. This can be accomplished even more easily when the foundation is portrayed as carrying out the scholarship mission of the national trade association and its success in that role is both applauded and highlighted. A wise association builds on the success of its affiliated foundation and promotes all of its fundraising initiatives; it does not detract from either the foundation or its initiatives. And a wise foundation executive links the foundation's missions to those of the association rather than distancing the foundation from the association. With this approach, both the association and the foundation will have a better chance of success in their separate fundraising activities.

The Foundation Question

If the foundation also takes the enlightened perspective, the foundation can address the question of whether an annual giving campaign can so closely follow a capital campaign. Again, the competition for dollars is not between the annual giving and the capital campaign but between all other opportunities for an individual donor to contribute to a cause. As the funding source is usually different, the foundation can highlight the difference even more with careful wording of the annual appeal letter.

The amount of the funds being requested is also different. Small requests of $50, $100, or $250 appear in annual appeal letters whereas these small amounts are almost nonexistent in a capital campaign. Correspondingly, while a capital campaign can receive millions of dollars from fewer than 100 donors, the number of donors in an annual appeal can be in the thousands. The annual appeal reaches out to the many persons who were not asked to join the successful capital campaign and offers them the opportunity to give. Everyone wants to be a part of something that is successful, and that can be the theme for giving to the annual campaign.

Donor Stewardship

The enlightened perspective says, "Do not leave the donors to a capital campaign out of your appeal for annual giving." This approach recognizes that donors will give to two separate campaigns because of their feelings for the organization, the people, the cause, or the recognition. If you don't ask those who gave to the capital campaign for an annual gift, you have failed in your stewardship responsibility. Donors want to be included, not excluded.

Good stewardship, though, does require the foundation to treat the capital campaign donors differently from other donors. The opening sentence in the appeal for annual giving to these donors must immediately thank them for their gifts to the capital campaign. The appeal should note that annual giving builds on the success of the capital campaign in which they were a part. It should suggest an individual gift theme to those who contributed from business funds and it should stress a business gift theme to those who contributed to the capital campaign from individual funds. If the leader of the annual appeal was someone who also contributed to the capital campaign, as is often the case, that should be highlighted to show the validity of what is being requested of all other prospective donors who contributed to the capital campaign. Providing this type of specialized information requires extra effort but will be of value and benefit in the end.

The Successful Conclusion for Both the Association and Foundation

More money will be available to both the association and the foundation if the image presented is one of cooperation and team spirit between the two organizations and not one of competition. By using the enlightened perspective, the association, the foundation, and donors to both will all be winners in the end.

Source: Courtesy of Douglas Viehland, Past President, American Hotel Foundation, Washington, DC.

Sample of an Association's Dues Notice with a Voluntary Contribution Checkoff to Support the Association's Foundation

APICS Vision and Mission Statement

VISION: Success through lifelong learning.

MISSION: APICS will continue to set the standard as the recognized global leader and premier provider of resource management education and information for individuals and organizations.

SIGs (OPTIONAL)

The APICS SIGs were created as a forum to enhance the APICS body of knowledge relative to specific interests. These volunteer groups are continuously researching the body of knowledge in their respective areas and producing educational materials and programs to assist the APICS membership and resource management community.

❏ Yes, I am interested in joining the following SIGs. I understand I must include with this invoice a $15 fee for each SIG membership.

(Check all that apply)

❏ Constraints Management (CM) ❏ Remanufacturing (REMAN) ❏ Repetitive Manufacturing (RMG)
❏ Process Industries (PI) ❏ Textile & Apparel (TA) ❏ Small Manufacturing (SM)
❏ Complex Industries (CI) ❏ Service (SVC)

Please total the amount due and add to "SIG/E&R" on the reverse side.

$ _____

EDUCATIONAL AND RESEARCH (E&R) FOUNDATION

Founded in 1965 as a 501(c)(3) not-for-profit organization, the APICS Educational and Research (E&R) Foundation, Inc., is the research arm of APICS and may receive tax-deductible contributions from corporations and individuals for research to support APICS education. The foundation directs contributions and earnings from several endowments to applied research grants. Each completed research project is published in the E&R Foundation's research paper series and made available through the *APICS Educational Materials Catalog* (item #01041).

By supporting the foundation and bridging the gaps in the APICS body of knowledge, your contribution is an investment in future productivity and can earn special recognition.

Please accept my gift of: ❏ $10 ❏ $50 ❏ $100 ❏ Other $ _____

❏ Please send me additional information on the APICS E&R foundation and its programs (items #04060 and #01025).

$ _____

Please total the amount due and add to SIG/E&R on the reverse side.

STUDENT MEMBERS (REQUIRED)

Student members must submit a copy of their current curriculum schedule and the signature and phone number of a university official. The official's signature confirms the student's full-time enrollment in resource management-related classes.

Univ. Name _____ Phone Number _____

Univ. Official Signature _____ Univ. Official Name (print) _____

If you are no longer a student, you may renew as a regular member. Please call (800) 444-APICS (2742) or (703) 354-8851 for specific chapter dues information.

PERF
- -

*Request for the *Production & Inventory Management Journal*

The *APICS Production and Inventory Management Journal (P&IM)*, is available to members upon request only. One request for the *P&IM Journal* entitles you to all four issues, every year, for the life of your membership.

If you would like to continue or start receiving quarterly copies of the *P&IM Journal*, place a "Y" in the box marked PLEASE SEND ME THE *P&IM Journal* on the reverse side of the notice and return with your payment, if you have previously requested the *P&IM Journal*, a "Y" should appear in the box.

Individual corporate members should make individual requests.

*MAIL LIST Inclusion

Safeguarding Member Privacy

As a professional organization, APICS is obligated to safeguard its members from exposure to unwanted mailings that may occur as a result of their membership. However, we are also authorized to use APICS mail lists to be responsive to customers and ensure the professional management of those mail lists.

APICS realizes many members appreciate the offers and information made available by showing outside sources access to APICS mail lists. However, if you no longer wish to receive these additional offers and information, you can have your name excluded from any rented or traded mail list by placing an "N" in the box marked KEEP ME ON YOUR MAIL LIST on the other side of this statement. If you have previously requested exclusion, an "N" should already appear in the box. NOTE: Exclusion from the mail lists will not affect the delivery of your normal APICS mail.

APICS. MAKING BUSINESS RUN BETTER

Source: Courtesy of the APICS—The Educational Society for Resource Management, Alexandria, Virginia.

Sample Association Foundation Annual Appeal Brochure

Please make your donation to the AIST Foundation using this card.

(Your Annual Fund gift is tax deductable where applicable.)

You may be able to double your gift at no cost to you. Check with your human resources department for your employer's matching gift!

Please accept my: ☐ Personal ☐ Corporate Annual Fund gift of $ _____

Name _____

Title _____

Address _____

City _____ State _____ ZIP Code _____

Phone _____ Fax _____ E-mail _____

Make check payable to AIST Foundation or charge:
☐ Check Enclosed (U.S. funds only)
☐ Visa ☐ MasterCard ☐ American Express

Card No. _____ Exp. Date _____

Signature _____
(if credit card is used)

Mail form to: AIST Foundation • 186 Thorn Hill Road • Warrendale, PA 15086-7528

SCHOLARSHIP program

Scholarships are awarded on an annual basis to talented and dedicated students to encourage them to pursue careers within iron and steel-related industries. Approximately $340,000 will be awarded in 2007–2008 through Foundation scholarships, endowment scholarships and Member Chapter scholarships.

AIST FOUNDATION Scholarships

- Ronald E. Lincoln Memorial Scholarship
- Willy Korf Memorial Scholarship
- Benjamin F. Fairless Scholarship
- William E. Schwabe Memorial Scholarship
- David H. Samson Scholarship (Canadian)
- Don Nelson Scholarship
- Ferrous Metallurgy Education Today (FeMET) Scholarship
- Steel Engineering Education Link (StEEL) Scholarship

AIST ENDOWMENT Scholarships

The AIST I.E. Madsen Scholarship is awarded and administered by the Massachusetts Institute of Technology. Visit www.mit.edu for more information.

The AIST Morrow Scholarship is awarded and administered by the University of Pennsylvania. Visit www.seas.upenn.edu for more information.

The AIST Farrington Memorial Scholarship is awarded and administered by the Rose-Hulman Institute of Technology. Visit http://fc.rose-hulman.edu for more information.

AIST MEMBER CHAPTER Scholarships

- AIST Detroit Chapter Scholarship
- AIST Globe-Trotters Chapter Scholarships
- AIST Mexico Chapter Scholarships
- AIST Midwest Chapter Scholarships
- AIST Northeastern Ohio Chapter Scholarships
- AIST Ohio Valley Chapter Scholarships
- AIST Pittsburgh Chapter Scholarships
- AIST San Francisco Chapter Scholarship
- AIST Southeast Chapter Scholarship

In total, there are 21 AIST Member Chapters, all of which strive to issue annual scholarships to qualified individuals within their local region. Visit www.aist.org to explore additional scholarship opportunities.

FUTURE programs

As our industry evolves, the AIST Foundation will strive to develop new and innovative programs to support the future of the iron and steel industry.

GIFT clubs

Carnegie Circle	$25,000+
Frick Society	$10,000–$24,999
Oliver Council	$5,000–$9,999
Schwab Associates	$1,000–$4,999
Morgan Guild	$250–$999

FERROUS METALLURGY education today initiative (FeMET)

The AIST Foundation teamed up with the American Iron and Steel Institute in 2005 to create the FeMET Initiative. Its three goals are to compel more students to choose metallurgy or materials science as their field of study; to recruit more of such graduates into the steel industry; and to increase the number of professors knowledgeable in steel in North American universities. The program's comprehensive strategy includes:

- Scholarship/Internship Program
Ten scholarships of US$5,000 each will be awarded to college juniors. Each scholarship includes a paid internship at a North American steel company during the summer and a second scholarship of US$5,000 in the student's senior year, based on satisfactory academic and internship performance.

- Design Grant Program
Proposals are solicited from North American universities for innovative designs/solutions to an industry-related design theme. The maximum allowable time for a project is one year. The maximum grant per award will be US$50,000.

- Curriculum Development Program
Proposals are solicited from professors of ferrous metallurgy or materials science at North American universities for funding for a curriculum development assistant who will enhance or update industry curriculum in ferrous metallurgy programs. The maximum allowable time for a curriculum development grant is five years. The maximum grant per award will be US$5,000 per year for five years.

STEEL ENGINEERING education link initiative (StEEL)

The AIST Foundation teamed up with the American Iron and Steel Institute in 2006 to create the StEEL Initiative. The program's goals are to increase the number of students studying engineering in North America, and to encourage such students to pursue careers in the iron and steel industry upon graduation.

The StEEL Scholarship/Internship portion of this initiative matches corporate sponsors with qualified engineering students who are awarded US$5,000 toward tuition in their junior year, a paid internship with the corporate sponsor during the summer, and an additional US$5,000 toward tuition in the second year of the program, based on satisfactory academic and internship performance.

For more information, visit www.femet.org.

Source: Courtesy of the AIST Foundation, Warrendale, Pennsylvania.

Memorandum of Understanding

This Memorandum of Understanding (Agreement) is between the American Society of Civil Engineers Foundation, Inc. (referred to as the "Foundation") and the American Society of Civil Engineers (referred to as the "Society") for the purpose of conducting sponsorship fundraising activities for the **Orlando 2007 ASCE Civil Engineering Conference**, October 2007 in Orlando, Florida (referred to as "the conference"). The fundraising goal for the Orlando Conference is $100,000.00.

1.0 Effective Date. This agreement shall be in effect for the period commencing November 1, 2006, and ending October 31, 2007.

2.0 Sponsorship Program. The Foundation agrees to conduct a fundraising campaign to secure sponsors for the conference. The Society agrees that no other individuals, agents, or organizations will be authorized to solicit or commit sponsors, or conduct any other fundraising for the conference.

3.0 Sponsorship Opportunities. By January 31, 2007, the Foundation and the Society shall agree upon the specific sponsorship opportunities, and the specific minimum financial contribution for each, to be offered. The Society shall prepare the preliminary list of opportunities, and the Foundation will respond by proposing a preliminary financial contribution for each opportunity. The Society agrees to fulfill at its expense the programmatic, printing, display, event or related activity associated with each sponsorship opportunity for which the Foundation secures a sponsor.

4.0 Fundraising Services. The Foundation agrees to: organize and manage a sponsorship fundraising campaign for the Conference; compile possible sponsors (from previous conferences and from sponsorship committee members) and research sponsor prospects; conduct weekly sponsorship committee conference calls (to be adjusted to meet the sponsorship committee's needs); invoice and receive all sponsorship contributions; send thank you letters with IRS notification; obtain electronic logos, etc. from sponsors; send a "Benefits E-mail" to sponsors prior to the Conference delineating sponsorship, date, time, room assignment (if known/applicable) and "benefits" of sponsorship; reviewing and editing of Preliminary and Final Program for sponsorship information; send an after Conference "Evaluation" e-mail to sponsors, compiling and sharing the results with the Conference Department; and coordinate the sponsorship program with the Conference Department's overall management of the meeting.

5.0 Sponsorship Contributions. The Foundation will convey all sponsorship contributions received to the Society.

6.0 Fundraising Expenses. The Society agrees to pay all direct expenses (long distance charges, overnight deliveries, reproduction, out of town travel, design and printing of a brochure to promote sponsorships, etc.) of the sponsorship fundraising activities, or to reimburse the Foundation for such expenses. In addition, the Society agrees to pay the Foundation a management fee of $15,000, with $7,500 due on March 31, 2007, and $7,500 due on August 31, 2007. If the $100,000 is surpassed, the fee charged will be based upon the rates in the attached document, ASCE Foundation Fundraising Rates.

7.0 Government Funds. Should the Society wish for sponsorships to be solicited from United States (federal or state) governments or from any of their subordinate agencies or entities, those solicitations shall be conducted in coordination with, but independent of, the Foundation.

8.0 Ethical Standards. The Foundation and the Society agree to adhere to the Donor Bill of Rights (Appendix A) and the Code of Ethical Principles and Standards of Professional Practice of the Association of Fundraising Professionals (Appendix B) in all matters related to activities under this agreement.

9.0 Authority. The sponsorship fundraising activities will be conducted under the authority of the ASCE Foundation Board.

Agreed to this _____ day of _____ 2007, by the Society and the Foundation.

For the Foundation: For the Society:

_____   _____
Jeanne G. Jacob, CFRE, CAE   Patrick J. Natale, P.E., F.ASCE, CAE
Executive Vice President   Executive Director
ASCE Foundation   ASCE

Source: Courtesy of American Society of Civil Engineers Foundation, Reston, Virginia.

Sponsorship Opportunities Summary
2007 ASCE Civil Engineering Conference and Exposition
November 1–3, 2007 • Orlando, Florida

More detail is available for individual sponsorship opportunities. BOLDED EVENTS are available for sponsorship at this time.

CATEGORY	AMOUNT	SPONSORSHIP OPPORTUNITIES AND RECOGNITION HIGHLIGHTS
PLATINUM	$20,000–and above	**ASCE Theme Party—$20,000 (may have multiples of $10,000 each*)** Ice Breaker Reception—$30,000 **General Sponsor—$20,000 and above (may have multiple sponsors)** *Recognition highlights:* *Event Sponsor—Receives 2 Full Registrations to Conference* *Event Sponsor—Receives 2 extra tickets to their sponsored event* *Event Sponsor—Opportunity to speak for 2 minutes "Welcome" at event* *Event Sponsor—Company Name on sign at your event* *Event Sponsor—Company Name shown with event in Program* *Event Sponsor—May have their own staff handout pre-approved item at event* *Attendee List provided to Sponsors to have a Room Drop of materials at Conference Hotel (sponsor is responsible for all costs associated with the hotel).* *Name/Logo on the ASCE Conference Website* *Hotlink on ASCE Conference Website to Sponsor's Home Page* *Name/Logo on the Conference Sponsors Signs* *Name/Logo and website in Sponsorship List in Conference Programs*
GOLD	$15,000–$19,999	**Attendee Gifts—$15,000** **Leadership Awards Program—$15,000** **Celebration of Leaders—$15,000** **General Sponsor—$15,000–$19,999 (may have multiple sponsors)** *Recognition highlights:* *Event Sponsor—Receives 1 Full Registration to Conference* *Event Sponsor—Company Name on sign at your event* *Event Sponsor—Company Name shown with event in Program* *Event Sponsor—May have their own staff handout pre-approved item at event* *Attendee List provided to Sponsors to have a Room Drop of materials at Conference Hotel (sponsor is responsible for all costs associated with the hotel).* *Name/Logo on the ASCE Conference Website* *Hotlink on ASCE Conference Website to Sponsor's Home Page* *Name/Logo on the Conference Sponsors Signs* *Name/Logo and website in Sponsorship List in Conference Programs*

CATEGORY	AMOUNT	SPONSORSHIP OPPORTUNITIES AND RECOGNITION HIGHLIGHTS
SILVER	$10,000–$14,999	**International Program (Dinner, Lunch, and Roundtable)—$10,000 (may have multiples of $5,000 each*)** **Opening Plenary—$10,000 (may have multiples of $5,000 each*)** **Badge Holders—$10,000** **General Sponsor—$10,000–$14,999 (may have multiple sponsors)** *Recognition highlights:* *International Program Sponsor—Receives 2 tickets each to their Dinner and Lunch* *Event Sponsor—Opportunity to speak for 2 minutes "Welcome" at Plenary* *Event Sponsors—Company Name on sign at your event* *Event Sponsors—Company Name shown with event in Program* *Event Sponsors—May have their own staff handout pre-approved item at event* *Attendee List provided to have a Room Drop of materials at Conference Hotel (sponsor is responsible for all costs associated with the hotel).* *Name/Logo on the ASCE Conference Website* *Name/Logo on the Conference Sponsors Signs* *Name/Logo and website in Sponsorship List in Conference Programs*
COPPER	$5,000–$9,999	**Breakfasts—Choice of three (3):** **1) Council of Presidents Program (Breakfast and Break)—$6,000 (may have multiples of $3,000 each*)** **2) Friday Opening Day Networking Breakfast—$6,000 (may have multiples of $3,000 each*)** **3) Saturday Networking Breakfast—$6,000 (may have multiples of $3,000 each*)** **General Sessions—Choice of 4:** **General Session I—$5,000 (may have multiples of $2,500 each*)** **General Session II—$5,000 (may have multiples of $2,500 each*)** **General Session III—$5,000 (may have multiples of $2,500 each*)** **General Session IV—$5,000 (may have multiples of $2,500 each*)** **Student Member Program—$5,000 (may have multiples of $2,500 each*)** **Younger Member Program—$5,000 (may have multiples of $2,500 each*)** **General Sponsor—$5,000–$9,999 (may have multiple sponsors)** *Recognition highlights:* *Breakfast Sponsors—Receives 2 tickets to their Breakfast* *Event Sponsors—Company Name on sign at your event* *Event Sponsors—Company Name shown with event in Program* *Event Sponsors—May have their own staff handout pre-approved item at event* *Name on the ASCE Conference Website* *Name on the Conference Sponsors Signs* *Name and website in Sponsorship List in Conference Programs*
BRONZE	$2,500–$4,999	**Student & Younger Member Luncheon (Saturday)—$4,000** **Session Breaks (choice of 2)—$4,000 each break** **General Sponsor—$2,500–$4,999 (may have multiple sponsors)** *Recognition highlights:* *Event Sponsors—Company Name on sign at your event* *Event Sponsors—Company Name shown with event in Program* *Name on the Conference Sponsors Signs* *Name and website in Sponsorship List in Conference Programs*

CATEGORY	AMOUNT	SPONSORSHIP OPPORTUNITIES AND RECOGNITION HIGHLIGHTS
BRASS	$1,000–$2,499	**Breaks—Choice of two (2):** 1) Session Breaks (choice of 2)—$2,000 each break 2) Student & Younger Member Break (Saturday, choice of 2)—$2,000 each **Guest Program (choice of 3 days)—$1,000 each day** **Student Registration Sponsorships (multiple)—$1,000** **Tours—Choice of four (4):** 1) Disney Tour—$2,000 2) NASA Space Center Tour—$2,000 3) Planned Growth Tour—$2,000 4) Transportation Tour—$2,000 **Student Tour—$2,000** **General Sponsor—$1,000–$2,499 (may have multiple sponsors)** *Recognition highlights:* *Event Sponsors—Company Name on sign at your event* *Event Sponsors—Company Name shown with event in Program* *Name in Sponsorship List in Conference Programs*
PEWTER	$250–$999	**General Sponsor—$250–$999 each** *Recognition highlights:* *Student Room Sponsor: Special Student Sponsors Sign at Conference* *Name in Sponsorship List in Conference Programs*

BOLDED EVENTS are available for sponsorship.

* *"Partial" event sponsors recognition category will be determined by the dollar amount paid and sponsored.*

Source: Courtesy of the American Society of Civil Engineers Foundation, Reston, Virginia.

Seven Habits of Highly Successful Foundations

#1 The Foundation has a clear mission and focus.
- The mission is clearly defined.   1 2 3 4 5
- The mission is shared by Foundation board and staff.   1 2 3 4 5
- The mission is compatible with the Association's mission.   1 2 3 4 5
- The mission "resonates" with Association members.   1 2 3 4 5
- The mission is reflected in the Foundation's strategic plan.   1 2 3 4 5
- The mission is reflected in the Association's strategic plan.   1 2 3 4 5
- The mission demonstrates a willingness to "stretch."   1 2 3 4 5

Average score   _____

#2 Volunteer leadership are active and committed.
- The Foundation Board supports the Foundation mission.   1 2 3 4 5
- The Foundation Board proactively supports the goals and objectives of the Foundation.   1 2 3 4 5
- Other Foundation volunteers are similarly invested.   1 2 3 4 5
- Foundation volunteers commit time and talent.   1 2 3 4 5
- Association leaders demonstrate their support of the Foundation's goals and objectives.   1 2 3 4 5
- Foundation leaders personally contribute financially.   1 2 3 4 5
- Association leaders personally contribute financially.   1 2 3 4 5
- The Foundation Board is respected by its constituents.   1 2 3 4 5

Average score   _____

#3 Foundation staff are competent and valued.
- Foundation staff are competent.   1 2 3 4 5
- Foundation staff are committed to the Foundation.   1 2 3 4 5
- Foundation staffing is sufficient.   1 2 3 4 5
- Foundation staff work well with Foundation volunteers.   1 2 3 4 5
- Foundation staff work well with Association volunteers.   1 2 3 4 5
- Foundation staff are respected and valued internally and externally.   1 2 3 4 5

Average score   _____

#4 The Foundation is visible within its "community."
- The Foundation has high visibility within the Association.   1 2 3 4 5
- The Foundation has a reputation for success.   1 2 3 4 5
- The Foundation has a strong public relations program.   1 2 3 4 5
- Foundation volunteers and staff are effective emissaries.   1 2 3 4 5
- Association volunteers and staff are effective emissaries.   1 2 3 4 5

Average score   _____

#5 The Foundation enjoys financial stability.
- The Foundation has a solid donor base.   1 2 3 4 5
- There is a reservoir of funding prospects.   1 2 3 4 5
- The Association demonstrates its support of the Foundation mission and
  accomplishments through its financial support.   1 2 3 4 5
- The Foundation is able to raise funds successfully.   1 2 3 4 5
- The Foundation's fund raising is cost effective.   1 2 3 4 5
- Volunteers provide meaningful funding contacts.   1 2 3 4 5
- Volunteers are actively involved in achieving funding goals.   1 2 3 4 5
- The Foundation's fund raising is viewed positively by the Association.   1 2 3 4 5
- The Foundation is a good steward of its contributions.   1 2 3 4 5

Average score _____

#6 The relationship between Association and Foundation is positive.
- There is an affirming relationship between Association and Foundation.   1 2 3 4 5
- The Foundation enjoys a positive relationship among Association staff, leadership
  and other constituents.   1 2 3 4 5
- The relationship between Foundation and Association is based on a shared vision.   1 2 3 4 5
- To a degree, there is overlap between the two missions.   1 2 3 4 5
- There is meaningful, ongoing communication between Association and Foundation.   1 2 3 4 5
- Association leaders sitting on the Foundation Board are actively supportive of the
  Foundation mission.   1 2 3 4 5

Average score _____

#7 The Foundation's contributions to the "community" are valued.
- The Foundation is seen as making a difference.   1 2 3 4 5
- Donors and others see value in becoming involved.   1 2 3 4 5
- There is a desire on the part of the Association membership to have the Foundation succeed. 1 2 3 4 5

Average score _____

Total average score _____

Source: Courtesy of James P. Gelatt, PhD, Graduate School of Management & Technology, University of Maryland University College.

Model Affiliation Agreement Between an Association and Related Foundation

THIS AGREEMENT (the "Agreement") is made and effective this _____ date of _____, 20 _____, by and between ABC Association, Inc., a _____ nonprofit corporation, with its principal place of business at _____ ("ABC"), and ABC Educational Foundation, Inc., a _____ nonprofit corporation, with its principal place of business at _____ ("AEF") (ABC and AEF are collectively referred to hereinafter as the "Parties" and individually as a "Party").

WHEREAS, ABC and AEF, while separate, distinct and independent corporate entities, have certain common goals and interests in _____, such goals and interests which are in furtherance of the tax-exempt purposes of both ABC and AEF;

WHEREAS, in furtherance of such common goals and interests, ABC and AEF may desire to coordinate certain complementary activities; and

WHEREAS, given such common goals and interests, the mutual desire of the Parties to maximize the opportunities available to them, and the mutual desire of the Parties to minimize their administrative expenses, the Parties desire to enter into this Agreement, under which ABC may provide, and AEF may accept, certain staffing, office space, office equipment, office furniture, office supplies, office services, and other administrative support, and under which ABC may license, and AEF may accept, certain intellectual property.

NOW THEREFORE, in consideration of the premises set forth above and the promises set forth below, the sufficiency and receipt of which are hereby acknowledged, the Parties hereby agree as follows:

I. TERM AND TERMINATION.

This Agreement shall be effective as of the date and year first written above and shall remain in full force and effect for a period of one (1) year from such date and year. Thereafter, this Agreement shall automatically renew for successive one (1) year terms without any further action by either Party. Notwithstanding the foregoing, this Agreement may be terminated by either Party for any reason upon written notice provided by either Party to the other Party no less than _____ (_____) calendar days prior to the effective date of any such termination. In the event of a material breach of this Agreement, this Agreement may be terminated by the non-breaching Party immediately upon written notice to the other Party, such termination which shall be contingent upon the breaching party failing to cure such breach within _____ (_____) calendar days of its receipt of such written notice from the non-breaching Party.

II. STAFFING, OFFICE SPACE, OFFICE SERVICES, AND OTHER ADMINISTRATIVE SUPPORT.

During the Term of this Agreement, as an in-kind donation to AEF and in furtherance of ABC's tax-exempt purposes, ABC agrees to make available and provide to AEF certain professional and administrative staffing, office space, office equipment, office furniture, office supplies, office services, and other administrative support, and to license to AEF certain intellectual property of ABC, as may be required by AEF and as agreed to by ABC in its sole discretion, subject to the following terms and conditions.

A. Professional Services and Staffing.

ABC shall provide AEF, at no cost to AEF, with the services of some or all of its employees as may be required by AEF from time to time and as agreed to by ABC in its sole discretion, such agreement by ABC which may be modified or withdrawn at any time in ABC's sole discretion. All ABC employees who perform services for or on behalf of AEF shall maintain contemporaneous written daily time logs reflecting the amount of time spent by such employees on AEF programs, activities and administration, as well as the amount and nature of all other time logged by such employees. The financial value of such time spent by ABC employees on AEF programs, activities and administration (i.e., the financial value of the allocable share of the relevant ABC employees' compensation, benefits and employment taxes, calculated, in part, by reference to the written daily time logs maintained by ABC employees) shall be treated by ABC and AEF as an in-kind donation from ABC to AEF.

B.   Office Space, Equipment, Furniture, Supplies, and Services.

ABC shall provide AEF, at no cost to AEF, with the use of office space within ABC's offices (the "ABC Offices"), which offices are presently located at _____. ABC shall provide such office space to AEF within the ABC Offices as may be required by AEF from time to time and as agreed to by ABC in its sole discretion, such agreement by ABC which may be modified or withdrawn at any time in ABC's sole discretion. ABC also shall provide AEF with the use of such office equipment, office furniture, office supplies, office services, and other administrative support as may be required by AEF from time to time and as agreed to by ABC in its sole discretion, such agreement by ABC which may be modified or withdrawn at any time in ABC's sole discretion. The financial value of such office space, office equipment, office furniture, office supplies, office services, and other administrative support shall be treated by ABC and AEF as an in-kind donation from ABC to AEF. Where possible and practical, the financial value of such services and support should be calculated, in part, by reference to the written daily time logs maintained by ABC employees (e.g., if five percent (5%) of all ABC employee time was spent on AEF matters during a given month, then five percent (5%) of the cost of ABC's mortgage/rental payment(s), utility payments, etc. for that month should be treated as an in-kind donation from ABC to AEF). Wherever the direct costs of providing such services and support can be readily ascertained (e.g., postage costs, overnight mail charges, courier service charges), such direct costs of ABC should be treated as an in-kind contribution from ABC to AEF.

III.   INTELLECTUAL PROPERTY LICENSE.

A.   Name and Logo.

During the Term of this Agreement, ABC grants to AEF a non-exclusive, limited license to use the service marks "ABC Association" and "ABC," the logo or logos of ABC, and all other marks consisting of letters, words or graphics in which ABC may have a proprietary interest or property right (collectively, "Marks"), in the name or description of AEF and in programs and activities undertaken by AEF, pursuant to the terms and conditions of this Section.

B.   Other Intellectual Property.

During the Term of this Agreement and unless otherwise reserved in writing by ABC, ABC grants to AEF a non-exclusive, limited license to use all other names, trademarks, service marks, certification marks, copyrights, and any such other intellectual property in which ABC may have a proprietary interest or property right (collectively, "Other Property"), including but not limited to all ABC mailing, telecopying and electronic mail lists.

C.   Sublicenses.

During the Term of this Agreement and unless otherwise reserved in writing by ABC, AEF shall have the limited right to sublicense ("Sublicense") any and all Marks and Other Property licensed to it by ABC to third parties ("Sublicensees"), provided that all such Sublicenses shall be subject to the same restrictions on use of such Marks and Other Property and the same confidentiality requirements as are imposed upon AEF under this Agreement. All Sublicenses shall require the prior written approval of ABC, such approval which may or may not be granted by ABC in ABC's sole discretion. AEF shall take all reasonable and prudent steps in order to ensure that all Sublicensees comply with the restrictions on use and confidentiality requirements imposed under this Agreement.

D.   Ownership of Marks and Other Property.

Notwithstanding any provision contained herein, AEF hereby recognizes the exclusive residual ownership by ABC of all rights, proprietary interests, and property rights in the Marks and Other Property.

E.   Restrictions on Use of Marks or Other property.

AEF shall not use, authorize others to use, or permit the use of Marks or Other Property except in programs and activities that are consistent with this Agreement and any written reservation of rights provided by ABC. AEF shall not use, authorize others to use, or permit the use of Marks or Other Property that would materially decrease the value of such Marks and Other Property or the goodwill or reputation associated with ABC. AEF shall take all reasonable and prudent steps to ensure that any use of the Marks or Other Property pursuant to the limited license granted herein, either by themselves or by an Subllicensee, shall contain the applicable copyright, trademark or service mark notices, pursuant to the requirements of any applicable laws or regulations and any other guidelines provided under this Agreement or that ABC may have heretofore or may hereafter prescribe in writing.

F. Notification of Claims; Assistance in Registration: Termination.

AEF shall promptly notify ABC of any claim related to or potentially affecting the ownership or use of the Marks or Other Property. AEF shall not object to, or impede registration by, ABC of the Marks or Other property, and shall provide all reasonable assistance requested by ABC in ABC's efforts to protect the Marks and Other Property and/or to avoid their unauthorized use. Upon any termination or expiration of this Agreement, all use by AEF and all Sublicensees of the Marks and Other Property shall cease immediately. AEF's obligations herein to protect the Marks and Other Property shall survive any termination or expiration of this Agreement.

IV. BOARDS OF DIRECTORS.

A. Election of AEF Board of Directors.

The Board of Directors of ABC, on an annual basis at a meeting of the Board of Directors of ABC, shall elect the members of the Board of Directors of AEF. Such election shall be by the affirmative vote of a majority of the Directors of ABC present at such meeting, provided a quorum (as set forth in the Bylaws of ABC) is present. The Board of Directors of ABC shall set forth procedures for the nomination of candidates for AEF's Directorships.

B. Board of Directors Meetings.

For reasons of convenience and cost efficiency, if reasonably feasible, the Annual Meeting of the Board of Directors of AEF should be held on the same or proximate date and at the same general location as the Annual Meeting of the Board of Directors of ABC. In addition, if reasonably feasible, all other in-person regular meetings, if any, of the Board of Directors of AEF should be held on the same or proximate date and at the same general location as regular meetings, if any, of the Board of Directors of ABC. All Board of Directors meetings of AEF shall be separate and distinct from Board of Directors meetings of ABC.

V. COORDINATED ACTIVITIES.

In the event that ABC and AEF mutually determine to coordinate certain activities, the Parties shall ensure that the separateness and independence of the Parties is respected at all times with respect to finances, marketing, assets, and in all other respects. The Parties also shall ensure that there is full accountability for the use by one Party of the services and assets of the other Party.

VI. SEPARATE ENTITIES.

The Parties further agree that they are, and shall remain, separate entities and that no partnership, joint venture or agency relationship shall be actually or constructively created under this Agreement.

VII. CONFIDENTIAL INFORMATION.

The Parties shall maintain the confidentiality of all of the confidential and proprietary information and data ("Confidential Information") of the other Party. The Parties also shall take all reasonable steps to ensure that no use, by themselves or by any third parties, shall be made of the other Party's Confidential Information without such other Party's consent. Each Party's Confidential Information shall remain the property of that Party and shall be considered to be furnished in confidence to the other Party when necessary under the terms of this Agreement. Upon the termination or expiration of this Agreement, each Party shall: (i) deliver immediately to the other Party all Confidential Information of the other Party, including but not limited to all written and electronic documentation of all Confidential Information, and all copies thereof; (ii) make no further use of it; and (iii) make reasonable efforts to ensure that no further use of it is made by either that Party or its officers, directors, employees, agents, contractors, or any other person or third party. Each Party's confidentiality obligations under this Section shall survive any termination or expiration of this Agreement.

VIII. INDEMNIFICATION.

Each Party hereby agrees to indemnify, save and hold harmless the other Party and the other Party's subsidiaries, affiliates, related entities, partners, agents, officers, directors, employees, attorneys, heirs, successors, and assigns, and each of them, from and against any and all claims, actions, demands, losses, damages, judgments, settlements, costs and expenses (including reasonable attorneys' fees and expenses), and liabilities of every kind and character whatsoever, which may arise by reason of: (i) any act or omission of the Party or any of its officers, directors, employees, or agents in their capacity as officers, directors, employees, or agents of the Party; and/or

(ii) the inaccuracy or breach of any of the covenants, representations or warranties made by the Party under this Agreement. The indemnity under this Section shall require the payment of costs and expenses by the liable Party as they are incurred. The Party seeking reimbursement or indemnity under this Section shall promptly notify the liable (other) Party upon receipt of any claim or legal action referenced in this Section. The indemnified Party shall not at any time admit liability or otherwise attempt to settle or compromise said claim action or demand, except upon the express prior written instructions of the indemnifying Party or upon the repudiation or denial of indemnification by the indemnifying Party. For purposes of this Section, a repudiation or denial of indemnification shall be deemed to occur if the Party seeking indemnification does not receive written confirmation of indemnification from the Party from whom indemnification is sought within thirty (30) calendar days of notice of the claim, action or demand by the Party seeking indemnification. The Party seeking indemnification shall make all reasonable efforts to provide the Party from whom reimbursement is sought with all information that may be useful in determining whether indemnification is proper. The provisions of this Section shall survive any termination or expiration of this Agreement.

IX. WARRANTIES.

Each Party covenants, warrants and represents that it shall comply with all laws and regulations applicable to this Agreement, and that it shall exercise due care and act in good faith at all times in performance of its obligations under this Agreement. The provisions of this Section shall survive any termination or expiration of this Agreement.

X. WAIVER.

Either Party's waiver of, or failure to exercise, any right provided for in this Agreement shall not be deemed a waiver of that or any further or future right under this Agreement.

XI. GOVERNING LAW AND JURISDICTION FOR DISPUTE RESOLUTION.

All questions with respect to the construction of this Agreement or the rights and liabilities of the Parties hereunder shall be determined in accordance with the laws of the State of _____. Any legal action taken or to be taken by either Party regarding this Agreement or the rights and liabilities of Parties hereunder shall be brought only before a federal, state or local court of competent jurisdiction located within the State of _____. Each Party hereby consents to the jurisdiction of the federal, state and local courts located within the State of _____.

XII. HEADINGS.

The headings of the various paragraphs herein are intended solely for the convenience of reference and are not intended for any purpose whatsoever to explain, modify or place any construction upon any of the provisions of this Agreement.

XIII. ASSIGNMENT.

Except as otherwise provided herein, this Agreement may not be assigned, or the rights granted herein transferred or sublicensed, by either Party without the express prior written consent of the other Party. Any attempted assignment in contravention of this Section shall be of no force or effect and shall not act to relieve either Party of any responsibility or liability under this Agreement. Any attempted assignment in contravention of this Section shall not act to convey, transfer or assign any rights to any third party and no such rights shall inure to the benefit of any such third party.

XIV. HEIRS, SUCCESSOR AND ASSIGNS.

This Agreement shall be binding upon and inure to the benefit of each Party, its subsidiaries, affiliates, related entities, partners, agents, officers, directors, employees, heirs, successors, and assigns, without regard to whether it is expressly acknowledged in any instrument of succession or assignment, notwithstanding Section XIII herein.

XV. SEVERABILITY.

All provisions of this Agreement are severable. If any provision or portion hereof is determined to be unenforceable in arbitration or by a court of competent jurisdiction, then the remaining portion of the Agreement shall remain in full force and effect.

XVI. ENTIRE AGREEMENT.

This Agreement: (i) constitutes the entire agreement between the Parties with respect to the subject matter hereof; (ii) supersedes and replaces all prior agreements, oral and written, between the Parties relating to the subject matter hereof; and (iii) may be amended only by a written instrument clearly setting forth the amendment(s) and executed by both Parties.

XVII. FORCE MAJEURE.

Neither Party shall be liable for failure to perform its obligations under this Agreement due to events beyond that Party's reasonable control, including, but not limited to, strikes, riots, wars, fire, acts of God, and acts in compliance with any applicable law, regulation or order (whether valid or invalid) of any governmental body.

XVIII. COUNTERPARTS.

This Agreement may be executed in one (1) or more counterparts, each of which shall be deemed an original and all of which taken together shall constitute one (1) and the same instrument.

XIX. NOTICE.

All notices and demands of any kind or nature that either Party may be required or may desire to serve upon the other in connection with this Agreement shall be in writing and may be served personally, by telecopier, by certified mail, or by overnight courier, with constructive receipt deemed to have occurred on the date of the mailing, sending or faxing of such notice, to the following addresses or telecopier numbers.

If to ABC: ABC Association, Inc.

                    _____

                    _____

                    <u>Attention</u>: President, ABC Association

                    Fax: (___) ___-___

If to AEF: ABC Educational Foundation, Inc.

                    _____

                    _____

                    <u>Attention</u>: President, ABC Educational Foundation

                    Fax: (___) ___-___

* * * * *

IN WITNESS WHEREOF, the Parties hereto have caused duplicate originals of this Agreement to be executed by their respective duly authorized representatives as of the date and year first above written.

ABC ASSOCIATION, INC.

By: _____

_____ (Name)

President

ABC EDUCATIONAL FOUNDATION, INC.

By: _____

_____ (Name)

President

DC1/106182

Source: Courtesy of Jeffrey S. Tenebaum, Venable, LLP, Washington, DC.

Association Foundation Fundraising Questions

Questions Frequently Asked by Prospective Donors with Answers / Responses

1. **Why should I contribute to the Foundation? I already support the Association with my dues.**

   - Associations and their related foundations exist for different purposes.
   - Associations are created to serve a profession or trade.
   - Associations exist to serve their members.
   - The money raised by associations typically comes from members:

     ➢ Dues
     ➢ Member services—such as conferences, group buying, publications
     ➢ Related organizations—insurance companies, for example

   - Foundations are created to raise funds.
   - Foundations exist for a 501(c)3 purpose—scientific, educational, or charitable
   - Foundations typically raise most of their funds from:

     ➢ Member contributions
     ➢ Dues check-off
     ➢ Members' companies via sponsorships for conferences, meetings, events, etc.
     ➢ Related companies and suppliers—those that provide products or services to association members
     ➢ Related organizations

   - The money raised through dues isn't always enough to support all of the Association's programs.

2. **I haven't heard much about what the Foundation does. Why should I give it my support?**

   - Provide a brief (one page) "case statement" for the Foundation that includes:

     ➢ The Foundation's mission
     ➢ Goals the Foundation has set for itself
     ➢ Tell how achieving those goals will be of interest to the average member.

   - Position the Foundation in terms of the value it adds:

     ➢ The Association serves the members year to year.
     ➢ The Foundation serves the members by helping them anticipate and prepare for the future through research, scholarships, and innovative ideas.

   - The Foundation can actually help control or reduce the amount of member dues by bringing in funds that would not be available to the Association.

3. **Why do we need to have two different organizations under the same roof? It just requires more overhead.**

   - Having two organizations provides a synergy that would not otherwise exist.
   - The Association board is comprised of people from the profession or trade.
   - The Foundation can draw on outside expertise, talent, and wealth for its board membership. It extends the boundaries of the Association.
   - The funding requires two different organizations—one that relies on dues and the commitment of members. The other expands the potential to reach out to new sources of funding.
   - Having two organizations makes it clear that there are two related but distinct missions—both of which, in the long run, make the profession or trade only stronger.
   - The Foundation, often times, can act more quickly on an idea than the Association because it is more nimble usually with fewer layers of bureaucracy.
   - Supporting Foundations help to provide long-term stability to their parent by building endowments.

4. **I'd like to support the Foundation, but I can't afford to now.**
   - A gift of any amount will help the Foundation and the Association.
   - Encourage a yearly gift to the Annual Appeal.
   - It is important to have their name on the donor list as this will encourage other members to make gifts.
   - Share information regarding "planned gifts"—suggest they make the Foundation a beneficiary on an IRA, gifts of property etc.

- Recognize all donors making planned gifts.
- Listen to what they are telling you. Is it really that they can't afford to make a gift or are there other reasons for their not giving.
- Be prepared to thank them for their time and note that you will look for a gift from them in the future. Then, sometime in the future after an appropriate passage of time, ask another member who is a colleague of theirs to approach them for a gift.

5. **I'd rather designate where my money will go.**

- Create categories that are consistent with Foundation programs—e.g., a Scholarship Fund, Research, Advancing the Future, or other specific programs.
- Acknowledge that gifts may be designated, but general support gifts allow the Foundation to be most responsive to needs as they arise.

6. **I give plenty of my time. Isn't that enough?**

- Giving of your time and your funding sends a positive message to others about your level of commitment.
- Volunteer time is vital to the success of the Foundation. But so, too, are donations of funding. It's the combination that allows the Foundation to reach its goals.
- Encourage donations in areas that seem to be of interest to the volunteer.

7. **I'd rather give locally, to my community, as opposed to a national organization.**

- Both are important. In the end, gifts to the Foundation are likely to have impact locally and regionally.
- In a very real sense, your Foundation is a community. It's a community of people not based on geography, but on shared values and goals.

8. **We already have an effective PAC to which I give and that will directly affect my day-to-day business.**

- The PAC plays an important role in influencing short-term objectives, such as the passage of legislation.
- The Foundation complements that short-term role by providing information and research that the PAC can use to inform and influence policymakers.
- It may make sense to support both. The PAC addresses immediate issues; contributions to it are not tax deductible. The Foundation provides for the future of the profession or trade. Both are essential to a healthy future for the profession or trade to which we are committed.

Source: Courtesy of James P. Gelatt, PhD, Graduate School of Management & Technology, University of Maryland University College.

Example of Letter Received by a Type 3 Supporting Foundation as a Result of Pension Protection Act of 2006

April 29, 2008

Goodwin House Foundation
4800 Fillmore Avenue
Alexandria, VA 22311

RE: File #0925338503

Ladies and Gentlemen:

AST Capital Trust Company is trustee for The U.S. Charitable Gift Trust™. Further information about us can be found at www.uscharitablegifttrust.org. We have a client who wishes to make a gift to your organization from a donor advised fund. Due to IRS regulations within the Pension Protection Act pertaining to donor advised funds, we are now required to confirm whether or not grant recipients are Supporting Organizations. Through our research, it appears your organization is a Supporting Organization. We request that you fax, mail, or e-mail the following information to us:

a. A copy of your organization's IRS Determination Letter.
b. A description of how officers, director, or trustees are selected.
c. Copies of your organization's governing documents and confirmation of the officer, director, and trustee selection process.
d. A list of who has "control" (as defined currently in Treas. Reg. §53.4942(a)-3(a)(3)) of the supported organization.

Please reference File #0925338503 when contacting us regarding this matter. We apologize for this inconvenience. Please do not hesitate to contact us if you have any questions or concerns regarding this request.

Thank you,

Robin Lupi

AST Capital Trust Company of Delaware
Trustee for The U.S. Charitable Gift Trust™
Phone: 800-664-6901

Frequently Asked Questions Regarding The U.S. Charitable Gift Trust™

The below questions and answers are designed to help you and your charitable organization better understand The U.S. Charitable Gift Trust™ and its request for information. As this is a summary, you may find more information by visiting our website at www.uscharitablegifttrust.org or by contacting our Trustee, AST Capital Trust Company of Delaware at 800-664-6901.

- What is The U.S. Charitable Gift Trust™?
  - The U.S. Charitable Gift Trust ("USCGT") is a 501(c) (3) public charity.

- What is its purpose?
  - ° USCGT is a Donor Advised Fund. Individuals or corporations (Donors) gift cash or publicly traded securities to USCGT and receive a tax deduction. Donors later recommend that USCGT grant monies to qualified charities from an account created by the donors' gifts.

- What is a "qualified charity"?
  - ° A qualified charity is deemed as either (i) religious organization, (ii) some municipalities, or (iii) 501(c)(3) public charities under section 509(a) of the Internal Revenue Code of 1986 as amended. As USCGT has already provided a tax receipt to the Donor, grants from USCGT may only be issued to charities that would provide the same tax receipt and benefit. In addition, all grants are subject to approval by the Board of Directors of USCGT.

- Why does USCGT ask for documentation?
  - ° Pursuant to IRS regulations, USCGT must confirm that the recommended organization is deemed a qualified charity prior to issuing a grant. To determine its eligibility, USCGT may ask the recommended charity for public information such as a copy of its recent tax filing (Form 990) or a copy of the organization's letter of designation from the IRS.

- What if the organization doesn't provide documentation to USCGT?
  - ° If USCGT cannot confirm if a charity is qualified, the grant cannot be issued to the recommended organization.

- Are there any restrictions on how the qualified charity allocates the grant?
  - ° The grant provided by USCGT may not be used to provide a private benefit (such as tuition or auction items) or to fulfill a pre-existing pledge.

- What if my organization receives a grant and it is intended to be used to provide a private benefit or to fulfill an existing pledge?
  - ° The letter accompanying the grant also provides the restrictions of the grant. By accepting the grant, your organization agrees to abide by these restrictions. If the grant will be used for either a private benefit or to fulfill a pledge, the organization must return the grant to USCGT or jeopardize its tax-exempt status.

- Provided the grant will not be used for a private benefit or to fulfill a pledge, how should the receiving charity direct the funds?
  - ° If the recommending Donor would like the grant to be used for a specific purpose within the organization (i.e. Building Fund, Annual Appeal, etc.), the accompanying letter will include this request. If no designation is requested, the charity may allocate the grant at its discretion.

- How can my organization receive a grant?
  - ° As USCGT is a Donor Advised Fund, all grants are initiated by a recommendation from a Donor of USCGT. Grant requests received from charities will not be honored.

- How can I learn the name of a Donor?
  - ° To protect the privacy of our Donors, we will not release the names of the recommending Donor until the grant has been approved and a check is mailed. Unless the Donor has requested anonymity, the name(s) and contact information of the recommending Donor will be provided in the letter accompanying the grant.

- If I can't send the recommending Donor a tax receipt, what can I do with the contact information?
  - ° As the grant was made possible by the Donor's recommendation, you may use the contact information to provide an acknowledgement that the grant was received. It is recommended that the acknowledgement indicate that it is not to be used for tax purposes.

- How can I learn more about The U.S. Charitable Gift Trust?
  - ° You may visit its website, www.uscharitablegifttrust.org or contact its Trustee, AST Capital Trust Company of Delaware at 800-664-6901.

Source: Courtesy of AST Capital Trust Company of Delaware, Trustee of the U.S. Charitable Gift Trust™ Use limited to publication only. All rights reserved.

Fundraising with Affiliates or Chapters

KEY VOCABULARY

- Advertising
- Affiliates
- Bottom-up Federation
- Branches
- Branding
- Chapters
- Federations
- Foundations
- Hybrid
- Marketing
- Memorandum of Understanding (MOU)
- National Organization
- Sections
- Student Chapters
- Subsidiaries
- Top-down Federation
- Umbrella Organizations

WHAT ARE AFFILIATES AND CHAPTERS?

Affiliates, chapters, or local entities are truly the heart and soul of associations or organizations. Whether they exist at the commu-nity, city, state, or regional level, the local experience can be the members' strongest, as well as closest, contact with the national association/organization. Local entities can be connected legally to the parent organization or have their own separate nonprofit status; however, for the individual member, these differences are often transparent and usually unimportant so long as the individual is receiving the benefits of affiliation they seek.

The names of affiliates or chapters often are used interchangeably even though they have clear legal and structural distinctions. Varying per organization, some use the term *affiliate* for their relationships with their chapters, even though not technically correct. While others have other names for their local groups—clubs, councils, branches, packs, sections, satellites, tribes, troops, forums, and units. It is important to understand what the relationship is legally, because the legal structure does dictate how decisions are made.

The word *affiliates* means the local entity is affiliated with, but not owned by, the national, parent, or umbrella organization. In addition, the parent organization owns less than 50 percent of the voting shares of the local entity or contributes equally to the financial investment, has board representation, and does not retain the sole right to dissolve the organization. Chapters, on the other hand, are an entity created or chartered by a parent organization or association that follows the same mission and usually identical by-laws. Chapters may or may not be incorporated and may have separate boards.

A membership association, for example, can have: one or more chapters in each state; a for-profit subsidiary that markets affinity products; a political action committee (PAC); and one or more affiliated or stand-alone nonprofit foundations.

It would surprise many to know that some of the larger, more well-known national organizations are large only because of the number of members/people supporting their chapters or clubs. For example, Rotary International in Evanston, Illinois, is known worldwide primarily for the work of their local clubs. Rotary International's headquarters didn't even have a dedicated membership division until 2000, and the change came only when their local clubs began losing members.

Another chapter-centric organization is the Grain Elevator and Processing Society (GEAPS) in Minneapolis, Minnesota. As the only individual-membership organization in the grain operations industry, it is an international professional society dedicated to providing its members with forums to generate leadership, innovation, and excellence in grain-related industry operations. It was in existence for more than 40 years with most of its 32 chapters (28 United States and 4 Canadian) chartered before its international organization was founded in 1973. This is an example of ideas flowing upward.

The National Association of Health Underwriters, headquartered in Arlington, Virginia, lets their local chapters run as their own entities and relies upon them to be in touch with its membership. They have 220 state and local chapters with 20,000 members. Larger chapters do their own fundraising, while smaller chapters receive assistance from the national organization or from other chapters.

No matter the legal structure or the titles assigned to local entities, usually there is a complex and often complicated relationship between national organizations and their local entities. For the purposes of this chapter, the term used to describe the international or national organization will be *national* and the term used to describe the local entities will be *affiliates* and/or *chapters*. Other definitions follow in Exhibit 17–1.

RELATIONSHIPS WITH AFFILIATES OR CHAPTERS

Generally, as national organizations needed delivery systems for their programs or fundraising, affiliates or chapters were created. Yet, sometimes, chapters preceded the national organization. No matter which came first, there are many different types of relationships between national organizations and their affiliates. Some national organizations fundraise for their chapters while with other organizations, just the opposite is true—the chapters provide the fundraising for the national organization. See Appendix 17–A for a brief overview of the American Library Association and how it interacts with its 57 chapters.

Exhibit 17–1 Many Definitions for the Relationship

A *national* organization means a group to which all individuals relate or belong. National organizations may have chapters, they may be part of a federation that bundles many chapters in a geographic area into a city/state/regional alliance, and they may have affiliates.

An *affiliate* means a group associated formally with an organization but is autonomous from the organization. For organizations with affiliates, the relationship is more complex. The national organization may provide resources to the affiliates, but the affiliates may also provide resources to the national organization and to other affiliates.

A *chapter* is a group that is formally related with a parent organization and is usually defined by geography as opposed to an area of special interest. For organizations with chapters, the parent organization is more likely to provide resources to the chapters, and chapters may have fundraising goals to support that parent group.

A *federation* is a group in which the organizations are the principal element or members. A *bottom-up federation* is one where the local organizations collect dues to be sent upward to the national level. A *top-down federation* is where the national organization has the primary role for programming, fundraising, memberships, and dues, for downward distribution. Federations are established to provide a more powerful force as a group (federation) than a sole institution would have.

Foundations are established as 501(c)(3) organizations to be the fundraising arm of associations, which usually are 501(c)(6) or 501(c)(4) organizations. Gifts made to foundations, the 501(c)(3)s, are tax deductible to the donors where money given to the associations are not. If chapters are not established as separate 501(c)(3)s, they will have to ask their donors to make the gifts to the national organization's foundation to be able to receive a tax deduction. As a service to the chapters, the foundation or national organization can capture the donors' names, acknowledge the gifts, and report the number and amount of gifts on a regular basis to the chapters.

A *subsidiary corporation* is owned by the national organization and usually has been set up to undertake profit-making endeavors. The monies a subsidiary corporation raises are taxable income. Subsidiaries can expand the parent organization's capacities and scope and also can shield the parent organization from legal risk.

Non-Dues Paying Locals

The American Red Cross, Susan G. Komen Breast Cancer Foundation, and Leukemia & Lymphoma Society, for example, all have local organizations/chapters that don't pay membership dues to the national organization. Instead, they organize local volunteer activities to raise money, provide specific materials needed for programs, or increase awareness of the cause. (They should not be compared with association chapters, though, as they are not membership organizations, but rather are local groups providing fundraising support.)

Komen's "Race for the Cure" and "Songs for the Cure" events raise money to help fight breast cancer and bring awareness of the disease to the forefront. The Leukemia & Lymphoma Society has national activities—"Light the Night Walk", "Team in Training," "The Leukemia Club Regatta," and "Hike for Discovery" to

"ALL THIS TIME I THOUGHT A MATCHING GIFT CAME IN THE SAME COLOR AND STYLE."

Source: Copyright © Mark Litzler.

raise funds for leukemia, lymphoma, and myeloma cures and to help fight blood-related cancers. The American Red Cross' program "Shop to Support" has formed partnerships with corporate partners to provide opportunities for shoppers to support the American Red Cross through the purchase of specific items such as: Christmas ornaments; apparel and other wearables; and household items such as moisture lotion, personalized checks, infant care products, and emergency radios.

In addition, all of these organizations provide support groups or survivor groups for those afflicted with the diseases, recovering from the diseases, or affected by natural disasters of some sort.

Dues Paying Locals

A second type of relationship is the membership societies that have local chapters/affiliates that pay membership dues to the national because they have the same programs, services, or products that are served at the national and local levels. Examples of this type are the American Society of Association Executives (ASAE) and the American Bowling Congress. For membership

organizations, dues paid to the national organization from local organizations is either a function of individuals paying a national dues rate with local dues included as an additional amount to be paid if they want to affiliate locally, or, in some cases, a local dues amount that includes a per capita amount that goes to the national, and if applicable, the state organization. Usually, an individual is required to join all levels under one dues amount, although some organizations allow membership at either the local or national level without belonging to the other. Appendix 17–B shows an example of a national association's dues renewal form that includes the cost of dues for a local chapter.

Umbrella Organizations

A third type of relationship is known as the *umbrella organization* where the national organization serves as an "umbrella" covering all of the needs of the local affiliates/chapters. They hold the tax exemption status, provide the training programs, undertake the fundraising, etc., as a resource to local chapters. Examples of this are the American Marketing Association and the National Conference of State Societies. The latter, located in Washington, DC, holds the 501(c)(4) status for all of the 50 state societies and 3 territorial societies.

Hybrid Organizations

Finally, there is the *hybrid* where the national supports the ability of locals to get their own tax status through a standardized set of bylaws and review of minimum annual standards—audited budget, annual meetings, etc.

WHO DOES THE FUNDRAISING?

It is important to remember that raising money to support most membership activities isn't the same as raising money for charitable purposes. The line is blurred when the parent association is both a membership association and a 501(c)(3) charitable organization. For example, the American Society of Civil Engineers is a 156-year-old membership organization that also is a 501(c)(3) organization. Thus, gifts given to it are tax deductible. Yet, ASCE still uses its Foundation, also a 501(c)(3), to raise money for the organization because ASCE's members clearly state that they would rather give to the ASCE Foundation than to the organization to which they are already paying their dues. The organization's chapters raise money for their own activities and don't use the Foundation except for occasional fundraising advice or training.

> *It is important to remember that raising money to support most membership activities isn't the same as raising money for charitable purposes.*

The concept of philanthropy may be universal, but its application will vary by location and culture. One of the challenges an organization or association with affiliates or chapters faces is embracing the different views of fundraising that may exist among the affiliates/chapters, especially if they are in widely separated locations. Chapter members in one area may embrace fundraising and take it on with fervor, whereas members in another chapter may not wish to undertake fundraising at all.

> *The concept of philanthropy may be universal, but its application will vary by location and culture.*

National Versus Affiliate/Chapter Fundraising

"There is no greater service a parent organization can offer its chapters than helping them grow" (Levine 2000). Mark Levine, in his article "Are Chapters Still Viable?" states,

> The dynamics of chapter-structured organizations are changing just as fast as the day-to-day lives of their members. . . . Computers and the Internet have forced our members to choose between chapter involvement or finishing a big (work) project on their home computers. . . . Work takes up so much time now that the choice is between their employers and their volunteer lives, and it's tough to win that fight. . . . The current leaders stay in positions for several years because no one is willing to take over. At some point, these leaders get burned out. When they leave, the chapter starts to struggle. . . . When a leader starts to get over worked and burned out, he or she loses the creativity that leaders need. . . . The long-term effect of this dearth of chapter leadership is that the chapters no longer do what they are supposed to do—provide continuing education, networking opportunities, and local representation for members. Parent organizations need to do some new things to help their chapters remain viable and productive. They also need to look at innovative ways to do some of the things they're already doing.

> *"There is no greater service a parent organization can offer its chapters than helping them grow."*

Does this mean that the parent organization or association assists the affiliate/chapter with fundraising? Not necessarily—this is a decision for each organization/association to make. Yet, helping affiliate/chapters may be as easy as providing the training necessary for local board members and other leaders to become effective fundraisers.

Often, the greatest service a national office can provide is teaching its affiliates/chapters to fundraise properly. This is particularly important if the local chapter utilizes the national 501(c)(3) tax status in generating dollars that are used locally. Each year, the American Society of Civil Engineers (ASCE) holds leadership conferences for the new officers of its sections, branches, younger member forums, and student chapters. In addition to learning all about the organization's structure and operations, they are provided with a training session on how to raise funds for their local operations and to do this within IRS guidelines. The national organization also provides examples of successful fundraising ideas undertaken by other sections, branches, younger member groups, and student chapters. See Appendix 17–C for a list of fundraising ideas, which were developed by ASCE at the local level, captured on paper by the national's foundation, and distributed free of charge to all of the local entities.

> *Often, the greatest service a national office can provide is teaching its affiliates/chapters to fundraise properly.*

Whose Donor Is It?

One of the greatest challenges facing nonprofits with affiliates is centered around fundraising and who owns the donors. Often when the national organization raises money, the local affiliates feel they are "taking money away" from them; however, experience shows that many donors are usually more interested in having their money stay locally. Handling this properly often can provide economies of scale to local organizations plus give national organizations the ability to help locals with more sophisticated donor development. The best service a national organization can provide is to train its locals in how to fundraise properly and to offer administrative services to the local chapters.

Yet, this requires trust between the parent and the chapters that their monies will be provided in a timely manner, accounted for, and the relationships with the donors will not be abused. The relationships developed at the local level should not become part of the national's fundraising efforts without the consent of the local chapter. Once this trust is violated, locals will stop sending in their donor information. Yet, there can be instances where the donor may not remain local. For example, a local entity may need assistance in working with a donor to bring the gift to fruition, or the donor may be interested in making a very large gift that could provide support to both the local and national organizations. Finally, the local donor may wish to sup-

port a program at the national level and not the local. Some organizations have established a system to provide some money to the local when a major gift comes into national with the assistance of the local. It is important to always put the interests of the donor first. See Exhibit 17–2 for a list of "Ten Tips for Fundraising with Chapters or Affiliates."

> *It is important to always put the interests of the donor first.*

Providing Revenue Streams

Often the role of a national organization in fundraising is to provide tested opportunities to its local affiliates/chapters so they may raise money locally. (Remember, selling a product is different from soliciting money from a donor.) Something as simple as selling wrapping paper or candy can raise large amounts of money for local groups. Many of these programs have been in operation for years and are clearly identified with a specific organization. For example, the Boys Scouts of America have worked for 25 years with a corporation called Trail's End,

Exhibit 17–2 Ten Tips for Fundraising with Chapters or Affiliates

1. Make the case local: The more local the reason for giving to a national organization, the more local chapters will raise money in support of that national organization's mission and programs.

2. The existing relationship between national organizations and their local chapters/affiliates should be evaluated regularly as part of the strategic planning process. This includes policies, governance, finance, legal, marketing, etc. There is no greater strength that can exist for each and no greater strain that can develop if this relationship is not clearly understood, nurtured, and administered. This evaluation should include a cost-benefit analysis, as the cost of servicing chapters can outpace the benefit if there is not a return on investment that meets national needs—either tangibly through dollars or intangibly through advocacy or volunteer efforts.

3. National organizations can provide an economy of scale fundraising administration that provides a service to local leadership by relieving them of databases, their management, and reporting which can drain volunteer time.

4. Economies of scale in designing fundraising events can provide successful models that can be carried out by local volunteers. National organizations that provide staffing to help first-year programs in planning and delivery will benefit from greater success and faster growth of a nationally-branded event.

5. National organizations that rely on or set goals for locals to raise specific dollars annually to support the national must have a consistently compelling case for support that resonates with the local volunteers. Otherwise, those national organizations

may find much-needed dollars directed elsewhere by their local chapter.

6. Local chapters want to raise money for local impact in their community. A national organization should find a way to help locals use at least a portion of the dollars raised at the local level for local benefit. If you have a national scholarship program, help your local chapter raise more funds by committing a relative portion of all scholarships given nationally to be given to qualified applicants in their community for every $ they raise. And, be sure they know how many people from their community have applied and could have been funded if national had the dollars.

7. Chapters should be encouraged and rewarded for sharing effective fundraising programs and techniques with their fellow chapters. To do this, national organizations should set up peer-mentoring networks, listservs, roundtables on fundraising at conventions, etc.

8. National organizations with professional development staff should reach out to include local members as part of their cultivation team, where appropriate.

9. National organizations, where the local chapters utilize the national's 501(c)(3) status, should brief local leadership annually on requirements for using it including an understanding of fair market value, acknowledgement and reporting requirements, use of funds, etc.

10. Local organizations should ask the national organization for support and resources if they are expected to carry out national programs and raise funds for the national organization.

Source: Courtesy of Sandra M. Walter-Steinberg, Chief Strategist, Sandra M. Walter & Associates Consulting.

which provides various popcorn products to help Scout councils and their units (troops, packs, dens) raise funds to expand their programs and activities. Beginning in 1981 with just seven Scout councils, Trail's End now serves more than 285 councils with more than $1 billion raised to support Scouting programs. Trail's End provides a training program, a Web site to support these efforts, and works with the individual Scout councils to build individual fundraising programs while the Scout councils provide the professional leadership and "boy power." More than 70 percent of the purchase price of the product goes to help boys in their local Scout councils.

Probably the most famous example of this type of fundraising is the Girl Scouts of the United States of America (GSUSA) cookie sales. It is difficult to find anyone who has not purchased a box of Girl Scouts cookies at some point in their lives. The national Girl Scouts organization formed the partnership with baking companies around the United States, and the local troops have the relationships with the purchasers. Advertising and marketing are done on the national level, and sales are done on the local level. The "cookie money," though, stays at the local level and is used for training, leadership development, and other special events.

In March of 2007, GSUSA celebrated it 95th anniversary sporting annual revenues of $120 million, while the Girl Scouts Cookie Program generated approximately $700 million annually. National considers the sale of cookies as an economic-literacy tool for teaching Scouts business skills, how to work as a team, and how to develop customer service skills. National's revenue comes from receiving a membership fee of $10 per Scout. In addition, national GSUSA put together a development office to focus on major gifts and annual giving that would bring additional resources to the national operations. Their goal is to contact the nearly 50 million women who were Girl Scouts before their 100th anniversary in 2012. Their tag line is "Reconnect with the premier organization for girls, the one that helped you become the successful woman you are today." Together with 10 local councils, they have developed a pilot program to create a bigger vision and to take fundraising to the next level. They are being careful, though, not to jeopardize what is being done locally to raise money. Cookie production is still strong, but the new fundraising efforts should make both the national GSUSA and its councils even stronger.

Revenue Sharing

To overcome the competitiveness in fundraising between national organizations and their affiliates/chapters, often there are agreements on how revenue will be shared between the two. The Association of Fundraising Professionals (AFP) has a revenue-sharing agreement with its chapters for its "Every Member Campaign." A chapter receives $.25 of every $1.00 contributed by their local chapter members if the chapter reaches the fundraising goal it has set.

"WE'VE FLOATED 'EDWARD THE KIND' AND 'EDWARD THE NICE' BUT THE PEOPLE WANT 'EDWARD THE GENEROUS.'"

Source: Copyright © Mark Litzler.

A different strategy used by another national organization is for the national to set the fundraising goal for the local/state chapters as the national organization holds the 501(c)(3), and all checks are written to that organization. Once the local/state chapter meets their goals, the national grants back at least 90 percent of the additional dollars raised above the initial goal for local projects. This process allows both the national and local fundraising efforts to be supported. The national provides the administrative economies of scale and the burden of the tax ID while the locals' work is recognized by the national through the awarding of grants.

When the Business and Professional Women's Clubs (BPW) did an assessment of its 600 chapters to see how they were raising funds and where the funds were going, they decided on a national fundraising effort that would be a win-win approach for everyone. National would take on all fundraising efforts with its expenses and then give back to the chapters what was raised. Thus, they maintained key messaging and kept all local organizations under one umbrella.

After Hurricane Katrina, the American Red Cross (ARC) found that many of their local chapters were nearly going broke as all of the Katrina gifts went to national. There were approximately 4 million first time donors to the ARC because of Katrina. To retain these donors, national implemented a direct mail campaign with each chapter receiving a percentage of the money received from the solicitation.

Another way ARC is providing support to its chapters is in the area of donor database management. Since ARC uses Raiser's Edge (RE) to manage its donor information, it is working with Blackbaud (RE's owner), located in Charleston, South Carolina, to develop a major new enterprise system for its chapters. ARC's South Carolina Chapter is acting as a Raiser's Edge hub for data entry, thank you letters, reports, etc. for other ARC chapters across the country. If implemented, the service will be undertaken for an annual fee per record.

Yet another example is the American Lung Association (ALA), whose state chapters conduct independent development programs from the national organization. In this case, the national provides support to ALA chapters by coordinating all direct response campaigns, conducting a program that allows chapters to apply for grants, and offering technical assistance on fundraising.

Other national organizations with local entities have similar programs with various revenue sharing agreements. Whatever the agreement between the national and the locals, it is imperative to have it in writing so there are no misunderstandings later.

> *Whatever the agreement between the national and the locals, it is imperative to have it in writing so there are no misunderstandings later.*

Sharing Special Events Ideas

In addition to partnerships with corporate entities designed to sell products, national organizations can provide affiliates or chapters with tested (tried and true) special events. The national organization also can layer on the branding necessary to give the event a uniform appearance, look, or brand.

When an event is found to be an effective fundraiser for one affiliate, it then can be offered to other affiliates, complete with how-to guides, training clinics at national meetings, knowledge sharing Web sites, collaborative marketing pieces that can be customized locally, etc. Such events might even have dedicated national staff working with local leadership to get the event off the ground its first year in new communities. This allows affiliates to try new programs or events with less fear of them not being successful, for the kinks have already been worked out by someone else. To help launch its newest chapter in Indiana, the Hospitality Sales and Marketing Association International looked to events that had met with much success in other areas such as Vail, Colorado, and Omaha, Nebraska.

Several good examples of events starting locally and then taking off like wild fire at other local levels are: "Race for the Cure" (Susan G. Komen Breast Cancer Foundation); "Chili Cook-Off" (National Kidney Foundation); and "Light The Night" (National Leukemia & Lymphoma Society).

ADVERTISING, BRANDING, COMMUNICATION, AND MARKETING

Branding and Marketing

For the Boys and Girls Clubs of America (BGCA), which has nearly 4,000 independent local clubs across the country, the national organization has to provide innovative approaches to fundraising and communications to support these clubs. Celebrating its 100th anniversary in 2006, the BGCA faced the difficulties of maintaining their brand while negotiating with its affiliates (clubs) over promotional activities and prospects and donors. BGCA's recent growth has been phenomenal. It took 92 years to open 2,000 clubs, but in the past seven years, 1,700 more clubs have been opened. Even more astounding, in the past four years, one new club has opened each day! Very few organizations, if any, can claim such growth.

These clubs are independent from the national organization, but look to national for new ideas they can implement at the local level. Like other nonprofits with chapters or affiliates, they also look to their national for their brand and general marketing. The national BGCA has 106 staff in its marketing and development offices working to ensure that what one hears about BGCA in Chicago is the same as in Boston or Los Angeles. The mission statement, the graphics, the logo, etc. are all the same. "We've succeeded in getting our clubs to sound alike, smell alike, taste alike, and to carry the message crafted by the national organization, so we're all saying the same thing," stated Kurt Ascherman, former senior vice president and chief marketing and development officer at BGCA.

Branding is important in that it ensures that all programs or publications connected with an organization or association have the same look. If the national organization has adopted a new logo, it does not want to have its affiliates using the old logo or an entirely different one from their own. It is important to remain uniform in messaging, especially when appealing

> *It is important to remain uniform in messaging, especially when appealing for donations.*

for donations. Donors can more easily identify with the organization and recognize it as one they support. The term brand loyalty not only applies to commercial products but to nonprofits as well.

If a national spokesperson has been selected for the organization, the chapters should also use the materials featuring this person to ensure continuity in message and to capitalize upon the investment made by the national organization. Most local

> *The term brand loyalty not only applies to commercial products but to nonprofits as well.*

affiliates just cannot afford the type and quality of advertising that is provided by their national.

If local affiliates print their own publications, they should plan their design to be the same or similar to the publications offered by the national organization. This allows any materials developed by national and used by the local to appear seamless—to look as though they were all from the same source. When donors consider gifts to a local affiliate, they want to know that it is operating as professionally as the national or vice versa.

For Easter Seals, based in Chicago, Illinois, it came as a surprise that donors were not exactly sure what Easter Seals did even though they had a great deal of trust in the organization, donated each year, and believed that Easter Seals did a lot of good. That led Easter Seals, founded in 1919 in Ohio to help crippled children, to revamp its logo to resemble the original stamps or seals with serrated edges that were first used in a 1934 campaign. This allowed donors to place the seals on letters to show their support of the organization. These seals were so popular and so identified with the organization that, in 1967, the organization decided to change its name from the National Society for Crippled Children to Easter Seals. This identification with the seal was so strong that the new logo, designed as a seal with the words "Easter Seals: Disability Services" is still used today by the organization.

Working with Safeway, their long time corporate partner, Easter Seals identified April as Easter Seals month and used Safeway stores all across the United States to promote Easter Seals' message and brand. The program being rolled out was its "Angels of Change" campaign, a promotion that raised $2.5 million for the charity and helped to build brand awareness for the organization and its affiliates. It also allowed the local affiliates to design other fundraising campaigns around this national campaign that fit their communities. In addition, Safeway offered a $100,000 challenge grant to be shared by the three affiliates who raised the most money in their local communities.

Easter Seals identified yet another need that is common in most organizations with affiliates—how the organization manages its constituent data. It is difficult to break out of the silo mentality that has both national and affiliates/chapters thinking in terms of "my donors." Due to this practice of not sharing donor information, donors often are not cultivated well because they do not receive current information about the organization. As Easter Seals attempts to become more donor-centric, they are working on the challenge of providing better quality stewardship of their donors.

Advertising

Another vital initiative employed at the national level is advertising. When the Boys and Girls Clubs of America launched an aggressive advertising campaign using Hollywood movie star Denzel Washington, a former BGCA kid, as its spokesperson, their local affiliates immediately benefited by the media attention this created. Not only did gifts increase to the national organization but to the local clubs as well.

In addition, other stories highlighting BGCA members were placed each week in such news vehicles as the *Wall Street Journal* and *USA Today*. Obviously, not all nonprofits are going to be able to afford this type of marketing/advertising, but most can undertake an organized marketing campaign at the local level with assistance from the parent organization. When with BGCA, Ascherman stated, "From a national perspective, our biggest challenge is helping our local clubs get better at business and development, that's the biggest challenge for nonprofits with affiliates."

> *"From a national perspective, our biggest challenge is helping our local clubs get better at business and development, that's the biggest challenge for nonprofits with affiliates."*

Communications

The American Lung Association views communications with affiliates as the key to a healthy relationship and to creating a culture of philanthropy. "They emphasize relationship building and integrated fundraising . . . to initiate a very consistent, friendly, informative, donor-centric relationship-building program." Karen Wertheimer, vice president and chief development officer for ALA notes, "The field/national split is a very real problem for national associations like the American Lung Association, and we have to continuously minimize that split with lots of communications, with lots of informational sessions, with lots of networking both ways."

The Association of Fundraising Professionals in Arlington, Virginia, knows that communicating with members is the key to the health of its chapters. Whether it is by print or electronic communications, AFP communicates regularly with its chapters and encourages its chapters to have newsletters in both print and electronic formats to inform members and prospective members about: upcoming luncheons, roundtables, celebrations such as National Capital Philanthropy Day, open position announcements, and to have a Listserv for members to communicate with each other to discuss issues of importance.

TRAINING

Often, a national organization can strengthen its relationships with its affiliate/chapters by developing and offering training programs for use at the local level. Whether fundraising training (as discussed previously) or other types of training, these programs are usually developed at the national level because national organizations have more funds to develop and test training modules, which they then can launch at the local level.

> *Donors are far more likely to respond to a call made from a local contact than from one made by a "stranger" at a national call center.*

Training can help locals become better fundraisers, which can then affect the outcome of any national campaigns being conducted at the local level. Donors are far more likely to respond to a call made from a local contact than from one made by a "stranger" at a national call center.

It can be difficult for the national organization to satisfy the changing needs of its local chapters, yet chapters rely upon their national organization to know what is current to their mission. Programs need to be up to date, but they also need to be tested. Once a need has been identified, the national can work together with its local leadership to design, develop, test, and launch training programs that can result in more professionally trained staff and volunteers. It is important to remember that not all local entities have offices and staff; many are organized by volunteers who need to be trained on a regular basis.

A perfect example of this type of cooperation was when the National Apartment Association (NAA), a federation with nearly 30,000 members affiliated with more than 150 state and local associations in the United States and Canada, decided to overhaul its training programs. NAA depends upon its local chapters for input into its training program as it is a bottom-up federation. Previously, the national organization provided the training curriculum, which the local chapters delivered. After a formal feasibility study, they discovered that they needed to change the process. Using the right product development team to test what the market wanted/needed, they were able to bring in subject experts to create the training programs requested at the local levels—classroom-style learning, individual programs, programs tailored to different learning styles, reasonably priced materials, and features to help nonprofessional trainers. The modules were field tested at their local affiliates' sites, which added to the "buy-in" by the local chapters. With materials that were tested by various chapters, it was much easier to launch the training effort with the others. Again, communication was the key. The entire program was laid out so that local chapters could see the advantages of the training to their operations and volunteers. Local leaders then could serve as advocates and spokespersons for the programs developed by national to their fellow chapter leaders.

The national organization also marketed the new training program by placing articles and ads in their national magazine, as well as featuring these training modules at their national conventions. For the local chapters, NAA developed ready-to-use electronic materials, which included course flyers and press releases. They also provided brochures and inserts to use in local and state publications.

The results of this training effort by NAA at the national level increased the rate of adoption at the local level; the rate of course completions; the sense that NAA helped to improve the local level quality; increased national visibility; and, the pride in the profession. NAA's credibility increased with its affiliate associations and its members through the use of the new training curricula.

HELPING AFFILIATES IDENTIFY AND RECRUIT TALENT

Another key role for the national organization is to help identify and recruit qualified staff professionals for its local affiliates. Nearly every issue of the *Chronicle of Philanthropy* will carry advertisements for staff positions at local chapters of national organizations. Whether it is the American Red Cross, the Cystic Fibrosis Foundation, or the American Heart Association, advertisements to fill staff positions that are placed in national newspapers are likely to provide a much larger talent pool with greater skills than ads placed in local papers by the affiliates/chapters. Appendix 17–D provides an example of an ad placed by the American Diabetes Association (ADA) seeking professionals for chapter positions open in more than 15 communities that ADA serves. The ad explains the ADA, promotes jobs in multiple communities from the executive director to special events managers, and defines working with ADA as a career.

> *Another key role for the national organization is to help identify and recruit qualified staff professionals for its local affiliates.*

Staff from one organization's affiliate/chapter may be interested in moving within the organization to fulfill a position at another affiliate/chapter's location. This not only keeps the investment made in training staff within the organization, it also helps to share talent and ideas among the affiliates. Those successful at fundraising in one city are most likely going to be successful in a new location. Having excellent communication skills, a proven track record of building relationships, and the ability to maximize fundraising opportunities certainly are transferable from one community to the next. The ADA states in their ad, "If you are a professional with sales, special events, and development skills and can manage/implement key fundraising activities at the community level—choose a career with us."

RESOLVING CONFLICTS

Working Together Peacefully and Productively

The relationship between nationals and locals should be mutually beneficial so that both can pursue their shared organizational mission at their respective levels. Usually, the most difficult part of maintaining good working relations between a national organization and its affiliates is having clearly defined operational roles. If the national is fundraising for the affiliates, the affiliates must know exactly what they will receive each year in funds so that they can budget accurately and effectively. If the affiliates or chapters are to raise the money and send it to the national organization, the goals must be realistic and achievable so the national organization can plan accordingly. Whatever the role for each, it is always best to have everything in writing.

Use Memoranda of Understanding (MOUs) or contracts to define the scope of work expected of each, and the end results can help to maintain good relations. Whether it is a contract for space or an MOU for which entity is to do the fundraising, clearly defined roles will eliminate much of the angst that exists when two or more different entities have to work together. When Robert Frost said in his poem *Mending Wall* that "good fences make good neighbors" he did not realize how this also could be applied to associations or organizations and their affiliates or chapters. When considering the role between national organizations and their affiliates or chapters, one would say, "good contracts make good working relationships." Although it is not a national/affiliate relationship, see Appendix 16–E in Chapter 16, Association Foundation Fundraising, for an example of a Memorandum of Understanding (MOU) between an association foundation and its national association regarding fundraising services to be provided by the foundation. See Appendix 17–E for an example of a model chapter/affiliate agreement.

REFERENCES

Association Foundation Group. 2003 membership survey. Washington, DC: Association Foundation Group.

Cox, J. 1997. Professional practices in association management, *Association Management.*

Levine, M. 2000. Are chapters still viable. *Association Management*, June, 81–90.

McKenna, D. 2007. Cover story—Smart cookies. *Fundraising Success Magazine*, April, 27–34.

Modelworks—A history of flexibility and support. 2006. *Associations Now*, April 27.

Motley, A. 2006. Retention in the ranks. *Associations Now*, September, 53–56.

Powell, K. and Krzmarzick, K. 2001. Redeveloping professional development—by revamping its training programs, a national association reinforced its ties with chapters and affiliates. *Association Management*, September, 33–39.

Rollender, N. 2006. Cover story–National Affiliates. *Fundraising Success Magazine*, March, 24–33.

Santicola, A. 2006. Wings of change. *Fundraising Success Magazine*, August, 28–37.

Santicola, A. 2007. Thinking Big(ger). *Fundraising Success Magazine*, January, 42–55.

Wertheimer, K. 2006. Keeping the line clear: A 5-minute interview. *Fundraising Success Magazine*, August, 16.

A History of Flexibility and Support—The Relationship Between the American Library Association and Its Chapters

intelligence

MODELWORKS

A history of flexibility and support

If you had to pick one word to describe how American Library Association, Chicago, manages its 57 chapters, "flexibly" should hit the mark. The organization's philosophy of flexibility—within necessary constraints—began when it first established chapter relationships in 1913. The relationship was not rigidly drawn by its founders, which has helped it to develop over time as needs change.

The ALA Constitution defines a chapter as "any legally constituted state, provincial, regional, or territorial library association." Its 57 chapters consist of 50 state library associations, councils, or federations; one such organization in

Washington, DC; one in Guam; one in the U.S. Virgin Islands; and four regional associations, including the Mountain Plains Library Association, New England Library Association, Pacific Northwest Library Association, and Southeastern Library Association.

While cross-membership is not automatic, ALA's framework is structured such that chapters and the national organization mutually benefit from one another. For example, though chapter members are not required to join the national ALA, local chapters help contribute to ALA's dues income by encouraging members to join ALA and by making available ALA membership information at the local level, and the chapters also are allowed to provide financial assistance to the Washington, DC office to aid in ALA's legislative efforts. The national organization provides chapters with a subscription to *American Libraries*; a copy of the *ALA Handbook of*

Organization and Membership Directory; a 10 percent discount on ALA publications; several headquarters services (such as joint membership, marketing, and advocacy efforts); and a seat on the ALA council, which ensures adequate geographical representation on ALA's governing body. There are 53 chapter councilors from all 50 states, the District of Columbia, Guam, and the U.S. Virgin Islands. Regional associations are not allowed a separate representative on the ALA council. Chapter councilors comprise approximately 30 percent of the 175-member ALA council.

Chapter status is a voluntary arrangement. Eligible library associations request chapter status, which is granted by action of the ALA council. Chapters may vote to withdraw, and, conversely, the ALA council can dissolve a chapter for inactivity or failure to comply with ALA bylaws. The basic requirements for chapters are dues (currently $110 annually) and the filing of chapter constitutions and bylaws, plus any amendments, with ALA headquarters.

ALA gives its chapters considerable latitude: For example, chapters have the final authority in determining all programs and policies that concern only their individual areas, so long as such actions are not inconsistent with the programs and policies established by the ALA council. Further, chapters can, with ALA, enter into "carefully planned and mutually beneficial" joint ventures.

Source: Courtesy of ASAE and the Center, *Association Now*, April 2006, Washington, DC.

Example of an Association Dues Renewal Notice with Chapter Dues Included

A Stronger Voice...A Stronger Profession: Count yourself among the thousands of fundraising professionals advancing in their careers and helping to advance the profession through membership in AFP.

AFP RENEWAL NOTICE

Please complete this entire form and return it with your dues payments in the enclosed envelope. To expedite your renewal, you can renew online at **www.afpnet.org** or fax this form to (703) 684-0540. **If your name does not appear below, please visit www.afpnet.org to join.**

1. CONTACT INFORMATION

Current Member Expiration Date:

The address listed above will serve as your primary address and will be listed in the online membership directory. Please verify your address and make any corrections or additions in the box below. ☐ Home ☐ Business

ADDRESS CHANGES:

CHAPTER(S):

2. ALTERNATE ADDRESS

Please indicate a home address or alternate address in the space provided below in order to insure that communication is maintained in case the primary address becomes invalid. ☐ Home ☐ Business

ADDRESS

CITY / STATE / ZIP

PHONE   FAX

EMAIL

3. AFP CODE OF ETHICS

I certify that I have read and subscribe to the *AFP Code of Ethical Principles and Standards of Professional Practice.* By virtue of signing this application, I accept the obligation to abide by the *Code* and acknowledge that a violation on my part may result in action by the AFP Ethics Committee.

SIGNATURE REQUIRED

4. CALCULATE YOUR PAYMENT

Member ID	Category	Association Dues	Chapter Dues	Credit Amt.	Total Due
☐ Voluntary Contribution to the AFP Foundation for Philanthropy				*Gift Amt.*	
☐ Is this Foundation Gift? ☐ Organizational ☐ Individual Contributions are tax-deductible to the full extent provided by law.				*New Total Due*	

Method of Payment:
☐ Check payable to AFP. Check # _____
☐ Credit Card:
     ☐ MasterCard   ☐ Visa
     ☐ American Express   ☐ Discover

ACCOUNT NUMBER

EXP. DATE

SIGNATURE REQUIRED FOR ALL CHARGES

For Income Tax Purposes, dues are not considered a charitable contribution. If you or your organization is permitted to deduct your dues from gross income under the U.S. Internal Revenue Code, AFP estimates that 3.9% of your dues are not deductible because of AFP's advocacy efforts. Voluntary contributions to the AFP Foundation for Philanthropy are tax-deductible to the full extent provided by law.

All dues are payable on an anniversary basis. This form is for RENEWALS only. Records are not transferable from one individual to another. If your name does not appear on this form but you would like to become a member, please call the AFP toll free number (800) 666-FUND.

$50 of your annual dues goes toward *Advancing Philanthropy* magazine.

(Over Please)

US RENEW-0308

5. MEMBERSHIP CATEGORIES

Active: Open to persons who have had at least one (1) year of experience as of the time of application, as fundraising professionals, are self-employed or associated with an organization, institution or firm and are compensated for his/her services. Active members hold some degree of responsibility directly for fundraising, subscribe to the *AFP Code of Ethical Principles and Standards of Professional Practice* ("Code") and its bylaws, promote *A Donor Bill of Rights* and, are employed or have been employed by an institution or organization that provides benefits to society.

Dues: $220.00 + chapter dues

Retired: May be extended to individuals who no longer practice as paid professionals in the field but have been Active members for the immediate past five (5) consecutive years and who subscribe to the *AFP Code of Ethical Principles and Standards of Professional Practice* and its bylaws, and promote *A Donor Bill of Rights.*

Dues: $75.00 + chapter dues

Introductory: Open to persons newly employed in the field, full-time students in a degree-granting, certificate or diploma program; members who work for grassroots organizations with an operating budget of $250,000 or less, executive directors who spend less than 25% of their time on fundraising related responsibilities and volunteers. All must subscribe to the *AFP Code of Ethical Principles and Standards of Professional Practice* and its bylaws and promote *A Donor Bill of Rights.* Membership in this category is limited to a two-year duration.

Dues: $100.00 + chapter dues (year one)
$150.00 + chapter dues (year two)

Associate: May be extended to persons who are engaged in fields related to fundraising, volunteers, or those who have mutual interests with fundraising professionals, and who subscribe to the *AFP Code of Ethical Principles and Standards of Professional Practice* and its bylaws; and promotes *A Donor Bill of Rights.*

Dues: $220.00 + chapter dues

6. HELP US SERVE YOU!

Please help us get to know and serve you better by completing the following:

1. How many fundraisers are employed with your organization? _____

2. How many are associated with AFP? _____

3. Is your organization paying for your annual dues?
   ☐ Yes ☐ No

PLEASE REMIT TO:
Association of Fundraising Professionals
P.O. Box 631989 • Baltimore, MD 21263-1989
(800) 666-3863 • Fax: (703) 684-0540
Online at **www.afpnet.org**

---

6. HELP US SERVE YOU! *Continued*

4. In what type of organization are you currently employed? *(check one)*

   ☐ Health   ☐ Public/Society Benefit
   ☐ Religious   ☐ Consultant
   ☐ Educational   ☐ Not Currently Employed
   ☐ Arts/Cultural/Humanities   ☐ Retired
   ☐ Human Services   ☐ Other _____

5. What areas are you interested in?

   ☐ Annual Giving   ☐ Internet Fundraising
   ☐ Direct Response   ☐ Fundraising Internationally
   ☐ Telemarketing   ☐ Fundraising Trends
   ☐ Planned Giving   ☐ Special Events
   ☐ Major Gifts   ☐ Ethics
   ☐ Capital Campaigns   ☐ Nonprofit Management
   ☐ Other *(please specify)* _____

6. Occasionally we make the membership list available for mailing by reputable companies. If you do not wish to have your name released for this purpose, please check here. ☐

The following information is not required, but your answers will assist us in serving you more effectively.

7. Gender ☐ Female ☐ Male

8. Date of Birth: _____ / _____ / _____
                      MM   DD   YY

9. Ethnic Background *(check one)*
   ☐ African American, not of Hispanic Origin
   ☐ Alaskan Native
   ☐ Native American
   ☐ Asian
      ☐ Chinese
      ☐ Japanese
      ☐ Filipino
      ☐ Korean
      ☐ Other *(please specify)* _____
   ☐ Pacific Islander
      ☐ Hawaiian
      ☐ Samoan
      ☐ Other *(please specify)* _____
   ☐ Caucasian, not of Hispanic Origin
   ☐ Hispanic/Latino
   ☐ Multi-Ethnic
      ☐ Other *(please specify)* _____

10. Are you fluent in any languages other than English? *(please specify)*
    _____

Source: Courtesy of the Association of Fundraising Professionals (AFP), Arlington, Virginia.

Sixty Fundraising Ideas for Local Chapters or Affiliates

AMERICAN SOCIETY OF CIVIL ENGINEERS

For Use by ASCE Section, Branch, Younger Member, and Student Leaders

1. **Career Fair**

   Seek companies to have a table/booth at a career fair. Call alumni, faculty, and student government representatives to coordinate the event. Seek donations from schools and businesses. Survey students to see what types of companies they want scheduled at the fair. Find company sponsorships for the table/booth space and acknowledge sponsorships in the career fair program.

2. **Golf Tournament**

   Hold a golf tournament. Get course donated. Seek sponsors for each hole and for hole-in-one, closest to the hole, longest drive, etc. Companies can provide sponsorships of $100.00 or more per hole. Ask golf course pro shop and local golf shops to make gifts of putters, drivers, towels, balls, etc. Ask local signage company to print signs and acknowledge their in-kind gift in the tournament program. Sell golf/polo shirts. Charge players an entry fee. Sell putt "mulligans." Sell tickets and have a drawing for a door prize for extra money.

3. **Outbid the Contractor**

   Offer to build something needed by the community at a cheaper rate than regular company sandboxes, swing sets, parking lot, etc. Seek an in-kind gift of guidance from a local civil engineering company who will manage the student team (for liability). Get materials donated or at cost. Chapters keep the profits.

4. **Raffle**

   Sell raffle tickets at a football game or other athletic games (check to see if legal in your location). Charge $1.00 or $2.00 per ticket. Ask local businesses for donation of prizes. The prizes could also be free student labor—car washing, dog walking, snow shoveling, etc.

5. **Battle of the Bands Block Party**

   Find a place on campus to have a concert. Get the PA system donated. Get local radio stations and companies to help advertise. Get refreshments either donated or at wholesale. Charge a cover fee. Charge for refreshments. Seek local company sponsorships and list sponsors on event banners or signage. Contact local recording studios to offer free recording session for winner.

6. **Silent Auction**

   Hold two similar events—one in the fall and one in the spring. Ask local companies, stores, alumni, and parents to donate items or vacation trip packages. Storage may be needed for gift items. Advertise at local games and in the school paper before each event. Place minimum bid amounts on all packages being auctioned off.

7. **Direct Mail Campaign to Alumni**

   Ask the Alumni Office for names and addresses of civil engineering alumni and civil engineering companies at which alumni work. Write to them seeking gifts to support the student chapter. Gifts should cover the cost of postage, paper, envelopes, and production of the letter.

8. **A Car Bashing**

   Obtain vehicles from junk yards or police pounds and paint them the colors of your rival school (for example, grey/red or blue/gold). Advertise on your local radio stations during the week before the "big game." Have several vehicles in key locations. Have civil engineering student teams managing the areas and collecting the money. Be sure to obtain permission from the University/College. Charge $2.00 to $5.00 per hit.

9. **Boat Race**

   Contest for local high school students to build boats out of plastic bottles. Then hold a race and award prizes. Work with civil engineering professors and student chapter to introduce high school students to engineering. Seek sponsorships from local companies. Get newspapers to cover the event. Charge entry fee and make money off concessions.

10. **Dance Club/Date Auction Theme Party**
Hold a theme party and auction-off date packages. Get students to volunteer to be auctioned. Students being auctioned can seek donations from local businesses to add to their date package. For example, the evening starts with complimentary limo service to a restaurant for dinner, and then off to a sporting event, followed by dessert and drinks before the limo drives each home. All items donated. Place minimum bids on the better packages. Get food and drinks for the evening donated. Charge $10.00 or $15.00 per couple for entrance and then end the evening with date auction.

11. **Kissing Booth**
Use as an "outreach" to student programs. Set up a booth for both men and women before a major event(s). Charge $5.00 per kiss. All money goes to the student chapter.

12. **Open House**
Hold open house for local students to give them an overview of the campus (and the civil engineering department). Charge $5.00 per student to attend.

13. **Laser Tag**
Use the engineering building to hold a laser tag contest. Staffed by faculty, use the hallways of the building during one evening for a contest of laser tag. Find corporate sponsors for the evening. Charge students $7.00 to $10.00 per person to participate.

14. **Formal Benefit Dinner**
Work with the student government and ask the university to donate a location. Contact local companies to donate food or money in return for acknowledging their gifts in the program. Charge $50.00 a plate and have ASCE section or branch members wait the tables for the students and their dates. All money goes to the chapter.

15. **Sell Used Engineering Books**
Buy students' used books at the end of each semester. Then, sell the used engineering books for less than the book stores would sell them. The difference (profit) would be kept by the student chapter.

16. **Elimination Dinner**
Dinner and open bar. Use tip boards (type of gambling, so must check it out with local authorities to see if it is legal). Eliminate tickets throughout the evening. The holder of the last ticket at the end of the night wins a cash prize. Charge $30 each.

17. **One-Stop Shopping**
Get a parking lot donated by the school for massages, manicures, food tables, etc. (all donated by local businesses), and a car wash. Students sell the food, wash the cars, etc. Professionals provide the massages, manicures, hair braiding, etc. Set a price for each item. All profits are kept by the student chapter.

18. **Students as Volunteer Workers at Events**
Students can work at various sports games or at local businesses taking inventory. The money they earn goes to the student chapter.

19. **Lunch or Errand Running**
For one week, volunteer to get lunches for workers at various local companies for a fee of $5.00 per person. Take orders, drive to food establishments, place orders, and then deliver the lunches for the $5.00 per person fee. All proceeds go to the student chapter.

20. **Jell-O Wrestling**
Hold a Jell-O wrestling contest. Open to all university students. Charge a fee for entrance to participate and to watch. Sell food and beverages that have been donated. Add an auction or raffle to earn more money. Student chapter keeps all money raised.

21. **Non-event Event**
Invite people to a Non-Event. Print classy invitations, but ask them not to show up. Instead have them donate the money it would have cost them to attend. Provide various giving levels.

22. **5K Run**
Host a 5K run with corporate sponsors. Ask the school to provide the facility for free. Entry fee is $30.00 to $40.00 per person. Seek donated prizes for winners.

23. **Olympics Day**
Invite students to compete in a variety of sports. Ask school to provide the facility for free. Seek sponsorships and food from local companies. Ask students to pay an entry fee of $10.00 or $15.00.

24. **PE Review Course**
Ask a professor to teach a PE review course. Advertise at other schools nearby. All money goes to the student chapter. Charge students $50.00 per session.

25. **Book Royalties**
Ask a professor to donate all of his/her book royalties for one year to the chapter.

26. **Work Concessions at School Events**
Civil engineering students volunteer to work the concessions at sporting events and concerts. The money goes directly to the student chapter instead of to the working individuals.

27. **Pie in the Face**
Ask a professor to volunteer to be auctioned off and be put in "jail" for a day. Set up a booth where people buy tickets

and get to throw pies at the professor. Pies can be whipped cream in a pie crust, so that there is no waste and expense is limited.

28. **Pink Flamingos**
Put 20 to 100 pink flamingos in the yard of a faculty member. Have them pay a set fee to get them removed. An additional fee can be paid to have them placed in someone else's yard. This also can garner great publicity if it is being done for the first time in your community. (Check with local police first.)

29. **Pizza Sale**
Get a restaurant to donate pizza and soda. Sell 2 slices and a soda for $4.00. Do this weekly on a set evening so students begin to depend on it while they are studying.

30. **Final Exam Care Package**
Provide boxes of goodies during exam time. Ask for donations from local businesses to defray costs. You can even sell these to parents by taking advanced orders. Charge $25.00 per box.

31. **Parking Spot Raffle**
Raffle-off a parking spot in the engineering building's parking lot. Raffles can be held monthly during the school year—nine opportunities to raise money.

32. **Chances to Kick a Field Goal**
Sell tickets for the chance to kick a field goal during half time at a university football game. Winner gets small cash prize, or a gift(s) can be donated by local merchants. Remainder of proceeds goes to student chapter.

33. **eBay Sales**
Get people to donate items such as textbooks, apartment furnishing, clothing, etc. List on eBay and collect the cash when they purchase the item.

34. **Phone-a-Thon**
Call alumni and businesses. Ask alumni for a $1.00 for every year that has passed since they graduated. Ask businesses to support the effort with either money or products which can be used later for a silent auction.

35. **Haunted House at Halloween**
Design a haunted house for the community's young children during October with donated materials from local merchants. Sell tickets and refreshments. This is great for publicity in the local papers.

36. **Student-Faculty Variety Show/Student vs. Faculty Athletic Event**
Arrange for a variety show or an athletic event to include both students and faculty. Sell tickets and refreshments.

37. **Concrete Canoe Bashing**
Obtain the concrete canoes that did not win the contest. Paint them the colors of your rival school. Advertise before a big game. Have civil engineering students manage the event. Charge $2 to $5 a hit. Obtain permission from the university first.

38. **Basketball Tournament**
Hold a Basketball Tournament at a local school or gym. Charge $xx per team. Set up groups of four teams and have them play each other. The team with the best record advances to the playoffs. Have prizes for most creative name. Have area businesses sponsor the event.

39. **Fishing Tournament**
Charge $xx per person. Have prizes for the largest fish, largest fish in each category, and fish of each kind.

40. **Penny Wars**
Set up jars in a common area and label them with either school names/departments/companies/etc. Each penny in the jar = +1 cent.
Each nickel = minus 5 cents
Each dime = minus 10 cents
Each quarter = minus 25 cents
Each dollar = minus 100 cents
Each participant wants to put pennies in their jar and any other remaining change in another school's/department's/company's jar. For example, a participant puts 30 pennies in his/her jar, giving his/her team 30 points and puts a nickel and a dime in another jar, giving that team minus 15 points. At the end of the competition, the team with the most pennies/points wins.

41. **Casino Night**
This can be either a casual or formal event. Charge an entrance fee that will encourage attendees. Piggy-back other fundraising events into the evening by holding a silent auction and/or a 50/50 raffle to raise even more money. Make sure you check with your local city officials to see if these are legal and if you have all of the permits required.

42. **Bowling Tournament**
Charge $130.00 per four-member team. Awards to the highest individual and team score. All money raised beyond prizes goes to whatever program you designate.

43. **Kickball Tournament**
Charge $xx per team. See golf tournament (#2) for details on how to organize.

44. **Softball Tournament**
Charge $xx per team. See golf tournament (#2) for details on how to organize.

45. **Coupon Book**
Buy coupon books for local area restaurants for $4.00 and resell them for $10.00. Proceeds go to whatever program has been designated.

46. **Happy/Sad Dollar**

Pass a bowl around at each meeting and each member drops in at least $1.00 for a happy/sad moment they share with the group.

47. **Cookbook**

Have each member bring in a favorite recipe, collect them, and bind them into a book to sell to family and friends or at the office. Price appropriate to the community. Make sure people know this is a fundraiser.

48. **Newsletter Ads**

In your ASCE newsletter, sell ads to local civil engineering companies and vendors. Amount you charge will vary upon the size of the ad.

49. **Photo Contest**

Have local high school and college students throughout the state or region take pictures of positive images of civil engineering. Award one prize for the best picture and then compile 12 of the best into a calendar that you can sell. Price appropriate to the community.

50. **"Free" Happy Hour**

Work with a local restaurant, hotel, or bar to secure a "free" happy hour even for ASCE younger members or students. Charge a set fee to attend or ask for donations to be made toward a program fund since they aren't paying for drinks.

51. **Skeet & Eat**

Fundraiser which combines shooting skeet and eating barbecue. The event features competition for all ages. Supports whatever age group—student chapters, younger member groups, branches, or sections.

52. **Name of Organization—Lock-Up**

"Lock-Up" business leaders, college professors, etc. by "sentencing" them to an hour (or shorter time period) behind bars as attendees raise bail money that will go to the organization. A jail can be built and placed in the center of a ballroom or gymnasium—wherever a dinner is held. Guests pay cash to the jailer or make pledges to "release" the "detainee."

53. **Festival of Wreaths**

Just in time for the holidays. Pick the perfect wreath to adorn your door during this three-week silent auction. Enjoy the ongoing holiday festivities in November and bid on a wreath that will be made and ready to deliver the first week in December. More than one wreath of the same type can be auctioned off, if the designer wishes to do so.

54. **Festival of Trees**

Similar to the Festival of Wreaths, but trees are theme decorated and placed in the silent auction.

55. **Services Auction**

Bid on the unusual and rare during this exciting auction of local services including: massages, walking tours, handyman services, dog walking or other pet related services; and more of whatever your group has to offer. Fees charged for each service and services can be sold more than once.

56. **Turkey Trot**

Get ready for that huge Thanksgiving Day dinner by running in a Thanksgiving morning race. This event can benefit any level of the organization. Pick any length/distance (5K or 10K) and invite the community to give-back on the day that they say thanks. Entry fees raise the money. Having friends and colleagues pledge money for each mile the entrant runs is another way to raise additional money.

57. **Reindeer Run/Walk**

Same concept as the Turkey Trot, but it can be held any time in December. Also, people can dress up in their costumes to run and to win prizes. Entrance fee is charged and pledges taken for distances run.

58. **Oyster Roast and Auction**

Great food and a silent auction to raise money for any organization. In addition to oysters, barbeque can be served. Tickets are sold and all money goes to support a student chapter.

59. **Bowling for Kids**

Whether you consistently bowl strikes or still need the bumpers, come out to the bowling alley to raise funds for the ASCE student chapter. Prior to game day, teams of five are asked to collect money and pledges with prizes given according to money raised.

60. **Cow Bingo Family Festival**

You and your family have never played bingo quite like this. Buy a square on the giant bingo field for $50.00 and watch as a cow chooses where to "drop a chip" and claim a $1,000.00 winner. The day also can include other kid friendly activities such as a jump castle, a giant water slide, moon bounce, etc. This is a perfect day of fun for the whole family. This is geared to younger member groups.

Source: Courtesy of the American Society of Civil Engineers Foundation, Reston, Virginia.

Example of a National Organization Assisting Local Affiliates with Personnel Recruitment

THE CHRONICLE OF PHILANTHROPY • APRIL 6, 2006

For over 60 years, the American Diabetes Association (ADA) has been serving as a solid backbone of support: raising funds, supporting research, educating, and fighting for the rights of people living with diabetes. And we'll continue improving the quality of their lives because of professionals like you.

If you are a professional with sales, special events, and development skills and can manage/implement key fundraising activities at the community level — choose a career with us.

Executive Director
Sacramento, CA • Baltimore, MD • Cincinnati, OH
Manage all activities in market, including recruiting/building relationships with volunteers, major gift cultivation, and coaching staff to success. Requires 8–10 years of related experience and the ability to travel throughout market. Relocation assistance may be available. Financial goals vary per market.

Fundraising and Special Events Director & Associate Director
Charlotte, NC • Houston, TX • Los Angeles, CA New York, NY • Philadelphia, PA • Wichita, KS • Chicago, IL
Act as a player/coach in managing a team that executes ADA signature events. Requires 5+ years of related experience and a thorough understanding of principles, concepts, and methodology associated with programs/events in a professional setting as well as cold calling experience. Financial goals vary per market.

Fundraising and Special Events Manager & Associate Manager
Boston, MA • Los Angeles, CA • Des Moines, IA • Rockford, IL Phoenix, AZ • St. Louis, MO • McAllen, TX
Organize/coordinate community fundraising events by recruiting participants, securing corporate sponsorship, and planning logistics for ADA signature events. Requires 2–4 years of experience. Financial goals vary per market.

Associate Director, Major and Planned Giving
Dallas, TX • Seattle, WA • San Francisco, CA
Renew/secure gifts of $5K+ through solicitation and cultivation of prospective donors.

Many other rewarding opportunities are available at nationwide locations.

When you join us, you can expect competitive salaries, comprehensive benefit programs, and a true focus on work-life balance. You can find all of this in an environment that promotes inclusion.

Please apply online at **http://careers.diabetes.org**. Although online applications are preferred, resumes can be mailed to: **American Diabetes Association - Employment Department, c/o Chronicle Response - [indicate position AND location], 1701 N. Beauregard Street, Alexandria, VA 22311, Fax - 703.299.5525.** NO PHONE CALLS PLEASE.

We are an Equal Opportunity Employer, M/F/D/V, which holds inclusion as one of our Core Values.

American Diabetes Association.
Cure • Care • Commitment

TAKE YOUR CAREER ON A MISSION!

http://careers.diabetes.org

Source: Copyright © 2006 American Diabetes Association, Alexandria, Virginia. Reprinted with permission from the American Diabetes Association.

Model Chapter Affiliate Agreement Between an Association and Its Chapters

THIS AFFILIATION AGREEMENT (the "Agreement"), is made this _____ day of _____, 20____, by and between _____ ("ASSOCIATION"), a _____ nonprofit corporation, with its principal place of business at _____, and _____ ("CHAPTER"), a _____ nonprofit corporation, with its principal place of business at _____.

NOW THEREFORE, in consideration of the premises set forth above and the promises set forth below, the sufficiency and receipt of which are hereby acknowledged, the parties hereby agree as follows:

I. GRANT OF CHARTER TO CHAPTER.

A. <u>Charter</u>. ASSOCIATION hereby grants to CHAPTER a non-exclusive charter to be a chapter of ASSOCIATION. In accordance therewith, CHAPTER is authorized to use the name [insert full name of ASSOCIATION]," acronym "[insert acronym of ASSOCIA-TION]," and logo of ASSOCIATION in or in connection with CHAPTER's name, acronym and logo, with the authority to use such marks in connection with CHAPTER's activities authorized under this Agreement, subject to the terms and conditions of this Agreement and any written guidelines attached hereto, otherwise incorporated herein, or subsequently provided to CHAPTER by ASSOCIATION.

B. <u>Term and Termination</u>. The Term of this Agreement shall commence on the effective date set forth above and shall continue until revoked by ASSOCIATION or surrendered by CHAPTER, pursuant to the terms of this Agreement for revocation and surrender.

C. <u>Territory</u>. CHAPTER shall represent ASSOCIATION as ASSOCIATION's affiliate in _____ (the "Territory"), pursuant to and in accordance with ASSOCIATION's mission and purposes as set forth in ASSOCIATION's Articles of Incorporation and Bylaws or as otherwise established by ASSOCIATION's Board of Directors. CHAPTER acknowledges that this designation is non-exclusive in the Territory and that ASSOCIATION may, in its sole discretion, designate other affiliates in the Territory or may sponsor or conduct programs, accept members, and perform other activities within the Territory.

D. <u>Authorized Activities</u>. ASSOCIATION specifically authorizes CHAPTER to conduct the following activities within the Territory: _____, _____, _____, _____, _____, and such other activities as may be consistent with the mission and purposes of ASSOCIATION and in which ASSOCIATION may from time to time authorize CHAPTER to engage.

II. MEMBERSHIP.

Members of CHAPTER also must be members of ASSOCIATION. The terms and conditions of membership in ASSOCIATION shall be determined exclusively by ASSOCIATION. The terms and conditions of membership in CHAPTER shall be determined exclusively by CHAPTER, and shall be set forth in CHAPTER's Bylaws. [All CHAPTER and ASSOCIATION membership dues shall be collected directly from members by ASSOCIATION. ASSOCIATION shall thereafter remit CHAPTER dues to CHAPTER.]

III. OBLIGATIONS OF ASSOCIATION.

ASSOCIATION's obligations under this Agreement shall include:

A. _____
B. _____
C. _____
D. _____
E. _____

IV. OBLIGATIONS OF CHAPTER.

CHAPTER's obligations under this Agreement shall include:

A. <u>Corporate and Tax Status</u>. CHAPTER warrants that it is incorporated as a nonprofit corporation in good standing, that it shall remain in good standing, and is and shall remain exempt from federal income tax under Section 501(c)(___) of the Internal Revenue Code. [Insert alternative requirements if CHAPTER is exempt from federal income tax pursuant to a group exemption.]

B. <u>Articles of Incorporation, Bylaws and Other Requirements</u>. As a condition of receipt of its charter as a chapter of ASSOCIA-TION, CHAPTER heretofore provided to ASSOCIATION, and ASSOCIATION provided its approval to, the ARTICLES OF INCOR-PORATION and BYLAWS of CHAPTER. Such CHAPTER Bylaws are, and shall remain, consistent in all material respects with the Model Bylaws attached hereto as <u>Exhibit A</u> and incorporated by reference herein. Any amendments to CHAPTER's Articles of Incorporation or Bylaws must first be submitted to, and approved by, ASSOCIATION. CHAPTER shall have as its purposes those set forth in the Model Bylaws attached hereto, shall conduct its activities at all time in strict accordance with such Bylaws, and shall comply at all times with all of the requirements set forth in ASSOCIATION's Bylaws and all other chapter-related policies, procedures, handbooks, or other written guidance heretofore or hereafter promulgated by ASSOCIATION (all of which are incorporated by reference herein).

C. <u>Compliance with Laws</u>. CHAPTER warrants that it is in full compliance with all applicable laws, regulations and other legal standards that may affect its performance under this Agreement, and shall remain in full compliance with, and otherwise conduct its activities at all times in accordance with, all applicable law, regulations and other legal standards. Further, CHAPTER warrants that it shall maintain at all times all permits, licenses and other governmental approvals that may be required in the Territory in connection with its performance under this Agreement. Furthermore, CHAPTER warrants that it shall make all required filings, such as annual corporate reports and tax filings, that may affect its corporate or tax status.

D. <u>Recordkeeping, Reporting and Inspection</u>. CHAPTER shall maintain all records related to its corporate and tax-exempt status and shall forward to ASSOCIATION copies of its Articles of Incorporation, Bylaws and tax exemption determination letter from the Internal Revenue Service, as well as any adverse notices or other correspondence received from any governmental agency (e.g., Internal Revenue Service, state Secretary of State or corresponding agency). CHAPTER shall maintain reasonable records related to all of its programs, activities and operations. CHAPTER shall submit regular written reports, no less than once per year, to ASSOCIATION summarizing its programs, activities and operations, including but not limited to budget and financial statements. Upon the written request of ASSOCIATION and at ASSOCIATION's expense, CHAPTER shall permit ASSOCIATION or ASSOCIATION's designated agent to review appropriate records of CHAPTER pertaining to its programs, activities and operations. Alternatively, CHAPTER shall send to ASSOCIATION copies of such records.

E. <u>Programs and Activities</u>. CHAPTER shall endeavor to sponsor and conduct programs and activities that further the purposes and objectives of ASSOCIATION, and shall use its best efforts to ensure that such programs and activities are of the highest quality with respect to content, materials, logistical preparation, and otherwise. CHAPTER shall endeavor to use, to the extent possible, materials available through ASSOCIATION in support of such programs and activities. CHAPTER shall send to ASSOCIATION on a regular basis a schedule of upcoming meetings, conferences and seminars, as well as other programs and activities that CHAPTER intends to sponsor or conduct. ASSOCIATION may, at its sole discretion, send representatives to observe such programs and activities.

F. <u>Government Affairs Efforts</u>. CHAPTER shall endeavor to conduct government affairs efforts within the Territory consistent with the purposes and objectives of ASSOCIATION. In performing this function, CHAPTER shall work with ASSOCIATION in order to ensure national consistency in these efforts.

F. <u>Other Obligations</u>:

1. _____
2. _____
3. _____
4. _____
5. _____

V. INTELLECTUAL PROPERTY AND CONFIDENTIAL INFORMATION.

A. <u>Limited License</u>. In accordance with ASSOCIATION's non-exclusive grant to CHAPTER to be a chapter of ASSOCIATION in the Territory, CHAPTER is hereby granted a limited, revocable, non-exclusive license to use (i) the name "[insert full name of ASSO-CIATION]," acronym "[insert acronym of ASSOCIATION]," logo of ASSOCIATION, and other ASSOCIATION trademarks, service marks, trade names, and logos (hereinafter collectively referred to as the "Marks"), (ii) ASSOCIATION's membership mailing, telephone, telecopier, and electronic mail lists with respect to past, current or prospective members of ASSOCIATION located within the

Territory (hereinafter collectively referred to as the "Mailing List"), and (iii) all copyrighted or proprietary information and materials provided by ASSOCIATION to CHAPTER during the Term of this Agreement (hereinafter referred to as the "Proprietary Information") (the Marks, Mailing List, and Proprietary Information are hereinafter collectively referred to as the "Intellectual Property") in or in connection with CHAPTER's name, acronym and logo and for other official CHAPTER-related purposes, with the limited authority to use the Intellectual Property solely in connection with the activities authorized under this Agreement, subject to the terms and conditions of this Agreement and any written guidelines attached hereto, otherwise incorporated herein, or subsequently provided to CHAPTER by ASSOCIATION.

1. The Intellectual Property is and shall remain at all times the sole and exclusive property of ASSOCIATION. The Intellectual Property may be used by CHAPTER of ASSOCIATION if and only if such use is made pursuant to the terms and conditions of this limited and revocable license. Any failure by CHAPTER to comply with the terms and conditions contained herein, whether willful or negligent, may result in the immediate suspension or revocation of this license, in whole or in part, by ASSOCIATION. Failure to comply, whether willful or negligent, also may result in the suspension or revocation of the charter of CHAPTER by ASSOCIATION. The interpretation and enforcement (or lack thereof) of these terms and conditions, and compliance therewith, shall be made by ASSOCIATION in its sole discretion.

2. ASSOCIATION's logo may not be revised or altered in any way, and must be displayed in the same form as produced by ASSOCIATION. The Marks may not be used in conjunction with any other trademark, service mark, or other mark without the express prior written approval of ASSOCIATION.

3. The Intellectual Property must be used by CHAPTER in a professional manner and solely for official CHAPTER-related purposes. CHAPTER shall not permit any third party to use the Intellectual Property without ASSOCIATION's express prior written approval. CHAPTER shall not sell or trade the Intellectual Property without ASSOCIATION's express prior written approval. Notwithstanding the foregoing, the Intellectual Property may not be used for individual personal or professional gain or other private benefit, and the Intellectual Property may not be used in any manner that, in the sole discretion of ASSOCIATION, discredits ASSOCIATION or tarnishes its reputation and goodwill; is false or misleading; violates the rights of others; violates any law, regulation or other public policy; or mischaracterizes the relationship between ASSOCIATION and CHAPTER, including but not limited to the fact that CHAPTER is a separate and distinct legal entity from ASSOCIATION.

4. CHAPTER shall maintain the confidentiality of the Mailing List and shall not sell, trade, transmit, or otherwise disseminate the Mailing List, in whole or in part, to any third party without the express prior written approval of ASSOCIATION.

5. In any authorized use by CHAPTER of the Intellectual Property, CHAPTER shall ensure that the applicable trademark and copyright notices are used pursuant to the requirements of United States law, the laws of the Territory, and any other guidelines that ASSOCIATION may prescribe.

6. ASSOCIATION shall have the right, from time to time, to request samples of use of the Intellectual Property from which it may determine compliance with these terms and conditions. ASSOCIATION reserves the right to prohibit use of any of the Intellectual Property, as well as to impose other sanctions, if it determines, in its sole discretion, that CHAPTER's usage thereof is not in strict accordance with the terms and conditions of this limited and revocable license.

7. Use of the Intellectual Property shall create no rights for CHAPTER in or to the Intellectual Property or its use beyond the terms and conditions of this limited and revocable license. All rights of usage of the Intellectual Property by CHAPTER shall terminate immediately upon the revocation, surrender or other termination of this Agreement. CHAPTER's obligations to protect the Intellectual Property shall survive the revocation, surrender or other termination of this Agreement.

B. <u>Confidential Information</u>. The parties shall maintain the confidentiality of all of the confidential and proprietary information and data ("Confidential Information") of the other party. The parties also shall take all reasonable steps to ensure that no use, by themselves or by any third parties, shall be made of the other party's Confidential Information without such other party's consent. Each party's Confidential Information shall remain the property of that party and shall be considered to be furnished in confidence to the other party when necessary under the terms of this Agreement. Upon any revocation, surrender or other termination of this Agreement, each party shall: (i) deliver immediately to the other party all Confidential Information of the other party, including but not limited to all written and electronic documentation of all Confidential Information, and all copies thereof; (ii) make no further use of it; and (iii) make reasonable efforts to ensure that no further use of it is made by either that party or its officers, directors, employees, agents, contractors, or any other person or third party. Each party's confidentiality obligations under this Section shall survive any revocation, surrender or other termination of this Agreement.

VI. RELATIONSHIP OF PARTIES.

The relationship of ASSOCIATION and CHAPTER to each other is that of independent contractors. Nothing herein shall create any association, joint venture, partnership, or agency relationship of any kind between the parties. Unless expressly agreed to in writing by the parties, neither party is authorized to incur any liability, obligation or expense on behalf of the other, to use the other's monetary credit in conducting any activities under this Agreement, or to represent to any third party that CHAPTER is an agent of ASSOCIATION.

VII. INDEMNIFICATION.

CHAPTER shall indemnify, save and hold harmless ASSOCIATION, its subsidiaries, affiliates, related entities, partners, agents, officers, directors, employees, members, shareholders, attorneys, heirs, successors, and assigns, and each of them, from and against any and all claims, actions, suits, demands, losses, damages, judgments, settlements, costs and expenses (including reasonable attorneys' fees and expenses), and liabilities of every kind and character whatsoever (a "Claim"), which may arise by reason of (i) any act or omission by CHAPTER or any of its subsidiaries, affiliates, related entities, partners, officers, directors, employees, members, shareholders or agents, or (ii) the inaccuracy of breach of any of the covenants, representations and warranties made by CHAPTER in this Agreement. This indemnity shall require CHAPTER to provide payment to ASSOCIATION of costs and expenses as they occur. CHAPTER shall promptly notify ASSOCIATION upon receipt of any Claim and shall grant to ASSOCIATION the sole conduct of the defense to any Claim. The provisions of this Section shall survive any revocation, surrender or other termination of this Agreement.

VIII. REVOCATION OR SURRENDER OF CHARTER.

A. Revocation of Charter. The charter granted by ASSOCIATION to CHAPTER hereunder shall remain in full force and effect unless and until revoked by ASSOCIATION or surrendered by CHAPTER in accordance with the provisions of this Agreement. ASSOCIATION, through its Board of Directors, shall have the authority to revoke the charter of CHAPTER if the Board of Directors determines that the conduct of CHAPTER is in breach of any provision of this Agreement. Any decision by ASSOCIATION to revoke CHAPTER's charter shall be initiated by sending written notice to CHAPTER specifying the grounds upon which the revocation is based; provided, however, that ASSOCIATION shall provide CHAPTER with _____ (___) days from the date of such notice to cure any alleged breach of this Agreement. In the event that ASSOCIATION determines, in its sole discretion, that CHAPTER has not corrected the condition leading to ASSOCIATION's decision to revoke CHAPTER's charter, ASSOCIATION shall so notify CHAPTER in writing. ASSOCIATION's decision shall become final unless, within _____ (___) days of its receipt of written notice from ASSOCIATION, CHAPTER delivers to ASSOCIATION a written notice to appeal such determination. Upon the filing of such an appeal notice, CHAPTER shall have the opportunity to present its case by written communication or in person, to the Board of Directors of ASSOCIATION pursuant to the applicable rules or procedures prescribed by ASSOCIATION's Board of Directors. The decision of ASSOCIATION's Board of Directors upon such appeal shall be final and not subject to further appeal.

B. Surrender of Charter. CHAPTER may surrender its charter by delivering to ASSOCIATION written notice of its intention to do so in less than _____ (___) days prior to the effective date of such surrender.

IX. MISCELLANEOUS.

A. Entire Agreement. This Agreement: (i) constitutes the entire agreement between the parties hereto with respect to the subject matter hereof; (ii) supersedes and replaces all prior agreements, oral and written, between the parties relating to the subject matter hereof; and (iii) may be amended only by a written instrument clearly setting forth the amendment(s) and executed by both parties.

B. Warranties. Each party covenants, warrants and represents that it shall comply with all laws, regulations and other legal standards applicable to this Agreement, and that it shall exercise due care and act in good faith at all times in performance of its obligations under this Agreement. The provisions of this Section shall survive any revocation, surrender or other termination of this Agreement.

C. Waiver. Either party's waiver of, or failure to exercise, any right provided for in this Agreement shall not be deemed a waiver of any further or future right under this Agreement.

D. Arbitration. Any and all disputes arising under this Agreement shall be subject to mandatory and binding arbitration. Said arbitration shall take place in the State of _____. Neither party shall have any right to bring an action relating to this Agreement in a court of law, except insofar as to either enforce or appeal the results of any such arbitration. In any such arbitration, and subsequent court action, the prevailing party shall be entitled to collect its fees and costs associated therewith from the non-prevailing party.

E. Governing Law. All questions with respect to the construction of this Agreement or the rights and liabilities of the parties hereunder shall be determined in accordance with the laws of the State of _____. Any legal action taken or to be taken by either party regarding this Agreement or the rights and liabilities of parties hereunder shall be brought only before a federal, state or local court of competent jurisdiction located within the State of _____. Each party hereby consents to the jurisdiction of the federal, state and local courts located within the State of _____.

F. Assignment. This Agreement may not be assigned, or the rights granted hereunder transferred or sub-licensed, by either party without the express prior written consent of the other party.

G. Heirs, Successors and Assigns. This Agreement shall be binding upon and inure to the benefit of each party, its subsidiaries, affiliates, related entities, partners, agents, officers, directors, employees, heirs, successors, and assigns, without regard to whether it is expressly acknowledged in any instrument of succession or assignment.

H. Headings. The headings of the various paragraphs hereof are intended solely for the convenience of reference and are not intended for any purpose whatsoever to explain, modify or place any construction upon any of the provision of this Agreement.

I. Counterparts. This Agreement may be executed in one (1) or more counterparts, each of which shall be deemed an original and all of which taken together shall constitute one and the same instrument.

J. Severability. All provisions of this Agreement are severable. If any provision or portion hereof is determined to be unenforceable in arbitration or by a court of competent jurisdiction, then the remaining portion of the Agreement shall remain in full effect.

K. Force Majeure. Neither party shall be liable for failure to perform its obligations under this Agreement due to events beyond its reasonable control, including, but not limited to, strikes, riots, wars, fire, acts of God, and acts in compliance with any applicable law, regulation or order (whether valid or invalid) of any governmental body.

L. Notice. All notices and demands of any kind or nature that either party may be required or may desire to serve upon the other in connection with this Agreement shall be in writing and may be served personally, by telecopier, by certified mail, or by overnight courier, with constructive receipt deemed to have occurred on the date of the mailing, sending or faxing of such notice, to the following addresses or telecopier numbers:

If to ASSOCIATION: _____
_____
_____
Attention: _____
Fax: (___) _____-_____

If to CHAPTER: _____
_____
_____
Attention: _____
Fax: (___) _____-_____

* * * * *

IN WITNESS WHEREOF, the parties hereto have caused duplicate originals of this Agreement to be executed by their respective duly authorized representatives as of the date and year first above written.

[Name of Association]

By: _____
Name: _____
Title: _____

[Name of Chapter]

By: _____
Name: _____
Title: _____

DC1DOCS1.108418

Source: Courtesy of ASAE and the Center, Washington, DC.

Chapter 18

Working with Consultants: Hiring and Using Consultants in Your Fundraising Programs

CHAPTER OUTLINE

- Determining the Need for a Consultant
- What Consultants Can Offer to a Development Operation
- How to Convince Your Board and Staff to Use a Consultant
- What to Expect from a Consultant
- How to Find a Consultant Who Can Work with You

- How to Hire a Consultant
- How to Develop Trust with a Consultant
- Determining the Amount to Pay Consultants
- The Contract
- Fees and Expenses
- Evaluating the Work of a Consultant
- Employee or Consultant According to the IRS

KEY VOCABULARY

- Giving Institute, formerly known as the American Association of Fundraising Counsel (AAFRC)
- Fundraising Consultant
- Paid Solicitor
- Request for Proposals (RFPs)

DETERMINING THE NEED FOR A CONSULTANT

Inevitably, at some point in a development officer's career, he or she will need to or want to employ a consultant to do the fol-

> *At some point in a development officer's career, he or she will need to employ a consultant.*

lowing: provide advice or consultation on an issue, actively steer a campaign, motivate a board, or provide needed expertise in some areas. Some of the best and most experienced development officers employ consultants on a regular basis. This does not mean that these officers are having fundraising difficulties or do not know their business. Instead, it just may be more cost-effective to use a short-term consultant rather than adding permanent staff to the payroll. Or it may be that board members or other volunteers need specific specialized training, something that the development officer does not have time to do or cannot do as well as a consultant or

that would be better presented by an outside party rather than staff. Appendix 18–A lists 12 reasons when it is wise to engage a consultant.

Individual consultants and consulting firms are hired to provide a variety of specialized services. In fact, an organization may use several firms at one time. One firm may produce an organization's special events, another firm may conduct the capital campaign, another may provide computer expertise, and another may provide strategic planning or board training. The use of consultants is increasing, and fundraising consultants have matured just as their field has.

There are many issues to consider when hiring a professional fundraising consultant. It is important for the organization to know the difference between a fundraising consultant and a paid solicitor. A fundraising consultant will not solicit or retain custody of the organization's contributions. A paid solicitor or solicitation firm that is employed to solicit contributions for a charity may have possession of the contributions before turning the money over to the organization. Many telemarketing firms work in this manner. Most states require paid solicitors to post bond before rendering their services. If a consultant is needed, most nonprofit organizations will want to hire a fundraising consultant and not a paid solicitor.

But first question if there is a need for a consultant at all. Ask yourself the following: What can a consultant do for me—generally and specifically? Do I need general advice about or specific assistance on a project? Should I use a large or small consulting firm or an individual contractor? How much will I have to pay a consultant or firm? Should I pay by the project or by the hour? How do I set priorities, goals, and objectives for the person or persons, and will I know how to evaluate the work produced by the consultant?

WHAT CONSULTANTS CAN OFFER TO A DEVELOPMENT OPERATION

Let's answer the basic questions first. What does a consultant do? Consultants bring a level of wisdom, expertise, and creativity to a fundraising effort. They may provide staff and board training, or strategic guidance to a capital campaign. They can furnish a sense of objectivity and candor, and they can *assist* you in raising money—*they do not raise it for you.*

According to Rutter (1994), "Fundraising consultants do not solicit funds for organizations in large part because of donor perception. Donors want a relationship with the cause they are considering helping rather than communication with a paid representative of the organization. Therefore, consultants manage the behind-the-scenes aspects of fund-raising campaigns, developing plans, surveying prospects, organizing committees, designing marketing strategies, and training volunteer leaders."

Exhibit 18–1 presents some of the considerable benefits a nonprofit organization can receive from using a consultant or consulting firm.

HOW TO CONVINCE YOUR BOARD AND STAFF TO USE A CONSULTANT

Often it is a member of the board who suggests bringing in a consultant to assist with a particular project or campaign. Staff should not feel threatened by this suggestion, because consultants can provide a fresh perspective to a department mired in its day-to-day operations. The familiar phrase "not being able to see the forest for the trees" often applies to staff. A consultant can relate issues to the senior management or board that staff cannot. Instead of fighting the prospect or opportunity of hiring a consultant, embrace it. Be glad that the board is open to using a consultant, and begin the search for the right consultant for the organization.

If board members need to be convinced that a consultant would be beneficial to their fundraising efforts, remind them that a consultant could provide valuable training for the board as well as for the current staff in areas in which they may lack expertise. Even though the consultant eventually will leave, the knowledge will stay behind. This is one of the major benefits of

---

Exhibit 18–1 Contributions of Fundraising Consultants

- **Experience**
  This can be especially helpful for an organization with a new or young development program. Even in instances when a nonprofit organization has a chief development officer with considerable experience, the development officer and his or her staff may lack experience in a specific program or area of development.
- **Objectivity**
  Frequently, development programs, even comparatively sophisticated programs, need an experienced outside observer whose viewpoint is not influenced by internal institutional politics or other considerations. Often, simply a fresh point of view is required.

  Objectivity is good in the creation and management of a capital campaign, but is particularly important when the organization is having a "development program audit."
- **Focus**
  This is especially important in a capital campaign. There is a clear distinction between the mindset that is "development" in approach and that which is "campaign" in approach. A development officer must keep the long-term future of the organization and its development programs in mind, whereas the campaign consultant focuses everyone's attention to the matter at hand.

  A campaign has an established time frame and a goal that must be met within the time allotted. Therefore, the consultant will keep the group's attention focused on the campaign process—as distinct from other details of a development operation.

  Regular development operations focus on the cultivation of the gift for the long-term enrichment of the institution. A cam-

paign requires a clear sense of urgency to meet a specific goal. Therefore, the consultant's job is to "hold everyone's feet to the fire," including the board and campaign committee, a task frequently outside the staff's capability.

  It almost always is necessary to create a group that is separate from the organization's board to oversee the operations of a campaign. The board may be concerned about facility maintenance, bonding, staff salaries, endowment management, etc. The campaign steering committee focuses on the operation and structuring of the effort at hand. A consultant can be decisive in selecting and organizing the best available committee from among a group's many constituencies.
- **Prospect Research**
  Few consulting firms will match large university development programs with staff and resources devoted to an established long-term research program. But a good consulting firm will make a commitment to research resources to which most organizations, except for the larger ones, will not have access. Also, a consulting firm's research resources will cover a wider variety of data and sources than the in-house programs of even the largest universities.
- **Breadth of Staff Resources**
  Staff of most consulting firms include several individuals with particular expertise. Although a particular skill may not be required for the entire course of the campaign, an individual with a critical skill can be brought aboard on an *ad hoc* basis, without requiring the institution to make a long-term commitment to new staff.

Source: Courtesy of Michael Y. Walters, Fundraising Consultant, Manchester, Kentucky.

hiring a fundraising consultant. See Exhibit 18–2, How to Persuade Your Board to Hire a Consulting Firm.

But keep in mind that there can be some negatives when working with consultants. If an organization hires only consultants or a consulting firm to do its fundraising and does not involve permanent staff, it may lose any sense of history when the contract is completed. Organizations need to be cautious about staffing a campaign entirely with consultants. Although

Organizations need to be cautious about staffing a campaign entirely with consultants.

many tasks, such as proposal writing, data entry, event coordination, and public relations, can be handled by consultants, it probably will not be in the best interest of the organization to have these done by consultants over the long run. After the consulting firm leaves, who will be trained to carry on with the work? Relationships developed with the volunteers and members may disappear when the consulting team departs. If permanent staff is used alongside the consulting team, then some permanent bonding may occur, with new relationships developing or old ones strengthening.

WHAT TO EXPECT FROM A CONSULTANT

Before any work begins, a written proposal should be submitted. Be sure that it includes the scope of work for which the consultant will be paid, what tasks will be performed for the consultant's fee, and on what dates they are to be completed. Spell out clearly who is responsible for incidentals such as postage, printing, mileage, etc. In addition, references, including telephone numbers, should be listed. Call all references listed and ask for more if necessary. Agree upon a fee and sign a contract before the consultant starts to work.

When hiring a consultant, look for qualities that complement the organization. The person or firm should meet the standards set by the organization. Seek a professional who can represent the organization well. Find someone who is able to mix well with the staff, who is experienced and knowledgeable, who is a specialist in the area in which the organization seeks help, who has a

good ability to present materials at all staff and volunteer levels, who is a good writer and communicator, and who is able to devote the full amount of time needed for the tasks at hand. Remember to seek a fundraising consultant, not someone who just solicits money for your cause—and, remember, there is a difference between the two.

HOW TO FIND A CONSULTANT WHO CAN WORK WITH YOU

Your first inclination when hiring a consultant may be to hire the person or firm that a board member recommends. Another potential mistake is hiring someone that looks and sounds like you, with whom you feel comfortable. Don't forget that what you are seeking is expertise, not necessarily a friend, buddy, or clone! The consultant may need to play the role of the "tough guy," the person who has to say "no" to board members, the person who has to "insist" that schedules be met during a campaign. If he or she is too close to you, or a friend of a member of the board, an important dynamic can be lost—that of separation. The consultant needs to be free to tell you what you need to know, not what you would like to hear!

Again, the best way to find a consultant that fits your and your organization's comfort level is to ask development staff members in other organizations similar to yours what consultants they have used and if they would recommend them. Appendix 18–B presents basic criteria for retaining fundraising counsel.

HOW TO HIRE A CONSULTANT

There are at least 60 major fundraising consulting firms in the United States, and each major city has at least that many independent consultants (i.e., not members of a firm). How do you know where to find a consultant or consulting firm? You might first want to contact the Giving Institute formerly known as the American Association of Fundraising Counsel for larger consulting firms and the Association of Philanthropic Counsel for smaller firms. Independent consultants likely will be members of the Association of Fundraising Professionals (AFP). All of these organizations require that their members adhere to a code of ethics.

Before hiring any consultant, at least three competitive bids should be received and reviewed. Previous and current references should be included in bids. Call these references before meeting with the consultant and ask them detailed questions concerning the work that the consultant did for them. Did the consultant complete the work on time, within budget, and successfully? Would they rehire the consultant? Would they recommend the consultant to others? See Exhibit 18–3, Four Steps to Hiring a Consultant.

A larger consulting firm may put a clause in the contract that prevents the organization from permanently hiring any person who at the time of the contract was employed by the consulting group or any of its affiliates. This prevents the organization from

---

Exhibit 18–2 How to Persuade Your Board to Hire a Consulting Firm

1. Experienced help can save you from jeopardizing your campaign and your organization.
2. A campaign feasibility study bares valuable truth for your planning.
3. Consultants can speak freely.
4. Rating prospects is best done by an objective outsider.
5. Consultants bring experience and tested solutions.
6. The net value outweighs the firm's cost.

Source: Reprinted with permission from David G. Phillips, President and CEO, Custom Development Solutions Inc., Mt. Pleasant, South Carolina.

Exhibit 18-3 Four Steps to Hiring a Consultant

1. Prepare a job description, including expected results.
2. Interview and select best candidates, fostering collaboration from the start.
3. Set clear consulting service agreements and determine shared responsibility.
4. Define measurements for success—both qualitative and quantitative.

Source: Reprinted with permission from Davida Hartman-Griffin, Hartman-Griffin Associates, Berkeley, California, in Hartman-Griffin, D. (2006). The Bottom Line. Advancing Philanthrophy, September, October, 28–40.

hiring account executives from the consulting firm without giving it some sort of remuneration.

It is recommended that an organization not use an open-ended contract to hire a consultant. There always should be a cancellation clause—the ability to terminate the contract. Any contract should be reviewed by legal counsel. Fees and reimbursable expenses should be spelled out in detail in the contract.

Before you sign a contract with a consultant or firm, there are six areas you should consider. They are listed in Exhibit 18–4, and Appendix 18–C presents the 18 advantages of a professional consultant. Both should be read thoroughly before signing a consulting contract.

HOW TO DEVELOP TRUST WITH A CONSULTANT

By clearly stating up front what you expect from the consultant or the consulting firm, much of the anxiety of both sides can be alleviated. Regular meetings with the consultant allow monitoring of the consultant's progress without presenting the "feeling" of too much supervision. Expect expertise, assistance, advice, and knowledge from the consultant in addition to quality workmanship. Treat the consultant with respect and fairness. Don't

Exhibit 18-4 Six Common Concerns About Hiring a Professional Consultant

1. ***The cost of professional fund counsel increases our fundraising costs. Will that turn off our donors?***
   Perhaps some people will be disappointed, but if you are honest with them, and the costs are reasonable, most people will understand. In fact, the net amount raised should be higher with counsel, making the cost per dollar raised (which is the most important factor) lower with counsel than without. And, there is nothing more costly for a nonprofit organization than a failed campaign.

2. ***Will counsel do an effective job—what if we fail?***
   While success is never assured, it is much more likely if professional fundraising counsel is involved. Even the most highly talented and well-trained musicians make more beautiful music when under the direction of a competent conductor. If your constituents do not care about your organization or if the board is unwilling to make the campaign a priority, you will likely struggle whether counsel is involved or not. Counsel has a contractual obligation to give you competent direction—otherwise you are not required to pay the fee.

3. ***Will paid professionals push too hard, alienating our members, volunteers, and even our donors?***
   This is a good question, but it is highly unlikely. Ethical considerations in the fundraising consulting industry long ago made working on a contingency or percentage basis unethical. Counsel has no incentive (financial or otherwise) to risk antagonizing volunteers or potential donors by pushing too hard. While counsel wants to motivate all parties to work toward success, they do not want to "bite the hand that feeds them," so to speak.

4. ***What if we do not like the resident director assigned to our account?***
   Within reason, fundraising counsel will want to ensure that you feel comfortable with your resident director. You will need to work closely with this person to reach your potential so it is im-

portant that they have your confidence. As reasonable people, however, clients must understand that it is very expensive to bring people in and out and that the most important thing is the director's experience and ability to get the job done effectively. A good firm only will assign you a highly qualified director. Thus, they will have taken much of the work out of the selection process.

5. ***If we use outside counsel on this campaign, how will we manage when they are gone or when we need to do our next campaign?***
   By working closely with your resident campaign director, you will learn much about planning and running a capital campaign. Most importantly, you will learn how to solicit major gifts efficiently and effectively and how to build a successful campaign organization. We have had clients who, after working with us on one campaign, turned around and ran another similar campaign by themselves. The key is that they had to free their development director from most other activities to be able to concentrate on the campaign—as does our resident director. When we at CDS leave a client, we leave them with a "historical file" or scrapbook, which contains all important campaign materials and documentation in chronological order. This file can serve as your roadmap for future campaigns.

6. ***Will this campaign require a large majority of management's time? How will we find the time to show our director everything and to teach them about the organization?***
   No! If board members and top management are willing to give the campaign several hours per week, on average, that will be more than enough time. And, with regard to spending time training the resident director, relax. Our directors are quick to study an organization to learn what we need to know. What they cannot learn from reading your marketing and internal material, they will learn from talking to management and board members and asking questions. They will not need you to "hold their hands." In fact, we expect that they will be holding your hands very quickly and offering you advice.

Source: Reprinted with Permission from David G. Phillips, President and CEO, Custom Development Solutions, Inc. (CDS), 268 West Coleman Blvd., Suite 1B, Mt. Pleasant, South Carolina 29464.

Right from the start, John knew this meeting with his consultants was not likely to be a productive one.

Source: Copyright © RSM McGladrey, Inc.

try to add on work that was not in the original contract. If more work is needed and expected, then add a rider to the contract spelling out the additional work and the additional fee. Treat the consultant as you would want to be treated. The consultant will then trust you, and you will trust the consultant.

DETERMINING THE AMOUNT TO PAY CONSULTANTS

Consulting fees vary depending on the size of the project or campaign and what the consultant thinks that the organization can pay. Fees usually cover the cost of the people involved, travel and living expenses, telephone, fax reproductions, copies, etc. Never allow consultants' fees to be based upon the goal of the campaign or a percentage of the development office's budget. Fees should be based upon the services provided to the organization. Also, never allow the fundraising firm to hold any of the funds being raised for the organization. Most established firms will

> *Never allow consultants' fees to be based upon the goal of the campaign or a percentage of the development office's budget.*

have a schedule for billing professional fees. Compare the fees of the persons or firms asked to submit bids. Are they in line with one another? If so, then look at the other areas of importance when deciding which consultant to hire.

It is suggested that three bids be obtained for each project being undertaken. Appendix 18–D shows a sample RFP—Request for Proposal. Any more than this can be counterproductive—more of your time is taken up in interviews than in getting the project completed. It is not necessarily wise to choose the lowest bid. Consider all aspects of the proposal and select the bid best suited to the organization and the work to be accomplished.

Hire a consultant for a specific fee to cover specific duties. AFP does not approve of hiring consultants who work on a percentage basis. This form of compensation does not meet its code of ethics for professional fundraisers. In this code, which is presented in full in Exhibit 18–5, the following is stated: "Members shall work for a salary or fee, not percentage-based compensation or a commission," and "Members may accept performance-based compensation such as bonuses provided that such bonuses are in accord with prevailing practices within the members' own organizations and are not based on a percentage of philanthropic funds raised."

Exhibit 18–5 AFP Code of Ethical Principles and Standards

AFP Code of Ethical Principles and Standards

AFP
Association of
Fundraising Professionals

ETHICAL PRINCIPLES • Adopted 1964; amended Sept. 2007

The Association of Fundraising Professionals (AFP) exists to foster the development and growth of fundraising professionals and the profession, to promote high ethical behavior in the fundraising profession and to preserve and enhance philanthropy and volunteerism. Members of AFP are motivated by an inner drive to improve the quality of life through the causes they serve. They serve the ideal of philanthropy, are committed to the preservation and enhancement of volunteerism; and hold stewardship of these concepts as the overriding direction of their professional life. They recognize their responsibility to ensure that needed resources are vigorously and ethically sought and that the intent of the donor is honestly fulfilled. To these ends, AFP members, both individual and business, embrace certain values that they strive to uphold in performing their responsibilities for generating philanthropic support. AFP business members strive to promote and protect the work and mission of their client organizations.

AFP members both individual and business aspire to:

- practice their profession with integrity, honesty, truthfulness and adherence to the absolute obligation to safeguard the public trust
- act according to the highest goals and visions of their organizations, professions, clients and consciences
- put philanthropic mission above personal gain;
- inspire others through their own sense of dedication and high purpose
- improve their professional knowledge and skills, so that their performance will better serve others
- demonstrate concern for the interests and well-being of individuals affected by their actions
- value the privacy, freedom of choice and interests of all those affected by their actions
- foster cultural diversity and pluralistic values and treat all people with dignity and respect
- affirm, through personal giving, a commitment to philanthropy and its role in society
- adhere to the spirit as well as the letter of all applicable laws and regulations
- advocate within their organizations adherence to all applicable laws and regulations
- avoid even the appearance of any criminal offense or professional misconduct
- bring credit to the fundraising profession by their public demeanor
- encourage colleagues to embrace and practice these ethical principles and standards
- be aware of the codes of ethics promulgated by other professional organizations that serve philanthropy

ETHICAL STANDARDS

Furthermore, while striving to act according to the above values, AFP members, both individual and business, agree to abide (and to ensure, to the best of their ability, that all members of their staff abide) by the AFP standards. Violation of the standards may subject the member to disciplinary sanctions, including expulsion, as provided in the AFP Ethics Enforcement Procedures.

MEMBER OBLIGATIONS

1. Members shall not engage in activities that harm the members' organizations, clients or profession.
2. Members shall not engage in activities that conflict with their fiduciary, ethical and legal obligations to their organizations, clients or profession.
3. Members shall effectively disclose all potential and actual conflicts of interest; such disclosure does not preclude or imply ethical impropriety.
4. Members shall not exploit any relationship with a donor, prospect, volunteer, client or employee for the benefit of the members or the members' organizations.
5. Members shall comply with all applicable local, state, provincial and federal civil and criminal laws.
6. Members recognize their individual boundaries of competence and are forthcoming and truthful about their professional experience and qualifications and will represent their achievements accurately and without exaggeration.
7. Members shall present and supply products and/or services honestly and without misrepresentation and will clearly identify the details of those products, such as availability of the products and/or services and other factors that may affect the suitability of the products and/or services for donors, clients or nonprofit organizations.
8. Members shall establish the nature and purpose of any contractual relationship at the outset and will be responsive and available to organizations and their employing organizations before, during and after any sale of materials and/or services. Members will comply with all fair and reasonable obligations created by the contract.

9. Members shall refrain from knowingly infringing the intellectual property rights of other parties at all times. Members shall address and rectify any inadvertent infringement that may occur.
10. Members shall protect the confidentiality of all privileged information relating to the provider/client relationships.
11. Members shall refrain from any activity designed to disparage competitors untruthfully.

SOLICITATION AND USE OF PHILANTHROPIC FUNDS

12. Members shall take care to ensure that all solicitation and communication materials are accurate and correctly reflect their organizations' mission and use of solicited funds.
13. Members shall take care to ensure that donors receive informed, accurate and ethical advice about the value and tax implications of contributions.
14. Members shall take care to ensure that contributions are used in accordance with donors' intentions.
15. Members shall take care to ensure proper stewardship of all revenue sources, including timely reports on the use and management of such funds.
16. Members shall obtain explicit consent by donors before altering the conditions of financial transactions.

PRESENTATION OF INFORMATION

17. Members shall not disclose privileged or confidential information to unauthorized parties.
18. Members shall adhere to the principle that all donor and prospect information created by, or on behalf of, an organization or a client is the property of that organization or client and shall not be transferred or utilized except on behalf of that organization or client.
19. Members shall give donors and clients the opportunity to have their names removed from lists that are sold to, rented to or exchanged with other organizations.
20. Members shall, when stating fundraising results, use accurate and consistent accounting methods that conform to the appropriate guidelines adopted by the American Institute of Certified Public Accountants (AICPA)* for the type of organization involved. (* In countries outside of the United States, comparable authority should be utilized.)

COMPENSATION AND CONTRACTS

21. Members shall not accept compensation or enter into a contract that is based on a percentage of contributions; nor shall members accept finder's fees or contingent fees. Business members must refrain from receiving compensation from third parties derived from products or services for a client without disclosing that third-party compensation to the client (for example, volume rebates from vendors to business members).
22. Members may accept performance-based compensation, such as bonuses, provided such bonuses are in accord with prevailing practices within the members' own organizations and are not based on a percentage of contributions.
23. Members shall neither offer nor accept payments or special considerations for the purpose of influencing the selection of products or services.
24. Members shall not pay finder's fees, commissions or percentage compensation based on contributions, and shall take care to discourage their organizations from making such payments.
25. Any member receiving funds on behalf of a donor or client must meet the legal requirements for the disbursement of those funds. Any interest or income earned on the funds should be fully disclosed.

Source: Courtesy of the Association of Fundraising Professionals (AFP), Arlington, Virginia.

Beware of the consultant who suggests the fee be open ended. It may be the invitation to paying open-ended bills. Ask for a proposal with a set fee for a specific scope of work. Also beware of the consultant who asks for a large advance. One month's fee or a quarter of the cost of the project upfront is acceptable. Establish a payment schedule upfront that is acceptable to both parties.

THE CONTRACT

All major agreements between a client and a consulting firm should be put in writing to avoid problems arising from a misunderstanding. It is important for the client to understand what the firm is capable of doing for the organization and at what price. It is equally important for the consulting firm to understand what the organization expects, wishes to keep in or a percentage of its own control, wants to have reported and at what intervals, expects to be charged, etc. Every contract should include some basics that protect both the client and the consulting firm. These basics are covered below and in the sample contract in Appendix 18–E.

> *All major agreements between a client and a consulting firm should be put in writing.*

FEES AND EXPENSES

The consulting firm must list all of the fees and expenses it expects to charge. This may mean developing a detailed budget for the assignment that the organization can review. Other projects may be detailed by task, with one sum covering all of the work to be performed. Then, if additional expenses occur during the course of the work, the expenses must be agreed upon before being incurred. A provision should be included that will address this issue. For example, before an expense can be incurred that is not already included in the agreed-upon budget, the organization and firm must both approve it. Flexibility must be built into a contract, because it is impossible to know exactly every charge that will occur. The important point to keep in mind is that there must be open communication between the organization and the firm. A consultant should never spend money that has not been agreed upon in advance!

> *A consultant should never spend money that has not been agreed upon in advance!*

As important as agreeing upon the price to pay is agreeing upon the method of payment. After obtaining competitive bids, selecting a firm, and agreeing upon a price, next negotiate the type of payment structure. Will the money for the work to be done be paid in advance? Will it be paid monthly, quarterly, or at the end of the contract? How will bills from other vendors be paid? Should these bills be given directly to the organization or go through the consulting firm first? All of these items should be discussed and placed in the contract. Make sure the issue of whether the consulting firm can receive any markup on these outside contracts is discussed and agreed upon in advance. For example, if the consulting firm has accounts with suppliers, caterers, or printers, should its discounted prices be passed along to the organization? Ask these questions before the contract is signed, not after.

Services

Spell out clearly what services will be provided by the consultant or firm, when they will be provided, and what happens if they are not provided on time. Also, clearly state to what the organization is obligated. For example, if the consulting firm is providing design work for a piece to be printed, will the organization or the firm own the artwork after the project is completed? This is particularly important if additional work is to be done at a future time using the same artwork. Resolve upfront who "owns" the art.

Determine ahead how many staff members will be assigned to the contract and where they will work. If the consulting staff is responsible for written materials, determine who on the organization's staff will be responsible for approving the work. Never allow any materials to be distributed or printed without the approval of the organization. The organization must have control of what is being said, how it is being said, and the frequency of the message being disseminated.

Termination Clause

Always build a cancellation clause into the contract for use by either party. Most would agree that a 30-day escape clause is reasonable, whereas 60- to 90-day clauses may be more reasonable when a contract involves direct mail, a capital campaign, or a major special event. Also, the longer time may be insisted upon when a consulting firm has made a large investment, such as covering the expenses of moving a consultant and his or her family to the organization's location.

Be wary of the consulting firm that wants to "manage" the organization's funds as it helps to raise them. This is dangerous, can be a direct conflict of interest, and most likely will not benefit the organization. Also, consulting firms may not always negotiate the best subcontracts for clients or exercise the best control over expenditures. Plus, the organization should not prefinance a project and should retain control over expenditures.

A consulting firm should be wary of the organization that expects to pay it only after it has raised money for the organization. Some organizations will want a firm to be paid a percentage of the money that the firm raises. This type of payment is not permitted for members of AFP, nor is it recommended for consulting firms or their clients. Payment should be based on services provided and should not be a percentage of funds raised. A consultant or consulting

> *Payment should be based on services provided and should not be a percentage of funds raised.*

firm may wish to delay payment for a few months while the campaign "gets off the ground" and then, when money starts to flow into the organization, begin to receive payments. The organization still would be responsible for the fees, even if the money raised wasn't as much as expected. Is a doctor not paid for services even if the patient dies? Fundraising is also a profession, and its professionals should receive reimbursement based on services rendered.

EVALUATING THE WORK OF A CONSULTANT

Evaluating a consultant's work should not wait until the end of the project. Regular progress reports from the consultant and a review of the work completed should be undertaken on an ongoing basis. Reports may be either written or verbal, but the important factor is that there is communication between the consultant and the organization. Weekly meetings between the staff and the consultant are a must. Taking the time to make sure that the consultant understands what is expected by the organization can prevent many mistakes from happening. Some organizations expect consultants to be a visible part of their staff, whereas others would prefer that a low profile be maintained. Whatever the case, one staff person should act as the liaison or contact with the consultant and provide the direction and guidance. Although the consultant may work with many staff members, the direction and monitoring must be done by one person. How the consultant is directed and guided through the maze of internal politics will make the difference between success and failure

and determine the organization's degree of satisfaction with the work produced.

Make sure that everything expected from a consultant is written in the initial contract. Also, indicate if a final written report is expected.

EMPLOYEE OR CONSULTANT ACCORDING TO THE IRS

An organization may have a consultant on its payroll for a long time, but what makes this person different from an employee? According to the Internal Revenue Service (IRS), if this person is consulting solely with this organization, works in the organization's office every day, and is supervised to the point of being able to exercise only limited independent judgment, then the consultant well may be considered an employee by the IRS. Be careful of this when hiring a consultant. Make sure that written contracts clearly indicate that these are independent contractors with federal tax identification numbers, that they pay quarterly income tax and FICA payments, and that they have other clients.

Exhibit 18–6 lists 20 questions based on IRS guidelines that can be asked to gauge whether a contractor should be considered an employee or a consultant. If the answer is yes to questions 1 through 14, 19, and 20, then the employer controls or has the right to control the manner in which services are performed. This generally indicates an employer–employee relationship and not an organization-consultant relationship.

Exhibit 18–6 IRS Guidelines to Determine Consultant Status

1. Do you require the worker to comply with another person's instructions about when, where, and how he or she is to work?
2. Do you provide training for the worker that indicates you want services performed in a particular method or manner?
3. Are the worker's services integrated into the business operation? That is, does the success or continuation of the business depend to an appreciable degree upon the services performed by the worker?
4. Do you require the worker to personally render his or her services? If so, you are demonstrating interest in the methods used to accomplish the work as well as in the results.
5. Does the person to whom the worker reports hire, supervise, and pay assistants?
6. Do you have a continuing relationship with the worker?
7. Do you establish set hours of work?
8. Does the worker devote substantial time to your business?
9. Is the worker required to perform his or her services on your premises?
10. Do you require the worker to perform services in a set order or sequence?

11. Do you require the worker to submit regular or written reports?
12. Do you pay the worker by the hour, week, or month?
13. Do you pay the worker's business or traveling expenses?
14. Do you furnish the worker with significant tools, materials, and other equipment?
15. Does the worker invest in facilities he or she uses to perform services that are not typically maintained by an employee, such as renting an office or setting up a home office?
16. Can the worker realize a profit or suffer a loss as a result of his or her services?
17. Does the worker perform work for several unrelated persons or firms at the same time?
18. Does the worker make his or her services available to the general public on a regular and consistent basis?
19. Do you have the authority to discharge the worker?
20. Does the worker have the right to terminate his or her relationship with you at any time without incurring liability?

Source: Reprinted with permission from A. Greenblat, Guiding Your Consultant, *Association Management*, © 1994, American Society of Association Executives.

REFERENCE

Rutter, E.J. 1994. Hiring a fundraising consultant—Sending shivers up the organization's spine. *The Funding Connection*, Winter.

Twelve Reasons to Use a Consultant

If any of the situations below apply to your organization, it is wise to consider using a consultant:

1. It is your first capital campaign.
2. The dollar amount to be raised is more than $500,000.
3. What you have been doing so far has not worked.
4. Key leaders are either not involved or are becoming disenchanted and may leave.
5. There is a conflict of views internally and no consensus.
6. The current campaign has stalled.
7. The time and talents required are not available in-house.
8. Objectivity is necessary to determine the true picture.
9. There is a desire or need for fresh ideas or new techniques.
10. Information needed can only be gathered confidentially.
11. You (the development professional) are pondering a job search.
12. Politics keeps the organization from consensus and advancement.

Source: Courtesy of Steve Moore, Moore and Associates, LLC, Columbus, Indiana.

Criteria for Retaining Fundraising Counsel

Your fundraising success will be a function of how much is known, rather than assumed, prior to launching a fundraising campaign. Fundraising counsel can provide many benefits and services for you and your organization: experience, proven methodology, information, professional representation, and strategic guidance, among others. If you are considering retaining fundraising counsel, here are some criteria to apply.

Experience

Keeping in mind that counsel will represent your organization with your current and expanded constituency, the broader the experience of your counsel, the better, since broader experience will provide greater perspective. Specifically ask about the counsel's experience with a wide variety of clients, not just in your field; actual inside (staff) fundraising/foundation experience as opposed to just consulting by the firm's professionals; and experience with your primary as well as *potential* constituency (foundations, corporations, or individuals).

Methodology and Approach

A team of people working on your project is far better than one person because a number of perspectives will counteract one person's preferences. Determine if the planning stage people and the implementation team overlap. Otherwise, you will be retraining (more costly) and resensitizing a new team. Confidentiality of information is another area that should be well understood.

Information and Analysis

Fundraising is more art than science, but your counsel should provide you with recommendations based on your unique situation, not generalities or what worked elsewhere. Therefore, you should have *all* the information upon which the firm relies rather than a sampling. Because your volunteers will need to understand it, the analysis and interpretation of the information to form a viable strategy is critical.

Product

The difference between a feasibility study and a *strategy* is the degree to which all nine factors that will determine your success are comprehensively assessed and addressed. Therefore, be sure you know what the final report will cover and that your expectations will be met. *What worked well for another, similar organization may not work for you at all.* Your report and its recommendations must reflect your environment and provide a clear foundation on which to base recommendations and on which to develop the steps required to match your needs with your capabilities.

Fees and Expenses

Whether the work is by fixed contract, hourly rate, or retainer, the fundraising counsel fee structure should be clear. Expenses connected with the work should be itemized, and costs should be shared if your counsel travels concurrently for your organization and another client. *In particular, inquire about fees related to the implementation phase of your effort.*

As much as 90 percent of your effort is in the initial assessment and strategy design phases. Thorough preparation is a must, even though your campaign fulfills self-interests. Fundraising in this environment is not just charitable giving, it is a unique opportunity for your organization to impact and better control its own future.

Source: Courtesy of Steve Moore, Moore and Associates, Columbus, Indiana.

Eighteen Advantages of a Professional Consultant

1. With fund counsel, you have an unbiased professional assessment as to your fundraising potential, enabling you to set a challenging, yet realistic goal;

2. You will realize much more money because of your access to professional advice and techniques;

3. The resident director is onsite to monitor progress, encourage activity, and make adjustments daily, where necessary;

4. Counsel gives you security, making you more confident in your ability to carry out a successful campaign;

5. Lower net cost—both in terms of fundraising cost per dollar raised, and in terms of money raised per hour of volunteer activity. With counsel involved, you get the most efficient and effective use of scarce volunteer time;

6. An effective solicitor to accompany you on calls and a professional to teach people at every level of your organization (board, management and volunteers) how to make an effective solicitation for your organization. This means more money raised for the organization than would be raised without counsel;

7. A professional to help you design the most effective campaign materials and to negotiate reasonable and cost effective prices;

8. Someone to prepare your plan and budget the amount required to run a successful campaign based upon many similar experiences;

9. Outside counsel is an unbiased third party whose sole responsibility is to help you run a successful campaign. That singular focus helps us move board members or donors who have been inflexible and unresponsive to the pleas of management and even other members of the board. We strengthen the position of management and board leaders by expressing our professional opinions about what a successful effort is going to require;

10. Counsel prepares your proposals for you, ensuring their accuracy and fundraising integrity;

11. Counsel is there to brief and debrief solicitors who are about to/or just made a request for funds—we are there to stop problems before they become trends;

12. Outside counsel knows the guidelines and giving officers of many local corporations and foundations. Our directors know where to go to get the most current prospect research information quickly and easily—often right online;

13. Counsel knows the hundreds of things that must be done in a successful campaign and how to prioritize these actions to create the most enthusiasm and build the most momentum;

14. Using counsel for a fixed period, you put the entire organization on notice that you have a campaign timetable, complete with specific action steps. For a very short time, you have professional help to enable you to achieve your goals. This greatly increases the motivation of volunteers and board members to act now, increasing your chances for success. Without this incentive to act immediately, campaigns drag on and lose the sense of urgency which is essential for a successful campaign;

15. As fundraising professionals, we know what makes an effective campaign chairman or a good campaign leader. We can help you identify the best candidates, help you convince them to join the campaign team (which they are more apt to do if they have professional help to reassure them), and we help you prepare these leaders to assume their roles successfully;

16. Counsel can help you accurately assess the giving potential of each prospective donor;

17. Outside counsel knows the logistical burdens placed upon the system by a campaign. We can help you anticipate these problems and streamline the solutions;

18. The resident director is there to encourage all parties involved and to push hard (though tactfully and tastefully) to ensure you succeed. If a board member or volunteer is upset by the assertive nature of our encouragement—any ill feelings associated with that unfortunate incident will leave with us when we go. Permanent staff is hamstrung by their need to get along and be well-liked.

Source: Courtesy of David G. Phillips, President and CEO, Custom Development Solutions, Inc. (CDS), Mt. Pleasant, South Carolina.

Sample Request for Proposals (RFPs)

SAINT MARY'S UNIVERSITY OF MINNESOTA

Request for Proposals

Saint Mary's University of Minnesota, a Catholic, Lasallian university, invites selected firms offering professional development counsel to submit a proposal to conduct a pre-campaign capacity study.

The university anticipates conducting a comprehensive capital campaign that will culminate during the celebration of its centennial in 2012. Based on identified and prioritized needs, the university anticipates that the primary—but not exclusive—focus of the campaign will be endowment expansion.

The only feasibility study commissioned by Saint Mary's was conducted in 1980. In advance of the proposed campaign, university leadership deems it prudent to retain counsel to conduct a capacity study that will provide:

- Feedback and informed reactions to the case for support.
- Identification of perceived obstacles to success.
- Identification of, and insight into, prospective volunteer campaign leaders.
- A reality check for trustees.
- Assessment of staff capacity, capability, and enthusiasm.
- Assessment of internal readiness and capacity.
- Identification of a pool of potential benefactors.
- Assessment of benefactor capacity and interest.
- An overall reaction to the proposed campaign.
- Estimate of fundraising potential (gifts and pledges) within the timeframe of the campaign.
- Strategic recommendations to be implemented going forward in the campaign.

While the university is open to creative suggestions and methodologies from development counsel, it anticipates that the firm selected will:

- Enjoy an impeccable reputation for providing ethical service to the philanthropic sector.
- Provide a detailed proposal, including methodologies, timeframe, personnel likely to be involved, study-related costs, and references.
- Use methodologies that provide constituent groups with a voice in shaping the eventual campaign and its core messages.
- Have the perspective that its interactions with university stakeholders are, in fact, cultivation opportunities.
- Conduct a series of interviews and focus groups with both internal and external stakeholders.
- Develop for those interviews and focus groups a customized questionnaire, unique to the specifics of the university and the proposed campaign.
- Have capital campaign experience providing counsel to private, preferably Catholic, colleges and universities.
- Be able to demonstrate success in similar endeavors.
- Be represented by one or more individuals with whom the President, development staff, and volunteers will enjoy positive chemistry.
- Prepare, submit, and present a final report that includes:
  - An evaluation of the findings from interviews, focus groups (or whatever methodologies are employed), and other research.
  - Recommendations for the financial goal of the campaign.
  - Recommendations for the substantive components of the case for support.
  - A campaign plan.

- ° A list of potential major benefactors (confidential appendix).
- ° A list of prospective campaign volunteer leadership (confidential appendix).
- ° A proposed operational budget and timeline for the campaign.

Saint Mary's University of Minnesota

Background
A fact sheet about Saint Mary's University of Minnesota is enclosed.

Fundraising History
Saint Mary's University of Minnesota (nee Saint Mary's College) has conducted four successful capital campaigns in the last quarter century:

	Goal	Result
• The Saint Mary's Design, 1980–1984	$5.9 million	$ 7.0 million
• Context & Vision, 1986–1990	$10 million	$12.5 million
• The Next Step, 1993–1996	$13 million	$15.0 million
• Legacy for Learning, 1999–2002	$30 million	$30.1 million

Each of the campaigns was comprehensive; dollar totals were inclusive of annual fund revenue; planned gifts were counted at present value.

The first two campaigns extensively and productively engaged volunteers. The two most recent campaigns were staff driven and led. The university seeks expanded volunteer leadership and engagement in the anticipated campaign.

Gift income totals for the most recent fiscal years at the university were:

- • 2005–2006 $4.5 million
- • 2004–2005 $5.4 million
- • 2003–2004 $8.5 million
- • 2002–2003 $6.5 million
- • 2001–2002 $4.0 million

In its history, the university has secured nine seven-figure gifts, eight of those from individuals. Of those eight individuals, four are deceased.

The primary locations of both the development office and the President's office are on the Winona (MN) campus.

Endowment
The university's endowment is approximately $35 million.

Alumni
The university has about 15,000 traditional undergraduate alumni and about 15,000 non-traditional alumni from its School of Graduate and Professional Programs. Identification, cultivation, and solicitation efforts directed at the non-traditional alumni are just beginning.

Software
The university's fundraising data base is Blackbaud's Raiser's Edge.
The university has electronic screening data for its undergraduate alumni and parent constituencies from Blackbaud Analytics.

Web Presence
The Web site of Saint Mary's University of Minnesota is http://www.smumn.edu.

Contacts

All questions, requests for clarification, and requests for additional information *prior* to submission of proposals should be directed to:

Tim Burchill, CFRE
Executive Director
The Hendrickson Institute for Ethical Leadership
Saint Mary's University of Minnesota

700 Terrace Heights #3
Winona, Minnesota 55987
Phone: 507.457.1750
E-mail: ethics@smumn.edu

Such calls will be welcomed.
Proposals should be addressed to:

Jeremy R. Wells
Vice President for Development and Alumni Relations
Saint Mary's University of Minnesota
700 Terrace Heights #30
Winona, Minnesota 55987

Please submit three (3) complete copies of your proposal.
Proposals must be received no later than **Monday, August 7, 2007**.

Source: Courtesy of Tim J. Burchill, CFRE, (deceased) Executive Director, Henrickson Institute for Ethical Leadershop, St. Mary's University of Minnesota, Winona, Minnesota.

Sample Contract Between a Consultant and an Association

WARE DEVELOPMENT CONSULTANTS
11478 Links Drive
Reston, Virginia 20198

I. Scope of Services

This agreement between Ware Development Consulting (WDC) and the ABC Association, Inc. (ABC) is for assistance in research, planning, training, and other services to be provided by WDC for the development of a Member Giving Program (the Program) for ABC. Services of WDC will be provided at the direction of ABC, on an "as needed" basis, over a period of approximately three months, and are estimated to require up to 112 hours of WDC assistance. It is understood that Molly Ware of WDC will personally provide all assistance requested by ABC under this agreement.

A. *Planning Services*

WDC shall provide planning assistance for the Program to the ABC Director of Development, which shall include assistance in the development of:

a) a management, operational, and marketing plan

b) an implementation plan; and

c) a full presentation of the Program plan to the Development Committee

B. *Writing Services*

WDC shall draft written material for the Program, to be submitted to ABC for approval, which shall include:

a) two promotional articles regarding the Program, for inclusion in an ABC Newsletter; and

b) model letters for use in response to prospective donors.

C. *Coaching and Training Services*

WDC, at the direction of ABC's Director of Development, shall provide the following training services as needed:

a) presentation training for ABC staff or others; and

b) coaching and strategic planning with staff for calls to prospective donors, and, if directed by ABC, will accompany staff on visits to prospective donors.

D. *Resource Assistance*

WDC shall assist ABC's Director of Development in promoting the Program to the ABC membership and shall advise the Director on all aspects of the Program's preparation, including:

a) selection of suppliers and the design and procurement of promotional materials;

b) selection of appropriate software programs;

c) appropriate responses to inquiries from potential donors; and

d) counsel on outside legal assistance for specific planned giving matters.

II. Fees, Schedule, and Payment

A. *Fees*

The services to be provided by WDC under this agreement are estimated to require the equivalent of fourteen days of work over a period of approximately three months. It is estimated that WDC will work in the offices of ABC one day per week during that time. WDC shall be paid by ABC at the rate of $125.00 per hour for services rendered, and WDC shall work only at the direction and approval of the Director of Development. The total fees to be paid to WDC under this agreement are estimated to be $14,000.00 but may be subject to change by mutual agreement as the needs of ABC are determined by the Director of Development.

B. Direct Costs and Reimbursable Expenses

In addition to the fees described above for services rendered, WDC shall be reimbursed by ABC for reasonable costs and expenses incurred in the completion of tasks assigned by ABC. These expenses may include costs related to printing, reproduction, delivery, telephone calls, postage, or local travel. Any expense exceeding $50.00 must be approved in advance by ABC.

C. Term

This agreement shall continue in force for a period of three months, beginning on July 28, 2008, and ending on October 28, 2008.

D. Payment

ABC shall pay WDC $4,000.00 at the initiation of work by WDC. This payment shall be credited against work to be performed by WDC on ABC's behalf. At the end of each month under this agreement, WDC shall submit an itemized invoice for services rendered and expenses incurred during that time period. ABC shall pay each invoice, after approval by the Director of Development, within ten days of approval.

E. Confidentiality

The work performed by WDC may involve confidential or proprietary information obtained from ABC or prepared by WDC for ABC. All work product submitted by WDC to ABC for payment shall become the property of ABC. WDC shall not disclose any confidential or proprietary information received from ABC or prepared for ABC to any other party without the express written permission of ABC.

F. Conflicts

During the term of this agreement, WDC shall not pursue objectives of other clients which may conflict with ABC objectives. Potential conflicts which arise shall be immediately disclosed to ABC and proper conflict avoidance shall be undertaken.

G. Additional Services

The parties may agree to modify the scope and amount of services to be provided by WDC under this agreement by mutual consent and in writing.

H. Extension

This agreement may be extended by mutual consent and in writing.

Agreed to _____
              (Date)

For: Ware Development Consulting   For: ABC Association, Inc.

By: _____   By: _____
Molly E. Ware, CFRE   John Q. Smith
Principal   Director of Development
Ware Development Consulting   **ABC Association, Inc.**
11478 Links Drive   1111 Old Town Road
Reston, Virginia 20198   Anywhere, USA 11111-1111

Source: Courtesy of Molly E. Ware, CFRE, Principal, Ware Development Consulting, Reston, Virginia.

Chapter 19

Fundraising as a Career

CHAPTER OUTLINE

- The Characteristics of a Successful Fundraiser
- Career Mapping
- Career Questions for All Disciplines
- Salaries
- Ethics in Fundraising
- The Fundraiser as a Donor Steward

- Growing Career Opportunities
- Conducting a Job Search
- The Importance of Networking
- Certification
- Education
- Turning Fundraisers into CEOs

KEY VOCABULARY

- Advanced Certified Fund Raising Executive (ACFRE)
- American Association of Homes and Services for the Aging (AAHSA)
- American Society of Association Executives (ASAE)
- Association for Healthcare Philanthropy (AHP)
- Association Foundation Group (AFG)
- Association of Fundraising Professionals (AFP)
- Certified Fund Raising Executive (CFRE)
- Chief Executive Officer (CEO)
- Council of Engineering and Scientific Society Executives (CESSE)
- Council for Advancement and Support of Education (CASE)
- Downsizing
- Ethics
- Fundraising
- Independent Sector
- Private Sector
- Public Sector
- Stewardship
- Third Sector

THE CHARACTERISTICS OF A SUCCESSFUL FUNDRAISER

Female or male, what is it that makes a good fundraiser? Why would someone want to become a fundraiser or development officer? Certainly, few of the older professional fundraisers today even knew of the profession when they were in college, let alone considered it as a career option. Today, many colleges and universities offer courses, certificates, and degrees in fundraising or nonprofit management. In fact, of the top four fields from which fundraisers enter the profession, school/student is ranked third and represents approximately 13 percent of those entering fundraising. See Exhibit 19–1.

> *Today, many colleges and universities offer courses, certificates, and degrees in fundraising or nonprofit management.*

Even some high schools are offering innovative courses on how to make money and how to give it away to local charities.

Exhibit 19–1 Top Four Fields from Which People Enter Fundraising

1) Business (17 percent United States and 18.3 percent Canada)
2) Public relations/marketing (16.8 percent United States and 20.6 percent Canada)
3) School/student (12.7 percent United States and 15.5 percent Canada)
4) Education (12 percent United States)

Source: Courtesy of the Association of Fundraising Professionals (AFP), Arlington, Virginia.

Working with a Junior Achievement affiliate and a local community foundation, the semester-long course taught students how to raise money through companies they created and then make grants to nonprofits after reviewing grant proposals. The money granted was matched by the local foundation.

Most everyone has done some fundraising at some stage of life. Whether selling Girl Scout cookies or asking relatives, friends, and neighbors to purchase wrapping paper or candy to help raise funds for a classroom, students are learning fundraising skills at a younger age than ever before. What, then, are the personality traits and skills that an individual should have to be a successful fundraiser?

In a survey of 1,800 fundraisers undertaken by the University of Pittsburgh, the most frequently mentioned traits or abilities associated with successful fundraising were good writing ability, the ability to work well with volunteers, and strong managerial skills. Others in the list were a flexible, adaptable personality; strong self esteem (without having an inflated ego); the ability to listen to others; integrity and honesty; strong leadership skills; attention to details; and a good sense of humor. If asked to put these in order of importance, it would be nearly impossible, but all of the traits listed in Exhibit 19–2 are absolute requirements of the successful development officer.

Having a good sense of humor may be the most important trait of all. One had better have a sense of humor in a profession where the workday can average 10–12 hours and the tenure of the job itself can be as short as 18 months. Plus, working with people with various personalities in itself can require an active sense of humor. A quick smile or hearty laugh at oneself can help to ease tensions, generate cooperation, and inspire confidence in your role as a leader in the organization.

CAREER MAPPING

If considering a career in fundraising, you can investigate the profession by (1) reading and doing research, (2) interviewing those currently in the profession, (3) volunteering, (4) joining the professional organizations, and (5) networking. Some individuals will do all of the aforementioned; some will choose one approach only. Whatever the method selected, make sure to thoroughly gather information. Remember, selecting a career or making a career change involves investments of time, energy, and money. Take time to thoroughly investigate this possible career path.

Deciding upon a career direction requires some introspection. What is it that you want to do with your life? What are your personal goals? What will make you happy—not just in the short run, but in the long run? Do you have any specific skills that could translate into a career track? Do you have any passions you wish to follow? Have you undertaken any volunteer work for a nonprofit that has given you a feeling of accomplishment and fits your personal values?

Many fundraisers state that one of their reasons for entering the field was that it provides the opportunity to do good works. Many choose to work for a particular organization because they believe in the cause of the organization. Although we would like to think that an orientation to public service is what brings people into the field, this is usually not the main reason. For the most part, people enter the field because they become genuinely enthusiastic about the mission of an organization or a cause that strikes their heart. If it is an emotional urge that draws a person to the profession, the individual should not lose sight of the practical side of the profession. Fundraisers have goals to meet, deadlines to keep, and a responsibility to the board, just like people in other professions. For a person to find a "fit" with an organization, he or she must find a connection between the organization's mission and his or her own personal values. If this match doesn't occur, there will not be much to keep the person working at the organization. A development professional must be able to promote the organization enthusiastically and honestly. If the professional cannot, then the organization is wrong for him or her.

In 2000 and 2001, many baby boomers, made wealthy by the stock market surge, retired much earlier than expected. Many turned to the nonprofit world for new and different volunteer or employment opportunities. Today, there is a trend for people to be offered "early retirement" by their employer. With the downsizing of the U.S. military and many government agencies, as well as many regional banks and U.S. firms such as IBM, AT&T, Xerox, and AOL, many middle-aged people faced the need to find new jobs or elected to retire. In many cases, they sought new career paths as well. In both instances, many of these individuals moved into the field of fundraising. They were well educated and committed people who thoroughly investigated the field and found that becoming a fundraiser offered a role that met their need to do something with their life that would benefit society and also offered opportunities for personal growth. They were not as concerned with upward mobility as they were with finding satisfaction. As more people entered the field, the development profession became more recognized. It is important that

---

Exhibit 19–2 Characteristics of a Development Professional

- Strong leadership skills
- Good writing skills
- Ability to work well with and motivate volunteers
- A flexible and adaptable personality
- Ability to listen to others
- Attention to details
- Strong managerial skills
- Strong self-esteem, but with the ability to give credit to others, especially when you've done all the work
- Integrity and honesty
- Sense of humor

those who enter the field bring to it the high standards that the profession requires.

As broad as the backgrounds are of those considering the field, there are just as many career opportunities for a person to investigate within the development profession. It is not likely that someone will enter the field at the senior level (vice president for advancement, chief development officer, director of development) unless he or she has had extensive nonprofit experience in a position that was involved with fundraising yet was not a development position. Rather, most will enter the field by working in a specific area of fundraising, such as direct mail, special events, corporate fundraising, major gift fundraising, the annual campaign, or planned giving. Yet, some, because of the stature of their past positions, will be able to enter at the most senior level because of the contacts they bring with them to the organization.

How do you decide on a particular field within the development profession? Begin by selecting an area in which you have an interest, in which you have some experience as a volunteer, or, at a minimum, about which you have some knowledge. Most individuals know little about planned giving, but if your background is in banking, the law, or estate planning, this may be the perfect area in which to begin your development career. Likewise, if you have worked extensively with senior corporate leaders and understand the corporate world, then perhaps corporate fundraising is where you should begin. Or if you have spent years coordinating dinners and other special events, then perhaps a position in the special events area is what you should seek.

While deciding on a career direction, a person may wish to volunteer at a nonprofit organization. This gives one the opportunity to experience the profession of fundraising first-hand and help determine the area that fits best. Whatever career path is selected within the development profession, a person will be challenged. To the novice, fundraising can be a strange but fascinating field. People frequently can feel exhilarated or exhausted. It can be the best job ever and it always will demand the highest quality work. To adapt a slogan of the Peace Corps, fundraising can be the toughest job you'll ever love!

CAREER QUESTIONS FOR ALL DISCIPLINES

What is the future of the fundraising profession? What types of people are entering the field? Who can be expected to enter the field tomorrow? Will the same skills be necessary?

Over the past 20 years, we have seen a shift from males dominating the fundraising field to females leading the fundraising efforts in nonprofit organizations. Women for years have managed volunteer organizations and learned how to develop the significant alliances needed to run a nonprofit. It is no surprise that they have taken these skills into the fundraising world. Also, women usually are more likely to help nurture younger colleagues in order to benefit the organization and the field.

Thus, more women are coming up through the ranks of fundraising.

Also, today, more fundraising leaders have a strong financial management background. Many come with an MBA degree, and even more enter the field as a second career, ready to give back to their communities after having made a substantial sum of money from the community. These new fundraisers are adept at managing large sums of money, skilled at speaking about transference of wealth, and have no qualms about asking a peer to make a six- or seven-figure gift because many have made gifts of these magnitudes themselves.

Finally, we are now seeing more young people entering fundraising directly out of college. These are children of parents who have worked in nonprofits, have been fundraisers, or have directed or been on boards of nonprofits. They have been raised to understand the need for fundraising and have known many people who have made their careers in fundraising. They have had role models to emulate, and courses and degrees in nonprofit management are now offered in their colleges and universities. The world of nonprofit management, including fundraising, is wide open to people of all ages, sexual orientations, and cultural diversities.

SALARIES

Salaries continue to rise for development professionals. In 2008, AFP released the results of its 2008 Compensation and Benefits Study. Those surveyed were AFP members in the United States and Canada. Of the AFP's 29,071 active members, 3,179 U.S. members responded to the survey. The study revealed the following information:

- The mean (average) salary for all respondents is $72,683. The median (middle value) salary is $63,000. The top 25 percent of respondent fundraisers earn more than $85,000, and the bottom 25 percent earn $48,000 less.
- There is a dramatic difference in the compensation of males and females. The average salary of male fundraisers is reported to be $88,071. Females are paid an average of $66,646.
- There is a strong correlation between years of experience and compensation. Fundraisers with less than 10 years of experience reported average salaries of $49,440–$70,580. Those with 10–14 years of experience reported average salaries of $74,840. Those with 30 or more years of experience averaged $114,545.
- Within the six regions of the United States, average salaries for all survey respondents ranged from $68,732 in the South Central area to $78,564 in the Northeast region.
- Fundraisers working in national and international organizations reported average salaries higher than those affiliated with local or state/regional entities.

"A pledge form on the back of a business card?
You must be a development director."

Source: Copyright © Mark Litzler.

- Expected strong positive correlations were noted between average compensation and the size of an organization's staff, its budget, and the amount of funds raised.
- There was also a strong positive correlation between average compensation and level of education. Those who reported holding a doctoral degree had the highest average compensation at $100,757. Only 228 individuals of the 3,179 respondents reported having less than a baccalaureate degree.
- The possession of a certification credential correlates positively with salary. In the United States sample, CFREs reported average salaries more than $19,000 higher than the average for respondents with no certification, and those who hold the ACFRE (Advanced Certified Fund Raising Executive) or FAHP (Fellow of the Association of

Healthcare Philanthropy) reported average salaries $48,000 higher than noncredentialed individuals.

Even though there are more women in fundraising today than ever before, the AFP study shows that they are still earning less than men, although some progress has been made in closing the gap. The salary gap is usually due to the type of institutions or organizations; women tend to work for smaller, local nonprofits that are arts, cultural, or social service related. Men tend to work for larger, consulting, educational, or religious organizations with larger budgets and staffs that raise significantly more money. It is thought that women do not negotiate their salaries and benefits as well as men do. Even though they are highly competent fundraisers, they haven't mastered the skills of asking for themselves.

Unfortunately, this trend doesn't seem to be changing as younger women enter the field. Considerations for family still tend to be more the responsibility of women, and today, even older women whose children have left home may now be caring for elderly parents. The result is that women often cannot move for more desirable jobs with higher pay, nor can they put in the longer hours necessary to advance their careers because of family responsibilities.

The NonProfit Times also does an annual salary survey. The *NPT 2008 Salary Survey* revealed that those responsible for raising money for nonprofit organizations can expect to see healthier pay hikes than their co-workers and even their non-development bosses. The greatest average increases of more than 1,400 organizations were for major gifts officer (6.38 percent), planned giving officer (5.10 percent), and development director (4.47 percent).

Like the AFP Study, the *NPT Salary Survey* also found that geographic location makes a difference in development director compensation with the highest average salary of $82,916 in the West and the lowest of $62,237 in the Central area, with the largest salary increases in the Southwest (6.8 percent) and South (6.56 percent). Exhibit 19–3 shows the effect of an organization's budget on development director salaries.

ETHICS IN FUNDRAISING

"Fund-raising executives are not merely raising money for the institutions that pay their salaries; they are a vital component of a sector that defines the very distinctiveness, indeed the uniqueness, of our society," says Dr. Joel Fleishman. In a recent lecture on philanthropy, Fleishman urged all fundraising executives to exert themselves to do the following:

- Shape the kinds of persons chosen to serve on the boards of your organization.
- Raise standards of accounting, planning, and stewardship in your organization.
- Have your organization report more fully to public authorities and to the public itself.

Exhibit **19–3** 2007–2008 Average Salary for Development Director by Budget Size

Overall Average:	$70,568–$73,725
Below $500,000:	$44,834–$45,288
$500,000–$999,000:	$50,065–$51,447
$1M–$9.9M:	$64,038–$66,359
$10M–$24.9M:	$81,337–$85,365
$25M–$49.9M:	$ 97,445–$101,504
$50M and above:	$104,595–$105,221

Source: Courtesy of the *NonProfit Times*, Morris Plain, New Jersey. www.nptimes.com

- Seek education and certification.
- Take pride in fundraising and volunteerism.

"You have every reason to demand accountability and propriety," says Fleishman. "Your capacity to produce funds for your employer or client depends directly on your organization's public reputation, a reputation that is likely to suffer damage as a consequence of any publicly noted failure of accountability."

Two scandals rocked the world of fundraising in the 1990s. The first was the downfall of the head of the United Way of America for improperly using the organization's funds. The second involved the fleecing of both donors and their nonprofit recipients by the head of the New Era Foundation.

Then, in the early 2000s, the public lost confidence in corporate America when the Enron corporation collapsed and several other corporations, including WorldCom and Arthur Anderson, were rocked with scandal. Unfortunately, all of these corporate scandals also drew negative publicity and attention to the field of fundraising, as many of these corporate leaders were heavily involved with local and national charities. The cloud of guilt from their illegal behavior in the corporate

> *It is imperative that the profession "police" itself and hold all who enter its doors to the highest of ethical standards.*

world carried over and tarnished the work they undertook in the nonprofit sector. Day after day, reading in the news and hearing on television about the fall of these officials, the general public tends to forget all of the honest, hardworking professionals and volunteers who make up the field. This is why it is imperative that the nonprofit world and fundraising profession "police" itself and hold all who enter its doors to the highest of ethical standards.

Increasingly, as more companies merge, downsize, or offer early retirement opportunities and more people consider fundraising as a career opportunity, the issues of how many employees are needed to raise funds and how much to pay them come to the forefront. The number of staff needed will be determined by the overall size of the organization and its fundraising plans, as will the level of staff salaries. Most development professionals work for small or mid-size organizations and do not receive large salaries. Some larger trade associations, universities, and hospitals offer very high salaries, but some of the less financially stable, nonprofit employers are asking fundraisers to take smaller salaries and work on commission for a percentage of what they raise. This creates ethical questions that need to be addressed.

Members of the Association of Fundraising Professionals (AFP) adhere to a code of ethics that prohibit them from working on commission (see Exhibit 18–5). They may accept performance-based compensation such as bonuses but not percentages of monies raised for an organization. Recently, salaries for directors of development with five years of experience have been listed in the $70,000 to $90,000 range. Senior level fundraisers have commanded salaries well into the six figures. A strong economy benefits fundraising as well as the rest of the professions.

Why is this important for a person entering the field to understand? If a person comes from the for-profit sector with a sales background, he or she may have been compensated based on the percentage of whatever it was that he or she sold that month or quarter. It may be difficult for this person to understand that this is not the practice in the development profession. For example, if a development officer was working with a major donor whose gift to the organization was to be in the six-figure range, would that donor still want to give as much if he or she knew that the development officer was going to receive 10 percent of the gift? Probably not. In addition, what would prevent a fundraiser from accepting money from a source not appropriate to the institution so he or she could receive a percentage of the gift? Would the American Cancer Society want a gift from one of the tobacco firms? Probably not. Yet if a person knew that a large gift from an inappropriate donor could be successfully solicited, the temptation to accept it would be great. Many other scenarios can be discussed, but AFP guidelines do not permit its members to work for a salary based on commission. If a person's sole interest is earning a great deal of money, then another profession should be considered. Although respectable salaries can be earned, development professionals should put the donor's interest above all other interests. It is imperative in our profession to "do the right thing!" Appendix 19–A discusses Seven Ethical "Dilemmas" in Philanthropic Fundraising.

THE FUNDRAISER AS A DONOR STEWARD

Fundraisers are continually being asked to build relationships with members of their board, donors, clients, staff, and the public in general. Probably the most important relationship to develop is that with the donor. Not only must donors be comfortable with the organization's mission, but they must trust the judgment of the organization's board and staff, who will be managing their contribution. After donors have chosen to make gifts to an organization, the board and staff must maintain contact with them to keep them informed of the activities of the organization and how their gift was used in support of the organization's mission. Donors should be sent reports on the use of their gifts at least annually. These may be letters re-thanking them for their gifts and may include a copy of the organization's annual report, calling their attention to whatever program they were supporting.

If there have been any changes in the mission, programs, or activities of the organization that will affect the intentions of a donor in making a gift, then the donor must be informed of the changes immediately. It is probably best to arrange a face-to-face meeting to discuss the changes and not to talk over the phone, especially if the gift is large. This becomes more difficult when an

organization decides to phase out a program that was established years before by an endowment fund and the original donor is deceased. It is still the responsibility of the organization to contact the remaining family or an official representative of the donor to inform them of the changes and then ask their permission to alter the use of the gift. This may even require a court order. It is unethical to use a donor's money for any purpose other than that initially specified unless permission to do so is received.

It is also important to understand that, upon accepting a gift, the organization becomes responsible for the proper investment of the funds. There should be no high-risk investment of donors' money placed in an endowment. The last thing an organization should want is to erode the corpus.

> *Upon accepting a gift, the organization becomes responsible for the proper investment of the funds.*

The financial committee of the board of the organization must establish written policies that will govern all gifts made to the organization. These should be published and made available to donors upon request. In fact, it may be useful to print them and use them when discussing possible major gifts with prospective donors.

AFP, along with the Giving Institute, formerly known as the American Association of Fundraising Counsel (AAFRC), the Association for Health Care Philanthropy (AHP), and the Council for Advancement and Support of Education (CASE), developed a Donor Bill of Rights to support donors in their desire to make gifts to nonprofit organizations and to help them feel that they have made the right decision in giving their money in support of a cause. The Donor Bill of Rights is included in its entirety in Appendix 1–A. It begins by stating, "Philanthropy is based on voluntary action for the common good. It is a tradition of giving and sharing that is primary to the quality of life. To assure that philanthropy merits the respect and trust of the general public, and that donors and prospective donors can have full confidence in the not-for-profit organizations and causes they are asked to support, we declare that all donors have these rights:"

In addition to the Donor Bill of Rights, AFP has included in its Code of Ethics (Exhibit 18–5) basic principles under which its members work when acting as stewards of a donor's money. According to the code, members shall, "to the best of their ability, ensure that contributions are used in accordance with donors' intentions" (Standard No. 14) and shall "ensure to the best of their ability, proper stewardship of charitable contributions, including timely reporting on the use and management of funds and explicit consent by the donor before altering the conditions of a gift" (Standard No. 15).

GROWING CAREER OPPORTUNITIES

Finding a job takes time; building a profession can take a lifetime. From the 1980s to today, the development profession has expanded rapidly. Membership in AFP increased from 3,559 in 1982 to more than 30,000 in 2008—an increase of 843 percent!

There are 197 AFP chapters represented throughout the United States, Canada, Mexico, and throughout the world. Expansion of the field was not only successful but necessary. More nonprofit organizations were formed to support new causes, and this required more people to raise money.

With the large increase in position openings, new names and titles were created for the fundraising executive. The most preferred term today seems to be *development officer,* but one can find advertisements for the following: advancement officer, fundraising executive, vice president, director of development, account executive, special events coordinator, major gifts officer, planned giving specialist, vice president for institutional development, annual gifts coordinator, director of resources development, and manager of organizational fundraising, among others. Whatever the titles listed for this vocation, those entering the field can expect to be challenged and be required to work for the right to use the title—it is one that has to be earned.

CONDUCTING A JOB SEARCH

If you have decided to pursue a career in fundraising, the next step is to determine for which type of institution you would prefer to work. Universities, colleges, hospitals, membership and trade associations, continuing care retirement communities, and almost all nonprofit organizations need fundraising and thus hire development professionals. The right place for you need not be found by chance. You can seek a new career or position in an organized way. Ask questions! Remember, it is your future.

First, look for an organization whose mission is of interest to you, something you can believe in, something you can support. Consider those organizations to which you already have given your time and/or money. Then look for organizations whose work is similar but with which you are not as familiar. For example, if you have been a supporter of the Sierra Club, you could then look into other environmental groups, such as the National Wildlife Federation, Conservation International, the Nature Conservancy, Defenders of Wildlife, The Wilderness Society, American Rivers, etc. If you attended and/or strongly believe in small liberal arts colleges, then you may not want to work for a development operation in a large university. Similarly, if you are attracted to liberal causes, you may not want to work for an organization that supports conservative programs.

Sooner or later, most development professionals will work in several of the many philanthropic areas—health, the arts, social science, education, association foundations, etc.—and will be

> *Sooner or later, most development professionals will work in several of the many philanthropic areas.*

required to know about all facets of the profession. Development professionals are often asked to relocate to secure the kind of job for which they are best suited and which they really desire. This is no different from

what occurs in most other careers. To be successful in a career, one may have to go to where the job is.

Second, determine whether the organization is legitimate. How many years has it existed? Who sits on its board? Is it legally incorporated? Does it have a worthy cause? What is its track record in its business and what is its record in fundraising? Ask for an annual report and other materials. Review its mission statement. Is it clear and understandable? Does it put forth the group's purpose and reason for existence? After all, if it doesn't communicate its mission clearly, is it a place where you will be comfortable working?

Third, review the volunteer leadership and executive management. Who heads the board? What is their commitment? Are they working members of the board or have they been asked to serve for use of their names only? Are these the types of individuals whose values and ethics coincide with yours? Could you work for a cause in which you did not believe even if you had the opportunity to "mingle with" Hollywood or Wall Street personalities? Also, considering that the responsibility of the board is to raise money, look at the board members critically. Do they have contacts? Do they have job descriptions that state the amount of money they are to bring yearly to the organization? Have they actively assumed financial oversight of the organization to provide it with stability? Have they made personal gifts to support the organization? Is there a long-range plan for the organization?

Fourth, review the professional staff and operations. How long have the staff members been employed by the organization? How is the organization structured? Where does the development operation fit in the overall structure? Does the head of development have direct access to the board? If not, beware! It is almost impossible to raise money for an organization if you are not directly working with or have access to its leadership.

Fifth, use your professional organizations and their resources to help you in your search. For example, AFP and CASE have created a database of individuals from culturally and ethnically diverse backgrounds to assist in networking and job placement. In addition, AFP offers a course in fundraising tailored to those entering the profession. More than 7,000 persons have participated in this course, which is offered online and through AFP chapters. AFP continues to attract thousands of people each year at its international conference, which is usually held in March or April. In addition, more than 80,000 people per year attend meetings of the local chapters of AFP or monthly luncheons, round tables, and seminars.

Sixth, ask who will be your supervisor and how that person manages daily activities. Is training provided for staff? Will the organization pay for your membership in your professional organization? Does the organization encourage attendance at professional meetings and monthly luncheons? How long has the current staff been employed by the institution? What is the institution's method for evaluating performance?

Upon completion of these tasks, the next important step is to make sure that others know that you are seeking a position in

"THE IDEAL FUND RAISING EXEC-UTIVE WILL KNOW A LITTLE BIT ABOUT ESTATE PLANNING, TAX LAW, MARKETING, AND HYPNOTISM."

Source: Copyright © Mark Litzler.

the development world, that your qualifications are superb, and that you wish to be referred to those who have positions open.

THE IMPORTANCE OF NETWORKING

Remember the old adage "It's not *what* you know, it's *who* you know"? Well, networking has its place in the field of fundraising just as it does in all other fields. Learning about the profession of fundraising can be as easy as becoming involved with fundraisers, their activities, and their professional organizations. Whether you select to volunteer for a specific organization's development office or attend conferences, monthly seminars, or weekly luncheons and round tables, opportunities are available for you to talk and work with those who are experienced in the field. See Appendix 19–B for more information on professional development.

Most development officers are members of and active in their professional organizations. Organizations to which fundraisers belong include the following:

- American Association of Homes and Services for the Aging (AAHSA)
- American Society of Association Executives (ASAE)
- Association of Fundraising Professionals (AFP)
- Association for Healthcare Philanthropy (AHP)
- Association Foundation Group (AFG)
- Council for Advancement and Support of Education (CASE)
- Council of Engineering and Scientific Society Executives (CESSE)
- EUCONSULT
- Giving Institute, formerly known as the American Association of Fundraising Counsel (AAFRC)
- Independent Sector
- Institute of Charity Fundraising Managers (ICFM)
- International Society for Third-Sector Research (ISTR)
- National Catholic Development Conference (NCDC)
- National Committee on Planned Giving (NCPG)
- National Council for Resource Development (NCRD)
- Southern Africa Institute of Fundraising (SAIF)
- United Way of America

To learn more about these organizations or other philanthropic-related organizations, visit a fundraising library, check out their

Web sites, or call to obtain more information regarding their membership requirements, costs, and benefits.

Another form of networking is selecting a mentor, someone who cares about you and your success. Meet with this person on a weekly or monthly basis and share your professional desires. Ask for direction and guidance. Your mentor should be someone you trust and respect.

CERTIFICATION

Once a development professional has five or more years of experience in the fundraising field, it may be time to consider certifi-

> *Once a development professional has five or more years of experience in the fundraising field, it may be time to consider certification.*

cation. AFP encourages certification and promotes the program for obtaining credentials as a Certified Fund Raising Executive (CFRE), which is considered "the ultimate mark of distinction for the profession." Appendix 19-B lists 10 reasons why someone should become a CFRE, how to obtain the CFRE, and the benefits of certification.

The certification process is administered by CFRE International, a 501(c)(6) organization located in Alexandria, Virginia, and founded in 2001 by AFP and AHP. The exam consists of 225 multiple choice questions, covering six major areas of fundraising: prospect identification, solicitation, donor relations, volunteerism, management, and stewardship. Prior to 1997, both AFP and AHP had their own certification programs—CFRE and CHAP, respectively. The two organizations merged to create the new board, and 15 other philanthropic organizations then joined the program (see Exhibit 19–4). Detailed information on why to become a CFRE, how to apply, and what distinguishes the designation also can be found in Appendix 19–B.

Exhibit 19–5 describes the differences between obtaining a certificate and being certified, and outlines how CFRE certification can benefit a fundraising professional's career, how to obtain the certification, and the criteria on which it is based.

A development professional can take the certification examination for the Advanced Certified Fund Raising Executive (ACFRE) after (1) being in the field a minimum of 10 years; (2) earning an undergraduate degree; (3) holding active CFRE certification status, with at least one renewal; and (4) taking management, leadership, and ethics courses. Details describing this opportunity for the advanced professional can be found in Appendix 19–C.

Also, development professionals working for associations may wish to obtain another certification—the Certified Association Executive (CAE), offered through the American Society of Association Executives (ASAE). Holding both a CFRE and a CAE can be the key to advancement in the association world.

Exhibit 19–4 CFRE Participating Organizations

CFRE International works with seventeen (17) leading philanthropic associations who endorse the certification process. These organizations are:

- Association for Healthcare Philanthropy (AHP)
- Association of Christian Development Professionals (ACDP)
- Association of Fundraising Consultants (AFC) (U.K.-based)
- Association of Fundraising Professionals (AFP)
- Association of Lutheran Development Executives (ALDE)
- Association of Philanthropic Counsel (APC)
- Canadian Association of Gift Planners*Association Canadienne des professionnels en dons planifies (CAGP*ACPDP)
- Council for Resource Development (CRD)
- Fundraising Institute—Australia (FIA)
- Fundraising Institute of New Zealand (FINZ)
- International Catholic Stewardship Council (ICSC)
- Institute of Development Professionals in Education (IDPE)
- National Catholic Development Conference (NCDC)
- New England Association for Healthcare Philanthropy (NEAHP)
- North American YMCA Development Organization (NAYDO)
- Philanthropic Service for Institutions (PSI)
- United Way of America

Source: http://www.cfre.org/cfre-participating-organisations.html.

EDUCATION

One's professional knowledge of fundraising can be expanded by taking educational courses offered by universities, colleges, nonprofit centers, etc. Most large cities offer these courses on a regular basis. In any city that has an AFP chapter or a Foundation Center, one will find fundraising classes being offered. The Foundation Center (www.fdncenter.org) provides lists of training centers across the country as well as other services vital to fundraisers, such as fundraising publications and newsletters, links to databases on grantmakers, libraries, etc.

Appendix 19–D lists the colleges and universities that specialize in the study of philanthropy. Many others offer continuing education courses and certificate programs in fundraising.

TURNING FUNDRAISERS INTO CEOS

After highly successful careers raising money, many fundraisers will seek other challenges. Many will pursue careers as the CEOs of nonprofit organizations. Prepared with the proper background, this can become the natural next step for a fundraising executive. Over the years of building a fundraising career, fundraisers will have worked closely with nonprofit executive committees and with the individual board members themselves, and will have become intimately involved with the organization's programs as they raised money for them. Plus, they understand their organizations' finances because they have worked closely with their finance departments to present the organization's financial situation to

Exhibit 19–5 Certification vs. Certificate

People ask, "What's the difference between certification and a certificate?" Take a look at the grid below. This can assist your communications with colleagues, organizational leadership, volunteers, donors, and prospects.

As stewards of the public trust, CFRE International *certifies* fundraising professionals. Unlike many certificate programs being offered by colleges and universities, CFRE International is practice-based. It is <u>not</u> intended to teach individuals how to effectively raise funds. Rather, it is designed to measure an individual's "knowledge-in-use"—the application of knowledge and skills by those with real-life experience in this role.

CFRE International promotes voluntary certification as the preferred alternative to licensure and/or government regulation.

Certification	Certificate
• Results from an *assessment* process	• Results from an *educational* process
• For individuals	• For individuals
• Typically requires some amount of professional experience	• For both newcomers and experienced professionals alike
• Awarded by a third-party, standard-setting organisation	• Awarded by educational programs or institutions
• Indicates mastery/competency as measured against a defensible set of standards, usually by application or exam	• Indicates completion of a course or series of courses with specific focus; is different than a degree granting program
• Standards set through a defensible, industry-wide process (job analysis/role delineation) that results in an outline of required knowledge and skills	• Course content set a variety of ways (faculty committee; dean; instructor, occasionally through defensible analysis of topic area)
• Typically results in a designation to use after one's name (CFRE, ACFRE, FAHP, CFP, APRA, CAE); may result in a document to hang on the wall or keep in a wallet	• Usually listed on a resume detailing education; may issue a document to hang on the wall.
• Has on-going requirements in order to maintain; holder must demonstrate he/she continues to meet requirements	• Is the end result; demonstrates knowledge of course content at the end of a set period in time

People also confuse *certification* and *credentials* and *designation*.

- *Credentials* attest to someone's knowledge or authority. Credentials can be a FBI agent badge; a letter of introduction from an ambassador to the President of the United States; a Ph.D. in physics and a list of published papers; or being called a Certified Fundraising Executive (CFRE).
- *Certification* is a process that results in credentials.
- A *designation* simply refers to the letters someone uses after their name (CFRE, Ph.D., M.D., CPA).

Source: Courtesy of CFRE International, 4900 Seminary Road, Suite 670, Alexandria, Virginia, http://www.cfre.org.

prospective donors. Thorough knowledge of all of these areas, plus others, is key to having the skills to fill a CEO position.

REFERENCES

Association of Fundraising Professionals. 2008. *2008 AFP Compensation and Benefits Study*. Arlington, VA.

Boice, J.P. 2006. Separate & unequal—A look at why men and women in the fundraising profession earn different salaries. *Advancing Philanthropy*, March/April.

Fleishman, J., Maurice G. Gurin, CFRE, Annual Lecture on Philanthropy.

Siska, D.M. 2006. Learning the business of philanthropy. *The Chronicle of Philanthropy*, May 18.

The Nonprofit Times. 2008. Nonprofit Times Salary Survey. Morris Plains, NJ.

Seven Ethical "Dilemmas" in Philanthropic Fundraising

By virtue of their missions, non-profits are often held to an even higher (some might argue, a different) standard of ethical performance than for profit corporations. While the overwhelming majority of non-profit leaders, both staff and volunteers, are persons of unimpeachable integrity, on occasion these good people make bad choices simply because they are unprepared to deal with the ethical complexities of their actions.

Over the years, I've observed what I've come to call the "Seven Ethical Dilemmas of Fundraising." These dilemmas are not obstacles to raising money, but they are issues about which all nonprofit leaders, governing boards, fundraisers, and donors need to be aware.

Dilemma #1: Tainted money—This concerns conflict between an organization's mission and the source of the contributed funds. For example, Mothers Against Drunk Driving would not accept money from Anheuser-Busch, because the company derives profits from the sale of alcohol. But an art museum or a historical society may have no issues with a gift from the same benefactor. An organization's mission always needs to be top-of-mind with its board and fundraising staff and never compromised.

Dilemma #2: Compensation—Nearly all associations of fundraisers and fundraising consultants have prohibitions in their codes of ethics against paying finder's fees and against fundraisers working on a commission basis. Nonetheless, the practice can be found, especially in small organizations that see this approach as "risk-free." Compensation for fundraisers and fundraising consultants should never be connected to the amount of funds raised. In the spirit of philanthropy, fundraisers are motivated by advancing the mission of their organizations, not by "earning" a percentage of funds raised.

Dilemma #3: Privacy—Organizations should neither obtain nor retain non-essential and highly personal information about donors in their paper or electronic files. Also, care must be taken to assure that development staff members do not take information about donors with them when they change jobs. Nonprofits need to be methodical stewards of personal information in an era where privacy concerns rightly run rampant.

Dilemma #4: Stewardship—Nonprofits must assure the public that the funds the organization raises are indeed being used for the purposes for which they were given. Non-profits must honor the spirit as well as the letter of donor intentions.

Dilemma #5: Honesty and full disclosure—Nonprofits must give people enough information to make informed giving decisions, not "sugarcoat" their organizations' stories to make them more attractive to a wider array of donors. Honesty with donors is the essential foundation of healthy benefactor relations.

Dilemma #6: Conflicts of interest—Non-profit organizations that "do business" with members of their governing boards must ensure that such transactions are completely transparent and are subject to the same rules (e.g., bidding process) as all other transactions. Other areas with potential for concern include fundraisers acting as executors for estates of their benefactors.

Dilemma #7: The appearance of impropriety—There are many things that fundraisers can do that are legal, but are unethical, such as a fundraiser benefiting personally from a benefactor's estate gift, bequest, or outright gift. The profession views such behavior negatively.

Awareness of the existence of these dilemmas can be the most important step in avoiding unethical behavior. There is no ethical dilemma when choices are clear-cut—when there is both a "right" and a "wrong" decision that can be made. However, there is an ethical dilemma inherent in choosing between two "rights." Using tainted money as an example: a school can benefit from a gift of $1 million to upgrade its technology; but the prospective benefactor is a convicted felon. Is the nature of the felony relevant? If the person has served a sentence and is rehabilitated does that matter?

Nonprofit institutions need to determine the values that are important to them (e.g., honesty, integrity, fairness, loyalty, compliance with the law, accountability, etc.). Whatever values they choose must be regarded as fundamental, but none of them are absolute. Ethical dilemmas will arise when the organization has to make a decision between two or more competing institutional values.

Making sound ethical decisions typically involves seeking counsel and perspective from other people prior to making such a decision. Practicing "Lone Ranger" ethics can be dangerous.

Source: Courtesy of Tim Burchill, CFRE, (deceased) Executive Director, The Hendrickson Institute for Ethical Leadership, Saint Mary's University of Minnesota, Winona, Minnesota.

TOP 10 REASONS TO BECOME CFRE-CERTIFIED

1. Certification grants you more credibility. CFRE certification serves as an impartial, third-party endorsement of your knowledge and experience against international standards in philanthropy. It adds to your credibility as a fundraiser and sets you apart from other professionals.

2. Certification can improve career opportunities and advancement. CFRE certification can give you the "edge" when being considered for a promotion or other career opportunities. CFRE certification clearly identifies you as an employee who has demonstrated mastery of fundraising principles and techniques based on accepted best practices.

3. Certification prepares you for greater on-the-job responsibilities. CFRE certification is a clear indicator of your willingness to invest in your own professional development. Certified professionals are aware of the constantly changing environment around their profession and possess the desire to anticipate and respond to change.

4. Certification improves skills and knowledge. Typically, achieving CFRE certification requires training, study and "keeping up" with changes. CFRE certification showcases your individual mastery by confirming proficiency and knowledge in the field. CFRE certification also requires recertification every three years, proving you stay ahead of the curve in fundraising.

5. Certification may provide for greater earnings potential. Many fundraising professionals who have become CFRE certificants experience salary and wage increases based on their certification status. Studies show that on average CFRE certificants earn 17% more than their non-certified counterparts. In addition, CFRE certificants are in high demand internationally.

6. Certification demonstrates your commitment to the fundraising profession. Receiving CFRE certification shows your peers, supervisors and, in turn, donors your commitment to your chosen career and your ability to perform to set standards.

7. Certification enhances the profession's image. CFRE certification programme seeks to grow, promote and develop certified professionals, who can stand "out in front" as role models in the fundraising field.

8. Certification reflects achievement. CFRE certification is a reflection of personal achievement because the individual has displayed mastery of his or her field by meeting requirements and standards set in philanthropy.

9. Certification builds self-esteem. CFRE certification is a step toward defining yourself beyond a job description or academic degree while gaining a sense of personal satisfaction.

10. Certification offers greater recognition from peers. As a CFRE certificant, you can expect increased recognition from your peers for taking that extra step in your professional career.

FOR MORE INFORMATION ABOUT BECOMING A CFRE, VISIT OUR WEBSITE AT WWW.CFRE.ORG OR CALL +1 703.820.5555

Source: Courtesy of CFRE International, Alexandria, Virginia.

What Distinguishes the CFRE Designation?

Certification Requires:

Fundraising Experience

Certificants have at least five years of paid, professional experience as a member of a philanthropic fundraising staff or as a consultant to a nonprofit bringing a significant knowledge base to any position.

Continuing Education

Certificants remain current with trends in best practices. Certificants are required to continue to obtain current professional development information, explore new knowledge in specific content areas, master new fundraising related skills and techniques, and conduct professional practice in an ethical and appropriate manner

Demonstrated Fundraising Performance

Certificants have a proven track record of performance with communications projects, management assignments, or front line fundraising experience with outcomes that directly impact the development function of their organisation and must demonstrate this throughout their certification.

Community Service

Certificants are personally and professionally invested in their community. Through participation in professional associations and/or community organisations (i.e., local church, youth groups, service clubs, etc.), members are active volunteers who care about their community.

Candidates adhere to the Donor Bill of Rights

Candidates pledge adherence to Accountability Standards

Now Is The Time To Become CFRE Certified

IN EVERY FIELD, the professionals who receive the best positions and the most respect are those who have obtained the relevant certification. The Certified Fund Raising Executive (CFRE) credential provides you with a way to demonstrate your achievements, integrity and mastery of the philanthropic fundraising profession. It also signals to your employer, colleagues, the community and potential donors that you have the knowledge and skills to be an effective fundraising executive.

In today's world, where the actions of more and more people in government and industry show an erosion of personal ethics, employers and donors want to know they are working with allies they can trust. The CFRE standard sends the message that you are committed to upholding the Donor Bill of Rights and a defined set of Accountability Standards. And it tells others you are committed to continuing your professional growth through ongoing education. That's a lot of credibility to be gained from one programme.

Does It Pay to Become Certified?

A major salary survey conducted by the Association of Fundraising Professionals (AFP), conducted in 2003, showed that fundraising professionals who are certified earned an average of 23% more than their non-certified counterparts.

What Other Colleagues Are Saying About Becoming Certified

"The certification process provided a personal challenge that tested my knowledge of the profession and gave me a tremendous feeling of accomplishment when I received the designation. I think it establishes your credibility among your peers and a standard by which to measure your own performance." — *Nan Selz, CFRE St. Vincent Foundation, Little Rock, AR USA*

"I got tired of people from other fields taking fundraising jobs. That's why I got my CFRE. It tells the world I'm a fundraiser. That I'm dedicated to the profession." — *Steve Thomas, CFRE Chairman and Creative Director, Stephen Thomas, Inc., Toronto, ON Canada*

Join Us On The Journey of a Lifetime

Fundraising is often a solitary endeavour. You are someone who has chosen not the easiest of professions; who has chosen not the easiest of topics (giving away money). You may find yourself walking lonely halls with no other development savvy professionals to support new ideas, stewardship decisions or even ethical frameworks. Yet, you have the power to transform the organisations you work for and connect it with its future.

You may never have to walk those lonely halls alone again. You are invited to walk in the company of giants - become a Certified Fund Raising Executive (CFRE).

Physicists have Planck and Bohr, psychologists Freud and Jung. These great thinkers developed theoretical constructs, tested concepts and forwarded results to make infinite universes understandable and applicable to everyday practitioners.

CFRE certificants, through our commitment to excellence, continued learning and growth in attaining and maintaining the CFRE, have Seymour and Rosso, Greenfield and Joyaux with us to affirm practice, buttress ethics, detail tactics and illuminate best practices. The CFRE credential demonstrates that you have that commitment, too.

The CFRE credential means a commitment to personal growth, not expediency, theory not conjecture as you emulate the great thinkers in the field and their knowledge, gleaned from countless years of experience and trial. CFRE certificants get a leg up on efficiency, effectiveness. CFRE certificants walk those lonely halls with a cadre of like-minded professionals connected by a common desire to do the most they can for their organisations.

You, too, can have the credibility the CFRE brings to fundraising. You can have the increased opportunities for employment and advancement. You can have the peer-recognition and personal satisfaction of meeting standards in your chosen career. You can have the company of nearly 4,800 fundraising professionals around the world who want to make the biggest impact for their donors and employers.

Becoming a Certified Fund Raising Executive (CFRE) has never been easier. Now with a computer-based exam providing immediate test results available in over 300 locations in North America and a new web-based application process, you don't have to wait.

Join the company of greatness. Become a CFRE today. **Visit www.cfre.org for complete details.**

Apply Online...Get Started Today!

THEY SAY THE BEST THINGS in life are free. That's why we've made starting your CFRE application absolutely free. Simply, go to www.cfre.org and click on **Apply Online Now**. You'll be taken through all of the steps to complete your application. When YOU'RE ready to take the test, that's when we'll collect the fees.

How Much Does the Exam Cost?

Individuals taking the computer-based exam in North America, who are members of a participating organization (ACDP, AFC, AHP, AFP, ALDE, APC, CAGP*ACPDP, CRD, FIA, FINZ, NAYDO, NEAHP, NCDC, ICSC, IDPE, PSI and United Way) pay a reduced fee of $520 USD. This is the application and computer-based exam fee. Individuals who are not members of the above organizations pay $770 USD.

Individuals outside North America, who are still taking the paper-and-pencil exam, pay $425 USD or $660 USD.

CFRE
Certified Fund Raising Executive   Setting Standards in Philanthropy

Certified Fund Raising Executive (CFRE) Online Application
Welcome to the CFRE online application.

If you are returning to complete an application you have already initiated, please complete the login information and proceed to your secure private account

If you are initiating an application, please complete the login and new user section and select "Create new account".

Home
Study Wizard
Apply Now
Library
0. Introduction
1. Personal Information
2. Memberships
3. Method of Payment
4. Demographic Questionnaire
5. Education
6. Continuing Education
7. Professional Practice
8. Professional Performance
9. Communications
10. Management
11. Actual Funds Raised
12. Service
13. Accountability Standards
14. Application Summary
15. Application Checklist
16. Permission to Notify Employer
Survey

Email:
Password: [Log in]
☐ Forgot Password

Retype password: (new users only)
Company: [Create new account]

info@cfre.org ~ 703/820-5555
All materials copyright 2001-2006. All Rights Reserved.

Advanced Certified Fund Raising Executive (ACFRE)

The Advanced Certified Fund Raising Executive (ACFRE) certification program of AFP is designed as a means for identifying superior mastery of the profession. It offers professionals a means to distinguish themselves, employers a way to identify advanced fund-raisers, and philanthropy an opportunity for enriched interactions between donors and advanced-level executives. The process involves an application, exam, portfolio review, and oral peer review.

ELIGIBILITY REQUIREMENTS

- Current employment in the profession.
- Current CFRE credential and having recertified at least once.
- Minimum of 10 years of full-time paid professional experience in the fundraising field.
- BS/BA or equivalent experience.
- Adherence to AFP's Code of Ethical Principles and Standards of Professional Practice.
- Membership and active participation in field related fundraising organizations with demonstrated volunteer service to other not-for-profit organizations.
- Participation as an attendee and/or instructor within the previous five years in at least 15 contact hours of senior-level organizational leadership courses, such as those offered by AAHSA, AFP, AHP, or CASE.

- Participation as an attendee and/or instructor within the previous five years in at least 15 contact hours of senior-level organizational management courses.
- Participation within the previous five years in at least five contact hours of ethics courses.

STEPS TO BECOMING AN ACFRE

1. Submit an Advanced Certification Application to and obtain approval by the ACFRE Board.
2. Achieve a passing score on the written examination, which covers general development, ethics, fundraising, management, and leadership skills.
3. Successfully complete a peer review by submitting a portfolio of development materials, with an emphasis on special skills areas, and a written synopsis of use and results.
4. Successfully complete an oral peer review evaluation by demonstrating competency in two areas, such as annual giving, direct mail, special events, corporate and foundation solicitation, capital campaigns, planned giving, not-for-profit management, etc.

Candidates must complete the entire ACFRE process within three years from the date the ACFRE application was approved by the ACFRE Board. Upon successful completion of all four steps, the ACFRE designation is conferred for life.

Source: About the Advanced Certified Fundraising Executive (ACFRE) program (http://www.afpnet.org).

College and University Centers Specializing in the Study of Philanthropy

A. NONPROFIT MANAGEMENT COURSES IN THE UNITED STATES—BY STATE

AL

Auburn University–Montgomery (Montgomery, AL)

University of Alabama–Birmingham (Birmingham, AL)

AR

University of Arkansas–Little Rock (Little Rock, AR)

University of Arkansas–Little Rock–American Humanics (Little Rock, AR)

AZ

Arizona State University (Tempe, AZ)

University of Arizona (Tucson, AZ)

CA

Alliant International University (San Diego, CA)

Azusa Pacific University (Azusa, CA)

California State Polytechnic University (Pomona, CA)

California State University–Hayward (Hayward, CA)

California State University–Los Angeles (Los Angeles, CA)

California State University–Los Angeles–Political Science (Los Angeles, CA)

California State University–San Bernardino (San Bernardino, CA)

California State University–Fresno (Fresno, CA)

California State University–Fullerton (Fullerton, CA)

California State University–Long Beach (Long Beach, CA)

Fielding Graduate Institute (Santa Barbara, CA)

Pepperdine University (Malibu, CA)

San Diego State University (San Diego, CA)

San Francisco State University (San Francisco, CA)

San Jose State University (San Jose, CA)

University of California–Berkeley (Berkeley, CA)

University of California–Irvine (Irvine, CA)

University of California–Los Angeles (Los Angeles, CA)

University of California–Riverside (Riverside, CA)

University of Judaism (Los Angeles, CA)

University of San Diego (San Diego, CA)

University of San Diego–American Humanics (San Diego, CA)

University of San Francisco (San Francisco, CA)

University of Southern California (Los Angeles, CA)

CO

Metropolitan State College of Denver (Denver, CO)

Regis University (Denver, CO)

University of Colorado–Colorado Springs (Colorado Springs, CO)

University of Colorado–Denver (Denver, CO)

University of Northern Colorado (Greeley, CO)

CT

Eastern Connecticut State University (Willimantic, CT)

Sacred Heart University (Fairfield, CT)

Southern Connecticut State University (New Haven, CT)

University of Connecticut (West Hartford, CT)

Yale University (New Haven, CT)

DC

Georgetown University (Washington, DC)

Howard University (Washington, DC)

The George Washington University (Washington, DC)

University of the District of Columbia (Washington, DC)

DE

University of Delaware (Newark, DE)

FL

Barry University (Miami Lakes, FL)

Florida Atlantic University (Ft. Lauderdale, FL)

Florida State University (Tallahassee, FL)

University of Central Florida (Orlando, FL)

University of Central Florida–American Humanics (Orlando, FL)

University of Florida (Gainesville, FL)

University of South Florida (Tampa, FL)

University of West Florida (Pensacola, FL)

Source: Updated from: Roseanne M. Mirabella, PhD, Department of Political Science, Seton Hall University, Nonprofit Management Courses in the United States, http://tltc.shu.edu/npo/, © 2006.

GA

Clayton College and State University (Morrow, GA)
Georgia College and State University (Milledgeville, GA)
Georgia State University (Atlanta, GA)
Kennesaw State University (Kennesaw, GA)
University of Georgia (Athens, GA)

IA

Graceland University (Lamoni, IA)
Luther College (Decorah, IA)
University of Iowa (Iowa City, IA)
University of Northern Iowa (Cedar Falls, IA)
University of Northern Iowa–American Humanics
    (Cedar Falls, IA)

IL

Aurora University (Aurora, IL)
DePaul University (Chicago, IL)
Illinois Institute of Technology (Chicago, IL)
Loyola University Chicago (Chicago, IL)
North Park University (Chicago, IL)
Northern Illinois University (De Kalb, IL)
Northwestern University (Evanston, IL)
Northwestern University School of Continuing Studies
    (Chicago, IL)
Roosevelt University (Chicago, IL)
Saint Xavier University (Chicago, IL)
Southern Illinois University–Edwardsville (Edwardsville, IL)
Spertus Institute of Jewish Studies (Chicago, IL)
University of Illinois at Chicago (Chicago, IL)
Western Illinois University (Macomb, IL)

IN

Indiana State University (Terre Haute, IN)
Indiana University–Bloomington (Bloomington, IN)
Indiana University–Center on Philanthropy (Indianapolis, IN)
Indiana University–Purdue University–Indianapolis
    (Indianapolis, IN)
University of Notre Dame (South Bend, IN)

KS

Kansas State University (Manhattan, KS)
Wichita State University (Wichita, KS)

KY

Murray State University (Murray, KY)
Western Kentucky University (Bowling Green, KY)

LA

Louisiana State University in Shreveport (Shreveport, LA)
Southern University (Baton Rouge, LA)
Xavier University of Louisiana (New Orleans, LA)

MA

Boston College (Chestnut Hill, MA)
Boston University School of Management (Boston, MA)

Boston University School of Social Work (Boston, MA)
Brandeis University (Waltham, MA)
Cambridge College (Cambridge, MA)
Clark University (Worcester, MA)
Harvard Business School (Boston, MA)
Harvard University (Cambridge, MA)
Lesley College (Cambridge, MA)
Tufts University (Medford, MA)
University of Massachusetts–Amherst (Amherst, MA)
Worcester State College (Worcester, MA)

MD

College of Notre Dame of Maryland (Baltimore, MD)
Coppin State College (Baltimore, MD)
Goucher College (Baltimore, MD)
Johns Hopkins University (Baltimore, MD)
University of Baltimore (Baltimore, MD)
University of Maryland–College Park (College Park, MD)
University of Maryland–University College (Adelphi, MD)

MI

Eastern Michigan University (Ypslanti, MI)
Grand Valley State University (Grand Rapids, MI)
Lawrence Technological University (Southfield, MI)
Michigan State University (Canton, MI)
Oakland University (Rochester, MI)
University of Michigan (Ann Arbor, MI)
University of Michigan School of Social Work (Ann Arbor, MI)
Walsh College (Troy, MI)
Wayne State University (Detroit, MI)
Western Michigan University (Battle Creek, MI)

MN

Hamline University (St. Paul, MN)
Saint Mary's University of Minnesota (Winona, MN)
St. Cloud State University (St. Cloud, MN)
University of Minnesota–Humphrey Institute (Minneapolis,
    MN)
University of St. Thomas–Center for Nonprofit Management
    (Minneapolis, MN)

MO

Lindenwood University (St. Charles, MO)
Missouri Valley College (Marshall, MO)
Park University (Kansas City, MO)
Rockhurst University (Kansas City, MO)
St. Louis University (St. Louis, MO)
University of Missouri–Kansas City (Kansas City, MO)
University of Missouri–St. Louis (St. Louis, MO)
William Jewell College (Liberty, MO)

MS

University of Southern Mississippi (Hattiesburg, MS)
University of Southern Mississippi–American Humanics
    (Hattiesburg, MS)

MT

The University of Montana (Missoula, MT)

NC

Duke University (Hillsborough, NC)
High Point University (High Point, NC)
North Carolina State University (Raleigh, NC)
Shaw University American Humanics (Raleigh, NC)
University of North Carolina–Greensboro (Greensboro, NC)
University of North Carolina–Chapel Hill (Chapel Hill, NC)
University of North Carolina–Chapel Hill–Social Work
     (Chapel Hill, NC)

ND

University of North Dakota (Grand Forks, ND)

NE

University of Nebraska–Omaha (Omaha, NE)

NH

Antioch University (Keene, NH)
Dartmouth College (Hanover, NH)
University of New Hampshire (Durham, NH)

NJ

Kean University (Union, NJ)
Rutgers University–Newark (Newark, NJ)
Rutgers University/Camden College (Camden, NJ)
Seton Hall University (South Orange, NJ)
The College of New Jersey (Ewing, NJ)

NV

University of Nevada, Reno (Reno, NV)

NY

Binghamton University (Binghamton, NY)
C.W. Post College (Brookville, NY)
Columbia University–Division of Executive Education (New
     York, NY)
Columbia University–Graduate School of Business (New York,
     NY)
Columbia University–School of International and Public Affairs
     (New York, NY)
CUNY–Baruch College (New York, NY)
CUNY–Hunter College (New York, NY)
Long Island University (Brooklyn, NY)
Marist College (Poughkeepsie, NY)
Marymount College (Tarrytown, NY)
New School University (New York, NY)
New York University–School of Continuing & Professional
     Studies–The George H. Heyman, Jr. Center for Philanthropy
     and Fundraising (New York, NY)
New York University–Wagner Graduate School (New York, NY)
Roberts Wesleyan College (Rochester, NY)
Siena College (Loudonville, NY)
SUNY College–Brockport (Brockport, NY)
SUNY College–Buffalo (Buffalo, NY)

SUNY College–Oneonta (Oneonta, NY)
SUNY College–Oswego (Oswego, NY)
SUNY University–Albany (Albany, NY)
SUNY University–Buffalo (Buffalo, NY)
Syracuse University (Syracuse, NY)
Yeshiva University (New York, NY)

OH

Case Western Reserve University (Cleveland, OH)
Cleveland State University (Cleveland, OH)
Franklin University (Columbus, OH)
Kent State University (Kent, OH)
Ohio State University (Columbus, OH)
The Union Institute (Cincinnati, OH)
University of Akron (Akron, OH)
Wright State University (Dayton, OH)
Youngstown State University (Youngstown, OH)

OR

Portland State University–Division of Public Administration
     (Portland, OR)
Portland State University–Social Work (Portland, OR)
Southern Oregon University (Ashland, OR)
University of Oregon (Eugene, OR)

PA

Bryn Mawr College (Bryn Mawr, PA)
Bucknell University (Lewisburg, PA)
Eastern University (St. Davids, PA)
Indiana University of Pennsylvania (Indiana, PA)
LaSalle University (Philadelphia, PA)
Marywood University (Scranton, PA)
Robert Morris University (Moon Township, PA)
Slippery Rock University (Slippery Rock, PA)
Temple University (Philadelphia, PA)
University of Pennsylvania (Philadelphia, PA)
University of Pittsburgh (Pittsburgh, PA)
Widener University (Chester, PA)

RI

Providence College (Providence, RI)
Rhode Island College (Providence, RI)

SC

Clemson University (Clemson, SC)
College of Charleston (Charleston, SC)
University of South Carolina–Upstate (Spartanburg, SC)

SD

South Dakota State University (Brookings, SD)
University of South Dakota (Vermillion, SD)

TN

Austin Peay State University (Clarksville, TN)
Crichton College (Memphis, TN)
LeMoyne-Owen College (Memphis, TN)
Maryville College (Maryville, TN)

Southern Adventist University (Collegedale, TN)
University of Memphis (Memphis, TN)
University of Tennessee–Chattanooga (Chattanooga, TN)
Vanderbilt University (Nashville, TN)

TX
Abilene Christian University (Abilene, TX)
Baylor University (Waco, TX)
Texas Tech University (Lubbock, TX)
University of Dallas (Irving, TX)
University of Houston (Houston, TX)
University of Houston–Victoria (Victoria, TX)
University of North Texas (Denton, TX)
University of Texas–Austin–Thompson Conference Center
    (Austin, TX)
University of Texas–Austin–Lyndon B. Johnson School of
    Public Affairs (Austin, TX)
University of Texas–San Antonio (San Antonio, TX)

VA
George Mason University (Fairfax, VA)
University of Richmond (University of Richmond, VA)
Virginia Commonwealth University (Richmond, VA)
Virginia Tech (Blacksburg, VA)

VT
Johnson State College (Johnson, VT)
School for International Training (Brattleboro, VT)

WA
Seattle University (Seattle, WA)
University of Washington MPA Program (Seattle, WA)
University of Washington School of Social Work
    (Seattle, WA)
University of Washington–Tacoma (Tacoma, WA)
Washington State University (Pullman, WA)

WI
Lakeland College (Plymouth, WI)
University of Wisconsin–Milwaukee (Milwaukee, WI)
University of Wisconsin–Madison (Madison, WI)
University of Wisconsin–Superior (Superior, WI)

WV
Salem International University (Salem, WV)
West Virginia University (Morgantown, WV)

B. PHILANTHROPIC COURSES OFFERED ONLINE— BY STATE

CA
California State University–Long Beach (Long Beach, CA)
University of California–Los Angeles (Los Angeles, CA)
University of San Francisco (San Francisco, CA)

CO
Regis University (Denver, CO)
University of Colorado–Denver (Denver, CO)

FL
University of Central Florida (Orlando, FL)

IA
University of Iowa (Iowa City, IA)

IL
North Park University (Chicago, IL)
University of Illinois–Chicago (Chicago, IL)

IN
Indiana University–Purdue University–Indianapolis
    (Indianapolis, IN)

MD
University of Maryland–University College (Adelphi, MD)

MI
Michigan State University (Canton, MI)

MO
Park University (Kansas City, MO)

TN
University of Memphis (Memphis, TN)

TX
University of Dallas (Irving, TX)
University of North Texas (Denton, TX)

VA
George Mason University (Fairfax, VA)

C. SCHOOLS OFFERING DOCTORATE DEGREES IN NONPROFIT MANAGEMENT—ALPHABETICALLY

CA
Fielding Graduate Institute (Santa Barbara, CA)
University of San Diego (San Diego, CA)

CO
University of Colorado–Denver (Denver, CO)

FL
Florida State University (Tallahassee, FL)

IL
Northern Illinois University (De Kalb, IL)

IN
Indiana University–Bloomington (Bloomington, IN)
Indiana University–Center on Philanthropy (Indianapolis, IN)

MA
Boston University School of Management (Boston, MA)
Brandeis University (Waltham, MA)
Harvard University (Cambridge, MA)

MO
St. Louis University (St. Louis, MO)
University of Missouri–Kansas City (Kansas City, MO)

NE
University of Nebraska–Omaha (Omaha, NE)

NJ
Rutgers University–Newark (Newark, NJ)

NY
New York University–Wagner Graduate School (New York, NY)
Syracuse University (Syracuse, NY)
Yeshiva University (New York, NY)

OH
Case Western Reserve University (Cleveland, OH)
Cleveland State University (Cleveland, OH)
The Union Institute (Cincinnati, OH)

OR
Portland State University–Division of Public Administration (Portland, OR)

PA
Indiana University of Pennsylvania (Indiana, PA)
Robert Morris University (Moon Township, PA)
University of Pittsburgh (Pittsburgh, PA)

TX
University of Texas–Austin–Lyndon B. Johnson School of Public Affairs (Austin, TX)

VA
Virginia Tech (Blacksburg, VA)

Compliance with Fundraising Laws and Regulations

A nonprofit organization is defined as an organization that pertains to or provides services of benefit to the public without financial incentive. Before soliciting tax-deductible gifts, the organization must first be qualified by the Internal Revenue Service (IRS) as a tax-exempt organization with the designation of 501(c)(3) from the federal tax code. Because of this special designation, nonprofit organizations are subject to certain federal, state, and local government laws and regulations. Of particular importance to development professionals are those regulations pertaining to charitable solicitations, proper filing of the Form 990, the organization's federal tax return, and fundraising administration. To assist nonprofit organizations, the IRS has developed a new Web site, *Stay Exempt: Tax Basics for 501(c)(3)s* (http://www.stayexempt.org), that offers online training in five key issues related to nonprofit operations including completing the redesigned Form 990, short summaries of each presentation, a glossary of tax terms, a list of frequently asked questions, and the appropriate forms and publications a nonprofit will need to use.

AT THE FEDERAL LEVEL

Filing the Form 990

The IRS is the main agency of the federal government involved in regulating fundraising administration. In 2008, the Form 990 was redesigned, the first major overhaul since 1979. It now includes a core form and a series of schedules that may need to be completed. The core form allows an organization to describe its exempt accomplishments and mission up-front and provides more opportunities throughout the form for the organization to explain its activities. A checklist of schedules also was added.

Some areas of major changes in reporting requirements from the 2007 Form 990 include a new governance section and substantial revisions to the reporting of the organization's compensation of officers, directors, trustees, key employees, and highest compensated employees. For example, PART VI, *Governance, Management, and Disclosure*, is a new section that asks questions about the organization's governance structure, policies and prac-

tices. The IRS considers such policies and practices for which information is sought generally to improve tax compliance. Part VII, *Compensation of Officers, Directors, Trustees, Key Employees, Highest Compensated Employees, and Independent Contractors*, also contains important changes, including new definitions of officer and key employee applicable to all organizations, and the extension of reporting compensation paid to the top five highest compensated employees and top five independent contractors to all organizations filing the Form 990, which now includes social welfare organizations, business leagues, trade associations, and social clubs. The additional compensation information is needed to more effectively administer the laws regarding inurement, exempt purpose, and private benefit, as applicable to these organizations. Visit http://www.irs.gov/charities/pub to see the final 2008 Form 990 core form and Schedules A–R.

It is very important for the development staff to be involved in preparing the organization's 990 given it reflects the organization's fundraising progress and is available for public inspection. At the very minimum, even if there is no role for them to help in its preparation, the senior member of the development or foundation staff should know what the 990 reports. This is true, too, for a nonprofit organization's board of directors. In the new Form 990's governance section, line 10 asks whether the Form 990 is provided to the governing body before it is filed with the IRS, and directs all organizations to describe in Schedule O the process, if any, the organization uses to review the form before or after it is filed with the IRS.

Tax Deductibility of Charitable Gifts

The IRS has two excellent, comprehensive and up-to-date publications to help nonprofit organizations and donors determine the tax deductibility of charitable gifts. Nonprofit organizations should refer to IRS Publication 1771—Charitable Contributions—Substantiation and Disclosure Requirements while donors should refer to IRS Publication 526—Charitable Contributions.

Substantiation

In a case of a donation of $250 or more, no charitable deduction is allowed unless the donor obtains written acknowledgment from the charity in a timely manner and keeps this document. The acknowledgment must describe and declare the value of any goods or services provided by the charity to the donor.

With this rule, it is no longer permissible to use a canceled check as documentation of a charitable gift of $250 or greater.

Disclosure of Quid Pro Quo Contributions

When a contribution exceeds $75 and the donor is receiving something of value in return, the charity must tell the donor that the only portion of the contribution that is tax deductible is the amount that exceeds the fair market value of whatever the donor received in return. The charity must also provide the donor with an estimate of the fair market value for the goods or services provided to the donor. If the organization has a gala for which tickets are $100 and where food and entertainment with a fair market value of $50 is provided, you must include on the solicitation materials a statement to the effect that only $50 of the ticket price is tax deductible, and that the fair market value of admission to the event (food and entertainment) is $50.

Sample language to use:

"No goods or services were received in exchange for this contribution."

"We very much appreciate your gift of $XXX (or description of property). In appreciation of your gift, we provided you with _____ (insert description), which has an estimated value of $ _____. The amount of your contribution that is deductible for federal income tax purposes is limited to the excess of your contribution over the value of goods and services we provided to you."

According to the IRS regulations, donors do not have to reduce the deductible amount of their donation when they receive low-cost items or items of "insubstantial" value. A donor's gift is fully deductible if the following occurs:

- The donor receives benefits having a fair market value of less than 2 percent of the amount of the contribution or $89, whichever is less; or
- The donor made a contribution of $44.50 or more and received a token benefit (such as a coffee mug, key chain, or bookmark) bearing the charity's name and logo that costs the charity $8.90 or less. For this purpose only, the measurement used is the actual cost to the charity to purchase the item, not the fair market value of the item.

The dollar amounts used above (tax year 2007) are adjusted annually by the IRS for inflation using the Consumer Price Index.

Here are some examples to help you see how to put these rules into practice.

1) A donor gives a gift of $2,500 and receives $125 worth of benefits (perhaps two people attending a special reception and dinner). The cost of the dinner is greater than either 2 percent of the value of the gift ($50) or $89; therefore, the actual amount of the charitable deduction is $2,375 (i.e., $2,500—$125).
2) A donor who gives a gift of $65 receives a coffee mug that costs the charity $5.00. The donor can claim the full amount of the contribution as a charitable deduction because the value is less than $8.90.

See Exhibit A–1 for a sample acknowledgement letter. Also see Exhibit A–2 for a sample sponsor acknowledgement letter.

Federal Tax Documents Available to the Public

Federal tax documents must be available for inspection by the public. The following federal tax documents should be available for inspection, upon request during normal business hours, at your principal office and any regional or district office with three or more full-time employees. Tax legislation enacted in 1996 also requires that you honor in-person or written requests for copies of these documents.

- The annual Form 990, for the preceding three years, including all attachments and schedules (except you may omit lists of names or addresses of contributors), and the Form 990-T for unrelated business tax.
- Form 1023 or 1024, the original application for tax exempt status, with all materials submitted in support of the application.
- The IRS's determination letter issued in response to your application for tax exempt status or any IRS letters issued in response to your annual tax return.

Documents must be provided free of charge, except that you may charge a reasonable fee for reproduction and mailing costs, e.g., $1.00 for the first page and $.15 for each additional page of copying. You may not require the person making the request to tell you the reason they wish to see the materials.

AT THE STATE LEVEL

Registration to Solicit Funds

Many states require registration of charitable organizations, fundraising counsel, and professional fundraisers (telemarketing and direct mail firms). In most states, registration for all three types of organizations is handled by the Secretary of State or the Attorney General. In a few states, registration is handled by the Department of Consumer Protection or the Department of Agriculture. The development department is responsible for seeing that the organization is in compliance with all state registration requirements. In addition, fundraising counsel, telemarketing, and direct mail firms that the organization employs also must be properly registered.

Exhibit A–1 Sample Acknowledgment Letter

June 15, XXXX

Name
Address
City, State Zip

Dear Mr./Ms. Last Name:

On behalf of the ASCE Foundation, please let me extend our thanks for your gift of $100.00 received on June 13, XXXX, to the Foundation's XXXX *Annual Appeal*. This gift, along with your previous gift of $100.00 received on December 8, XXXX, brings your total contribution to the XXXX *Annual Appeal* to $200.00. We will be pleased to recognize your gifts at the Patron Level in the next issue of the *ASCE Foundation News*.

The IRS requires that the ASCE Foundation, a 501(c)(3) organization, provide contemporaneous acknowledgment of all gifts and include the fact that the Foundation provided no goods or services in exchange for these contributions. This letter serves not only to acknowledge this gift, but also to notify you that no goods or services were given by the ASCE Foundation in return for your gift of $100.00. This is your official tax receipt. Please retain it for tax-filing purposes.

Please know that your generosity serves as an important example to other ASCE Members, their colleagues, and friends, and helps to establish a strong base of support for the Foundation and civil engineering philanthropy.

Again, thank you for your most generous gift.

Sincerely yours,

Jeanne G. Jacob, CAE, CFRE
Executive Vice President
ASCE Foundation

Since the definitions of those who need to register vary state by state, it is best that inquiries be made directly to appropriate state regulatory agencies. Generally, charitable organizations are 501(c)(3)s, plus some other organizations. Fundraising counsel are those individuals that give advice, counsel, or assistance on any type of fundraising campaign; they never have possession or control of client funds and are not authorized to expend client funds without prior approval. Professional fundraisers are those who conduct fundraising campaigns including telemarketing and direct mail firms; also included are those who have possession or control of client funds or are authorized to expend client funds without prior approval of client.

As for exemptions from registering, virtually all states have exemptions for religious organizations, organizations that raise less than $25,000 per year, hospitals, and educational institutions. Other types of exemptions vary greatly state by state. There are no exemptions for fundraising counsel and professional fundraisers. As for application procedures, approximately 39 states accept the uniform registration statement for charities. To see which states accept the form and to download a copy of the form, visit http://www.nonprofits.org/library/gov/urs. There are no uniform applications for professional fundraisers and fundraising counsel.

Registration in all appropriate states where your organization solicits charitable contributions will consume a significant amount of staff time to compile the necessary information for the preparation of registration applications and the subsequent filing of campaign reports. All states require renewal on an annual basis; however, compliance with registration requirements is required. Remember, it is not an option. Failure to comply with a state's registration requirements before fundraising in that state could result in significant fines to the organization and even the personal liability of corporate officers and staff to any state in which the organization failed to register.

Exhibit A–2 Sample Sponsor Acknowledgment Letter

March 24, XXXX

Name
Title
Firm
Address
City, State Zip

Dear Mr./Ms Last Name:

On behalf of the ASCE Foundation and the Society it serves, please let me extend our thanks to FIRM NAME for its gift of $20,000.00, received on March 22, XXXX. This completes payment on your pledge for sponsorship at the Diamond Circle for the American Society of Civil Engineering's OPAL Awards Dinner, being held at the Ronald Reagan Building and International Trade Center, Washington, D.C., on April 25, XXXX.

The IRS requires that the ASCE Foundation, a 501(c)(3) organization, provide contemporaneous acknowledgment of all gifts and include whether or not the Foundation provided goods or services in exchange for these contributions. This letter serves not only to acknowledge this gift, but also to notify FIRM NAME that it will receive 16 tickets at $275.00 per ticket, of which $115.00 is taxable, for a total of $1,840.00 in goods or services in return for its gift of $20,000.00. This document is your official tax receipt. Please retain it for tax-filing purposes.

The OPAL Awards recognize the best of civil engineering. We are delighted that you will be joining us for the presentation of these most prestigious awards.

Again, thank you to FIRM NAME for sponsoring ASCE's OPAL Awards Dinner.

Sincerely yours,

Jeanne G. Jacob, CAE, CFRE
Executive Vice President
ASCE Foundation

Further, the failure to register could ultimately result in a court injunction, which permanently prohibits the charity, professional fundraiser, or fundraising counsel from carrying out any operations in that state, and, in some circumstances, has resulted in the forced dissolution of fundraisers, counsel, and even charitable organizations.

The amount of resources required to comply with registration requirements is not insignificant, but any fundraising organization that fails to comply with the appropriate state registration requirements is putting its continued existence at risk. To find firms or companies that will assist nonprofits for a fee in complying with their registration requirements, see the listing in the services section of each *Chronicle of Philanthropy*.

The following provides a sampling of state regulations.

CALIFORNIA

STATE REGULATORY AGENCY: Registry of Charitable Trusts
CHARITABLE ORGANIZATIONS:
REGISTRATION/LICENSING: State accepts unified registration form.

Initial registration for organizations located, doing business, or conducting fundraising in state. Foreign charitable organizations must obtain certificate of authority and franchise tax exemption. $25 fee. Over 200 cities and counties have solicitation ordinances that may require registration. Contact Registry of Charitable Trusts for more information.

REPORTING DATES/REQUIREMENTS: Form RRF-1 due annually four and one-half months after fiscal year end. $25–$300 fee based on gross revenue scale. Form 990 due annually four and one-half months after fiscal year end. Audited financial statements required if gross revenue equals $2,000,000 or more.

SOLICITATION DISCLOSURE REQUIREMENTS FOR CHARITABLE ORGANIZATIONS: None

GEORGIA

STATE REGULATORY AGENCY: Secretary of State, Business Services and Regulation

CHARITABLE ORGANIZATIONS:

REGISTRATION/LICENSING: State accepts unified registration form.

Registration, $25 fee.

REPORTING DATES/REQUIREMENTS: Annual report due on organization's renewal date. $10 fee.

Certified financial statement required if proceeds are $1,000,000 or more; independent CPA review required for proceeds of $500,000 to $1,000,000; file form 990 if proceeds are under $500,000, late fee, $25.

SOLICITATION DISCLOSURE REQUIREMENTS FOR CHARITABLE ORGANIZATIONS: Organization must disclose to donor names of solicitor and organization. If telephone solicitation, solicitor must disclose his or her location and that full description of the charitable program and the financial statement are available upon request.

ILLINOIS

STATE REGULATORY AGENCY: Attorney General, Charitable Trusts Bureau

CHARITABLE ORGANIZATIONS:

REGISTRATION/LICENSING: State accepts unified registration form. Initial registration, $15 fee.

REPORTING DATES/REQUIREMENTS: Annual financial report due within 6 months of fiscal year end. $15 fee. CPA opinion must accompany report if revenues exceed $150,000 or if professional solicitor is engaged and contributions exceed $25,000. $200 late registration fee. $100 late annual financial report fee.

SOLICITATION DISCLOSURE REQUIREMENTS FOR CHARITABLE ORGANIZATIONS: None.

NEW JERSEY

STATE REGULATORY AGENCY: Division of Consumer Affairs, Charities Registration Section

CHARITABLE ORGANIZATIONS:

REGISTRATION/LICENSING: State accepts unified registration form. Annual registration. Fee scale: $30 to $250, depending on annual gross receipts.

REPORTING DATES/REQUIREMENTS: Annual financial report due within 6 months of fiscal year end. Late fee $25, if registration submitted more than 30 days after due date. File audited financial statement if gross revenue exceeds $250,000.

SOLICITATION DISCLOSURE REQUIREMENTS FOR CHARITABLE ORGANIZATIONS: Printed solicitations, written confirmation, receipts, or written reminders issued by a charitable organization, independent paid fund raiser, or solicitor must contain the following statement, which must be conspicuously printed. Solicitation disclosure statement: "Information filed with the attorney general concerning this charitable solicitation and the percentage of contributions received by the charity during the last reporting period that were dedicated to the charitable purpose may be obtained from the attorney general of the state of New Jersey by calling 201-504-6215 and is available on the Internet at www.state.nj.us/lps/ca/. Registration with the attorney general does not imply endorsement."

Disclosure Requirements

Charitable organizations must comply with each state's regulation to include a required disclosure statement in all fundraising solicitations and receipts. An organization must decide where the language should be printed. One acceptable place is on the back of the response card. For some states, no editing of their text is permitted. Example:

> "[Name of Organization] was established in [state] on [date] and incorporated on [date]. Organization has a 501(c)(3) classification from the Internal Revenue Service and donations are tax deductible. You may send a written request for our annual report to: [name and address of organization]. Or, in the alternative, residents of the following states may request information from the offices indicated: registration with any state does not imply endorsement by that state. A copy of the latest financial statement and/or registration statement for [organization] may be obtained by contacting us at [address and telephone number], or by contacting the state agencies as noted below. [Organization] is in compliance with all state registrations required."

Specific text required by each state would follow this disclosure statement.

REFERENCES

Giving USA Foundation. Annual Survey of State Laws Regulating Charitable Solicitations as of January 1, 2007. *Giving USA Quarterly*, Issue 1, 2007.

Internal Revenue Service (IRS). Web site, http://www.irs.gov.

Maryland Association of Nonprofit Organizations. *Public Policy Alert, Disclose It!* (revised January 2007).

Fundraising books, periodicals, and directories

ANNUAL GIVING

Dove, Kent. *Conducting a Successful Annual Giving Program.* San Francisco: Jossey-Bass, 2001.

Greenfield, James M. *Fundraising Fundamentals: A Guide to Annual Giving for Professionals and Volunteers, Second Edition* (AFP Fund Development Series). New York: Wiley Publishers, 2002.

McKinnon, Harvey. *Hidden Gold: How Monthly Giving Will Build Donor Loyalty, Boost Your Organization's Income & Increase Financial Stability.* Chicago: Bonus Books, 1999.

Rich, Patricia, and Dana Hines. *Membership Development: An Action Plan for Results.* Sudbury, MA: Jones and Bartlett Publishers, 2002.

Seiler, Timothy. *Developing Your Case for Support* (Excellence in Fundraising Workbook Series). San Francisco: Jossey-Bass, 2001.

Williams, Karla A. *Donor Focused Strategies for Annual Giving.* Sudbury, MA: Jones and Bartlett Publishers, 2004.

BOARDS AND VOLUNTEERS

Association of Fundraising Professionals (AFP). *Building an Effective Board of Directors,* AFP's Ready Reference Series. Arlington, VA: AFP.

BoardSource. Publications for board members and chief executives.

Bowen, William. *Inside the Boardroom.* New York: John Wiley & Sons, 1994.

Carlson, Mim, and Cheryl Clarke. *Team-Based Fundraising Step by Step: A Practical Guide to Improving Results Through Teamwork.* San Francisco: Jossey-Bass, 2000.

Carver, John. *Boards That Make a Difference, Third Edition.* New York: Wiley Publishers, 2006.

Carver, John, and Miriam Carver. *Reinventing Your Board, Revised Edition.* New York: Wiley Publishers, 2006.

Carver, Miriam, and Bill Charney. *The Board Member's Playbook: Using Policy Goverance to Solve Problems, Make Decisions, and Build a Stronger Board.* New York: Wiley Publishers, 2004.

Cochran, Alice Collier. *Roberta's Rules of Order: Sail Through Meetings for Stellar Results Without a Gavel.* San Francisco: Jossey-Bass, 2004.

Eadie, Doug. *Extraordinary Board Leadership: The Seven Keys to High-Impact Governance.* Sudbury, MA: Jones and Bartlett Publishers, 2001.

Ellis, Susan. *The Volunteer Recruitment (and Membership Development) Book, Third Edition.* Philadelphia, PA: Energize, 2002.

Gifford, Gayle. *How Are We Doing: A 1-Hour Guide to Evaluating Your Performance as a Nonprofit Board.* Medfield, MA: Emerson & Church Publishers, 2005.

Grace, Kay Sprinkel. *Fundraising Mistakes That Bedevil All Boards.* Medfield, MA: Emerson & Church Publishers, 2004.

———. *The Ultimate Board Member's Book.* Medfield, MA: Emerson & Church Publishers, 2006.

Howe, Fisher. *The Nonprofit Leadership Team: Building the Board-Executive Director Partnership.* San Francisco: Jossey-Bass Publishers, 2004.

Joyaux, Simone. *Strategic Fund Development: Building Profitable Relationships That Last, Second Edition.* Sudbury, MA: Jones and Bartlett Publishers, 2001.

Lansdowne, David. *Fund Raising Realities Every Board Member Must Face.* Medfield, MA: Emerson & Church Publishers, 2007.

———. *Getting Your Board to Accept the Fund Raising Challenge.* Medfield, MA: Emerson & Church Publishers.

Light, Mark. *The Strategic Board—The Step-By-Step Guide to High Impact Governance.* New York: John Wiley & Sons, 2001.

Lysakowski, Linda. *Nonprofit Essentials: Recruiting and Training Fundraising Volunteers.* New York: Wiley Publishers, 2005.

O'Connell, Brian. *The Board Member's Book*. New York: The Foundation Center, 2003.

Panas, Jerold. *Asking: A 59-Minute Guide to Everything Board Members, Volunteers, and Staff Most Know*, Medfield, MA: Emerson & Church Publishers, 2006–2007.

_____. *The Fundraising Habits of Supremely Successful Boards*. Medfield, MA: Emerson & Church Publishers, 2006.

Perry, Gail. *Fired-Up Fundraising: Turn Board Passion into Action* (AFP Fund Development Series). New York: Wiley Publishers, 2007.

Robinson, Andy. *Great Boards for Small Groups*. Medfield, MA: Emerson & Church Publishers, 2006.

Robinson, Maureen K. *Nonprofit Boards That Work: The End of One Size Fits All Governance*. New York: Wiley Publishers, 2001.

Scott, Katherine Tyler. *Creating Caring and Capable Boards*. San Francisco: Jossey-Bass Publishers, 2000.

Wagner, Lilya. *Leading Up: Transformational Leadership for Fundraisers*. New York: Wiley Publishers, 2005.

CAPITAL CAMPAIGNS

Association of Fundraising Professionals (AFP). *Getting Ready for a Capital Campaign*. AFP's Ready Reference Series. Arlington, VA: AFP.

Bancel, Marilyn. *Preparing Your Capital Campaign* (Excellence in Fundraising Workbook Series). San Francisco: Jossey-Bass Publishers, 2000.

Dove, Kent E. *Conducting a Successful Capital Campaign, Second Edition*. San Francisco: Jossey-Bass Publishers, 2001.

Kihlstedt, Andrea. *Capital Campaigns: Strategies That Work, Second Edition*. Sudbury, MA: Jones and Bartlett Publishers, 2005.

Newman, Diana. *Nonprofit Essentials: Endowment Building*. New York: Wiley Publishers, 2005.

Novom, Martin L. (ed.). *The Fundraising Feasibility Study: It's Not About the Money* (AFP Fund Development Series). New York: Wiley Publishers, 2007.

Schumacher, Edward. *Building Your Endowment* (Excellence in Fundraising Workbook Series). San Francisco: Jossey-Bass, 2003.

Walker, Julia Ingraham. *Nonprofit Essentials: The Capital Campaign*. New York: Wiley Publishers, 2004.

Weinstein, Stanley. *Capital Campaigns from the Ground Up: How Nonprofits Can Have the Buildings of Their Dreams*. New York: Wiley Publishers, 2003.

CORPORATE, FOUNDATION, AND GOVERNMENT SUPPORT

Barbato, Joseph. *How to Write Knockout Proposals*. Medfield, MA: Emerson & Church Publishers, 2004.

Carlson, Mim. *Winning Grants Step by Step, Second Edition*. San Francisco: Jossey-Bass Publishers, 2002.

CD Publications. Various newsletters, reports, publications and Web-based resources on funding sources, fundraising, and nonprofit management. Silver Spring, MD. http://www.cdpublications.com

Clarke, Cheryl. *Storytelling for Grantseekers: The Guide to Creative Nonprofit Fundraising*. New York: Wiley Publishers, 2001.

Clarke, Cheryl, and Susan Fox. *Grant Proposal Makeover: Transform Your Request from No to Yes*. New York: Wiley Publishers, 2006.

The Foundation Center. *Corporate Foundation Profiles*. New York: The Foundation Center.

_____. *The Foundation Directory*. New York: The Foundation Center. Updated annually.

_____. *The Foundation Directory, Part 2*. New York: The Foundation Center. Updated annually.

_____. *The Foundation Directory Supplement*. New York: The Foundation Center. Updated annually.

_____. *Foundation Fundamentals, Eighth Edition*. New York: The Foundation Center.

_____. *Foundation Giving Trends*. New York: The Foundation Center.

_____. *Foundation Growth and Giving Estimates. Current Outlook*. New York: The Foundation Center.

_____. *Foundation Yearbook: Facts and Figures on Private and Community Foundations*. New York: The Foundation Center.

_____. *The Foundation Center's Guide to Proposal Writing, Fifth Edition*. New York: The Foundation Center.

_____. *The Foundation Grants Index Quarterly*. New York: The Foundation Center.

_____. *The Foundation 1000*. New York: The Foundation Center. Updated annually.

_____. *Grant Guides* on various topics. New York: The Foundation Center. Updated annually.

_____. *Guide to Funding for International and Foreign Programs*. New York: The Foundation Center

_____. *Guide to U.S. Foundations, Their Trustees, Officers, and Donors*. New York: The Foundation Center.

_____. *National Directory of Corporate Giving*. New York: The Foundation Center.

_____. *National Directory of Grant Making Public Charities*. New York: The Foundation Center.

_____. *National Grant Guides* on select topics. New York: The Foundation Center.

Grantmakers for Effective Organizations. *Funding Effectiveness: Lessons in Building Nonprofit Capacity*. San Francisco: Jossey-Bass, 2004.

New, Cheryl Carter, and James Aaron Quick. *How to Write a Grant Proposal*. New York: Wiley Publishers, 2003.

Orosz, Joel J. *The Insider's Guide to Grantmaking: How Foundations Find, Fund & Manage Effective Programs*. San Francisco: Jossey-Bass Publishers, 2000.

Plinio, Alex, and Joanne Scanlan. *Resource Raising: The Role of Non-Cash Assistance in Corporate Philanthropy*. Washington, DC: Independent Sector.

Quick, James Aaron, and Cheryl Carter New. *Grant Winner's Toolkit*. New York: Wiley Publishers, 2000.

Reif-Lehrer, Liane. *Grant Application Writer's Handbook, Fourth Edition*. Sudbury, MA: Jones and Bartlett Publishers, 2005.

Robinson, Andy. *Grassroots Grants: An Activist's Guide to Grant-seeking, Second Edition*. New York: Wiley Publishers, 2004.

Sheldon, K. Scott. *Successful Corporate Fund Raising: Effective Strategies for Today's Nonprofits*. New York: Wiley Publishers, 2000.

Teitel, Martin. *"Thank You for Submitting Your Proposal."* Medfield, MA: Emerson & Church Publishers.

Ward, Deborah. *Writing Grant Proposals That Win, Third Edition*. Sudbury, MA: Jones and Bartlett Publishers, 2006.

DATA AND PROSPECT RESEARCH

Birkholz, Joshua. *Fundraising Analytics: Using Data to Guide Strategy*. AFP Fund Development Series. New York: Wiley Publishers, 2008

Hogan, Cecilia. *Prospect Research: A Primer for Growing Nonprofits, Second Edition*. Sudbury, MA: Jones and Bartlett Publishers, 2008.

Leadership Directories. *Corporate Yellow Book, Federal Yellow Book, Law Firm Yellow Book*. New York: Leadership Directories, Inc. Published annually.

Nichols, Judith E. *Pinpointing Affluence in the 21st Century, Second Edition*. Bonus Books, Santa Monica, CA, 2001.

DEVELOPMENT PLANNING, OPERATIONS, AND FINANCES

American Society of Association Executives (ASAE). *Generating and Managing Nondues Revenue in Associations—A Benchmarking Guide*. Washington, DC, 2002.

Association of Fundraising Professionals (AFP). *Bringing a Development Director on Board*. AFP's Ready Reference Series, Arlington, VA: AFP

———. *Developing Fundraising Policies and Procedures: Best Practices for Accountability and Transparency*. AFP's Ready Reference Series, Arlington, VA: AFP.

———. *Establishing Your Development Office*. AFP's Ready Reference Series, Arlington, VA: AFP.

Blazek, Judy. *IRS Form 990: Tax Preparation Guide for Nonprofits, Revised Edition*. New York: Wiley Publishers, 2004.

———. *Nonprofit Financial Planning Made Easy*. New York: Wiley Publishers, 2008.

———. *Tax Planning and Compliance for Tax-Exempt Organizations, 2008 Cumulative Supplement: Rules, Checklists, Procedures, Fourth Edition*. New York: Wiley Publishers, 2008.

Dove, Kent. *Conducting a Successful Development Services Program*. San Francisco: Jossey-Bass, 2001.

Dropkin, Murray, Jim Halpin, and Bill La Touche. *The Budget-Building Book for Nonprofits: A Step-by-Step Guide for Man-agers and Boards, Second Edition*. New York: Wiley Publishers, 2007.

Robinson, Andy. *Selling Social Change (Without Selling Out): Earned Income Strategies for Nonprofits*. New York: Wiley Publishers, 2002.

Lysakowski, Linda. *Nonprofit Essentials: The Development Plan (AFP Fund Development Series)*. New York: Wiley Publishers, 2007.

Ruppel, Warren. *Not-for-Profit Accounting Made Easy, Second Edition*. New York: Wiley Publishers, 2007.

———. *Not-for-Profit Audit Committee Best Practices*. New York: Wiley Publishers, 2005.

Sumariwalla, Russy. *Unified Financial Reporting System for Not-for-Profit Organizations—A Comprehensive Guide to Unifying GAAP, IRS Form 990, and Other Financial Reports Using a Unified Chart of Accounts*. San Francisco: Jossey-Bass, 2000.

Tenenbaum, Jeffrey. *Association Tax Compliance Guide*. Washington, DC: American Society of Association Executives (ASAE).

DIRECT MAIL/TELEMARKETING

Association of Fundraising Professionals (AFP). *Reviving Your Donor File*. AFP's Ready Reference Series, Arlington, VA: AFP

Hitchcock, Stephen. *Open Immediately: Straight Talk on Direct Mail Fundraising*. Medfield, MA: Emerson & Church Publishers.

Johnston, Michael. *Direct Response Fund Raising: Mastering New Trends for Results*. San Francisco: Jossey-Bass Publishers, 2000.

Lautman, Kay. *Direct Marketing for Nonprofits: Essential Techniques for the New Era*. Sudbury, MA: Jones and Bartlett Publishers, 2001.

Lister, Gwyneth. *Building Your Direct Mail Program* (Excellence in Fundraising Workbook Series). San Francisco: Jossey-Bass, 2001.

Warwick, Mal. *How to Write Successful Fundraising Letters, Second Edition*. San Francisco: Jossey-Bass, 2008.

———. *Raising $1,000 Gifts by Mail*. Medfield, MA: Emerson & Church Publishers.

———. *Revolution in the Mailbox: Your Guide to Successful Direct Mail Fundraising*. San Francisco: Jossey-Bass, 2004.

———. *Testing, Testing 1, 2, 3: Raise More Money with Direct Mail Tests*. San Francisco: Jossey-Bass, 2003.

ETHICS AND ACCOUNTABILITY

Fischer, Marilyn. *Ethical Decision Making in Fund Raising*. New York: Wiley Publishers, 2000.

Petty, Janice Gow. *Ethical Fundraising: A Guide for Nonprofit Boards and Fundraisers*. AFP Fund Development Series. New York: Wiley Publishers, 2008

Josephson, Michael. *Preserving the Public Trust*. Los Angeles, CA: Josephson Institute, Center for Public Service Ethics, 2005.

Nish, Steve. *Good Ideas for Creating a More Ethical and Effective Workplace.* Los Angeles, CA: Josephson Institute, Center for Public Service Ethics, 2005.

Svara, James H. *The Ethics Primer for Public Administrators in Government and Nonprofit Organizations.* Sudbury, MA: Jones and Bartlett Publishers, 2007.

FUNDRAISING, MANAGEMENT, AND THE LAW

American Society of Association Executives (ASAE). Principals of Association Management. Washington, DC.

Cox, John. *Professional Practices in Association Management.* Washington, DC: American Society of Association Executives (ASAE), 1997.

Fleishman, Joel. *The Foundation: A Great American Secret: How Private Wealth Is Changing the World.* Cambridge, MA: Public Affairs, 2007.

Glassie, Jefferson. *International Legal Issues for Nonprofits.* Washington, DC: American Society of Association Executives (ASAE), 1999.

Hopkins, Bruce. *Bruce C. Hopkins' Nonprofit Counsel.* New York: Wiley Publishers. Published monthly.

————. *Charitable Giving Law Made Easy.* New York: Wiley Publishers, 2006.

————. *The Law of Fundraising, 2008 Cumulative Supplement, Third Edition.* New York: Wiley Publishers, 2008.

————. *The Law of Tax-Exempt Organizations.* New York: Wiley Publishers. Supplemented annually.

————. *650 Essential Nonprofit Law Questions Answered.* New York: Wiley Publishers, 2005.

————. *Starting and Managing a Nonprofit Organization: A Legal Guide, Fourth Edition.* New York: Wiley Publishers, 2006.

————. *The Tax Law of Associations.* New York: Wiley Publishers, 2006.

Jacobs, Jerald. *Associations and the Law.* Washington, DC: American Society of Association Executives (ASAE), 2003.

————. *Association Law Handbook, Third Edition.* Washington, DC: American Society of Association Executives (ASAE), 2007.

Niven, Paul. *Balanced Scorecard Step-by-Step for Government and Nonprofit Agencies.* Hoboken, NJ: John Wiley & Sons, 2003.

GENERAL INTEREST

Periodicals

Advancing Philanthropy. Association of Fundraising Professionals (AFP). Bimonthly journal.

AHP Journal. Association for Healthcare Philanthropy.

Associations Now. Published by the American Society of Association Executives (ASAE).

Case Currents. Council for Advancement and Support of Education (CASE).

The Chronicle of Philanthropy. Trade publication published twice a month.

Contributions Magazine. Contributions. Bimonthly trade publication.

Fundraising Success. Published monthly by North American Publishing Co., Inc.

Grassroots Fundraising Journal. Published bimonthly by Grassroots Fundraising, Inc.

New Directions for Philanthropic Fundraising. San Francisco: Jossey-Bass. Quarterly journal.

The NonProfit Times. Monthly trade publication.

Stevenson Consultants' monthly newsletters—*Successful Fund Raising, Volunteer Management Report, Major Gifts Report, Special Events Galore, Nonprofit Communications Report, Membership Management Report.* Sioux City, Iowa.

Books

Alexander, Douglass, and Kristina Carlson. *Essential Principles for Fundraising Success.* New York: Wiley Publishers, 2005.

Bray, Ilona. *Effective Fundraising for Nonprofits: Real World Strategies That Work.* Berkeley, CA: Nolo, 2005.

Brinckerhoff, Peter C. *Social Entrepreneurship: The Art of Mission-Based Venture Development.* New York: Wiley Publishers, 2000.

Connors, Tracy Daniel. *The Nonprofit Handbook: Management, 2002 Supplement, Third Edition.* New York: Wiley Publishers, 2002.

Covey, Stephen. *The 7 Habits of Highly Effective People—Powerful Lessons in Personal Change.* New York: Simon & Schuster, 1989.

Dove, Kent. *Conducting a Successful Fundraising Program.* San Francisco: Jossey-Bass, 2003.

Flanagan, Joan. *Successful Fundraising: A Complete Handbook for Volunteers and Professionals, Second Edition.* New York: Contemporary Books, 2002.

Gary, Tracy, and Melissa Kohner. *Inspired Philanthropy: Your Step-by-Step Guide to Creating a Giving Plan, Third Edition.* New York: Wiley Publishers, 2007.

Giving USA Foundation. *Giving USA.* Indianapolis: Center on Philanthropy at Indiana University. Updated annually.

Grace, Kay Sprinkel. *Beyond Fund Raising: New Strategies for Nonprofit Innovation and Investment, Second Edition.* New York: Wiley Publishers, 2005.

————. *Over Goal! What You Must Know to Excel at Fundraising Today, Second Edition.* Medfield, MA: Emerson & Church Publishers, 2006.

Greenfield, James M. (ed.) *The Nonprofit Handbook: Fundraising, Third Edition.* New York: Wiley Publishers, 2001.

Klein, Kim. *Fundraising for Social Change, Fifth Edition.* San Francisco: Jossey-Bass, 2006.

————. *Fundraising in Times of Crisis.* San Francisco: Jossey-Bass, 2003.

Lansdowne, David. *The Relentlessly Practical Guide to Raising Serious Money, Second Edition.* Medfield, MA: Emerson & Church Publishers, 2005.

Petty, Janice Gow. *Cultivating Diversity in Fundraising* (AFP Fund Development Series). New York: Wiley Publishers, 2001.

Roth, Stephanie, and Mimi Ho. *The Accidental Fundraiser: A Step-by-Step Guide to Raising Money for Your Cause.* New York: Wiley Publishers, 2005.

Seltzer, Michael. *Securing Your Organization's Future.* New York: The Foundation Center, 2001.

Tempel, Eugene R. (ed.). *Hank Rosso's Achieving Excellence in Fund Raising, Second Edition.* New York: Wiley Publishers, 2003.

Weinstein, Stanley. *The Complete Guide to Fundraising Management, Second Edition.* New York: Wiley Publishers, 2002.

MAJOR GIFTS

Association of Fundraising Professionals (AFP). *Asking for Major Gifts.* AFP's Ready Reference Series, Arlington, VA: AFP

Burnett, Ken. *Relationship Fundraising.* New York: Wiley Publishers, 2002.

———. *The Zen of Fundraising: 89 Timeless Ideas to Strengthen and Develop Your Donor Relationships.* New York: Wiley Publishers, 2006.

Campbell, Bruce. *Listening to Your Donors.* New York: Wiley Publishers, 2000.

Dove, Kent. *Conducting a Successful Major Gifts and Planned Giving Program.* San Francisco: Jossey-Bass, 2002.

Fredricks, Laura. *The Ask.* New York: Wiley Publishers, 2006.

———. *Developing Major Gifts: Turning Small Donors into Big Contributors.* Sudbury, MA: Jones and Bartlett Publishers, 2001.

Hart, Ted, and James Greenfield. *Major Donors: Finding Big Gifts in Your Database and Online.* New York: Wiley Publishers, 2006.

Irwin-Wells, Suzanne. *Planning and Implementing Your Major Gifts Campaign* (Excellence in Fundraising Workbook Series). San Francisco: Jossey-Bass, 2001.

Panas, Jerold. *Mega Gifts: Who Gives Them, Who Gets Them, Second Edition.* Medfield, MA: Emerson & Church Publishers.

Robinson, Andy. *Big Gifts for Small Groups.* Medfield, MA: Emerson & Church Publishers.

Walker, Julia Ingraham. *Nonprofit Essentials: Major Gifts* (AFP Fund Development Series). New York: Wiley Publishers, 2006.

MARKETING AND COMMUNICATIONS

Ahern, Tom. *How to Write Fundraising Materials That Raise More Money.* Medfield, MA: Emerson & Church Publishers.

———. *Raising More Money with Newsletters Than You Ever Thought Possible.* Medfield, MA: Emerson & Church Publishers.

Ahern, Tom, and Simone Joyaux. *Keep Your Donors: The Guide to Better Communications & Stronger Relationships.* New York: Wiley Publishers, 2007.

Barbato, Joseph. *Attracting the Attention Your Cause Deserves.* Medfield, MA: Emerson & Church Publishers.

Burk, Penelope. *Donor-Centered Fundraising.* Chicago: Cygnus Applied Research, 2005.

Daw, Jocelyne. *Cause Marketing for Nonprofits: Partner for Purpose, Passion and Profits.* (AFP Fund Development Series). New York: Wiley Publishers, 2006.

Feinglass, Art. *The Public Relations Handbook for Nonprofits: A Comprehensive and Practical Guide.* San Francisco: Jossey-Bass, 2005.

Taylor, Caroline. *Publishing the Nonprofit Annual Report.* New York: Wiley Publishers, 2001.

PLANNED GIVING

Barrett, Richard D., and Molly E. Ware. *Planned Giving Essentials: A Step by Step Guide to Success, Second Edition.* Sudbury, MA: Jones & Bartlett Publishers, 2002.

Jordan, Ronald R., and Katelyn L. Quynn. *Planned Giving: Management, Marketing, and Law, Third Edition.* New York: Wiley Publishers, 2007.

Planned Giving Today. G. Roger Schoenhals (ed.) Newsletter.

Schoenhals, G. Roger. *19 Handy Articles You Can Use to Inspire Planned Gifts.* Seattle, WA: Planned Giving Today, 2004.

Sharpe, Robert F. Jr. *Planned Giving Simplified.* New York: Wiley Publishers.

Stelter, Larry. *How to Raise Planned Gifts by Mail.* Medfield, MA: Emerson & Church Publishers.

Valinsky, David, and Melanie Boyd. *Raising Money Through Bequests.* Medfield, MA: Emerson & Church Publishers.

White, Douglas E. *The Art of Planned Giving: Understanding Donors and the Culture of Giving.* New York: Wiley Publishers.

SPECIAL EVENTS

Armstrong, James. *Planning Special Events* (Excellence in Fundraising Workbook Series). San Francisco: Jossey-Bass, 2001.

Association of Fundraising Professionals (AFP). *Making the Most of Your Special Event.* AFP's Ready Reference Series, Arlington, VA: AFP.

Freedman, Harry A., and Karen Feldman. *Black Tie Optional: A Complete Special Events Resource for Nonprofit Organizations, Second Edition.* New York. Wiley Publishers, 2007.

IEG LLC. *The Special Events Report.* Chicago: International Events Group. Biweekly.

Wendroff, Alan. *Special Events: Proven Strategies for Nonprofit Fundraising, Second Edition.* New York: Wiley Publishers, 2003.

STRATEGIC PLANNING

Allison, Michael, and Jude Kaye. *Strategic Planning for Nonprofit Organizations.* New York: Wiley Publishers, 2005.

Bryson, John M. *Strategic Planning for Public and Nonprofit Organizations, Third Edition.* New York: Wiley Publishers, 2004.

Collins, Jim. *Good to Great.* New York: HarperCollins Publishers, 2005.

Crutchfield, Leslie, and Heather McLeod Grant. *Forces for Good: The Six Practices of High-Impact Nonprofits*. New York: Wiley Publishers, 2007.

McLaughlin, Thomas A. *Nonprofit Strategic Positioning: Decide Where to Be, Plan What to Do*. New York: Wiley Publishers, 2006.

Shapiro, Andrea. *Creating Contagious Commitment—Applying the Tipping Point to Organizational Change*. Hillsborough, NC: Strategy Perspective, 2003.

Wilcox, Pamela J. *Exposing the Elephants: Creating Exceptional Nonprofits*. New York: Wiley Publishers, 2006.

TECHNOLOGY AND THE INTERNET

Grobman, Gary M., and Gary Grant. *Fundraising Online: Using the Internet to Raise Serious Money for Your Nonprofit Organization*. Harrisburg, PA: White Hat Communications.

———. *The Wilder Nonprofit Field Guide to Getting Started on the Internet*. Danbury, CT: Amherst H. Wilder Foundation.

Hart, Ted, James Greenfield, and Michael Johnston. *Nonprofit Internet Strategies: Best Practices for Marketing, Communications and Fundraising Success*. New York: Wiley Publishers, 2005.

Hart, Ted, James Greenfield, and Sheeraz D. Haji. *People to People Fundraising: Social Networking and Web 2.0*. New York: Wiley Publishers, 2007.

Podolsky, Joni. *Wired for Good: Strategic Technology Planning for Nonprofits*. San Francisco: Jossey-Bass, 2003.

Stanionis, Madeline. *Raising Thousands (if Not Tens of Thousands) of Dollars with Email*. Medfield, MA: Emerson & Church Publishers.

The Foundation Center. *Guide to Grantseeking on the Web*. New York: Foundation Center.

Woodward, Jeannette. *Nonprofit Essentials: Managing Technology*. New York: Wiley Publishers, 2006.

WORKING WITH CONSULTANTS

Association of Fundraising Professionals (AFP). *So You Want to Be a Consultant*. AFP's Ready Reference Series. Arlington, VA: AFP.

Lukas, Carol. *Consulting with Nonprofits: A Practitioner's Guide*. Danbury, CT: Amherst H. Wilder Foundation, 1998.

Glossary

AAFRC *n.* American Association of Fundraising Counsel; a professional organization for fundraising consultants.

AAHSA *n.* American Association of Homes and Services for the Aging; a professional organization whose members work in healthcare or retirement communities.

ACFRE *n.* Advanced Certified Fund Raising Executive.

AFG *n.* Association Foundation Group; a professional organization whose members are the executive directors or fundraisers in a supporting foundation—a foundation that supports an association or other like organization such as a Continuing Care Retirement Community (CCRC) or hospital.

AFP *n.* Association of Fundraising Professionals; a professional organization whose members are fundraisers for nonprofit organizations. Formerly known as the National Society of Fund Raising Executives (NSFRE).

accountability *n.* the responsibility of a donee organization to keep a donor informed about the use of the donor's gift.

accounting policy *n.* a systematic routine that determines how the financial transactions of an organization are recorded and reported, such as how income (whether earned or a gift) is received and recognized, how expenses are authorized and paid, and how assets and liabilities are presented on the organization's financial statements. Such policies should be established by the organization's trustees in consultation with outside auditors and should conform to generally accepted accounting principles (GAAP).

acknowledge *v.t.* to express gratitude for (a gift or service) in written or oral form, communicated privately or publicly; *n.* **acknowledgment**.

acknowledgment form *n.* standardized form used to acknowledge a contribution.

acknowledgment letter *n.* type of correspondence used to thank and acknowledge a contribution.

acquisition *n.* the process or act of acquiring new donors.

active phase *n.* the period of public solicitation during a campaign that usually follows the successful completion of a campaign's nucleus fund and the establishment of a pattern of giving. This phase consists of solicitation activity in contrast to campaign planning. Also **intensive phase**.

ad hoc *adj.* and *adv.* for a specific purpose or situation, such as an ad hoc committee.

advance gift *n.* a donation, often from a trustee or director of an organization, that demonstrates a commitment to a campaign and provides momentum at the outset before external solicitations are undertaken. Also **initial gift**; **nucleus gift**; **strategic gift**; or **leadership gift**.

advocacy *n.* the presentation of a cause in order to influence the course of events.

advisory board *n.* a group of usually influential and knowledgeable people that offers counsel and prestige to the organization or cause with which it is associated, but that usually does not have any fiscal or policy authority.

advisory committee *n.* see **advisory board**.

AHP *n.* Association for Healthcare Philanthropy; a professional association of healthcare development professionals, formerly known as National Association for Hospital Development.

analyze *v.* to make an analysis of, such as fundraising data.

annual giving *n.* 1. an amount given annually; 2. a fundraising program that generates gift support on an annual basis. Also *(Austr.)* **budget fundraising**.

annual report *n.* a yearly report of the financial and program status of an organization or institution.

anonymous gift *n.* a gift that is not publicly attributed to the donor.

appreciated security *n.* a security with a market value greater than its original tax basis.

APRA *n.* Association of Professional Researchers for Advancement; a professional organization whose members provide research to support the fundraising efforts of staff and volunteers in development offices and supporting foundations.

articles of incorporation *n.* a document that, when filed with and approved by an appropriate state agency, establishes the legal status of a corporation.

asset *n.* 1a. something that has value or an advantage; 1b. an item of value, such as real estate, cash, a security, or patent; 2a. (**assets**) a all items of value (such as real estate, cash, inventories, securities, and patents), owned by a person or a business, that constitute the resources of that person or business; 2b. an organization's holdings including current assets and fixed assets.

audit *n.* 1. an examination and evaluation of an organization's accounting and financial affairs by an accountant, who issues a statement of the organization's financial standing and legal compliance as of a certain date; 2. an evaluation and examination of an organization's fundraising practices, policies, and results, usually performed by an outside consultant, who issues a report on the effectiveness of the organization's fundraising program. This report may also include recommendations for enhancing the program.

back up *v.t.* to copy (information) from the hard drive of a computer to either a compact disk (CD), DVD, or flash drive: also known as **memory key**.

back-up *n.* 1. the procedure for making security copies of computer data; for example, from a hard drive to either a CD, DVD, or flash drive; 2. the disk or information copied.

bellwether *n.* 1a. a gift, action, or other leading indicator in a movement or campaign; 1b. anything that sets a standard for a campaign.

benefactor *n.* a generous donor, usually at the highest gift level.

benefit *n.* 1. something of value; 2. a social event from which net proceeds are designated as a donation to one or more causes.

bequest *n.* 1. the act of bequeathing; 2. something bequeathed; also **legacy**.

bequest society *n.* a membership group made up of donors who informed an organization of their intention to provide financially for the organization in their will.

bleed *v.i.* of text or an illustration or embellishment, to be extended into the margin of a trimmed printed page; *v.t.* 1a. to extend (such material) into the margin; 1b. to print so that this occurs; *n.* any printed material that bleeds.

blog *n.* short for Weblog; a blog is basically a journal that is available on the Internet and typically updated daily.

blue line *n.* in printing, the final corrected pages of a print job, used as a review before printing.

board *n.* 1. governing board; 2. an advisory board; 3. in printing, material that is camera-ready (also mechanical).

board member *n.* one who serves on a governing or advisory board.

board of trustees *n.* another name for a governing board.

BRE *n.* see **business reply envelope**.

brand equity *v.* a composite process that involves: evaluating a particular brand of a product as a separable asset when it is sold or included on a balance sheet; measuring the strength of consumer interest in the brand; and describing consumer opinions about the brand, including any loyalty toward it. See also **brand image**.

brand image *n.* the impression of a product in the minds of current or prospective consumers that is typically created by its manufacturer to convince users that this product is superior to other brands of the same product, although it may be technically identical to other brands. See also **brand equity**.

branding *n., v.t.* the fact, process, or act of creating a brand image.

bricks and mortar campaign *n.* (informal) a capital campaign to meet the financial needs for constructing a physical plant, including facilities and furnishings.

briefing *n.* a formal or informal report prior to or subsequent to an event or situation that either prepares a participant or that reports or relates the outcome.

brochure *n.* a printed pamphlet or booklet used to promote an organization and/or its programs.

bulk rate mail *n.* second, third, or fourth class mail that qualifies for special postage rates that are lower than first-class rates. This mail is presorted by an organization or a mailing service before going to the post office.

business reply envelope (BRE) *n.* a self-addressed, return envelope with postage paid by the receiving organization or institution. Also **postage-paid envelope; return remit**.

campaign analysis *n.* a report on the results and effectiveness of a campaign. The report may include a quantitative and qualitative review of income and expense, number and size of gifts, and other considerations. See **evaluation**.

campaign brochure *n.* a summary statement most often accompanied by a pictorial depiction of an organization's case for support—the relevance of its mission, the urgency and legitimacy of its needs, and the compelling reasons for campaign goals.

campaign chair *n.* the overall volunteer leader of a campaign organization who is in charge of all volunteer forces.

campaign director *n.* a fundraising executive, from either a consulting firm or an organization's staff, who is assigned to direct a campaign.

campaign leader *n.* a volunteer who helps recruit and motivate other volunteer members of a campaign organization and who sets the pace for the giving of gifts and active participation in a campaign.

campaign management *n.* the administration and implementation by appointed staff of the overall operations of a campaign.

campaign organization *n.* a chart or table delineating the responsibilities and relationships among fundraising committees.

campaign staff *n.* paid personnel who perform clerical, research, record keeping, and other coordination and support functions essential to campaign operations under the supervision of the campaign director.

capital campaign *n.* an intensive fundraising effort to meet a specific financial goal within a specified period of time for one or more major projects that are out of the ordinary, such as the construction of a facility, the purchase of equipment, or the acquisition of endowment.

carrier envelope *n.* an envelope, containing an appeal letter and other material, that is attached to a direct mail package.

CASE *n.* Council for Advancement and Support of Education; a professional organization for individuals working in higher education.

case statement *n.* a presentation that sets forth a case; *adj.* **case-stating.**

cash gift *n.* a contribution made by writing a check or giving cash.

cause-related marketing *n.* marketing in which a for-profit organization, by using the name of a not-for-profit organization, promotes its product and in return provides financial support to the organization according to a predetermined formula based on sales and purchases.

CD-ROM *n.* compact disk read-only memory; an information storage device capable of storing large amounts of material read by a specially equipped computer.

Certified Fund Raising Executive (CFRE) *n.* 1a. a designation, conferred by CFRE International, that is awarded to a professional fundraiser who has met specified standards of service, experience, and knowledge; 1b. a person who has earned this designation.

CFRE International *n.* an organization (headquartered in Alexandria, VA) that is a collaboration of the following fundraising service organizations: Association for Healthcare Philanthropy (AHP); Association of Lutheran Development Executives (ALDE); Council for Resource Development (CRD); Fundraising Institute-Australia, Ltd. (FIA); International Catholic Stewardship Council (ICSC); National Catholic Development Conference (NCDC); North American YMCA Development Organization (NAYDO); and Philanthropic Services for Institutions (PSI). The organization certifies, through a voluntary certification process, fundraising professionals who demonstrate the knowledge, skills, and commitment to the highest standards of ethical and professional practice in serving the philanthropic sector. See also **certified fund raising executive.**

challenge gift *n.* a gift donated by a person made on condition that other gifts or grants will be obtained using some prescribed formula, usually within a specified period of time, with the objective of encouraging others to give.

challenge grant *n.* a challenge gift donated by an organization, corporation, or foundation.

charitable *adj.* 1a. giving to those in need; 1b. giving for benevolent purposes; 2a. for or pertaining to charity; 2b. for or pertaining to a charity or charities.

charitable deduction *n.* the portion of a gift to a qualified charity that is deductible from a person's or corporation's federal income tax, a person's gift tax, or a person's estate tax.

charity *n.* 1. that which is given in willingness to aid those in need; 2. a not-for-profit organization or institution that is active in humanitarian work and supported entirely or in part by gifts.

closed-face envelope *n.* a type of envelope that does not have a window through which the address on the enclosed letter can be seen.

cold list *n.* a list of prospects that has not been previously tested or contacted.

cold prospect *n.* a potential donor that has never contributed to or been contacted by a particular organization.

community foundation *n.* a not-for-profit organization that receives, manages, and distributes funds including any income from endowed funds, for charitable purposes, typically in a specific geographic area.

communication audit *n.* a review to determine the effectiveness of an organization's public relations program in reaching a specific target audience with the desired material.

communication program *n.* the transference of an organization's ideas, concepts, and purposes to its constituency.

constituency *n.* people who have a reason to relate to or care about an organization. Such people typically fall into customary groupings, such as faculty, alumni, medical staff, users, parents, and donors.

consultant *n.* a person with expertise in a specific field of knowledge who is engaged by a client to provide advice and services.

consulting firm *n.* fundraising counsel.

contribution *n.* a gift or donation.

control package *n.* a direct mail package used as a model against which a different mailing package is tested.

corkage fee *n.* the fee charged by vendors, hotels, or other establishments to open wine, hard alcohol, or other beverages and provide the glasses and other necessities for service when the beverages have been donated and not purchased from the vendor or hotel.

corporate foundation *n.* a private foundation, funded by a profit-making corporation, whose primary purpose is the distribution of grants according to established guidelines.

corporate-giving program *n.* 1. a grant-awarding program established and controlled by a profit-making corporation; 2. an organization's activities to solicit donations from a corporation.

corporate philanthropy *n.* support from corporations and corporate foundations through gifts of cash, equipment, supplies, and other contributions.

corporate sponsorship *n.* financial support of a project by a corporation in exchange for public recognition and other benefits. Also **corporate underwriting.**

corporate underwriting *n.* see corporate sponsorship.

cost per dollar raised *n.* a measure of the productivity of a fundraising program calculated by dividing the expenses incurred in raising the funds by the total dollars raised.

cost-benefit analysis *n.* 1a. a process by which an organization judges the effectiveness of its expenses in relationship to its objectives; *v.* 1b. an instance of doing this.

council *n.* a group of people, usually volunteers, organized to act on organizational issues and offer direction on policy and programs.

cultivate *v.t.* to engage and maintain the interest and involvement of a donor, prospective donor, or volunteer with an organization's people, programs, and plans. *n.* **cultivation.**

cultivation event *n.* a special event (such as a dinner, meeting, or similar affair) to enhance interest in and enthusiasm for the work of an organization.

database *n.* indexed information held in computer storage from which a computer user can summon selected materials. In a database, data are organized so that various programs can access and update information.

decoy *n.* a name and address placed in a database file to monitor use of the file.

deferred gift *n.* a gift (such as a bequest, life insurance policy, charitable remainder trust, charitable gift annuity, or pooled-income fund) that is committed to a charitable organization but is not available for use until some future time, usually after the death of the donor.

demographics *n.* the study of the characteristics of human populations, such as size, growth, density, distribution, and vital statistics.

designated gift *n.* a gift, the use of which is designated by the donor. This gift is either a temporarily restricted gift or a permanently restricted gift.

desktop publishing (DTP) *n.* a personal computer software program capable of producing printed documents, including such as advertising and magazines to a publishable standard of typesetting, layout, and design.

development *n.* the total process by which an organization increases public understanding of its mission and acquires financial support for its programs.

development audit *n.* an objective evaluation, sometimes conducted by professional fundraising counsel, of an organization's internal development procedures and results.

direct mail *n.* 1. mass mail sent by a not-for-profit organization directly to prospects; 2. the soliciting by this method of donations, product sales, or subscription sales.

diversity *n.* 1a. a broad representation of experiences, perspectives, opinions, and cultures, with an effort toward creating an environment of inclusiveness; 1b. the quality or state of encompassing all people; 1c. the quality or state of being different from one another; *adj.* diverse; *adv.* diversely; *v.* diversify.

donor *n.* a person, organization, corporation, or foundation that makes a gift. Also **contributor.**

donor acquisition *n.* the process of identifying and acquiring new donors.

donor list *n.* a listing of donors who give to an organization.

donor profile *n.* 1a. detailed information, compiled through research, about an individual donor; 1b. a statistical description of the characteristics of all donors to an organization.

donor pyramid *n.* a diagrammatic description of the hierarchy of donors by size of gifts. The diagram reflects that as the size of donations increases, the number of donations decreases; as the number of years a donor is asked to renew increases, the number of donors decreases; as campaign sophistication progresses from annual giving to planned giving, the number of donors decreases; as donor involvement increases, the size of the donor's contribution increases and the response to campaign sophistication increases. Also **pyramid of giving.**

donor recognition *n.* the policy and practice of providing recognition to a donor, by a personal letter, a public expression of appreciation, a published list of donors, or in another appropriate way.

downsizing *n.* the decision by businesses, nonprofits, and the government to reduce the number of persons being employed.

download *v.* in computers, to transfer (a program or file) from one system in a network to be processed by another that is lower in the control hierarchy. Compare **upload.**

e-commerce *n.* conducting business through transactions over the Internet.

electronic funds transfer (EFT) *n.* 1a. a process or act by which a person may authorize automatic and periodic deductions from his or her bank account to be credited to another account, as to a not-for-profit organization; 1b. money transferred in this way.

electronic screening *n.* the process or act of comparing an organization's database to national databases to gain address, telephone, and household information to be added to an organization's records. The process also usually involves ranking prospects by both capacity and likelihood to make gifts.

endowment *n.* a permanently restricted net asset, the principal of which is protected and the income from which may be spent and is controlled by either the donor's restrictions or the organization's governing board.

entrepreneurial philanthropist *n.* major donors from the high technology industry whose approach to giving combines the principles of entrepreneurial business development and financing and applies them to charitable giving.

e-philanthropy *n.* the act of making a contribution over the Internet.

evaluation *n.* examination, judgment, appraisal, or estimate; 1. an act or fact of evaluating; 2. campaign analysis; 3. prospect rating.

face-to-face solicitation *n.* the soliciting in person of a prospective donor. Also **personal solicitation.**

fact sheet *n.* a brief statement of an organization's purposes, programs, services, needs, plans, and other pertinent information prepared in summary form for use by volunteers involved in a campaign.

family foundation *n.* a foundation funded entirely by one family.

feasibility study *n.* an objective survey, usually conducted by fundraising counsel, of an organization's fundraising potential. The study assesses the strength of the organization's case and the availability of its leaders, workers, and prospective donors. The written report includes the study findings, conclusions, and recommendations.

federated campaign *n.* a unified fundraising program administered by a not-for-profit organization that distributes funds to similar agencies. The United Way is an example of a federated campaign.

fiduciary *n.* 1. a person, such as a trustee or executor, responsible for the affairs or the estate of another person (such as a beneficiary or donor) or organization; *adj.* 1a. of or pertaining to a person who holds something in trust for another; *adv.* 1b. held in trust; fiduciarily. 2. a person, such as a company director or an agent of a principal, who stands in a special relation of trust, confidence, or responsibility to another or others.

financial report *n.* a report, for a not-for-profit organization, that includes a balance sheet and activity statement.

501(c)(3) *n.* the section of the Internal Revenue Service Code designation that exempts certain types of organizations (such as charitable, religious, scientific, literary, and educational) from federal taxation and permits these organizations to receive tax-deductible donations. For information about other 501(c) organizations, see the IRS Tax Code.

font *n.* in printing, a complete set of type of one size and style (or face).

foundation *n.* 1. an organization created from designated funds from which the income is distributed as grants to not-for-profit organizations or, in some cases, to people. 2. a nonprofit organization created to raise funds for another organization or group, i.e., a supporting foundation.

full disclosure *n.* 1. the written or verbal disclosure of fundraising or administrative costs, or both, to a person or to the public; 2. the disclosure of actual or potential conflict(s) of interest.

fundraiser *n.* 1. a person, paid or volunteer, who plans, manages, or participates in raising assets and resources for an organization or cause; 2. an event conducted for the purpose of generating funds.

fundraising *n.* the raising of assets and resources from various sources for the support of an organization or a specific project; *adj.* **fundraising.**

fundraising counsel *n.* a person or firm contracted to provide service to not-for-profit organizations seeking advice, evaluation, or planning for the purpose of fundraising. Also **consulting firm; development counsel; professional counsel.**

fundraising goals *n.* number of gifts, donors, and total dollars to be raised.

fundraising tripod *n.* the three components of a fundraising program: the case, volunteer leadership, and sources of support.

general gift *n.* 1. a gift derived from a general appeal; 2. a gift within the lower range of giving in a campaign.

general ledger *n.* a book containing the master accounts of all money transactions, both debit and credit, that an individual or business conducts. The information from a ledger is used in composing a financial statement.

generally accepted accounting principles (GAAP) *n.* the conventions, standards, rules, and procedures that define a responsible practicing of accounting. These principles are currently under the domain of the Financial Accounting Standards Board.

general-purpose foundation *n.* an independent, private foundation that awards grants in many different fields of interest.

gift *n.* donation; *v.t.* to endow or present with a gift.

gift-acceptance policy *n.* the rules and regulations developed by a donee organization to determine which types of gifts should or should not be accepted.

gift-in-kind *n.* a gift of a service or a product rather than a cash or stock gift.

gift opportunities *n.* a list of campaign needs, usually within a range of donation levels, that are used in an appeal to the various special interests of prospective donors.

gift planning *n.* a systematic effort to identify and cultivate a person for the purpose of generating a major gift that is structured and that integrates sound personal, financial, and estate-planning concepts with the prospect's plans for lifetime or testamentary giving. A planned gift has tax implications and is often transmitted through a legal instrument, such as a will or trust. Also **planned giving.**

gift processing *n.* a procedure by which a donation is received, recorded, transmitted for deposit, receipted, and acknowledged.

gift receipt *n.* an official acknowledgment, required by the Internal Revenue Service, issued to a donor by a recipient organization in response to a donation of (currently) $250 or more, requiring information naming the charity, the asset donated, and any benefits received by the donor in exchange for the gift. This can be done in a letter which is more personal.

gift range table *n.* a projection of the number of gifts by size (in descending order: leadership gift, major gift, general gift) so as to achieve a particular fundraising goal.

giving club *n.* one of various donor categories that are grouped and recognized by a recipient organization on the basis of the level of donations. Also **gift club.**

grant *n.* 1. a financial donation given to support a person, organization, project, or program. Most grants are awarded to not-for-profit organizations; 2. *informal (incorrectly for)* a grant proposal; *v.t.* to give or confer (such as the ownership or a right) by a formal act.

graphic artist *n.* a designer who provides art work either hand done or by computer for brochures or other publications.

hardware *n.* the mechanical, electrical, and structural apparatus that make up a computer system, including processor, printer, and screen. Compare **software**.

homepage *n.* see **Web site**.

honorary chair *n.* a person of prominence or influence who agrees to lend his or her name to a campaign organization.

honor roll of donors *n.* a method of showing appreciation of donors, a list of which may be published annually or quarterly or placed on a wall or special plaque at the organization or elsewhere.

identify *v.* (with object) to ascertain, through investigation, research, and analysis (those candidates who appear to be the most promising as prospective leaders, workers, or donors).

identification *n.* the first phase in the fundraising process.

incremental budgeting *n.* a process of budgeting using a percentage increase or decrease in prior-year figures. Compare **zero-based budgeting**.

Independent Sector (IS) *n.* an alliance (headquartered in Washington, DC) of donors and donees that promotes the interests of the independent sector. The organization is composed of memberships from corporations and foundations with national giving programs, as well as from national, not-for-profit organizations concerned with philanthropy.

indicia *n.* (singular, *indicium*) markings printed on bulk mail in place of stamps, metered postage, or other postmark. Often used to carry a tagline.

initial gift *n.* advance gift.

ink-jet printer *n.* a printer that uses an ink spray to print the characters on a sheet of paper.

institutional readiness *n.* the combination of several specific components in an organization or institution that impact its fundraising capability, including a case statement, donors, prospects, volunteers, and adequate staffing.

Internet *n.* in computers, a global computer network consisting of a loose confederation of interconnected networks. The Internet provides many services, such as file transfer, research, electronic mail, electronic journals and other publications, discussions, and community information service.

kick off *v.t.* to begin an official, public launching of (a campaign), usually at a special event to which major prospects have been invited and where major funds, committed or already in hand, are announced.

kind *n.* similarity in sort or type, in the phrase **in kind**; *adv.* gifts of goods or services, not of money, such as a contribution of equipment, supplies, space, or staff time. The donor may place monetary value on such a contribution for tax purposes; *adj.* in-kind (as in in-kind contribution).

L-A-I (*l*inkage, *a*bility, *i*nterest) *n.* the three factors, when considered together, that are indicators of the likelihood of success when soliciting a major gift. Linkage is the association with the organization or constituency; ability is the capacity

for giving; interest is the concern about the cause, need, or project.

lapsed donor *n.* a donor who has contributed at any time prior to the current year.

laser printer *n.* a printer that uses a laser beam to print the characters on a sheet of paper.

leadership gift *n.* a gift, donated at the beginning of a campaign, that is expected to set a standard for future giving.

letter shop *n.* a commercial enterprise that addresses, inserts, sorts, bags, ties, and delivers a mailing to a post office. Printing services are also frequently available.

leverage *n.* 1. the ability of one or more people in leadership positions to influence or persuade others to take a specific action, such as to serve in a campaign or make a certain financial commitment; 2. a concept, practiced by some foundations, in which a grant is given with the express purpose of attracting additional funding; *v.* (with object) to negotiate based on the interests of a prospective donor or business partner.

life-income gift *n.* a gift arrangement by which a donor makes an irrevocable transfer of property to a charity while retaining an income interest to benefit the donor and any other beneficiary for life or a specified period or years, after which the remainder is distributed to the charity.

list broker *n.* a commercial firm that buys, sells, and rents mailing lists; *adj.* **list-brokering**; *n.* **list-broking**.

list exchange *n.* the exchange of constituent lists between two or more organizations, often on a name-for-name basis, that enables each organization to mail to the other's constituency.

lock box *n.* an address, usually at a banking institution, where mailed donations are received, envelopes opened, results recorded, funds deposited, and transactions reported to the organization.

logo *n.* two or more letters, a figure, symbol, or other identifying representation associated with an organization or other enterprise.

mail house *n.* a commercial business that addresses, inserts, sorts, bags, and delivers a mailing to a post office. See **letter shop**.

mailing list *n.* a list of donors or prospective donors to receive a mailing.

mailing package *n.* a package that usually contains an appeal letter, a brochure, and a response device.

major gift *n.* a significant donation to a not-for-profit organization, the amount required to qualify as a major gift being determined by the organization.

marketing *n.* 1a. a process designed to bring about the voluntary exchange of values between a not-for-profit organization and its target market, such as the transfer of a donation in exchange for addressing a social need, recognition, or a feeling of good will; 1b. the process or act of fostering such an exchange in a market. See also **Cause-related marketing**.

marketing plan *n.* a plan used in the field of marketing that encompasses an organization or any part of it. The plan includes a situational analysis, budget, action plan, problems and opportunities, goals, strategies, and monitoring systems.

matching gift *n.* 1. a gift contributed on the condition that it be matched, often within a certain period of time, in accordance with a specified formula; 2. a gift by a corporation matching a gift contributed by one or more of its employees.

memory *n.* computer's temporary data storage area.

merge-purge *v.t.* to both combine (two or more computer files) into one file and delete duplicate records; *n.* the process, act, or an instance of doing this.

mission statement *n.* a statement about a societal need or value that an organization proposes to address.

modem (*mo*dulator + *dem*odulator) *n.* a computer attachment that, when used either with a telephone or on a direct line, transmits data by converting outgoing signals from one form to another and converting incoming signals back again.

monitor *v.* (with object) to check in order to control or observe something; *n.* 1. any device that monitors; 2. a device onto which images (such as text or graphics) generated by a computer's video adapter are displayed, used for viewing information. Also **screen**.

multi-tasking *n.* 1. the capability of some applications to run several other applications or several documents at one time. The user can switch between applications or documents instead of exiting and reloading. 2. The capability of an individual to manage multiple tasks at one time.

needs assessment *n.* the study of an organization's program or situation to determine what activity or activities should be initiated or expanded to satisfy a need.

network *n.* 1. in computers, a system that accommodates a series of computer terminals, all remote from one another, with each having the ability to link into commonly held files in a file server or a mainframe computer; 2a. a chain of broadcast stations linked up for carrying the same program; 2b. a nationwide broadcast company; 2c. broadcast companies collectively; 3. a group of people sharing the same interest or cause who meet informally to provide professional support. Also **net.** *v.* (with object) 1. to broadcast simultaneously over a network of radio or television stations; 2. to link (computers and terminals) together to form a computer network. *v.* (no object) to acquire or exchange information through one's membership in a commercial or other computer network system.

nine ninety (990) *n.* an Internal Revenue Service financial information return submitted annually by most tax-exempt organizations and institutions, except religious.

nixie, nixy *n.* (*plural,* nixies). *Informal.* an undeliverable piece of mail returned to the sender because of incorrect address, illegibility, or other reason.

nonprofit sector *n.* any not-for-profit or tax-exempt organizations collectively that are specifically not associated with any government, government agency, or commercial enterprise. Also **independent sector; not-for-profit sector; third sector.**

not-for-profit *adj.* that pertains to or provides services of benefit to the public without financial incentive. A not-for-profit organization is qualified by the Internal Revenue Service as a tax-exempt organization. Also **nonprofit**.

NGO *n.* nongovernmental organization usually used internationally for a nonprofit organization.

NPO *n.* nonprofit organization.

online databases *n.* databases of information retrieved by a computer.

operating foundation *n.* a private foundation that, rather than making grants, conducts research, promotes social welfare, and engages in programs determined by its governing body or establishment charter.

operating support *n.* contributions that are used so that the organization can operate. It funds salaries, utilities, supplies, travel expenses, etc.

operating support grant *n.* a grant to cover day-to-day expenses.

outsourcing *n.* contracting work to be done outside of the office by another firm and not by staff of the organization. Most often used to save the organization money by not hiring full-time staff and not paying their salaries and benefits. Outsourcing can also produce a high-quality product, decrease costs, and reduce stress on the staff.

pace-setting *adj.* 1a. (said of gifts) that set a standard for all subsequent gifts; 1b. related to the gift range table of anticipated giving. Also **pattern-setting**.

package *n.* 1. a proposal for support incorporating a combination of gift opportunities; 2. all components of a mailing package; *v.* (with object) to create into a package; *adj.* packageable; *n.* packager.

paid solicitor *n.* a person who fundraises for compensation by a fee or salary for time and effort.

personal solicitation *n.* face-to-face solicitation.

philanthropy *n.* 1. love of humankind, usually expressed by an effort to enhance the well-being of humanity through personal acts of practical kindness or by financial support of a cause or causes, such as a charity (e.g., the Red Cross), mutual aid or assistance (service clubs, youth groups), quality of life (arts, education, environment), and religion; 2. any effort to relieve human misery or suffering, improve the quality of life, encourage aid or assistance, or foster the preservation of values through gifts, service, or other voluntary activity, any and all of which are external to government involvement or marketplace exchange; *adj.* **philanthropic, philanthropical**; *adv.* **philanthropically**; *n.* **philanthropist**.

Phone/Mail® *n.* 1a. (*trademark*) a simulation of face-to-face solicitation techniques used in a mass solicitation procedure utilizing a carefully orchestrated sequence of telephone and mail contacts; 1b. the process or act of using Phone/Mail.

piggyback mailing *n.* (*informal*) a letter or other communication that accompanies a mailing but covers a different topic.

piggybacking *v.* the act of raising additional money by including the request or opportunity along with a request for another purpose. For example, mailing a dues renewal to a member and including a request for funding of a new project, or selling t-shirts, mugs, caps, etc. at a charity dinner in addition to charging money for the ticket in order to raise additional funds.

planned giving *n.* a systematic effort to identify and cultivate a person for the purpose of generating a major gift that is structured and that integrates sound personal, financial, and estate-planning concepts with the prospect's plans for lifetime or testamentary giving. A planned gift has tax implications and is often transmitted through a legal instrument, such as a will or a trust. Also **gift planning** or **deferred giving**.

planned giving committee *n.* a group of volunteers who assist an organization in planning, promoting, and implementing a planned giving program. Members usually include attorneys, accountants, insurance agents, certified financial planners, etc.

planning *v.t.* formulating a scheme or program for the accomplishment or attainment of a goal.

planning study *n.* a fundraising study that places emphasis upon the development of a plan to implement a campaign.

pledge *n.* 1a. a promise that is written, signed, and dated, to fulfill a commitment at some future time; specifically, a financial promise payable according to terms set by the donor. Such pledges may be legally enforceable, subject to state law; 1b. the total amount of such a pledge; 2. a verbal pledge; *v.t.* to commit (a specified amount of money) as a pledge. Also **promise to give**.

pledge card *n.* a printed form used by a donor as a response to an appeal.

podcasting *n.* a method of publishing files to the Internet, allowing users to subscribe to a feed and receive new files automatically by subscription, usually at no cost.

pooled-income fund *n.* a trust to which a donor transfers property and contributes irrevocably the remainder interest to the charity that has established the trust, retaining a life-income interest for one or more beneficiaries. The transferred property is commingled (pooled) with gifts made by other donors, and each income beneficiary receives a pro rata share of the net income earned by the fund each year. Upon the death of the beneficiary, the fund's trustee severs from the fund an amount equal to the value upon which the beneficiary's associated income interest was based and distributes that amount to the charity.

postage-paid envelope *n.* see **business reply envelope**.

precampaign *adj.* of or pertaining to the period preceding the launching of a campaign.

premium *n.* 1. goods or services, or both, offered as an inducement to a prospective donor to make a donation; 2. a payment made on an insurance policy.

press kit *n.* a packet of informational materials, usually used for supporting a news release, an organization's program, or a particular situation within an organization.

private foundation *n.* as designated by federal law, a foundation whose support is from relatively few sources and typically from a single source (usually a person, family, or company) and that makes grants to other not-for-profit organizations rather than operating its own programs. Its annual revenues are derived from earnings on investment assets rather than from donations. Private foundations are subject to more restrictive rules than public charities. Also **family foundation**.

private inurement *n.* the receiving (by such as a board member, staff member, stockholder, or business owner) of financial benefit of the net profits from an endeavor. Not-for-profit organizations cannot legally provide private inurement to any entity.

private phase *n.* the phase of a campaign that precedes the public announcement of the campaign. The private phase is also called the "quiet phase," the "dark phase," and the "prepublic" phase.

private sector *n.* the area of a nation's economy and civic enterprise that is under private, rather than any governmental, control.

professional ethics *n.* standards of conduct to which members of a profession are expected to adhere.

program officer *n.* a staff member of a foundation who reviews grant proposals and makes recommendations for action.

progress report *n.* a report prepared periodically during a campaign for distribution to leaders and workers of the campaign organization as well as for the record.

proposal *n.* a written request or application for a gift, grant, or service.

prospect *n.* any potential donor whose linkages, giving ability, and interests have been confirmed; *v.t.* to identify (a prospect).

prospect list *n.* a listing of those individuals who are evaluated to be candidates for making contributions to an organization.

prospect profile *n.* a research report detailing the pertinent facts about a prospective donor, including basic demographic information, financial resources, past giving, linkages, interests, potential future giving, and such.

prospect research *n.* 1. the continuing search for pertinent information on prospects and donors; 2. identification of new individual, foundation, and corporate prospects. *n.* **prospect researcher**.

prospecting *n.* the act of performing prospect research.

PSA *n.* public-service announcement.

public charity *n.* as designated by federal law, a foundation that, during its most recent four fiscal periods, has received one-third of its support from donations from individuals, trusts, corporations, government agencies, or other not-for-profit organizations, provided no single donor gives 2 percent or more of the total support for the period. Normally, the charity must receive no more than one-third of its support from investment income. A public charity escapes the stringent rules that apply to a private foundation.

public sector *n.* the area of a nation's economy that is under governmental, rather than any private, control.

pyramid of gifts *n.* a reference to the distribution of gifts by size to a capital campaign within the context of the principle that larger gifts, although limited in number in relation to the total gifts received, will account for a larger and disproportionate share of the total objective; the classic gift pattern for a campaign that, graphically represented, resembles a pyramid.

renewal rate *n.* the rate at which members renew their membership, which is ordinarily between 80 and 95 percent for multi-year members, and between 45 and 50 percent for first-year members, with an overall renewal rate of between 70 and 80 percent.

reinstated donor *n.* a donor who reinstates his or her support after a period of not contributing.

rejection letter *n.* the term used to describe the letter sent by a funder when a gift request is turned down. This denial letter is sent by many funders to applicants explaining why the gifts the applicants requested were not made.

research *n.* the second phase in the fundraising process.

resource development *n.* the practice of identifying, cultivating, and securing financial and human support for an organization.

restricted gift *n.* a former accounting term for a temporarily restricted gift or a permanently restricted gift.

return on investment (ROI) *n.* 1a. a measure of the efficiency of an organization or program, calculated as the ratio of net income received to the expended funds; 1b. the monetary amount derived by this calculation.

rollout *n.* the extension of an earlier test program, such as a direct mail appeal, to a larger number of people on a given list or within a given population.

rule of thirds *n.* a formula for constructing a gift range table for a capital campaign, based on the premise that ten donors account for the first third of funds raised, the next hundred donors for the next third, and all remaining donors for the final third.

Rich Site Summary (RSS) *n.* an XMP format for sharing content among different Web sites.

screening and rating sessions *n.* volunteers and staff members gathering together to identify individuals they know from prepared lists of names and to evaluate or rate each individual's ability to give at certain levels.

seed money *n.* an early gift by a donor used for launching a program, thereby establishing credibility and momentum for that program.

segment *v.t.* to subdivide (such as donors or prospects) into smaller groups with similar characteristics; *n.* a segmented portion or group.

self-mailer *n.* a package for mailing that requires no separate carrier envelope or reply envelope.

sequential solicitation *n.* a cardinal principle of capital campaign fundraising that gifts should be sought "from the top down,"—that is, the largest gifts in a gift range table should be sought at the outset of a campaign, followed sequentially by the search for lesser gifts.

site visit *n.* a visit by a potential donor to inspect a project or review a program for which donations are being sought.

slug *n.* a device used with a postage machine that will imprint a message to the left of the printed postage each time an envelope is put through the postage machine. This message can be changed to promote an organization's many causes.

social entrepreneur *n.* a term used to describe the new philanthropists who combine the principles of entrepreneurial business development and financing and apply them to charitable giving.

software *n.* 1a. the instructions, programs, routines, symbolic languages, and any other related documentation required for operating a computer; 1b. a particular brand of software.

solicit *v.t.* 1a. to ask (a person or group) for a contribution of money, resources, a service, or opinion; 1b. to request or try to acquire (such a contribution); *v.* (no object) to make a request or appeal as for such a contribution; *n.* solicitation.

solicitor *n.* a person, paid or volunteer, who asks for donations on behalf of an organization or a cause.

solicitor's kit *n.* a packet of materials to be used by volunteers when doing personal solicitations. The kit contains general information about the organization, the case for support, brochures about the organization, materials for making a gift such as pledge cards, and envelopes.

special event *n.* a function designed to attract and involve people in an organization or cause.

special gift *n.* a gift among the higher ranges of the gift range table.

special-purpose foundation *n.* a public foundation that focuses its grantmaking activities on one or a few special areas of interest.

sponsor *v.t.* 1. to endorse (an organization or cause); 2. to agree to assume the financial responsibility of (all or part of the cost of a special event or a special event or a special program or activity); *n.* a person or corporation that sponsors.

steering committee *n.* a committee of top volunteer leaders who oversee and manage a campaign or other fundraising effort. This committee is often composed of the chairmen of other working committees.

stewardship *n.* 1. a process whereby an organization seeks to be worthy of continued philanthropic support, including the acknowledgment of gifts, donor recognition, the honoring of donor intent, prudent investment of gifts, and the effective and efficient use of funds to further the mission of the organization; 2. the position or work of a steward.

strategic plan *n.* decisions and actions that shape and guide an organization while emphasizing the future implications of present decisions. This plan usually employs the SWOT (Strengths, Weaknesses, Opportunities, Threats) analysis.

stretch gift *n.* 1. a donation that fulfills a donor's optimum capacity to give; 2. a gift that is larger than a donor originally intended to make.

surge protector *n.* a device that protects both hardware and software from being damaged by a surge in power through the electrical or telephone wires. Some will even maintain a power supply for up to 30 minutes.

suspect *n.* a possible source of support whose philanthropic interests appear to match those of a particular organization but whose linkages, giving ability, and interests have not yet been confirmed.

target *n.* 1. a specific objective in a fundraising program or campaign; 2. a campaign goal; 3. a prospective donor; *v.t.* to identify, single out, or make as a target.

tagging *v.* occurs when a user categorizes data on a specialized Web site that gives others access to it. There is photographic tagging as well.

teaser copy *n.* the wording or phrase found printed on the carrier envelope of a direct mail fundraising solicitation letter.

technology consultant *n.* a consultant who specializes in database management and computer technology.

telemarketing *n.* the raising of funds or the marketing of goods or services by volunteers or paid solicitors, using the telephone.

telethon *n.* a television program in which entertainment features are integrated with a fundraising message that is broadcast over a television station. During the program, viewers are asked to call and make pledges.

third sector *n.* independent sector.

three G's *n.* give, get, or get off; the phrase attributed to a board member's ability to raise money for an organization.

three W's *n.* work, wisdom, and wealth; the phrase that describes what board members can bring to an organization.

thumbnail *n.* mini mock-ups of a design project that are literally thumbnail size.

token gift *n.* a gift considerably below the capacity of the donor.

trust *n.* 1. an arrangement establishing a fiduciary relationship in which a trustor conveys property to a trustee to hold and manage for the benefit of one or more beneficiaries. Trusts can be revocable or irrevocable; 2. something (such as property or financial securities) managed by a trustee for someone else's benefit. In the phrase **in trust**, in the care or possession of a trustee.

typeface *n.* in printing; 1a. the printing surface of a piece of type; 1b. a single design of type; 1c. all the characters of a single design of type.

typeset *v.t.* to set (copy) into printing type.

unrestricted gift *n.* a gift made without any condition or designation.

upgrade *v.t* 1. to increase or attempt to increase (the level of donor giving); 2. to reconfigure (a computer) to increase its computing power; *n.* 1. donor upgrade; 2. a new release of a brand of computer software, usually containing major changes.

upload *v.* in computers, to transfer (a program or file) from one system in a computer network to be processed by another that is higher in the control hierarchy. Compare **download**.

user friendly *adj.* (said of computer software) designed with easily understood commands and instructions.

vendor *n.* a manufacturer, wholesaler, or retailer who sells a product or service.

venture philanthropist *n.* one who approaches charitable giving as an investment much like a venture capitalist.

venture philanthropy *n.* the term used to cover a wide range of funds, from those that raise money from technology millionaires, i.e., Social Venture Partners in Seattle, Washington, to those that make sustained, closely managed grants to charities to help them generate revenue, much in the way a venture capitalist would do.

vision statement *n.* a statement about what an organization can and should become at some future time.

volunteer *v.i.* to work without compensation in behalf of an organization, cause, benefit, etc; *n.* a person who volunteers. Also *n.* **worker, volunteerism.**

wallet envelope *n.* a contribution envelope with a large flap that can be used for giving information about a requested contribution.

Web site *n.* in computers, a location connected to the Internet containing information about an organization, its mission and services, often with links and other relevant information.

Webcasting *n.* similar to broadcasting, Webcasting involves communicating to multiple computers at the same time via the Internet or an intranet by "streaming" live audio and/or live video. A Webcast also can be simulcast. It is also possible to Webcast to a selected group of recipients, which is also known as "narrowcasting" or "multicasting."

Wiki *n.* a Web site or similar online resource that allows users to not only add content, as on an Internet forum, but also edit content collectively. Wiki also refers to the collaborative software used to create such a Web site.

will *n.* a legally executed statement of a person's wishes about what is to be done with the person's property after his or her death; also **last will and testament**; *v.t.* to give or dispose of by a will.

window envelope *n.* an envelope with a window through which you can read the name and address of the recipient; commonly used for pledge reminders and receipts.

World Wide Web (www) *n.* a system of Internet servers that support specially formatted documents that support links to other documents, as well as graphics, audio, and video files. Not all Internet servers are part of the World Wide Web. Also **Web.**

XML Extensible Markup Language *n.* A flexible way to create common information formats and share both the format and the data on the Internet, intranets and elsewhere.

year-end gift *n.* a gift made in the last two months of a calendar year.

zero-based budgeting (ZBB) *n.* a system in which the budget of an organization, government, etc. is evaluated anew without regard to any previous year's budget. Compare **incremental budgeting.**

Source: Copyright 2006, Association of Fundraising Professionals (AFP), formerly NSFRE. All rights reserved. Reprinted with permission, http://www.afpnet.org.

Index

Note: Italicized page locators indicate a photo/figure; tables are noted with a *t*.